W9-BMZ-767

Orlando &
Central Florida

Orlando & Central Florida

Sandra Friend & Kathy Wolf

The Countryman Press ✳ Woodstock, Vermont

First Edition
Previously published in 2004 by The Countryman Press as *Orlando, North & Central Florida: An Explorer's Guide*

No entries or reviews in this book have been solicited or paid for.

ISBN 978-0-88150-813-0

Maps by Mapping Specialists, Ltd., Madison, WI
Text and cover design by Bodenweber Design
Composition by PerfecType, Nashville, TN
Front cover photograph © John Athanason, Weeki Wachee Springs
Interior photographs by the authors unless otherwise indicated

Published by The Countryman Press,
P.O. Box 748, Woodstock, Vermont 05091

Distributed by W. W. Norton & Company, Inc
500 Fifth Avenue, New York, NY 10110

Printed in the United States of America

10 9 8 7 6 5 4 3 2 1

DEDICATION

Remembering Sunny, for bringing us together,
and Ethel Palmer, for sharing her memories

"If there were no mystery left to explore, life would get rather dull, wouldn't it?"
—Sidney Buchman

Also by Sandra Friend
50 Hikes in North Florida
50 Hikes in Central Florida
50 Hikes in South Florida
Along the Florida Trail
Florida
The Florida Trail: The Official Hiking Guide
Hiker's Guide to the Sunshine State
Sinkholes

Also by Sandra Friend and Kathy Wolf
North Florida and the Florida Panhandle: An Explorer's Guide
South Florida: An Explorer's Guide

EXPLORE WITH US!

Welcome to the first edition of *Orlando & Central Florida: An Explorer's Guide*, the most comprehensive travel guide you'll find on the middle of the Sunshine State. All of the attractions, accommodations, restaurants, and shopping have been included on the basis of merit (primarily close, personal inspection by your authors) rather than paid advertising. The following points will help you understand how the guide is organized.

WHAT'S WHERE

The book starts out with a thumbnail sketch of the most important things to know about traveling in Florida, from where the best small town getaways are to which beaches you should head to first. We've included important contact information for state agencies and advice on what to do when you're on the road.

LODGING

All selections for accommodations in this guide are based on merit, and most were personally inspected by us or by a reliable source known to us. No businesses were charged for inclusion in this guide. Many B&Bs do not accept children under 12 or pets, so if there is not a specific mention in their entry, ask them about their policy before you book a room. Some places have a minimum-stay requirement, especially on weekends.

Rates: Rates quoted are for double occupancy, one night, before taxes. When a range of rates is given, it spans the gamut from the lowest of low season (which varies around the state) to the highest of the high season; a single rate means the proprietor offers only one rate year-round. Rates for hotels and motels are subject to further discount with programs like AAA and AARP, and may be negotiable depending on occupancy.

RESTAURANTS

The distinction between *Eating Out* and *Dining Out* is based mainly on price, secondarily on atmosphere. Dining in Florida is more casual than anywhere else in the United States—you'll find folks in T-shirts and shorts walking into the dressiest of steak houses. If a restaurant has a dress code, it's noted.

Smoking is no longer permitted within restaurants in Florida if the bulk of the business's transactions are in food rather than drink. Many restaurants now provide an outdoor patio for smokers.

KEY TO SYMBOLS

- ☙ **Special Value.** The special value symbol appears next to lodgings and restaurants that offer quality not usually enjoyed at the price charged.
- ⌁ **Certified Green Lodging.** This property meets or exceeds the standards of the Florida Department of Environmental Protection Green Lodging Program, which holds hotels accountable to eco-friendly standards in construction and daily operation.

✎ **Child-friendly.** The crayon symbol appears next to places or activities that accept children or appeal to families.

  Handicapped access. The wheelchair symbol appears next to lodgings, restaurants, and attractions that provide handicapped access, at a minimum with assistance.

🐾 **Pets.** The pet symbol appears next to places that accept pets, from B&Bs to bookstores. All lodgings require that you let them know you're bringing your pet; many will charge an additional fee.

∞ **Weddings.** The wedding symbol appears next to venues that are experienced with hosting weddings.

((↑)) **Wi-Fi.** Locations that offer wireless Internet.

Prices for lodgings and restaurants are subject to change, and shops come and go. Your feedback is essential for subsequent editions of this guide. Feel free to write us at Explorer's Guide, PO Box 424, Micanopy, Florida 32667, or e-mail eg@genuineflorida.com with your opinions and your own treasured finds. See www.genuineflorida.com for updates to properties listed in this book.

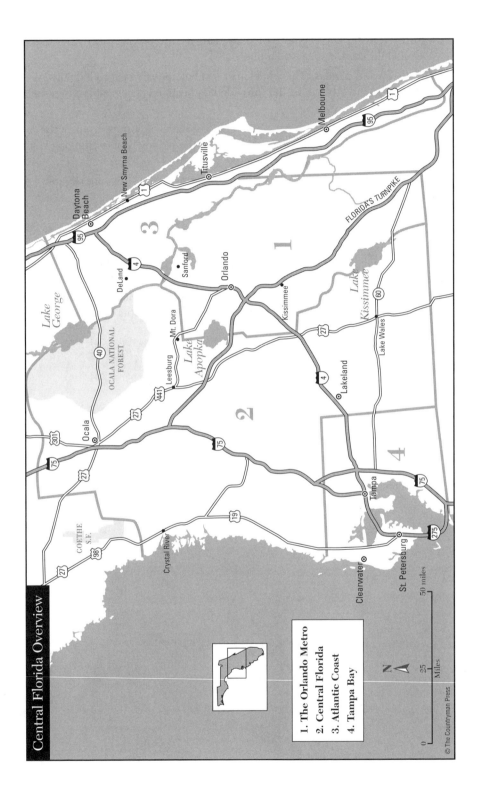

Central Florida Overview

1. The Orlando Metro
2. Central Florida
3. Atlantic Coast
4. Tampa Bay

© The Countryman Press

CONTENTS

INTRODUCTION

Welcome to *Orlando & Central Florida: An Explorer's Guide*! Kathy Wolf and I collaborated on the initial edition, and were able to spin off North Florida and the Panhandle into its own book last year. This truly new edition of our Central Florida guide builds on the original foundation while pulling more places to stay, eat, and see, and folding in a crucial part of the I-4 corridor: Tampa Bay, the southernmost section of Central Florida.

This is my home, and I'm happy to share the best of it with you. Central Florida is home to some of the state's oldest tourist attractions (Cypress Gardens, Silver Springs, and Weeki Wachee) as well as its newest theme parks. We have wonderful wild places, sweet little small towns, and two major cities, Orlando and Tampa. I took my first steps on Florida sand at the tender age of three and moved here with my family in the 1970s before settling here permanently after college. Thanks to my involvement with the Florida Trail Association and the *50 Hikes* guides, I've poked around every wild nook and cranny of this state. Reviewing travel destinations is a whole different ballgame. But I've always loved the genuine side of Florida, places like Mount Dora and Plant City, Tarpon Springs and New Smyrna Beach, and to dig into them in detail brought out the best in our small towns to me. As for Orlando—for all the years I worked and played there, I never took the time to appreciate our resources the way I did while researching this guide. I knew about the art scene and the theme parks, but hadn't made the deep connection with its history and architecture. It just goes to prove that you can be a tourist in your own backyard! Marrying an Orlando native didn't hurt, either; I met my husband while researching the original version of this book, and he gave me my first tour of downtown Orlando. Now, I almost know it by heart.

Given the historic importance of tourism to Florida's economy, there is no way to capture the breadth and depth of what this region of the state has to offer in a single book. Rather, Kathy and I delved into what we, as residents, appreciate the most: Florida's natural and cultural heritage, especially on the backroads and in small towns and downtowns, and our outdoor recreation opportunities. As I've served for several years on a state advisory committee for nature-based tourism, I'm glad to see that more and more visitors to Florida spend time outdoors enjoying our trails, springs, and forests.

I think you'll be pleased with our finds, and you'll use this book as a launch pad for your own exploration of Florida. In some cases our picks lead you into off-the-beaten-path places that are worthy of note in their entirety, like the lakeside towns of Mount Dora and McIntosh. In other cases, exploration means getting past the outer rim of strip malls and chain restaurants to discover the beauty in a city's heart—which is the certainly the case for cities like Orlando, Ocala, and Lakeland.

Having watched tourism shift from the roadside attractions of the 1960s to the slick theme parks of today, I take my Florida with a good dose of nostalgia, reflecting on the thousands of years of human settlement and five centuries of European culture that shape our towns and cities, the unique botanical wonders of our state, and its geological oddities. Welcome to my backyard—and enjoy!

ACKNOWLEDGMENTS

Building on a fine foundation from the many, many people who helped us pull together the first edition, I'd like to thank the following folks for their assistance as I updated this guidebook:

John Athanason, Weeki Wachee Springs
Captain Reg and Judy Bale, Premier Boat Tours
Carlene Barrett and Dianne Redd, Florida State Parks
Ebe Bower, Clearwater Chamber of Commerce
Tangela Boyd, Daytona Beach Area Convention & Visitors Bureau
Leon Corbett and Paul Kayemba, VISIT FLORIDA
Danielle Courtney, Orlando-Orange County Convention & Visitors Bureau
Mary Craven and Tracie Conti, Citrus County Convention & Visitors Bureau
Mary Deatrick, Deatrick Public Relations
Fred Gaske, Florida Division of Historical Resources
Christie Gregovich, YPartnership
Doug Kelly and Tommy Thompson, Florida Outdoor Writers Association
Dina Marie Lomagno and Rose Valdez-Keyes, The Belleview Biltmore
Katy Martin, Central Florida Visitors & Convention Bureau
Leslie Menichini and Jon Bloom, Rosen Shingle Creek
Kathy Pagan, Debi Dyer, and Greg Mihalic, Lake County Department of Tourism
Ken Hamilton and Cindy Phillips, Palm Pavilion Beachside Grille
Rob Pici and Kathy Masterson, The Plaza Resort & Spa
Kelly Grass Prieto, Hayworth Creative Public Relations
Marian Ryan, Friends of Polk County Parks
Susan Rupe, Hernando County Tourism
Jesse Smith and Monso Tatum, Pioneer Settlement for the Creative Arts
Ann Sternal, Ocala/Marion County Convention & Visitors Bureau
Laurilee Thompson, Dixie Crossroads
Georgia Turner, Georgia Turner Group
Ron Woxberg, St. Johns River Cruises

Thanks, too, to the innkeepers and restaurateurs who took the time to provide me a personal tour of their premises. I do not always announce my intent to review when I visit, so for those of you who remember helping me—thank you!

In my travels, I shared many a scouting trip or restaurant review with friends who suggested new places to visit, facilitated my visit, or just shared the experience with me, including Tex Ann Ivey Buck and Bob Buck, Grace Chewning, Jim Fern, Lorinda Gilbert, Sioux Hart, Herb Hiller, Sandy Huff and Logan Fowler, Joan Jarvis and Jon Phipps, Mayor Carl T. Langford and Tom and Pam Langford, Tim O'Keefe and Linda Sykes, Beth Kelso, Ann Sabo, G. K. Sharman, James Saunders, John Stephens, my sister Sally White and her husband Randal and their children Logan and Sydney, my brother-in-law Jeff Smith and father-in-law Bob Smith, my niece Amber Friend, and my parents Philip and Linda Friend. I salute my co-author Kathy Wolf, who was fighting an illness that neither of us knew about while we worked together on our first few books; she is now on the road to recovery and cheering from the sidelines. But above all, my biggest supporter has been my husband, Rob Smith Jr., who took on a huge chunk of work from me in the way of phone calls, site visits, and historical research.

WHAT'S WHERE IN FLORIDA

ADMISSION FEES If an admission fee is $7 or less, it's simply listed as "fee." Fees greater than $7 are spelled out. Although fees were accurate when this book went to press, keep in mind that yearly increases are likely, especially for the larger attractions and theme parks.

AIRBOAT RIDES Airboats are an exciting way to get out in the backcountry of Florida. These shallow boats can skim over only a few inches of water. Boat sizes range from small four-seaters to massive floating buses holding up to 30 people and dictate the type of experience you can expect.

Kissimmee-St. Cloud Convention & Visitors Bureau

The smaller, intimate boats will be more one-on-one, will get into tighter places, and may be more expensive. Most of the larger boats provide handicapped assistance. A ride in any airboat requires hearing protection, which is provided by the operators.

AIR SERVICE Major airports in the region covered by this book include the **Greater Orlando International Airport** (407-825-2001; www.state.fl.us/goaa), **Orlando Sanford International Airport** (407-322-7771; www.orlandosanfordairport.com), **Daytona Beach International Airport** (386-248-8069; www.flydaytonafirst.com), and **Tampa International Airport** (813-870-8700 or 1-800-767-8882; www.TampaAirport.com). Smaller regional airports served by commuter flights are listed in their respective chapters.

ALLIGATORS No longer an endangered species, the American alligator is a ubiquitous resident of Florida's lakes, rivers, streams, and retention ponds. Most alligators will turn tail and hit the water with a splash when they hear you coming—unless they've been fed or otherwise desensitized to human presence. Do not approach a

NASA/Dimitri Gerondidakis

sunning alligator, and never, ever feed an alligator (it's a felony, and downright dangerous to do) in the wild. Nuisance alligators should be reported to the Florida Fish and Wildlife Conservation Commission (352-732-1225; www.floridaconservation.org).

AMTRAK Two daily Amtrak (1-800-USA-RAIL; www.amtrak.com) trains make their way from New York/Washington, DC, to Florida: the **Silver Service/Palmetto**, ending in either Tampa or Miami, and the Auto-Train, bringing visitors (and their cars) to Sanford. Stops are noted in *Getting There*.

ANTIQUES While **Mount Dora** is the state's top destination for antiques collectors, you'll also find **Dade City, Deland,** and **Plant City** worth at least a full day for antiques browsing. Since 1985, the free magazine *Antiques & Art Around Florida* (352-475-1336; www.aarf.com) has kept up with the trends throughout the Sunshine State; pick up a copy at one of the antiques stores you visit, or browse their Web site to do a little pretrip planning. I've found some unexpected bargains in **Bartow, Lake Alfred, Winter Haven,** and downtown **Lakeland**. No matter what you're collecting, it's out there somewhere!

ARCHEOLOGY Florida's archeological treasures date back more than 10,000 years, including temple mound complexes such as those found at the **Crystal River Archeological Site State Park,** and thousands of middens (prehistoric garbage dumps) of oyster shells found along the state's rivers, streams, and estuaries. Of the middens, the most impressive in size in Central Florida are those at **Philippe Park** in Safety Harbor and **Mosquito Lagoon** in Canaveral National Seashore. More recent archeological finds focus on the many shipwrecks found along Florida's coasts and in its rivers, protected by underwater preserves. For information about archeological digs and shipwrecks, contact the **Florida Division of Historical Resources, Bureau of Archeological Research** (www.flheritage.com/archaeology).

ART GALLERIES Florida is blessed with many creative souls drawing their inspiration from our dramatic landscapes, working in media that range from copper sculpture and driftwood to fine black-and-white photography, giclée, and watercolor. Artists gravitate into communities, so you'll find clusters of art galleries in places like **Cocoa, Deland, Sanford, St. Petersburg,** and **Mount Dora**.

ARTS COUNCILS Many cities and counties have public art displays (such as "art in the parks" in Orlando, Bartow, Cocoa, Lakeland, and Melbourne) thanks to their local arts councils. The **Florida Cultural Affairs Division** (www.florida-arts

.org) offers resources, grants, and programs to support the arts throughout Florida; its Florida Artists Hall of Fame recognizes great achievements in the arts.

AVIATION While Florida may not be the birthplace of aviation, it is definitely its nursery school and post-doctorate program. Florida's aviation history includes the many World War II training bases and the birth of naval aviation in 1914; the first scheduled commercial airline flight from St. Petersburg to Tampa was also in 1914, and the first nonstop flight across the nation came soon after. The rocket technology of NASA brings modern aviation into the space age. Visit the **St. Petersburg Museum of History** (727-894-1052; www .stpetemuseumofhistory.org) for a full rundown on the history of commercial aviation

BALLOONING, GLIDING, AND PARA-SAILING The unique topography of the Florida peninsula makes it ideal for aerial sports, since strong thermals rise down the center of the peninsula. **Orange Blossom Balloons** in Orlando (see "Theme Parks") offers a splendid ride over the treetops, where you can watch the sunrise over the Magic Kingdom and downtown Orlando. Near Clermont, the **Seminole Gliderport** gives unique trips in unpowered gliders, where you feel like a bird as you catch a thermal to climb thousands of feet in the air. Parasailing floats you over lakes or ocean from the back platform of a boat. And hang-gliding was invented right here in Central Florida at Cypress Gardens. Nearby, the folks at **Wallaby Ranch** will tow you high up so you can soar like a bird.

BASEBALL Florida is home to Major League Baseball's annual spring training, and although most teams train in the southern portion of the state, you'll catch players hanging out in Central Florida, including the **Atlanta Braves** at Disney's Wide World of Sports. Polk County is a hot spot for spring training, with the **Toronto Blue Jays, Detroit Tigers,** and **Kansas City Royals** playing exhibition games in venues around the county, and in the Tampa Bay area, the **New York Yankees** and **Philadelphia Phillies** have their spring Grapefruit League and year-round farm teams. Some of the teams have announced intent to bolt to Arizona, so check Web sites before showing up at a stadium.

BEACHES Where to start? Florida's 2,000-mile coastline means plenty of beaches for every taste, from the busy social scene at **Daytona Beach** to the remote serenity of **Caladesi Island**. The north end of **New Smyrna Beach** has broad strands with serious wave action for surf fanatics. **Cocoa Beach** is Surf Central, where the annual Easter competition packs in the college crowd. Public lands are your best places to enjoy pristine

Sandra Friend

dunes and uncluttered beachfronts, from quiet **Fort Island Park** near Crystal River to **Sebastian Inlet State Park** at the southern tip of the Space Coast.

BED & BREAKFASTS Given the sheer number of B&Bs throughout Florida, we do not cover them all; we reviewed those available for a visit during our travels in this vast region, and selected from them accordingly. There is a mix of historical B&Bs, working ranches, rustic lodges, and easygoing family homes. Some, but not all, are members of associations such as **Superior Small Lodging** (www.superiorsmall lodging.com) or the **Florida Bed & Breakfast Inns** (281-499-1374 or 1-800-524-1880; www.florida-inns.com), both of which conduct independent inspections. All of the B&B owners I stayed with were eager to tell their story; most have a great love for the history of their home and their town. I find B&B travel one of the best ways to connect with Florida, and strongly encourage you to seek out the experiences listed throughout the book. Some motels will offer breakfast so that they can list their establishment as a B&B. I have tried to note this wherever possible, as Internet sites can be misleading.

BICYCLING Bike Florida (www.bike florida.org) is your gateway to statewide bicycling opportunities. Regional groups have done a great job of establishing and maintaining both on-road bike routes and off-road trails suitable for mountain biking, and information on these routes and trails is listed in the text. Check in with the Office of Greenways and Trails (see *Greenways*) for information on rail-trail projects throughout the state.

BIRDING As the home to millions of winter migrants, Florida is a prime destination for bird-watching; see the *Great Florida Birding Trail*. The Florida Game and Fresh Water Fish Commission (www.floridaconservation .org) has a bird-watching certificate program called **Wings Over Florida**. My top pick for birding: **Merritt Island National Wildlife Refuge**. If you can fit no other visit into your schedule, go there during the winter months to see a vast variety of birds, including the elusive bright pink roseate spoonbills feeding on the mudflats.

BLACK HERITAGE TRAIL In 1990, the Florida Legislature created the Study Commission on African-American History in Florida to document African-American contributions to Florida history and culture. To promote these sites for tourism, the Florida Department of State and Visit Florida created the **Florida Black Heritage Trail** program (www.fl heritage.com/services/trails/bht) and guidebook, which is available online or through the Department of State.

NASA/Ken Thornsley

BOAT AND SAILING EXCURSIONS

Exploring our watery state by water is part of the fun of visiting Florida, from the blasting speed of an airboat skipping across the marshes to the gentle toss of a sailboat across Clearwater Harbor. Many ecotours rely on quiet electric-motor pontoon boats to guide you down Florida's rivers and up to its first-magnitude springs. I greatly recommend a cruise on **Silver Springs's classic glass-bottomed boats**, but you'll find almost any boat tour you take a delight.

BOOKS To understand Florida, you need to read its authors, and none is more important than **Patrick Smith**, whose *A Land Remembered* is a landmark piece of fiction tracing Florida's history from settlement to development. A good capsule history of Florida's nearly 500 years of European settlement is *A Short History of Florida*, the abbreviated version of the original masterwork by **Michael Gannon**. To see through the eyes of settlers who tried to scratch a living from a harsh land, read the award-winning books of **Marjorie Kinnan Rawlings**, including *The Yearling*, *Cross Creek*, and *When the Whipoorwill*. For insights into the history of African American culture in Florida, seek out novelist **Zora Neale Hurston**; her works *Their Eyes Were Watching God* and *Jonah's Gourd Vine* touch the soul. For a taste of frontier Florida, try the Cracker western novels of **Lee Gramling**, which draw deeply from Florida's history.

To understand Florida culture, read *Palmetto Country* by **Stetson Kennedy**, a Florida icon who worked to compile Florida's folklore with the 1940s WPA project and went on to fight for civil rights throughout the South. For a glimpse of Florida's frenetic development over the past century, *Some Kind of Paradise: A Chronicle of Man and the Land in Florida*, by **Mark Derr**, offers serious insights. All visitors to Florida who love the outdoors should read *Travels* by **William Bartram**, a botanist who recorded his adventures along the St. Johns River during the 1700s, as well as the *A Thousand-Mile Walk to the Gulf* by **John Muir** and *A Naturalist in Florida: A Celebration of Eden* by **Archie Carr**. *River of Lakes: A Journey on Florida's St. Johns River* by **Bill Belleville** is a wonderful celebration of our state's mightiest river. When you plan your outdoor activities, don't forget that Florida has more than 2,500 miles of hiking trails—and I've walked a large percentage of them while compiling *50 Hikes in Central Florida* and six other hiking guides.

BUS SERVICE Greyhound (1-800-229-9424; www.greyhound.com) covers an extensive list of Florida cities; see their Web site for details and the full schedule. Stops are noted in the text under *Getting There*. Where useful for travelers, local bus service is noted.

CAMPGROUNDS Rates are quoted for single-night double-occupancy stays; all campgrounds offer discounts for club membership as well as weekly, monthly, and resident (6 months or more) stays, and often charge more for extra adults. If pets are permitted, keep them leashed. Also see the *Green Space* section of each chapter for campgrounds at state and county parks. Florida State Parks uses Reserve America (1-800-326-3521; www.reserveamerica.com) for all campground reservations; a handful of sites are kept open for drop-ins. Ask at the gate.

CHILDREN, ESPECIALLY FOR The crayon symbol ✐ identifies activities and places of special interest to children and families.

CITRUS STANDS, FARMER'S MARKETS, AND U-PICKS Citrus stands associated with active groves are usually open seasonally Nov–Apr. I've listed permanent stands as well as places you're likely to see roadside fruit and vegetable sales (often out of the backs of trucks and vans) from local growers. All U-pick is seasonal. Florida's growing seasons run year-round with citrus in winter and spring, strawberries in early spring, blueberries in late spring, and cherries in early summer. Don't pick citrus without permission: it's such a protected crop in Florida that to pluck an orange from a roadside tree is a felony. The **Florida Department of Agriculture** provides a full listing of farmer's markets around the state at www.florida-agriculture.com/consumers/farmers_markets.htm; for u-pick locations, see www.florida-agriculture.com/consumers/upick.htm.

CIVIL WAR As the third state to secede from the Union, Florida has a great deal of Civil War history to explore. Although most battle sites are in North Florida and the Panhandle, skirmishes and raids occurred in places like **Brooksville, Homosassa Springs, Narcoossee**, and **Ocklawaha** and are commemorated annually. See **Florida Civil War Reenactors Event Roster** (www.floridareenactors online.com/EventRoster.htm) for a

calendar of reenactments held throughout the state.

CRABBING From mid-October through May, it's perfectly legal for you to dive offshore to collect stone crab claws—if you can stand the thought of removing them from their owners. The good news is, the crabs grow them back, so take only one from each critter. Limits set by the Florida Fish and Wildlife Conservation Commission (www.florida conservation.org) are 1 gallon of claws per person (2 gallons per vessel), and all claws must be a minimum of 2¾ inches from elbow to tip. Divers must fly a diver-down flag.

CRABS Florida can lay claim to some of the freshest crabs anywhere in its seafood restaurants, with blue crabs and stone crabs caught along the Gulf Coast; some restaurants, like **Pecks Old Port Cove** in Ozello, raise their own crabs in the Gulf's salty waters. Eat your crab legs with melted butter for optimum appeal.

DIVE RESORTS Dive resorts cater to both open-water and cave divers, with an on-site dive shop. They tend toward utilitarian but worn accommo-

Sandra Friend

dations—wet gear can trash a room! Lodgings categorized under this header will appeal to divers because of their location.

DIVING Certification for open-water diving is required for diving in Florida's rivers, lakes, and streams; certification in cave diving is required if you plan to enter the outflow of a spring. Expertise in open-water diving does not translate to cave diving, and many experienced open-water divers have died attempting to dive Florida's springs. Play it safe and stick with what you know. A DIVER DOWN flag is required when diving.

THE DIXIE HIGHWAY Conceptualized in the 1910s by Carl Graham Fisher and the Dixie Highway Association as a grand route for auto touring, the Dixie Highway had two legs that ran along the East Coast of the United States into Florida, both ending in Miami. Since it ran along both coasts of Florida, you'll find OLD DIXIE HIGHWAY signs on both US 1 and US 17 on the east coast and along US 19, 27, and 41 on the west coast, and even US 441 in the middle—the highway ran through places as diverse as Jacksonville, Daytona Beach, Melbourne, Tallahassee, Micanopy, Ocala, downtown Orlando, and Fort Meade. The original brick pavement that still exists on the Old Tampa Highway in Loughman was part of the Dixie Highway route.

EMERGENCIES Hospitals with emergency rooms are noted at the beginning of each chapter. Dial 911 to connect to emergency service anywhere in the state. For highway accidents or emergencies, contact the **Florida Highway** Patrol at °FHP on your cell phone, or dial 911.

FACTORY OUTLETS You've seen the signs, but are they really a bargain? Several factory outlets, particularly in the Orlando area, offer brand and designer names for less, but you may also get great deals at smaller shops and even the local mall. I've listed some factory outlets that I found particularly fun to shop at that also had a nice selection of eateries and close access to major highways.

FERRIES Florida has few remaining ferryboats; in the region covered by this book, you'll find the **Fort Gates Ferry** crossing from the Ocala National Forest to Welaka.

FISH CAMPS An important Florida tradition, fish camps are quiet retreats for anglers to relax along a lake or river and put in some quality time fishing. Sometimes the family comes along, too! Accommodations listed under this category tend to be older cabins, mobile homes, or concrete block structures, sometimes a little rough around the edges. If the cabins or motel rooms at a fish camp are of

Kathy Wolf

Sandra Friend

superior quality, I list them under those categories.

FISHING The **Florida Fish and Wildlife Conservation Commission** (www.floridaconservation.org) regulates all fishing in Florida, offering both freshwater and saltwater licenses. To obtain a license, visit any sporting goods store or call 1-888-FISH-FLO for an instant license; you can also apply online at www.florida conservation.org; choose from short-term, annual, 5-year, or lifetime options. No fishing license is required if you are on a guided fishing trip, are fishing with a cane pole, are bank fishing along the ocean (varies by county), or are 65 years or older.

FLORIDA GREEN LODGING PRO-GRAM Established in 2004 by the Florida Department of Environmental Protection, this innovative program recognizes lodgings that go the extra mile to protect Florida's natural resources by lessening their environmental impact. The program is entirely voluntary and encompasses not just

linen reuse but energy efficiency, waste reduction, clean air, and communications. There are several levels of achievement for which lodgings earn one-, two-, or three-palm ratings. Designated Green Lodgings are marked with a ⊷ symbol in this guide; to date, 66 lodgings statewide have earned this honor. To learn more about the program, visit www.dep .state.fl.us/greenlodging

FLORIDA TRAIL The Florida Trail is a 1,400-mile footpath running from the Big Cypress National Preserve north of Everglades National Park to Fort Pickens at Gulf Islands National Seashore in Pensacola. With its first blaze painted in 1966, it is one of only eight congressionally designated National Scenic Trails in the United States, and is still under development—but you can follow the orange blazes from one end of the state to the other. The Florida Trail and other trails in state parks and state forests, known as the **Florida Trail System**, are built and maintained by volunteer members of the nonprofit Florida Trail Association (352-378-8823 or 1-877-HIKE-FLA; www.floridatrail .org), 5415 SW 13th St, Gainesville 32608; the association is your primary source for maps and guidebooks (written by yours truly) for the trail.

FORESTS, NATIONAL There are three national forests in Florida (Apalachicola, Ocala, and Osceola), administered out of the **US Forest Service** (850-523-8500; www.fs .fed.us/r8/florida) offices in Tallahassee. Established in 1908 by President Theodore Roosevelt, **Ocala National Forest** is the oldest national forest east of the Mississippi River.

FORESTS, STATE The Florida Division of Forestry (www.fl-dof.com) administers Florida State Forests, encompassing thousands of acres of public lands throughout Florida; **Withlacoochee State Forest** is one of the largest. Each forest offers an array of outdoor activities from hiking, biking, trail riding, and camping to fishing, hunting, and even motocross and ATV use. Most (but not all) developed state forest trailheads charge a per-person fee of $1–4 for recreational use. For $30, you can purchase an annual day-use pass good for the driver and up to eight passengers: a real bargain for families! There are many state forest campgrounds, and they are cheap options for tent campers, running $5–15 per night depending on amenities and location. If you're a hiker, get involved with the **Trailwalker** program, in which you tally up miles on hiking trails and receive patches and certificates; a similar program is in place for equestrians, called the **Trailtrotter** program. Information on both programs can be found at trailhead kiosks or on the Florida State Forests Web site.

GAS STATIONS Gas prices fluctuate wildly around the state—and not in proportion to distance from major highways, as you might think. You'll find your best bargains for filling your tank along US 441 between Tavares and Apopka, along US 27 south of Clermont through Polk County, along US 19 from Crystal River to Clearwater, and in the Oviedo–UCF area of Orlando. The highest prices cluster around Lake Buena Vista and Walt Disney World.

GENEALOGICAL RESEARCH In addition to the excellent resources found in some local genealogical libraries like the Quintilla Geer Bruton Archives Center in Plant City, check the **State Library of Florida, Florida Collection** (www.flgenweb.net) for the Florida GenWeb project, census data, vital records, pioneer families, and links to the state's many historical societies.

GENUINE FLORIDA After writing more than ten guidebooks to Florida, I realized that what I cared about the most were the honest-to-goodness down-home experiences that often get lost in the shuffle when visitors are looking for what's hot and new in the Sunshine State. My husband and I started Genuine Florida (www.genuineflorida.com) with the intent of promoting these rural, natural, and cultural heritage gems, and we keep an active blog (www.genuineflorida.com/blog) featuring Florida book reviews, roadside Floridiana, and our funky finds as we travel within our home state.

GOLFING Golfing is a favorite pastime for many Florida retirees, and there are hundreds of courses across the state, impossible for me to list in any detail; a good resource for research is **Play FLA** (www.playfla.com), the state's official golf travel Web site. I've covered courses that are particularly interesting or feature exceptional facilities. Florida is home to both the PGA and LPGA headquarters.

GREAT FLORIDA BIRDING TRAIL The Great Florida Birding Trail (www.floridabirdingtrail.com), supported by the Florida Fish and Wildlife Conservation Commission, provides guidance to birders on the best overlooks, hiking trails, and waterfront parks to visit and which species you'll find at each location. Sites listed in the regional Great Florida Birding Trail brochures are designated with brown road signs displaying a stylized swallow-tailed kite. Certain sites are designated "Gateways" to the Great Florida Birding Trail, where you can pick up detailed information and speak with a naturalist. In the region covered by this guidebook, these sites include Merritt Island National Wildlife Refuge and Tenoroc Fish Management Area.

GREENWAYS Florida has one of the nation's most aggressive greenway programs, overseen by the Office of Greenways and Trails (www.dep .state.fl.us/gwt), which administers the state land acquisition program under the Florida Forever Act and works in partnership with the Florida Trail Association, Florida State Parks, water management districts, and regional agencies in identifying crucial habitat corridors for preservation and developing public recreation facilities.

HANDICAPPED ACCESS The wheelchair symbol ⅃ identifies lodgings, restaurants, and activities that are, at

a minimum, accessible with minor assistance. Many locations and attractions provide or will make modifications for people with disabilities, so call beforehand to see if they can make the necessary accommodations.

HIKING I note the best hiking experiences in each region in the *Hiking* section, and you can find additional walks mentioned under *Green Space*. The most comprehensive hiking guides for this portion of Florida include my *50 Hikes in Central Florida* (Backcountry Guides), *The Florida Trail: The Official Guide* (Westcliffe Publishing), and *A Hiker's Guide to the Sunshine State* (University Press of Florida).

HERITAGE SITES If you're in search of history, watch for the brown signs with columns and palm trees that mark official Florida Heritage Sites—everything from historic churches and graveyards to entire historic districts. According to the Florida Division of Historical Resources (www.flheritage .com), to qualify as a Florida Heritage Site a building, structure, or site must be at least 30 years old and have significance in the areas of architecture, archeology, Florida history, or traditional culture, or be associated with a significant event that took place at least 30 years ago.

HISTORIC SITES With nearly five centuries of European settlement in Florida, historic sites are myriad—so this book's coverage of Florida history is limited to sites of particular interest. For the full details on designated historic sites in Florida, visit the state-administered **Florida's History Through Its Places** (www.flheritage .com/facts/reports/places) Web site. Historic sites that belong to the

Gary Rothstein

Florida Trust for Historic Preservation (www.floridatrust.org), PO Box 11206, Tallahassee 32302, honor the Florida's Historic Passport program, in which membership (www .floridatrust.org/membership) offers to member sites—some for free, others for discounted admissions.

HURRICANES Hurricanes can strike anywhere in Florida, and in 2004, our state suffered four hurricanes in just six weeks. I live about as far from both coasts as you can get, and while my home, protected by ancient live oaks, was spared damage, all of my neighbors lost parts of their roofs. While traveling during hurricane season (June through October), be aware of hurricane evacuation routes from coastal areas and keep daily tabs on the weather forecasts. If a landfall is predicted, do not wait until the last minute to evacuate the area: Be proactive and get out fast. Better safe than sorry, even if it means a radical change to your vacation plans.

HUNTING Hunting is regulated by the Florida Fish and Wildlife Conservation Commission (www.florida conservation.org), with general gun season falling between Oct and Feb in various parts of the state. Check the Web site for specific hunt dates, the wildlife management areas (WMAs) open to hunting, and hunting license regulations.

INFORMATION Along the interstates, kiosks and roadside billboards will entice you to come in for vacation deals. Most are tied to time-shares or are operating in their own interest. True visitors centers will offer information without trying to sell you something. At the beginning of each section under *Guidance* I have listed the visitors' bureaus and chambers with no commercial affiliation.

INSECTS Florida's irritating insects are myriad, especially at dawn and dusk during summer months. We love our winters when they get chilly enough to kill the little buggers off. If you don't like DEET and you can't stand citronella, you'll spend 99 percent of your time indoors. Flying annoyances include the mosquito (which comes in hundreds of varieties), gnat, and no-see-um; troublesome crawling bugs are the chigger (also known as redbug), a microscopic critter that attaches itself to your ankles to feed; the tick, which you'll find in deeply wooded areas; and red ants, invaders that swarm over your feet leaving painful bites if you dare step in their nest. Bottom line—use insect repellent, and carry an antihistamine with you to counter any reactions you might have to communing with these native residents.

JELLYFISH At almost any time of the year you will find jellyfish in the ocean and washed up on the shore. Take particular care with the blue man o'war jellyfish; the sting from this marine creature is excruciatingly painful. Do not touch the dead ones on the beach, as their venom is still potent. Contrary to popular belief, they won't chase you down, but in case you do get stung, consider carrying a small bottle of white vinegar in your beach bag; this seems to help alleviate some of the pain. Then seek medical attention. Just as with bee stings, reactions vary.

THE KINGS HIGHWAY Established between 1763 and 1819 to connect coastal communities south from Brunswick through Cow Ford (Jacksonville) and St. Augustine to New Smyrna, this military trail is now approximated by the route of US 1; you will see KINGS HIGHWAY signs on historic sections of the road that are not part of US 1, most notably between Dupont Center and Ormond Beach.

MANGROVES The mangroves that grow along our barrier islands and coastline provide a natural anchor for sand and sediment, which build up to expand the land. During a storm they serve as a buffer between the raging water and the coastal habitats. Three types of mangroves grow in Florida: black, white, and red. Red mangroves have a distinct network of prop roots, roots that look like arches holding up the tree, and tend to be the "island builders." Black mangroves are broader and are surrounded by a network of short breathing roots that protrude from the soil under the plant and look like miniature cypress knees. White mangroves look the most treelike, with light green, oval leaves (the other mangroves have dark green, elliptical leaves).

MARITIME HERITAGE In a state where many still pull their living from the sea, it's only appropriate that we have a **Florida Maritime Heritage Trail** (www.flheritage.com/archae ology/underwater/maritime) that ties together the these elements of our history: working fishing villages such as Tarpon Springs; coastal fortresses built to defend Florida from invasion; lighthouses; historic shipwrecks; and endangered coastal communities such as the coastal pine flatwoods and coastal scrub. Visit the Web site for a virtual travel guide.

MOTELS, HOTELS, AND RESORTS We've included resorts with motels and hotels for this guide, since many properties refer to themselves as resorts but do not offer everything you need to stay put on the property, such as an on-site restaurant, shopping, and tours. In general, chain motels and hotels are not listed in this guide because of their ubiquitous nature; however, we've included a handful that are either the only lodging options in a particular area or happen to be outstanding places to stay.

MUSEUMS Explore our centuries of history: The **Florida Association of Museums** (850-222-6028; www .flamuseums.org) provides a portal to more than 340 museums throughout the state. Their Web site also provides a calendar of exhibits in museums around the state.

NATIONAL WIDLIFE REFUGES Founded by President Theodore Roosevelt on March 21, 1903, with the dedication of Pelican Island National Wildlife Refuge in Florida's Indian River Lagoon, the National Wildlife Refuge system protects lands used by migratory birds and vanishing species. When visiting a National Wildlife

Sandra Friend

Refuge, keep in mind that all animals and plants are protected—visitors have been arrested and fined for removing tree snails, orchids, and bromeliads from these preserves.

OYSTERS Nowhere in the United States can compare to Apalachicola and its oysters, pulled fresh from the Gulf estuaries along the Panhandle. A lack of industrial pollution and a small population mean the waters are clean and the oysters prime; ask for them at your stops for seafood.

PADDLING Canoeing and kayaking are extraordinarily popular activities in Florida, especially during the summer months, with sea kayaking a favorite along the barrier islands and the Indian River Lagoon. Most state parks have canoe livery concessions, and private outfitters are mentioned throughout the text. Under development, the **Circumnavigational Saltwater Paddling Trail** (www.florida dep.org/gwt/paddling/saltwater.htm) offers 1,600 miles of sea kayaking along the edges of our state. Portions of the trail are already in place as Blueways, mentioned in the text. Thanks to our interconnecting chains of lakes, you'll find freshwater Blue-

ways, waymarked and with tent platforms or campsites, in some interior counties as well, such as Lake County.

PARKS, STATE The Florida State Parks system (www.floridastateparks .org) is one of the United States' best and most extensive state park systems, with more than 150 to explore. All Florida state parks are open 8 AM–sunset daily. If you want to watch the sunrise from a state park beach, you'll have to camp overnight. Camping reservations are centralized through Reserve America (www .reserveamerica.com) and can be booked through each individual state park Web site. Walk-in visitors are welcome on a first-come, first-served basis. An annual pass is a real deal if you plan to do much traveling in the state: Individual passes are $40 plus tax; family passes are $80, plus tax, per year. The family pass is good for up to a maximum of eight people in one vehicle. These passes are honored at all state parks except Madison Blue Spring, Homosassa Springs, and the Sunshine Skyway Fishing Pier, where they are good for a 33 percent discount. Pick up a pass at any state park ranger station, or order through the Web site.

PETS The dog-paw symbol 🐾 identifies lodgings and activities that accept pets. Always inform the front desk that you are traveling with a pet, and expect to pay a surcharge.

PARROTS A favorite pet of the early 1990s, Quaker parrots were thrown into the eco-mix after Hurricane Andrew in 1992. The loud, lime green birds put on an impressive and often humorous display, and are frequently seen in flocks of a dozen or more

NASA

Sandra Friend

throughout the Tampa Bay area and along the Atlantic Coast.

POPULATION According to the 2000 federal census, Florida's population is closing in on 16 million people. What's scary to those of us who live here is that there continues to be a net gain of 800 people moving into Florida every day—which means an increasingly serious strain on our already fragile water resources.

RAILROADIANA Florida's railroad history dates back to 1836 with the **St. Joe & Lake Wimico Canal & Railroad Company,** followed shortly by the 1837 opening of the mule-driven **Tallahassee & St. Marks Railroad,** which brought supplies from the Gulf of Mexico to the state capital. Railroad commerce shaped many Florida towns, especially along David Yulee's **Florida Railroad** (circa 1850) connecting Fernandina and Cedar Key, and the later grandiose efforts of Henry Plant and the **Plant System** (later the Seaboard Air Line) on the west coast and Henry Flagler's **Atlantic Coast Line** on the east. This category notes sites of interest to railroad history buffs.

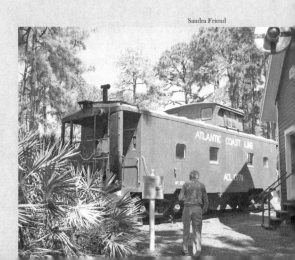

Sandra Friend

RATES The range of rates provided spans the lowest of low season to the highest of high season (which varies from place to place), and does not include taxes or discounts such as AARP, AAA, or camping club.

RIVERS Central Florida's rivers have two distinct beginnings: either flowing forth from a first or second magnitude spring (**Silver River, Homossasa River, Crystal River,** and the like) or rising up from a mosaic of wetlands to form a river (**Withlacoochee, Peace, Ocklawaha, Hillsborough, St. Johns**). Both the **St. Johns** and **Ocklawaha Rivers** form "rivers of lakes" on their northward journey, flowing through enormous lakes formed from the river's flow. Three state Water Management Districts oversee this region's water resources and provide information on recreational opportunities on their lands: the **St. Johns Water Management District** (www .sjwmd.com) covers the St. Johns River basin on the east coast; **Southwest Florida Water Management District** (www.swfwmd.state.fl.us) covers rivers emerging from the Green Swamp, including the northflowing Withlacoochee River; and the

South Florida Water Management District (www.sfwmd.gov) covers the Kissimmee River basin, with its headwaters at Shingle Creek near Orlando.

SCENIC HIGHWAYS The Florida Department of Transportation oversees the Florida Scenic Highway (www.dot.state.fl.us/emo/scenichwy/designated.htm) program, used to call attention to areas of significant natural and cultural heritage throughout the state. Each scenic highway is charged with developing its own resources for visitors, typically a Web site; these are listed in the text. In Central Florida, these include the **Florida Black Scenic Byway, River of Lakes Heritage Corridor, Indian River Lagoon Scenic Highway, Green Mountain Scenic Byway, Ormond Scenic Loop and Trail, Suncoast Scenic Parkway, Courtney Campbell Scenic Highway,** and **The Ridge Scenic Highway.** In addition to these state-level routes, you'll find local designations, such as county-designated **canopy roads** in places like Marion County and Volusia County, where the dense live oak canopy overhead makes for a beautiful scenic drive.

SEASHORES, NATIONAL Between New Smyrna Beach and Titusville, Canaveral National Seashore protects a slender strip of coastal strand just outside the Kennedy Space Center.

SEASONS Florida's temperate winter weather makes it ideal for vacationers, but we do have a very strong tropical delineation of wet and dry seasons, which strengthens the farther south you venture. Daily thundershowers are an absolute in summer from Ocala southward. Winter is generally dry and crisp, with nighttime temperatures falling as low as the 30s and 40s in Central Florida.

SHARKS Yes, they are in the water. At any given time there are a dozen or more just offshore, but for the most part they will leave you alone. To avoid being bitten, stay out of the water if there is a strong scent of fish oil in the air, which means that fish are already being eaten and you may be bitten by mistake. You will also want to avoid swimming near piers and jetties, which are active feeding zones.

SHRIMP You'll find different types of shrimp fried, broiled, sautéed, and blackened up and down both coasts. The most sought after are red, white, pink, rock, "brownies," and "hoppers," all of which are served at Shrimp Central—**Dixie Crossroads**.

THE SUNSHINE STATE The moniker "Sunshine State" was an effective 1960s advertising slogan that was also required on motor vehicle tags; it became the state's official nickname in 1970 by a legislative act.

TAXES Florida's base sales tax is 6 percent, with counties adding up to another 1.5 percent of discretionary sales tax. A raise of both taxes is under discussion right now in our legislature. In addition, a tourist development tax of up to 12 percent is levied on lodgings (including campgrounds) in almost every city and county, so factor that into your budget.

THEME PARKS Florida is the birthplace of the theme park, starting with glass-bottomed boats drawing tourists

courtesy Universal Studios

ber, under state law, riders utilizing trails on state land must have proof with them of a negative Coggins test for their horses. If you're interested in riding, hook up with one of the many stables listed in the text. Under state law, equine operators are not responsible for your injuries if you decide to go on a trail ride.

VISIT FLORIDA (www.visitflorida .com), the state's official tourism marketing agency, is a clearinghouse for every tourism question you might have. Their partners cover the full range of destinations, from the sleepy hamlets of the Nature Coast to the snazzy new hotels along I-Drive in Orlando. Utilize their Web site resources to preplan your trip, and share your experiences about your stay.

to **Silver Springs** in 1878. But the real heyday in Central Florida came with Dick Pope's water ski and botanical garden wonder called **Cypress Gardens**, circa 1932, followed by **Weeki Wachee Springs**, the "Spring of Living Mermaids," in 1947. The 1950s and 1960s saw an explosion in roadside attractions and zoos like **Gatorland**, and fancier parks like **Rainbow Springs** and **Homosassa Springs** showing off Florida's natural wonders. But when Walt Disney started buying up Osceola County in the 1950s, Florida tourism changed forever. After **Walt Disney World** opened in 1971, most of the old roadside attractions that made Florida so much fun in the 1960s folded. If you want to see all the manmade attractions today, you'll need at least 2 full months for the Orlando area alone.

TRAIL RIDING Bringing your own horses? You'll find working ranches and B&Bs with boarding stables listed in this guide, and believe it or not, some hotels will put up your horse— the **Ocala Hilton** (www.ocalahilton .com) offers free boarding for your horse with your stay, and some B&Bs have stables as an amenity. Remem-

WATERFALLS AND RAPIDS Yes, Florida has natural waterfalls and rapids! They're mostly in the North and Panhandle due to topography, but at **Hillsborough River State Park**, the rush of water over limestone rock is especially picturesque. I've been told the southernmost natural waterfall in Florida is in **Lakeland Highlands Scrub**, Polk County, which

Kathy Wolf

straddles the Lake Wales Ridge, but I have yet to find it myself.

WEATHER Florida's weather is both our greatest attraction and our greatest heartache. Balmy winters are the norm, with daytime temperatures in the 70s and evenings in the 50s common for Central Florida. Frost and snow happen, but are rare. Our summers are predictably hot and wet, with thunderstorms guaranteed on a daily basis and temperatures soaring up to the 90s in Central Florida. Our thunderstorms come up fast and carry with them some of the world's most violent and dangerous lightning. It's best to get indoors and out of or off the water should you see one coming. Hurricane season runs June–Nov, and when the big winds from Africa start moving across the Atlantic, it pays to pay attention—follow public announcements on what to do in the event of a tropical storm or hurricane.

WHERE TO EAT We've limited our choices to local favorites and outstanding creative fare, avoiding the chains seen everywhere across America. Several Florida-based chains deserve a mention, however; you'll enjoy their cuisine when you find them. **Hooters** got its start in Clearwater, and **Fred Fleming's Barbecue** hails from St. Petersburg, as does **Outback Steakhouse**. **Shells** is a family seafood restaurant serving ample portions for reasonable prices; **R.J. Gators** appeals to the sports-bar crowd with great Florida seafood on tap. **Buddy Freddy's**, based in Plant City, serves up the fine, farm-fresh, country-style food for which that town is famous. **TooJay's**, a New York–style deli, shines with big breakfasts, stellar sandwiches, and its yummy Mounds Cake. You'll also find the Stuart-based **Ice Cream Churn**, with 28 flavors of homemade ice cream, tucked away inside convenience stores throughout the state.

WI-FI The Wi-Fi symbol "ĭ" indicates places that provide wireless Internet access, which may or may not be free. The forward-thinking city of Sanford (see "North of Orlando") offers free Wi-Fi throughout the entire downtown area—sit on a park bench and check your email.

WINERIES Florida's wineries run the gamut from small family operations to large production facilities, and some partner together to provide a storefront in a high-traffic region while the growing, fermenting, and bottling is done in an area more favorable for agriculture. Native muscadine grapes are the cornerstones of the state's wines. For an overview of Florida wineries, contact the Florida Grape Growers Association (www.fgga.org).

The Orlando 1
Metro

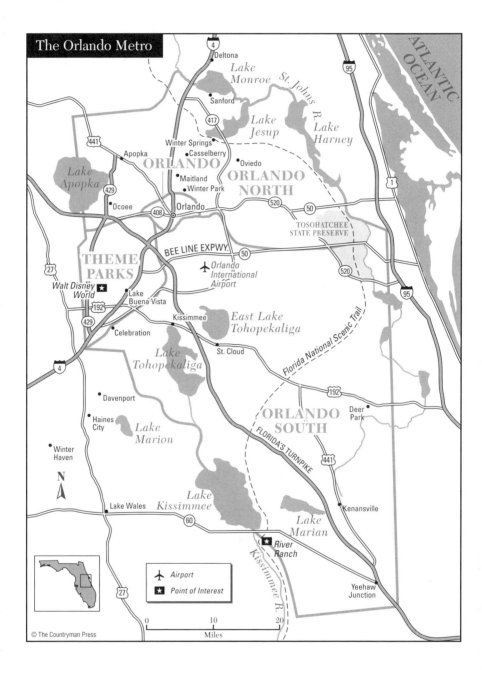

The Orlando Metro

THE ORLANDO METRO

Rich in history, the Orlando metro is the vibrant heart of Central Florida, centered on a frontier town that grew up to shape the space age. It all began during the Second Seminole War in the 1830s, when a string of fortresses were built by the US Army to push the Seminoles southward: Fort Christmas and Fort Mellon (on the St. Johns River, in what is now Sanford) were the first. Built in 1838 along the military trail to Fort Mellon, Fort Gatlin formed the core of a new settlement in Central Florida. To accelerate the removal of the Seminoles from Florida, the US Armed Occupation Act offered settlers on the Florida frontier up to 160 free acres as long as they would build a home and maintain a farm for at least 5 years. Aaron Jernigan moved to Fort Gatlin in 1843 with 700 head of cattle, becoming Mosquito County's first resident; the settlement around his spread along Lake Eola was called Jernigan. After Florida achieved statehood in 1845, Mosquito County was renamed Orange County (the better to attract settlers), and Jernigan served as the county's first representative in the state legislature. By 1856 the county required a permanent seat, and the name decided upon was *Orlando*. One account claims frontier Judge James G. Speer named the town for his appreciation of Shakespeare's *As You Like It*. Another credits Orlando Rees, an army officer who died on the shores of Lake Eola during a Seminole attack in 1835; "Orlando's Grave" became a stopping point along the military trail.

Spreading out from its city core in Orange County, the Orlando metro encompasses Seminole and northern Osceola Counties, with commuters coming in to work from adjoining Lake, Volusia, and Polk Counties. More than a million people live in this bustling region, where the population exploded during the 1940s—more than 100,000 servicemen were stationed in Orlando at various bases, receiving military training during World War II. After the war, the space race began, and the defense and aerospace industries started to grow, with what is now Lockheed Martin becoming an anchor employer in the northern suburbs.

In the late 1950s animator Walt Disney came to town, quietly buying up land. As early as 1967, accounts in local publications touted the coming wonder that was Walt Disney World, and the opening of the Magic Kingdom in 1971 triggered explosive growth on the southern edge of the metro area—hotels, restaurants, and more theme parks. The Orlando metro area now hosts the largest number of tourists in the world, with more than 43 million visitors arriving annually to the undisputed center of Florida tourism.

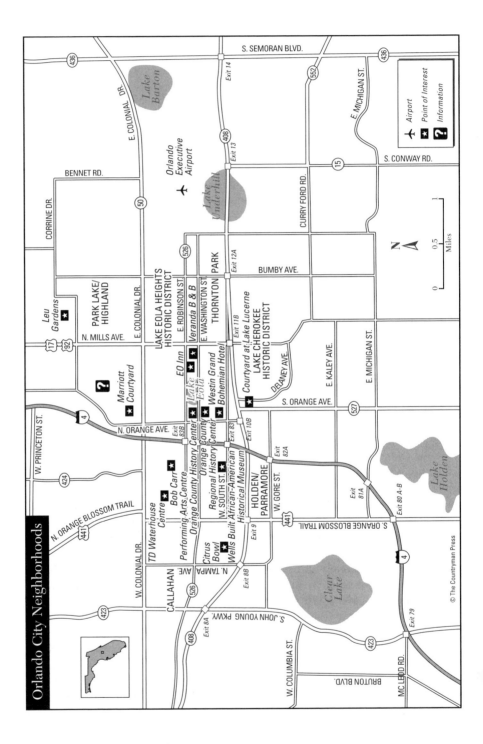

Orlando City Neighborhoods

S. SEMORAN BLVD.

E. MICHIGAN ST.

Lake Barton

E. COLONIAL DR.

BENNET RD.

CORRINE DR.

Orlando Executive Airport

Lake Underhill

S. CONWAY RD.

Point of Interest
Airport
Information

Leu Gardens

PARK LAKE/ HIGHLAND

N. MILLS AVE.

E. COLONIAL DR.

LAKE EOLA HEIGHTS HISTORIC DISTRICT

E. ROBINSON ST.

Veranda B & B

E. WASHINGTON ST.

THORNTON PARK

CURRY FORD RD.

BUMBY AVE.

N

0   0.5   1
Miles

Marriott Courtyard

EO Inn

Lake Eola

Westin Grand Bohemian Hotel

Courtyard at Lake Lucerne

LAKE CHEROKEE HISTORIC DISTRICT

DELANEY AVE.

E. KALEY AVE.

E. MICHIGAN ST.

W. PRINCETON ST.

N. ORANGE AVE.

Exit 83B

Orange County History Center

Exit 83

Exit 10B

S. ORANGE AVE.

Exit 82A

Lake Holden

N. ORANGE BLOSSOM TRAIL

Bob Carr Performing Arts Centre

TD Waterhouse Centre

Orange County Regional History Center

W. SOUTH ST.

Wells Built African-American Historical Museum

HOLDEN/ PARRAMORE

W. GORE ST.

Exit 81A

Exit 80 A-B

W. COLONIAL DR.

CALLAHAN

N. TAMPA AVE.

Citrus Bowl

Exit 8B

Exit 9

S. ORANGE BLOSSOM TRAIL

Clear Lake

S. JOHN YOUNG PKWY.

Exit 8A

W. COLUMBIA ST.

BRUTON BLVD.

MC LEOD RD.

Exit 79

© The Countryman Press

CITY NEIGHBORHOODS

With nearly 200,000 residents within its city limits, Orlando is a vibrant modern city with deep roots in Florida's long and storied history. As part of a string of defenses for the US Army, Fort Gatlin was built in 1838 near the Council Oak, a meeting place for the Seminoles. Soon after, Aaron Jernigan moved to what was then Mosquito County to set up a homestead and start cattle ranching near the fort; he served as a volunteer in the army as the settlement grew. By 1854 there was a sawmill and trading post along **Lake Eola**, and a steady stream of settlers picked out spreads around the region's many lakes: the Hugheys on Lake Lucerne, the Patricks and Barbers on Lake Conway, and the Speers on Lake Ivanhoe. It was a rough-and-tumble frontier town, the "Wild West" of Florida—cattle rustling from the free-range herds was common, and the herds were indeed the cash cow of the region, as the Spanish would pay in gold for Florida beef to be shipped to Cuba. Drovers stopped at **Fern Creek** on their way south to water the herds. Florida's top cattle baron, Jacob "King of the Crackers" Summerlin, settled his family in Orlando in 1873 to take advantage of its central location along his cattle-droving route from St. Augustine to Punta Rassa; he built a large home on Main Street and purchased the 200 acres surrounding Lake Eola. In a power struggle with General Henry Sanford over the location of the county seat, Summerlin offered to front $10,000 to build a proper county courthouse if the seat would remain at Orlando; the courthouse became reality, as did the incorporation of the village of Orlando, a mile square surrounding the courthouse.

The 1880s ushered in the region's railroad era, when the newly incorporated Florida Southern Railroad brought in tourists and settlers entranced by the descriptions of the area written by promoter W. W. Harney. The influx of visitors created a need for hotels and services. Many newcomers planted their land as citrus groves. The old frontier ways yielded to a more genteel class of people attracted by the growing citrus industry; the cows were officially herded out of downtown (by law) in 1882, and sidewalks went in. Jacob Summerlin donated the land that became Lake Eola Park. By 1885 more than 600,000 crates of oranges were shipped north from the region, which saw a wave of British investment in land from afar, based on descriptions of the "outdoors life" that residents enjoyed. Mule-drawn streetcars provided transportation downtown. In the first 6 years that the railroad connected Orlando to the outside world, the population increased 20-fold, and the city was dubbed "The Phenomenal City," its rows of shops and businesses generating business "equal to a city three times its size." A passenger coach was sent to the 1893 Columbian Exposition, filled with Florida's fabulous citrus and tropical fruit products, exhibiting the best of Florida to the citizens of Chicago. And the people continued to come.

The big freeze of 1895 dealt a harsh blow to the region's burgeoning citrus industry. As the century turned, interests were diversified to lumbering and turpentine; banking and real estate speculation began to boom. Ravaged by fires, the old wooden buildings of the city were replaced with edifices of brick and stone. As subdivisions began to radiate away from downtown, new communities like **Colonialtown** appeared. At his factory at Orange Avenue and Princeton Drive, Dr. Phillip Phillips developed a rotary juice press and a method of pasteurizing orange juice that introduced consumers to a safer, better-tasting product, leading to expanded exports for the citrus industry. After the post–World War I economic downturn, the subsequent 1920s Florida land boom brought new growth to the region. But World War II accelerated the city's population growth to epic proportions. In 1940 an Army Air Corps training field opened, and military personnel and their families moved in. The year 1941 ushered in the Pine Castle Air Force Base, which served as Strategic Air Command for B-52 bombers. More than 100,000 servicemen were stationed in Orlando. The boom continued after World War II, with industries tied to military weaponry and the defense contractor The Martin Company (today's Lockheed Martin) moving into the suburbs, and a naval training center opening in 1968. In conjunction with the population explosion, downtown's urban renewal programs changed the Orlando skyline. Skyscrapers sprouted in the 1960s in the wake of the CNA Building, and now the tallest tops 30 stories.

Outside of downtown, city neighborhoods sprang up around social and economic centers. **Parramore** was the heart of swing in the 1950s, when giants like Count Basie and Ella Fitzgerald stopped in to play at the South Street Casino. **College Park**, a very distinct community within the city, arose during the 1920s land boom as the city of Orlando's limits were extended to Par Street. After Edgewater High School opened in 1952, the area saw another big growth boom. Streets perpendicular to north–south Edgewater Dr (the community's "Main Street") are named for major universities.

On the south shore of Lake Eola, **Thornton Park** has become the city's tony place to live, dine, and shop. **North Orange Avenue** and **Virginia Drive** define the cultural and antiques districts within the city; cultural offerings cluster around Loch Haven Park as well. Since the 1980s, Hispanic immigrants from South

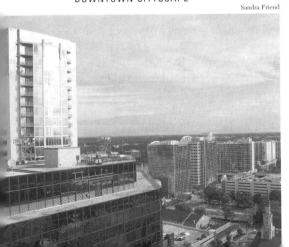

DOWNTOWN CITYSCAPE

Sandra Friend

America and the Caribbean have been moving into the southeastern neighborhoods, redefining them with businesses and cultural events that reflect the lifestyles of their homelands.

GUIDANCE In advance of your trip, get general information from the **Orlando/Orange County Convention & Visitors Bureau** (407-354-5586; www .orlandoinfo.com), 6700 Forum Dr, Suite 100, 32821; they can also help with hotel bookings and provide the free Orlando Magicard (1-888-799-1425), a passport to discounts on attractions, accommodations, transportation, and shopping throughout the region.

For directions to city neighborhoods, parks, and downtown sites, as well as information on the city's culture and history, visit the **City of Orlando** Web site (www.cityoforlando.net). For a full calendar of downtown Orlando's festivals and special events, contact the **Downtown Development Board** (407-246-2555; www.downtownorlando.com), 100 S Orange Ave, 32801.

For tickets to events held at the Florida Citrus Bowl, Bob Carr Performing Arts Centre, and TD Waterhouse Centre, contact the **Centroplex Box Office** (407-849-2020; www.orlandocentroplex.com).

GETTING THERE *By car:* Two major arteries bisect the heart of Orlando: **I-4** and **FL 408** (a toll road also known as the **East–West Expressway**).

By air: To the south, the **Greater Orlando International Airport** (407-825-2001; www.state.fl.us/goaa) serves the world with hundreds of flights daily on 89 different carriers; check their Web site for contact information on the many airlines servicing Orlando. To the north, **Orlando Sanford International Airport** (407-322-7771; www.orlandosanfordairport.com) hosts many foreign charters and offers regular commuter service on Pan Am.

By bus: **Greyhound** (1-800-229-9424; www.greyhound.com) has a major terminal on John Young Parkway between FL 408 and FL 50.

GETTING AROUND *By car:* The **Orange Blossom Trail** (US 441, US 17-92) and **Colonial Drive** (FL 50) are the major thoroughfares through the city; expect wall-to-wall strip malls and traffic lights along both. **Edgewater Drive**, off West Colonial Drive, forms the main road through College Park, which can also be reached from I-4 off Par Street or Princeton Avenue. Keep in mind that most downtown Orlando streets are one-way; Orange and Magnolia Aves and Central Blvd and Pine St are the major crossroads.

By bus: Downtown, **Lymmo** is a free bus service on a 3-mile loop, with no longer than a 5-minute wait at the sheltered stations. It operates Mon–Thu 6 AM–10 PM, Fri 6 AM–midnight, Sat 10 AM–midnight, Sun 10–10. Beyond, **Lynx** (407-841-8240; www.golynx.com) offers 57 routes throughout the tri-county area; fare is $1.75.

By bicycle: To step back in time to the neighborhoods that show the true character of Orlando, leave the main roads and amble down the slower routes like Central Blvd. College Park in particular is bike-friendly, with a bike lane running down Edgewater Blvd. A network of bicycle paths runs throughout the city; see *Bicycling* for details.

By pedicab: In the evenings, free pedicabs roam downtown looking for "fares" (they rely on tips to survive, so be generous).

By taxi: You'll rarely be able to hail a taxi along the street, but you will find taxi stands outside major hotels and restaurants. To summon a taxi, call **National Cab** (407-678-8888) or **Yellow Cab** (407-699-9999).

By rental car: Primarily located at Orlando International Airport—though rentals can be arranged through some hotels—rental agents include **Alamo** (1-800-327-9633), **Avis** (1-800-831-2847), **Budget** (407-850-6700), **Enterprise** (1-800-736-8222), **Hertz** (1-800-654-3131), and **National Car Rental** (1-800-227-7368).

PARKING You won't find much in the way of street parking in downtown Orlando; your best bet is to hit one of the nine downtown garages, such as the **Market Garage** at 60 W Pine St, Church Street at 150 S Hughey, or the **Library Garage** at 112 E Central and 119 Pine St. There is limited 2-hour metered parking on downtown streets. At Mills and Colonial, the shops have parking behind them. In the Virginia and Mills antiques districts, some shops have lots and street parking is free; along North Orange Ave, you'll find some short-term spaces, but the shoppers well outnumber the spaces. Instead of fighting for street parking, look for the **P** sign at Orange and Highland; turn onto Alden Rd and leave your vehicle at the **Lake Highland Sports Complex**—unlimited free parking. College Park has free 2- and 3-hour on-street parking, and some of the businesses have parking lots behind them, accessed via alleyways.

MEDICAL EMERGENCIES The region is well staffed for medical emergencies. Within city limits, you'll find **Florida Hospital East Orlando** (407-303-8110), 7727 Lake Underhill Rd; **Florida Hospital Orlando** (407-303-6600), 601 E Rollins St; and **Orlando Regional Medical Center** (407-841-5111), 1414 S Kuhl Ave—the only Level 1 Trauma Center in Central Florida.

✳ To See
ART GALLERIES

Downtown
Gallery at Avalon Island (407-803-6670; www.galleryatavalonisland.com), 39 S Magnolia Ave, inside the historic Rogers Building (see *Historic Sites*), features public interaction with modern impressionism, with new shows opening each month and the O'Town Art Café (see *Coffee Shops*) to keep things humming. Tue–Sat 12–6, free.

Orlando City Hall Galleries (407-246-2221), Orange Ave and South St. Rotating exhibits in the ground-floor gallery and the third-floor gallery outside the mayor's office have selected works from their permanent collection. Mon–Fri 8–9, Sat and Sun noon–5; free.

At the Westin Grand Bohemian (see *Lodging*), the **Grand Bohemian Gallery** (see *Selective Shopping*) showcases regional and national artists; wander upstairs (check at the front desk first) for a look at the fifth-floor galleries, including rotating single-artist exhibits in one meeting space and the **Orlando Room**, with its paintings of the city's mayors and the city skyline.

Orange Ave

Fredlund Gallery (407-898-4544; www.fredlundgallery.com), 1219 N Orange Ave, features five permanent Florida artists such as Dee Smith (who paints roseate spoonbills in Audubon's style) and Peter Pettigrew with his oils of Florida waterways, as well as other changing exhibits.

Maria Reyes Jones Gallery (407-893-9878; www.mariareyesjones.com), 1810 N Orange Ave, has her vivid pop art palm trees and florals that just scream Florida—I can't wait to own one!

Virginia Dr

Gallery on Virginia (407-898-8343), 1003 Virginia Dr, is a cooperative representing the works of the Artist League of Orange County, with 23 artists displaying their creative pottery, art glass, batik, turned wood, jewelry, and paintings in a bright gallery space.

HISTORIC SITES

Downtown

To know the real Orlando, walk the city streets (see *Walking Tours*) in search of historic sites. The core of old Orlando dates back to the late 1800s, typified by the **Rogers Building**, 39 South Magnolia Avenue, circa 1886, a former British tearoom and performance venue that is the oldest remaining building downtown. Stamped tin decorates the building inside and out; it is considered the best example of preserved sheet-metal construction in the state. Just down the street is the city's first doctor's office, the **Dr. McEwen Building** at 108 East Central Boulevard. When it was constructed between 1921 and 1923, competing for customers with the grand San Juan Hotel (demolished 1981), the **Angebilt Hotel** (now an office complex with an incredible atrium) on Orange Avenue was, at 11 stories, Orlando's first skyscraper. The **Downtown Historic District** stretches from Magnolia Avenue toward I-4, containing buildings dating back to the early 1900s, including the **Bumby Arcade** on Church St and the **Orlando Railroad Station** (see *Railroadiana*) circa 1900.

THE ROGERS BUILDING

Sandra Friend

Overlooking Lake Lucerne, the 1893 painted lady Victorian **Dr. Phillips House** is now part of the Courtyard at Lake Lucerne (see *Lodging*), but stands on its original location and is one of Orlando's oldest homes; the city's oldest home, the **1883 Norment-Parry House**, is part of the complex as well, which falls within the **Lake Cherokee Historic District**. The district encompasses a neighborhood of stately homes between Lake Lucerne and Lake Cherokee.

The **Lake Lawsona Historic District**, with its beautifully canopied brick roads and 1920s homes, is bounded by Summerlin Avenue, South Street, Hampton Avenue, and Robinson Avenue, and includes historic **Fern Creek**, a place where cattle drovers stopped to water their herds. Three other residential historic districts within city limits also celebrate the city's classic architecture, from the late 1800s to the 1930s: the **Lake Copeland Historic District**, which centers on Lake Copeland; the **Lake Eola Heights Historic District**, which sits between Lake Eola and East Colonial Drive and encompasses more than 480 buildings of historic merit; and the **Colonialtown South Historic District** between Concord Street, Ridgewood Street, and Shine Avenue.

Built in 1927 with a facade mimicking the New York Public Library (minus the lions), the **Orange County Courthouse** hosted the infamous trial of Ted Bundy; his initials can be seen scratched into the courtroom table. With the opening of a new courthouse, the building now hosts the Orange County Regional History Center (see *Museums*).

South Orlando

The **Fort Gatlin Monument** is on Gatlin Avenue just a few feet east of the intersection of Summerlin Street in south Orlando, commemorating the location of the 1838 US Army fortress that attracted settlers to the region.

College Park

Dating back to 1882, the **Erricsson-Harper House**, 19 W Princeton St, was built by a Union soldier who received a homestead land grant for his military service. Orlando's own astronaut, John Young, is commemorated with a plaque outside his birthplace along Princeton Avenue; he grew up in College Park. There is no plaque outside the **Kerouac House** (www.kerouacproject.org) at 1418 Clouser Avenue, but literature buffs make the pilgrimage anyway to pay homage. Sleeping under the stars, when the mood struck him, beneath the grand old live oak tree in the front yard, Jack Kerouac spent a year in an apartment in the back of his mother's house penning *The Dharma Bums*. This 1920s cottage now serves as a writer's retreat, with a memorabilia exhibit in the back room; the home is open for tours during the annual **Central Florida Book & Music Festival** (see *Special Events*).

MURALS Look for a colorful **mural of lizards and flowers** climbing up a picket fence on the side of the parking garage at Central Boulevard and Rosalind Avenue. A **Wyland sea life mural** graces the side of a shop along East Colonial Dr near Mills Ave, and a mural commemorating the **history of the telephone** is on the side of the AT&T building across from the historic Orange County Courthouse. A historic **Coca-Cola advertising mural** graces the side of the redbrick building housing Parky's Deli at 71 E Church St.

Downtown

♂ & **Orange County Regional History Center** (407-836-8500; www.the
historycenter.org), 65 E Central Blvd, in the historic Orange County Courthouse, uses bold graphics and engaging interactive displays to tell the story of
Orlando. Start your tour with the multimedia presentation in the Linda W.
Chapin Theatre and move on to ancient cultures and geology; I loved the
human-sized Winter Park Sinkhole that you can stand in and examine closely.
Sounds and aromas bring the outdoors inside, with tactile exhibits like logs,
cowhide, and mattresses stuffed with Spanish moss. Walk through the history of
the cattle and citrus industries and on to the kingdoms—those of Henry Sanford,
the Florida land boom, and Disney. Mon–Sat 10–5, Sun 12–5, $10 adults, $3.50
ages 3–12, $6.50 students and seniors.

Orlando Fire Museum (407-898-3138), 814 E Rollins St. Built in the 1920s to
house horse-drawn steamer trucks, this historic firehouse is now a newly renovated museum showcasing antique fire equipment such as ladder trucks, steam-
ers, and pumpers. Free.

Wells' Built Museum of African American History (407-245-7535; www
.pastinc.org), 511 W South St. Dr. William M. Wells was a prominent African
American musician and owner of the
South Street Casino, where Count
Basie, Ella Fitzgerald, Cab Calloway,
and hundreds of other regulars
played during segregation. The Well-
s' Built Hotel opened next door to
house acts and visitors. The museum
traces the history of Orlando's
African American community and
displays African art on loan. Open
Mon–Fri 9–5; free.

Mills Ave

Loch Haven Park is the one-stop
cultural center of Orlando, the up-
and-coming Alden Arts District, with
the Orlando Science Center, Shakespeare Festival, Folk Art Museum,
Mennello Museum, Orlando Museum
of Art, and Civic Theatre Complex.
Whimsical art is scattered along the
winding paths throughout the park;
brightly colored Adirondack chairs
invite you to stay and sit a spell along
the lakes.

THE ORANGE COUNTY HISTORY CENTER

Sandra Friend

Mennello Museum of American Folk Art (407-246-4278; www.mennello museum.com), 900 E Princeton St, shows off the city's collection of southern folk art and the lifework of Maine sea captain Earl Cunningham (1893–1977), whose nautical folk art oils on Masonite simply glow; look carefully to note the tremendous depth of detail on each piece. Some of the museum's galleries are dedicated to rotating exhibits on world folk art. Open Tue–Sat 11–5, Sun noon–5; fee.

Founded in 1924, the **Orlando Museum of Art** (407-896-9920; www.omart .org), 2416 N Mills Ave, covers a broad spectrum of art, from American classics to African, ancient Americas, and exhibits by contemporary artists. Open Tue–Fri 10–4, Sun noon–4; fee.

✧ ♿ Kids can be kids at the four-story **Orlando Science Center** (407-514-2000 or 1-877-208-1350; www.osc.org), 777 E Princeton St, where interactive fun rules, in themed areas like Science City, Body Zone, and Kidstown (where you must be under 48 inches to enter). At 123 Math Avenue, exhibits make it easy to understand how math works at home, and Physics Park lets you build bridges and roller coasters. On the bottom floor, NatureWorks focuses on Florida habitats, with alligators swimming across a cypress swamp, mangroves marching along a shoreline, and sinkholes forming (as they do) in Orlando roads. There were lines out the door for a peek through the observatory telescope when Mars drew close to the earth, and the eight-story Dr. Phillips CineDome offers one of the top IMAX experiences in the state. Be sure to stop in the Science Store for the coolest toys and books for kids. The "Unlimited Ticket" offers admission to the exhibit halls, planetarium, observatory, and CineDome films for one price: $23 adults, $21 seniors, $18 ages 3–11. Open Sun–Thu 10–6, Fri–Sat 10–9.

THE ORLANDO RAILROAD STATION ON CHURCH ST

Sandra Friend

RAILROADIANA At the **Orlando Railroad Station**, 76–78 W Church St, see the original brick South Florida Railroad depot, dedicated Jan 14, 1900. Built in the Queen Anne style, it was part of the Plant System. To add to the picturesque view, a steam train has been parked here for years—it was part of the show at the now-defunct Church Street Station.

SPORTS The **Orlando Predators** (407-447-7337; www.orlandopredators.com) are an arena football team playing in the TD Waterhouse Centre, 600 W Amelia St, downtown. Sharing the space during basketball season is the popular **Orlando Magic** (1-800-338-0005; www.orlandomagic.com), playing Nov–Apr.

Originally built in 1936, the **Florida Citrus Bowl Stadium** (407-849-2001; www.fcsports.com), 1610 W Church St, has been revamped several times over the decades, and hosts the annual New Year's collegiate football game, the Florida Citrus Bowl, plus events like the Superbowl of Motorsports and UCF Knights football. Adjoining **Tinker Field**, 287 S Tampa Ave, is a 5,500-seat baseball stadium hosting amateur and semipro baseball games; it's used as an alternate site for some major-league spring training.

✳ To Do

BICYCLING Explore the city via the **Orlando Bikeway System** (www.cityoforlando.net/planning/transportation/bikeways/default.htm), a network of dedicated bicycle paths and bike routes that includes the popular Cady Way Trail (see *Greenways*). In College Park you can rent a bike from **Orange Cycle** (407-422-5552), 2204 Edgewater Dr.

BOAT EXCURSIONS Drift across downtown's Lake Eola in a showy **swan boat** (407-232-0111), the lake's signature craft, with rentals at Lake Eola Cafe—$12 per half hour, Mon–Fri 12–8, Sat–Sun 10–8, three people per boat, closed in bad weather.

FAMILY ACTIVITIES ✿ For a big list of fun family things to do in the city of Orlando, visit the **City of Orlando Recreation Bureau** Web site (www.cityoforlando.net/fpr/net/index.aspx), where you can pull up lists of activities that you and the kids can do together in parks around the region. One specialized park is **Orlando**

SWAN BOATS AT LAKE EOLA

Sandra Friend

Skate Park (407-898-9600; www.actionparkalliance.com/orlando.htm), Central Blvd near Primrose Dr, which offers fun for skateboarders in a flow course and giant bowl, a virtual swimming pool without water; bring your own safety gear or rent theirs. It costs $6 for a 3-hour session. Nearby **Colonial Lanes** (407-894-0361), 400 N Primrose Dr, is a great place to take the family out bowling; open daily 9 AM–midnight or later.

FISHING Thanks to a partnership between Orange County Parks and Recreation and the Florida Fish and Wildlife Conservation Commission known as **Fish Orlando!** (407-317-7329; www.floridafisheries.com/fishorlando), some city parks are stocked with top-quality channel catfish and largemouth bass; get a copy of their brochure for a list of more than 50 regional destinations. At **Shadow Bay Park** (407-296-5191), 5100 Turkey Lake Rd, you can borrow fishing equipment and teach the kids to fish at Lupine Pond; catch-and-release encouraged, limit one catfish over 30 inches per day. **Turkey Lake Park** (see *Parks*) offers fishing in a fully rigged Tracker Bass Boat sponsored by Bass Pro Shops, available Thu–Sun 7–11 AM, fee.

GOLF Boggy Creek Golf Club (407-857-0280), 3650 Eighth St, offers golfing on a mostly flat nine-hole public course with wide-open fairways and small greens; a driving range and putting green are available.

For a taste of golfing the genteel Old South, play the historic **Dubsdread Golf Course** (407-650-9558; www.golfdubsdread.com), 549 W Par St, established in 1924 by Carl Dann Sr. "in the middle of nowhere." The city grew to encompass the course, which is now a ribbon of green shaded by ancient live oaks, stretching from College Park toward Winter Park. During World War II the facility became the unofficial officers' club, and it retains that proper feel; the Tap Room at Dubsdread (see *Dining Out*) is a fine place for a special meal. The 18-hole course just underwent a 16-month renovation back to its former glory.

HIKING Enjoy more than a mile of hiking at **Turkey Lake Park**, where you'll walk through oak hammocks and along wetlands fringing the shore of Turkey Lake. Other brief city nature walks can be taken in a semi-wilderness setting at **Dickson Azalea Park** and **Langford Park**. See *Parks*.

SCENIC DRIVES For a real taste of old Orlando, follow Central Blvd east out of downtown toward the Orlando Executive Airport, where grand old live oaks dwarf modest 1920s homes along brick streets in the **Lake Lawsona Historic District** (see *Historic Sites*). Past Fern Creek and Langford Park, turn left on Mills Ave to return to the endless strip mall that is E Colonial Dr (FL 50).

SPAS The **Urban Spa** (407-481-8485; www.eoinn.com) at Eo Inn (see *Lodging*) provides a full menu of delightful pampering, from indulgence packages including facials and full-body massage to couples massage, aromatherapy wraps, salon services, and waxing. Services start at $15 for waxing and pedicures, $45 for skin treatments (including wraps) and reflexology massage.

Downtown

Pick up a copy of the **Historic Downtown Orlando Walking Tour** brochure
at the Orange County Regional History Center (see *Museums*), where your 13-
point tour of downtown history begins. Presented by the Historical Society of
Central Florida, each of the Orlando Remembered exhibits along the route
depicts city history with a montage of paintings, period photographs, and artifacts like doorknobs and tambourines. Interested in knowing more about **Orlando City Hall**? Call the office of the city clerk (407-246-3308; www.cityoforlando
.net), 400 S Orange Ave, to arrange a tour. The Orlando Parks Bureau (407-246-
2827), 195 N Rosalind Ave, can set up tours of Lake Eola Park and historic sites
within the city.

College Park

An annual **College Park Neighborhood Association Historic Homes Tour**
(407-898-2946; www.collegeparkorlando.org), held in Dec, opens the doors of
College Park's most interesting homes, which are nestled in oak-canopied subdivisions dating back to the 1920s. Donation.

✳ Green Space

BEACHES Warren Park (407-858-3289), 3406 Warren Park Dr, north of FL 528
on Daetwyler Rd. A small sand beach along the lake is a perfect place to take the
tots to build sand castles. Open 8–8 summer, 8–6 winter.

GARDENS Dickson Azalea Park (407-246-2283), 100 Rosearden Dr, between
Central Blvd and Robinson Blvd, is a linear park that follows historic Fern Creek,
crossing the winding tree-shaded waterway several times on bridges. Park your
car at the Langford Park Neighborhood Center and walk along the creek to enjoy
hundreds of azaleas dripping pink and magenta blooms in February.

✑ ⅄ **Harry P. Leu Gardens** (407-246-2620; www.leugardens.org), 1920 N Forest Ave. Nestled along Lake Rowena in a residential area shaded by grand old
live oaks, the nearly 50 acres of
botanical gardens are broken up into
themed areas such as Native Wetlands, Rose Garden, Annual Garden,
and the North and South Woods, with
more than a mile of paved paths
meandering through the gardens. My
favorite place is the Tropical Stream
Garden, completed in 2000, lush with
banana trees, ginger, ferns, palms,
orchids, and bromeliads along bur-
bling streams. Opened in 1962, Leu
Gardens owes its spectacular collection of camellias (one of the largest in
the country) and tropical plants to

DICKSON AZALEA PARK

Sandra Friend

Harry P. Leu, a businessman and horticultural enthusiast who traveled world-wide to collect seeds and plants; the Leus' 1880s home, now the Leu House Museum, is open to the public for tours as part of the garden's admission. Civic and cultural groups meet regularly at the Garden House, where you might catch folk musicians or the Orlando Symphony; this is one of the most popular venues in the region for weddings. The gift shop at the Garden House offers an excellent selection of books on botany, gardening, and Florida history. Open 9–5 daily; Leu House closed in July. Fee.

GREENWAYS ᵬ **Cady Way Trail** (407-836-6160), 1360 Truman Rd, is a 3.8-mile urban greenway with a paved bicycle path connecting the Fashion Square Mall on East Colonial Drive with the Cady Way Pool in Winter Park; you'll find trailhead parking at both ends of the trail.

PARKS The city of Orlando has 83 public parks, mostly small neighborhood playgrounds and green space with picnicking. If you love the outdoors, here are some you shouldn't miss:

Tiny **Big Tree Park**, 930 N Thornton Ave, protects a live oak more than 500 years old; its branches shade almost the entire park.

Lake Eola Park (407-246-2827), 195 N Rosalind Ave, dominates downtown Orlando and enjoys special protection as part of a land grant left to the city by Florida cattle baron Jacob Summerlin, who settled here in 1873. The lake is the site of the first encampment by US Army troops entering the area during the Second Seminole War, and is encircled by beautifully landscaped grounds and a paved walking trail. Stop to enjoy a bench in the shade, catch a play at the Walt Disney Amphitheatre, or feed the ducks and swans at the Chinese "Ting" gazebo. Elegant swan boats ply the waters; to rent one, stop by the Lake Eola Cafe (see *Boat Excursions*).

Lake Fairview Park (407-246-2288), 2200 Lee Rd, provides access to Lake Fairview with a boat ramp and public beach, picnic and playground facilities, and athletic fields.

Major Carl T. Langford Park (407-246-2150), 1808 E Central Blvd, has playgrounds, ball fields, boardwalks over marshes, and winding paths under the old oak trees; don't miss the swinging bridge across Fern Creek. It's one of the few places in the city you'll see wildlife—I encountered a Florida box turtle along my walk.

LAKE EOLA

Sandra Friend

⚓ At **Turkey Lake Park** (407-299-5594), 3401 Hiawassee Rd, take the family out for a picnic, kayak on the lake, get out your bike and take on more than 2 miles of trails, or hike around the 300-acre preserve. Kids will love the Cracker farm with its barnyard animals, and you can even rent a fully equipped bass boat (see *Fishing*) to try your luck on the lake.

In addition, the city owns and maintains **Orlando Wetlands Park** (see "North of Orlando") near Christmas.

✳ Lodging

BED & BREAKFASTS

Downtown 32801

❝⟊❞ ∞ **The Courtyard at Lake Lucerne** (407-648-5188; www .orlandohistoricinn.com), 211 N Lucerne Circle E. Few cities let you sleep with their history, but at the Courtyard, you can relax in Dr. Phillips's bedroom and mull over his contributions to Florida's citrus industry. The Dr. Phillips House is a masterpiece of grand Victorian archi-tecture circa 1893, faithfully restored by the Meiner family and tastefully decorated with period furnishings and special touches. Guests especially enjoy the two romantic turret rooms—Room 405, with a sleigh bed and brick fireplace, and Room 406, with a fireplace and Jacuzzi—for their sweeping views of Lake Lucerne. I've stayed here several times in different parts of the complex and enjoyed relaxing in the oasis of tropical gar-dens connecting the four historic buildings. $150–225.

Thornton Park 32801

🐾 ∞ **The Veranda** (1-800-420-6822; www.theverandabandb.com), 115 N Summerlin Ave. With 12 lavish rooms ($99–139), a cottage ($169), and a honeymoon suite ($189) arranged around a large oak-canopied court-yard, this is a fabulous place to stay right in the middle of Thornton Park. Every room is unique. Two of the more modern rooms, the Magnolia and Washington, feature four-poster bed and Jacuzzi, and overlook

bustling Pine Street. Breakfast is served family style in the dining room adjoining the office.

HOTELS, MOTELS, AND RESORTS

Downtown 32801

⤳ ❝⟊❞ 🐾 ♿ In its own shady oasis, the **Courtyard by Marriott** (407-996-1000; www.marriott.com), 730 N Magnolia, is a relaxing getaway geared towards business travelers, with an executive work desk in every room ($119 and up). A breakfast buffet ($10) is served in the restaurant each morning, and the lobby bar is open in the evenings. Relax around the pool or keep fit in the workout room. Some rooms have hydromassage tubs, and

DR. PHILLIPS HOUSE, THE COURTYARD AT LAKE LUCERNE

Sandra Friend

the king suites are like a small apartment, perfect for extended stays.

"1" ♿ **Embassy Suites** (407-841-1000; www.embassysuites.com), 191 E Pine St. A seven-story indoor atrium lends light to 167 two-room suites ($150 and up), each with separate bedroom and living room; the hotel is in the thick of the action, within walking distance of all downtown Orlando. Guests receive a cooked-to-order breakfast as part of their room rate.

"1" ∞ ♿ From the ebony pillars and gilded moldings to the textured Italian tile underfoot, the grandeur of the Renaissance meets the sleek lines of today at the **Grand Bohemian Hotel** (407-313-9000 or 1-866-663-0024; www.grandbohemianhotel .com), 325 S Orange Ave. Marvel at more than 200 original paintings and sculptures handpicked by owner Richard Kessler and showcased throughout the hotel—from the formal Grand Bohemian Art Gallery off the lobby to the pieces (all for sale, just ask) hanging on the walls of your room, in the common areas, and even in the public restrooms. Each spacious guest room (from $250) extends the luxury of a pillow-topped bed, fluffy duvet, and piles of pillows to in-room Starbucks coffee, a Bose CD player, a mini bar, high-speed Internet access, and surroundings appealing to the artist within. Every room has an evening view of the city lights, and you're right in the thick of the action in the Orange Avenue club district. At night patrons pack the hotel's Boheme restaurant for the finest food, and the Bösendorfer Lounge and Klimt Rotunda for martinis, live entertainment, and conversation; the richly appointed Bösendorfer piano is one of only two in the world.

Thornton Park 32801

"1" 🐾 **Eo Inn** (407-481-8485 or 1-888-481-8488; www.eoinn.com), 227 N Eola Dr. Formerly a youth hostel, this restored 1923 boutique hotel has sleek lines and simple hues that resonate with art lovers like myself. Its 17 rooms ($139–229) are a delight for working travelers—each has a built-in cubbyhole work space for setting up your laptop. Some rooms come with Jacuzzi or garden tub, or a balcony overlooking a shady courtyard. On the rooftop you'll find an exclusive urban spa (see *Spas*); downstairs, a Panera Bread. The complex is an easy walk around Lake Eola from downtown, and just up the street from fine dining in Thornton Park.

✳ Where to Eat

DINING OUT

College Park

🦞 **The Tap Room at Dubsdread** (407-650-0100; www.taproomatdubs dread.com), 549 W Par St. Talk about an Orlando classic. Steve Allen performed here. Folks still come in and tell the manager, "We got married in the dining hall 58 years ago. Mind if we take a look?" Warm wood walls accent this comfortable restaurant with its fabulous view of the Dubs-dread Golf Course. The menu offers Orlando's best burger (according to the *Orlando Sentinel*) and creative salads ($7–9) at lunch, with entrées like filet mignon, alpine chicken, and pot roast moving to the menu in the evening ($12–22).

Downtown

♿ Off the lobby of the Grand Bohemian (see *Hotels and Motels*), **The Boheme** (407-313-9000, www .grandbohemianhotel.com/theboheme) offers intimate four-star dining in a favorite venue for City Hall power lunches. Their eclectic cuisine mixes French and Asian influences, with entrées such as grilled portobella cannelloni and Thai spiced duck breast starting around $25. Open for all meals. Reservations are suggested; appropriate dress is a must.

Manuel's on the 28th (407-246-6580; www.manuelsonthe28th.com), 390 N Orange Ave. On the 28th floor, you expect an excellent view of the city skyline—and you're not disappointed. Manuel's tops the Bank of America building and is a favorite of the late-night crowd, serving dinner entrées like fennel-roasted rack of lamb and steamed lobster, $18 and up, 6–10 PM Tue–Sat. Reservations recommended, jackets suggested.

East Colonial

Barney's Steak and Seafood (407-896-6864; www.barneyssteakhouse .com), 1615 E Colonial Dr. Sometimes I get a major craving for steak, and if I'm nearby, I seek out Barney's, an Orlando landmark since 1975. Their New York strip smothered in mushrooms is simply delightful, and with a huge salad bar and fast service, it rivals its competitors for the money. Many of the entrées are offered "light size" for a bargain price, and the early-bird specials are the best around. Open for lunch and dinner; entrées $18–50.

Orange Ave

🌸 **La Coq Au Vin** (407-851-6980), 4800 S Orange Ave. I can forever thank my former boss for taking the staff here for a Christmas party; we had my farewell party here, too. Owners Louis and Magdalena Perrotte are used to hosting private parties, as well as most of their competitors—this is

the place that area chefs come to dine. It's fabulous and unpretentious French cuisine, from their signature coq au vin to the scrumptious chocolate mousse; entrées start around $14. Lunch served Tue–Fri 11:30–2, dinner Tue–Sat 5:30–10 and Sun 5–9.

Thornton Park

Cityfish (407-849-9779; www.city fishorlando.com), 617 E Central Ave, is the new haute cuisine choice along Central Blvd, serving sushi and the freshest fish from every corner of the globe. On any given day, oyster po'boys may share the menu with Alaskan king crab legs, fried Ipswich clams, and Maine lobster roll.

Like its counterpart in Winter Park, **Dexter's** (407-648-2777; www.dex wine.com), 808 E Washington Ave, is a place to see and be seen, with food worth waiting for ($18–25). Hang out on the patio and enjoy the view.

With a name like **Fifi's** (407-481-2250), 100 S Eola Dr, I was expecting poodles, but what I found was a sumptuous repast ($15–30) shared with friends. After a grilled romaine wedge, my bowl of handcrafted but-

HUE, THORNTON PARK'S SOURCE FOR PAN-ASIAN FUSION FOOD AND JAZZ

Sandra Friend

ternut squash ravioli, with a hint of toasted butter and sage, was a lavish follow-up. Paired with the perfect wine, it made for a memorable meal.

Hue (407-849-1800; www.huerestau rant.com), 629 E Central Blvd, is the hip and happening place in Thornton Park, where jazz and modern art meet over pan-Asian fusion food ($22 and up) like oven-roasted Chilean sea bass with Asiago tapenade and wok-seared ahi tuna with a sesame ginger glaze. At lunch try the sirloin burger or lemon pappardelle pasta.

EATING OUT

Downtown
Wicker sofas and flickering candle-light sets the tone at **Brix Eurobistro** (407-839-1707), 151 E Washington St, where viscous entrées ($7–12) in the form of soups, bisques, and fondues provide an array of textures and tastes. Pair Granny Smith slices with beer cheese fondue, or sup on mush-room and Brie bisque. It's a creative concept, and with a sidewalk café right across from Lake Eola, a popu-lar evening destination.

&. In an upscale urban atmosphere dropped right in from Tokyo, **Ichiban Japanese Restaurant** (407-423-2688), 19 S Orange Ave. offers sushi and traditional bento box lunches (a great bargain) for $5 and up; open for dinner, too.

Looking for take-out for a lakeside lunch? **Metro Espresso Pizza Cafe** (407-422-5282), 417 E. Central Blvd, may be up your alley. Serving pizza by the slice and a simply super Greek salad along with hot Italian subs ($2–7), it's a worthy lunch or dinner break and just a block from Lake Eola.

College Park
🍴 Celebrating 50-plus years of serving up subs, **Gabriels Sub Shop** (407-425-9926), 3006 Edgewater Dr, is right next to the high school my hus-band graduated from, and it's certain-ly where the kids stop in after class. Catch them at a quieter time to enjoy their famous subs ($4–7), of which meatball and cheesesteak are hot sell-ers, but I love the stacked ham and cheese with provolone, lettuce, onions, pickles, and oregano. Eat in or carry out; closed Sun.

When I worked nearby, one of my lunch standards was the **Princeton Diner** (407-425-5046), 3310 Edgewa-ter Dr, where meatloaf and mashed potatoes went great with a freshly made chocolate milkshake; serving breakfast and lunch for under $7.

🍴 **Shakers** (407-422-3534), 1308 Edgewater Dr. Vintage salt and pep-per shakers crowd shelves and table-tops in this great family restaurant, where the breakfast selections (start-ing at $3) include goodies like almond pancakes and Greek omelets, and lunch salads, and quiches; specialty sandwiches ($5–10) include Mom's Meatloaf, spinach salad, and the tasty Orlando Grill with spinach, mush-rooms, tomatoes, and provolone grilled on pumpernickel, topped with a special dressing. Yum!

West Colonial
O'Boys Real Smoked Barbecue (407-425-OBOY; www.oboysbbq.net), 924 W Colonial Ave. Serving up mounds of real smoked barbecue (starting under $8) to an overflowing lunch crowd, O'Boys is an institution in the Edgewater area. If you're wary of ribs but want to give the taste a try, their riblets will tickle your fancy. My top pick: the overly generous chef

salads topped with a choice of barbecue beef, pork, or chicken, laced with a heaping helping of homemade barbecue sauce and your choice of dressing.

East Colonial

🍴 An Orlando classic that my generation grew up on, **Beefy King** (407-894-2241; www.beefyking.com), 424 N Bumby Ave, serves up slow-cooked real roast beef sandwiches fit for a king, chicken sandwiches with the slaw on top, and thick orange shakes: It's what fast food ought to be. Grab a meal for $4 and up.

With its distinctive bit of roadside Americana (the giant fork), **Hot Dog Heaven** (407-282-5746; www.hot dogheaven.com), 5355 E Colonial Dr, beckons with all-beef hot dogs. Try the southern-style dog with slaw, the New York–style with onions and mustard, or the Chicago-style ($3 and up) with onions, peppers, and relish. Great root beer floats, too!

When I worked nearby, **Little Saigon** (407-423-8539; www.little saigonrestaurant.com), 1106 E Colonial Dr was a great lunch stop with a menu made up of photographs—if you don't know Vietnamese food, it certainly helps! Their hearty noodle-thick soups ($6) can't be beat, and I would often make an inexpensive meal of their massive summer rolls (spring rolls with a twist—wrapped in rice paper rather than fried), served with tasty peanut dipping sauce ($3).

A favorite of downtown workers, especially for the folks across the street at the *Orlando Sentinel*, **Mama B's Giant Subs** (407-422-7353), 692 N Orange Ave, serves up massive New York subs hot and cold.

🍴 Wrapped in wall murals of Asia, **Viet Garden** (407-896-4154; www

.vietgardenorlando.com), 1237 E Colonial Dr, is a Thai and Vietnamese restaurant I've patronized time and again. At either lunch or dinner ($8 and up), settle back and enjoy fresh garden rolls, chicken cashew nut, and a tall glass of Thai iced tea.

Orange Ave

At **Cecil's Texas Style Barbecue** (407-423-9871), 2800 S Orange Ave, you dish your own side dishes—pile it on! Hickory-smoked BBQ ($5–12) is the centerpiece of the meal. I'm partial to the pork, and won't miss the cheesy au gratin potatoes. U-serve soft serve ice cream included with every dinner!

A fun stop for dessert—with homemade sundaes, shakes, and pies—**Shannon's Casual Cafe** (407-855-9995), 4401 S Orange Ave, also offers great burgers and club sandwiches.

Step into **White Wolf Cafe** (407-895-9911; www.whitewolfcafe.com), 1829 N Orange Ave, a classy antiques-bedecked bistro with marble-slab tables, and savor some of the best salads Orlando has to offer, served up with unique fresh breads. My favorites: the White Wolf Waldorf, the Greek salad with real kalamata olives, and the vegetarian plate with mango-almond tabouli and black bean hummus. They serve lunch and dinner (except Sun), with entrées $9–12, and daily flatbread pizzas.

Semoran Blvd

🍴 I love Thai food, and **Royal Thai** (407-275-0776), 1202 N Semoran Blvd, never disappoints, no matter whether I'm ordering spring rolls and tom yum goong or a full entrée ($8–14) like pa-nang or drunken noodles. If you order your entrée hot, it will be fiery.

Virginia Dr

In the antiques and arts district, snazzy **Logan's Bistro** (407-898-5688), 802 Virginia Dr, offers tasty quesadillas, daily quiches, and entrées ($15 and up) like free-range chicken, chicken pot pie, and Veal Shank Redemption.

Thornton Park

Sit beneath the canopy at **Anthony's Pizzeria and Restaurant** (407-648-0009; www.anthonyspizza.com), 100 Summerlin Ave. and savor the aroma of fresh-baked dough as you enjoy hearty slices of authentic New York pizza. One of their specialties is the VIP Stuffed Pizza ($29), with cold cuts wedged between layers of veggies and melted mozzarella cheese inside a crispy crust. Pasta and Italian entrées $9–15.

Wildfires BBQ (407-872-8665), 700 E Washington St, is an upscale barbecue and grill where they take gator bites and drizzle them with roasted garlic aioli; oak-grilled sandwiches and house-smoked barbecue (served with a colorful side of tortilla chips and watermelon) make great lunch choices, and it's fun to sit on the patio and watch the world go by. Entrées $7 and up.

BAKERIES, COFFEE SHOPS, DELIS, AND ICE CREAM

Downtown

In the historic Rogers Building (see *Historic Sites*), the **O'Town Art Café and Wine Bar** (407-620-6344), 37 Magnolia Ave, is a relaxing coffee klatch hangout by day, a buzzing bar by night, where microbrews and fine wines can be savored in surroundings that include original art—and no smoking.

"**I**" A neighborhood grocery and deli, **903 Mills Market** (407-898-4392; www.millsmarket.com), 903 S Mills Ave, is right in the middle of a residential district and thus a gathering place for friends out on the patio. Creations include the usual Reubens and Cubans and then stray into the offbeat, like the Grateful Bread—roasted turkey, cranberry mayo, blue cheese stuffing, and red onions on wheat. Sandwiches, wraps, salads, and breakfast items, $4–8; open daily.

Dover Gardens

In 1971, veteran baker Charlie Hawks left the famed Wolfie's in South Beach to start his own shop in Orlando, **Charlie's Gourmet Pastries** (407-898-9561; www.charliesgourmet pastries.com), 3213 Curry Ford Rd. It's the sweet stuff my husband grew up with; no birthday was complete without a cake from Charlie's. All the goodies are full of butter and sugar in recipes passed down through three generations—well worth a little detour for a taste.

Thornton Park

In a coffee-colored cottage circa 1922, the **Aroma Coffee and Wine Bar** (407-426-8989), 712 E Washington St, is a cozy retreat to sip a latte or other Italian delight off their *lista dei caffe*. They passed my husband's Snickers test—one complicated coffee drink down pat. Panini and antipasto make their debut at lunch, and decadent desserts are available all the time.

The lemon gelato is sharp and tart, just like I like it, and it's one of the simpler flavors at **il Gelatone** (407-839-8825; www.ilgelatone-usa.com), 8 N Summerlin Ave, an authentic Italian gelataria where creations run toward Nutella Brownie Caffé, Hot Pepper Chocolate, and Panna Cotta; savor each tiny nibble, starting at $3.25.

FARMER'S MARKETS The **Downtown Farmer's Market** in the plaza in front of the Orange County Regional History Center happens every Saturday morning 7–1; amble through and follow your nose to tasty baked goods and fresh-cut flowers. Streets are blockaded so residents can browse fresh produce at the weekly **College Park Farmer's Market**, downtown College Park along Edgewater between Princeton and Smith, Thu 6:30–7:30 PM.

✳ Selective Shopping

College Park

At **Acacia Collectibles** (407-872-2374), 1313 Edgewater Dr, look for fuzzy blueware, antique pottery, and costume jewelry.

Beyond Words (407-316-8622), 1315 Edgewater Dr, offers a fabulous selection of children's books, plus home decor items like wreaths and candles.

The original dress shop on this block a decade ago, **Bijou's Boutique** (407-841-9728; www.bijousboutique.com), 2501 Edgewater Dr, features fancy purses and dressy clothing with a French flair.

Step into the soothing world of **Drema's Gallery of Dreams** (407-236-7878), 2525 Edgewater Dr, for delightful works of art and decor items in a melding of New Age and Asian influences, where you'll find frogs and mermaids, angels and fairies, pillows cloaked in Rajasthani fabrics, and soap-bubble-like witch balls; ask about their drumming circles and yoga classes.

My Secret Garden (407-246-1975), 2300 Edgewater Dr, carries floral soaps and gift items.

Truffles and Trifles (407-648-0838), 711 W Smith St, is a fine gourmet kitchen shop that will tempt you in with gourmet foods in the window; it's a great place to look for cookbooks.

Corrine Dr

The **Bead Lounge** (407-894-8941), 2912 Corrine Dr, has all the raw materials you need for inspired creations—strings of colorful precious gems and clay beads—and the place to sit down and make your own necklaces on the spot.

It's got that heavy-metal grunge warehouse look inside, but **Park Avenue CDs** (407-629-5293), 2916 Corrine Dr, has a darn good selection of everything from pop to world and especially blues and jazz. Mix of used and new CDs.

What a surprise to find **Orlando Outfitters** (407-896-8220; www.orlandooutfitters.com), 2814 Corrine Dr, in this decidedly urban setting! While I was able to pick up some technical clothing for hiking off the sales rack, their stock-in-trade here is fly fishing, with an enormous selection of materials to stand here and tie your own flies; they'll even help you arrange fly-fishing trips and they offer fly-tying classes.

Downtown

At **Art Angels Market** (407-872-3884), 430 E Central Ave, shimmering glass draws the eye to a delight of shiny gift objects, including veils, feather boas, scarves, and little glass angels.

Grand Bohemian Gallery (407-581-4801), 325 S Orange Ave. Befitting the grandeur of its setting in the Westin Grand Bohemian (see *Lodging*), this gallery showcases massive works by local artists, including Yuri

Maiorov, the ribbon-clad flier of Cirque du Soleil, who photographs his fellow performers in black and white, and Todd Lundeen, with his haunting images of Nepal. In addition to photography, enjoy the grand oil paintings, soapstone carvings, art glass, and fine selection of handcrafted jewelry.

Nightly "wine flights" draw a crowd at the **Eola Wine Company** (407-481-9100; www.eolawinecompany.com), 500 E. Central Ave, where these specialized tastings include 2-ounce samples of several of the featured wines. Hang out in the bar for a bit of chatter, or simply savor the luxury of shopping more than 200 wines.

Mills Ave

Colonial Photo & Hobby (407-841-1485), 634 N Mills Ave, is where I head for consultations on camera equipment and for next-day slide developing; they also carry a large stock of professional films. Half the store is devoted to models (airplanes, trains, cars, boats), so it's fun for the kids, too.

Ritzy Rags (407-897-2117), 928 N Mills Ave, is your glam stop for funky clothing, be it vintage duds or dress-up for a masquerade party.

Orange Ave

At **Boom-Art** (407-281-0246; www.rainfall.com/boom-art), 1821 N Orange Ave, artists Glenn and Sandy Rogers create "recycled art," vibrant and affordable pop art pieces with comic-book flair; they'll keep you in touch with your inner child.

In **The Fly Fisherman** (407-898-1989), 1213 N Orange Ave, shop for upscale outdoor clothing and fishing tackle in a relaxed atmosphere.

In the green brick house, **Golden Phoenix Antiques** (407-895-6006),

1826 N Orange Ave, melds the exotic and commonplace, with garden wicker and floral-print dishes next to brass trays from Turkey.

Humbugs Antiques, Furniture, and Non Sense (407-895-0155), 1618 N Orange Ave, has fine furnishings with Asian and European influences, and interesting ephemera.

Step back into the 1960s at **Rock & Roll Heaven** (407-896-1952; www.rock-n-rollheaven.com), 1814 N Orange Ave, and browse through Orlando's largest collection of vintage vinyl, cassettes, and eight-tracks.

Tim's Wine Market (407-895-8463; www.timswine.com), 1223 N Orange Ave, had that rare Inniskillin ice wine I've been on the lookout for, plus hundreds of other options at reasonable prices. Tim hosts regular wine tastings and seminars; call for reservations.

Thornton Park

Fashionistas will appreciate the selection at **Marie-France** (407-835-8855; www.marie-franceinc.com), 716 E Washington St, where imported casual wear comes from designers with flair. They commission their own line of vintage jewelry, so the selection is superb.

❦ **Urban Think! Bookstore** (407-650-8004; www.urbanthinkorlando.com), 625 E Central Blvd, plays off its name with mod surroundings decked out with fine art from local artists, a coffee bar with comfortable chairs, and urban glamour mags. In an age where independent booksellers truly struggle, I salute Jim Crescitelli for providing his city's literati a place to hang out and discuss philosophy or pore over the newest in literary fiction.

Designer duds shine at **Zou Zou Chic Boutique** (407-843-3373; www.zouzouboutique.com), 2 N Summerlin Ave, where creations by Ella Moss and Rebecca Taylor rub shoulders with Lexi Lu jewelry.

Virginia Dr
Atlantis Art Glass Studio, Inc. (407-896-9116), 809 Virginia Dr. Creative multilayered stained-glass pieces decorate the front room of this studio, where you can pick up supplies and take classes on the art.

Flag World (407-895-9245; www .aflagworld.com), 728 Virginia Dr. If you need a flag—any flag—this is the place. Pick your country and size; they sell seasonal house banners and pennants.

✳ Entertainment

FINE ARTS **The Dr. Phillips Center for the Performing Arts**, 1111 N Orange Ave, hosts performances of the Orlando Ballet (407-426-1739; www.orlandoballet.org) Sep–May, and the **Orlando Opera Company** (1-800-336-7372; www.orlandoopera .org), with three main-stage and four minor productions each year.

Southern Ballet Theatre (407-426-1733), for two decades Central Florida's only professional troupe, performs seasonally at the Bob Carr Performing Arts Centre, as does the **Orlando Philharmonic Orchestra** (407-896-6700; www.orlandophil.org) and its guest symphonic orchestras during the annual Festival of Orchestras (407-896-2451; www.festivalof orchestras.com).

THEATER From Broadway shows to symphony performances, high-ticket entertainment stops at the **Bob Carr Performing Arts Centre** (407-849-2001; www.orlandocentroplex.com), 401 W Livingston St,. on tours.

At the **John and Rita Lowndes Shakespeare Center** (407-477-1700), 812 E Rollins St, the play's the thing! It wasn't until I started attending the Orlando-UCF Shakespeare Festival (www.shakespearefest.org) that my background in English lit actually meant something . . . to see Shakespeare performed means so much more than just reading the words. I was blown away by *The Taming of the Shrew*. The venue's the thing, too—what an incredible location, with the old John Young Science Center renovated to provide three different theaters for various-sized plays. And if you'd rather enjoy the Bard outdoors, try Shakespeare in the Park under the bandshell along Lake Eola every Apr.

Mad Cow Theatre (407-297-8788; www.madcowtheatre.com), 105 E Pine St, presents off-off-Broadway versions of modern classics and contemporary plays in an intimate downtown venue with regular productions.

Orlando Theatre Downtown (407-841-0083; www.theatredowntown .net), 2113 N Orange Ave. During *A Streetcar Named Desire* chills went down my spine when Stanley threw his meal at Stella; they were so close I wanted to scream at him for treating her that way. Great shows and an intimate setting (125 seats) surrounding the stage make this an outstanding venue. Studio Theatre (407-872-2382; www.orlandotheatre.com), 398 W Amelia St, provides another intimate theater experience with seats right next to the stage.

Plaza Theatre (407-228-1220; www .theplazatheatre.com), 425 N Bumby Ave. This Orlando landmark from the 1960s, the former Rocking Chair Theatre, draws appreciative crowds for its variety of shows.

UCF Civic Theatre (407-896-7365; www.icflorida.com/community/groups /civic), 1001 E Princeton St, offers theater productions on three stages throughout the year, as well as classes for children and adults.

COMEDY ✨ SAK Theatre Comedy Lab (407-648-0001; www.sak.com), 380 W Amelia St. Orlando's long-standing hot spot for improv is hot—just ask Wayne Brady, an alumnus who moved on to bigger and better things. These folks are serious about perfecting their craft, not selling drinks: They put on a PG-only show, and no alcohol is served.

NIGHTCLUBS I dare say no other city in Florida is as packed with nightclubs at its core. It's not my scene, but I know they're out there, catering mainly to a college-age crowd. You'll find wall-to-wall bars and clubs along Orange Avenue near Wall Street and Church Street, and they do come and go; among the more crowded on the Saturday night I strolled by were **Zinc Bar** (407-246-1755), 13 S Orange and **Big Belly Brewery** (407-649-4270), 33 W Church St. Take a late-night stroll through the district; with more than 30 choices, you'll find one to suit your tastes.

✳ Special Events

February: **Central Florida Fair** (407-295-3247; www.centralflorida fair.com), 4603 W Colonial Dr, is the region's big traditional county fair, with rides, music headliners, and more at the Orange County Fairgrounds.

February–April: **Firelight Fridays at Lake Eola Park**. Sunset, second Sat. Savor the city skyline at sunset while listening to live jazz, opera, and classical music as you stroll with your sweetheart around Lake Eola.

March: **Festival of Speed** (www .festivalofspeed.org), second weekend. One of the country's top cycling events brings nearly 500 cyclists into town for 2 days of racing. On Saturday enjoy live entertainment, food, arts, and games; see the Web site for location and times.

April: The **Central Florida Book & Music Festival**, College Park, features live concerts, tours of the Kerouac House (see *Historic Sites*), arts and crafts, and a huge book sale.

Spring Fiesta in the Park, first weekend, Lake Eola Park. Browse through 175 booths of regional arts and crafts during this spring arts festival, which includes live entertainment and food vendors.

May: **Orlando International Fringe Festival** (407-648-0077; www .orlandofringe.com), 398 W Amelia St. Ten days in May devoted to nearly 500 performances of street theater, performance art, and cabaret, creatively pulled together in downtown Orlando noon–midnight. $5 cover charge; most performances held indoors.

October: **Festival Calle Orange**, last Sat, wraps 10 blocks of downtown Orlando in festive Latino music, dance, and arts, with more than 50,000 participants flocking to the city to salsa and merengue in the streets.

October–April: At the **Downtown Arts Market** (407-356-8626; www .orlando.arts), Florida artists display their creations in a juried arts show on the second Saturday of every month Oct–Apr. It's held on Wall Street adjacent to the Orange County Regional History Center (see *Museums*).

NORTH OF ORLANDO

SEMINOLE AND ORANGE COUNTIES

When I lived in this area some years ago, I was delighted to discover shady avenues and sparkling cypress-lined lakes, public gardens and thickly forested wilderness places—a stark contrast to the not-so-appealing overdeveloped open prairies that characterize the south end of the metro area, which, on my drives to the airport, I'd always assumed was what all of the Orlando metro looked like. Not so. The original communities of this region have deep roots, harking back to 1820s territorial Florida, when eager families came by steamboat and train to eke out a life on a new homestead.

Seminole County, established in 1913, follows the meandering course of the St. Johns River. Its towns reflect Florida's pioneer and boomtown history. **Oviedo** is Old Florida, settled in the 1870s, its quaint downtown now surrounded by a sea of suburbia spreading from Orlando. Although they're rapidly vanishing under developers' bulldozers, you can still find citrus groves and cattle ranches toward **Geneva** and **Chuluota**. Perusing an 1890 map of the region, I was surprised to see Crane's Roost Lake and **Altamonte Springs** listed; while there are plenty of restaurants and mall-type shopping spots in the area, you won't find anything left of the original settlement. But drive a few miles north, and it's a delight to discover the picturesque historic district of **Longwood**, established in 1878, just off FL 434. Incorporated in 1877, **Sanford** grew out of 1830s Mellonville, a settlement around Seminole War–era Fort Mellon; founder Henry Sanford devel-

ORANGE GROVES IN OVEIDO

Sandra Friend

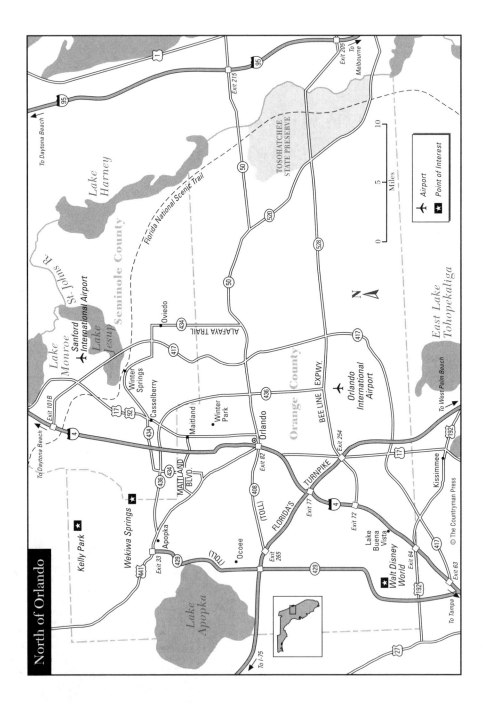

North of Orlando

oped a planned community with green space, and today most of the residential neighborhoods are fully canopied by ancient live oaks. Sanford envisioned the town, a place where rail and river transportation converged, as the gateway city for South Florida.

Orange County (which includes the city of Orlando) was once the heart of Florida's citrus industry. The settlements of **Oakland**, **Winter Garden**, **Ocoee**, **Apopka**, **Zellwood**, and **Tangerine** around the shores of Lake Apopka date back to the late 1800s and early 1900s, founded along the rail lines during the industry's heyday. Although the town of **Christmas** is best known for its busy post office, it picked up its name from Fort Christmas, completed on Dec 25, 1837, as a US Army outpost during the Second Seminole War. Similarly, **Maitland** sprang up around Fort Maitland and adjacent **Eatonville**, the nation's first free black community, incorporated in 1887. And then there's cosmopolitan **Winter Park**, founded in 1882 and so much a little city that I almost included it in the "City Neighborhoods" chapter. But it's staunchly outside the Orlando city limits and proud of it. Although its downtown is a shopper's delight, with Ann Taylor, Williams-Sonoma, and the Pottery Barn jostling for space with local art galleries and liberal arts Rollins College, Winter Park still finds the time and space for a Saturday morning farmer's market.

GUIDANCE

Seminole County
❝ℹ❞ I was thrilled to discover the **Historic Sanford Welcome Center** (407-302-2586), 230 First St, on my last trip to downtown Sanford—just the place for a visitor on foot to get her bearings. In addition to racks of brochures, restrooms, and a helpful attendant to point you in the right direction, this former post office building also has a gift shop with city-themed items, local books, quilts, images of the city, and arts and crafts from local artisans. Best of all, they're open when you're most likely to visit: Tue–Fri 11–5, Sat 9–5, and Sun 12–5, in tune with the surrounding shops. Even better, all of downtown is wired for Wi-Fi. For more about the county, contact the **Seminole County Convention & Visitors Bureau** (407-665-2900 or 1-800-800-7832; www.visitseminole.com), 1230 Douglas Ave, Suite 116, Longwood 32779.

Orange County
Orlando/Orange County Convention & Visitors Bureau (407-354-5586 or 1- 800-972-3304; www.orlandoinfo.com), 6700 Forum Dr, Suite 100, Orlando 32821.

GETTING THERE *By air:* Not just one, but two international airports cover the region. **Greater Orlando International Airport** (407-825-2001; www.state .fl.us/goaa) serves the world with hundreds of flights daily; check their Web site for contact information on the many airlines servicing Orlando. **Orlando Sanford International Airport** (407-322-7771; www.orlandosanfordairport .com) hosts many foreign charters but also offers regular commuter service on Pan Am.

By car: The region is bisected by **I-4** and **FL 417** (the Greeneway, a toll road) and bounded on its southern edge by FL 50 (**Colonial Dr**) and FL 408 (the **East–West Expressway**, another toll road).

By train: The southern terminus of the Amtrak (1-800-USA-RAIL; www.amtrak .com) **Auto-Train** is in Sanford.

By bus: **Greyhound** (1-800-229-9424; www.greyhound.com) has a major terminal on John Young Pkwy between FL 408 and FL 50.

GETTING AROUND *By car:* Everyone uses I-4 to access the northern and eastern suburbs, which is why it's a parking lot in rush hour. But **US 17-92**, **Semoran Blvd** (FL 436), and the **Orange Blossom Trail** (US 441) make great alternative routes: Despite the lights, traffic usually moves at a steady clip. E Colonial (US 50) takes you out past the University of Central Florida, while W Colonial heads to Winter Garden. Paralleling this busy road are the two toll roads on which you can make great time through the middle of Orlando: FL 408 between Ocoee and Goldenrod, and FL 417, which connects the UCF area with Oviedo and Sanford.

By bus: The Orlando metro area is served by the **Lynx** bus system (407-841-8240 in Orange County; 407-628-2897 in Seminole County), with 56 routes; look for the paw-print bus stop signs. Exact change $1.75 fare. Service runs 5:45 AM–10 PM or later.

By taxi: To summon a taxi, call **National Cab** (407-678-8888) or **Yellow Cab** (407-699-9999).

THE HISTORIC SANFORD WELCOME CENTER
Sandra Friend

By rental car: Primarily located at Orlando International Airport—but rentals can be arranged through some hotels—rental agents include **Alamo** (1-800-327-9633), **Avis** (1-800-831-2847), **Budget** (407-850-6700), **Enterprise** (1-800-736-8222), **Hertz** (1-800-654-3131), and **National Car Rental** (1-800-227-7368).

PARKING Most of Orlando's outlying communities have free surface lots and street parking, although you'll find vast metered parking lots (2- to 3-hour time limits) and parking garages just a block off Park Ave in Winter Park.

PUBLIC RESTROOMS You'll find public restrooms in Maitland, adjacent to the Maitland Art Center at **Lake Sybelia**, and in **Lake Lily Park** next to the Garden Club, and in Sanford at the new **Sanford Visitor Center** in the old Post Office.

MEDICAL EMERGENCIES There are many major hospitals in the region, including **Health Central** (407-296-1000; www.health-central.org), 10000 W Colonial Dr, Ocoee; **Florida Hospital Apopka** (407-889-1000; www.floridahospital .com), 201 N Park Ave, Apopka; **Central Florida Regional Hospital** (407-774-0455; www.centralfloridaregional.com), 916 N FL 434, Longwood; and **Florida Hospital Altamonte** (407-303-4321; www.floridahospital.com), 601 E Altamonte Dr, Altamonte Springs.

☀ To See
ART GALLERIES

Maitland
Maitland Art Center (407-539-2181; www.maitlandartcenter.org), 231 W Packwood Ave. From the street it looks like a Mayan temple complex, perfectly fitting its setting under fern-draped live oaks and lush greenery around Lake Sybelia. And indeed, a maze of outdoor courtyards leads you past works of art across the street from the art gallery and classroom space designed in the late 1930s by artist Andre Smith; the gallery showcases rotating exhibits of works of art from the permanent collection, and there's an excellent art shop. Open Mon–Fri 9–4:30, Sat and Sun noon–4:30; free.

Sanford
The exterior of the **Jeanine Taylor Folk Gallery** (407-740-0991; www.jtfolkart .com), 211 First St, will give you pause—it's a three-dimensional mural full of found objects, including dominoes and a key ring, seashells and photos and pieces of glass, all artfully arranged by "Mr. Imagination." This new venue for the gallery is its best yet. Showcasing contemporary folk artists from the Deep South, they also provide studio space to artists, so you can watch them at work. Each studio, whether occupied when you visit or not, is open for your inspection and has a bio of the current occupant and examples of his or her work. The gallery curates four to eight shows per year in its central space. Free.

Florida artists are the key to **Beth's Friends** (407-302-4664), 301 First St, which features not just the creativity of Lockhart native Beth Lawson but that of her imaginative friends as well. Robert Boynton's nature photos extend beyond their frames, while Sanford photographer Jim Rucquoi captures intimate moments in historic Sanford. A new artist is featured every month, and everyone helps out.

DOWNTOWN SANFORD

Sandra Friend

UCF

University of Central Florida Art Gallery (407-823-5203; www.art.ucf.edu), 4000 Central Florida Blvd. In the Visual Arts Building, this gallery features rotating exhibits with a focus on local and student artists. Free.

Winter Park

Creadle School of Art (407-671-1886), 600 St. Andrews Blvd. Founded in 1965, this nonprofit school of the arts incorporates several indoor and outdoor gallery spaces with a collection of lakeside studios. Follow the path through the sculpture gardens to the Jenkins Gallery, and check out the rotating exhibits. Classes are offered on a regular schedule; call for details. Open Mon–Thu 9–5, Fri and Sat 9–4; free.

HISTORIC SITES

Eatonville

Follow the walking trail through the **Eatonville Historic District**, circa 1887, when Joseph E. Clarke purchased the land from Josiah Eaton and established the nation's first incorporated black community. Interpretive markers trace the history of buildings such as the **Hungerford School** and the **St. Lawrence AME Church**.

Longwood

With more than 30 historic buildings, the **Longwood Historic District** showcases what the villages of Central Florida looked like during Reconstruction. The walking tour brochure (see *Walking Tours*) touches on such gems as the **1873 Inside-Outside House**, 141 W Church Ave, probably the oldest prefabricated house in the United States—and it was put together wrong when reassembled in Altamonte Springs. It was moved to its present site in 1973. The **Clouser Cottage**, 218 W Church Ave, is an original board-and-batten pioneer home from 1881. But two structures dominate the old village—the **Longwood Hotel**, 300 S CR 427, opened as the Waltham in 1886, and the **Bradlee-McIntyre House** (407-767-1636), 130 W Warren St, lovingly restored to its 1885 glory; the Central Florida Society for Historic Preservation offers tours through the house the second and fourth Wed and Sun 11–4, $3 donation.

Maitland

In 1915 Orange County paved the old military road between Fort Mellon in Sanford and Fort Gatlin in Orlando, creating **the first grouted brick road in Florida**. In 1925 the road became part of the Dixie Highway; walk the restored highway at Lake Lily Park past the historic **Waterhouse Residence**, built 1883, and its adjoining carpentry shop; both are open as museums (see *Museums*).

Ocoee

Built in 1884, the **Withers-Maguire House**, 16 E Oakland Ave, is a two-story frame vernacular home built by Kentuckian William T. Withers, who wintered in Ocoee. Restored to a house museum, it's open to the public Sat and Sun 2–4. Free.

Oviedo

Settled by northerners looking for a winter haven, the **Lake Charm District** (centered on Lake Charm) dates back to the late 1800s. The **Lawton House**, 200 W Broadway, built in 1890, houses the Oviedo Chamber of Commerce and the Oviedo Historical Society.

Sanford

Downtown Sanford is loaded with historical structures dating to 1877–1924, well worth a walking tour (see *Walking Tours*) to catch highlights like the **Whalers Saloon** and the **Pico Hotel**, built in 1877 for Henry Plant's railroad. A separate **residential historic district** lies south between Magnolia and Park Aves. Circa 1913, **the St. James AME Church**, 819 Cypress Ave, is an anchor structure for Georgetown, an African American community created by Henry Sanford with its own commercial district. During the early 1900s, Sanford gained fame as "Celery City" because of the abundant crops shipping from its port. A stone marker at Mellonville Ave and Second St marks the site of **Fort Mellon**, constructed during the Second Seminole War. Florida's first Swedish community, **New Upsala**, was established in 1871 with Swedish immigrants who worked in Henry Sanford's orange groves; the cemetery on Upsala Rd remains. The Orlando Sanford International Airport occupies the grounds of the former **Sanford Naval Air Station**, an operational base 1942–1968; historical exhibits and vintage aircraft are on display at the airport.

Winter Garden

The completion of the West Orange Trail (see *Bicycling*) revitalized historic **downtown Winter Garden**. Plant St is lined with cozy coffeehouses, arts and antiques shops, and several historic museums. Don't miss its Italianate fountain with mosaics depicting citrus-packing labels.

Winter Park

Established in 1885 on the site of a former sawmill, **Rollins College** (407-646-2000; www.rollins.edu), 1000 Holt Ave, is the oldest independent college in Florida. Stroll the campus and discover architectural gems like the **Knowles Chapel**, designed by Ralph Adams Cram, the renowned Gothic architect whose work also graces Rice University, West Point, and Notre Dame, its entrance topped with a scene of the Spanish landing at St. Augustine; a piazza connects the chapel with the **Anne Russell Theatre**, circa 1931. Don't miss the state's top art collection at the **Cornell Fine Arts Museum** (see *Art Galleries*). At the north end of Park Ave, **Casa Feliz** (www.casafeliz.us) is now open as a house museum Sunday 12–3 and by appointment. A 1933 Spanish-influenced masonry farmhouse designed by noted architect James Gamble Rogers II, the home—all 750 tons of it—was moved in 2001 just 300 yards to its current spot to avoid demolition. It took artisans five years to restore it to its former glory. Two blocks west of Park Ave, the **Hannibal Square District** is Winter Park's historic African American neighborhood.

Apopka

Museum of the Apopkans (407-703-1707; www.apopkamuseum.org), 122 E Fifth St. A slab of limestone shot through with solution holes and an old red tractor sit outside a new log cabin in downtown Apopka that houses more than a century's worth of historical artifacts and records. In terms of presentation and depth of material, it's one of the more interesting local history museums in the region. A research library with hundreds of scrapbooks and historical documents houses genealogical material as well. Free; donations appreciated.

Christmas

✒ ⛬ **Fort Christmas Historical Park and Museum** (407-568-4149), 1300 Fort Christmas Rd. Housed in a replica of Fort Christmas (the original Seminole War–era log fortress sat less than a mile north on Christmas Creek), this historical museum covers regional history, 1835–1940. Seven historic structures around the park are open during daily guided tours—check out slices of Florida frontier history like the Beehead Ranch House, circa 1917, a hunt lodge formerly in Tosohatchee State Reserve, and the Yates and Simmons Houses, excellent examples of rural Cracker homesteads. Museum open Tue–Sat 10–5, Sun 1–5; park open daily.

Eatonville

Zora Neale Hurston National Museum of Fine Arts (407-647-3307; www.zoranealehurston.cc), 227 E Kennedy Blvd. From her searing novel *Their Eyes Were Watching God* to her 1940s work with the WPA, collecting oral history and folktales throughout Florida, Zora Neale Hurston's contributions to African American literature and culture are inestimable. In her honor, this small gallery provides a space for rotating exhibits from artists of African American descent, and sells copies of her many books. Donation.

Geneva

Geneva Museum (407-349-5697), 165 First St. This small historical society museum covers life in Geneva during its periods of cypress logging, citrus growing, turpentining, and cattle ranching. Open the first Sunday of the month, May–Oct, 2–4.

Goldenrod

Goldenrod Station & Museum (407-677-5980; www.goldenrodchamber.org), 4755 Palmetto Ave. In the 1890s settlers started a thriving orange industry; the Florida land boom brought "suburban homes" to Aloma Ave. Learn this and more at this museum of local history, housed in a former fire station.

Maitland

Holocaust Memorial Resource & Education Center (407-628-0555; www.holocaustedu.org), Jewish Federation of Greater Orlando Community Campus, 851 N Maitland Ave. The sculpture *The Deportation* at the entrance to this important memorial touched me deeply, and my education continued as I walked along the museum's permanent exhibit wall, a timeline of the history of the Jews in Europe, the Nuremberg Laws, the ghettos, the concentration camps, complete with photos and video of the horror. A Gentile unschooled in the Holocaust, I walked away with tears in my eyes and a deeper appreciation of the Jewish struggle. Open Mon–Thu 9–4, Fri 9–1, Sun 1–4. Free; donations appreciated.

✦ **Maitland Historical Museum** (407-644-2451; www.maitlandhistory.com), 221 W Packwood Ave. Rotating exhibits showcase facets of Maitland's long history, from its role in the Seminole Wars of 1838 to its settlement in 1872 as a citrus grove community around Lakes Faith, Hope, and Charity to today. Behind the main building is the Telegraph Pioneers Museum, with the largest exhibit of historic telephone equipment in Florida. Best of all—the switching equipment works! The docents have fun showing off how rotary phones kick off the switches, and how the first magneto telephones (no dial, just a speaker) connected to the switchboards. Central Florida's first telephone service began in 1909 when the Galloway family of Maitland had lines installed so their customers could place orders. Everyone had a three-digit phone number. The company grew and evolved into the Winter Park Telephone Company, then continued as a rare family-owned operation until 1976. Open Thu–Sun noon–4; fee.

Historic Waterhouse Residence and Carpentry Museum (407-644-2451), 820 Lake Lily Dr. The scent of roses drifts from a nearby garden as you walk up Florida's first brick road (see *Historic Sites*) to this 1883 home, restored with period furnishings as a house museum. Open Thu–Sun noon–4; fee.

Sanford

✦ **Sanford Museum** (407-302-1000; www.ci.sanford.fl.us/cf03.html), 520 E First St. Did you know that Henry Sanford was the head of the US. Secret Service in Europe during the Civil War, and that he spied on the Confederate Army? You'll uncover this and a lot of other unique facts about the town's founder and the region as you explore the exhibits in this waterfront museum, from sports and agricultural history to artifacts from Fort Mellon. Talk to the curator for the full story, including Sanford's extensive archives and library. Open Tue–Fri 11–4, Sat 1–4; free.

Housed in the poor farm, circa 1926, the **Museum of Seminole County History** (407-665-2489; www.seminolecountyfl.gov/lls/museum), 300 Bush Blvd, illuminates this county's extensive history in a rambling expanse of exhibit rooms. Learn about iceman John Wesley Woods's role in establishing the Sanford Zoo, view 1920s antiques in the period rooms, and see relicts from Fort Mellon circa 1837. Call for hours; the museum was recently shuttered due to a county budget crunch, awaiting volunteer support.

✦ **Student Museum** (407-320-0520), 301 W Seventh St. The oldest school building in the region (circa 1902) is a working educational center and museum exploring pioneer Florida, the Timucua, and life in the early 1900s. Open weekdays 1:30–4.

UCF

Artifacts from Central Florida war veterans are showcased at the **National Vietnam War Museum** (407-601-2864; www.nwmvocf.org), 3400 N Tanner Rd, where you can walk through a full-scale replica of a firebase and see a US Navy River Patrol Boat, among other exhibits. Open Sat 9–5, Sun 1–5; donation.

Sandra Friend

THE CENTRAL FLORIDA RAILROAD
MUSEUM

Winter Garden

✎ Central Florida Railroad Museum (407-656-0559; www.cfcnrhs.org), 101 S Boyd St. Perhaps the finest collection of railroad memorabilia in Florida—including a renowned collection of dining car china—is tucked away inside the former Tavares & Gulf railroad depot, managed by the Central Florida chapter of the National Railway Historical Society.

✎ Winter Garden Heritage Museum (407-656-5544), 1 N Main St. Inside the 1918 Atlantic Coast Line passenger depot, exhibits recount the history of this vibrant citrus-packing town. Outside, kids can pose with a Ford F-750 pumper truck and a 1907 citrus spray wagon, or the Chessie caboose parked on a siding. Daily 1–5; free.

Winter Garden History Center (407-656-3244), 32 Plant St. Exhibit cases and walls of photos tell the story of Winter Garden's rise to citrus fame, with a stronger focus on local people and places than the heritage museum. Free.

Winter Park

Albin Polasek Museum and Sculpture Gardens (407-647-6294; www.polasek .org), 633 Osceola Ave. A Czech-born sculptor of the human form whose heyday spanned the 1920s through the 1940s, Polasek retired to this 3-acre estate along Lake Osceola in 1949 and established working studios and a gallery. Docent-led tours take you beyond the art gallery to walk through Polasek's home and chapel, which contain treasures like the A.D. 100 bust of a centaur from Pompeii and a late-18th-century icon of St. Spiridon; enjoy a stroll through the beautifully landscaped outdoor sculpture gardens, with his whimsical multiheaded Slavic gods and soaring religious images. Open Tue–Sat 10–4, Sun 1–4; fee.

Cornell Fine Arts Museum (407-646-2546; www.rollins.edu/cfam), 100 Holt Ave. One of Florida's true art treasures hides on the campus of Rollins College, where rotating and permanent exhibits showcase the college's incredible collection of European and American art of more than 6,000 pieces dating back to 1380. On a leisurely stroll through the galleries, I found myself lost in the details of paintings like *A Mosque in China* (Alberto Pasini, 1882) and *Moonlight Seascape* (Thomas Moran, 1892). Open Tue–Fri 10–5, Sat and Sun 1–5; fee.

Morse Museum of American Art (407-645-5311; www.morsemuseum.org), 445 Park Avenue N. A private museum founded in 1942 with collections built over 50 years by the McKean family, this incredible celebration of art glass features the world's most comprehensive collection of the works of Louis Comfort Tiffany; the showpiece is the Glass Chapel that Tiffany installed at the 1893 World's Columbian Exhibition in Chicago. It's a don't-miss stop for art lovers;

you'll see works from Maxfield Parrish and others. Open Tue–Sat 9:30–4, Sun 1–4, and until 8 on Fri Sep–May; fee (free on Fri after 4).

Winter Park Historical Association Museum (407-647-8180), 200 W New England Ave, provides an overview of this old Florida boomtown, its architecture and its growth, with a photographic timeline of early Winter Park. Open Thu–Fri 11–3, Sat 9–1, Sun 1–4. Free, donations appreciated.

RACING Prepare to be shaken up at **Speed World** (407-568-5522; www.speed worlddragway.com), 19442 E Colonial Dr, Bithlo, a real contrast to the cultural offerings of suburban Orlando. Home of the Crash-o-rama, Florida's only school bus demolition derby, Speed World hosts stock car racing on Fri evenings at 8 and drag racing 3 nights a week. The adjacent **Orange County Raceway** (407-568-6693), 19444 E Colonial Dr, has several different earthen tracks, hosting motocross, BMX, and mud-bogging. Admission runs $15 and up; call for a schedule of events.

RAILROADIANA One of Florida's last local short lines, the **Florida Central Railroad**, has its shops and yard along US 441 at the north end of Apopka at the **Seaboard Air Line Railway Depot**, 36 E Station St, circa 1918. Driving past, you'll see both rolling stock and engines; the **Orlando–Mount Dora Railroad** stores its passenger cars here. In Winter Garden the town's two original passenger depots are now historical museums—railfans shouldn't miss the **Central Florida Railroad Museum** (see *Museums*) and the **Chessie caboose** parked along Plant St. At the **Seminole County Museum** in Sanford, see railroad relics like switches and signs. Along Lake Virginia at Rollins College (see *Historic Sites*), the **Dinky Dock** marks one terminus of the narrow-gauge Dinky Line, circa 1888, that brought cypress cut in Oviedo to a sawmill on this site.

ZOOLOGICAL PARKS AND WILDLIFE REHABILATION

Bithlo
With a mission of rehabilitating and releasing animals back to the wild, the nonprofit **Back to Nature Wildlife Refuge** (407-568-5138; www.btn-wildlife .org), 18515 E Colonial Dr, takes in more than 2,000 animals every year, primarily birds. Stop and tour their roadside zoo of exotic animals and permanent residents; free admission, donations appreciated. Open daily 9–4, closed major holidays.

Christmas
Jungle Adventures (407-568-1354; www.jungleadventures.com), 26205 E Colonial Dr. Don't let the roadside-attraction exterior fool you: Jungle Adventures is about conservation. Yes, you enter through the maw of Florida's largest alligator sculpture, a true piece of old-time kitsch that was the original owner's home, and is said to be the "largest gator in Florida" at 200 feet long—worth a stop just for the photo. But once inside this nearly 40-year-old former alligator farm, now a 20-acre preserve, I walked the Jungle Nature Trail and met some of the most knowledgeable guides I've ever encountered at a commercial attrac-

tion. They wowed their guests with extraordinary detail on Florida habitats, endangered species programs, and Native American culture. In the floodplain of the St. Johns River, the park offers several pleasant boardwalk loops, a boat ride, and some of the largest alligators I've ever seen, as well as four daily wildlife shows featuring endangered Florida panthers. Open daily 9:30–5:30; $20 adults, $17 seniors, and $11 ages 3–11.

Maitland

✄ ♿ **Audubon Birds of Prey Center** (407-644-0190; www.audubonofflorida .org/who_centers_CBOP.html), 1101 Audubon Way. Centered on a 1924 bunga- low along 2.5 acres on Lake Sybelia, this special refuge was established in 1979 for the rehabilitation and release of injured raptors, with a large raptor trauma clinic, a walking trail around aviaries that house birds unable to be released to the wild, and a small research library and gift shop. Home to the state's Eagle- watch program, the facility has rehabbed and released more than 200 bald eagles since it opened in 1979. Open Tue–Sun 10–4; fee.

Sanford

✄ ♿ **Central Florida Zoo** (407-323-4450; www.centralfloridazoo.org), 3755 NW US 17-92. The entrance road to this acclaimed zoological park tells the story: You're stepping into a place that blends perfectly with its natural sur- roundings, the floodplain forests of Lake Monroe. Visitors utilize a series of boardwalks to connect the buildings and enclosures; past alligators and bald eagles, a Florida nature walk meanders through the forest. The key focus, of course, is conservation and the reproduction of endangered species like Grand Cayman rock iguanas and wreathed hornbills. A herpetarium shows off Florida's venomous snakes as well as endangered species like the Aruba Island rat- tlesnake, king cobra, and Amazonian palm viper. But the kid in you (or your kids) gets to play, too. At Zoofari Outpost, feed and pet llamas, goats, zebu, and cows; a hand-washing station is thoughtfully provided. And I was almost tempted by the retro "make your own souvenir" plastic injection Mold-A-Rama, with its aroma pulling me back to the 1960s. Ever conscious of its audience, the zoo hosts special kids' events like the Zoo Boo Bash, a gentle trick-or-treat for young- sters. Spend an afternoon and get to know the 300-plus animals hidden through- out the 116-acre park; it's a great retreat. Open daily 9–5; $10 adults, $8 seniors, $6 children 3–12. New "Behind the Scenes" tours offer encounters with chee- tahs and elephants, with reservations required; call for rates.

✳ To Do

AIRBOAT RIDES With the St. Johns River making a mazy meander along the eastern edge of the region, this is prime airboat territory. My first-ever airboat outing was with **Bill's Airboat Adventures** (407-977-3214; www.airboating .com); Captain Bill Daniel takes you on a truly educational journey through the marshes where the river flows toward Lake Monroe, pointing out Indian mounds and cypress swamps while giving you background about Florida's unique aquatic habitats. Fares run $45 adult, $30 child, minimum 4 on a trip; tours by appoint- ment only. In Christmas, **A-Awesome Airboat Rides** (407-568-7601; www.air

boatride.com) departs from the St. Johns River bridge on FL 50 just east of Christmas to take you on a spin up through Puzzle Lake or down along the fringe of Tosohatchee Reserve, where Captain Bruce points out the region's wildlife. At Black Hammock Fish Camp (see *Eating Out*) in Oviedo, hop **Gator Ventures** (407-977-8235) for a spin around the alligator-rich Lake Jesup.

BICYCLING Orlando's suburbs boast numerous dedicated paved bicycle trails, as well as marked routes for bicycles in both urban and rural areas. While the eventual intent is to have the **Cross Seminole Trail** cross the entire county, it presently has paved segments open between Oviedo and Winter Springs and Lake Mary and Longwood, including a fancy suspension span carrying the trail across I-4 (see *Greenways*). Hikers on the Florida Trail share this route through suburban Orlando. Look for green BIKE ROUTE signs in other parts of the county for quiet back-road trips.

If you're interested in biking the popular 22-mile **West Orange Trail**, which passes right through downtown Winter Garden and crosses a bridge over US 441 in downtown Apopka on its way out to Kelly Park, check out the rentals at West Orange Bike (407-877-8884), 6 E Plant; Abbott's Bicycles (407-654-0115), 36 E Plant; and Bikes & Blades (407-877-0600; www.orlandobikerental.com), 17914 FL 438. Most shops are closed Sun.

For off-road biking, see Wekiwa Springs State Park in *Parks*.

BIRDING The region's top spot for birding is **Orlando Wetlands Park** (see Parks), where vast human-made wetlands filter treated water flowing into the St. Johns River floodplain. Walk the Berm Trail for an eagle's-eye view of the marshes and the many wading birds that call it home. Looking for eagles in the wild? Stop at **Black Hammock Trailhead** (FL 434 at FL 417) on the Cross Seminole Trail (see *Greenways*) and walk in to the trail junction (left fork); look up and to your left. This eagle pair has been nesting in the pines for nearly a decade. Of course, you'll find herons and egrets hanging out at most regional parks, and one splendid osprey nest sits right at the end of the point at Black Hammock Fish Camp (see *Eating Out*).

BOAT EXCURSIONS Step back into another era with a boat trip from Sanford, the ♿ **Rivership *Romance*** (407-321-5091 or 1-800-423-7401; www.rivership romance.com), 433 N Palmetto Ave, on a delightful cruise along the St. Johns River. Sanford was the last port of call up the St. Johns for turn-of-the-20th-century steamships, which brought tourists and settlers to Central Florida until the railroads gained a strong foothold in the 1920s. Your ship is a refurbished 1940s Great Lakes steamer, which glides across Lake Monroe and up the St. Johns with ease. Of course, what would a cruise be without dining? The dining room, all red velvet and windows, feels like an elegant palace, and your choice of five entrées includes prime rib and roasted herb-crusted grouper. The helpful wait staff will make suggestions on meals and drinks, and your "cruise director" lines up activities (like dancing and a narrated ecotour) on the 2- to 3-hour cruise. Tickets $38–49; $54 for moonlight dining and dancing cruise held Fri and Sat evenings.

✍ ♿ Drift across Winter Park's placid lakes on a 12-mile, 1-hour excursion you won't forget: the famed **Winter Park Scenic Boat Tour** (407-644-4056; www .scenicboattours.com), 312 E Morse Blvd, established in 1938. I knew about the lakes, the gardens, and many of the homes of the wealthy gentry who settled in Winter Park in the 1920s, but I was surprised and delighted at the passages between the lakes—the canals are narrow and shaded. The captains know their stuff, and will give you a great history lesson while talking about the backgrounds of local families and their historic upscale homes. Tickets $10 adults, $5 for ages 2–11.

FAMILY ACTIVITIES ✍ Play mini golf at **Congo River Golf** (407-682-4077), 531 W Semoran Blvd, Altamonte Springs, where you can feed the live gators out front! At Flea World (see *Selective Shopping*) on US 17-92, Sanford, you'll find ✍ **Fun World**, offering carnival rides and shows; when I drove by, a Chinese acrobatic troupe was strutting their stuff. Open Fri–Sun 10–7. Stop by the **RDV Sportsplex** (407-916-2442), 8701 Maitland Summit Blvd, to see the Orlando Magic (www.nba.com/magic) and other teams practice.

GAMING **Orlando Jai Alai** (407-331-9191), US 17-92 and FL 436, Casselberry. Wager on players' performance in this high-speed cousin to lacrosse, where athletes hurl the ball back and forth at speeds up to 150 mph. They offer horse racing telecasts as well. For more racing, just up US 17-92 is the **Sanford-Orlando Kennel Club** (407-831-1600), 301 Dog Track Rd, Longwood, with greyhound racing.

GOLF **Casselberry Golf Club** (407-699-9310; www.casselberrygolfclub.net), 300 S Triplet Lake Dr, Casselberry, is an interesting 18-hole public course—built in 1947, the par-69 course winds like a slender ribbon through residential communities. It's a local favorite, and it doesn't hurt that green fees (including golf cart) run $12–27.

WINTER PARK'S SCENIC BOAT TOURS TAKE YOU THROUGH NARROW CANALS.
Sandra Friend

HIKING Hikers on the eastern side of Orlando are blessed with an almost infinite array of trails to choose from; an explanation of them all would merit another book. Is it any wonder that one of the largest Florida Trail Association chapters (Central Florida) meets in Orlando? Pick up a flyer from Seminole County (see *Parks*) for an excellent sampling, or thumb through the St. Johns River Water Management District recreation guide (available online at http://sjr.state.fl .us), and get yourself a copy of *50 Hikes in Central Florida* (Backcountry Guides), which covers more than a dozen hikes in this region in detail. My top picks not included in that first edition: the **Florida Trail Little Big Econ section** between Chuluota and Oviedo, a scenic segment following the Econlockhatchee River, and the trails at ✧ **Spring Hammock Preserve** (fun for kids), which lead out to some of the oldest cypresses in Florida along Lake Jesup.

PADDLING Kings Landing (407-886-0859; www.kingslandingfl.com), 1014 Miami Springs Rd, rents canoes and kayaks for paddlers to head down Rock Springs Run to the Wekiva River ($30, includes transportation), as does **Wekiva Adventures** (407-321-7188; www.wekivaadventures.com), which also does guided trips. You'll find these waterways busy on summer weekends; a good alternative is the Econlockhatchee River from Bithlo to Oviedo. Check with **Hidden River Park** (407-568-5346), 15295 E Colonial Dr, where they not only rent canoes and kayaks but also run guided paddling trips of 9 to 12 miles; some include overnight camping. **Riverquest Kayaks** (407-834-4040), 4099 Orlando Ave, Casselberry, rents kayaks-to-go and does free demos in Lake Katherine behind the store. **Travel Country Outdoors** (see *Selective Shopping*) runs kayak clinics, leads guided trips, and rents kayaks and canoes. For a unique urban paddle past million-dollar homes down the scenic canals of Winter Park, check in at the **Winter Park Scenic Boat Tour** (see *Boat Excursions*) for canoe rentals.

SAILING Fun Maritime Academy (1-866-320-SAIL; www.funma.com), 531 N Palmetto Ave, A Dock. Offers sailing instruction and boat rentals on vast Lake Monroe. Instructional courses start at $85 and range up to $800 for multiday bareboat chartering instruction. The American Sailing Association certifies the instructors. They rent boats, too: pontoons, runabouts, and sailboats for use on Lake Monroe.

SCENIC DRIVES In such an urban setting, you wouldn't expect much in the way of scenic drives, but there are a few beauty spots worth noting. Heading east of Sanford toward the coast, **FL 46** parallels the sprawling wetlands of the St. Johns River, with expansive views. US 17-92 cleans up nicely as it rounds the bend at Sanford, heading north as **Lakeshore Dr** along the oceanlike expanse of Lake Monroe. For a nice historic district trip, drive Oak St west from downtown Sanford, or check out the beauty of old homes tucked under a canopy of ancient live oaks on Park Ave between US 17-92 in Maitland and Winter Park.

SWIMMING Swim within sight of Lake Apopka at **Farnsworth Pool**, a community swimming pool in Winter Garden, or jump into the icy fresh spring water of Rock Springs Run at **Kelly Park** and **Wekiwa Springs** at Wekiwa Springs State Park (see *Parks*).

TRAIL RIDING Visit **Devonwood Farms** (407-273-0822; www.devonwoodfarms .com/), 2518 Rouse Rd, between FL 50 and University Blvd, for horseback riding lessons and trail riding, and to watch competitions that are scheduled throughout the year.

TUBING Head out to ✐ **Kelly Park** (see *Parks*) for Central Florida's only *natural* tubing experience: a real lazy river amid ferns and palms. Rock Springs Run gets its start as the spring splashes out of a rocky cliff, forming a crystal-clear stream flowing toward the Wekiva River. Tubing starts right in front of the caves from which the river flows, and continues along a gentle crystalline course for a mile. Tubes must be rented outside the park; several vendors on Park Ave will let you take tubes with you, and they'll pick up the tubes at the park each evening.

WALKING TOURS Pick a copy of the **Sanford Historic Downtown Walking Tour** at the Sanford Museum (see *Museums*) for a stroll through Sanford's historic business district, where several of the downtown blocks date back to 1887. The **Longwood Historic District Walking Tour** touches on 33 points of interest; pick up a brochure at city hall or visit the City of Longwood Web site (www.longwoodfl.org). Pick up a **Walking Tour of Eatonville, Florida** at the town hall or the Zora Neale Hurston National Museum of Fine Arts (see *Museums*), with details on 10 significant sites in the town's history, and **Historic Properties of Maitland Florida**, a booklet from the Maitland Historical Society, to check out homes dating back to the 1880s.

✳ Green Space

GARDENS Behind a screen of cypresses fringing the shore of Lake Maitland, **Kraft Azalea Gardens** (407-599-3334; www.ci.winter-park.fl.us/2005/depts/parks/kraftazalea.shtml), along Alabama Dr (off Palmer Ave), Winter Park, has spectacular fragrant blooms January–March. According to local legend, if you stand in the circle of columns in the replica Parthenon and whisper at the wall, your voice will echo back.

♿ Part wilderness, part formal gardens, **Mead Garden** (407-262-2049; www.meadgarden.org) 1300 S Denning Dr, Winter Park, offers 1.5 miles of gentle walking trails (including a Braille Trail) around well-groomed natural areas along a clear creek linking lakes in Orlando and Winter Park; slip away to this lovely urban oasis for a quiet walk in the woods. Named for pioneer Florida horticulturalist Dr. Theodore L. Mead, the 55-acre former botanical garden opened to the public on Jan 14, 1940.

University of Central Florida Arboretum (407-823-3146; www.arboretum.ucf.edu), UCF campus. This little-known tranquil oasis encompasses gardens of both native and exotic plants. Follow the 30- to 45-minute trail through the bromeliad sanctuary, cycad garden, and palm collection, or wander for an hour through Florida's natural habitats of pine flatwoods, oak hammock, cab-

FLOATING DOWN ROCK SPRING RUN IN KELLY PARK

Sandra Friend

bage palm flatwoods. marshes, and scrub. Park next to the Stockyard Conservatory Greenhouse; open sunrise–sunset daily. Free.

GREENWAYS Greenways (primarily old railroad beds converted to paved trails) crisscross the entire Orlando metro area, providing miles of comfortable biking. The **West Orange Trail** (407-654-5144; http://parks .onetgov.net/index.htm) runs 22 miles from a trailhead near Monteverde through downtown Winter Garden, heading through Apopka over a showy bridge over US 441 and east toward Sorrento. The **Little Econ Greenway** (407-249-4586), 2451 Dean Rd, links the UCF area with the **Cady Way Trail** coming out of the city of Orlando, and the **Cross Seminole Trail** (407-665-2093) connects

Sandra Friend
KRAFT AZALEA GARDENS

Oviedo with Winter Springs, Longwood, Lake Mary, and Heathrow, with parts still under construction. The 14-mile **Seminole-Wekiva Trail** links Altamonte Springs and Winter Springs with the Wekiva River corridor, and features a fancy bridge over I-4 at Heathrow. Efforts are actively under way to link together the region's network of greenways with those in adjoining Volusia, Lake, and Polk Counties to eventually provide hundreds of miles of protected cycling throughout Central Florida.

PARKS Communities north of Orlando are blessed with a large number of urban parks, far too many to cover here. Enjoy a walk around **Lake Lily Park** in Maitland, where you can watch turtles from the boardwalk. Sedate **Lake Lotus Park** (407-293-8885) off FL 414 provides an immersion into a sliver of wilderness along the Little Wekiva River. Several pleasant community parks provide scenic views of and boat ramp access to Lake Apopka, like **Trimble Park** in Tangerine and **Loughton Park** in Winter Garden. On the Winter Springs–Longwood border, **Big Tree Park** on General Hutchinson Pkwy protects the South's elder statesman, an ancient bald cypress known as The Senator, thought to be more than 2,000 years old. **Crane's Roost Park** behind the Altamonte Mall, FL 436, appeals to the urban Altamonte Springs crowd as a place to see and be seen while power walking and jogging around the lake. For full information on the region's parks, contact **Orange County Parks & Recreation** (407-836-6200; www .orangecountyparks.net), 4801 W Colonial Dr, Orlando 32808, and **Seminole County Parks & Recreation** (407-665-7352; www.seminolecountyfl.gov/parks), 264 W North St, Altamonte Springs 32714, for their respective brochures.

Clarcona Horseman's Park (407-886-6255), 3535 Damon Rd, is a unique 40-acre public equestrian facility off CR 435 with dressage show rings, judging towers, and horse stalls. Connects to the West Orange Trail's equestrian path; RV camping available.

Orlando Wetlands Park (407-246-2213), 25155 Wheeler Rd, Christmas, provides miles of biking and hiking trails around human-made impoundments where nearly 2,000 acres of wetlands naturally filter treated wastewater before it is released to the St. Johns River. Restrooms and picnic tables at trailhead; closed Oct–Jan 20. The Florida Trail follows the perimeter. Free.

✔ Encompassing nearly 8,000 acres along the wild and scenic Wekiva River, **Wekiwa Springs State Park** (407-884-2008; www.floridastateparks.org/wekiwa springs), 1800 Wekiwa Circle, Apopka, has a crystalline spring for swimming, more than 10 miles of hiking and off-road biking trails, canoe rentals for launch, and a large family camping area with electric and water hookups, dump station, and restrooms. Fee.

NATURE CENTERS Oakland Nature Preserve (407-656-1117; www.oakland naturepreserve.org), FL 438. With 95 acres of wetlands and uplands along Lake Apopka, this living laboratory has a boardwalk down to the lake and 2 miles of

✔ **Kelly Park** (407-889-4179), 400 E Kelly Park Rd, Rock Springs. Picture a grotto where ferns and mosses dangle over the dark entrance, where a glassy stream emerges from the earth and flows away over ancient slabs of limestone. Rock Spring is a magical place, a water park as designed by Mother Nature (with a little help from her friends)—the natural spring run twists and winds through the forest under a heavy canopy of trees before reaching an island buttressed with concrete; the waterway splits in two. Take your choice; both sides of this lazy river spill out into a broad pool that serves as the park's main swimming area. Bream and killifish sparkle in the depths as you float over aquatic gardens of tapegrass. Caught up in the gentle flow, you leave the busy swimming hole and float back into the forest to reach the take-out point after a mile. Yes, the park can be overrun on weekends—the trouble with many of our natural places is they're loved to death. Better to visit on a quiet afternoon or early morning, when you can slowly snorkel or tube (see *Tubing*) with the current without bumping into anyone else. In addition to its watery wonders, Kelly Park has extensive shady picnic grounds, several generations of playgrounds, pleasant pathways paralleling the run, and a campground (see *Campgrounds*). Paddlers can launch their craft just down the road at Kings Landing (see *Paddling*) for a trip down this wild and scenic river, one of the few unspoiled waterways in Central Florida. Open 9–7 in summer, 8–6 in winter. Fee.

interpretive trails winding through the uplands. Volunteers recently began construction of the environmental center, a replica Cracker homestead. Free.

WILD PLACES Despite being one of Florida's most densely populated counties, Seminole County offers excellent wilderness getaways thanks to the **Seminole County Natural Lands program** (407-665-7352; www.co.seminole.fl.us/natland). Some of the better-known preserves include the **Chuluota Wilderness Area**, 3895 Curryville Rd, Chuluota, with 625 acres of densely wooded hammocks and floodplain forest with hiking trails; the **Econ River Wilderness Area**, 3795 Old Lockwood Rd, Oviedo, protecting shoreline and lowlands along the scenic Econlockhatchee River; the **Geneva Wilderness**, 3501 N CR 426, Geneva, where you can take a short hike through scrub and flatwoods around ponds dotted with lilies; the **Lake Jesup Wilderness**, 5951 S Sanford Ave, Sanford, 490 acres with wetlands along vast Lake Jesup, part of the St. Johns River chain of lakes; **Lake Proctor Wilderness**, 920 E FL 46, Geneva, with its beautiful ponds amid the sand pine scrub; **Black Hammock Wilderness Area**, end of Howard Ave, Oviedo, with a boardwalk leading out into the floodplain forest; and **Spring Hammock Preserve**, FL 419, Winter Springs, one of my favorite places in the region for its ancient cypress stands along the edge of Lake Jesup. For maps and directions to all of these natural areas, visit the county's Web site. Free.

The **St. Johns Water Management District** (407-893-3127; http://sjr.state.fl.us) also does its part to preserve wild lands along the St. Johns River floodplain, with hiking and equestrian trails, seasonal hunting, fishing, and paddling permitted in their conservation areas. **Hal Scott Preserve**, Dallas Rd off FL 520, offers hiking and trail riding through vast palmetto prairies along the Lower Econlockhatchee River; **Lake Jesup Conservation Area** in Oviedo and Lake Mary encompasses several wetland areas along Lake Jesup, with some picturesque but soggy hiking trails; **Lake Monroe Conservation Area** off FL 46, Sanford, includes hiking and camping in the Kratzert Tract, and canoe-in campsites on Brickyard Slough; **Seminole Ranch Conservation Area** in Christmas, adjoining Orlando Wetlands Park, includes a portion of the Florida Trail running through jungle-like hydric hammocks dense with cabbage palms; and the **Wekiva River Buffer Conservation Area** in Longwood has the Sabal Point Trail, a hiking trail along a cypress-logging tramway that takes you into the floodplain forest without getting your feet wet.

GENEVA WILDERNESS

Sandra Friend

The Little-Big Econ State Forest (407-971-3500; www.fl-dof.com/state
_forests/index.html), CR 426, Oviedo, protects the floodplain of the Econlock-
hatchee River, with its palm hammocks and sandy beaches; the Florida Trail and
a series of bike trails run through the forest. Fee.

Off FL 46, the truly wild **Lower Wekiva River Preserve State Park** (407-
884-2008; part of Wekiva Basin Geo Park) has only one short nature trail intrud-
ing into the landscape, which protects the confluence of Blackwater Creek and
the Wekiva River. Several Timucuan shell mounds sit along the river's edge.
Free.

South of FL 50 at Christmas, the 28,000-acre **Tosohatchee State Reserve**
(407-568-5893), 3365 Taylor Creek Rd, stretches along 19 miles of the St. Johns
River floodplain, providing vast marshes for wintering birds and hammocks of
ancient oaks enjoyed by backpackers on the reserve's two loop trails and the
Florida Trail; deer and turkey hunters share the woods. Fee.

✳ Lodging

BED & BREAKFASTS

Oviedo 32765

🌺 ¹ Enjoy genteel old Oviedo at
Kings Manor (407-365-4200; www
.kingsmanorbb.com), 322 King St, a
two-story Victorian with a classic
Florida dogtrot design, built in 1884
by George Browne, Florida's Speaker
of the House. Hosts Roberta and Paul
McQueen restored this beauty to its
full glory, with five original fireplaces
and their mantels accented by period
furnishings; the light-button system is
also original to the house. Three massive guest rooms ($119–129) feature
romantic appointments like sleigh
beds and soft white robes as well as
practical amenities like Internet
access. Sit on the front veranda of
Master John's Green Room and soak
in the grandeur of the live oak
canopy, or enjoy the common area,
including the large screened back
porch. Full breakfast served.

Maitland 32789

¹ **Thurston House** (407-539-1911
or 1-800-843-2721; www.thurston
house.com), 851 Lake Ave. Innkeeper
Carole Ballard has one of the best-
kept secrets in metro Orlando: a
beautiful 1885 Victorian overlooking
Lake Eulalia, convenient to everything and yet privately tucked away,
surrounded by several acres of gardens and forests. Mingle with other
guests on the porch, relax in the spacious parlor, or simply enjoy one of
four spacious rooms ($180) with read-
ing area, desk with phone and dataport, and comfortable bed; popular
with business travelers. The rate
includes continental or full breakfast,
your choice.

Sanford 32771

∞ **Higgins House** (407-324-9238;
www.higginshouse.com), 420 S Oak
Ave. Steeped in history, this 1894 Victorian home of the first railroad super-
intendent in Sanford has a 1902
Kimball piano dominating the grand
parlor; guests partake of a full three-
course breakfast (dietary restrictions
honored) overlooking the "Secret
Courtyard" backyard. A two-bed mas-
culine-themed room and The Pub, a
TV lounge with stocked fridge, make

this B&B popular with the guys, but there's also a romantic bridal suite with a country feel. Three rooms, $125–155.

HOTELS, MOTELS, AND RESORTS
There is no lack of lodging in the northern Orlando metro area. At every exit off I-4, you'll find a variety of major chain hotels with a wide range of amenities, such as **Springhill Suites by Marriott** (407-995-1000) in Sanford 32771, **Homewood Suites Orlando North** (407-875-8777) in Maitland 32751, and **La Quinta Inn & Suites** (407-805-9901) in Lake Mary 32746. The newest options are clustered around the business parks at Lake Mary and UCF.

Maitland 32751
& "I" ∞ **Lake of the Woods Resort** (407-834-7631 or 1-800-544-1266; www.lakeofthewoodsresort.net), 8875 S US 17-92. Renovated by local owners, this 38-unit motel complex with banquet center offers pleasant, spacious rooms, kitchenettes, and suites ($78–95) overlooking the placid waters of Lake of the Woods, with a beautiful lakeside pool.

Sanford
🐾 "I" ∞ & **The Palms Island Resort and Marina** (407-323-1910 or 1-800-290-1910; www.palms-resort.com), 530 N Palmetto Ave, Sanford 32771, has a commanding waterfront on Lake Monroe, adjacent to the marina; you could cast a line right out your front door. Older rooms ($79) have the usual amenities but show a little wear thanks to their proximity to the water. Newly remodeled rooms run $90 and up. The swimming pool overlooks the massive lake, and there's always a breeze.

At the 1950s **Slumberland Motel** (407-322-4591), 2611 S Orlando Dr, Sanford 32773, Lee and Yong Li offer clean nonsmoking efficiencies ($45) with older furnishings and paneled walls; a sparkling pool sits outside the appealing exterior.

UCF
& "I" **Comfort Suites** (407-737-7303; www.comfortsuites.com/hotel/fl061), 12101 Challenger Pkwy, Orlando 32826. These roomy suites ($119–129) add a sofa and dedicated work space for road warriors to the traditional motel room layout. In-room amenities include fridge, microwave, and free high-speed Internet access; convenient to UCF and FL 50, with a small pool, business center, and large common breakfast area.

♂ & "I" **Hilton Garden Inn** (407-992-5000; www.orlandoeastucf.gardeninn.com), 1959 N Alafaya Trail, Orlando 32826. This pleasant chain hotel adjacent to UCF hums on the weekdays but is quiet on the weekends. In addition to the usual in-room amenities you'd expect at a Hilton, like refrigerator, microwave, coffeemaker, and high-speed Internet access in each room and junior suite ($99–205), enjoy the pool and hot tub outside; kids stay free with adult guests.

Winter Park 32789
Enjoy 1920s elegance in an intimate setting at the **Park Plaza Hotel** (407-647-1072 or 1-800-228-7220; www.parkplazahotel.com), 307 Park Ave S, where an old-fashioned elevator takes you up to a series of high-ceilinged rooms and suites ($130–300) with original pine floors and classy touches like sleigh beds and writing desks; the

tiled bathrooms are original. In the popular Balcony Suites, guests can enjoy their coffee in an outdoor balcony garden overlooking Park Ave.

WORKING RANCH

Chuluota 32766
⤷ ⊙ **Big Oaks Ranch** (407-629-1847; www.bigoaksranch.com), 615 Grand Chenier Cove. Relax in the shade of an oak hammock in a gorgeous two-story log cabin along the banks of Mills Creek on this 720-acre working beef cattle ranch, where longhorns and Herefords roam the fields in the distance. Featuring five uniquely decorated rooms, including a children's room, the spacious cabin is popular for on-site wedding packages but can also be rented for a minimum of 2 nights, no credit cards; reservations required.

CAMPGROUNDS

Apopka 32712
🎣 ♂ **Kelly Park** (see *Parks*) has a well-shaded 24-site campground with electric hookups within walking distance of Rock Springs; resident rangers are on-site. $20 for family campground sites with hookups, $4 per person for primitive tent sites.

Christmas 32709
Christmas Airstream RV Resort (407-568-5207), 25525 E Colonial Dr. With deeply shaded sites tucked under a canopy of tall cabbage palms and pines, and a sparkling swimming pool out front, this is one very appealing campground, with three meeting halls with kitchen facilities. Electric and water hookups, on-site dump station; rates start at $15. No tents.

Winter Garden 34787
The **Stage Stop Campground** (407-656-8000), 700 W FL 50, offers easy access to the theme parks, and features full-hook-up spaces ($25 day, $150 week) with concrete patios and picnic tables, a game room with pool tables, and an Olympic-sized swimming pool; tent campers welcome.

✳ Where to Eat
DINING OUT

Apopka
♿ Several meals out at the **Captain and the Cowboy** (407-886-7100; www.captainandthecowboy.com), 604 E Main St, convinced me I'd never get through everything that looked good on the menu. The imposing, historic 1905 Eldrege House sits high on a hill above a busy interchange (where FL 436 and US 441 merge), so it was heartening to see it restored and reopened when I lived nearby. Entrées ($15–35) change frequently, with Asian fusion steak and seafood showcasing the talents of executive chef and co-owner Henry Gong; the fried shrimp, for instance, is corn-dusted and accompanied with wasabi aioli, mango sauce, and Thai chili sauce. A "Wonders of the World" appetizers ($4–12) are always on the menu, with choices like French baked Brie, fried green tomatoes with chipotle remoulade, and Apopkan sweet potato pie topped with pecan streusel and marshmallows. Share enough of these and you won't need dinner.

Casselberry
♿ **Enzo's on the Lake** (407-834-9872; www.enzos.com), 1130 S US 17-92, in a class by itself, is the crème de la crème of Italian restaurants in this region, where dresses and suits are de rigueur and the prices match

the atmosphere; expect to drop $19–39 on refined Italian entrées like veal scaloppine sautéed with capers, artichokes, tomatoes, and white wine.

Cypriana Greek Restaurant (407-834-8088; www.silveroid.com/cypriana.htm), 505 Semoran Blvd, is a little slice of Greece, with murals wrapping the dining area in scenes of the islands, blue-and-white-checkered wicker chairs, and Greek newspapers at the counter. Enjoy a fine dining menu that extends beyond ordinary Greek specialties to entrées ($9–15) like shrimp Mykonos, lamb chops, and chicken Aegean, or stop in at lunch for a shish kebab or marinated Greek sausage.

Longwood
Ali Baba (407-331-8680; www.aliba barestaurant.info), 1155 W FL 434. It's like stepping into a temple complex, the vast space decorated with tiles and tapestries. Ali Baba is Orlando's only Persian restaurant, and your best bet here is to hit the daily buffets. In addition to offering a great sampler of Middle Eastern cuisine (entrées $10–17), the buffet is a fabulous deal. On weekends expect entertainment from belly dancers. A small shop at the cashier's station offers Middle Eastern imports, including an array of exotic foods.

Mona Lisa Ristorante (407-265-8246), 135 W Jesup Ave. The aromas of Italy permeate this comfortable bistro, which serves up Italian country entrées like *maccheroni alla chitarra, penne amatriciana,* and *veal saltimbocca alla romana* ($13–25). Lunch and dinner, reservations recommended.

Maitland
Antonio's La Fiamma Trattoria (407-645-5523; www.antoniosonline

.com/AntoniosLaFiamma.asp), 611 S Orlando Ave. Enjoy fine dining above Antonio's Cafe (see *Eating Out*), with refined Italian entrées like *penne al forno, bistecca tagliata,* and *pollo carciofi* ($11–35).

Buca di Beppo (407-MACRONE; www.bucadibeppo.com), 1351 S Orlando Ave. Adopt your very own Italian family at this Italian comfort-food haven, where the food comes in platters serving a crowd (singles beware!)—or dinner for two. For greatest fun, reserve the Kitchen Table, a booth right in the middle of the action, where you can watch the chefs at work.

Sam Snead's Tavern (407-622-8800; www.samsneadstavern.com), 1801 Maitland Blvd. It's a natural for sports fans visiting the RDV Sportsplex, with decor honoring golfer Sam Snead. And the food is superb: I enjoyed the best-ever steak sandwich of my life at this particular location. They serve lunch and dinner in a cozy tavern atmosphere, with sandwiches and burgers starting around $11, steak and seafood entrées $15 and up.

UCF
Michael's Italian Restaurant (407-273-3631), 12309 E Colonial Dr. There aren't a lot of restaurants that have been on this strip for 20-plus years, but Michael's keeps the customers coming back with good Italian home cooking for a fair price. Pleasant surroundings and excellent service (staff are quite willing to explain the entrées to you) accent classy Italian dishes like *pollo vitello* and *zuppa di pesce*, prepared to order ($15–21); choose your *carne, pollo,* or *pesce alla cacciatore*, Parmigiana, or Milanese. My grilled vegetable ravioli was per-

fect, with a hint of herbs and plenty of garlic dressing up fresh marinara sauce.

Winter Park

Del Frisco's Steakhouse (407-645-4443; www.delfriscosorlando.com), 729 Lee Rd. It's a classy old-fashioned steak house with a refined 1940s feel; you'd expect Frank Sinatra to step out of the shadows. Serving some of the region's best USDA prime steaks and seafood for dinner, including filet mignon, porterhouse, swordfish, and salmon (entrées, $21–35). Appropriate dress and reservations suggested—it's a popular date-night spot with live music on weekends.

Dexter's on the Square (407-629-1150; www.dexwine.com), 558 W New England Ave. Great wine, great art: That's the theme at Dexter's, a classy corner bistro where I've enjoyed many a party with friends. I'm partial to the Bourbon Street. Jambalaya, but their chicken tortilla pie is tasty, too. Lunch and dinner entrées start around $9.

EATING OUT

Altamonte Springs

&. **Bahama Breeze** (407-831-2929; www.bahamabreeze.com), 499 Altamonte Dr. It looks a little incongruous, this breezy beachfront-style restaurant parked in the front lot of the Altamonte Mall. And normally I wouldn't list a chain restaurant—this is part of the Darden's family (Red Lobster, Olive Garden, and the like). But the chain started here at this mall, and this place is fun, with "Floribbean" offerings like paella, coconut curry chicken, and pina colada bread pudding; it'll tickle your taste buds like it did mine. Serving dinner, with entrées $12 and up.

A standout amid the sea of chain restaurants around it, ❧ **Kohinoor** (407-788-6004), 249 W Semoran Blvd, hides in a strip mall behind TGI Fridays. I've visited India, and appreciate this restaurant's authenticity, particularly the *kormas* and chicken *biryani*, with almonds and raisins mixed into the aromatic rice, and tandoori specialties like chicken tikka masala. Open for lunch and dinner, with buffet specials; entrées start around $8 for vegetarian specialties.

It doesn't look like much more than a little roadside shack along Semoran Blvd, but looks can be deceiving. **Uncle Jones Bar-B-Que** (407-260-2425), 1370 E Altamonte Dr, offers up some of the best ribs in the region.

Apopka

❧ &. When asked where I wanted to go for Valentine's Day, I didn't hesitate—**The Catfish Place** (407-889-7980 www.mycatfishplace.com), 311 S. Forest Ave, has awesome fried green tomatoes and a delicious seafood platter served up with grits. The filet mignon is magnificent, too. Lunch items run toward the lighter side, and yes, you can get gator, and frog legs too. Entrées, $10-19.

❧ **Roma Ristorante** (407-886-2360), 730 Orange Blossom Trail. Since 1964, Maria and her family have created Italian specialties for the pleasure of patrons, and patrons and owners pass into a second generation with the founder's children running the business. Featuring homemade egg noodle pastas, including fettuccine, lasagna, and spaghetti, as well as Italian classics like veal marsala and shrimp scampi; dinners $11–17.

Casselberry

Dinner in a cozy Aspen lodge—that's the theme at the **Colorado Fondue Company** (407-767-8232; www .coloradofondue.com), corner of Red Bug Rd and Semoran Blvd, where you cook your own meal in a fondue pot or atop a sizzling hot rock while relaxing in a slice of the Rocky Mountains. Appetizers (primarily fondues) $9–11, entrées $11–20; fixed price Colorado Fondue for Two, $45. Melted chocolate desserts, too!

At **Rolando's** (407-767-9677), 870 E Semoran Blvd, Cuban art in a bistro atmosphere accents hearty Cuban food like *papas rellena* (stuffed potatoes), *ropa vieja* (shredded beef), and *arroz con pollo* (chicken and rice). Lunch and dinner served daily, $6 and up.

Lockhart

Where city meets suburbs near the Lockhart Post Office, **Thai Cuisine** (407-292-9474), 5325 Edgewater Dr, surprised me when they opened a few years ago—hidden behind an Oriental store, you could hardly tell they were there. But I stopped in when I saw the sign, and discovered authentic Thai curries and entrées ($7–9) that are fabulous and inexpensive. If you order it hot, it will be hot!

Longwood

Kobe (407-389-1888; www.kobesteak house.com), 1231 Douglas Ave. There's something about the spectacle of having a Japanese chef prepare dinner in front of you that I just adore—it's creative and it's fun. I've always enjoyed my visits to Kobe, where as much as I love their sushi (rolls $4–10) I always have to have something prepared on the table, usually Tori Chicken Teriyaki or Sirloin &

Shrimp. Entrées ($15–55) and tempura come with salad and rice.

Korea House (407-767-5918), 977 FL 434 (at Rangeline Rd), was Central Florida's first authentic Korean restaurant, and my friends who've traveled in Korea vouch for the food, especially the kimchi; lunch and dinner entrées $8–27.

It's a pleasure to dine at **Mykonos** (407-788-9095; www.mykonoscfl .com), 2401 W SR 434, where the owners hail from Paleokastritsa along the shore of one of my favorite Greek islands, Corfu. The recipes are spot-on, with favorites like moussaka and gyro balanced with authentic *marithes* (fried smelts) and *garides Ellinikes* (Greek-style shrimp) at lunch and dinner, $12–20.

Maitland

Antonio's Café (407-645-1039; www .antoniosonline.com), 611 S Orlando Ave. On the lower floor of this restaurant complex enjoy a bustling casual atmosphere amid an Italian store and deli, where the aroma of baking from the wood-burning oven will have you salivating for classic Italian calzones and pizza topped with portobello mushrooms and fresh tomato slices; lunch and dinner $10–20.

🦑 🐟 A Maitland landmark, **Kappy's** (407-647-9099), US 17-92, is an old-fashioned drive-in with all-beef hot dogs, Philadelphia hoagies, New York heroes, and "super rich & thick" jumbo shakes; grab lunch or dinner (except Sun) for $3–8.

Ocoee

Positano (407-291-0602), 8995 W Colonial Dr. It's an Italian restaurant with a twist: Order a sub or pizza at the counter, or sit down in one of the spacious booths for a more upscale meal. Most folks come here for their excellent daily lunch buffet, which gives you a sampling of entrées like veal scaloppine, ravioli, and several types of salad; entrées $9–28.

Oviedo

🌹 **Bill's Elbow South** (407-365-2435; http://billselbowsouth.com), 1280 Oviedo Marketplace Blvd. Imagine this concoction: a biscuit topped with cinnamon and sugar, a dollop of vanilla ice cream, more cinnamon and sugar, and cornflakes. It's called the King of Oviedo, and according to the gal who met me at the door of this popular Oviedo landmark, she and her friends would drive miles just to split one of these desserts. Bill's occupies spacious accommodations at the Oviedo Marketplace Mall, but they still have the same fabulous food they did at their former location (lunches $4–10, dinners $10–34), and paintings by local artists decorate the walls—including the famous free-range Oviedo roosters that hang out by Popeye's Fried Chicken, go figure!

🌹 🐚 **Black Hammock Fish Camp** (407-365-2201; www.blackhammock.net), 2536 Black Hammock Fish Camp Rd. Only Glenn Wilson could

stroll through the Sanford Airport security checkpoint with an alligator on a leash and not raise any eyebrows. A fixture in Oviedo, Glenn is the heart and soul behind this funkiest of fish camps, where you can watch baby gators crawl around in an aquarium and get your picture taken with one while chowing down on the best catfish and farm-raised alligator in Central Florida (entrées $11–17). This is the place I take my friends for a taste of authentic Florida. Before dinner, you can grab an airboat ride on Lake Jesup; afterward, hang out at the waterfront bar and listen to the house band jam.

Toucan Willie's (407-366-6225; www.toucanwillies.com), 829 Eyrie Dr. Taking on the popular "Floribbean" theme seen commonly in South Florida, Toucan Willie's does a nice job with atmosphere, from the faux Key West front porch dining room with rattan furnishings to the Caribbean and Jimmy Buffett music drifting through the air. While appetizers such as fried mushrooms or coconut shrimp may tease you, leave room for the seafood gumbo, a spicy, thick, and creamy rendition with an almost gravy-like texture. Served with a side of mustard dipping sauce, the fried oysters have a subtle breading and are honest-to-God fresh. Nice and flaky, the crab cakes boast much more crab than breading. The top value on the menu is Willie's Deal Meals, satisfying smaller portions at $11 with veggies, side, and salad included. The dining room stays open until 10 most evenings, 11 Fri and Sat.

The Town House Restaurant (407-365-5151), corner of Central and Broadway. Sip your morning coffee

KAPPY'S, A MAITLAND LANDMARK

Sandra Friend

and watch the town of Oviedo come alive through the picture windows in this local institution, the pride of an Athenian family with attention to detail. Enjoy a great breakfast value with a stack of fluffy pancakes with bacon (one of two daily specials), or give the corned beef hash a whirl. Lunches include Greek favorites like gyros and Greek salad as well as more traditional fare, from BLTs to burgers.

Sanford—Downtown

The Colonial Room (407-323-2999), 115 E First St, has been the town's favorite breakfast spot for more than 25 years, serving up home-style southern cooking like the big Country Breakfast (where stewed apples or grits or potatoes come with your eggs, toast, and meat). Serving lunch and dinner, too ($3–9); no credit cards accepted.

We met up with friends for a pre-Christmas lunch at **Hollerbach's Willow Tree Cafe** (407-321-2204), 205 E First St, and it was such a delightful experience. The menu is laden with authentic German cuisine like schnitzels and strudels in addition to tasty salads and deli sandwiches, and the freshly baked German breads are not to be missed. Surrounded by murals of Europe, it feels like a slice of the Old Country, especially when you order a slice of Black Forest cake. Live music begins Saturday afternoon out on the patio and continues into the evening.

The **Hot Spot Café** (321-578-1436), 108 S Magnolia, serves a shrimp po'boy made with popcorn shrimp and provolone as one of several hot grilled sandwiches; their "mile high" sandwiches and wraps ($6-7) have healthful fillings like hummus, sprouts, spinach, and avocado.

Little Fish Huge Pond (407-321-2264), 512 S Sanford Ave, is the only place I know where you can order a Spam sandwich fried and complete with pineapple, like Mom used to make. Not that I want one, but you might! This artsy café offers unusual stuff ($5–13), including fried bologna, salami with smelly pickles, and a pitcher of tater tots. Closed Sun.

Sanford—Riverside

Gator's Riverside Grill (407-688-9700; www.gatorsriversidegrille.com), 4522 Peninsula Pt. Overlooking the St. Johns River, this cozy seafood shack offers snook (a rare find on a menu) as well as gator bites, tuna bites, grouper sandwiches, and other seafood goodies in baskets and sandwiches; $4–14, serving lunch and dinner.

Captains Cove Restaurant and Poolside Bar (407-323-3991; www.boattree.com), 4380 Carraway Place at BoatTree Marina, is the only restaurant I know that has its own pool. No motel, but there is a poolside bar. Bring your bathing suit! Sunday brunch, 11–2; $13 adults, $6.50 children. Live entertainment on Saturday and Sunday afternoons, a Thursday comedy night, and karaoke Tuesdays!

Sanford—US 17-92

Colorado's Prime Steaks (407-324-1741), 3863 Orlando Ave. Step into a virtual Aspen eatery for a taste of Colorado beef: My girlfriends brought me here for the Dark Horse Saloon steak sandwich ($9), which was certainly tender, but I think the fire-grilled burgers ($8–9) are a better lunch choice.

UCF

At **Anmol Fine Indian Cuisine** (407-384-8850), 12239 University

Blvd, I was pleased to find authentic chicken tikka masala, one of my favorite dishes, to be prepared to perfection. The extensive menu includes many vegetarian options and a cross-section of Indian cuisine with *biryani*, *dopiaza*, tandoori, and *makhani* ($8-15) among the presentations.

⚓ Greeted by a gator and a pink pig, you know you'll have fun at **Bubbalou's Bodacious BBQ** (407-423-1212; www.bubbalous.com), one of the area's best for barbecue ribs and pork. I used to live around the corner from their original (and now gone) Winter Park location; this spacious restaurant seems downright upscale by comparison. But the great food hasn't changed one bit. Bodacious sandwich platters, combos, and dinners, $5–14; try a fried pickle on the side.

Winter Garden

Downtown Brown's (407-877-2722; www.downtownbrowns2004.com), 126 W Plant St. A real soda fountain with retro seats and the original floor, where you can enjoy "eats & sweets" like fresh fruit salads, Belgian waffles, stuffed baked potatoes, and, of course, sundaes. Breakfast under $5; daily blue-plate lunch special. It's a popular hangout for bikers on the West Orange Trail.

Winter Park—Downtown

⚓ **Bakely's Restaurant and Bakery** (407-645-5767), 345 W Fairbanks Ave, serves breakfast all day, but what draws the crowds is their fresh baked goods and comfort foods, including hand-dipped shakes and pot roast sandwiches. Sparkling blue and yellow tile sets a French country atmosphere, but the food is very Greek. The Alexandrou family took the diner through a major remodel and added

specialties like moussaka, *pastitsio*, *stifado*, and kebab to the menu, made with their very own olive oil imported from their grove in Greece. Entrées ($8–16) served after 4 PM include not just Greek and classic American food but their own creations like Pork Bakely's—a filet of pork sautéed then flambéed in sherry, served with a sauce of mushrooms, onions, cheese, and cream.

At **The Briarpatch Restaurant** (407-628-8651), 252 Park Ave N, order shakes at the old-fashioned marble-topped ice cream counter, or settle back in the casual country setting for a Park Avenue Salad with mandarin oranges, praline pecans, Gorgonzola, and grilled chicken on a bed of romaine. Breakfast omelets include sage sausage frittata and pear and Gorgonzola; lunch salads and sandwiches; dinner entrées like pesto-crusted salmon; $8–15.

I know of no place in the region better than **Fiddler's Green Irish Pub & Eatery** (407-645-2050; www .fiddlersgreenorlando.com), 544 Fairbanks Ave, to nab a steaming bowl of potato leek soup and a shepherd's pie; entrées $8–13. Most evenings, you'll catch an entertainer or two strumming in the front room.

Winter Park—Semoran Blvd

🍴 **Greek Flame Taverna** (407-678-2388; www.greekflametaverna.com), 1560 N Semoran Blvd, is my old local favorite for just plain good Greek food—moussaka, *dolmades*, and gyros; lunch and dinner $7–11. Leave room for one of the great pastries in the front case.

Winter Park—US 17-92

At **Chamberlin's Market & Cafe** (407-647-6661; www.chamberlins

.com), expect top-quality vegetarian and organic offerings from this hometown health-food grocer; the café (open for lunch and dinner during store hours) is fun to dine in, and serves up great hummus, veggie pitas, and a tasty vegetarian chili, $6 and up.

🍲 **Fuji Sushi** (407-645-1299; www.fujisushiwinterpark.com), 1449 Lee Rd. Booths gracefully decorated with Japanese paintings accent this classic sushi bar that my friends agree is the best in Orlando. Choose your roll: vegetarian, spicy, house special, or perhaps Fuji's exclusive, $5–11. Not into fish? Happy Cat still smiles down on you. Have a hot teriyaki entrée, kettle dish, or curry. Lunch served Mon–Fri, dinner daily.

Thai Place (407-644-8449), 501 N Orlando Ave. When I lived nearby, I stumbled across this restaurant en route to the movies and have been coming ever back since. The owners treat you like family, and the intimate setting makes it a perfect place to meet a friend for a meal. I love the house peanut dressing, and recommend the *pad med mamuang*, made with cashew nuts. House specials include Siamese duck, grouper, chicken, and shrimp in several choices of preparations; entrées $10–14.

Winter Springs
Villa Capri (407-388-7766), 5661 Red Bug Lake Rd. My friends highly recommend this comfortable Italian bistro where family-size portions are the norm; the attentive wait staff will recommend their favorites, like the tomato and mozzarella Caprese salad. Expect to take some of your massive lunch or dinner ($12–21) entrée home.

Altamonte Springs
♿ **Too Jays** (407-830-1770), 515 E Altamonte Dr. Got a craving for pickled tomatoes? A real Reuben? This is as close as Central Florida gets to a New York deli, and this successful small chain has since spread across neighborhoods of displaced New Yorkers all over southeast Florida. Have some potato pancakes, authentic blintzes, or herring in cream sauce; they serve the best Reubens around (sandwiches $7–9, dinner entrées $10–14). And don't forget dessert—the baked goods at the checkout will have you salivating. My fave: the Mounds Cake, a heady concoction of chocolate and coconut with a rich chocolate icing.

Longwood
☕ **Volcanoes Coffee Bar** (407-260-8845; www.volcanoscoffee.com), 1901 W FL 434, in Longwood Village, was a favorite of mine when I lived nearby, a great place to grab creative coffee drinks and a gelato while journaling.

Sanford
☕ Chill out with friends at **Eberwine's Arthouse Coffeegallery** (407-321-3112), 417 S Sanford Ave, in the historic Stokes Fish Market building.

Winter Park
Lacomka Bakery & Deli (407-677-1101; www.lacomka-orlando.com), 2050 N Semoran Blvd, is a unique Russian grocery with authentic lunch offerings ($3–8) like *pirozhki, blinchiki, pelmeni,* and borscht; the napoleon with traditional Russian cream is an incredible delight.

FARMER'S MARKETS AND FRESH PRODUCE

Goldenrod

Visit the Goldenrod Station (see *Museums*) for the **Goldenrod Farmer's Market** (407-677-5980), every Saturday 8–1, for fresh produce, baked goods, candles, honey, and plants from local farmers and vendors.

Maitland

Hollieanna Groves (407-644-8803 or 1-800-793-7848), 540 S Orlando Ave. While Maitland's orange groves have vanished under the developers' bulldozers, Hollieanna, an old family operation, still offers ready-to-ship citrus during the growing season. It's not only a storefront, but a packing house as well—you can peek right in and watch the sorting and boxing going on.

Oviedo

Pappy's U-Pick Strawberries, Fruit and Produce (407-366-8512) is one of the last remaining pick-your-own farms in what used to be a busy celery-growing district. Follow the signs

HOLLIEANNA GROVES

Sandra Friend

from FL 434 along De Leon Ave to Florida Ave.

Sanford

Downtown Sanford hosts a **weekly farmer's market** every Saturday 9–2 at Magnolia Square. Not only will you find the freshest from local growers, there are baked goods, honey, and fresh-cut flowers to add to your market basket.

Winter Park

Every Saturday morning 7–1, stop in Winter Park for the **Winter Park Farmer's Market** (407-599-3358), corner of Lyman and New York Ave, where you'll find exotic spices and freshly baked pies next to ferns and flowers, homemade jellies, and, of course, farm-fresh produce.

Zellwood

Farm Fresh Produce, Laughlin Rd and US 441, sells sweet Georgia peaches and produce from local farms (including the famed Zellwood corn, in-season) at a permanent roadside stand.

Long & Scott Farms (352-383-6900; www.longandscottfarms.com), CR 448A, is the last remaining grower of Zellwood corn; many farmers' fields have turned to housing developments throughout this area. Stop here in springtime for their fun Corn Maze and to pick up a bushel of the sweetest corn in Florida.

✳ Selective Shopping

Altamonte Springs

Travel Country Outdoors (407-831-0777 or 1-800-643-3629; www.travelcountry.com), 1101 E Semoran Blvd. Being an avid hiker, this is one of my frequent stops in the Orlando area; it's the most extensive backpacking and paddle sports outfitter in the region. This is where all of my friends come from around the state to get fitted for insoles for their hiking boots and proper sizing for backpacks.

Apopka

When **Mosquito Creek Outfitters** (407-464-2000; www.mosquitocreek .com), 170 S Washington Ave, opened up near my house, I was thrilled to have a gear source nearby. The focus is mostly on technical clothing, but they also carry hunting and fishing, hiking and backpacking, and canoe and kayak supplies.

Christmas

Country Craft Christmas (407-568-8084), 25250 E Colonial Dr. What would Christmas be without Christmas? This large new shop represents more than 20 area crafters with country craft items, a Victorian room, and, of course, a room brimming with Christmas ornaments and home decor. Open daily.

Lockhart

3 Flea Market, US 441 at Overland Rd. Right at the county line, this small flea market is a gathering place for folks who are emptying their attics and garages, selling their wares off tables behind their trucks. You'll wade through a lot of stuff, but there's always the chance of an excellent bargain! Sat and Sun, rain or shine.

Longwood

The Apple Basket (407-332-1700), 218 W Church Ave. Primitive furniture, country chic, vintage china, and collectibles like Dept 56 in a home more than a century old.

Culinary Cottage (407-834-7220), 141 Church Ave. Gourmet food, gift items, and reasonably priced art glass

fills the 1870 Inside-Outside House (see *Historic Sites*), where each room offers up new gift ideas.

Judy's Dolls (407-332-7928), 280 W Warren Ave. Featuring a popular "newborn nursery" (one of only two in Florida) and "create a doll," plus a doll repair "hospital," this cute little shop is the perfect place to pick out the perfect doll.

Legible Leftovers (407-339-4043; www.legibleleftovers.com), 1111 N Ronald Reagan Blvd, is a browser's delight, with room after room filled with well-organized used books. Plenty of paperbacks (trades welcome) and nice depth in areas like philosophy, travel, and cooking. Open daily at 9:30. The **Cat's Meow** gift shop takes up a tiny corner of the store with crafts and home decor items; don't let the cats out! Opens at 9:30 AM Tue–Sat.

Sweet William Antiques (407-831-1657), 216 W Warren Ave. Inside a historic home, you'll find beautiful stained-glass windows along with Victorian antiques, books, dolls, and jigsaw puzzles. Outside, a landscaped garden of young plants and pottery (all for sale) fill the space between this shop and the adjoining Enchanted Cottage.

Maitland

Cram-packed with antiques and collectibles, **Bestnwurst Antiques** (407-647-0533), 145 S Orlando Ave, has delighted customers for nearly 20 years with great finds in glassware, furnishings, silver flatware, and costume jewelry.

At **Cranberry Corners Antiques** (407-644-0363), 203 E Horatio Ave, country primitives fill the rooms, mingling antiques like restored quilts from the 1880s with home decor such as quilted pillows, homemade soaps by Granny Greer, jam and chutney, and scented candles.

With more than 85 dealers, **Halley's Antique Mall** (407-539-1066), 475 S Orlando Ave, has an excellent diversity in stock—from fine china and paintings to vintage ads and books—and reasonable prices. Open daily.

Voted "Best in Florida," the **Orange Tree Antiques Mall** (407-622-0600), 150 Lake Ave, has been around for more than a decade, filled with rooms of collectibles, antiques, and fine art, with a heavy emphasis on glassware and art glass. In the Highwaymen Room, I saw paintings by Sam Newton I wished I owned, and found a classic streetcar sign in another corner. Take your time; you'll browse for hours!

Ocoee

In downtown Ocoee, **The Book Rack** (407-905-0279), 125 W McKay St, features stacks of gently used paperbacks at half retail, with trade-ins encouraged.

Oviedo

The Artistic Hand (407-366-7882), 353 N Central Ave. Dwarfed by an ancient live oak tree, this little purple house with white trim holds a fairyland of treasures created by artisans from all over Florida. Established in 1992 by Barbara Walker-Seaman, the Artistic Hand overflows with the work of more than 200 artists in an appealing variety of media, from fine art paintings to collage, sculpture, traditional pottery, textiles, glass, and so much more. Browse the bright rooms and you're sure to come up with a suitable gift for the art lover in your family, since the prices range right on down to downright reasonable.

Sanford—Downtown

Sanford is an antiques and arts mecca, definitely worth a day for browsing; there are plenty of dining options, too. Shops and galleries line First Ave; these are just a few of the many.

This is a first! Man-tiques. Yup, you read that right. At **An Acquiring Mind** (407-302-8224), 218 E First St, Mike's Man-tiques appeals to the grown-up boy with model planes, trains, and other old-fashioned toys. That's one in a bunch of dealer booths with a heavy emphasis on glassware but a little bit of everything, like postcards, comics, and '70s kitsch kitchen clocks.

Magnolia Square (407-322-7544), 201 E First St, is the oldest antiques shop in town, and it has a special draw—an ice cream parlor serving locally made homemade ice cream. The owners take several buying trips a year, filling the large, open rooms with a fresh stock of collectibles, jewelry, and dishes.

Maya Books & More (407-321-6504), 205A E First St, displays its Florida books and a good selection of used tomes in comfy digs; if you're looking for record albums, you'll find them here, too.

A nicely arranged library of books and albums makes it **Something Special** (407-323-5332), 105 E First St, where you'll also find glassware, jewelry, toys, and home decor.

At **The Treehouse** (407-936-2394), 222 E First St, it's like walking into a furnished house, with everything in suite groupings. The Indonesian frog with parasol seemed a bit odd next to ceramic roosters and Depression glass, but most everything is vintage, including handmade wooden table and chair sets and desks.

Sanford—US 17-92

Flea World (407-330-1792, ext 224; www.fleaworld.com), US 17-92. This massive 1,700-booth complex claims to be the largest flea market in the world, although the one in Webster (see "Nature Coast") gives them a run for the money. Nonetheless, you'll find everything you're looking for and a lot of stuff you're not. Open Fri–Sun 9–6.

Winter Garden

Shirley's Trailside Antiques (407-656-6508), 12 W Plant St. Local handicrafts, Victorian furniture, classic advertising, and a whole lot more—this place is packed with goodies.

Webb's Antique Mall (407-877-5921; www.webbsantiquemalls.com), 13373 W Colonial Dr, hidden in a strip mall next to the Kmart, provides a dizzying array of dealer booths and row upon row of display cases showcasing gems like antique pottery, fine art, and jewelry. Disney collector note: This store's proximity to the source means tons of Disney-employee-only goodies show up on the shelves.

Winter Park—Downtown

Like its New York counterpart, **Park Ave** is where tony Orlando comes to shop. In addition to upscale chains, you'll find plenty of local gems along this elegant thoroughfare, including a nice selection of consignment art galleries. Don't forget to stroll down East Morse Ave, which is also crowded with shops.

Kathmandu (407-647-7071), 352 Park Ave, deals in imports like ceremonial masks, Rajasthani tapestries, and jewelry as well as incense and New Age items.

Since the 1960s, the **Miller Gallery** (407-599-1960), 348 Park Ave S, has displayed exceptional fine arts from around the globe, with one-of-a-kind pieces of art for your home; one section always focuses on Florida artists.

I love **Ten Thousand Villages** (407-644-8464; www.tenthousandvillages .com), 346 N Park Ave, for their indigenous handicrafts and fair trade partnerships with craftspeople in faraway lands. It's easy to find fun little gifts here, from bamboo platters to fiber creatures.

In addition to the most extensive collection of handcrafted jewelry in the United States, **Timothy's Gallery** (407-629-0707; www.timothysgallery .com), 212 Park Ave N, has inspirational and playful art pieces like turned wood bowls, kaleidoscopes, and vibrant art glass from more than 350 nationally renowned artists.

Winter Park—US 17-92

Like its sister shop in Maitland, the **Orange Tree Antiques Mall** (407-839-2863), 853 S Orlando Ave, has an incredible array of vintage items to explore. Take your time!

Chocoholics will delight in **Schako-lad Chocolate Factory** (407-677-

WINTER PARK'S PARK AVENUE

Sandra Friend

4114), hidden in Winter Park Village at 480 N Orlando Ave, where third-generation chocolatier Edgar Schaked presents fine handmade chocolates and truffles beyond description.

✳ Entertainment

Maitland
With indie films every evening at 7:30 and 9:30, the **Enzian Theatre** (407-629-0054; www.enzian.org), 1300 S Orlando Ave, is Orlando's hot spot for film buffs. The best part? Dinner and a movie in one seating.

Sanford
The **Helen Stairs Theatre** (407-321-8111; www.helenstairstheatre.com), 203 S Magnolia Ave, is a revitalized theater from 1922. The Milane, where Rachmaninoff performed in 1928 and Tom Mix delighted kids in 1933, was restored and renamed in 2000. It's again showcasing live acts as diverse as Lee Greenwood, *The Marriage of Figaro*, and *The Nutcracker*.

Kick up your heels while line dancing at **The Barn** (407-324-2276; www.thebarninsanford.com), 1777 S French Ave, with country music at its foot-stomping finest; opens 7 PM Wed–Sun; $7 cover.

Orlando Theatre Project (407-328-2040; www.otp.cc), Seminole Community College, 100 Weldon Blvd. This small Actors' Equity group presents American classics like *The Death of a Salesman* and *Grapes of Wrath*, as well as original plays by local playwrights. Three plays presented Nov–May.

Winter Park
A walk though the bistros of Winter Park will yield plenty of weekend entertainment, primarily live jazz and blues at places like **Dexter's** and **Fiddler's Green** (see *Eating Out*).

At the **Annie Russell Theatre** (407-646-2145; www.rollins.edu/theatre), 1000 Holt Ave, enjoy dance and theater events as well as the Bach Festival Society (407-646-2182; www.bachfestivalflorida.org), which holds an annual concert series that spans the gamut from piano recitals and philharmonic orchestras to African drumming and dance.

✳ Special Events

January: **Central Florida Scottish Festival and Highland Games** (407-I-AM-SCOT; www.flascot.com), third Sat, Central Winds Park, Winter Springs. After more than 30 years, those men in kilts are still tossing cabers and throwing hammers, dancing Highland dances and playing the pipes. Join in the fun as a participant or spectator!

Zora Neale Hurston Festival of the Arts and Humanities (407-647-3959 or 1-800-972-3310; www.zoranealehurstonfestival.com), 227 E Kennedy Blvd, Eatonville, last week. Celebrating the legacy of Eatonville's best-known resident, this renowned African American festival, now nearly 20 years old, focuses on the arts and humanities, featuring a juried street festival of the arts, live music, film screenings, and more.

March: The **Florida Film Festival**, held mid-Mar and centering on the Enzian Theatre in Maitland (see *Entertainment*), features the finest in independent filmmaking from Florida studios, with at least 150 films screened in four regional venues, plus informative seminars from the filmmakers. Free.

Fort Christmas Militia Encampment (407-568-4149), late Mar and Nov. Soldiers in 1840 US Army regalia demonstrate life during the Seminole Wars.

Thousands flock annually to the **Winter Park Sidewalk Art Festival** (407-647-5557). One of Florida's largest arts festivals, it encompasses the downtown district. In addition to juried competitions, arts vendors, and food, enjoy live music all day and jazz headliners at night.

April: **Rajuncajun Crawfish Festival**, (http://www.crawfishcoofcentral flainc.com/), third Sat, Isle of Pines. For 20 years, this fun Cajun food festival has raised money for the Central Florida Children's Home and presents live Cajun and zydeco performers like the Porchdogs. All-you-can-eat buffet and entertainment, $40 advance; kids 7–12 are $20, under 7 free.

In its 16th year, the **Maitland Festival of the Arts** (407-644-0741), third weekend, Maitland Civic Center, brings in renowned artists in all media.

A **Taste of Oviedo** (407-365-6500; www.oviedochamber.org). After a decade of treating participants to the best food that Oviedo restaurants have to offer, this annual festival is going strong.

May: Love corn-on-the-cob? Then don't miss the **Zellwood Sweet Corn Festival** (407-886-0014; www .zellwoodsweetcornfest.org), 4253 W Ponkan Rd, an annual event that celebrates this rural community's best-known export. Marvel at the boiler Big Bertha—cooking 1,650 ears of corn every 9 minutes in 350 gallons of boiling water. Arts and crafts vendors, live music, and more.

November: **Fort Christmas Militia Encampment** (see Mar).

SOUTH OF ORLANDO

KISSIMMEE–ST. CLOUD

Osceola County was created in 1886 with sections of Brevard and Orange Counties and was named in honor of Seminole chief Osceola. Only 18 miles from downtown Orlando and less than an hour's drive to the Atlantic Ocean, the area has long been known as an important crossroads. **Kissimmee**, the county seat, was once Central Florida's largest shipping port. As headwaters to the Florida Everglades system, Lake Tohopekaliga still serves as the launch point for boats, which travel through a series of locks to Lake Okeechobee and onward to either the Atlantic or Gulf. Trains have been rolling through with supplies since the shipbuilding heyday with the Florida East Coast, Seaboard, and Amtrak systems still in operation.

Before the area became the gateway to Walt Disney World and other Central Florida attractions, the cattle industry dominated the land. Osceola County's rich cattle history still has not diminished. Except for the northwest quadrant, the area remains one of the largest cattle-producing counties in the state, which is why you'll see so many steakhouses around **St. Cloud**, long the gateway to the vast ranches of Osceola County. Acres of open land also provide an excellent habit for wildlife. The rich forests, vast prairies, and clear lakes are home for many endangered species, as well as some of the best fishing in the world. The Kissimmee chain of lakes is where you'll find world-class bass fishing and the largest concentration of nesting bald eagles in the continental United States.

Please note: Attractions, lodgings, and restaurants in the theme park areas, which straddle Osceola and Orange Counties, are listed in the "Theme Parks" chapter under Kissimmee-St. Cloud subheadings.

GUIDANCE **Kissimmee–St. Cloud Convention & Visitors Bureau** (407-847-5000; www.floridakiss.com), 1925 E Hwy 192, Kissimmee 34742.

St. Cloud Chamber of Commerce (407-892-3671; www.stcloudflchamber .com), 1200 New York Ave, St. Cloud 34769.

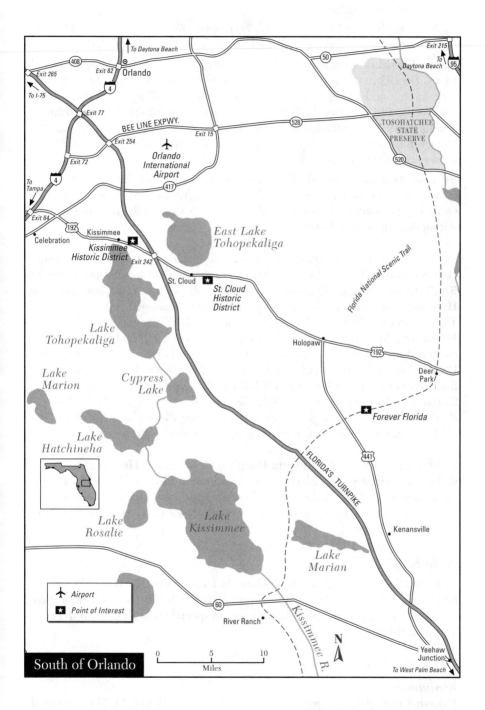

South of Orlando

GETTING THERE *By air:* **Greater Orlando International Airport** (407-825-2001; www.state.fl.us/goaa/).

By bus: **Greyhound Lines** (407-847-3911; www.greyhound.com), 103 E Dakin Ave, Kissimmee, has service near the historic district, just off US 192.

By car: **Florida's Turnpike** and **I-4** both have exits to **US 192** and the **Osceola Pkwy**. US 192 runs though the heart of Osceola County, with plenty of shops, restaurants, and lodging—but traffic jams are common. For a faster east–west connection, use the Osceola Pkwy, US 522 (toll), then get off on either **John Young Pkwy** or the **Orange Blossom Trail**. Both run north to south, with the Orange Blossom Trail making a pass through the Kissimmee historic district before connecting to the parkway.

By train: **Amtrak** (1-800-872-7245; www.amtrak.com) provides regularly scheduled service to Kissimmee, near US 192 and the historic district, and metro Orlando, just north of the theme parks. Coach USA vans will take you from the station directly to your hotel.

GETTING AROUND **US 192** weaves through the heart of the tourist area, from Holopaw and St. Cloud, through Kissimmee, past Walt Disney World, and out to FL 27. Once you reach Kissimmee, the road is also known as the **Irlo Bronson Hwy** and is marked with brightly lit guide markers at about 1-mile intervals. These markers coincide with businesses listed in the Kissimmee–St. Cloud Resort Area Map of US 192 Guidemarker Locations; you'll find a long stretch of chain restaurants, economy motels, and fast-food and dine-in eateries here. On US 192, you know you've entered the "Disney Zone" near the main gate when the lampposts turn purple. Jump off I-4 (exit 26C) or Florida's Turnpike (exit 249) to the **Osceola Pkwy**, (US 522, toll), for a direct route into Walt Disney World without the stop-and-go traffic. **John Young Pkwy** also connects to Osceola Pkwy and will take you directly into the heart of Kissimmee.

MEDICAL EMERGENCIES **Florida Hospital Celebration Health** (407-764-4000; www.celebrationhealth.com), 400 Celebration Place, and **Florida Hospital Kissimmee** (407-846-4343; www.floridahospital.com/locations/kissimmee), 2450 North Orange Blossom Trail, Kissimmee, are located near Disney and the US 192 attractions.

✳ To See

ART GALLERIES The gallery at the **Osceola Center for the Arts** (407-846-6257; www.ocfta.com), 2411 E Irlo Bronson Hwy (US 192), Kissimmee, features local and national artists and is host to several special events. Open Mon–Fri 10–5, Sat 9–12.

HISTORIC SITES

Kissimmee
Bataan-Corregidor Memorial (407-846-6131), 461 W Oak St. This memorial in honor of the Americans and Filipinos who fought in World War II depicts scenes from the 1942 Bataan Death March.

The **1916 Colonial Estate** at 240 Old Dixie Highway is worth a drive by just to see the colossal Ionic columns supporting a full entablature. But don't knock on the door—it's a private residence.

Makinson's Hardware Store (407-847-2100) 308 Broadway Ave. Opened in 1884 by W. B. Makinson Sr., this is the oldest operating hardware store in the state of Florida. A glorious mural depicting a bygone era is on the south side of the building.

The **Monument of States**, 300 Monument Ave. Built in 1943, this impressive 50-foot tower, representing every state and 20 foreign countries, contains more than 1,500 stones, meteors, and stalagmites, as well as petrified wood, teeth, and bones. Conceived by Dr. Bressler-Pettis, the monument soon received national attention; tourists, governors, and even a US president furnished stones for its inclusion. The tower also contains fragments from the original Washington Monument's base. Dr. Bressler-Pettis's ashes are buried at the site.

Old Holy Redeemer Church, 120 N Sproule Ave. A single-story Gothic Revival facility, circa 1912, with a battlemented entrance porch and stained-glass windows. Originally Catholic, it now serves the Hispanic community as a First United Methodist church.

One of the state's oldest courthouses (circa 1886), and the only one continuously in daily use, the **Osceola County Courthouse** (407-343-2275; www.osceola .org), 1 Courthouse Square, continues to retain its architectural integrity and is listed on the National Register of Historic Places. Dedicated May 6, 1890, it once had a cow pen in front of it, where lost cows were held until their owners claimed them.

St. Cloud
Mount Peace Cemetery (407-957-7243), 755 E 10th St. Final resting place for more than 300 Civil War Union veterans set amid the serenity and grandeur of centuries-old live oak trees.

Yeehaw Junction
On the National Register of Historic Places, the **Desert Inn** (see Eating Out) was established in the 1880s as a watering station for a railroad built through the region to enable lumberjacks to cut grand old cypress out of the swamps along the Kissimmee River basin. As cattle drovers moved their herds south along the route, this was the only "watering hole" for the men between the cities of St. Cloud and Okeechobee. In the 1930s, "Dad" Wilson fixed up the property and added gas pumps for travelers along US 441. In the 1950s, when this rural crossroads needed a name for its Florida's Turnpike exit, Yeehaw Junction was chosen from several alternatives, including Desert Inn.

MUSEUMS

Kissimmee
✐ I spent an afternoon under the live oaks at the **Osceola County Historical Society & Pioneer Museum** (407-396-8644), 750 N Bass Rd, watching the blacksmith at work, marveling at the ingenuity of make-do Florida pioneers in

outfitting their home, and enjoying the trails through the nature preserve. The complex includes a genealogy library of Osceola County residents and a museum filled with local ephemera. Open Thu–Sat 10–4, Sun 1–4; fee.

St. Cloud

⚓ The Cannery Museum (407-892-3728), 901 Virginia Ave, is run by fourth-grade students from Michigan Ave Elementary as part of their Florida history studies. Learn about life in the 1930s on a tour—complete with living history—through the Depression-era cannery, blacksmith shop, and one-room schoolhouse. Call for hours.

Grand Army of the Republic Museum (407-892-6146), 1101 Massachusetts Ave. Built in 1914, this building, on the National Register of Historic Places, houses Civil War items and GAR memorabilia. Guided tours available; fee. Open Mon, Tue, and Thu 10–4.

&. **Historical Museum of St. Cloud & Osceola County** (407-892-3671; www .stcloudflchamber.com), 1200 New York Ave. Artifacts, photographs, and collectibles housed in St. Cloud's oldest commercial building, the First National Bank, circa 1910. Also home to the St. Cloud Chamber of Commerce; open Mon–Fri 9–4.

REPTILE VIEWING ❀ ⚓ &. **Reptile World Serpentarium** (407-892-6905), 5705 E Irlo Bronson Hwy (FL 192). Since 1972, this working research facility, operated by George Van Horn and his wife, Rosa, has supported more than 400 research labs and supplies venom proteins for three antivenin companies. The facility houses 600 to 700 snakes; 50 or so are on display. From the enormous anaconda to the camouflaged Madagascar leaf nose, the natural history of reptiles is displayed in clean, indoor exhibits. Daily, at approximately noon and 3, you can watch George and Rosa milk venomous snakes such as albino monoclid cobras, eastern diamondback rattlesnakes, and Florida's cottonmouth, while you are safely outside the glass enclosure. Those too squeamish to watch the venom milking can spend time outside with the turtles and gopher tortoise, green iguanas, American alligator, and various birds. Open Tue–Sun 9–5:30, closed in Sep; fee.

GEORGE VAN HORN MILKS AN EASTERN DIAMONDBACK AT THE REPTILE SERPENTARIUM

Kathy Wolf

✷ To Do

AIRBOATS ♿ Hop on one of the **Boggy Creek Airboat Rides** (407-348-4676; www.bcairboats.com). West location on Lake Tohopekaliga, 2001 E Southport Rd, Kissimmee; east location on East Lake Tohopekaliga, 3702 Big Bass Rd, Kissimmee. Continuous 30-minute guided tours in 18-passenger airboats around the marshy edges of the Toho lakes. Custom and night rides on six-passenger boats available. Open daily 9–5:30. $23 adults, $18 ages 3–12 for a standard tour; $35 and $30 for a one-hour night tour—the best way to see alligators eyes gleam in the swamp after dark! Call for reservations.

AVIATION **Orlando Helitours** (407-397-0226; www.orlandohelitours.com), 5519 W US 192, Kissimmee, flies air-conditioned 206 Jet Rangers, which seat up to four people. If you've never ridden in a helicopter, this one is like a Land Rover for the air. You'll want to take it for an aerial view of the Disney properties; Blizzard Beach looks like Santa's village from the air. A "ride" ($15) is barely worth it—you'll go up, bank a turn, and come back down in 2 or 3 minutes. Opt for the $40 tour, which gets you over part of Disney and back in 7 to 9 minutes, or—for the ride of your life—go for 12 to 15 minutes ($75) and see all of Disney. Charter flights can take you anywhere you want for as long as you want.

Stallion 51 (407-846-4400; www.stallion51.com), 3951 Merlin Dr, Kissimmee. I watched as a man in his mid-80s climbed into the cockpit of the Crazy Horse, his wife waving him good-bye as he closed the bubble canopy. The former P-51 pilot had flown this aircraft for real in World War II and now, as a birthday gift, he was taking it up again. For about an hour he took to the skies and performed maneuvers like he did so long ago. His hands were still steady; it all came back to him high up in the clear blue skies. As he taxied back to the hangar and deplaned, he burst into tears. This had been his dream, and his loving wife had made it a reality. Off they went for parts unknown after what I suspect was his best birthday gift ever. If you mention P-51 to anyone who knows planes, they will immediately say Ohhh! and get starry-eyed. Only a few of these "Cadillacs of the Skies" were ever made, and even fewer are still in operation. The rare Crazy Horse at Stallion 51 is one of only 12 dual-control Mustangs in the world. This highly maneuverable warbird delivers heart-stopping performance with exceptional vertical and horizontal capabilities. The half-hour or 1-hour orientation tour will have you flying the plane 90 percent of the time. No flight experience is necessary, but this trip will cost you. Still, it's worth every penny for those who dream to fly the very best.

♿ Slip into the front cockpit and take to the skies in a real World War II fighter at **Warbird Adventures, Inc**. (407-870-7366 or 1-800-386-1593; www.warbird adventures.com), 233 N Hoagland Blvd, Kissimmee. Take your "wingmate" with you in another plane and do some formation flying. Yes, you can fly tip to tip and experience all the aerobatic maneuvers used by the aces. Loop, dip, roll, fly upside down, and capture every screaming bit of it on video with their three-camera system. No flying experience is necessary; your instructor will walk you through each maneuver as you fly a real North American T-6 TEXAN. $195 for 15 minutes (no aerobatics); $340 for a half hour (aerobatics option, $375); $590

WARBIRD ADVENTURES' PLANES FLY IN
FORMATION

for an hour (includes aerobatics and positive-g maneuvers). Add-ons include three-camera video or still pictures with each level of flight. Flight instruction and formation flying (with your buddies, scheduled at the same time) available, too. Reservations strongly suggested.

ECOTOURS

Holopaw

Forever Florida (407-957-9794 or 1-866-854-3837; www.foreverflorida .com and www.floridaeco-safaris.com), 4755 N Kenansville Rd. This working cattle ranch and 4,700-acre nature preserve is a loving tribute to the owners' son, Allen Broussard, a conservationist who passed away at age 29. The untouched, unspoiled wilderness is unsurpassed for seeing the Florida where cowmen and Cracker cattle roamed for more than a century. You'll travel through nine ecosystems by either elevated swamp buggy or horseback (see *Trail Riding*), through the Broussards' Crescent J. Ranch and the Allen Broussard Conservancy, where you'll see Cracker cattle, longhorn steer, alligators, eagles, and more. The knowledgeable guides will tell you all about the local flora and fauna, and discuss land management—including the effects of lightning and the necessity of controlled burns—in this informative and entertaining adventure, which includes a stop at a boardwalk for a stroll under ancient cypress to the floodplain of Bull Creek. Kids will like the petting pen near the main lodge, and hikers will enjoy the natural paths; 6 miles of the statewide Florida Trail stretch through the heart of the property. Eco-safaris on the Safari Coach are offered daily at 10 and 1, $25 adults, $20 ages 6-12. Reservations are required for the horseback safaris, which range from one hour excursions ($38) to three-day, two-night trail rides including campouts on the Florida prairie ($300). Open daily 9–6.

FISHING

Kenansville

& Fish Lake Kissimmee from **Middleton's Too Fishcamp** (see *Fish Camps*), where your guide is 35-year veteran lunker-hunter Captain Rob Murchie (1-800-FISH-007; www.all-florida-fishing.com), who knows the backwaters and marshes of this massive Central Florida lake. Half day $225, 6 hours $275, full day $325 for up to two anglers; add a third person for an extra $50. License and bait extra. Bait shop right at the fish camp.

Kissimmee

& Founded by Captain Tony Weatherman, a consortium of full-time professional guides offer their services as **Champion Pro Guide Services Central Florida**

(407-288-0087; www.championbass.com), 2317 Emperor Dr. Bass fishing on the Kissimmee chain of lakes—not to be missed, given the size of the lunkers here—runs $275 half day, $325 for 6 hours, or $375 for 8 hours for up to two people; license and bait extra.

Florida Guidelines (321-777-2773 or 1-888-800-9794; www.flguidelines.com), covering the state of Florida. My friend and fellow outdoor writer Rodney Smith, a Florida native and outdoor photojournalist, will help you plan a memorable fishing excursion. His consortium of experienced guides will help you locate the trophy fish of your dreams, whether on Lake Toho or out on the Indian River Lagoon. Sightseeing trips also arranged. Rates run $300 for 4 hours, $350 for 6 hours, or $400 for a full day for up to two anglers.

GOLF Omni Orlando Resort at ChampionsGate (321-677-6664; www.omni hotels.com/FindAHotel/OrlandoChampionsGate/Golf.aspx), 1500 Masters Blvd, Orlando (see *Lodging*). Two phenomenal 18-hole, par-72 championship golf courses designed by Greg Norman are set amid Florida's natural beauty. Special care was taken to create a natural environment. You'll tee off while hot-air balloons soar overhead nearby, and then chip one in on the green while a pair of sandhill cranes honk their approval. The challenging international course resembles the great links of Scotland, and also boasts the highest course rating in Florida—76.3! Before you tee off, perfect your swing with lessons from the David Leadbetter Golf Academy; you might just find David himself wandering the grounds.

SPA Slip into luxury at the **Fitness Centre & Day Spa at Celebration Health** (407-303-4400; www.celebrationfitness.com), 400 Celebration Place, Celebration. Enjoy the fitness facilities, indoor lap pool, sauna, and steam rooms before or after your treatment. The Aromatherapy Massage ($80) takes you through a botanical journey with essential oils extracted from healing herbs. The Warm Stone and Paraffin Massage ($130) removes all your tension as warm paraffin coats your entire body, softening your skin; then warm stones glide over your body, melting away your stress. For the best buy after walking through the theme parks, opt for the Anti-Fatigue Leg Treatment ($30). A full menu of day-spa treatments, like facials, sea scrubs, manicures, and pedicures, awaits you.

TRAIL RIDING

Holopaw
Forever Florida (407-957-9794 or 1-866-854-3837, www.floridaeco -safaris.com), 4755 N Kenansville Rd. See the real Florida while riding several hours on horseback through nine ecosystems. You can take your choice of the 1-hour ($38), 2-hour ($57), or—if your seat can take it—the 3-hour ($73) tour; all rides are walk only and the 3-hour trip includes a

CONTINUING A RANCHING TRADITION AT FOREVER FLORIDA

Sandra Friend

Sandra Friend

A CRACKER PONY

lunch. Ask for the tour through Bull Creek, where your horse will go belly deep while crossing this beautiful wetland wilderness. You might even pass a sunning alligator—but don't worry, the horses are used to them. For an adventure you'll never forget, join the City Slickers Roundup, where you'll be part of a working cattle drive as they move their herd across the Crescent J Ranch. Or go for the half-day Rawhide Roundup. For a true immersion into the genuine Central Florida wilderness of palmetto prairies and cypress domes, sign up for an overnight (two-day, one-night, $199) or weekend (three-day, two-night, $299) guided trip, minimum two riders. The roundups and overnight trips must be reserved in advance.

Kissimmee

For years I wondered where I could go horseback riding near Orlando—and there was a great stable just down the street! Get off US 192 and head a few miles down Orange Blossom Trail, where a sign will point you to **Horse World Riding Stables** (407-847-4343; www.horseworldstables.com), 3705 S Poinciana Blvd, with more than 700 acres of wooded trails tucked back off the road. Wildlife appears on cue in this natural environment; ducks, alligators, eagles, and deer don't seem to mind the horses. Depending on the time of year, you may even see a newborn foal with its mom. Three levels of riding are offered: Nature Trail (walk) is a relaxing ride along gentle sandy trails and is great for families with kids or those with no prior riding experience; the Intermediate Trail (walk/trot) will take you under a beautiful canopy of live oaks and contains a lot of trotting. You'll want to have some riding experience for the Advanced Trail (walk/trot/canter), which is a great workout, lasting about 1½ hours. These horses are well groomed and well behaved. I selected the Intermediate ride, and when my horse got to the "canter" section, her ears perked up waiting for my guide's signal. When none was given, she continued on with the trot, but I felt like I had dashed her hopes—she would have responded if I'd asked for more. Such control is a testament to exceptional horses; where you often find trail ponies racing for the barn, you'll see none of this here. Special thanks to my guide, Austin Roberts, who took me on an incredible ride through a magical land. Nature Trail: $39 adults and children 6 and over; $17 ages 5 and under, riding double with adult. Intermediate: $47 adults and children over 10. Advanced: $69 adults and children over 10, by reservation only. Weight limit 250 pounds for trail rides; 50 pounds for pony rides. Open daily 9–5.

WATER SPORTS **Buena Vista Water Sports** (407-239-6939; www.bvwater sports.com), located on Lake Bryan on FL 535, Lake Buena Vista. Come on in, the people are friendly and the water is clean and warm. This is the place to go for waterskiing, Jet Skis, and wakeboarding. Rentals and rides from $50. Open daily.

✳ Green Space

BEACHES **Ralph V. Chisholm Park** (407-892-2397), 4700 Chisholm Park Trail, off Narcoossee Rd (FL 15), St. Cloud. Set along the shoreline of Lake Narcoossee, this large county park provides a pleasant public beach and boat ramp for fishing access plus vast acreage for trail riding; walk the open fields, and you'll see sandhill cranes. Free.

NATURE CENTERS **Osceola District Schools Environmental Study Center** (407-870-0551), 4300 Poinciana Blvd, Poinciana. Protecting 200 acres of the Reedy Creek Swamp, this environmental center opens your eyes to the beauty of the cypress forest; walk the boardwalk out to Reedy Creek to see ancient cypresses, one topped with a bald eagle nest. The Indian Mound Trail leads through a floodplain forest to a midden along the creek. Open Sat 10–5, Sun noon–5; free.

PARKS At the north end of Lake Tohopekaliga, Kissimmee's **Lakefront Park** features a lighthouse, fishing pier, boat ramp, picnic tables, playground, and children's water play area.

Moss Park (407-273-2327), 12901 Moss Park Rd, Orlando, is a 1,500-acre Orange County park popular for camping and picnicking. A hiking trail through a wetlands area good for birding connects this park with Split Oak Forest Mitigation Park (see *Wild Places*). Fee.

Peghorn Nature Park (407-957-7243), Peghorn Way, St. Cloud. Two hiking trails wind through a variety of ecosystems in this 58-acre urban park.

WILD PLACES

Holopaw
Bull Creek Wildlife Management Area (407-436-1818; http://www.sjrwmd.com/recreationguide/s02/index.html), Crabgrass Rd off US 192. The Florida Trail creates a 17-mile loop through this vast wilderness of pine flatwoods and prairies along Bull Creek, with several primitive campsites; take a scenic drive through the forest on the 8-mile Loop Rd. A shorter hiking loop is available on the Triple N Tract, separate entrance off US 192. Trail riding and hunting are also permitted. Free.

THE KISSIMMEE LIGHTHOUSE

Kathy Wolf

Kenansville

Three Lakes Wildlife Management Area (407-436-1818), 1231 Prairie Lakes Rd off Canoe Creek Rd. Protecting wet prairies along the southern edge of Lake Kissimmee, this preserve offers a figure-8 loop of the Florida Trail with 12 miles of hiking; an observation tower gives a bird's-eye view of the Kissimmee prairies. Trail riding and hunting also permitted. Free.

Kissimmee

Makinson Island (407-892-2397), in the northern third of Lake Tohopekaliga, is a 132-acre island preserve accessible only by boat, with a 3.5-mile hiking trail. Kayaker camping permitted. Free.

Narcoossee

Split Oak Forest Mitigation Park (407-892-2397), located on Clapp-Simms-Duda Rd just north of the intersection of FL 15 and Boggy Creek Rd. Protecting acreage along Lake Hart for sandhill crane habitat, this massive wilderness park centers on a significant botanical feature, an ancient oak tree that split in two and continued to grow. A network of 7 miles of hiking trails encircles the park: the North Loop passes through scrub, flatwoods, and oak hammocks along the lake, while the South Loop meanders through vast, open, wet prairies. Day use only, no camping permitted; visit adjacent Moss Park (see *Parks*), connected via the Swamp Trail, for camping. Free.

A NASA ROCKET LAUNCH SPIED FROM THREE LAKES WMA

Sandra Friend

Poinciana

Disney Wilderness Preserve (407-935-0002), 2700 Scrub Jay Trail, located off Poinciana Blvd. Administered by The Nature Conservancy, this 12,000-acre preserve along pristine cypress-lined Lake Russell protects vast pine flatwoods, bayheads, and cypress domes. Walk the 4.5-mile outer loop for the big picture, or take an easy stroll on the interpretive trail. September–June, take a swamp buggy ride (fee) out into the boggy ecosystems. Open daily 9–5; fee.

St. Cloud

Lake Lizzie Nature Preserve (407-892-2397), Midland Dr, is a 918-acre nature preserve with a network of hiking and equestrian trails that lead through the pines to Lake Lizzie and Trout Lake. From US 192, follow Pine Grove Rd to Bass Hwy to find Midland Dr. Free.

HOTELS, MOTELS & RESORTS As the spillover zone for travelers visiting the theme parks (see "Theme Parks"), the Irlo Bronson Highway (US 192) is simply lined with chain hotels, motels, and resorts. These are some of the more unique offerings outside the Theme Parks area.

Celebration 34737

& ∞ ⁙ At the intimate **Celebration Hotel** (407-566-6000 or 1-888-499-3800; www.celebrationhotel.com), 700 Bloom St, there are only 115 rooms and suites, so you'll feel like you're in a country inn or bed & breakfast. Owner Richard Kessler personally selects many outstanding pieces of art: the life-sized Indian sculpture located on the lakeside terrace, the stuffed alligator in the lobby, and you'll want to see if you can find Chief Osceola in the mural. Staff treat you not like guests, but like family. As your room is literally steps from the shopping and dining establishments, you won't need a car. When you want some privacy, enjoy sunning and swimming at the heated pool overlooking a lovely lake, or explore the nature preserve, with miles of walking trails. Enjoy a culinary experience in The Plantation Room Restaurant or listen to live music Thu–Sat in the lobby bar. High-season rates start at $235 for rooms, $335 for suites; low-season (June–Sep) start at $175 rooms, $255 suites.

Champions Gate 33896

& ∞ ⁙ After a stay at the Mediterranean-style **Omni Orlando Resort at ChampionsGate** (407-390-6664; www.omnihotels.com), 1500 Masters Blvd, for a major convention, I can vouch to the immense size of the place—I got a good workout walking back and forth from my room to the convention center. The plush accommodations helped me relax in the evenings after a long day's work, and folks who are here just to relax have their pick of possibilities—nature and jogging trails, a 10,000-square-foot European Spa, a pool surrounded by cabanas, a family activity pool with water slides, and my personal favorite—an 850-foot lazy river that winds through a tropical paradise. Rates start at $169.

Kenansville 34739

✍ **Heartbreak Hotel** (407-436-1284 or 407-436-0208; www.heartbreak hotelkenansville.com), 1350 S Canoe Creek Rd. Well off the beaten path, this old-fashioned hotel along the railroad tracks in Kenansville charms with its historic exterior and four nicely appointed, roomy suites ($100–125), each with wooden floors, a full kitchen, and a porch with rocking chairs. Closes during the summer months, so call ahead.

HEARTBREAK HOTEL

Sandra Friend

VACATION HOMES One of the more budget-conscious ways to visit the region is to rent a vacation home, and there are many to choose from in Osceola County. Rates vary by location, size, and season.

With more than 200 properties in stock, **Alexander Holiday Homes** (407-932-3683 or 1-800-621-7888; www.floridasunshine.com), 1400 W Oak St, Kissimmee 34744, can offer you plenty of choices, all the way up to 7 bedrooms. The privacy makes a peaceful escape from the resort areas and an ideal way to relax and soak up the Florida sunshine.

American Vacation Homes (407-847-0883 or 1-800-901-8688; www.americanhomesavh.com), 1631 E Vine St, Kissimmee 34744, offers more than 250 fully furnished individually owned homes scattered through several housing developments; capacities of 6 to 14 guests make these rentals an ideal option for families on vacation. Pick your size and amenities (high-end rentals include pools), and they'll figure out the rates.

One of the largest suppliers of fully furnished homes, the folks at **ResortQuest Orlando** (407-396-2262; www.magicalmemories.com), 7799 Styles Blvd, Kissimmee 34747, can select which home will be right for you, from condos in resort-style settings to portfolio homes with private pools. By the day, week, or month.

FISH CAMPS, RV PARKS, AND MARINAS

Kenansville 34739
Cypress Lake RV and Sports Club, LLC (407-957-3135), 3301 Lake Cypress Rd. Restaurant, bait and tackle, RV sites, cabin rentals, and airboat rides.

Lake Marian Paradise Marina (407-436-1464), 901 Arnold Rd. Bait and tackle, RV sites, and motel and cabin rentals under $70.

& Get right out on Lake Kissimmee at **Middleton's Too Fishcamp** (407-436-1966 or 1-800-347-4007; www.mfctoo.com), 4500 Joe Overstreet Rd, which has 10 RV hook-up sites ($24), campers available for rent ($60), and basic tent sites ($8). Find them at the end of Overstreet Rd off Canoe Creek Rd.

Kissimmee 34744
Big Toho Marina (407-846-2124; www.bigtoho.com), 101 Lake Shore Blvd, rents out boats, tackle, bait, rods, and reels so that you can explore Lake Tohopekaliga on your own, or ask about the many fishing charters and professional bass fishing guide services available in the area. Open daily from 5:30 AM.

At **East Lake Fish Camp** (407-348-2040; www.eastlakefishcamp.com), 3705 Big Bass Rd, settle in for a spell. Car-camping tent sites under the old oaks are $18, RV sites $22, and cabins—complete with linens, dishes, and maid service—just $65. Head out for a day of fishing, rent a Jet Ski, or take an airboat ride. The on-site East Lake Restaurant cooks Cracker cuisine, including frog legs, gator tail, and catfish (see *Eating Out*).

At **Southport Park** (407-933-5822; www.bcairboats.com/accomodations.shtml), 2001 E Southport Rd, home of Boggy Creek Airboat Rides (see *Airboats*), you can pitch your tent for $12 a night or pull in your RV for $19–24. Enjoy the lakefront picnic pavilions and put your boat in at the ramp. Wet and dry storage available.

St. Cloud

Open dawn to dusk, the **St. Cloud Fishing Pier and Marina** (407-957-7243), 1105 Lakeshore Blvd, provides anglers access to East Lake via the pier and boat ramp.

✳ Where to Eat

DINING OUT

Celebration

The atmosphere at **Cafe D'Antonio** (407-566-CAFÉ; www.antoniosonline.com/CafeDAntonio.asp), 691 Front St, is fun and relaxed. The meals—Italian! Sample the dozen pasta dishes with meats, seafood, lobster, and fresh herbs, or entrées ($11–28) where the main course is pollo, scaloppine, or pesce. The restaurant is an extension of the famed original Antonio's in Maitland (see "North of Orlando").

Dark rich wood and New England hospitality surround you at **Celebration Town Tavern and Boston Garden** (407-566-2526; www.thecelebrationtowntavern.com), 721 Front St. They actually fly in all the seafood, as well as their secret breading. You'll get to taste Ipswich clams ($23) and real clam "chowdah"—which passed this Mainer's test. One- and 2-pound lobsters are reasonably market priced; entrées $16 and up. Complete your meal with none other than a Boston cream pie!

Having dined here for a friend's birthday, I concur that **Charley's Steak House** (407-239-1270), 2901 Parkway Blvd, while a chain—considered among the best of steakhouses—presents a mighty fine meal. Pair a glass of wine off the extensive wine list with USDA prime and choice beef, aged 4 to 6 weeks and cooked over mesquite in an open pit. Expect a leisurely

meal, and budget a good $50 per person for the experience.

Kissimmee

They grow 'em big in cattle country, and the family-owned **Kissimmee Steak House** (407-847-8050; www.kissimmeesteakhouse.com), 2047 E Irlo Bronson Hwy (US 192), serves up the biggest with a 32-ounce porterhouse ($30) and 24-ounce top sirloin ($18). Smaller appetites will want the 6-ounce fillet ($20) or the 12-ounce New York strip ($21). If you must have fish in a steakhouse—they have that, too. Casual dress. Open 4:30–10 daily.

EATING OUT

Celebration

Serving breakfast, lunch, and dinner, the **Market Street Cafe** (407-566-1144), 701 Front St, is always bustling. Savor peach or banana-nut pancakes for breakfast ($3.50 for short stack) or meet a friend for lunch over crab quesadilla ($6.50) and their famous cream of mushroom soup ($3.50). Burgers and salads are part of the mix too, and don't forget to save room for a hot fudge sundae!

For that afternoon cup of tea, check out **Sherlock's** (407-566-1866; www.sherlocksofcelebration.com), 715 Bloom St, which has an extensive selection of traditional exotic teas, coffees, wines, and imported beers. Their menu is mainly organic and vegetarian, and they do an afternoon high tea complete with petits fours and savories.

Holopaw

Cypress Restaurant at Forever Florida (407-957-9794), 4755 N Kenansville Rd. Whether you're here to explore the working cattle ranch or just passing through, stop by for a quick lunch of gator bites ($8), chicken fingers ($6), Cypress Burger ($6), or fresh garden salad ($3). That's the entire menu, but you'll enjoy it either inside a beautiful lodge or outside on the porch surrounded by the natural landscape.

Kissimmee

Located next to Boggy Creek Airboats East, **East Lake Restaurant** (407-348-2040; www.eastlakefishcamp .com), 3705 Big Bass Rd, serves up a tasty Florida platter of gator tail, frog legs, and catfish along with fresh salads, steak and seafood dinners ($7–15), as well as beer and wine in a rustic setting. Don't miss the all-you-can-eat buffets on weekends! They serve breakfast and lunch, too.

My Family's Pizza (407-346-6747), 3297 S John Young Pkwy, tucked inside the Citgo station. This local favorite serves up 20-inch pizzas ($12 and up), calzones and strombolis, subs and gyros. Best bargain is a pizza burger. Call ahead and Alex can customize your order, going way beyond pizza.

Susan's Courtside Cafe (407-518-1150), 18 South Orlando Ave. Friendly country atmosphere in a historic home. Light breakfast fare, with fresh coffee roasted on the premises and sold by the pound. Lunch ($5–8) includes a selection of salads and sandwiches, personal-sized gourmet pizza, homemade cakes, pies, and cookies. Open Mon–Fri for breakfast, lunch, and dinner.

St. Cloud

& For a taste of frontier Florida, chow down at **The Catfish Place** (407-892-5771), 2324 13th St (US 192), a laid-back family restaurant that I visit every time I can. The murals of natural Osceola County are just plain stunning, and the menu is full of favorites that date back decades—choice Delmonico, never-ending plates of all-you-cat-eat Lake Okeechobee catfish, mounds of fresh Florida seafood, and the Florida Cracker Special of catfish, frog legs, turtle, and gator, all from local lakes. Everything is always fresh, and the veggies are home-grown. And yes, you can get cheese grits with that. It's always a pleasure to stop here for an authentic dining experience, dinners $8–22.

Yeehaw Junction

The **Desert Inn** (407-436-1054; www.desertinnrestaurant.com), 5570 South Kenansville Rd, just west of exit 193 off Florida's Turnpike at US 441, is not your typical listing on the National Register of Historic Places. This late-1800s watering hole served railroad workers, moonshiners, traders, cowboys, and Indians—some of whom are still here today. Dig into hearty burgers, red beans and rice, and other home-style favorites. Open 7 days for breakfast, lunch, and dinner.

THE DESERT INN, YEEHAW JUNCTION

Kathy Wolf

✳ Entertainment

The **Osceola Center for the Arts** (see *Art Galleries*) showcases great Broadway productions for $15–20.

✳ Selective Shopping

Celebration

The whole town of Celebration is one great place to shop, with quaint streets like Market, Bloom, and Front winding along the lake. But my favorite place was **Day Dreams** (407-566-1231; www.daydreamsdolls.com), 603 Market St. And I couldn't get out without a big dent in my credit card. This is the place all grandmothers should go for that oh-so-special grandchild—and they are all that special. All the old favorites are here, along with few new ones, like Madame Alexander, Susan Wakeen, and Lee Middleton. You'll find bunnies and bears from Boyd and Hermann, and other creatures from one of the best Steiff collections around. The selection of quality books is outstanding, with some from Wise and Lang that I just couldn't put back once I had them in my hand.

The **Camera Outlet** (407-397-9800), Parkway Pavilion, 2901 Parkway Blvd (across from Celebration off US 192), has European PAL systems.

🐾 **Dog Bark Bakery** (321-939-1334; www.dogbarkbakery.com), 660 Celebration Ave, Suite 120, spoils your pooch with precious gourmet treats like peanut-butter bones and Parmesan-cheddar sticks. Try Fifi out in some RuffWear, or fit Blaze out with a doggie backpack. Open daily.

If you're an avid reader like me, it'll take more than an hour to browse through **Reading Trout Books** (321-939-BOOK; www.readingtroutbooks

.com), 671 Front St, Suite 110. This independent bookseller has a mix of new and used titles, with a special emphasis on Disneyana. Open daily.

Kenansville

The ground floor of the historic **Heartbreak Hotel** (see *Lodging*) features a great gift shop with gourmet foods, Yankee candles, Christmas ornaments, and a selection of nicely priced antiques in the back room. Open Sat–Sun.

Kissimmee

Remember when you could walk into a clothing store and get unsurpassed personal service at a great price? Well, you still can at **Shore's** (407-847-4747), 201 Broadway. Manager George Cross will help choose from a selection of quality clothing and Florsheim shoes; he'll even rent you a tuxedo for that special night out.

For more than 30 years, **Lewis Music** (407-847-6397), 117 Broadway, has offered musical instruments and an extensive selection of sheet music with lots of old American favorites.

For antiques, jewelry, and fine furniture, go to **Lanier's Historic Down-**

ANTIQUE SHOPPING IN KISSIMMEE
Kissimmee–St. Cloud Convention & Visitors Bureau

town **Marketplace** (407-933-5679; www.laniersantiques.com), 108 Broadway—if you can't find it there, then you're not looking.

You'll find great cameras, accessories, and, of course, film at **Cameras Unlimited** (407-787-3535), 5039 W Irlo Bronson Hwy (US 192).

Superheroes will want to stop by the **Coliseum of Comics** (407-870-5322), 22 Broadway, open for nearly 20 years; browse through the titles inside the vintage brick walls. In the back of the building is the oldest ele-

vator in Central Florida. Down the street is **Comic Books & Collectibles** (407-870-0400), 17 W Monument Ave, for even more colorful fun.

FLEA & FARMER'S MARKETS There are more than 900 vendors at the **Osceola Flea and Farmer's Market** (407-846-2811), 2801 E Irlo Bronson Hwy (US 192), so get ready to do some digging. There's a heavy emphasis on cheap Asian goods, but dig deep and you may find a col-

---

✏ ♿ FEBRUARY: One of nation's oldest (since 1944) and top rodeos, **Silver Spurs Rodeo of Champions** (407-847-4052; www.silverspursrodeo.com), literally rides into town (down US 192) in this semiannual event at the new 2003 Silver Spurs Arena in Osceola Heritage Park. The precision skills coupled with an incredible air-conditioned indoor arena make this the largest rodeo east of the Mississippi and a must-see for everyone—from all walks of life. You'll witness 60 of the top cowboys and cowgirls from all over the world compete for over $50,000 in prizes and accolades while performing everyday ranching tasks, from tie-down calf roping to Xtreme Bulls, in this nationally televised event. One of the more beautiful displays is the popular Silver Spurs Quadrille Team, riding a type of square dance on horseback and performed by eight couples decked in their western finest.

For those who think this can't be good for the animals, let me set the record straight. As a staunch defender of animal rights, I entered the world of cowhunters and bullwrestlers with hesitation and an open eye. So down on the arena floor I went to get up close and personal with the wranglers of today in this exhibition of ranch skills. What I found was that the bulls and horses, and even the calves, are treated better than the family dog. A closer inspection revealed animals with rich shiny coats comparable to champion thoroughbreds at the Kentucky Derby. When not being ridden (for 8 seconds or less), even the bulls were social. Any why shouldn't they take good care of these animals? Training is lengthy, and the championship livestock is expensive—even the equipment to transport them (in air-conditioned comfort) rivals a recreational RV. A different world? Yes. But one that is full of emotion and excitement, with no evidence of animal abuse and sanctioned by the Professional Rodeo Cowboys Association.

lectible treasure or timeless antique. Free parking and admission, open Fri–Sun.

Farmer's Market Downtown Kissimmee, 201 E Dakin Ave, Kissimmee. Selections of locally grown fruits, vegetables, herbs, and baked goods are marketed in the downtown historic district on Thursday morning 7–1 in the civic center parking lot.

✳ Special Events

❀ *February*: **The Posh Pooch Celebration** (407-566-2200; www.celebration.fl.us), for dogs and their human companions, features live music, demonstrations and doggy info, contests, and even dog weddings! Great food includes special menu items just for dogs.

March: **St. Cloud Life** (www.stcloudfl chamber.com), held the 2nd weekend at the St. Cloud Civic Center, 3001 17th St, wraps up some tasty treats in events like the Dessert Fest, the Beer Fest, and Taste of St. Cloud.

Since 2002, the **Osceola Sportsmen's Show** (www.osceolasportsman .com) at Sods Farms has treated festival-goers to down-home traditional sports like rodeo, archery, sporting clays, hunting and fishing, and swamp buggy rides. Held mid-March, Kenansville, $10 admission.

April: **The Great American Pie Festival** (407-566-2200; www.pie council.org/great.htm), Celebration. Pie making and eating, games and crafts, and did I mention eating? Get ready for the "Never-Ending Pie Buffet." Third weekend.

Spring Art Festival (407-566-2200; www.celebrationtowncenter.com), Celebration. Fine-art festival on Market, Front, and Bloom Sts.

The whole town participates in the spring and fall cleaning of garages and attics for the **Celebration's Semi-Annual Yard Sale** (407-566-2200; www.celebrationtowncenter.com). One day only in both Apr and Oct.

Oct: **Celebration of Fall Festival** (407-566-2200; www.celebrationfl .com), Celebration. Leaves fall on Market St, live entertainment and hayrides. For Celebration's Semi-Annual Yard Sale, see April.

November: The Annual **Osceola Art Festival** (www.ocfta.com) in historic downtown Kissimmee features local and nationally known artists, live entertainment, food, and more. Free.

Get your handcrafted holiday gift at the Annual **Osceola Crafter's Holiday Gift Gallery**, Osceola Center for the Arts.

December: **Now Snowing** (407-566-2200; www.celebration.fl.us), Celebration. Snow falls, with carolers and holiday merriment throughout the town. Kids and pets can take photos with Santa.

BUCKING BRONCO AT THE RODEO
Kissimmee–St. Cloud Convention & Visitors Bureau

THE THEME PARKS

I t seems like the theme parks have been here forever, but my generation still remembers a Florida when Orlando was a sleepy citrus and cattle town and the state's tourist attractions centered on its springs, beaches, and lakes. That changed forever in 1971, when Walter Elias Disney unveiled the Magic Kingdom and a handful of truly different themed resorts, ushering in the phenomenon that is Walt Disney World. As vacationers shifted to this new take on entertainment, businesses followed: Hotels mushroomed along US 192 and in Lake Buena Vista, restaurants moved in to feed the steady stream of visitors, and other large entertainment entities took note and opened their own attractions, bringing SeaWorld and Universal Studios Orlando to life over the late 1970s and early 1980s. The 1990s saw explosive growth along International Drive (referred to locally as I-Drive) with the creation of the massive Orange County Convention Center complex and the establishment of Celebration, a planned-by-Disney residential community. From a playful re-creation of California's Disneyland in the rural prairies southwest of downtown Orlando, the theme park region has taken on a life of its own, pushing Orlando to the crest of the tourism wave, a top destination for travelers from around the world.

GUIDANCE Before your trip, get in touch with the **Orlando/Orange County Convention & Visitors Bureau** (407-354-5500; www.orlandoinfo.com), 6700 Forum Dr, Suite 100, Orlando 32821. **Walt Disney World** (407-WDW-INFO; www.disneyworld.com) offers an extensive Web site for trip planning, as do **Universal Studios Orlando** (1-800-711-0080; www.univacations.com) and **SeaWorld** (1-800-224-3838; www.seaworldvacations.com). You'll want the **International Drive Resort Area Official Visitors Guide** (407-248-9590; www.internationaldriveorlando.com), 7081 Grand National Dr, Suite 105, Orlando 32819, which will direct you to all the manmade wonders along this curvilinear stretch of Touristville.

GETTING THERE *By air:* **Greater Orlando International Airport** (407-825-2001; www.state.fl.us/goaa) serves the world with hundreds of flights daily; check their Web site for contact information on the many airlines servicing Orlando.

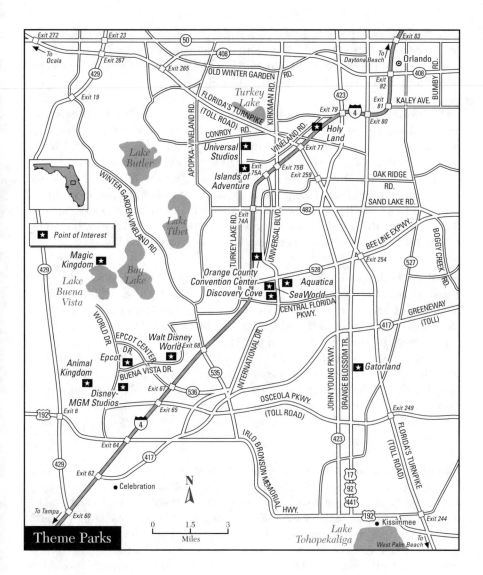

Theme Parks

0   1.5   3
Miles

By bus: **Greyhound Lines** (407-292-3440; www.greyhound.com), 555 N John Young Pkwy, Orlando.

By car: **I-4** runs though the heart of the theme park district, with plenty of signs to instruct you as to where to exit. However, it's Orlando's busiest highway. From the Orlando International Airport, the **Beeline ("Beachline") Expressway** and **FL 417** (toll) provide quick access to the area. Use the Osceola Pkwy (toll) to drive straight into Walt Disney World, with easy access to Wide World of Sports, Downtown Disney, but be aware that the speed limit drops to 45 mph the moment you hit the Disney property; pay attention to signage, which, instead of standard highway green, turns purple.

By train: **Amtrak** (1-800-872-7245; www.amtrak.com) provides regularly sched-uled service to metro Orlando, just north of the theme parks, and to Kissimmee, to the south of the theme parks. **Coach USA** (407-826-9999) provides door-to-door shuttle van service from Amtrak's Orlando station.

GETTING AROUND I-Drive (aka **International Drive**) parallels **I-4** between Universal and Lake Buena Vista and is "Entertainment Row," with hundreds of restaurants, shops, hotels, and small attractions lining the busy street; look for pedestrian traffic. Worth noting is that I-Drive connects to South I-Drive by way of FL 536. South I-Drive will take you straight to US 192. On US 192 you know you've entered the "Disney Zone" near the main gate when the lampposts turn purple; Black Lake Rd provides a back entrance to the Animal Kingdom area. **Turkey Lake Rd** and **Palm Pkwy** provide an alternate to I-Drive on the north side of I-4, a quiet way to slip between the theme parks. **FL 535** runs north–south through Lake Buena Vista.

& **I-Ride Trolley** (407-354-5656; www.iridetrolley.com) travels through the International Drive resort area. The easy-to-understand 10-foot-high markers along both sides of the road designate trolley stops. The Main Line route serves the I-Drive resort area north and south every 20 minutes. The Green Line serves Universal Blvd every 30 minutes. There are only a few spots to transfer between the lines: Main Line (32 N, 32 S, 14 N) and Green Line (10 N, 10 S, 2 N). Fares: single $1, senior 25¢. Exact change required. Unlimited ride passes ($3 for 1 day, $5 for 3 days, $7 for 5 days) are not sold on trolleys and must be purchased at any of the 90 locations along I-Drive. Kids ride free with a paying adult. Trolleys are handicapped accessible with an ADA-specified hydraulic lift system.

PARKING The theme parks sock you for a hefty parking fee, which is what makes staying "on property" and using their free transportation a huge allure. Disney hotels charge only for valet parking; Universal's hotels and the park charge $11 daily for self-parking, $18 for valet. Parking fees run $11 daily for Disney's four major theme parks; free parking at Downtown Disney and the water parks and for self-parking guests at the resorts (valet parking extra). Parking at SeaWorld will cost you $9, but at their Discovery Cove it's free. Parking garages provide the only parking for I-Drive attractions, but those rates are more reasonable. There are no parking fees at area malls.

MEDICAL EMERGENCIES **Florida Hospital Orlando** (407-303-5600), 601 E Rollins St, **Florida Hospital East Orlando** (407-303-8110), 7727 Lake Under-hill Rd, and **Sand Lake Hospital** (407-351-8500), 9400 Turkey Lake Rd, cover the metro area and I-Drive. **Florida Hospital Celebration Health** (407-764-4000), 400 Celebration Place, and **Florida Hospital Kissimmee** (407-846-4343), 2450 N Orange Blossom Trail, Kissimmee, are located near Disney and the US 192 attractions. For minor emergencies, stop by the **Main Street Physi-cians Walk-In Emergency Clinic** (407-370-4881), 8324 International Dr.

ART GALLERY Inside Rosen Shingle Creek (see *Lodgings*), **The Gallery at Shingle Creek** showcases the original and limited edition works of a dozen or so artists from Florida and California in pieces with vibrant color and texture, like the close-ups of zebras painted by Luis Sottil on massive canvases. Dan Mackin's blue and green Caribbean scenes are especially inviting. And I appreciate seeing the macro images of Central Florida flora shot by Garritt Toohey, whose work appears all throughout the hotel, for sale here as well. Open daily until 5.

ATTRACTIONS 𝒪 ♿ After more than half a century, **Gatorland** (407-855-5496 or 1-800-393-JAWS; www.gatorland.com), 14501 S Orange Blossom Trail, remains the undisputed Alligator Capital of the World, home of cinematic stars that appeared in *Indiana Jones and the Temple of Doom*. Remember those snapping jaws beneath the collapsing bridge? Filmed here! Let me dispel the myth that this is a cheesy roadside attraction—the late Owen Godwin started this park in 1949, and his family still runs it today. It's grown with the times from a serpentarium and alligator farm to an amazing eco-friendly wildlife preserve. You can cover the park in just a few hours or stay all day enjoying the relaxing natural environment—set inside a Central Florida cypress and bayhead swamp—and the many educational shows and exhibits. Stroll the incredibly clean walkways past massive gators and crocodiles set in a natural environment. Gatorland wants you to learn about these prehistoric beasts, so four great shows get you up close and personal. Find out about the parts and personality of the alligator, and then cross over a bridge and sit on a real 8-footer at the **Gator Wrestlin' Show**. Discover "what's in that box" at the **Upclose Encounters**, and take the little ones to the interactive **Critters on the Go** experience, which features cute and cuddly non-reptilians. But don't miss the headliner show, **Gator Jumparoo**, where alligators and the most enormous crocodile you'll ever see (his name is Alf) will jump to new heights. If you want to get behind the scenes, join the Trainer for a Day program ($129, includes park admission), a 2-hour trip around the park with a reptile expert, learning their ever-changing duties. Prepare to get muddy and arrive early (starts 8 AM), open only to ages 12 and up.

FEEDING TIME AT GATORLAND

Sandra Friend

The shiny **Gatorland Express**, which debuted in 1965 as the Iron Horse, circles the park, providing a fun train ride with a different take on the animal enclosures ($2 extra). **Gator Gully Splash Park**, a little water park, will keep the wee ones happy with getting wet (no live gators involved, honest). For hands-on fun, you can pet and feed deer, tortoises, emus, llamas, goats, and exotic birds at **Allie's Barnyard**. For more birds, enter the **Very Merry Aviary** to feed the colorful and curious lorikeets. To get a bird's-eye view of more than 100 alligators in their natural habitat, climb the three-story observation tower and look over the 10-acre breeding marsh and bird rookery—an official part of the Great Florida Birding Trail. For a scary take on this walk, try the **Gator Night Shine Tour** ($19 adults, $17 children), where you will see those hundreds of eyes glowing in the marsh . . . and realize that a lot of Florida lakes look like that after dark. Open daily 9–5. Admission $23 adults, $15 children ages 3–12, with discounts for tickets ordered online.

Bringing a little piece of the Middle East to Central Florida, the **Holy Land Experience** (407-367-2065 or 1-866-872-4659; www.holylandexperience.com), 4655 Vineland Rd, reflects the devotion of Robert and Judith Van Kampen, who wanted a place to display their growing collection of biblical and archeological artifacts. Entering through a traditional Middle Eastern medina, visitors encounter large-scale replicas of Christ's tomb at Calvary, the Temple of Jerusalem, and other biblical sites, with regularly scheduled plays and pageants bringing the pages of the Bible to life. Interpretive signs explain the biblical significance of plantings in the lush gardens. At the **Shofer Auditorium Jerusalem AD 66**, expect an entertaining talk on biblical history. The **Dead Sea Qumran Caves** is a replica of the site where the Dead Sea Scrolls were found. But the real centerpiece of the park is the **Scriptorium**, through which you'll walk on a 1-hour "guided" tour (at the pace of the museum's narrative and lighted sets) through five exhibit areas featuring the world's largest private biblical collection, with pieces dating back to cuneiform tablets from the city of Ur, 2000 B.C. In chronological order, each of the themed areas ushers you through an era of the history of the Bible, from its origins on papyrus to hand-copied scriptoria from the 12th through 15th centuries, through the Wycliffe gospels and Gutenberg press to today. It's a fascinating walk through history, with only a little bit of sermonizing along the way. At the end of the tour, the **Ex Libris** bookshop has an excellent selection of Bibles and historical and religious tomes. There are thematic food stands and gift shops scattered throughout the park. Admission $35 adults, $30 seniors, $20 ages 6–12; Jerusalem Gold Pass $120 provides annual admission. Modest dress (no shorts, please) is expected of guests; the park is popular with church groups. A limited number of people are permitted in daily, so purchase tickets in advance online to ensure you can visit the day you want. Open 10–6, closed Sundays.

BASEBALL Catch the **Atlanta Braves** during spring training at Disney's Wide World of Sports (407-828-FANS; www.disneyworldsports.com) Feb–Apr 1, with tickets starting at $14.50 for "bring your own lawn chairs."

MARCHING DUCKS ♪ **Famous Peabody Ducks at the Peabody Orlando** (407-352-4000 or 1-800-PEABODY; www.peabodyorlando.com), 9801 International Dr. A Peabody tradition since 1930, the world-famous Peabody Mallard Ducks march to much pomp and circumstance from their "penthouse," down the elevator, and across a red carpet into the hotel's beautiful lobby fountain, where they spend the day splashing and grooming. Young and old alike will enjoy the antics of the drake and his four ladies-in-waiting as the official Duckmaster and the Honorary Duckmaster (or -mistress) escort them to their place of honor. Kids and famous celebrities have enjoyed being honorary Duckmasters, and you can, too. Call well in advance of your trip if you would like to be one. Daily at 11 and 5. Free.

MUSEUM An indoor garden, waterfalls, and 12-foot-high mountains set the scene for 14 model railroad trains and more than 30 trestles and tunnels at the **Trolley & Train Museum** (407-363-9002), 8990-A International Dr. Climb aboard a California Victorian-style trolley or small replica of an 1880 locomotive. Open daily 9:30–7, $8 adults, $6 children.

SHRINE **Mary, Queen of the Universe Shrine** (407-239-4010; www.maryqueenoftheuniverse.org), 8300 Vineland Ave, was built to accommodate the spiritual needs of the vast number of visiting Catholic tourists. Completed in 1986, the 2,000-seat church and 22-acre sanctuary are open to all and a welcome respite after a day spent shopping or at the theme parks. At the center of the tranquil Rosary Garden, overlooking a small pond, sits an 1875 statue of Mary holding the divine infant; in the Mother and Child Chapel, a bronze statue honors the universal symbol of motherhood; and the shrine's museum houses many Marian art treasures, including a 17th-century oil painting of *The Assumption of the Blessed Virgin* by Spanish artist Bartolomé Murillo. The extensive gift shop displays a fine selection of quality religious gifts. Open daily.

✷ Theme Parks

♿ **DISCOVERY COVE** (407-370-1280 or 1-877-4-DISCOVERY; www.discoverycove.com), 6000 Discovery Cove Way. If you've been wondering if it's worth the $169 admission to visit SeaWorld's little sibling, let me do the math for you. First there's admittance to an amazing paradise set among white sandy beaches, blue lagoons, and grottoes and filled with dolphins, rays, tropical fish, and exotic birds. Then there's a freshly prepared lunch that rivals any of those at the fancy resorts. This has got to be the best bargain around, but the real bonus is how you'll feel after spending a day there. I can only describe it as having been to a spa and experiencing all that it might have to offer.

A MOTHER AND DAUGHTER TAKE PART IN THE DOLPHIN EXPERIENCE, DISCOVERY COVE.

Discovery Cove

Each day, only 1,000 guests are permitted to enter this oasis, so you won't find the usual rushing-to-get-there-first dash from the parking lot—which is so small, you won't need the valet, but they have one anyway. And there's no need to arrive any more than 15 minutes before the park opens. It's just not necessary. Check-in is a breeze inside the exotic open-air lodge. Then, instead of squeezing through turnstiles, you'll walk out onto a terrace where you'll sip Florida orange juice and hot

THEME PARK TIPS

Take it from a lifelong hiker—you will do a lot of walking while visiting the theme parks. While I've been tempted to carry a GPS to clock it, rest assured you will walk between 2 and 10 miles a day, from crossing the massive parking lots to the tram that whisks you to the gates to wandering across the vast acreage encompassed by each park. Prepare accordingly, just as if you were going on a hike. Wear comfortable shoes, go lightweight (leave as much baggage as you can in the car; it will be faster through the new security checkpoints), wear sunscreen and a hat, and carry water bottles! Water fountains are tough to find, and bottled water is especially pricey once you enter the park gates. It's far too easy to dehydrate when you're outdoors in the Florida sun, so you need to make a point of drinking water frequently while strolling around and standing in line. Carry energy bars as emergency food; it's too tempting to skip meals when you're caught up in parades, rides, and the like. And don't forget raingear—you'll be glad you brought that cheap plastic poncho along when Central Florida's daily afternoon thundershowers hit, June–Oct.

• **Beware of bottlenecks.** You'll stand in three lines at each park's gate unless you buy tickets in advance: one for a security check (try not to carry a purse or backpack unless you truly need one), one for a ticket purchase, and one to get through the gate. And then there are the lines for the rides, some of which can take an hour or more. At Disney, use the Fastpass, and at Universal, the Express, to nab fixed-time tickets for the more popular rides; that'll cut your wait down to 10 minutes or less. Traveling solo? Take advantage of the "singles" line on rides such as Test Track and Mission: Space at Epcot; it'll give you a big jump ahead of the crowd. Keep alert for parade routes, as daily parades can block access to certain parts of the park!

• **Don't try to fit it all in.** It's just not possible. To see all the attractions in the Orlando area, you'd need 67 full days. The major theme parks are designed so it'll take you two or three days per park to see and do every little thing. Make a plan beforehand and stick to it. Despite the popularity of Park Hopper passes at Disney, the single-day Park Hopper isn't worth your time and coffee. Pet the drowsy-eyed sloth and take a hint from this furry creature—this is the place to chill out and relax. Meander down a winding tropical path while a guide explains all the wonderful amenities. Slip on a wetsuit and grab a towel and snorkel gear, then stow your extra items in the locker rooms stocked with fluffy towels, toiletries, and hair dryers. You won't even need your camera, as staff photographers discreetly wander the property taking reasonably priced photos.

effort unless you're spending the morning at one park and then heading to Epcot for some fine international cuisine for dinner. You'll eat up a lot of time in transportation between the parks when you try to switch venues midday. Alternatively, if you're staying at or near a park, remember that this is a vacation. Take the opportunity to nip out to your hotel or B&B during the heat of the day for a siesta, or take a leisurely boat tour before plunging back into activities in the evening. At the Walt Disney World Resort, guests staying "on property" have access to free transportation via buses, monorails, and boats; however, the buses are time consuming. Plan an hour or more each way from your room to the park gate.

• **Have a plan.** If your group decides to split up, pick a specific place and time to meet—and stick to it. These parks are vast, and it's easy to lose a toddler or a teen left alone for a few seconds. I've seen families use walkie-talkies and cell phones to keep track of each other. If you make meal reservations, stick to them precisely, since Disney will charge you $10 or more if you don't show up.

• **Outfit your kids with a journal** to serve as an autograph book—they'll have plenty of photo ops with theme park characters, so have each character sign a blank page, and paste the child's photo into the book after the trip as a special bit of memorabilia.

• **Bargain hunting?** Despite billboards you'll see around Florida, park admission prices are non-negotiable; those operators are selling you tickets at a discount in exchange for something, usually your presence at a time-share presentation. For the best prices on rooms, shoot for the low-attendance times: February, September, and between Thanksgiving and Christmas. The best ticket bargains are now appearing online, so get that mouse moving. Most of the time you can get the best hotel rates by contacting the hotels directly and not through the kiosks peppered around town or off the highway. These visitors' info centers have great maps, but again will want you for a time-share presentation. If you have the extra 4 hours or so to go to a presentation, you will get the freebies they have offered, and some of the time-shares are well worth the investment. We only list the "official" visitor centers in this book.

So what's to see and do? Swim as long as you want in the Coral Reef, where you'll be surrounded by tropical fish, leopard rays, and even barracudas as they hover from under a sunken shipwreck. Spend hours floating down the heated Tropical River discovering ancient artifacts. If you time it just right, you'll get to feed the sting-less rays in the Ray Lagoon, while they'll tickle your body begging for more food. For the best experience, snorkel motionless in the water and let these gentle water pilots come to you. Those having a Dolphin Experience will have an assigned time period with a group of about six or eight other swimmers. During the 45-minute adventure, you'll spend time getting to know your dolphin by doing some behavioral training; when you and your dolphin have bonded, hang on and take an unforgettable ride around the lagoon.

A fabulous meal starts around 11 and continues to about 3, so there's no rush here, either. The lavish selection includes salads (from greens to macaroni), entrées (from giant burgers and steak fries to baked fish with steamed veggies), desserts (from pudding to red velvet cake), and soft drinks, iced tea, and coffee. There's a small fee for tropical drinks, beer, and wine. After lunch, take in some sun or shade while lounging around on comfy beach chairs, cabanas, or secluded hidden hammocks. Walk through the tropical free-flight aviary and get acquainted with toucans, hornbills, or hundreds of other exotic birds. You'll want to slide your feet so as not to step on these little feathered friends.

The beauty of this place will astound you, and you'll remember the feeling long after you're gone.

Tickets to Discovery Cove are all inclusive, change seasonally, and are subject to change without notice; reserve in advance. Special rates are occasionally available to Florida residents; check their Web site for details. Single-day, general admission runs $169–189; with dolphin swim, $269–289. Multiday and combination passes are available (linking up admittance to SeaWorld and Busch Gardens), and the special Trainer for a Day package is $468–488. Open daily 8:30–5:30.

SEAWORLD ADVENTURE PARK ORLANDO (407-363-2613; www.seaworldorlando .com), 7007 SeaWorld Dr. Founded in 1964 by four graduates of the University of California—Los Angeles (UCLA), SeaWorld began as a small 22-acre marine zoological park along the shores of San Diego. The larger Orlando park opened in 1973, but was still small compared to the other Central Florida theme parks. Working with other marine facilities, SeaWorld maintained its focus on its founding principles of conservation, research, education, and entertainment, eventually growing into the most respected marine zoological collection in the world and accredited by the American Zoo and Aquarium Association (AZA). In 1989 Anheuser-Busch Companies, Inc., purchased the parks to complement their Busch Gardens attractions, bringing with them state-of-the-art adventure rides. SeaWorld Adventure Park is still based primarily on educational exhibits and ecoconservation shows, but now you'll experience thrills and chills from furry polar bears in the frigid waters of the Arctic to dicey drops on Kraken.

One of the things I noticed first was shade, lots of it. Fully mature trees create a cool, breezy canopy over most of the pathways, leaving you refreshed throughout the day. For further refreshment, take your seat in the Soak Zone at any show that involves salt water. These zones are clearly marked and should be avoided unless you really want to be doused by a wall of water. Even sitting near this area you'll get a bit of a splash, so protect your camera.

SeaWorld is set up so you can wander and explore. Take your time; there's a lot to see and do. And while they'll tell you it can be done in one day, you'll want to schedule two to really see it properly. At the Key West at SeaWorld you can feed dolphins in **Dolphin Cove** or touch stingrays at **Stingray Lagoon**. See the newest calves and their moms at the **Dolphin Nursery** and learn how these mammals are born. Over at the **Key West Dolphin Fest** you'll be entertained surfside by Atlantic bottle-nosed dolphins and *Pseudorca crassidens* (false killer whales) as they perform spectacular behaviors to a tropical beat. See **Manatees: The Last Generation** and learn of this endangered animal's plight. Six thousand pounds of snow fall daily inside the **Penguin Encounter**, where the temperature is a chilly 30 degrees. More than 200 penguins, like the 3-foot-tall king penguin and the rockhopper, sporting a yellow crest of feathers, romp with puffins in the icy waters of the Antarctic. Go to the north end of the globe at **Wild Arctic**, where a simulated jetcopter takes you on a fast and bumpy expedition over the frozen tundra, then under the sea in search of beluga whales and polar bears. Experience the same show without the ride, in the walk line. Stop by the **Clydesdale Hamlet** to pet the world-famous Budweiser Clydesdales. Touch tropical fish, sea urchins, and starfish at the **Caribbean Tidepool**. Denizens of the deep surround you as you pass through a 60-foot underwater tunnel in **Shark Encounter**.

SHAMU AND DIVER

SeaWorld Orlando

Check your show schedule for **Believe**, starring SeaWorld's famous killer whales choreographed to an original score performed by the Prague National Symphony Orchestra. At **Shamu Rocks**, Shamu shakes to a rock-and-roll beat. **Clyde and Seamore Take Pirate Island** is a high-seas buccaneer adventure. Laugh to the crazy antics of sea lions, otters, and an adorable walrus as their swashbuckling high jinks unfold. Don't miss **Pets Ahoy**, where the animals not only steal the show, they run it. Watch while pets rescued from local animal shelters perform amazing and hilarious skits. Then go home and train your pet to do the same. **Blue Horizons** is a beautiful production featuring dolphins, false killer whales, and tropical birds with costumed divers and aerialists, and **Odyssea** transports you underwater through special effects and the artistry of its performers.

When you ride the mythical sea creature **Kraken**, make sure you tie your sneakers tight, as Kraken has no floor. This intense roller coaster is one of the world's highest and fastest. You'll climb 149 feet, then drop down 144 feet and go through seven inversions at speeds of up to 65 mph—only for those with guts of steel. The unique water coaster **Journey to Atlantis** is not to be missed! This water ride through the lost city of Atlantis has spectacular special effects, and then plunges everyone down one of the steepest flume drops in the world. Just when you think the ride is over, you hear a voice say, "Leaving so soon? I don't think so . . ." and the boat becomes a roller coaster, dipping and curving then plunging you back in the water.

Behind-the-scenes and interactive encounters cost extra above your entrance ticket but provide a broad range of educational experiences you just can't find elsewhere. Learn about the realm of the shark at an add-on close encounter, as you snorkel or scuba inside a real shark cage on the 2-hour **Sharks Deep Dive**, limited to two guests. While you can swim with dolphins at Discovery Cove, Sea-World lets you swim with whales! Conduct animal training sessions in this one-on-one **Beluga Interactive Program**, limited to only a few people daily. The 8-hour **Marine Mammal Keeper Experience** is perfect for those thinking about a career in marine fields or for those who want an unforgettable day. Your adventure doesn't have to end when the park closes, either: Have dinner over at the **The Waterfront's SeaFire Inn** as the **Makahiki Luau** (see *Dinner Shows*) entertains you with a celebration of the ancient customs of the Pacific Islands.

SeaWorld opens at 9 AM year-round, with extended hours during summer, holidays, and special events. Admission presently costs $70 for ages 10 and up, $60 ages 3–9 (subject to change without notice). There are many options for discounts, including ordering online in advance, printing your own tickets at home (just like airline e-tickets!); AAA and AARP members, seniors, military personnel, and guests with disabilities also receive discounts. Active military, with up to three direct dependents in tow, are granted a free single-day admission. Florida residents can purchase a SeaWorld Fun Card for the same price as a single day admission and use it all year long. You may also build-your-own passport, including various lengths of visits to SeaWorld, Busch Gardens, and Discovery Cove.

UNIVERSAL ORLANDO RESORT (407-363-8000; www.universalorlando.com). So popular was the Universal Studio Tour in Hollywood, California, that they decided to duplicate it in Orlando's growing entertainment center. The working studio and theme park was pitched as a partnership to Paramount, where none other than Michael Eisner was acting studio chief. Paramount passed on the project, and it was a few more years before Universal Studios Florida was ready to set up shop. Then they got lucky and landed Academy Award–winning producer-director Steven Spielberg as creative consultant. The king of family action-adventure films, Spielberg was a perfect fit for the motion-picture-themed park. Opening in 1990, only a year after Eisner's launch of MGM Studios, the modest action-adventure park had some problems and took a few more years to get its bearings. Almost from the beginning, though, the concept of Islands of Adventure was being developed. In 1999 the adrenaline-pumped adventure park, the entertainment complex CityWalk, as well as on-site resorts, became a reality.

The 2,300-acre resort and amusement complex is all in one neat geographic area, making navigation a snap. And the close proximity means there's no need for monorail or bus transfers. Once you park your car at Universal, you'll travel on moving sidewalks, then enter the exciting **CityWalk**, where you'll find restaurants, nightclubs, cinemas, and lots of shops. The **Islands of Adventure Port of Entry** is just a few more steps to your left, while **Universal Studios** is equidistant to your right.

These are no kiddie parks. At Universal Studios things blow up, sharks lunge at you, and laser guns zap nasty aliens. At Islands of Adventure most of the rides are for extreme thrill-seekers, making it a great place for teens bored with warm and fuzzy parks. For high-speed thrills, 3-D excitement, and nonstop adventure, this is the place to get pumped up.

Universal opens at 9 AM, with earlier access if you're staying at one of the on-site resorts (see *Hotels and Motels*). Both adventure parks close at the same time, with CityWalk (see *Eating Out* and *Entertainment*) staying open to the wee hours. In winter the parks can close as early as 6 PM or as late as 8 PM, with summer hours extending to 9 or 10 PM. Make sure to call in advance, as closing times seem to change depending on the season, special events, or during spring break. Special events, such as Halloween Horror Nights, have additional admission fees.

Ticket options include deep discounts if you purchase in advance online. The best value is the 2-park Unlimited Admission Ticket, providing unlimited access to Universal Studios and Islands of Adventure for 7 consecutive days, $80 advance booking or $90 for immediate use, only available online. A 2 parks–1 day pass available at the park gate is $83 adult, $73 child, or $75/$65 if ordered in advance online. Add-ons include the Express Plus Pass that jumps you to the front of the lines and special vacation packages, or tickets to the Blue Man Group (see *Entertainment*). Florida residents receive deep discounts, but they really do want you to use their Web site to book ahead, so do so to receive the best prices all around. All prices are subject to change.

Islands of Adventure

This is where the rides are! At the **Port of Entry**, on the far left side of City-Walk, you'll enter five islands set along exotic coastlines, where you might enter a comic-book city full of superheroes and old favorites, or a strange architectural land full of Seussian characters, then continue on to a jungle where dinosaurs rule and a mythical island full of legendary gods and dragons. If you collected comic books as a kid or were first in line for such movies as *Jurassic Park* and *Spider-Man*, then this is the place for you. If you don't like adrenaline thrill rides, then head back over to Universal Studios, where there's still plenty of excitement without the white-knuckle chills. On **Marvel Super Hero Island**, **The Amazing Adventures of Spider-Man** takes you on a 3-D adventure while you help fight the Sinister Syndicate in your transport vehicle. Beware: The action-packed simulator moves along a track, but the drops will feel real. On **Doctor Doom's Fearfall** the 150-foot drop *is* real. For more even more heart-pounding action, the **Incredible Hulk** launches you out of a purple tunnel at 40 mph, then immediately inverts and plunges 105 feet toward the lagoon—only to loop around and do it again.

On **Jurassic Park River Adventure**, take a water ride back 65 million years through the jungles of the Jurassic period; then the velociraptors escape and anything can happen. You'll be refreshed (and wet) after being plunged 85 feet into total darkness while escaping *T. rex*. The little ones will enjoy **Pteranodon Flyers** soaring high above the prehistoric jungle and **Camp Jurassic** play-ground. Make sure to walk down the **Triceratops Discovery Trail** to see what's in the veterinary paddock. Over on the **Lost Continent**, twin serpents, Fire and Ice, pass within inches of each other during their roller-coaster dogfight on **Dueling Dragons**. My daughter still hasn't forgiven me for chickening out. So for the timid there's **The Flying Unicorn**, a junior roller coaster set in an enchanted forest. Sounds tame, but this one still had enough twists and drops to tickle my belly. The walk-through **Poseidon's Fury** showcases the king of the sea's power with water and fire explosions, including an impressive wave tunnel.

Get your towel out for the wacky water rides in **Toon Lagoon**. Help Popeye save Olive Oyl at **Popeye & Bluto's Bilge-Rat Barges**, a white-water adven-ture, then take care of Snidely Whiplash once and for all on **Dudley Do-Right's Ripsaw Falls**. The two-step waterfall near the end is one of the steepest of any flume rides anywhere. The young and young-at-heart will enjoy **Seuss Landing**, complete with a spin on **The Cat in the Hat**, and an odd variety of Seuss char-acters on the **Caro-Seuss-El** that even the adults will want to ride. More Seuss-ian characters can be found at **If I Ran the Zoo**, a great place for parents to sit while kids climb around the interactive play area. As you head out of the park you'll still be exhilarated, so hang around CityWalk for dinner, movies, or night-club action. The day has only just begun.

Universal Studios Florida

✍ ♿ If you just can't get enough of Steven Spielberg's productions *Jaws, E.T., Men in Black, Shrek, Twister,* and *Back to the Future* (yes, they were all his), then turn right at CityWalk and "ride the movies." The old standby, **Jaws**, is still here (and still just as exciting), along with new 3- and 4-D shows, rides, and adventures. Universal's rides are without a doubt thrilling, but you won't need nerves of steel to go on anything at this park. Some jolt you around a bit, though thankfully not one of them features death-defying drops; those rides are over at Islands of Adventure. But hold on: Just when I thought it was safe to wander around, I find out Kong's Penn Station was turned into **Revenge of the Mummy**, a screaming roller-coaster ride with pyrotechnics, computer animation, Egyptian sets, and space-age robotics—all indoors, and with those creepy scarab beetles to freak you out.

Go **Back to the Future** in your own time-travel vehicle. This simulator ride jolts you left, right, up, down, back, and forth while you hurtle through the past, present, and future in this Sensurround adventure. Board your own rocket and blast off on a wild chase on **Jimmy Neutron's Nicktoon Blast**. The individual simulators make this ride even more realistic in its out-of-control cartoon adventure. I waited for over an hour to see **Shrek 4-D**, and it was worth it. I just can't give away the 4-D part—it would spoil the adventure. Don't wait until the end of the day to see this one, or Jimmy Neutron, both on the exit path. **Terminator 2: 3-D Battle Across Time** merges live action and actors with 3-D special effects. Don't forget to take your 3-D glasses off during the live-action sequences. You'll have to fight off aliens in the interactive **Men in Black Alien Attack**. And you'll want to do it again and again, as the ending is different, depending on how many aliens you terminate while spinning around and at times moving backward—it's one of the most unusual rides in the park. The new **Disaster! A Major Motion Picture Ride . . . Starring You!** replaced Earthquake in 2008 and uses high-tech virtual imagery to prepare you as an extra for the disaster movie *Mutha Nature*, in production at Disaster Studios; at the end, you show up in the movie trailer. For more natural disasters, head over to **Twister**. To get the most out of this walk-on adventure, get into the story line, and then hold on as a real vortex whips into town. It's even got cows! Take a trip back to 1975 on a boat ride through Amity, but be warned: You'll never know when **Jaws** will charge the boat. You'll want to bring a change of clothes for the kids, and then head over to **Woody Woodpecker's Kid Zone** for water-based fun where **Curious George Goes to Town**. Climb the 30-foot spiderweb or twist and turn down the 200-foot water slide at **Fievel's Playland**. Jump into a crate and hang on for a wild and nutty roller-coaster ride through a nut factory on **Woody Woodpecker's Nuthouse Coaster**.

Don't forget that Universal Studios is a working studio. You never know what show may be shooting on the day you arrive, or what celebrities may be wandering about. Stroll through the **Street Sets** in the New York and Hollywood sections, where a walk-through exhibit honoring America's favorite redhead is at **Lucy: A Tribute**. You'll need to arrive at least 15 minutes before showtimes for ***Beetlejuice's Graveyard Revue***, ***The Blues Brothers***, and the ***Universal Horror Make-up Show***. Make sure you pick up a show schedule, as some shows have only two performances a day. For soundstages, head over to Production Central for a peek at Stage 54 and Nickelodeon Studios. If you love anything on film, Universal Studios is the place to be. Toward the end of the day, I had just enough time to slip into the **E.T. Adventure**. And I'm so glad I didn't miss it. After taking a walk through tall woods, I boarded my "bike" and flew off to the stars to help E.T. save his world. This gentle, rolling ride is full of great scenes and not to be missed. After all, it was one of Spielberg's own favorites. What I can't wait for next is the **Wizarding World of Harry Potter**, a "theme park within a theme park" based on J.K. Rowling's books, due to open here in 2009.

WALT DISNEY WORLD RESORT The epicenter of Florida tourism, the **Walt Disney World Resort** (407-WDW-INFO; www.disneyworld.com) consists of a 47-square-mile complex of theme parks, resorts, shopping centers, and wilderness, a city unto itself with its own police force, fire and rescue, and transportation system. From Walt Disney's original vision in the 1950s, the world-renowned entertainment complex has grown in directions that he probably never expected, hosting baseball spring training, race car driving, and one of the world's best circus performances. Each of these "on property" venues is discussed.

Hours vary daily at the Disney theme parks. When you arrive, request the current two-week calendar that shows park hours, parades, and special events. In general, Animal Kingdom closes the earliest (5 PM) and Epcot the latest (9 PM), but there are often exceptions for special events; the parks generally open at 9 AM, but guests staying in the Walt Disney World Resort hotels are offered earlier entrance to certain parks on a rotating basis.

Tickets to the four major parks follow a fixed price structure (subject to change without notice). A base ticket starts at $60 for ages 3–9, $71 for ages 10 and older for a single day, single theme park. You can purchase a length-of-stay ticket for up to 10 days, with the price capping out at $187 and $225 (bringing the per-day price down to $22.50 per day). Then there are add-ons. For an additional $45, your ticket becomes a Park Hopper—useful for multiday stays. For an additional $50, you receive 2 to 10 visits (depending on days on ticket) to the Disney water parks. All tickets expire within 14 days unless you buy a "No Expiration" add-on as well . . . guess I can't cash in those old E Tickets I have from 1972 in my collectibles chest! Annual passes are now $395 for ages 3–9 and $448 for ages 10 and up, covering the four theme parks. A Premium Annual Pass throws in the water parks, Pleasure Island, Wide World of Sports, and Disney Quest for $510 and $579. Florida residents get the best bargain with a Florida Resident Seasonal Pass, with blackout dates during peak periods, for $203 and $230. Best of all? Annual pass holders get free parking.

Disney's Animal Kingdom

Education about conservation with a side of entertainment—that's Animal Kingdom, the 500-acre theme park that staunchly claims it's "not a zoo" but nevertheless presents animals in natural habitat enclosures, melding nature and art. Themed regions radiate from **Safari Village**, where art is everywhere: more than 1,500 hand-painted wooden folk art animal carvings crafted in Bali decorate the buildings, and the enormous Tree of Life dominates the skyline. It's an incredible work of art, with 325 animals carved into the structure, and houses the 3-D film ***It's Tough to Be a Bug***—a performance that'll get a rise out of you. In the surrounding garden, animals like axis deer and green peafowl roam, each identified with an interpretive sign adorned with a poem about the creature, information on the animal, and a map of its habitat. **Camp Minnie Mickey** presents live shows—most notably the ***Festival of the Lion King***, a grand Broadway-style performance of artistic pageantry that you won't want to miss— and offers kids chances for character photos and autographs. The din of the crowd in **Harambe** mingles with live music and echoes off the buildings, creating an atmosphere like a busy African village, gateway to **Kilimanjaro Safaris**, a popular bumpy ride through re-created African forests and savannas where herds of antelope, rhinos, and elephants roam. I enjoy strolling down the **Pangani Forest Trail**, watching the troop of lowland gorillas wander through their habitat. **Rafiki's Planet Watch** requires a train ride out to the complex; en route, you'll see the animals from a different perspective, including within their nighttime digs. The complex is Animal Kingdom's nerve center, with veterinarians looking after rare species and a nursery for new additions to the animal families. In **Anandapur** stroll the Maharajah Jungle Walk, where a 900-pound Malayan tapir lazes beneath the bamboo, Rodrigues fruit bats and Malayan flying foxes dangle from the trees, and female Bengal-Sumatran tigers loll about beneath flapping prayer flags in the temple ruins. **Kali River Rapids** is the thrill-seeker's destination for this section of the park, and you will get wet on this ride. **Expedition EVEREST** whisks you down the Himalayas on a runaway mountain railway past the yeti. At **DinoLand USA**, step into campy 1950s fun with the giant **Boneyard** for kids to dig through; **Chester & Hester's Dino-Rama**, a midway carnival/amusement park with the popular Primeval Whirl; and **Dinosaur!**, a bumpy time-travel trip past marauding dinosaurs as meteors fall to earth. Tie it all together by watching the artsy daily parade at 4 PM, with beautifully costumed critters stealing the show from Minnie and Mickey.

Disney's Hollywood Studios

Dropping their relationship with MGM Studios kicked off a transformation of this movie-themed park, where you're whisked away to the back lots and studios of Tinseltown, Disney style, with 1940s art deco setting the tone. It's full of feel-good movie-themed rides and shows like ***The Great Movie Ride*** and ***Jim Henson's Muppet Vision 3D*** (where I can never get enough of Statler and Waldorf bickering in the balcony), but many of the themes reveal the 1989 opening of this park, like **Star Tours** and the **Indiana Jones Epic Stunt Spectacular** (which, thanks to the new movie, is enjoying a resurgence of popularity). I encourage you to walk through **Walt Disney: One Man's Dream**, a multimedia museum of Walt's life and the evolution of his empire from *The Wonderful World of Disney* to the Walt Disney World of today; it's a great primer on what Walt was all about. Thrill-seekers gravitate to the **Twilight Zone Tower of Terror**, a 13-story sudden drop, and the **Rock 'n' Roller Coaster**, where Steven Tyler and Aerosmith lead you through a recording studio into a parking garage for a blastoff from 0 to 60 mph in 2.8 seconds followed by a blitz through the dark—think Space Mountain on a caffeine buzz. Families stand in even longer lines for **Toy Story Mania!**, an re-do of Buzz Lightyear's Space Ranger Spin, a 3-D mobile shooting gallery where you "shrink" to the size of a toy to play. Live theater shows that will captivate the kids include ***Beauty and the Beast*** and the ***Voyage of the Little Mermaid***; ***Fantasmic!*** draws upon Mickey's performance in *Fantasia*, with a limited-seating outdoor light-and-sound show to close out each evening.

EPCOT'S MISSION: SPACE

Sandra Friend

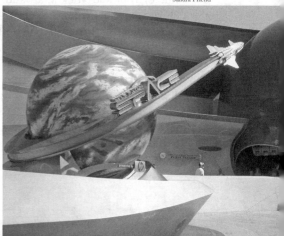

Epcot

It's extraordinary the influence that Epcot had on my family: One year, my sister joined in a street performance in Morocco; the next, she was braving her way to Marrakech for real. It's a theme park for adults, a virtual trip around the world for those who haven't yet set foot outside the United States, very much like the World's Fairs of my youth—with shopping! With their focus on future technologies, the pavilions of **Future World** remind me of those old World's Fair pavilions, right down to the corporate sponsorship. **Spaceship Earth,** the imposing entrance structure, contains a freshly updated ride through the history of technological change, depositing you into a new interactive playground presented by Siemens, **Project Tomorrow**. Ride beneath a 5.7-million-gallon artificial reef in **The Seas**, or take a guided boat trip through working greenhouses in **The Land**; let the kids play in **ImageWorks** and **Innoventions**. In **Wonders of Life**, a script straight from *Fantastic Voyage* comes to life in **Body Wars**, a high-speed trip through the immune system. You'll need the Fastpass for the top two rides in the park—**Test Track**, the mile-long General Motors simulator that speeds you through automobile tests, and the impressive **Mission: Space**, which uses NASA technology to propel you and your team into space, where you feel like you've left earth's gravitational pull. My usual reason for visiting Epcot, however, is to stroll around the 4-acre **World Showcase Lagoon** to shop and eat. Movies and rides in the country pavilions add to the fun, but I enjoy the cultural exhibits the best, like the **Animales Fantisticos** "spirits in wood" from Oaxaca at Mexico, and the **Gallery of Arts and History in Morocco**, a reverent mosque-like museum filled with treasures from their national museum. Of course, I still get chills when I see Ben Franklin walking through **The American Adventure**, and it's hard to pass up the beauty of **Impressions de France**, but visiting World Showcase is about soaking up atmosphere. I've seen and done it all many, many times, but I'll always come back for dinner and the unique imports filling the shops, especially during the annual **Food & Wine Festival** (see *Special Events*).

Magic Kingdom

With the top theme park attendance in the world, the **Magic Kingdom** is the core of the Disney empire, encompassing Walt's original vision of bringing fantasy and imagination to life. Start off with a walk down **Main Street USA** to reach the statue of Walt and Mickey, around which all of the themed areas radiate. I've always loved **Adventureland**, with its funky Caribbean atmosphere; laugh your way down the classic **Jungle Cruise**, slip down into the dark watery corridors of **Pirates of the Caribbean**, or sing along with the birdies in the **Enchanted Tiki Room** (albeit under new wisecracking management; I miss the 1960s feel). In adjoining **Frontierland**, motorized rafts float visitors to **Tom Sawyer Island**, one of the most fun "natural" attractions in the park, where kids can play in Fort Langhorn—a frontier fort that looks suspiciously like Fort Christmas—and sneak through catacomb-like caves. My favorite thrill rides at the park are **Big Thunder Mountain Railway**, a runaway train, and **Splash Mountain**, a dressed-up log flume that'll have you whistling zip-a-dee-doo-dah through vignettes populated by critters from the Uncle Remus stories of Joel Chandler Harris. **Liberty Square's** big draw is the ever-creepy **Haunted Mansion**, while behind the Bavarian facades of **Fantasyland** lie the busiest rides in the park—make sure you get a Fastpass for **Peter Pan's Flight**, the new 3-D **Mickey's PhilharMagic**, and the incredibly popular **Many Adventures of Winnie the Pooh**, where you drift through scenes of the A. A. Milne books in a giant honey jar. **Tomorrowland** is a campy 1950s sci-fi version of the future dominated by **Space Mountain.** I still love the **Carousel of Progress** ("Now is the time . . . now is the best time . . . now is the best time of your life"), a vision of the future from the past—I first saw it at the 1964–65 New York World's Fair, where it debuted. The youngest part of the Magic Kingdom, **Mickey's Toontown Fair**, is a cartoon village

Sandra Friend

CINDERELLA'S CASTLE AT THE MAGIC KINGDOM.

and county fair rolled into one, with Minnie and Mickey's houses, the **Barnstormer** at Goofy's Wiseacre Farm (a gentle roller coaster), and lots of opportunities for character photos and autographs at the **Toontown Hall of Fame** tent. Tie it all together with a ride around the world on the **Walt Disney World Railroad**, featuring classic steam engines that were model railroader Walt's pride and joy.

✳ To Do

AVIATION **Air Florida Helicopters** (407-363-9002; www.airfloridahelicopters .com), 8990 International Dr, is one of the longer-standing helicopter ride providers in the area, operating from their oh-so-visible helipad on I-Drive, from which they buzz over my friends' nearby home every few minutes or so. Tour prices start at $25 adult, $20 child for the quick eight-mile circuit over the heart of I-Drive and SeaWorld, and can get as extensive as a trip out and over Lake Apopka (Florida's second largest lake), including a flyover of all of the theme parks, for $355 adult, $325 child.

BICYCLING At Walt Disney World rent **old-fashioned tandem bikes** at Disney's Boardwalk and Port Orleans Resort (see *Resorts*), or grab a **standard road bike** or mountain bike at Fort Wilderness (see *Campgrounds*) to hit the many miles of paved trails under the pines.

BALLOONING Visitor interest in ballooning has, well, ballooned substantially over the last decade, leading to stiff competition among a number of operators who'll take you up, up, and away to see the Disney property gleaming from the air. However, one operator stands head and shoulders above the crowd. Since 1983, the pilots at **Orange Blossom Balloons** (407-894-5040; www.orangeblossomballoons.com) have taken off at daybreak daily (weather permitting) to drift across the Orlando skies. I'd never been in a balloon before, and was a bit frightened at the concept—I don't do well with heights. So it amazed me to find that we were several hundred feet in the air and I'd never felt us lift off. There is no sensation of movement, except the breeze blowing through your hair; you look down, and it's as if you're walking on air—or as my captain put it, "It's like standing above the earth and having it moved below you."

The duly promised spectacular sunrise over the Magic Kingdom and downtown Orlando was soon eclipsed by the beauty of watching our two sister balloons in colorful flight below and above us. Our captain skimmed the treetops to put a spin on our descent so we'd end up in an open space after the hour-long flight, which was soon followed by a traditional champagne toast and all-you-can-eat breakfast buffet. Cost? $175, including breakfast and postflight champagne; save $10 by booking online.

SHORTLY AFTER TAKEOFF AT ORANGE BLOSSOM BALLOONS

Sandra Friend

BIRDING Visit **Tibet-Butler Preserve** (see *Nature Center*) to listen to the ospreys cry over Lake Tibet; keep alert to identify warblers in the palmetto scrub.

BOATING ✍ **Walt Disney World** (407-WDW-PLAY) boasts the **world's largest fleet of rental watercraft**, more than 500 boats ranging from mini Watermouse powerboats (safe for teens) to pontoon boats. Skim the surface of Bay Lake or paddle down miles of canals; check in at the Polynesian Village Resort, Contemporary Resort (see *Resorts*), or Fort Wilderness (see *Campgrounds*) for details.

International Drive

Pirate's Dinner Adventure (407-248-0590; www.piratesdinneradventure.com), 6400 Carrier Dr. The preshow opens with an appetizer buffet set in an old seaport village. You'll have plenty of time to visit the local merchants or stop by the **Pirate's Maritime Museum**. Developed by Mel Fisher, the museum portrays pirate life through historical artifacts and examples of pirate crimes and punishments. The main show features a full-sized replica of an 18th-century Spanish galleon set in a large lagoon. Ship's mates defend the vessel with special effects, swashbuckling swordplay, and aerial acrobatics from 70-foot masts. This show is full of loud explosions and pyrotechnics, so it may be too much for the little ones. The feast includes salad, marinated chicken, roasted seasoned pork, shrimp with lobster sauce, West Indies yellow rice, steamed vegetables, and warm apple cobbler. Complimentary beer, wine, soft drinks, and coffee are offered only during the main show, but you may enjoy sticking around for the Buccaneer Bash Dance Party immediately following. One show nightly. $55 adults, $35 ages 3–11.

⅃ Not quite up for a full-scale extravaganza with more crowds? The **Outta Control Magic Show** (407-351- 8800; www.wonderworksonline.com) inside Wonderworks (see *Funhouses*) is just the place to unwind. This intimate dinner show is 90 minutes of high-energy comedy and improvisation. You'll wonder how only two guys and a gal can keep you so entertained. They are fabulous and funny! There's no preshow, but lots of audience participation. A simple dinner of unlimited hand-tossed pizza, popcorn, beer, wine, and soda will more than satisfy you. $25 adults, $17 ages 4–12 and seniors, offered at 6 and 8 PM nightly.

⅃ Who did it? That's the question you'll be asking yourself all night. **Sleuth's Mystery Dinner Theater** (407-363-1985 or 1-800-393-1985; www.sleuths .com), 7508 Universal Blvd, offers nine different comedy-mysteries, so you can come back again and again and never really know whodunit. Put your investigative talents to the test while interacting with cast members to solve the crime. Listen carefully, take notes, and ask questions—you might be chosen for a cameo role. Full-course dinner is served with hors d'oeuvres; salad; a choice of Cornish hen and baked potato, lasagna and meatballs, or prime rib and baked potato; vegetables; a delicious "mystery" dessert; and unlimited beer, wine, soft drinks, coffee, and iced tea. Nightly. No preshow. $50 adults, $24 ages 3–11.

Kissimmee–St. Cloud

⅃ A family business for more than 15 years, **Arabian Nights** (407-239-9223; www.arabian-nights.com), 6255 W Irlo Bronson Hwy, presents a breathtaking performance: 60 horses and 30 performers in a dazzling area of magical scenes. I kept forgetting to eat my dinner while riders and horses swept past for nearly 2 hours, weaving together the story of a royal wedding while showcasing the talents of 16 different breeds and one extra-special horse, Walter Farley's Black Stallion, who performs "at liberty"—no rider! The three-course dinner includes unlimited beer and wine. $46 adults, $21 ages 3–11. For an extra $11, the VIP tour provides an extra hour of interaction with the horses on the arena floor and

THE INSIDE DISH ON DINNER SHOWS Themed dinner shows have their own special appeal, and each production is unique. From the comedy of vaudeville revues, to interactive detective mysteries where you solve the crime, to full-scale productions with horses and pyrotechnics, you'll love them all. After a long day at the parks, you might think that a late night out may be too much for the kids, or for you, but much to my surprise everyone remained wide awake throughout the entire show. I like the idea that I didn't have to wait in line, my seats were reserved, I didn't have to order anything, and in some shows beer and wine were free, and free flowing.

There is an order to the way things work at dinner shows. First, unless noted, there is a preshow about an hour before the scheduled performance. This gives you a chance to arrive on time, and for them to hawk their souvenirs. For whatever you paid for your ticket, plan at least half that for trinkets and memorable goblets and mugs. Not that you should come late; the preshows are as entertaining as the main event, and help set the mood. Once inside you will sit with other guests—at long benches facing the action at the larger shows, and around community tables at the mystery and comedy shows. Except for buffet dinners, your meal will come in stages and you'll have no control over what it is or when it appears, although all the shows handle serving seamlessly.

Depending on the show, expect to spend anywhere from 90 minutes to 3 hours being entertained; all shows require reservations, although last-minute tickets can often be purchased. Admission fees can range from $16 upward to a whopping $50 and more. Almost all the shows have discount coupons on their Web sites with additional coupons in flyers and kiosks around town—some as much as half off. The admission does not include gratuity, and the servers expect one, as it's really their main paycheck. So do you tip on the full ticket price or what you think the food portion would cost? Most servers are happy with $5 per adult and $2–3 for each kid. Guests with allergies to hay and animals should take the necessary precautions at live animal shows.

a private tour of the stables, plus preferential seating in the first three rows. Reservations recommended; although the arena holds 1,300 guests, it does sell out!

The longest-running dinner show in the area, **Medieval Times Dinner & Tournament** (407-239-0214, 407-396-1518, or 1-800-229-8300; www.medieval times.com), 4510 W Irlo Bronson Hwy (US 192), is an institution. Arrive early and go back in time to the 11th century at the Medieval Life Village (the only such living history exhibit in the United States), where you'll walk through buildings and learn about life in the Middle Ages. The extra fee to see the medieval torture room is worth it and a real eye-opener—each historical artifact is explained in full, graphic detail (it's not for the squeamish or little ones). Over at the castle, enter the great hall, where you'll meet the royal court prior to the show and shop for costumes and accessories, dragon goblets filled with grog, and souvenir collectibles. As noble lords and ladies you will be assigned a brave knight who will fight on your behalf while defending the kingdom. Experience the adventure and romance as stunning Andalusian stallions perform amazing displays, much like the great Lipizzaner, while valiant knights compete in tournament games and jousting matches until only one knight remains. $57 adults; $36 ages 12 and under.

Set in a 1930s speakeasy, **Capone's Dinner & Show** (407-397-2378 or 1-800-220-8428; www.alcapones.com), 4740 W Irlo Bronson Hwy (US 192) comes alive in Gangland Chicago with comedy and Broadway-style musical productions. Surrounded by mobsters and molls at Al Capone's secret hideaway, you'll dine on Mama Capone's Italian American buffet during song and dance performed by some of the area's best professionals. Don't be surprised if the "Feds" raid the place. The buffet has more food than you can load on your plate—and you can go back for seconds. You'll also enjoy unlimited beer, sangria, rumrunners, and soft drinks served by your very own mobster. No preshow. $48 adults, $30 ages 4–12; check their Web site for deeply discounted coupons.

Lake Buena Vista

& Saturday nights are just deadly at **MurderWatch Mystery Dinner Show** (407-828-4444; www.murderwatch.com) at the Regal Sun Resort on the mezzanine level, 1850 Hotel Plaza Blvd. Dreamland Productions has been putting on interactive murder mysteries for nearly 20 years, and only on Saturday nights. The variety of scripts, written and directed by members of Mystery Writers of America, keeps well-cast professional actors fresh and audiences begging for more. This total immersion in interactive theater has nonstop action. You'll need to pay attention—all is not what it seems. Just when you think the murder has been solved, think again; there just might be a twist! This is your chance to sport your nicer clothes, unlike the other shows; this one is in an elegant ballroom, and hands down the best food of any dinner show. The lavish buffet is prepared by Disney resort chefs and includes everything you'd expect from a top resort, including roast prime rib of beef and desserts to "die" for. Quality wine, beer, soda, and coffee are complimentary and unlimited, with mixed drinks available for a fee. Two shows on Sat night only. No preshow. $50 adults, $15 ages 9 and under.

SeaWorld Orlando Resort

& **Makahiki Luau** (407-363-2613 or 1-800-327-2424; www.seaworldorlando .com). Enter the exotic South Seas at this exciting luau celebration of ancient rituals, and rhythmic music and dance, presented on stage in authentic costumes of native Pacific Islanders. At the pre-show, the island chief arrives amid lots of dancing and drumming. Here you'll get a complimentary drink; inside, you'll have to pay for beer, wine, and tropical drinks. Soft drinks, coffee, and tea are free and unlimited. The Polynesian fare is more than you could ever eat, and the pause in entertainment while the meal is served is well thought out, so you have time to enjoy your family's company. Adults will enjoy tropical salad, Hawaiian chicken, Polynesian-style barbecued spareribs, mahi-mahi in piña colada sauce, fried rice, stir-fried vegetables, and dessert—all served family style with extras on request. Children will get a meal of chicken fingers or hot dogs in a souvenir bucket. You'll need to pay the adult fee if your kids will be eating the adult meal. This is one of the earliest dinner shows, with the pre-show starting at 6 and your meal hitting the table around 7:15. You'll be out by 9, and directly after the show you can enjoy a brief admission to SeaWorld during extended hours. $46 adults, $29 ages 3–11; under 3 free, but mention them when you make reservations. Admission to the park is not required to attend this show.

Universal Orlando Resort

Participate in an extravagant Hawaiian feast and dinner show at the **Wantilan Luau** (407-503-DINE) at the Royal Pacific Resort (see *Resorts*). Suckling pig roasts in a pit in the midst of a tropical garden; Hawaiian dancers perform as servers bring around tropical fruit salad, tropical fruitcake, and ahi tuna poke salad. Sat night, $50 adults, $29 children 12 and under; reservations required.

FAMILY ACTIVITIES ✐ Beyond the attractions, the family can unwind with a round of miniature golf in any one of many venues. In the Walt Disney World resort, the popular **Fantasia Gardens**, with its scale replicas of renowned golf holes, is at the Epcot Resort Area. **Disney's Winter Summerland** course, with a North Pole theme, adjoins Blizzard Beach. Along International Drive, **Congo River Golf** (www.congoriver.com/orlando) near Wet 'n Wild follows the footsteps of African explorers while offering 36 holes; you can stop and feed the (real) gators. Open 10 AM–11 PM Sun–Thu, til midnight Fri–Sat; $11 for one course or $15 for both. Swashbucklers can head to **Pirate's Cove Adventure** (407-352-7378; www.piratescove.net/location/5), 8501 International Dr, open 9 AM–11:30 PM daily. Their 36-hole adventure is $14 with shorter options for less.

✐ Many midway attractions offer just good wholesome fun. Drive go-carts the old-fashioned way, on elevated wooden racks, at **Magical Midway** (407-370-5353; www.magicalmidway.com), 7001 International Dr, where you pay for rides à la carte. The Avalanche track has a 30-degree drop off the top of the arcade building. Experience free fall from the **Space Shot Tower**, then face off against your friends on the bumper boats and cars. Over at **Fun Spot Action Park** you'll drive go-carts around twists and turns on a concrete track. The park also offers an arcade and small selection of midway rides. Down US 192, **Old Town** is a great place to hang out after the parks have closed, especially on Friday and Saturday nights when classic cars cruise the strip. Stroll down brick streets browsing 75 specialty shops, eight restaurants, and an assortment of midway rides, including the world's tallest slingshot. The **Windstorm roller coaster**, with 80-degree banked turns and a g-force of 4.7, gives thrills as good as the coasters at the big parks.

FISHING ✐ Yes, you can **cast for bass** in the shadow of Cinderella's Castle at Walt Disney World (407-WDW-PLAY) on a 2-hour guided trip on Bay Lake, with all tackle and cold drinks provided. Catch-and-release only; no fishing license required.

FUNHOUSES

Downtown Disney

DisneyQuest is Florida's ultimate funhouse, with five floors of interactive fun and games. Yes, you can plunk the kids down in front of Skee-Ball and other classic arcade games, or play Space Invaders until midnight. But I got hooked on virtual reality: Design your own roller coaster, then ride it in a simulator on Virtual Space Mountain—and if it isn't hard-core enough for you, the attendant will conjure up a wild ride! Or grab a paddle and go white-water rafting on the Virtual Jungle Cruise, dodging dinosaurs and lava flows while the waves splash your face. It's a perfect rainy-day destination (complete with restaurants and snack bars), or you can spend your entire evening having a blast; $37 adults, $31 ages 3–9.

International Drive

Ripley's Believe It or Not Odditorium (407-345-0501; www.ripleysorlando .com) stays open late to catch the curious with displays of Robert Ripley's international finds that made the phrase "Believe it or not!" famous. Like its original St. Augustine counterpart, the walk-through 16-gallery attraction has its bizarre displays strung together by funhouse favorites like spinning tunnels and warped mirrors. Of course, I love the fact that it's slipping into a sinkhole. Open daily 8 AM–1 AM; $19 adults, $12 ages 4–12.

♪ **Wonderworks** (407-351-8800; www.wonderworksonline.com), 9067 International Dr. It first catches my eye as I drive up I-Drive. It looks as though a secret laboratory, housed in a three-story ancient structure, has crash-landed upside down! I cautiously enter through a rising mist as the building creaks and moans. My first clue that this is no ordinary funhouse comes when I pass over a bridge while an optical illusion spins around the walls and ceiling. I actually have to hang on and close my eyes to get across. Stepping off the bridge, I enter the laboratory where testing is being done on earthquakes and hurricanes. Hang on tight, real tight, in either of these experiments. The 1989 San Francisco earthquake, measuring 5.3 on the Richter scale, is re-created at your kitchen table, while over in a subway car, winds rip through at 65 mph. Heading up to the second floor, enter a scientific world of imagination. More than 100 interactive exhibits range from realistic to virtual reality. Design your own roller coaster and then ride it. Dance like you've never danced before as your psychedelic shadow grooves with you. Find out what you will look like in 25 years with computer aging, or try out the many "face-lifts." Strike a pose and leave your shadow behind. Climb a rotating wall. Stand your hair on end on the Bridge of Fire. Play a tune on the big piano keyboard. Challenge a 7-foot basketball player as you are immersed into a virtual-reality court, or avoid the sharks and barracudas as you swim under the sea. Optical illusions are everywhere. I was told to allow two hours for the experience, but I stayed for five! The time flew by so fast I missed the laser tag and arcade games on the third floor. Open daily 9 AM–midnight. $20 adults, $15 ages 4–12 and seniors. Magic Combo package ($39) includes Wonderworks and admission to the Outta Control Magic Show (see *Dinner Shows*).

Kissimmee–St. Cloud

You'll have chills running up your spine in the three-story **Grimm Haunted House** in Old Town. This old-fashioned fright house, with lots of stairs and hallways, is customized to your fright level, so it's okay for adventurous young ones. Open daily, Sun–Thu noon–11, Fri and Sat noon–midnight. $10 adults, $8 ages 10 and under.

GOLF Central Florida is a golfer's paradise, with more than 100 courses radiating out from the theme park area. Without driving all over creation, how can you choose the one for you? Contact **Tee Times USA** (1-888-465-3356; www.tee timesusa.com), a free golfer's matchmaker service, if you will, that helps you pick a course and make reservations. Walt Disney World Resort courses (407-WDW-PLAY) include **Eagle Pines**, **Osprey Ridge**, and **Lake Buena Vista**, where you might rub elbows with Tiger Woods and other top golfers taking on their 99 holes. At Rosen Shingle Creek (see *Resorts*), the **Shingle Creek Golf Club** is a David Harman–designed 18-hole course winding along natural areas at the headwaters of the Everglades; the Brad Brewer Golf Academy runs out of the very popular pro shop tucked inside A Land Remembered steakhouse along the links.

MOTORCYCLING I know you were Born to Ride! At **Harley-Davidson Real Riding Adventure** (407-423-0346 or 1-877-740-3770; www.orlandoharley.com), 3770 37th St, you'll first listen to important safety instructions and then gradually get to know the 500cc Buell Blast. This personalized 1½-hour course teaches you how to shift gears, turn corners, slalom, and then come to a rolling stop. The one-on-one course is offered twice a week, and you get a really cool certificate at the end. No motorcycle license necessary, but you'll need further instruction to get one. Reservations are a must. Wear hard shoes and bring a long-sleeved shirt. $199. Have your own bike? Orlando Harley also teaches basic and experienced courses and offers official examinations for the Florida DMV.

RACE-CAR DRIVING Learn to handle a 600-horsepower stock car on the three-corner track of the **Richard Petty Driving Experience** (1-800-BE-PETTY) at Walt Disney World, where professional race-car drivers offer you experiences ranging from a three-lap ride-along ($109) to 40 laps driving on your own ($2,999). Overheard from one satisfied customer: "The car sticks to the track like glue!" Open daily 9–5, reservations suggested. For drive-your-own experiences, you must be 18 or older with a valid driver's license, and able to drive a manual transmission.

Rev your engines while the lights count down red–yellow–green, then go. Strap into the life-sized race cars at **G-Force** (407-397-2509), next to SkyCoaster (see *Skydropping*) off US 192, and hold on for one wild ride. You and your passenger will race on a straight track alongside another car. Once you hit the pedal, the car launches like a jet fighter, and in less than 2 seconds you'll reach 120 mph.

It's all over in less than 2 seconds, but you'll feel the adrenaline for hours. Make sure to get the video for instant replays. Open daily noon–11:30 PM. $30 for driver, $10 for passenger.

SCUBA DIVING AND SNORKELING At **The Seas** pavilion in Epcot, visitors will wave and point as you drift through a 6-million-gallon saltwater aquarium, getting to know the loggerheads and sergeant majors on the coral reef. Certified divers are welcome to dive on the Epcot DiveQuest programs (407-WDW-PLAY); rates ($150, which does not include park admission) include equipment, so leave your dive gear at home. You'll spend 3 hours on this experience, 40 minutes of it in the water.

Visitors to Disney's **Typhoon Lagoon** (see *Water Parks*) snorkel above leopard and nurse sharks and schools of tropical fish at Shark Reef, included in the park's admission.

SKATEBOARDING ✐ Skaters from beginners to advanced take to the 31,000-square-foot **Vans Skate Park** (407-351-3881; www.vans.com/vans/skateparks), 5220 International Dr, in the Festival Bay Outlet Mall. The wood-and-concrete bowl reaches depths up to 8 feet, with ramps surfaced in Finland birch.

SKYDIVING ✐ That funky blue building towering off Universal Blvd and I-Drive beckons you to come inside for the ride of your life. I wish I had gone to Sky Venture **Skydiving Wind Tunnel** (407-903-1150; www.skyventure.com), 6805 Visitors Circle, before actually taking the plunge from 13,500 feet. Knowing then what I know now would have enhanced the experience, and taken away some of the tenser moments. You'll still feel real skydiving flight, but this time from only a few feet off the ground. And you'll get an incredible workout. It's amazing just how many muscles it takes to balance on a column of air pushing 120 mph winds at you. After only two one-minute flights, I was sore for several days.

SHERRI LEMON RECEIVES FLIGHT INSTRUCTIONS AT SKY VENTURE.

Kathy Wolf

Check in with Ron Landon at the office and get a taste of what's to come on the live-feed monitors, then head up the steps for a preflight briefing where flight instructors, like Ron Henderson and Dan Perry, tell you how to hold your body and what hand signals you'll need while in the tunnel. Then you'll gear up in a real flight suit, goggles, and helmet and head to the observation room, where you might see real skydiving teams practicing their routines. Once inside the tunnel you'll sit comfortably in a waiting area with about 12 other fliers. When it's your turn, you'll come to the door of the tunnel and just fall in. It's that easy. The air immediately catches you, and you're airborne. You'll have a real-time flight of about one minute while your instructor helps you position your body for turns and higher altitude, but more importantly keeps you from banging into the wall. Depending on your body position, you fly about 4 to 6 feet off the wire mesh base. Don't worry, the fans won't suck you up, but if you catch the wind just right you can get as high as 15 feet. Wildman Dan showed me just how high, as he caught the air, shot upward, did a few somersaults, dived, and flipped into a sitting position.

Two minutes are all you'll need. I sent my daughter back in again and again for photos, and after the fourth minute she was done. With the recent upgrades of bigger motors and wind controls, wind speed can now be changed in two to three seconds to accommodate any size or skill of fliers. And instead of tiny windows, your friends and family can now watch you through 9-foot acrylic panels from the comfortable observation area. Whether you plan to do a real skydive or not, you should at least try this Peter Pan experience. Adults need to be in relatively good shape and under 250 pounds. Kids can fly, too—sometimes better than the adults. The little ones I saw there had the time of their life. Open weekdays 2–midnight, weekends noon–midnight. Reservations strongly recommended. $39 adults, $34 ages 5–12. Videos available for $16.

SKYDROPPING Just off US 192 next to Old Town, two vertical columns reach toward the sky. Then you notice something dropping from them. What's going on here? Sometime back in the early 1990s, bungee jumping morphed into a safer version of the vertical drop, and **Skycoaster** (407-397-2509), 2850 Florida Plaza Blvd, Kissimmee, became an instant hit among thrill-seekers around the globe. The newest version tops out at 300 feet, the tallest of all the skycoasters. It's so high, in fact, that it requires aircraft beacons. Fitted with an FAA-approved flight suit and skydiving harness, I was attached to a cable and then winched backward and upward. Climbing to 100 feet, you'll get a great view with Disney just off to the northwest. At 200 feet, uh . . . what did I get myself into? At 300 feet my head began to spin and I just wanted to get down. A pull of the cord accomplished that, and I dived headfirst screaming as I raced toward the pond below. At 76 mph I leveled out and swung back and forth, skimming the treetops. At night you'll get an amazing view of city lights and area attractions. Single rider $37, two riders $64, three riders $81. Don't forget the $16 video. You'll want to capture this one for the grandkids.

SPAS With so many luxury hotels wrapped around the theme parks, this area is becoming a hot spot for spas, and I promise that by next edition, I'll take the time to savor and report on them all. Meanwhile, at **Canyon Ranch Spa at Gaylord Palms** (407-586-205; www.gaylordhotels.com), 6000 W Osceola Pkwy, your journey begins with a eucalyptus steam bath and shower, and then you'll relax in the waiting room while cool cucumbers soothe your eyes. An attendant escorts you to your private sanctuary for personalized body treatments like their signature Euphoria for the best in stress relief, with warm sage and geranium oils, or the Endless Energy Pedicure for those tired feet. Avoid end-of-the-day appointments so that when your treatment is over, you'll have time to relax in the co-ed tearoom with a cup of selected herbs, lunch in the Everglades Atrium, or enjoy a swim in Gaylord's outdoor pool. Open daily 8–9.

A tour of the **Spa at Shingle Creek** (www.spaatshinglecreek.com) has me convinced that a follow-up for a treatment is in order. The facility overlooks the pool and golf course and beyond, a sweep of native cypress stands that is the headwaters of the Everglades. Their signature scent, citrus and cedar, is born of Florida essences that us outdoorsy types encounter often, and is used for massage, shampoos, and body revitalization. Another natural essence is in the Everglades Wrap, natural marine mud that smells like the mangrove shores of South Florida. Treatments and massages start at $110, with packages available. Appointments recommended.

SWIMMING In addition to the water parks, all of the area's resort hotels feature elaborate swimming pools, from the 750,000-gallon mini water park with shipwreck at **Disney's Yacht Club Resort** to the intimate winding stream with cozy little nooks for sipping a piña colada at the **Hyatt Regency Grand Cypress**. No matter where you're staying, expect the pool to be a focal point of activity on hot afternoons.

TRAIL RIDING ✐ **Disney's Fort Wilderness** (407-WDW-PLAY) offers trail rides on mellow Paso Finos, quarter horses, and others gentle enough for the kids, following a beaten track for 45 minutes through a remnant of pine flatwoods where you will almost always see deer. At **Grand Cypress Equestrian Center** (407-239-1938 or 1-800-835-7377; www.grandcypress.com/equestrian), 1 Equestrian Dr (off FL 535, 4 miles northwest of I-4 at Lake Buena Vista), participate in a riding academy approved by the British Horse Society, with leisurely Western-style wilderness trail rides starting at $45.

WATER PARKS ✐ **Aquatica** (www .aquaticabyseaworld.com) is the newest entry to the water park lineup, with a South Seas theme. For swimmers who like to sun and dunk, twin wave pools (**Cutback Cove** and

A FORT WILDERNESS TRAIL RIDE

Sandra Friend

Big Surf Shores) let you choose between wild or mild surf. If you love water-slides, you won't find ones like these anywhere else in the world. The **Dolphin Plunge** has twin tubes that sail you underwater in a clear tube past a pod of live dolphins. **Walhalla Wave** and **HooRoo Run** send you six stories up in an elevator to plunge down through a maze of twists and turns to ground level. A float on the **Loggerhead Lazy River** can start with a whip through the **Tassie Twister**, where you and your tube shoot into a giant bowl for a seemingly never-ending spin cycle before you drop back into the river. Take the wee ones to **Kata's Kookaburra Cove** for splashy fun with waterspouts. There's too much to handle in one day, and under the hot summer sun, you'll find yourself hanging out here a lot. Single day admission costs $39 adult, $33 child, with many combination options available (adding on SeaWorld, Busch Gardens, Discovery Cove, multiday passes, and more), and discounts for Florida residents. Open 10 AM, closing times vary.

✔ **Disney's Blizzard Beach**. Native pine trees poke out of snowcapped faux Rocky Mountains, giving the place a surreal Colorado feel; even the bathhouses, gift shops, and restaurants look like they belong at an Aspen ski resort. The ski theme extends to a chairlift that carries you up to the highest peak with the most intense water slides. Open daily 10–5; $39 adults, $33 ages 3–9. Free parking.

✔ **Disney's Typhoon Lagoon**. If I could pick only one water park to visit in all of Florida, this would be the one. Lush tropical plantings usher you in to a world of watery fun, centering on a massive wave pool with sporadic waves. Secret trails lead up and over rocky mountains, across swinging bridges, and through caves; visitors can snorkel across Shark Reef, or grab a tube and drift down a lazy river under the blooming raintrees all day. Open daily 10–5; $39 adults, $33 ages 3–9. Across from Downtown Disney; free parking.

✔ You'll have something to scream about at **Wet 'n Wild** (407-351-3200; www .wetnwild.com), 6200 International Dr, with exciting thrill rides down a water pipeline, through a twisting dark tunnel, down a 76-foot vertical drop, or "flushed" around and around in a giant bowl. When it's time to take it easy, float down the Lazy River or splash around the ocean-like beach. Open daily. $40 adults, $34 ages 3–9.

✳ Green Space

NATURE CENTER ✔ Hiding just beyond touristy Lake Buena Vista, **Tibet-Butler Preserve** (407-876-6696), 8777 CR 535, protects a precious 440 acres of pine flatwoods, bayheads, and scrub along the shore of Lake Tibet; 3.5 miles of well-maintained interpretive hiking trails wind through the forest. Kids and adults alike will enjoy the exhibits at the environmental center.

PARK ✔ At **West Beach Park**, 9227 Winter Garden–Vineland Rd (FL 535), shaded picnic pavilions overlook the sweep of cypress-lined Lake Tibet, and the playground has a big canopy over it—great shelter from those afternoon rains! Open 8–7 daily.

✳ Lodging

BED & BREAKFAST

Lake Buena Vista 32836

Sixteen acres of solitude, just 10 minutes from Disney—that's the big secret that is **Perrihouse** (1-800-780-4830; www.perrihouse.com), 10417 Vista Oaks Court, where owners Matt and Becky Manganella pride themselves on creating a comfortable nest for their guests, a quiet retreat near Lake Tibet. Each of the eight rooms ($109–139) has its own bath and exterior entrance; guests share a warm den lined with birdhouses and filled with books and videos, a pool and hot tub, and gardens designated a backyard urban bird sanctuary. There's also a new "Villa de Perri" with full kitchen, master suite, and living/dining area; sleeps 6. I couldn't ask for a more perfect place to kick back with a novel and take a break poolside between hours on my feet at Disney.

HOTELS, MOTELS, AND RESORTS

Walt Disney World

&. ✐ With 30 uniquely themed resorts, **Walt Disney World** (407-W-DISNEY; www.disneyworld.com) has nearly 28,000 rooms scattered across their property, separated into several tiers of pricing: value (from $82), moderate (from $149), deluxe (from $225), and home-away-from-home (from $265). As my family has discovered over the years, you can wrangle a better deal (see *Theme Park Tips*), but it takes some work. The most popular resort groupings are clustered near Animal Kingdom, Epcot/Hollywood (within walking distance), Magic Kingdom (travel by monorail or boat), and Downtown Disney (travel by boat). An extensive bus system links the resorts and theme parks. Room sizes range from very small (at the All Star Resorts, $82–151) to extremely spacious (Polynesian Resort, $340–860). If you plan to stay "on property," the chart on page 140 has my top picks from past personal stays, all with enough room for a family of four. Room rates drop as you set up package deals and multi-day stays.

International Drive

&. ⊕ ✾ ✐ "Ψ" One of Richard Kessler's Grand Theme hotels, the **Doubletree Castle** (407-345-4511 or 1-800-95-CASTLE; www.doubletree castle.com), 8629 International Dr, 32819, is an unmistakable landmark amid the high-rises. It's big, pink, and gaudy on the outside, but on the inside, prepare to step into an elegant world with designer interiors and gracious service. Public spaces are decorated with European art and complemented by Renaissance music. It's hard to believe it's a part of the Hilton family, but it is. Rooms ($99–229) come equipped with Sony PlayStations, pillow-top mattresses, and a stereo system; suites include a microwave, executive desk, wet bar, and queen sleeper sofa for the kids.

&. ⊕ "Ψ" **The Peabody Orlando** (407-352-4000 or 1-800-PEABODY; www.peabodyorlando.com), 9801 International Dr, is only one of two hotels in the Orlando area receiving the Mobil Four-Star Award, and it gets my vote as well. From the very moment you drive up under the covered entrance you'll be greeted with the friendly valet staff, most of them long-timers with tenures of up to 20 years. What makes this group so special is that they are direct employees of the hotel and not a vendor concession.

Resort	Price	Why?
Animal Kingdom Lodge	$225–540	Rooms surround an African savanna with live animals; fabulous African decor in common areas
Boardwalk Inn	$325–790	Surrounded by nightlife; walk to Epcot and Hollywood
Contemporary Resort	$270–795	Right in the middle of the action, with a monorail down the middle; great views of Bay Lake
Coronado Springs Resort	$149–240	Sprawling complex centered on a large lake, with an Aztec pyramid dominating the swimming area
Grand Floridian Resort & Spa	$385–990	Genteel Old Florida beach atmosphere with spectacular lake frontage
Polynesian Resort	$340–860	Immersed in a tropical wonderland, complete with splashing waterfalls; walk to monorail transportation
Port Orleans Riverside	$149–240	Lazy bayou feel with natural landscaping; boat to Downtown Disney
Shades of Green	Varies	Official US Armed Forces Recreation Center; vacationing servicemen and -women pay according to their rank
Wilderness Lodge	$225–730	Patterned after national park lodges of the Pacific Northwest, with a faux Yellowstone swimming area; boat transportation to Magic Kingdom

I hope they don't change that. Once inside, the staff continues to generate southern hospitality. Don't miss the famous Peabody Marching Ducks (see *Marching Ducks*) as they parade down the red carpet at 11 and 5 each day. Rooms start at Superior and rise in cachet from there; rates are $250 and up, but travelers will find bargains during the holiday season when conventions wane.

🦢 🖊 ♿ ⊗ Now here's a makeover worth mentioning. The very 1970s **International Plaza Resort & Spa** (1-800-327-0363; www.intlplaza resort.com), 10100 International Dr, is undergoing rejuvenation therapy, bit by bit. With more than 1,100 rooms on 28 acres, this property dates back to my teenage visits to SeaWorld and the now-defunct Stars Hall of Fame. Transforming the resort, located across the street from Aquatica (see *Water Parks*), into thematic groupings will take several years, but the new rooms are just plain "wow!" with Decola bowl sinks, sliding bath shutters, some wooden floors, high-thread count sheets, and snazzy Balinese-style decor. The complex has three pool areas and is shaded by mature pines and oaks. Rates run from $89–169 now, the least expensive options being the older, rather 1970s standard motel rooms.

Lake Buena Vista 32830

Most major motel chains are represented on Palm Parkway, which is a quieter and less congested place to stay than the entertainment complex that is International Drive; most of the properties are new or newly refurbished, and an easy drive to Disney's "back door" via Downtown Disney. Here are a few I recommend:

🦞 ♿ ⇝ ⁕↑⁕ I have it on the best authority (my sister, a former Hilton employee) that the **Hilton in the Walt Disney World Resort** (407-827-4000; www.hiltonworldresorts .com/Resorts/WaltDisneyWorld/index .html), 1751 Hotel Plaza Blvd, rocks. Just as at the Disney Resort hotels, you're treated to an early entrance to the theme parks, and it's an easy stroll to Downtown Disney. The spacious four-star accommodations include top-notch amenities like dual-line telephones, mini bar, coffeemaker, and double vanities in the bathroom. Rates start at $92, depending on season; family suites and multiday package deals available.

✎ ♿ The super-kid-friendly Holiday Inn Family Suites has morphed into **Nickelodeon Family Suites** (407-387-5437 or 1-877-387-KIDS; www .nickhotel.com), 14500 Continental

Gateway, a family-friendly and safe environment. This all-suite hotel features themed Kid Suites that gives kids their own special space complete with entertainment center and bunk beds, with cartoon-themed wrap-around scenes from SpongeBob Squarepants, Johnny Neutron, and more. Parents can stretch out in their own king- or queen-bedded room, and the whole family will enjoy the family room and full kitchen. Take the kids down to the water park or mini-golf, or treat your girls to the Kid's Spa. An adorable place for families, this resort has a lot of excitement; travelers without children may find it overwhelming. Two- and three-bedroom suites range $246 and up, with special rates about $50 less.

♿ ⊚ ⁕↑⁕ At the **Hyatt Regency Grand Cypress** (407-239-1234; www.grandcypress.hyatt.com), 1 Grand Cypress Blvd, it's not a hotel, it's an experience. With 1,500 acres to roam and an incredible list of on-site activities, it's a wonder that anyone ever leaves to go to a theme park. Swim in a waterfall-fed canyon, bike along tropical nature trails, or visit the world-class equestrian facility for riding lessons. Four on-site restaurants offer fabulous cuisine: Coquina (see *Dining Out*) is one of Orlando's top fine-dining choices. Amenities include what you've come to expect from top-notch hotels: dataport, mini bar, in-room movies, and a private balcony. Rooms start around $169, and include shuttle transportation to the theme parks, bicycle rental, pitch 'n' putt, court time at the racquet club, use of the driving range, water sports on Lake Windsong, and use of the fitness center. Not a bad deal!

🦜 🐾 ♿ 🐾 The giant pineapple at the **Orlando Vista Hotel** (1-800-521-3297; www.orlandovistahotel.com), 12490 SR 535, is an unmistakable landmark, and with the bold primary colors and funky toon-like chairs in the lobby, there's no mistaking this is fun for the family! The casual first-floor dining spaces include an Au Bon Pain and Edy's Ice Cream, and niche round tables with dataports enable business visitors to hang out and get some work done. The hotel has been a Walt Disney World Good Neighbor for more than 23 years, which means their rooms undergo the same rigorous random inspections by Disney that the Disney hotels do. There are 246 rooms with playful decor, a colorful desk and table, and Hilton Sweet Dreams bedding (this was formerly a Doubletree). Thirteen of the rooms are Kid Suites, massive spaces with a room within a room containing three beds for the kids and their own TV. Larger rooms and suites come standard with a mini fridge, microwave,

and coffeemaker; guests can request them if they are not in the room. A game room, fitness room, and pool and spa will keep the family busy on-site, and there are free shuttles to Disney to keep you busy! Rooms $79–99, include breakfast.

🦜 🐾 ♿ The **Sheraton Safari Hotel** (407-239-0444), 12205 Apopka-Vineland Rd, just looks like fun—walk inside, and you're immersed into an African theme. Spacious, comfortable rooms provide in-room safe, coffeemaker, dataport, and more. The kids will love being spit out of the mouth of a 79-foot python into the swimming pool, and you'll love relaxing with a cool tropical drink at the Zanzibar lounge. The hotel is a certified Walt Disney World Good Neighbor, too. The 489 family-priced units include standard rooms and large suites, $99 and up.

Osceola Parkway

♿ 👓 ✈ "❶" Once you arrive at the **Gaylord Palms Resort & Convention Center** (407-586-2000; www .gaylordhotels.com), 6000 W Osceola Pkwy, you'll forget about the outside world. The stately resort, situated on 63 acres and visible from I-4, is centrally located to all the area attractions. Step inside; you'll be greeted with the ambience of an Old Florida mansion. Experience the unique geographic areas of Florida under the resort's 4.5-acre atrium, where the climate is always a perfect rain-free 72 degrees. The resort's showpiece is a replica of the Castillo de San Marcos, the historic Spanish fort in St. Augustine. Climb up the stairs and wander through archways, or drink from the "fountain of youth" in this smaller version of the famous stronghold. In the Key West section you'll find a 60-

THE GRAND FLORIDIAN RESORT AND SPA
Sandra Friend

foot sailboat sitting in a coral reef surrounded by a re-creation of Mallory Square, including a nightly sunset celebration. On the west side of the atrium, the "river of grass" comes to life in the Everglades, where swamp walkways take you through misty fog in search of animated alligators—or are they? **Emerald Bay** is a boutique hotel within the resort and offers upscale amenities and services. Like the atrium, each geographic section is mirrored in the guest rooms and suites. The Key West rooms are bright and colorful, capturing the festive island spirit. Nature enthusiasts will like the Everglades rooms, saturated with earthy colors, wicker furnishings, and flora and fauna, including whimsical dragonflies. St. Augustine accommodations evoke old-fashioned elegance with rich sepia tapestries and authentic artifacts. I loved the 18th-century map design in the bedskirts. Each evening your turndown service includes a bedside Florida Fact card, giving you something to ponder before dropping off to sleep. This doesn't feel like your typical cookie-cutter resort. The architectural and interior designers brought out their very best when they fashioned each room, right down to the custom carpets. You'll be impressed with the employees as they greet you with friendly smiles and take care of your needs at lightning speed. I still can't get over how fast my maid straightened my bathroom while I sat typing at my computer. You'll feel like you're at a bed & breakfast, and you'll love it! Rates from $299.

Universal Resort Orlando 32819

&. ❀ **Hard Rock Hotel** (407-503-ROCK), 5800 Universal Blvd. Want to rub elbows with a rock star? So do most visitors to Orlando, making this themed Loews Hotel—a virtual "Hotel California"—a favorite hangout on the last Thursday of each month during Velvet Sessions, when members of world-renowned bands like Cheap Trick, Twisted Sister, and the Lovin' Spoonful stop in for a jam. Rock and roll permeates the grounds, even underwater in the swimming pools! Bedecked with memorabilia, it's one sizzling place. Rates start at $229–329, depending on season.

&. ❀ **Portofino Bay Resort** (407-503-1000), 5601 Universal Blvd. Drifting into this Italianate resort for a corporate Christmas dinner, I felt as if I'd stepped into a Mediterranean village—the scene is a ringer for the real Portofino, with luxurious villas spilling down to the edge of the harbor. Dine at one of the many romantic restaurants, or retreat to your room and savor a sensual evening with the pampering only Loews provides. Rates start at $259–359, depending on season.

&. ❀ ⁙ The **Royal Pacific Resort** (407-503-3000), 6300 Hollywood Way, is lavishly themed around post–World War II South Pacific travel, when arriving by airplane or steamship was an experience unto itself. I walked

A ROOM AT THE HARD ROCK HOTEL
courtesy Universal Studios

&. 🖉 ⊛ "↑" ⇸ My introduction to the new **Rosen Shingle Creek** (407-996-6338 or 1-866-996-6338; www.shinglecreek resort.com), 9939 Universal Blvd, came during a very special event—the launch of Expedition Headwaters, a journey from the northernmost source of water feeding the Everglades down the Kissimmee River to Lake Okeechobee. When veteran Orlando hotelier Harris Rosen purchased this property and started to build a hotel, he didn't know that Shingle Creek, a sluggish stream amid the prairies and ragged young cypress, was the headwaters of the Everglades. But when

Sandra Friend

A PADDLE INTO THE EVERGLADES' HEADWATERS

he learned, he built his resort around a theme of natural Florida. As an active voice for nature-based tourism in Florida, I'm pleased to report he's done a stupendous job of melding the expected amenities of an upscale hotel with a not quite preachy (but always in your peripheral vision) celebration of Central Florida's natural and cultural heritage. Built from the bottom up as a green lodging, the complex includes features that guests never see, but which make an immense impact on eliminating the waste associated with the typical hotel. For instance, the staff does most of their business transactions online, avoiding printing paper except when necessary. Brochures and other materials in your room are printed on recycled paper with high post-consumer content. Lights turn on and off automatically in work areas as people enter and exit. And cooking oils are recycled as biodiesel fuel, used in the golf course maintenance carts at the Shingle Creek Golf Club (see *Golfing*). Runoff from the golf course channels through a series of settling ponds separated by locks and weirs to clean the waters before they reach Shingle Creek.

In the design of the hotel, the use of Florida's natural light is superb. Even in the massive convention halls, skylights and niche gardens bring the outdoors in. Behind the reception desk, a floor-to-ceiling glass wall is a portal into a tropical garden. Florida finches chatter in a giant birdcage in the lobby. Walking through the hotel, look for sculptures in corners by the restaurants and lounges—they depict natural Florida scenes and are entirely handcrafted in chocolate (often decorated with a dusting of colored cocoa powder). Florida art by University of Central Florida students decorates the main halls, and in the common spaces and in your room are photos of wild Central Florida captured by Garritt Toohey, the vice president of Rosen Hotels & Resorts—macro shots of air plants, broad views of cypress domes—a constant reminder of where you are. Yet for its size, the hotel feels intimate. There are spaces to gather and enjoy a latte with friends, quiet corners to read a book, and acres to roam on nature trails, all the way to Shingle Creek. Parents will appreciate Swamp Camp, open Thu–Sat for ages 4–14, with age-appropriate indoor and outdoor activities. Teens will have fun the in video arcade with its pinball machines and a classic Ms. Pac-Man! On the ground floor, Café Osceola is a large buffet restaurant, perfect for feeding the kids, and nearby there's an ice cream parlor and the 24-hour 18 Monroe Street Market, filled with healthful food (salads and deli to go), wines, soft drinks, and snacks, and the hotel's own signature Alligator Drool beer. Wander out toward the convention center and you'll find an arcade of upscale shops with sundries and resort wear, an art gallery, the Headwaters Lounge, and Smooth Java, a coffee shop filled with pastry delights made on-site. For more upscale dining, consider the lovely Calla Bella, an Italian restaurant overlooking Shingle Creek, or the very Florida-themed A Land Remembered (see *Dining Out*).

In each room ($375–425) the decor is Spanish revival, but the comfort is in sinking into the Egyptian cotton sheets and calling it a night. Each room has a host of amenities, from the 32-inch flat-screen TV (with connections for camera, iPod, or laptop) and business desk, to a safe big enough for a laptop, a mini fridge, plush robe, and enticingly scented citrus and cedar soaps from the in-house Spa at Shingle Creek (see *Spas*).

ROSEN SHINGLE CREEK RESORT

Sandra Friend

around under the Balinese umbrellas feeling like I'd bump into Bob Hope, Bing Crosby, and Dorothy Lamour; 1940s music pervades the on-site restaurants. Subtle touches such as high-thread-count sheets, dimmer switches, and free postcards that look like old steamship trunk stickers add to the comfort of each well-appointed room, which comes standard with a coffeemaker, ironing board, hair dryer, Playstation, Wayport high-speed Internet access, safe, and mini bar. In the Loews tradition, the hotel also lets you borrow comfort or necessity items from two long lists of choices, including a down pillow, an air purifier, a sound machine, personal exercise equipment, even travel guides. If you're looking for a place to relax amid the hubbub of the theme parks, this is it. Rates $199–299, depending on season.

VACATION HOMES

Kissimmee 34744
American Vacation Homes (407-847-0883 or 1-800-901-8688; www.americanvacationhomes.us), 1631 E Vine St, offers more than 250 fully furnished individually owned homes scattered through several housing developments; capacities of 6 to 14 guests make these rentals an ideal option for families on vacation. Pick your size and amenities (high-end rentals include pools), and they'll figure out the rates.

CAMPGROUNDS

Clermont 34771
Along US 192 just west of the Disney complex, **Encore SuperPark Orlando** (863-420-1300 or 1-888-558-5777; www.rvonthego.com), 9600 US 192 W, is a massive campground with paved pads and patios, full hookups, pull-through sites perfect for your big rig, and sunny spaces amid pleasant landscaping. This park offers great on-site amenities, including two swimming pools, recreation center, and tennis courts. Thirty- and 50-amp service; rates start at $32.

Walt Disney World
Fort Wilderness Resort and Campground (407-824-2727), 4510 N Fort Wilderness Trail, Lake Buena Vista 32830. For $42–111, pitch your tent or pull up the trailer under the shade of Florida pines in this back-to-nature campground, where you can walk for miles on pleasant footpaths or grab a bus or rent a golf cart if you're in a hurry. The Wilderness Cabins, essentially upscale park models that sleep up to eight (or more, if the kids are small), have a full kitchen and outdoor grill, with rates starting at $255.

✳ Where to Eat

DINING OUT **Dining at Walt Disney World** Most restaurants do not have individual phone numbers. For priority seating, call 407-WDW-DINE.

Downtown Disney
&. **Fulton's Crab House** (407-934-2628), Pleasure Island. On the paddle-wheeler *Empress Lily*, Dungeness crab cakes and Fulton's seafood boil come accompanied by unexpectedly exquisite breads and salads; every nuance of my meal here was sheer perfection, including the impeccable service. I'd choose this place for a date anytime. Reservations recommended, entrées $21–52.

Epcot
&. Always humming with activity, the **Chefs de France** are a perennial favorite, serving specialties like salade

Nicoise and slowly braised leg o' lamb, with dinner entrées $19–32. For a savory, inexpensive treat, stop in for an appetizer—the tomato and goat cheese tart is divine. Hidden upstairs, the intimate **Bistro de Paris** appeals for a quiet romantic dinner, with pan-seared lobster, filet mignon, and a spectacular wine list. Dinner entrées $29–43, or a *menu dégustation*, five courses, $120 with wine pairings or $75 without; reservations recommended.

 ♭ **Coral Reef Restaurant**, The Seas. Seafood with an aquarium view: Immersed in The Seas, diners stare out over the faux reef as they chow down on blackened catfish, grilled mahi-mahi, and pumpkin risotto. Serving lunch and dinner, $17–32.

 ♭ **Akershus Royal Banquet Hall**, Norway. In the past 25 years I've dined at most of the World Showcase restaurants, and I think none holds a candle to the uniqueness of this traditional Scandinavian smorgasbord in Norway, which has now been turned into character dining "with princesses." Since I'm of Scandinavian descent, it could be a genetic attraction to the cuisine, but prior to my visit, I'd never before had pickled herring or mashed rutabagas. I was smitten by the array of seafood and potato-based salads. Dinner $30 adults, $15 ages 3–11, with breakfast and lunch served also.

 ♭ **Restaurant Marrakesh**, Morocco. Hidden in the warren of alleyways that make up the souk at Morocco, this truly exotic restaurant offers fare ($21–36) you're not about to find elsewhere—shish kebab, couscous, roast lamb, and more; for an introduction to the cuisine, I suggest the Marrakesh Royal Feast ($42), each a

sampler of exotic delights. Belly dancing and Moroccan music accent the experience.

 ♭ **San Angel Inn**, Mexico. Now, this is a place for romance: a dimly lit virtual movie set of Mexico inside a giant Aztec pyramid, with a cantina overlooking a waterway and jungle along the edge of a bustling village, where mariachi bands stroll by. Granted, it's a fantasy, but a pleasant one, and the food offered here—from one of Mexico City's finest restaurants—is genuine Mexican cuisine like *mole poblano* (chicken in a bitter chocolate and hot pepper sauce) and *camarones con fideos* (grilled shrimp on angel-hair). Serving lunch and dinner, entrées $20 and up.

Magic Kingdom

 ♭ ♯ **Cinderella's Royal Table**. What princess wouldn't want to feast in Cinderella's castle? Mornings offer a character breakfast ($34 adults, $23 ages 3-9); for lunch and dinner (fixed price $41 and up), savor roast prime rib, pork tenderloin, or a less regal but nonetheless tasty smoked turkey breast focaccia sandwich (lunch only). Reservations required, characters always on hand.

Disney's Hollywood Studios

 ♭ A replica of the famous Tinseltown celebrity hangout, The **Hollywood Brown Derby** is all about glamour; caricatures of the famous grace the walls. Center-stage entrées ($18–32) include the creative Thai noodle bowl with coconut-crusted tofu, grilled Atlantic salmon, and hijiki-crusted ahi tuna. For lunch, don't miss their signature Brown Derby Cobb Salad, $14.

Walt Disney World Resorts

 ♭ **Artist's Point**, Disney's Wilderness Lodge. I love the name and the memories it evokes: of standing on Artist Point, a rock ledge at Colorado National Monument, overlooking vast red-rock canyons. Capturing nature's artistry each evening, this restaurant has a Frank Lloyd Wright feel and adventuresome offerings (entrées $20–42) like grilled buffalo sirloin and potato chive potstickers, as well as a wine list showcasing Pacific Northwest vintages.

& **California Grill**, Disney's Contemporary Resort, 15th floor. Featuring a show kitchen so you can watch the chefs prepare market-fresh beef and seafood, this classy restaurant has great offerings for vegetarians and is the ultimate spot to catch fireworks exploding over the Magic Kingdom. The menu changes frequently, attuned to fresh local ingredients. Enjoy sushi (deluxe platter $24), Sonoma goat cheese ravioli ($11), and more; entrées $28–35.

& **Kimonos Sushi Bar** (407-934-1621), Walt Disney World Swan. This authentic Japanese restaurant soothes with bamboo, black lacquer, and rice paper lanterns setting the ambience. Sushi rolls or à la carte selections ($5–11), and tempura and salads with a side of—yes!—karaoke.

& **Shula's Steak House**, Walt Disney World Dolphin. Classic Sinatra tunes set the tone for what critics call the top steakhouse in Orlando, serving choice cuts of certified Angus beef ($23 and up)—prime rib, porterhouse, filet mignon, New York strip— and succulent fresh seafood. My goodness, they even have a linebacker-worthy 48-ounce porterhouse ($75).

& **Victoria & Albert's** (407-939-7707), Disney's Grand Floridian Beach Resort. Elegant and intimate, it's Disney's top restaurant, and more an experience than a dinner. Expect to drop at least $125 per person for an ever-changing prix fixe menu of the finest gourmet food, with extra for wine pairings. The Chef's Table in the kitchen is booked up to 6 months in advance.

DINING OUT

Central Parkway

& Chef Norman Van Aken (I knew him when . . .) of Key West and South Florida fame brings his Floribbean cuisine to Orlando at **Norman's** (407-392-4300; www.grandelakes.com), 4040 Central Parkway in the Ritz-Carlton at Grand Lake. Van Aken, a pioneer of the New World Cuisine, has been waking up our taste buds ever since with creations like yucca-stuffed crispy shrimp, Mongolian marinated and grilled veal chop with Chinese eggplant and Thai fried rice, and whole roasted chicken with savory bread pudding, cinnamon maduros, and pumpkin-chicken jus. Prix fixe dinner around $60.

& **Primo by Melissa Kelly** (407-393-4444; www.grandelakes.com) 4040 Central Parkway in the J. W. Marriott at Grand Lake. When Melissa Kelly's staff called me I just about dropped the phone! Melissa is known all over my home state, Maine, with her original restaurant, Primo in Rockland. So when they asked me to dinner I couldn't find a date fast enough. The folks over at J. W. Marriott found a real gem when they convinced Kelly to re-create her concept of "Italian sensibility" here in Florida. And now she and partner, Price Kushner, Primo's pastry chef and co-owner, split their time between Maine and Florida. I missed her by a delayed flight, but got to meet her chef de cuisine, Kathleen Blake, who with grace and style balances her culinary career with four children; and general manager Suzanne Bonham, who will knowledgably pair your dining selections with the appropriate wines. This talented group of women really do it all in a culinary world long dominated by men. The trendy restaurant lacks the "attitude" prevalent in other upscale restaurants, and while nice clothes are a good idea, you don't need to dress to the nines. Presentation is everything at Primo, with tables set comfortably apart and a sound system that will make you think live musicians are around the corner. Food is prepared with not only fresh ingredients, some grown on the property, but also with as many organic ingredients as possible. Start with a salad of roasted organic beets wrapped around fresh goat cheese; your entrée selection might be seared Maine scallops with caramelized Vidalia onion vinaigrette, morels, and summer truffles. Finish off your meal with a trio of crème brûlée: black-and-white, lemon verbena, and lavender, which had me calling back to get take-out later that same night.

Dr. Phillips

🌸 In my former corporate life, the engineers and I descended on **Memories of India** (407-370-3277 or 1-866-271-0967), Bay Hill Plaza, 7625 Turkey Lake Rd, an authentic Indian restaurant, for our Friday lunch, when you can pick up any of 18 different thalis—entrées with basmati rice, nan, raita, pickle, papad, and dessert—for a song ($6–10). My fave: dal makhani; the guys would always go for vindaloo, the hotter, the better. Prices climb at dinner ($10 and up),

but the quality remains superb. Even though my old office moved 10 miles north, they still call here for take-out. A most excellent standout among Indian restaurants in Orlando: nay, in all of Florida. Don't miss it.

♿ The strip of Sand Lake Road north of I-4 near Universal Resort Orlando hosts a parade of high-end chains, such as Roy's, Stonewood Grill, the Samba Room, Seasons 52, and and Ruth Chris' Steak House. I enjoyed **Timpano Chophouse & Martini Bar** (407-248-0429; www.timpano chophouse.net), 7488 W Sand Lake Rd, a classy supper club and martini bar where Sinatra is always playing and the Italian food is freshly prepped in an open kitchen. The whisper-thin flatbread appetizers are savory with every bite and make a meal in themselves; the wild mushroom pasta was a perfect texture, with just a hint of cream sauce. It's quieter at lunch ($6–15), but dinner ($14–36) is where they shine—dry-aged, hand-cut prime steaks and chops are the centerpiece of the menu, and the martins ($9 and up) are just plain fun. Think Lemon Drop, Chocolate, and one I've never seen before, Sex on the Baby Grand, which pairs Ketel One vodka with one of my favorite rarities, Inniskillin ice wine from Ontario, garnished with grapes. And yes, there's a baby grand in the room. Ask for a table overlooking Sand Lake, one of the sights most folks driving Sand Lake Road never see.

International Drive

♿ There's nothing like going to **Café TuTu Tango** (407-248-2222; www .cafetututango.com/orlando) 8625 International Dr, with a passel of artists. They'll draw on and play with everything. It's that kind of place:

upscale but not (T-shirts acceptable), urban grunge meets fine art, with food that echoes tapas, best experienced with a whole bunch of friends who each get a plate or two and you all pass it around. We shared goodies ($5–12) like roasted pears on pecan crisps, sesame grilled chicken salad, seared salmon skewers, sun-dried tomato pizza, and alligator bites with fruit chutney, and it was so much fun. Their motto is "Food for the Starving Artist." Sound and sight and aromas meld to create a full-bodied experience for mind and appetite. My husband occasionally performs here as a caricaturist, so treat the artists well!

Universal Boulevard

& One of my most enjoyable steakhouse experiences has been **A Land Remembered** (1-866-996-6338; www .landrememberedrestaurant.com), 9939 Universal Blvd, at Shingle Creek Resort (see *Resorts*). First, the name: it comes from my favorite work of fiction recounting the history of Florida, written by author Patrick Smith, whom I've had the pleasure to meet many times, and who caught the attention of hotelier Harris Rosen for his straightforward depictions of the cattlemen's life in Florida and the broader historical sweep of change throughout the state. The intimate restaurant draws on this rustic Florida theme, echoed in the decor, right down to Clyde Butcher photography from the Everglades and hefty menus with the feel of a book and cover engravings that reflect the story. Overseeing the orchestra of the open kitchen is Chef James Slattery, who left a career in analytical chemistry to follow his passion for cooking, starting as a butcher for Emeril and working his way up to executive sous chef at

Tchoup Chop (see below) before taking this position. Slattery's innate feel for how foods work together means superb results for diners, with starters such as the Angel City Oysters, cornmeal crusted and served with baked spinach and Gruyère, and a Shingle Creek flatbread of cold smoked salmon and wild mushrooms with baked Parmesan, green and yellow pea tendrils, and white truffle oil. The meat of the meal is in the meat; my picky-about-steak husband proclaimed his New York strip superb, and my filet mignon with roasted garlic, served flanked with fried green tomatoes, was by far the best I've had—trimmed tightly and soft as butter. We shared a bowl of baked sweet potato with honey butter, and that could make a dessert in itself, but I had to taste the Dark Chocolate Filet—chocolate mousse is my downfall—with raspberry, chocolate cake, and chocolate shortbread, it was downright decadent. Dinner here is an experience to be savored, slowly, and reservations are a must. Enjoy an intimate evening with your spouse or a friend; even without wine pairings, a leisurely full-course meal for two will run about $125; all items are à la carte.

Universal Resort Orlando

& Business is always brisk at **Emeril's Tchoup Chop** (407-503-CHOP; www.emerils.com), 6300 Hollywood Way at the Royal Pacific Resort (see *Resorts*), the second of Emeril's Orlando restaurants. Looking out over lush tropical gardens, diners enjoy the "kick it up a notch" choices, like macadamia nut-encrusted Atlantic salmon, and Kiawe grilled New York strip entrée ($20 and up). Classy dress required, reservations recommended.

Singles, find a friend to pair up with, or you'll be asked to sit at the bar.

EATING OUT Eating Out at Walt Disney World

Most Walt Disney World restaurants do not have individual phone numbers. For priority seating, call 407-WDW-DINE.

Disney's Animal Kingdom

From the shrimp lo mein at **Yak and Yeti** (Anandapur) to fresh fruit and juices at the **Harambe Fruit Market**, Animal Kingdom provides a healthful variety of good food in their snack bars and chow wagons; it's possible to nab food and a drink for under $15.

✍ ♿ **Rainforest Cafe** (407-938-9100). Strategically placed at the front entrance, this chain restaurant provides tasty food and naturally themed entertainment for the kids. It's noisy once the crowds show up—with gorillas grunting, elephants trumpeting, and a faux rainstorm every 15 minutes or so, and the din of diners around you, you won't be able to hold a conversation—but it's the less crowded option of the two locations at Disney, especially in the midafternoon. I'm partial to the Volcanic Cobb salad, Cyclone Crab Cakes, and Tribal Salmon, and Dad loves the mushroom-shaped juice bar with its fresh carrot juice. Open 11–5, $20–40; reservations taken at the door.

Creative fare makes dining a pleasure at **Tusker House Buffet**, Harambe, where you can feast on grilled salmon, rotisserie chicken, and turkey wraps; $20 lunch, $27 dinner. My pick—the grilled vegetable sandwich with hummus spread and fresh fruit.

Disney's Hollywood Studios

On Sunset Blvd, **Anaheim Produce** has fresh fruit displayed in big produce bins, with a side of frozen lemonade ($4). Adjoining the Hollywood Brown Derby, the **Starring Rolls Cafe** offers fresh tasty treats ($1–5) like cream puffs, tiramisu, and, my favorite, the Bavarian fruit tart with blueberries, mandarin orange, kiwi, and strawberries atop Bavarian cream.

♿ **50's Prime Time Café** (near the Indiana Jones show). Most restaurants don't have a waitress nagging you like Mom did—"Eat your vegetables!"—but that's part of the charm of this cozy café that takes me back to my childhood, right down to the tables and flour bin from my family kitchen. It's a meat-and-potatoes menu of meatloaf, pot roast, and the like complemented by gourmet dishes like glazed salmon; $13–21, lunch and dinner.

Mama Melrose Restaurant Italiano (near Muppets 3-D). A comfortable Italian family restaurant infused with the aroma of their wood-fired oven. Choose from flatbread pizzas or main courses like wood-grilled salmon or eggplant Napolean with sun-dried tomatoes. Lunch and dinner, $12–22.

THE DINING ROOM AT EMERIL'S TCHOUP CHOP

courtesy Universal Studios

Downtown Disney

Bongos Cuban Cafe. Savor the salsa of South Beach at this restaurant created by Emilio and Gloria Estefan, where the food goes beyond Cuban sandwiches to encompass lunch and dinner favorites like *paella de mariscos* (seafood paella) and *ropa vieja*, $16–29.

✍ **Ghirardelli's Soda Fountain & Chocolate Shop**. Hey, it's chocolate and ice cream—how can you pass this one by? I certainly can't. World-famous hot fudge sundaes and enough varieties of ice cream that you'll find something you'll love; I'm nuts about the chocolate-and-raspberry Fog Horn sundae. It's open late, too, with fancy creations for $4–7, not counting the insane eight-scoop Earthquake mega banana split for $25.

House of Blues. Dan Aykroyd's dream restaurant serves up tasty Cajun cuisine, with Louisiana crawfish, pan-seared southern Voodoo shrimp, Creole jambalaya, and homemade banana bread pudding in a bayou atmosphere pulsing with Mississippi Delta music; serving lunch and dinner, $14–27, with frequent live music inside and on the patio. A special Sunday gospel brunch ($33 adults, $17 ages 3–9) includes all-you-can-eat southern fixin's followed by a foot-stompin' church meeting.

✍ ♿ **Rainforest Café** (407-827-8500). My favorite casual eatery in Downtown Disney—it's fun, and the portions are huge. Set inside a giant volcano that rumbles and belches a column of smoke, this is a place to take the kiddies, not a quiet getaway, as the cavernous setting echoes every sound. The wait to get in can be ridiculously long, but if you plan to do some shopping, no big deal. Just like

the venue at Animal Kingdom, a large retail store with a rainforest theme shares the space; the menus are identical.

Epcot

What fun to graze around the World Showcase, sampling ethnic foods and tasty treats. First stop: a wet burrito ($8) and frozen margarita ($8) at **Cantina de San Angel**, where ibises try to steal the food off your table. Move on to Norway's **Kringla Bakeri Og Kafe** for some lefse ($2) or a berry tart ($3), or the **Lotus Blossom Café** in China for potstickers ($5) and ginger ice cream ($3)—a tough choice over the massive mint chocolate chip soft serve ice cream cones ($4) at **Refreshment Outpost**. Grab a Tokyo sushi roll ($7) or miso soup ($2) at **Yakitori House** in Japan, and shawarma sandwich platters ($10-14) at the **Tangierine Cafe** in Morocco. And it's impossible to walk past the **Boulangerie Patisserie** in France without peeking in at the elegant tarts, chocolate mousse, and meringues ($2–4).

✍ **Biergarten**, Germany. Pile on the sauerbraten and Wiener schnitzel at this all-you-can-eat German buffet, with one of my favorite desserts— Black Forest cake—included. Lunch costs $11 children, $20 adults; dinner $13 children, $27 adults.

🍴 *✍* ♿ **The Garden Grill Restaurant**, The Land. Home cooking served family style, with heaping mounds of grilled flank steak, country-style catfish, and a never-ending bowl of home-grown salad; vegetarians will appreciate the zesty roasted vegetable stew. The restaurant rotates as you eat, and Disney characters come to call, making this a fun experience for the kids at lunch and dinner.

Lunch $12 children 3–11, adults $21; dinner $14 and $29.

Rose & Crown, Britain. I've savored many a shepherd's pie out on the patio of this unpretentious offering from the British Isles, where the accents are authentic and the food knocks the stuffing out of the old stereotypes about English cooking. Meat and potatoes are the strong points here along with Harry Ramsden's famous fish-and-chips. Reserve ahead if you want to sit inside, but you'll catch the best view in the park of parades and fireworks from the shaded patio. Serving lunch and dinner, with entrées $16–25; leave room for a sticky toffee pudding, $5.

Magic Kingdom

The Magic Kingdom is full of delightful little places for casual eating, if you know just where to look. Unfortunately, my favorites seem to shut down whenever attendance sags, but they serve (in my opinion) the best fare. At **Aunt Polly's Dockside Inn** on Tom Sawyer Island, sip lemonade or indulge in an apple pie sundae ($4) while watching the riverboats steam by from the comfort of a shaded rocking chair—it's heaven for those wanting to get away from the crowds. **El Pirata y el Perico** in Adventureland offers tacos and taco salad ($6–7) in the **Plaza del Sol Caribe**. For fresh fruit, fruit juice, and frozen fruit swirls, try **Aloha Isle** (near the Swiss Family Treehouse), **Sunshine Tree Terrace** (adjoining the Enchanted Tiki Birds), the **Enchanted Grove** (by the Mad Tea Party), and the **Toontown Farmers Market**. Grab an ice cream at the **Plaza Ice Cream Parlor** on Main Street, where they serve up my dad's favorite, butter pecan.

& **Liberty Tree Tavern**. Sit in a slice of New England and enjoy hearty lunch fare like a Pilgrim's Feast of turkey and mashed potatoes ($15); I'll always savor the Colony Salad ($14) with Washington apples, sweet pecans, applewood smoked cheddar, and grilled chicken. Characters come to greet the kids for a special fixed price buffet dinner ($29, $14 ages 3–11) of carved beef, smoked pork loin, macaroni and cheese, and more.

Walt Disney World Resort

& & **Boatwright's Dining Hall**, Disney's Port Orleans Riverside. A shipbuilding theme permeates this comfortable family restaurant, where I've never been disappointed by a meal, especially the heaping helpings served up at breakfast. Try the banana-stuffed French toast or their signature sweet potato cakes. Serving all day, $9–30.

& **Boma**, Disney's Animal Kingdom Lodge. Expand your culinary horizons: Immerse yourself in the colors and aromas of an African marketplace, where you'll find quinoa porridge, brioche, pap, and bobotie next to the bacon and eggs at this serve-yourself set of buffet stations. Breakfast buffet $17, $10 ages 3–11.

& **'Ohana**, Disney's Polynesian Resort. When my family stayed here in the 1970s, the Papette Bay Verandah was one of our favorites around Bay Lake, where I learned what South Seas cooking entailed. The all-you-care-to-eat 'Ohana replaces this old favorite, with skewers of chicken, beef, and veggies grilled over flaming open pits; desserts extra. $27 adults, $13 ages 3–11.

& **Spoodles**, Disney's Boardwalk. I love Spoodles. When I brought my

brother-in-law (who's an executive chef) here, even he was impressed by the tasty selection of breads and spreads brought to our table while we decided on exactly what sort of Mediterranean cuisine tickled our fancy. Try a handful of tapas (tiny appetizers) and pass them around, or order one of the big bowls of pasta. A little bit of everything, from Portuguese and Spanish to Moroccan, North African, and Greek, teases your taste buds. Serving breakfast and dinner, entrées $15–23.

🦆 ♂ **Trail's End Buffeteria**, Fort Wilderness. A family favorite for many years, this rustic-themed buffet next to the Hoop-de-Doo Musical Revue offers all-you-can-eat breakfast, lunch, and dinner, with barbecued chicken and ribs, salad bar, and tasty cobblers. Prices top out at $18 adults, $10 ages 3–11.

♂ **Whispering Canyon Cafe**, Disney's Wilderness Lodge. Whoop it up under the grand rafters of this western-themed lodge with wait staff who urge you and the kids out of your seats for rocking horse races and other madcap fun, while they bring out platter upon platter of barbecue and chicken in the all-you-can-eat Canyon Skillet ($23); you may also order à la carte items like meatloaf and vegetarian pasta ($14–21). Serving breakfast, lunch, and dinner.

International Drive

🦆 It's a rare breed for this part of town, family owned and operated for more than 35 years, and it has a dedicated following. The **Black Angus Steakhouse** (407-354-3333; www.blackangusorlando.com), 6231 International Dr, offers meals prepared in a family-friendly, casual, Western-themed atmosphere with superb

attention to quality. From an 8-ounce prime rib or filet mignon up to a 32-ounce porterhouse, you'll find a slab of beef to fit your appetite and budget, or a seafood selection to savor ($13–35). Angus steakburgers come with a side of tasty, thick-cut Angus fries, just the way steak fries should be, and for picky eaters, there's pizza on the menu. Annie's Pies Cake Bakery features delights like the tuxedo bombe, chocolate mousse, bourbon cake, and tiramisu served in a martini glass. And then there's the bounteous breakfast buffet for under $6—no wonder the parking lot is full at 10 AM! Additional locations at 12399 State Road 535 in Lake Buena Vista and 7516 W Irlo Bronson Hwy in Kissimmee.

B-Line Diner (407-352-4000; www.peabodyorlando.com), 9801 International Dr in the Peabody Hotel (see *Resorts*), open daily 24 hours. Stop by this 1950s diner inside the Peabody Hotel before or after watching the Peabody Duck March. At this unusual eatery, it feels like the dining car just drove in: Gray booths, cream walls, checkerboard floor, and lots of sleek chrome take you back in time. For breakfast ($5 and up) try the gingerbread-like sweet potato pancakes served with pure maple syrup, chicken-apple sausages, and spiced pecans or the tropical stuffed French toast with pineapple, strawberries, mango, and macadamia nuts. For a lean lunch ($7 and up), try the farm-raised ostrich burger served on cranberry sage focaccia with sun-dried cherry and cranberry relish and fruit cup. "Feelin' Ducky" menu items offer up healthy selections low in cholesterol, fat, and sugar, but high in fiber. Just don't expect to find duck served here!

With its all you can eat buffet of lobster, sushi, crab legs, and prime rib, the **Boston Lobster Feast** (407-248-8606; www.bostonlobsterfeast.com), 8731 International Dr, is always packed, so come early and take advantage of the early-bird specials until 6 PM.

Lake Buena Vista

Kitty O'Sheas Irish Pub (407-238-9769; www.kittyosheaspub.com), 8470 Palm Pkwy. Gather around the big-screen TV for *Monday Night Football,* or sink the eight-ball in the billiards tables. This comfortable Irish-gone-sports pub with deep booths serves up entrées ($8–10) like a great shepherd's pie, bangers and mash, and beer-battered fish-and-chips. The full bar features such Irish drinks as the Leprechaun and Irish Car Bomb. Oh, and yes—they have plenty of Guinness!

Pebbles (407-827-1111), 12551 FL 535, one of several locations in town, offers creative California cuisine for lunch and dinner at moderate prices, $8–28. Expect outrageously sized portions—I wish I could have taken the other half of my wild mushroom and pesto pasta ($13) home.

Founded in 1981 by Frank Crail in Durango, Colorado, **Rocky Mountain Chocolate Factory** (407-465-1002), 8200 Vineland Ave, has become one of the fastest-growing companies satisfying sweet teeth all over the world. With over 250 locations, they still don't have a shop near me. Come on, Frank! So I make regular trips to the Orlando Premium Outlets location (see *Selective Shopping*) and watch Brian and the gang whip up some fudge in copper kettles, then mold the creamy mixture on cool marble slabs. After which they let me sample the pralines—and you can, too.

Universal Boulevard

🐟 **Flipper's Pizza** (407-351-5643), 7480 Universal Blvd near Wet 'n Wild, (407-345-0113) at 6125 Westwood Blvd near SeaWorld, and (407-397-9509), 5770 W US 192 inside Old Town (see *Family Adventures*). Eat in or call for delivery. This old-fashioned pizza shop makes terrific pizza with special attention to fresh ingredients and home-style sauces, and will even deliver! Terrific pizza ($11–20) with special sauce and fresh ingredients makes this spot a crowd pleaser. I sampled their Neapolitan-style Sonoma pizza with sun-dried tomatoes, red onions, artichoke hearts, and spinach. My friends loved the penne pasta with meatballs topped with mozzarella cheese ($9).

Universal Resort Orlando

Islands Dining Room (407-503-3463; www.universalorlando.com) at Royal Pacific Resort (see *Resorts*). Looking out over the sparkling pool, with palm frond paddle fans slowly rotating overhead, you can sink back and imagine yourself in the South Pacific in the 1940s while choosing from a pan-Asian menu that'll tickle any gourmet's taste buds. The attentive waitstaff bring out a virtual bouquet of creative breads as you wait for your salad or entrée ($26–30), with choices that include ahi tuna; gently fried potato rounds complement the subtle smoky flavor. Save room for dessert—when the fellow across the room received his plateful of java brownie sundae, I thought he'd faint, contemplating the size of the task in front of him. Open for breakfast, lunch, and dinner, with daily specials and a children's own dining room so they can have fun while you eat in peace, and only $4 per child for a meal!

You'll have a hard time choosing among the great eateries at CityWalk at Universal Orlando (407-363-8000; www.universalsorlando.com). At **Emeril's Restaurant Orlando** you'll find a sophisticated menu with a New Orleans twist; lively Florida fare at **Jimmy Buffett's Margaritaville**; steaks, chops, and BBQ at **NASCAR Café**; and rockin' burgers at the largest **Hard Rock Café**.

✳ Selective Shopping

Disney's Animal Kingdom

As you sweep clockwise around the park, look for **Creature Comforts** near the Tree of Life, with a nice selection of stuffed animals. In Harambe, **Mombasa Marketplace** has several booths and a great shop, **Ziwani Traders**, with intriguing African wood chimes, straw baskets, ornamental masks, sculptures, and figurines in clay—a wonderful variety of art. In Safari Village, **Outfitters Gift Shop** brings it all together, setting an artistic tone with tapestries, copper art, and carved totem poles surrounding all the bits and pieces of unique art from around the park.

Disney's Hollywood Studios

On Sunset Boulevard, **Legends of Hollywood** has a focus on Winnie the Pooh, with perfect gifts for toddlers and fans of Pooh Bear. The **Muppet Stuff Shop** next to Muppets 3-D sells Kermit and friends, including videos and DVDs of the classic Muppet Show and movies. And of course, I had to stop in **The Writer's Stop** at Stage 14, a snazzy little coffee shop lined with books—not just Disney titles, but best-sellers and local interest, too!

Downtown Disney

Whimsical gifts abound at **Hoypoloi**, where fun art glass jostles for space with pottery and ceramics that just cry out to come home with me.

If you're obsessed with refrigerator magnets, then **Magnetron** is the store for you—that's all they stock. Finish off that state magnet collection, or start a new egg-shaped one.

Looking for an exotic Barbie, or a set of Lincoln Logs? Check out **Once Upon a Toy**, where they stock our childhood classics in addition to the usual Disney stuff.

Commander Data's uniform takes center stage at **Starabilias**, a movie memorabilia extravaganza dealing in everything from posters of classic flicks to clothes worn by the stars.

Thank you, Richard Branson, for bringing the **Virgin Megastore** (www.virginmega.com) to Orlando, elevating our music and movie choices to world-class standards. I love being able to pick up a new release from my favorite Greek pop artist, or finding a complete selection of Peter Sellers movies on DVD. With two stories of music, movies, and books to choose from, you will walk out with something!

Epcot

At Epcot's **World Showcase**, it's more a matter of where not to shop—you'll find enchanting gifts under every roof. Bargain hunters will find inexpensive exotic gifts in the **Yong Feng Shangdian Shopping Gallery**, China, where you can pick up fragrant soaps for a dollar; it's also a great place for books on philosophy, elegant silks, and fine furnishings. I've found warm fleece jackets at the

Puffin's Roost, Norway, and delicate glass ornaments in **Glas und Porzellan**, Germany. Pause as you pass **Village Traders** to watch African artists carving original art in soapstone and wood; the unique musical instruments demand attention as well. At Morocco, slip into a maze of alleyways to browse authentic metalworking, rugs, and clothing in the **souk**. But my favorite shopping stop is **Mitsukoshi** in Japan, where I get lost in the artistry of rice bowls and sushi trays.

Magic Kingdom

I love the **Zanzibar Trading Company** in Adventureland—it's set up like a Moroccan souk, broad and meandering, selling safari wear, oil lamps, turned wood, handwoven baskets, Moroccan drums, bullwhips, and other exotica. On Main St, the **Market House** features glassblowing and Austrian crystal glasses and vases, and it's tough to pass by the **Main Street Confectionary**, with its copper-kettle fresh-fudge kitchen. Right next to City Hall, the **Main Street Gallery** showcases fine Disney art, including animation cels and limited-edition bisque figurines.

International Drive

Stop by **Global Camera Gallery** (407-477-0089), 11025 International Dr, for NTSC and European PAL conversions.

You're a long way from the ocean, but don't let that stop you. The surf is up 24/7 at **Ron Jon Surf Shop** (407-481-2555; www.ronjons.com), 5160 International Dr, where you can find colorful surf clothing and browse through stacks of bodyboards, skateboards, and yes indeed, surfboards.

Orlando Harley-Davidson Historic Factory Dealership is one place to stop for any motorcycle enthusiast (see *Motorcycling*). The largest Harley dealership in Florida showcases the company's history, including a replica of the original building. Take a tour of the real factory and watch them assemble your very own "hog."

MALLS AND OUTLETS If the attractions are the number one tourist destination here, then number two is shopping. So get out your credit cards: Orlando offers every type of shopping experience, from discount outlets to upscale malls. Here are some of the major players worth checking out.

Factory Stores at Lake Buena Vista (407-238-9301; www.lbvfs.com), 15591 FL 535, offers factory-direct pricing on name brands commonly found at your local mall.

Festival Bay (407-351-7718; www.belz.com), 5250 International Dr. This Belz conglomerate makes its mark by merging shopping and entertainment in one complex. Look for Bass Pro Shops Outdoor World, Vans Skate Park (see *Skateboarding*), Ron Jon Surf Shop, Cinemark 20 Theatres,

HANDHELD DRUMS MAKE DELIGHTFUL GIFTS AT THE MAGIC KINGDOM

Sandra Friend

Sheplers Western Wear, and Steve and Barry's, the largest college and pro sports apparel store in Florida.

Mall at the Millenia (www.mallat millenia.com), 4200 Conroy Rd. New in 2003, this is Central Florida's only Bloomingdale's, Macy's, and Neiman Marcus. Features upscale shops and boutiques, including Tiffany, Chanel, Hugo Boss, Lladro, Louis Vuitton, Gucci, and such US staples as Gap, Banana Republic, Tommy Bahama, and Crate and Barrel. Not an outlet, but bargains can be found in this classy atmosphere. Seven full-service restaurants provide fine-dining options. Free live music on first Friday. Valet, foreign currency exchange, and multilingual concierge available.

Orlando Premium Outlets (407-238-7787; www.premiumoutlets.com), 8200 Vineland Ave. A Mediterranean-style village of 110 upscale outlet stores: Coach, Escada, Kenneth Cole, Burberry, and Polo Ralph Lauren, to name just a few. Stop by the Rocky Mountain Fudge Factory (see *Eating Out*) for some of the best fudge and pralines in town!

Pointe Orlando (407-248-2838; www.pointeorlando.com), 9101 International Dr. The open-air shopping, dining, and entertainment environment is in the heart of International Drive and offers a broad range of apparel shops, including the popular Florida-based Chico's, and some fun shops like Artsy Abode, full of trendy home decor and handbags.

✳ Entertainment

Downtown Disney

Run, do not walk. Get yourself a ticket to the **Cirque du Soleil** show **La Nouba** now. If you do nothing else at

Disney, you must see this show. It's simply the most whimsical, artistic performance you'll ever experience. Yes, there are acrobats and clowns and high-wire acts, but it's not a traditional circus; it transports you to another dimension. Tickets (407-939-7600) start at $65 adults, $52 ages 3–10. Skip a day at a theme park, if you must, to fund your expedition.

Top rock, blues, and country artists play the music hall at the **House of Blues** (407-WDW-2NITE); enjoy live blues in the restaurant. Thu–Sat starting at 11 PM.

International Drive

The entertainment venues in **Pointe Orlando** (see *Selective Shopping*) will keep you up past midnight. You'll dance in a stunning surreal world in **Matrix** (407-370-3700), featuring futuristic techno and hip-hop beats. **Metropolis** (407-370-3700; www .metropolismatrix.com) has all the glitz and glamour of a Victorian parlor, but they still kick it up to contemporary sounds of the 1980s and 1990s. Cover varies nightly, but includes access to both clubs. Go to the extreme at **XS Orlando** (407-226-8922) in the land of virtual reality, with simulators to keep you busy for hours.

Universal Resort Orlando

& The **Blue Man Group** (www .universalorlando.com) has come to Orlando, and this Vegas-style high-energy production blends humor with hard-driving rhythms and artistry. Tickets $59–74 adult, $49–64 child; not recommended for young children.

The nightlife at **CityWalk at Universal Orlando** (407-363-8000; www .universalorlando.com) will keep you hopping long after the parks close.

You'll be jammin' to live reggae at **Bob Marley: A Tribute to Freedom**. At **Pat O'Brian's** you'll experience Mardi Gras 365 days a year. **City Jazz** brings you high-energy funk, R&B, blues, soul, and jazz, and at **the groove** you'll be dancing to hits from the 1970s and 1980s.

✳ Special Events

March–June: One of the best times to see Epcot is during the Annual **Epcot International Flower & Garden Festival**. Colorful blooms, elaborate gardens, and topiaries are shown at their best throughout the park. Take a tour or go behind the scenes and learn how they do it at gardening workshops where guest speakers with the greenest of thumbs share their secrets.

September–November: **Epcot Food & Wine Festival**. Nibble on ethnic goodies as you stroll around the World Showcase, trying foods and wines from more than 25 countries (not just the ones represented permanently at the park). Prices start as low as $1 for a taste, so it's a cheap way to graze. All month long, the festival includes special seminars on wine and beer, exhibits on regional foods, and temporary marketplaces selling wine and gourmet foods.

November–January: **ICE! at the Gaylord Palms Resort** (407-586-0000; www.gaylordpalms.com/ice) showcases a whimsical winter wonderland with interactive displays and more than 5,000 blocks of carved ice. Different types of ice are carved with hand tools (no chain saws for these elves) and look like either flawless crystal or compacted snow. The larger-than-life frozen sculptures depict scenes from the North Pole and the Nativity in the coolest attraction in town. This incredible event sells out fast, so make your reservations early.

Central Florida 2

Sandra Friend

POLK COUNTY

Built on citrus, cattle, and phosphate mining, Polk County owes its legacy to hardy settlers who followed the military trails south through Florida's 1820 frontier to rolling hills and wide-open prairies. The ancient spine of Central Florida, the Lake Wales Ridge, has the peninsula's highest hills, up to 300 feet; these high, dry relict sand dunes seemed ideal for the cultivation of citrus. Flat prairies around its 554 lakes perfect for cattle. And thus grew settlements like **Fort Meade**, Polk County's oldest town (circa 1849), which also has the unusual distinction of being the geographic center of the *population* of Florida (circa 2003). **Lake Alfred** sprang up around Fort Cummings, a Second Seminole War fortress, and in 1867, the town of **Bartow** was named as the county seat. As the South Florida Railroad pushed south in 1911, land speculators created towns like **Dundee**, **Haines City**, and **Lake Wales**. When a devastating freeze trashed citrus groves across Florida in 1896–1897, a small area was uniquely insulated; this was appropriately named **Frostproof**. Florida's fourth largest county, Polk County is a whopper—its landmass is equal in size to Delaware.

The 1920s Florida land boom transformed the region forever, bringing a broad brush of elegance and culture to the emerging towns of **Winter Haven**, **Auburndale**, and **Lakeland**. Nowhere is this reflected better than downtown Lakeland's classy promenade around Lake Mirror, and the world's largest collection of Frank Lloyd Wright buildings at Florida Southern College. A cosmopolitan art scene permeates Lakeland's elegant downtown district.

Take a spin down US 27 or US 17-92 to discover the magic of this landscape of orange groves and cattle ranches, of homes clinging to steep slopes above picturesque lakes, of historic downtowns brimming with antiques and art, a patchwork of agriculture and settlement less than an hour from metro Orlando.

GUIDANCE **Central Florida Visitors & Convention Bureau** (863-298-7565 or 1-800-828-7655; www.visitcentralflorida.org), P.O. Box 8040, Cypress Gardens 33884. For maps and materials and a touch of regional tourism history, stop in at **Polk Outpost 27** (www.visitcentralflorida.org/polkoutpost27), their brand-new welcome center along US 27 just south of I-4 at Davenport. It's not your typical "pick up a handful of brochures" place—there's a virtual hot-air balloon ride, a

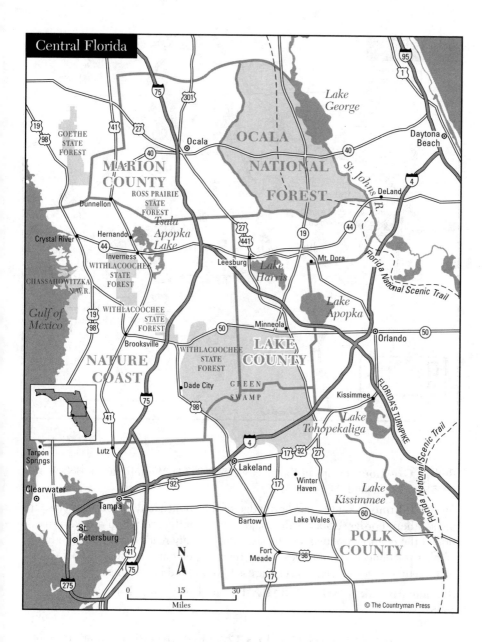

Central Florida

booth where you can e-mail photo greetings to friends, a putting green, and more! Open daily.

GETTING THERE *By air*: Polk County lies equidistant from the **Orlando International Airport** (see "Orlando") and **Tampa International Airport** (see "Tampa and Hillsborough County")

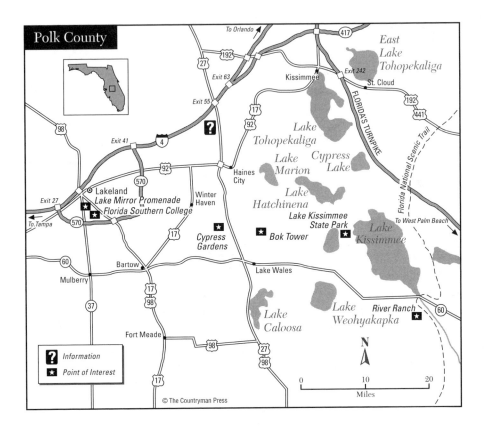

By bus: **Greyhound** stops in Bartow (863-553-2774), Winter Haven (863-293-5935), and Lakeland (863-682-3107).

By car: **I-4** runs along the northern edge of the county, and **SR 60** runs close to the southern border. **US 27** is the major north–south corridor on the eastern side of the county. A network of twisty, windy county roads circles the hundreds of lakes to connect communities. More than 80 percent of visitors to Polk County drive their own vehicles, as rural areas have limited bus service.

By train: **Amtrak** (1-800-USA-RAIL) stops in downtown Lakeland (863-683-6368).

GETTING AROUND Use **US 27** and **US 17-92** to drive north and south through major population areas. **US 92** and **US 98** connect communities to the east and west.

PARKING Winter Haven has free on-street parking, 2-hour limit; **Lakeland** offers the same but also has metered municipal lots, parking garages, and one small free 4-hour parking lot on Kentucky between Pine and Trader's Alley in the antiques district, plus the Oak Street Park & Ride. All of the smaller towns offer unlimited free parking in their downtowns.

MEDICAL EMERGENCIES This county is large, so there are quite a few hospitals with emergency rooms: **Bartow Memorial Hospital** (863-533-8111; www .bartowregional.com), US 98, Bartow; **Heart of Florida Regional Medical Center** (863-422-4971; www.heartofflorida.com), 40100 US 27, Davenport; **Lakeland Regional Medical Center** (863-687-1100; www.lrmc.com), 324 Lakeland Hills Blvd, Lakeland; **Lake Wales Medical Center** (863-676-1433; www.lakewalesmedicalcenter.com), 410 S 11th St, Lake Wales; and **Winter Haven Hospital** (863-293-1121; www.winterhavenhospital.org), 200 Ave F NE, Winter Haven.

✳ To See

ART GALLERIES

Davenport

Professional artist Lori Sanchez (863-424-0070), at **Wallaby Ranch** (see *Hang Gliding*), creates awesome hang-gliding art using the techniques of the Old Masters. Bright blue and red gliders pepper the sky, a hang glider crosses a valley in the beautiful style of Van Gogh, and even Picasso's cubism is represented. You'll find these extraordinary artworks on posters, T-shirts, and notecards, and maybe, just maybe, she'll part with an original. Whether or not you're a hang-gliding enthusiast, you'll be sure to appreciate Lori's humor and style.

Frostproof

The tiny **Frostproof Art League & Gallery** (863-635-7271; www.polkarts alliance.org), 12 E Wall St, is home to more than 50 local artists' creations featuring Florida wildlife, landscapes, and floral paintings in oil, acrylic, and watercolor. Classes scheduled throughout the year are open to the public. Open Mon, Tue, Thu, and Fri 9–4.

Lakeland

Arts on the Park (863-680-2787, www.polkartsalliance.org), 115 N Kentucky Ave. Sculpture, Florida landscapes, and wildlife art dominate this Lakeland Creative Arts Center with monthly receptions and six annual juried shows; the nonprofit arts organization also manages the annual Fall Festival of Art in Munn Park. Open Tue–Sat noon–4; free.

Imperial Art Gallery (863-603-4663; www.imperialartgallery.com), 128 S Kentucky Ave, is a cooperative of Lakeland artists working in all media, like Jeanne Barker's watercolors of trilliums and lady's slippers, and Madeline Lay's acrylics of swans drifting across Lake Morton, a favorite theme for local artists. Gift cards and postcards are an inexpensive way to take home an original design. Mon–Fri 10–5, Sat 10–4.

Lake Wales

✦ The **Lake Wales Arts Center** (863-676-8426; www.lakewalesartscenter.org or www.cityoflakewales.com), 1099 SR 60 E. Built in 1927 as the Holy Spirit Catholic Church, this Spanish Mission–style facility was named to the National Register of Historic Places in 1990 and is open to the public Mon–Fri 10–4 for musical performances, tours, lectures, classes, art exhibitions, and an annual arts

Sandra Friend

WATERSKIERS AT CYPRESS GARDENS

ATTRACTIONS 🏊 ♿ It opened in 1936 as Florida's first intentional theme park, and it's back in action, to the delight of millions, with a slightly tweaked name and a *lot* more to experience—**Cypress Gardens Adventure Park** (863-324-2111; www.cypressgardens.com), 6000 Cypress Gardens Blvd, Winter Haven. In the interest of full disclosure, I'm indirectly related to the new owners, who I am very proud of for preserving and restoring this Florida icon, with support from the Trust for Public Land and the local community. My sister's husband oversees the fine southern-style cooking that now permeates the park's many eateries, and I'll brag that the barbecue is worth the visit. Cypress Gardens has touched my life since I was just a few years old; it was one of my parent's favorite destinations on our annual vacations, thanks to the extensive tropical botanical gardens and the perennial waterskiing show, which is what started it all. Founder Dick Pope knew he had a goldmine when visiting servicemen started showing up just to see this newfangled idea called *waterskiing*. His wife, Julie, choreographed the show, his kids and their friends put it on, and Pope mined that vein for all it was worth. A tireless promoter, he called on movie studios and television executives to film in the tropical gardens and among the ancient cypresses lining Lake Louise, and they did, in droves, earning him the nickname "Mr. Florida" for his contributions to the state's tourism. In 1940, Julie needed to hide a showy plant damaged by frost and came up with the idea for the Southern Belles, women who still stroll the park in antebellum dress to add to the beauty. By the time I made my first visit to the gardens, Dick Pope Jr. ran the show. You could take the whole family's photo in a mirror reflecting gardens, gazebo, and Southern Belles, climb on giant storybook creatures, and make a phone call from an AT&T phone "room," a real first of its day.

Today's Cypress Gardens reflects three generations of care and creativity. As you enter the park through Jubilee Junction (formerly Crossroads Village), you're in the world of Dick Pope Jr., who added the village of shops and eateries and its zoological section, which includes **Nature's Way**, a boardwalk through grand old cypress down to **Lake Louise**, a free-fly interactive aviary with tropical birds, and the tucked in a corner but not to be missed **Pirates** show. Overshadowing it all, literally, is the **Sunshine Sky**

Adventure, the only such ride of its kind in North America, a rotating open-air platform that lifts you 16 stories in the air with the gentle touch of a hot-air balloon—and amazing views, including a clear sight of the Bok Tower on Iron Mountain, the high point of Florida's peninsula. The **Wings of Wonder** butterfly house showcases these ephemeral beauties amid tropical plants; **Planes, Trains, and Automobiles** houses an enormous HO model railroad display.

Leave the bustle of Jubilee Junction—down the steps or across the lawns and you transition into the original Cypress Gardens through **Topiary Trail**, which leads through a garden with oversized creatures and waterfalls. The **waterskiing spectator stadiums** flank the lakeshore, and it's here you'll see the stuff of legend. The current show pays homage to the past, showing off some of the original costuming, water ballets, and the famous pyramid alongside top-ranked skiers and wakeboarders being pulled by drivers who know their way around tight turns. The sport of hang gliding got its start right here, and you'll see a glider pulled up by tow rope and then sail back into shore. Directly past the stadiums is the entrance to the **botanical gardens**, a stroll you should not miss. While the 2004 hurricanes took down some of the older trees, grand cypresses still line the waterways and unusual species such as the sausage tree grow tall. Look for two different two-headed cabbage palms amid the colorful plantings, and pause at the **Florida Pool**, shaped like the state and built for a water ballet scene in the Esther Williams film *Easy to Love* (1953). The **Oriental Garden** offers a quiet place for reflection, but my favorite spot in the gardens is the **banyan tree** that Dick Pope planted in 1938—and look at it now. It's a forest unto itself, with orchids and bromeliads added for ornamentation.

The "Adventure Park" part of the name comes from the newest addition to Cypress Gardens. Prior owner Kent Buescher imported amusement park rides from around the world, and even purchased the about-to-be-demolished Skyliner, Florida's first roller coaster, from a closed attraction in Panama City Beach. The result? Cypress Gardens now has the finest classic amusement park in Florida, on par with the old-time amusement parks of the Northeast that are only open in summer. This year-round family park, with its shady byways and good old-fashioned rides like Tilt-a-Whirl, the Paradise Sky Wheel, a two-story Boardwalk Carousel, and Bugsville, a whole section devoted to children's amusement rides, will keep a family busy all day. My favorites are the roller coasters—two wooden, three steel—with names like "Okeechobee Rampage" and "Swamp Thing." The Skyliner, built in 1962, is a woodie imposing enough it requires modern-day restraint systems to keep you in your seat; I like the Triple Hurricane, a more sedate but still fun woodie with lots of hills, the best. Adjoining the amusement park area is the concert stage, where performers like Wayne Newton and the Oak Ridge Boys are regulars.

Cypress Gardens Adventure Park opens at 10 AM daily, and depending on special events and concerts, may close at 5 or as late as midnight. Summer visitors get full access to the adjoining waterpark, Splash Island (see *Water Parks*), with their admission. $40 adults, $35 for over 60 and ages 3–9; a Golden Passport good for a full year is only $80 adult, $70 senior, $60 child.

THE LANDMARK BANYAN TREE AT CYPRESS GARDENS

Sandra Friend

show. Local and national artists' work can be purchased in the fine arts and crafts gift shop (see *Selective Shopping*).

Original art from local artists can be found at **The Gallery and Frame Shop** (863-676-2821; www.thegalleryandframeshop.com), 249 E Stuart Ave, which also offers limited-edition prints and artist supplies. Open Mon–Fri 9:30–5:30, Wed & Sat 9:30–noon.

Winter Haven
Ridge Art Association (863-291-5661; www.ridgeart.org), 210 Cypress Gardens Blvd. More than 50 years old, this nonprofit fine arts organization has monthly juried and invitational art exhibitions. Open Mon-Fri 12:30–4.

✈ ✇ Aviation takes on a new sparkle at **Fantasy of Flight** (863-984-3500; www.fantasyofflight.com), 1400 Broadway Blvd, Polk City, a unique attraction that bills itself as the "World's Greatest Aircraft Collection" but is much, much more. Hosted by aviator and aviation collector Kermit Weeks, two-time winner of the US National Aerobatics Championship, it's an immersion in the history of flight; the skillful use of multimedia, mirrors, and movie makes you feel part of the action. Free fall over Polk County's farms and fields, participate in a B-17 bombing mission, or take off in a flight simulator for a dogfight over the Pacific. The walk-through history lesson and hands-on simulators are so entertaining they're well worth the price of admission. Of course, there's the museum component, too, with two hangars of classic aircraft to explore, including a Martin B-26 Marauder, a P-51 Mustang, and a flying boat, the Short Sunderland. All of the planes displayed are airworthy, which makes many of them one-of-a-kind. Grab a bite at the retro art deco Compass Rose restaurant (see *Eating Out*), and browse the aircraft models in the gift shop. Open daily 10–5 (closed Thanksgiving and Christmas), $29 adults, $15 ages 6–15. For an additional fee, take off in a hot-air balloon (see *Ballooning*), or fly the friendly skies in a 1930s biplane (see *Aviation*).

BASEBALL Spring means the return of the **Detroit Tigers** (863-686-8075) warming up at Joker Marchant Stadium in Lakeland. Grapefruit League teams play their exhibition games in March, and tickets range $5–25, depending on the team and location. Games typically begin at 1:05 PM. See the full schedules at www.visitcentralflorida.org/cool.php or call 800-828-7655 for more information.

HISTORIC SITES

Bartow

The Colonial Revival **A. A. McLeod Residence**, 395 S Central Ave, circa 1922, is now a law office. The story goes that city officials wanted to cut down an old oak tree on the south side of the house. The elderly Mrs. McCleod sat bearing a shotgun and refused to have her stately tree cut down. The city acquiesced, and the tree remains to this day.

The two-and-a-half-story neo-Gothic **Associate Reformed Presbyterian Church**, 205 E Stanford St, was built in 1926 and is one of the largest churches in Bartow.

One of the most architecturally significant homes today is the **Benjamin Holland Residence**, 590 E Stanford St. The 1895 home was placed on the National Register of Historic Places in 1975. Benjamin Holland's son, Spessard L. Holland, became governor of Florida and was a US senator.

One of the first two churches in Bartow, the **First Methodist Church**, 310 S Broadway, is a stunning representation of Richardsonian Romanesque architecture and was built in 1906 for only $16,000.

CLASSIC AIRCRAFT ON DISPLAY AT FANTASY OF FLIGHT

Sandra Friend

L. B. Brown (863-534-0100), 470 Second Ave. Home of the Neighborhood Improvement Corp. of Bartow, Inc. Born into slavery around 1856, Lawrence Bernard Brown rose above his roots and settled in Bartow, building a meticulously crafted two-story structure in an unusual Z layout. The circa-1892 home has leaded-glass transoms, gingerbread trim, turned posts, unique picturesque millwork, and a Palladian window. The foundation rests on 13 brick piers and 18 huge pine tree trunks and showcases a superior level of craftsmanship indicative of the late 19th century.

One of the oldest African American churches, the 1893 **Mount Gilboa Missionary Baptist Church**, 1205 Martin Luther King Blvd, is one of the oldest churches in Polk County. The current two-and-a-half-story building was constructed in 1928.

The neoclassical brick **Swearington-Langford Residence**, 690 E Church St, was built in 1925 for John J. Swearington, a state senator and prominent attorney. Placed on the National Register of Historic Places in 1982, it has served as location for a movie and several commercials.

The two-story **Windsweep** home at 935 Oak St was featured in the movie *China Moon*, which starred Madeleine Stowe and Ed Harris.

The **1908 Thomas Lee Wilson Residence**, 555 E Stanford St, was used in another movie, *My Girl*, staring Jamie Lee Curtis, Dan Aykroyd, and Macaulay Culkin. The two-and-a-half-story wood frame residence is now open to guests as the Stanford Inn (see *Bed & Breakfasts*).

The Wonder House, 1075 Mann Rd, was featured in a Ripley's Believe It or Not cartoon. The unique 1925 residence has a natural air-conditioning system and a system of mirrors that allows the residents to see who is at the front door from several locations throughout the house.

Homeland

Once a farming community centered on the **Bethel Methodist Church**, the town of Bethel was renamed in 1885 by a young Irishman who felt the area looked like his native Ireland. Several pioneer buildings sit on the 5-acre **Homeland Heritage Park** (863-534-3766; www.bartowchamber.com/homeland.htm), dedicated to preserving educational, religious, and cultural history and located at the intersection of Church Ave and Second St. Go 4 miles south of Bartow on SR 60 to SR 17 S, then FL 640 W; turn south on Hibiscus Ave to the intersection. The one-room **Bethany School**, built of cypress wood in 1878, was the first building rescued. Initially enrolling only 5 children, the school grew to 75 pupils within the first year, becoming the county's largest at that time. The **1887 Homeland Methodist Church** was moved from across the street, and during restoration in 1987, beautiful stained-glass windows were discovered hidden by a dropped ceiling. Two 19th-century Polk County economic stations are depicted: an original log cabin, and the typical rural homestead of an affluent family. This park often hosts events, such as the Cracker Story Telling Festival each Oct (see *Special Events*). Open Mon–Sat 9–5. Tours available. Free, except for special events.

Lakeland

Frank Lloyd Wright Buildings at Florida Southern College (863-680-4110; www.flsouthern.edu/fllwctr), 11 Lake Hollingsworth Dr. Architecture aficionados should not miss the largest collection of Wright buildings anywhere on earth— 18—clustered on the campus of Florida Southern College. Stop by the Frank Lloyd Wright "Child of the Sun" Visitor Center and Esplanade Gift Shop (closed Mon) for a walking tour brochure before starting your stroll around campus. Some of the characteristic Wright designs easily stand out, like geometric forms, colored-glass accents, and clerestory windows. But you'll be surprised at how pervasive the Wright touch is—even including the planetarium, the only one Wright ever designed. Open daily; free.

Lake Mirror Promenade & Park, off E Main, Orange St, and Lake Mirror Dr. Modeled after the 1893 Columbian Exposition Court of Honor, this restored 1928 gem designed by Charles Wellford Levitt looks as sparkling new as the day it opened. An ornate balustrade lined with lamps makes this a comfortable, romantic stroll well into the evening.

Pick up a walking tour brochure (see *Walking Tours*) for a detailed explanation of downtown's architectural landmarks, from the **1927 Polk Theatre** (see *Entertainment*) to the **1903 Clonts Building**, a Richardsonian Romanesque former dry goods store at 228 E Pine St, and **Munn Park**, established in 1884 as Lakeland's downtown square.

Lake Wales

A stroll through **Historic Downtown Lake Wales** (www.historiclakewales.com) will remind you of the exciting 1920s. Browse through the quaint collections of shops and galleries in one of Florida's Main Street cities, placed on the National Register of Historic Places in 1990. You find fascinating architecture, vintage charm, and fun nightlife along Central, Stuart, Park and Orange Aves, Scenic Hwy, Market St, and N First St. Pick up a self-guided walking tour at the **Depot Museum** (see *Museums*), which also lists the many beautiful murals depicting the bygone era. On Friday 8–2 stop by the **farmer's market** in the MarketPlace between Park and Stuart (see *Selective Shopping*).

Pinewood Estate at Historic Bok Sanctuary (see *Gardens*; www.bok sanctuary.org/visiting/pinewood.html). Step into the 1930s Mediterranean Revival mansion and you'll want to move right in. The 20-room home of C. Austin Buck features antique furnishings, Latin-inspired tile, intricate woodwork, awe-inspiring architecture, and a secret staircase. The best time

PINEWOOD ESTATE

Sandra Friend

to see this home is during the holiday season for Christmas at Pinewood (see *Special Events*). Open daily and included with Bok Sanctuary admission. Tours ($6 adults, children free) are offered Mon–Sat 12–3 and Sun 12–2 except for 3 weeks in Nov.

Loughman

In 1930 the **Old Tampa Highway** opened, connecting Orlando with Tampa through Lakeland. A mostly forgotten chunk of the original brick-and-cypress highway remains intact off Ronald Reagan Parkway at the eastern border of the county; look closely at the imposing 1930 concrete Polk County boundary monument along the old brick highway for a sculptor's faux pas. Matching monuments (minus the error) stand at the county boundaries along US 92 en route to Plant City and US 98 en route to Dade City.

MUSEUMS

Bartow

Polk County Historical Museum (863-534-4386; www.polk-county.net), 100 E Main St. Learn about the early pioneers and Seminole Indians though exhibits depicting stories of the cattle, citrus, and phosphate industries, as well as local military history and a children's discovery room. Tours available. Open Tue–Fri 9–5, Sat 9–3; free.

Dundee

The Dundee Depot (863-439-1312), 103 Main St, features the history of Dundee and the Atlantic Coast Line railroad, since the town attributes its establishment to the rail line. Artifacts date back to 1911. Open Thu and Sat 10–3; donation.

Fort Meade

At the **Fort Meade Historical Museum** (863-285-7474), Broadway and Tecumseh, browse through 1800s newspapers and marvel at artifacts from the pioneer settlers of Florida's frontier; the region marked the northern boundary of Seminole Tribal Lands in the 1840s. A railroad car contains displays. Open 9–12 weekdays, 10–4 Sat; free.

THE DUNDEE DEPOT, HISTORIC STOP ON THE ATLANTIC COAST LINE.
Sandra Friend

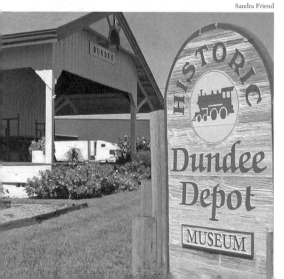

Frostproof

Frostproof Historical Museum (863-635-7865), 210 S Scenic Hwy, shares the early years of this citrus town through the memorabilia of pioneer families—clothing, photos, books, vintage household items, and other ephemera, including the town's first movie theatre's ticket booth and painted curtain. Open 1–4 Tue, Thu, Sat; free.

Lake Alfred

The **Lake Alfred Historical Museum** (863-956-3937) 210 N Seminole Ave at the Chamber of Commerce, contains exhibit cases with historical photos and ephemera, such as an 1839 map of the region's original wagon roads; Mon–Thu 10–2. Across the street, the fire station has vintage pieces of firefighting equipment.

Lakeland

🐾 ♿ **Florida Air Museum** (863-644-0741; www.sun-n-fun.org), 4075 Doolittle Rd, adjoining Lakeland Regional Airport, is the center stage for the annual Sun 'n Fun Fly In (see *Special Events*), showcasing more than 45 vintage and exotic aircraft like a 1912 Sopwith Camel and a Pitts S-1 special stunt plane with tooled leather seats; the variety of methods used to mount wings and engines testifies to the creativity of aircraft designers. One exhibit space pays homage to Howard Hughes's contribution to aviation; Hughes's personal memorabilia were given to the museum for a permanent display. Mon–Fri 9–5, Sat 10–4, Sun noon–4; donation of $8 adults, $6 seniors, $4 ages 8–12.

🐾 ♿ Nine galleries, two floors: hundreds of pieces of art. The **Polk Museum of Art** (863-688-7743; www.polkmuseumofart.org), 800 E Palmetto St, has it all. A permanent pre-Columbian collection includes hands-on activities for kids; a brick waterfall dominates the eclectic sculpture garden. If you're looking for whimsical educational gifts for the kids, don't miss the Museum Shop. Tue–Sat 10–5, Sun 1–5; fee.

Lake Wales

Lake Wales Depot Museum & Cultural Center (863-678-4209; www.cityof lakewales.com/depot), 325 S Scenic US Alt 27. Since the extension of the Atlantic Coast Line Railroad in 1911, the Lake Wales junction played an important role in the town's early development. Providing easy access from north, south, east, or west, the railroad soon brought pioneers seeking new lifestyles. Listed on the National Register of Historic Places, the restored 1928 Atlantic Coast Railroad station features a 1916 Pullman car, a 1926 Seaboard Air Line caboose, and assorted railroad memorabilia. Several exhibits display the history and early industries of Lake Wales, including a beautiful collection of quilts. Test your trivia knowledge by trying to identify over 70 dolls on display in the Celebrity Doll Challenge. Don't miss the Annual Pioneer Days and quilt show in the fall (see *Special Events*). Open Mon–Fri 9–5, Sat 10–4. Donations appreciated.

Florida's Natural Grove House Visitor Center (863-676-1411 or 1-800-237-7805; www.floridasnatural.com), 20160 US 27, is a half-mile north of SR60. Central Florida's Polk County produces more citrus crops than the entire state of California. This is as close to the groves as you can get (tours in the actual groves are no longer offered), and Florida's Natural is as fresh as it gets. This "not-from-concentrate" company is owned entirely by local growers. Learn about Florida orange growers at this educational visitors center. The short film on the citrus industry is well worth watching. Sample juices while browsing the citrus-themed gift shop or sit at the picnic tables under several varieties of orange trees. Open Mon–Fri 10–5, Sat 10–2 (seasonally); free.

Mulberry

✐ **Mulberry Phosphate Museum** (863-425-2823; www.mulberrychamber
.org/attractions.htm), 101 SE First St. Florida's mineralogical wealth is phosphate, used in products ranging from hair color and dog food to fertilizer.
Housed in a historic railroad depot and railcars, the museum explores phosphate mining and use, the spectacular fossil record uncovered by phosphate mining, and Florida's railroad history. Rockhounds and kids alike will delight in digging through the freshly mined pile of limestone outside in search of fossils and phosphate nuggets. Open Tue–Sat 10–4:30; donation.

Polk City

& **AWSEF Water Ski Experience** (863-324-2472; www.waterskihalloffame
.com), 1251 Holy Cow Rd. From the early days of waterskiing (1922, Lake Pepin, New York) through Esther Williams and Corky the Clown at Cypress Gardens to the US Water Ski Team, this one-of-a-kind museum and hall of fame covers it all; interactive displays (including a special exhibit on disabled waterskiing) show you what happens when you're out on the water. Educational clinics and exhibitions are held in the lake out back. Open Mon–Fri 10–5, fee.

RACING **USA International Raceway** (1-800-984-RACE; www.usaspeedway
.com), along FL 33 north of Lakeland, is a 0.75-mile high-banked oval stock car racing track, home of the Hooters Pro Cup Series. Racing events are held nearly every week; check the Web site for a schedule.

RAILROADIANA In Haines City the **1923 Seaboard Coast Line passenger station** with a couple of vintage baggage carts out front adjoins **Railroad Park**.
Built in 1912, the **Dundee Passenger Depot** was the first depot on the Haines City–Sebring line of the Atlantic Coast Line; it remained active until 1975. An **ACL caboose** sits outside the small historic museum. The 1899 **ACL freight and passenger depots** in Mulberry house the Mulberry Phosphate Museum (see *Museums*), with several pieces of historic rolling stock on site.

ZOOLOGICAL PARKS AND WILDLIFE REHABILITATION **Genesis Zoological & Wildlife Rehabilitation Center** (863-965-8706; www.genesiszoological.org) sits behind the International Market World (see *Selective Shopping*) flea market on US 17-92. This small rehab center hosts, among other animals, full-grown white Siberian tigers—the type popularized by Siegfried & Roy in Las Vegas—though its unclear pure white Siberians exist. All white tigers in the US are thought to be descendants of a white male Bengal tiger trapped in India in 1951; Siberians can cross-breed with Bengals, so such white hybrids may be the result. Volunteers care for these cats, and panthers and leopards as well. Open on weekends; donation.

✷ To Do

AVIATION At Fantasy of Flight (see *Attractions*), hang on to your hat on a 20-minute flight in the world's oldest New Standard 1929 open-cockpit biplane.
Pilot and proud owner Rob Lock of **Waldo Wright's Flying Service** (www
.waldowrights.com) takes you airborne in a special sky ballet befitting this grand

old barnstormer, the only antique D-25 capable of carrying four passengers. Flights run Oct–Aug, $65 for 15-minute Barnstorming Adventure, $229 for 30-minute hands-on WWII Stearman Flight.

Jack Brown's Sea Plane Base (863-956-2243; www.gate.net/~ seaplane), 2704 US 92 W, Winter Haven. What better way to get your seaplane license than while learning on Florida's "Land of 1000 Lakes"? In just 2 days you'll be able to take off, land, and sail, along with mastering techniques necessary for rough or glassy waters. Land license required.

BALLOONING Fantasy of Flight (see *Attractions*) offers crack-of-dawn balloon trips with one of their local pilots, who also lifts off from Town Manor B&B (see *Lodging*) for romantic getaway flights. 3-hour flights cost $175 per person, or $475 for an exclusive flight for two, and must be reserved in advance; weight limits apply. Call Mon–Fri 9–5 at 863-984-3500 ext. 288.

BICYCLING Options for cyclists have exploded in the past several years as the county has actively acquired old rail corridors and turned them into paved pathways that extend up to 30 miles, connecting various communities. One of the newest is the 8-mile **Fort Fraser Trail** between Bartow and South Lakeland, paralleling US 98 with a trailhead with facilities at Highland City. Oak hammocks and shaded benches help cool you down. The 6-mile **Auburdale TECO Trail** almost, but not quite, connects with the **Van Fleet State Trail** (see *Greenways*), which starts in Polk City and heads north into Sumter County, providing nearly 30 miles (each way) of on-pavement cycling. In Dundee ride a pleasant 1.8-mile paved loop, the **Lake Marie Bike Path**, overlooking rolling hills topped with citrus. Another scenic ride is the **Lake Wales Trailway**, a linear 1.7 mile path through residential areas overlooking Lake Wailes, connecting a park and the downtown area.

BIRDING Surprisingly, the **Eagle Ridge Mall** retention ponds on US 27 are a popular stop for birders, but you'll also find fabulous birding in most of the region's parks, especially **Lake Kissimmee State Park** (see *Parks*), where I've spotted Florida scrub-jays, crested caracaras, sandhill cranes, wild turkeys, and bald eagles all in one day's visit. On **Lake**

ALONG THE VAN FLEET TRAIL

Sandra Friend

LAKE HOLLINGSWORTH

Morton and **Lake Wire**, you'll find Lakeland's famed swans (wings are clipped, so they don't fly away) and hundreds of other waterfowl; nearby **Lake Hollingsworth Municipal Park** has a more natural community of wading birds passing through. **Pine Ridge Nature Preserve Trail** at Bok Tower Gardens (see *Gardens*) is home to 126 wild bird species.

BOATING With 554 lakes in Polk County, imagine the possibilities; you'll find public boat ramps off every major road and along quite a few minor roads as well. A promotional slogan for the county is the "Central Florida Lakes District." The county's largest lakes include **Kissimmee**, **Hatchinhea**, and **Pierce**, all extremely popular destinations for anglers. **Cherry Pocket** and **Jennings Resort** (see *Fish Camps*) are just two of many fish camps catering to anglers with bait and tackle, boat ramps, and live wells.

DRIVING TOURS Solve the mystery of **Spook Hill** (863-676-3445; www.historic lakewales.com/spookhill), N Wales Dr, as you defy gravity. Early settlers traveling around Lake "Wailes" noticed their mule-drawn wagons struggling with their loads as they moved downhill. Years later, residents noticed that their cars would roll uphill in this same spot—all by themselves. Test this phenomenon for yourself. I did, and it worked! Drive to the white line at the base of the hill, put your car in neutral, and watch it roll backward, uphill. Watch for cars behind you, as this is a one-way road. Free.

FAMILY ACTIVITIES

Lakeland

♂ 🎨 ⛄ If you have young children, don't miss **Barnett Family Park** (www .lakelandgov.net/parkrec/parks/Barnettfamilypark.html), 121 S Lake Ave, adjacent to Hollis Garden (see *Gardens*) and the Lake Mirror Promenade (see *Historic Sites*). It's compact but full of fun, offering giant spiderwebs to climb on, flying saucers to swing, giant Florida critters to scramble over, and a big wet play area where water squirts, dances, and pours across colorful mosaics of pond life (and the watchful eye of Blinky the alligator) as your kids get soaking wet (water playground Tue–Sun 10–5). Open daily dawn to dusk, free.

♂ ⛄ **Explorations V Children's Museum** (863-687-3869; www.explorations v.com), 109 N Kentucky Ave, Lakeland, offers small children one of the most fun hands-on experiences I've encountered in Florida. Kids play dress-up with clothing and props that let them be a television weather forecaster, a policeman, a fireman, a construction worker, and various other professionals. A miniature Publix supermarket lets the tots get the hang of shopping, and they can withdraw play money from an ATM. In the basement, older kids will enjoy internationally themed sets with challenging puzzles. The museum is open Mon–Sat 9–5:30, closed major holidays; fee.

✐ **Family Fun Center** (863-644-1728; www.TheFamilyFunCenter.com), 4825 S Florida Ave, Lakeland, also has miniature golf and arcade games; right up the street you can take the family bowling at **AMF Lakeland Lanes** (863-646-5791; www.amf.com/lakelandlanes), 4111 S. Florida Ave.

Winter Haven

✐ **Admiral's Cove** (863-326-5588; www.bestwesternadmiralsinn.com/minigolf .html), 5665 Cypress Gardens Blvd, in front of Admiral's Best Western in Winter Haven, offers miniature golf on a challenging little course with a pirate theme, replete with waterfalls and a replica pirate ship.

FISHING ♿ In addition to hundreds of sparkling lakes shimmering with sunfish and bass, you'll find two excellent stocked venues for fishing near Lakeland: **Tenoroc Fish Management Area** (863-499-2421; www.myfwc.com/Fishing/ offices/tenoroc-home/index.html), 3829 Tenoroc Mine Rd, and **Saddle Creek Park** (see *Parks*). Both provide managed impoundments with plenty of bank fishing and special fishing opportunities for youngsters and the disabled. For guided bass fishing on Lake Kissimmee, contact Bass Champions (1-800-826-0621; www.grapehammock.com/Guide.html) and ask for Johnny Doub; he and his guides work out of Grape Hammock Fish Camp (see *Fish Camps*).

GENEALOGICAL RESEARCH **Polk County Historical and Genealogical Library** (863-534-4389; www.polk-county.net), East Main St, in the east wing of the 1908 neoclassical courthouse, downtown Bartow. This comprehensive research facility stocks family history for residents of the southeastern United States, with full-time staff on-site for assistance. Open Tue–Sat 9–5.

GOLF **Lekarica Golf Course** in Highland Park Hills (863-679-9478; www.lekarica.com), 1650 S Highland Park Dr, Lake Wales. The par-72, 18-hole golf course, built by Stiels and VanKleek in 1927, was designed for the way golf was meant to be played: relaxed and uncrowded. The sweeping, rolling hills have a challenging elevation change of 111 feet. After several years of renovations, the course is better than ever.

For computerized swing analysis and lessons, stop by **GQ Golf, Inc.** (863-676-8628), Eagle Ridge Mall, 468 Eagle Ridge Dr, Lake Wales. They also carry golf accessories and apparel.

SPLASHING AROUND AT BARNETT PARK
Sandra Friend

HANG GLIDING Thought you needed mountains to hang glide? Not so! In fact, we were hang gliding here in Florida before anyone ever jumped off a mountain attached to one (see *Cypress Gardens*), so it's no surprise the first aerotow hang-gliding flight park in the world is here, too. On 200 secluded acres of field and forest, just a few miles south of the theme parks, you'll find a relaxed community of hang gliders at **Wallaby Ranch** (863-424-0070 or 1-800-WALLABY; www .wallabyranch.com), 1805 Dean Still Rd, Davenport. Sample a tandem flight, or learn to fly solo or how to tow gliders with an ultralight at this full-service flight park. Owner and USHGA-certified tandem instructor Malcolm Jones will take

FLYING HIGH AT WALLABY RANCH At some time in our lives we have all dreamed that we were flying—soaring high in the sky like Superman. Given any excuse to take to the skies, I'm there. Researching every possible air venue, I found that you can hang glide in the flatlands of Florida, and subsequently made a call to Wallaby Ranch (see *Hang Gliding*). So at the crack-o-doodle-dawn, my daughter Sherri and I headed down US 27 toward Davenport. A short drive down a country road brought us to the entrance of the ranch, and there stretching out across the open field, the mist still lingering, we were greeted by a pair of sandhill cranes honking their hellos. Barefoot and smiling, owner Malcolm Jones sauntered over and proclaimed it an awesome day for flying. "You going up? Well, let's go!" We filled out a few papers and got our official hang-gliding card, then headed out to the center of the 45-acre field.

Malcolm instructed us in flight safety, and we snuggled into the comfortable horizontal harness, which looked much like a sleeping bag. As the aero-tug started to pull us along, I got a dog's-eye view of the grassy field. Then we were airborne, just a few slight feet off the ground. A deer raced alongside us until we were well above the trees. Climbing higher and higher, I breathed in the view of the 250-acre ranch below. At 2,000 feet, Malcolm released the tug-line and we were flying on our own. Really flying! Searching out rising air, he had me pull the bar toward my hip, shifting my weight, and we banked a turn. I had wings—real wings that worked exactly like the ones in my dreams! Slowing the glider by slightly pushing the bar out and shifting my weight again, we circled around and around; I spotted the deer now ambling down a trail.

The time went by much too fast, and soon we were setting up our approach. I felt a rush of adrenaline as we increased our speed heading toward terra firma. And then we were skimming just inches above the field, touched down, and gradually rolled to a stop. Of all the air sports, this is the one that keeps you up the longest. The ranch record is 6½ hours. It's also the least expensive for those who want to learn solo and pilot their own bird. So guess what's on my Christmas list?

you up to 2,000 feet so that you can soar just like the birds. Arrive early while the air is still and calm, as most tandem flights end by 10 AM. After your flight, hang around and grab a cup of coffee and cool conversation in the screened-in rec barn, or wander the property's many hiking trails. Tandem instruction flights start at $120. Experienced gliders pay $25 per tow, and you can bring your own glider or rent one, starting at $20 per flight or $60 per day. Their pro shop sells new and used gliders, harnesses and parachutes, aerotow equipment, and clothing, featuring Lori Sanchez's whimsical Fine Art of Hang Gliding series, depicted in the style of such classic masters as Picasso (see *Art Galleries*). Open daily, 7:30–sunset, with flights dependent on weather. Spectators welcome.

HIKING A county-wide program called **Trek Ten Trails** (www.visitcentral florida.org/do/outdoors/trektentrails.php) is getting residents and visitors out to see and appreciate dozens of new trails that have opened up on county natural lands over the past few years (see *Wild Places*). *50 Hikes in Central Florida* covers the best of the original regional hikes, with **Lake Kissimmee State Park** (see *Parks*) and the loop trail systems at **Lake Wales Ridge State Forest** being my top recommendations for backpackers. You'll also find trails in places like **Saddle Creek Park** (see *Parks*) or in Nature Conservancy and state forest lands along Lake Wales Ridge.

PADDLING Starting at the **Fort Meade Outdoor Recreation Area** (see *Parks*), the 67-mile **Peace River Canoe Trail** is a serene float trip down a slow-moving tannic river with sand bluffs, floodplain forests, and dense pine forests. Contact the **Canoe Outpost** (863-494-1215 or 1-800-268-0083; www.canoeoutpost.com) in Arcadia for shuttles; the state Office of Greenways and Trails (850-245-2052 or 1-877-822-5208; www.dep.state.fl .us/gwt) can provide specific details and a map of the route.

SKYDIVING **Florida Skydiving Center** (863-678-1003; www.florida skydiving.com), Lake Wales Airport, 440 Airport Rd. This drop zone is host for many world-record skydiving events and the best novice training center around, with a stadium-seat theater where you can review tapes of teams or get critiques on your own video-recorded flight. A Twin Otter takes you 2.5 miles in the air for a tandem free fall at 120 mph, relative work, accelerated free fall (AFF), or free flying, capturing it all with professionally edited video and photographs. Not quite ready to jump? Sit in the hangar on an eclectic selection of

A SWANSATION SCULPTURE IN LAKELAND
Sandra Friend

comfy couches and watch the experts pack chutes. Bring your sunscreen, lawn chair, and binoculars to watch pros from around the world gather for the Annual Easter, Thanksgiving, and Christmas Boogies. Jump 'N' Jacks is right there in the hangar for after-jump snacks and light meals. First tandem jump $185, and if you want to go back up the same day it's only $125. Tandem jumpers must be 18 and weigh less than 230 pounds.

SWAN SPOTTING The **swan motif** you see around Lakeland commemorates the city's long history of swans drifting across its lakes; the original pair lived on Lake Bonny in 1926. In 1954 the queen of England presented two mute swans to Lakeland, descendants of a pair presented from Queen Beatrice to Richard

GARDENS

& ⊙ ✏ In 1929, Pulitzer Prize–winning author Edward W. Bok, a Dutch immigrant and humanitarian, made an incredible gift to the American people—the **Bok Tower Gardens** (863-676-1408; www.boksanctuary.org), 1151 Tower Blvd. Residing at Mountain Lake Colony, a 1920s subdivision adjacent to the current gardens, Bok roamed the top of Iron Mountain frequently. He commissioned renowned landscape architect Fredrick Law Olmsted—who was inspired by gardens being planted beneath the ancient oaks at Highlands Hammock near Sebring—to create "a spot of beauty second to none in the country." At 298 feet, the view from the highest point in the Florida peninsula, framed by grandfather live oaks, is breathtaking. Groups of carefully planned plantings and gardens usher visitors uphill from the visitor center (where you'll learn the history of the gardens, and do take the time to watch the video) toward the sanctuary. It's a masterful and functional piece of landscape art serving as a carillon tower (one of only two in Florida) and as a monument at Bok's gravesite. It's sculpted of 4 million tons of Georgia marble, faced with ceramics from Enfield Pottery, and contains 60 bells weighing 61½ tons, the largest 12 tons by itself. The carillon rivals those heard in Europe, and plays for 45 minutes at 1 and 3. The tower is reflected in the Mirror Pool, where swans glide across the surface. This core portion of the sanctuary, however, is only the beginning. Part of the property includes Pinewood, an estate designed by a member of Olmsted's staff, William Lyman Phillips, and notable as the most complete Mediterranean Revival home in the United States. There is a separate tour fee for Pinewood, but you can roam its gardens for free; there are grottos, outdoor rooms, and sweeping views amid the trees and shrubs. Along the pathways you'll discover specialty gardens, including the vastly important Endangered Plant Garden, which is part of a nationwide program to preserve endangered plant species and repopulate them in the wild. In its center, an analemmatic sundial lets you tell the Lion-Hearted during the Crusades. You'll see several generations of swans gliding across Lake Morton, as well as elegant swan sculptures that are part of "Swansation," a project encompassing 62 unique works of art scattered around the region.

WALKING TOURS

Bartow
You'll find hundreds of beautifully restored historic homes and commercial buildings throughout the city of Bartow. A map reveals 36 of these homes in a self-guided walking tour from the visitors center at 510 N Broadway (or call 1-800-828-7655).

the time using your own shadow. Children and birders will love the Window by the Pond, an indoor blind that lets you watch wildlife. Continue along the pathways to the Pine Ridge Trail for a ¾-mile ramble through native scrub and flatwood habitats along the edge of the gardens. Before you leave, stop in the gift shop, which offers a wide variety of gifts and books relating to gardening, nature, and Florida topics. Look for the children's hidden garden arbor nearby. The park is open daily 8–6 (last admission at 5), and offers occasional concerts as well as workshops for gardeners and naturalists. It's also a very popular destination for weddings, and they have a wedding coordinator on staff. Admission $10 adults, $3 ages 5–12; half-price discount offered for entrance between 8–9 AM Saturday; wheelchairs and motorized personal mobility cart available.

OUTDOOR ROOM AT PINEWOOD ESTATE

Sandra Friend

Lakeland

Check with the City of Lakeland Community Development Department (863-834-6011), 228 S Massachusetts Ave, for **A Walking Tour of Downtown Lakeland**, a brochure that leads you past 44 sites of historic and cultural interest around Lake Mirror, Munn Park, and the antiques district. **Touring the City of Haines City: Walking Guide to Historic Downtown** details 24 historic sites of this citrus industry boomtown, established in 1883.

Lake Wales

Roam around downtown Lake Wales (see *Historic Sites*) and stop by the **Lake Wales Depot Museum** (see *Museums*) to pick up a map of historical and cultural sites, including several well-executed murals.

WATERSKIING AND WAKEBOARDING It all began here in Polk County, the craze to skim the surface of lakes at high speed. If you're game to try it yourself, winter instruction camps are held by pro Dave Briscoe at Briscoe's Ride Center (863-521-1076; www.thewakeboardcoach.com), 77 Paine Dr, Winter Haven, with dorm-style accommodations available on site at the "House of Paine."

✳ Green Space

∞ Like a formal English garden, Lakeland's small but beautiful **Hollis Garden** (863-603-6281), 702 E Orange St along Lake Mirror, is sectioned off into themed "rooms" that grow increasingly ornate and manicured as they flow downhill toward the lake. Rocky grottoes with lily ponds yield to serene presentations of red, yellow, and green flora around sod centers. Pieces of sculpture and fountains accent the formal gardens, which can be rented for weddings. Open Tue-Sun 10–6. Free.

GREENWAYS Running for nearly 30 miles along a former railroad bed, the **Gen. James A. Van Fleet Trail State Park** (352-516-7384; www.dep.state.fl.us/gwt/state/van) provides a ribbon of pavement for bikers, in-line skaters, and hikers to traverse rural Polk, Lake, and Sumter Counties, with enough adjoining green space for equestrians to ride. Four trailheads provide access; the Polk City Trailhead is near the junction of FL 33 and CR 665. For more rail-trails on slimmer greenways, see *Biking*.

NATURE CENTERS ♪ **Babson Park Audubon Center** (863-638-1355; www.ridgeaudubon.org), FL 17 in Babson Park, protects 3.5 acres of longleaf pine sandhill on the Lake Wales Ridge and offers educational programs for all ages, but especially the kids—they can dress up as the creatures of the ridge and put on puppet shows. You'll also find a bookstore and library in the center. The **Caloosa Nature Trail** circles the building, giving you a personal introduction to "Florida's desert," the scrub.

Street Audubon Nature Center (863-324-7304; www.lakeregion.net), 115 Lameraux Rd, Winter Haven. Centered on the Mabel Howe House, which has a library with interpretive information on Florida habitats, this 42-acre tract is crisscrossed with nature trails that lead out through hardwood forests to the "Window on Lake Ned" bird blind.

PARKS **Fort Meade Outdoor Recreation Area** (863-285-9562), US 98 east of the bridge, provides access to the Peace River for anglers and canoeists, a short nature trail along the river, sports facilities, and picnic pavilions; it also hosts a country music jamboree (fee) the second Saturday of every month.

Lake Kissimmee State Park (863-696-1112; www.floridastateparks.com/lake kissimmee), 14248 Camp Mack Rd. On the western shore of Lake Kissimmee, this vast state park encompasses prairies and oak hammocks, pine flatwoods and scrub, and is one of the top places for wildlife-watching in the state: In a single weekend here, I counted 26 deer, two caracaras, a box turtle, a flock of turkeys, alligators, several sandhill cranes, and numerous wading birds. Set up base camp at the campground (water and electric hookups) or hit the backpacking loops (16 miles of trail) for primitive camping. The park also has boat access to Lake Kissimmee, a marina and camp store, and a unique living history 1876 Cracker Cow Camp open on weekends. Fee.

West of Lakeland on US 92, **Saddle Creek County Park and Campground** (863-665-2283; www.saddlecreekpark.com) has a chain of former phosphate pits heavily stocked with fish to attract area anglers; tent and trailer campers will appreciate the simple but peaceful surroundings of the small campground. A 1.2-mile hiking trail follows Saddle Creek along the eastern edge of the park.

WILD PLACES Despite its name, the **Green Swamp** is not an extraordinarily wet place. Covering 860 square miles (including a large chunk of northern Polk County), it's the headwaters of four major rivers and a crucial natural resource for Central Florida, a place where rainfall percolates through flatwoods, sand-hills, and cypress domes to replenish the Floridan Aquifer, the state's primary freshwater resource. Along US 98 north of Lakeland, **Gator Creek Reserve** provides a place for a short walk out into this interesting melange of habitats; follow Rock Ridge Rd north from US 98 to Green Swamp West WMA for access to backpacking along the Florida Trail.

When the rest of Florida was under a few feet of water in Miocene times, long, thin dune-capped islands stood well above the waves—the **Lake Wales Ridge**. As a result, strange and unusual plant species evolved; the ridge has the highest concentration of rare and endangered plants in the continental United States. These are the "mountains" of peninsular Florida, rising up to 300 feet. Several preserves permit access on foot via hiking trails; tread gently. **Lake Wales Ridge State Forest** (863-635-7801; www.fl-dof.com/state_forests/lake_wales_ridge.html), 452 School Bus Rd, includes nearly 14,000 acres around Frost-proof, including the Arbuckle Tract with its 20-mile Florida Trail backpacking loop; several Polk County Environmental Lands provide access off CR 17, and The Nature Conservancy (863-635-7506) manages **Tiger Creek Preserve**, with trails off Pfundstein Rd in Babson Park and CR 630 south of Lake Wales.

I'm amazed at the rapid growth of the **Polk County Environmental Lands Program** (863-534-7377; www.polk-county.net) over the past several years, as

I've watched hiking trails open up on newly acquired public lands that still retain a rustic wilderness feel: A parking lot (and maybe a portable toilet) is all you get, but the trails are well marked with a map at the trailhead, and are perfect for day hikes. Dig through the Enviromental Lands Web site for a list; some of my favorites include **Crooked Lake Scrub**, **Hickory Lake Scrub**, **Lakeland Highlands Preserve**, and **Sumica**, but there are many, many more.

✷ Lodging

BED & BREAKFASTS

Auburndale 33823

Town Manor on the Lake (863-984-4008; www.townmanor.com), 585 FL 559. Live R. J. Straw's 1930s life of luxury in his historic home, where relaxation comes easy in the hammock on the screened back porch overlooking Lake Juliana, or swaddled in a soft robe in an even softer feather bed. Period furnishings and original fixtures accent the imported Brazilian hardwood floors and Italian tiled baths. Innkeeper Nandy makes you feel right at home with fresh lemonade and pastries on arrival; sit by the pool and watch the ducks waddle past, or keep an eye on the lake as a fellow guest comes in for a seaplane landing. I rate this as one of the top B&B experiences in Florida; I started referring my friends here the day after I arrived. The five rooms run $179–299, with romantic getaway, honeymoon, and ballooning packages available, and Wi-Fi and fax for an additional charge.

TOWN MANOR ON THE LAKE

Sandra Friend

Bartow 33830

The Stanford Inn (863-533-2393; www.thestanfordinn.com), 555 E Stanford St. Located in the historic district, this charming turn-of-the-20th-century neoclassical home was featured in the movie *My Girl* and is within a short walking distance of all the downtown shops and restaurants. Four rooms, a cottage, and a carriage house, decorated with antique beds, plush quilts, fireplaces, and romantic details, are available starting at $95 a night. The Victorian Rose Room features an 1855 wood-carved Victorian queen-sized bed, private bath, separate shower, and Jacuzzi. The carriage house and cottage have full kitchens. This is one of the few B&Bs with a pool, which is surrounded by a sundeck and lush tropical landscaping, so bring your beach towel.

HOTELS, MOTELS, AND RESORTS

Older motels with budget prices cluster around the interchange of US 27 and I-4 at Davenport and at US 98 and I-4 in Lakeland. Around many of the region's lakes, you'll find old-fashioned 1940s–1960s cottages and family motels along the major highways; they vary greatly as to quality.

Lake Wales 33898

The brand new 40-room **Liar's Lodge Motel** (1-800-243-8013; www.campmack.com/LiarsMotel.asp), 14900 Camp Mack Rd, is on the grounds of Camp Mack's River Resort (see *Fish Camps*) and has a rocking chair waiting for you. Quilted log-frame beds and wood furnishings give an outdoorsy feel to the rooms ($79); efficiencies ($89) include mini fridge, sink, and coffeemaker. It's built to standards for anglers, which means 60-foot parking spaces outside the door and electric hookup for your battery or live well. The motel is just up the road from Lake Kissimmee State Park, making it an excellent choice for hikers, kayakers, and wildlife watchers who don't like to camp.

Lakeland 33811

LeMans Suites (1-800-647-7929; www.lemanssuites.com), 1501 Shepherd Rd, south of downtown, offers furnished one-story apartments with all linens and housewares. Rates run $52–79, depending on size, amenities (whirlpool tubs available), and length of stay (2-day minimum, and rates drop as stay increases).

& ∞ In 1924, **The Lakeland Terrace Hotel** (863-688-0800 or 1-888-644-8400; www.terracehotel.com), 329 E Main St, a high-rise overlooking Lake Mirror, was at the top of its class—a year-round destination, a rarity in those days. Extensively renovated in 1998 to showcase its 1920s charm, the hotel offers 73 comfortable rooms and 15 suites ($189–209), each with a spacious desk with dataport, in-room safe, ironing board, and hair dryer, and what I truly needed after several days on the road: a soft robe and the best set of aromatherapy lotions and potions I've encountered in my travels, perfect for unwinding with a nice soak in the tub.

River Ranch 33867

Westgate River Ranch (1-800-785-2102; www.westgateriverranch.com), 24700 SR 60 E. Situated on 1,700 pristine acres on the Kissimmee River, this new and improved resort offers a main lodge, cabins, water-front town homes, and golf villas, with rates starting as low as $99. Most guests book in for a week or more, since there's plenty to do—airboat and swamp buggy rides, horseback riding, barbecue and hayride Friday and Saturday nights, American Championship Rodeo Saturday night featuring bull riding, barrel racing, and a kids calf scramble, river cruise/pontoon boat rides, trap and skeet range, petting farm, tennis and basketball courts, nine-hole golf course, swimming pool, pony rides, bike and golf cart rentals, catch-and-release fishing, guided nature walks Friday and Saturday afternoons, and hiking the Florida Trail, which passes through the resort, down to the historic Kicco ghost town. The resort also has a 5,000-foot lighted runway with future plans for airport houses and private hangars. On site, their Fisherman's Cove Restaurant serves breakfast, lunch, and dinner 7–9; there is also a snack bar, and their western saloon features local country bands every Friday and Saturday night.

Winter Haven 33384

🦐 Although it's an older motel, the **Lake Roy Beach Inn & Suites** (1-866-557-6994 or 863-324-6320; www.lakeroybeachinn.com), 1823 Cypress Gardens Blvd, has serious curb appeal—it overlooks sparkling Lake Roy and has a pool right on the lake. The spacious rooms are in great shape and have nice furnishings, with your choice of suites or single rooms for $78–118, including continental breakfast.

The Best Western Admiral's Inn (863-324-5950 or 1-800-247-2799; www.bestwesternadmiralsinn.com), 5665 Cypress Gardens Blvd, offers a variety of newly renovated and very classy deluxe rooms ($141 and up) with wood floors (perfect for those of us with allergies), Roman-style tubs, and chic furnishings. As they're in the midst of their changeover, traditional carpeted motel rooms ($81 and up) are available, too. The hotel adjoins Cypress Gardens, with some rooms looking out over the amusement park and botanical gardens.

VACATION HOMES 🐾 𝒜 ⬤ **Sunsplash Vacation Homes** (863-287-5846; www.sunsplash.com), off CR 54, Davenport. One of the cheapest ways to take the family on vacation is to rent one of the nearly 3,000 vacation homes in Central Florida. Sunsplash homes are individually owned and decorated by host families, who rent out these spacious, airy houses when they're not living in them. Each has a large full kitchen with all utensils and linens. Some include a screened pool, and smokers and pets can be accommodated. Rates start at $150 per day or $900 per week for a three-bedroom house, and the 75 units on this property are within a 30-minute drive of Disney World. There is an additional "departure fee" for cleaning of $65 and up.

FISH CAMPS

Haines City 33844
Jennings Resort (863-439-3811), 3600 Jennings Rd, off Canal Rd east

of Dundee. Anglers will love this century-old beauty spot with RV and tent spaces ($15–20) and concrete block cottages ($62–68) tucked under cabbage palms and oaks on the edge of sparkling blue Lake Pierce; a brand-new screened pool overlooks the expanse of the lake. On-site bait and tackle, fish-cleaning house, and camp store. Cottages have two beds, a small bath, and kitchenette, plus outdoor seating and grill. Book well in advance if you plan an in-season (Jan–Apr) visit.

Lake Wales 33898
Enjoy a bit of Old Florida recently "duded up" at **Camp Mack's River Resort** (863-696-1108; www.camp mack.com), 14900 Camp Mack Rd, a traditional Florida fish camp with easy access to Lake Kissimmee. Bring your RV and tuck it under the oaks ($36), rent a pretty log cabin or park model ($90–120), or take a room in the Liar's Lodge, a brand-new 40-room motel (see *Motels*).

Cherry Pocket Fish Camp (863-439-2031; www.cherrypocket.com), 3100 Canal Rd, is a 1947 classic on Lake Pierce, with 55 RV spots (mostly booked in snowbird season), eight old-time cabins, a marina, bait and tackle, and one of the best Old Florida restaurants (see *Eating Out*) you'll ever set foot inside. RV spots $22, cabins $60.

Off FL 60 just before the Kissimmee River bridge, **Grape Hammock Fish Camp** (863-692-1500; www.grape hammock.com), 1400 Grape Hammock Rd, offers direct access to both Lake Kissimmee and the Kissimmee River in a hammock shaded by ancient live oaks. Tent camping along the Lake Kissimmee shoreline is only $12, RV spaces $20–28, and cabins

$60–125; they have trailers for rent, too. A boat ramp lets you put in, and the small camp store has some basic supplies. Airboat trips and guided fishing available.

CAMPGROUNDS

Davenport 33836
Deer Creek RV Golf Resort (1-800-424-2931), 42749 US 27, is a massive campground with its own golf course and pleasant landscaping preserving natural pines. Paved spaces ($35 summer, $40 winter) have full hook-ups, and most winter visitors use golf carts to zip around the property. One- and two-bedroom park model units available, $55–75.

Right along I-4 at US 27, **Fort Summit KOA** (863-424-1880 or 1-888-562-4712; www.fortsummit.com), 2525 Frontage Rd, offers quick access to both corridors but lets you plan an affordable family outing. It's big—nearly 300 sites—and offers free shuttle service to Disney World. Sites $28–42, cabins $59–69.

Lakeland 33811
Saddle Creek Park (see *Parks*) offers an inexpensive place to camp in a natural setting not far from downtown Lakeland and I-4. Campsites $7, add $2 for electric, $2 for air conditioning (if you're running one, that is), and $5 for dump station. Maximum stay limited to 14 days per quarter.

✳ Where to Eat
DINING OUT

Lakeland
✿ **Antiquarian** (863-682-1059), 211 E Bay St. Fine art, smooth jazz, and good food, all set in a bold and playful former Studebaker showroom with

changing exhibits from Florida artists. Chef Gary Schmidt's French influence coaxes forth delightful lunches ($10 and up) and entrées (starting at $22) like shrimp and blue crab in caper-dill mayonnaise, Bay Street gumbo, salmon of the day, and roast duck confit in a raspberry-chili sauce with caramelized onion cilantro reduction. Leave room for a slice of lemon chess cake, two-layer chocolate torte, or any of the six dessert choices of the evening. Enjoy live jazz Sat evenings and a Saturday lunch lecture series.

Terrace Room (1-888-644-8400; www.terracehotel.com/terrace -dining.php), 329 E Main St. Gourmet taste buds will delight at the creative entrées ($18–32) like pan-seared ahi tuna and lavender-crusted lamb, which come accompanied by your choice of three different salads. Try the goat cheese salad, as I did, for an unexpected taste sensation of caramelized bananas and nuts with the baby greens and fried ball of cheese. Five entrées, including two steaks, are straight off the wood grill, the enticing aroma of which pervades the hotel's lobby. For picky eaters, they make a mean meatloaf. Finish off your meal with a delicate chocolate mousse served in a chocolate cup, or a house-special Key lime pie. Befitting the elegant surroundings, proper dress is required. Serving all meals daily; dinner reservations recommended.

Lake Wales
At **Chalet Suzanne** (863-676-6011 or 1-800-433-6011; www.chalet suzanne.com), 3800 Chalet Suzanne Dr, the Hinshaw family has been creating an aura of romance and culinary delights since 1931. Astronaut Jim

Irwin, a regular here, first brought their "Moon Soup" aboard Apollo 15, and it has been a staple on several flights since. Sit and relax while you gaze across Lake Suzanne as several varieties of turtles amuse you with their water "ballet." Classical music plays in the background, seemingly to their movements. Only two dishes are served at breakfast ($17), but it was still hard to decide—they were both so good. Scrambled eggs were touched with a bit of chives and accompanied by delicate Swedish pancakes served with real maple syrup, or in true Scandinavian style with wild lingonberries. A choice of baked ham or sausage patties completes this dish. Or you can have perfectly poached eggs Benedict with thinly sliced ham and homemade hollandaise, served on a puff pastry. Four-course luncheon entrées ($29–34) and traditional six-course dinners are an event in themselves ($59–79), with courses featuring their trademark broiled grapefruit, romaine soup, lemon ice, and artichoke salad as starters to your selection of entrée and dessert. Check the Web site for coupons. Open 7 days.

EATING OUT

Auburndale

In the heart of the historic downtown, **The Magnolia Tea Room & Gift Shop** (863-965-1684; www.magnolia tearoomandgiftshop.com), 212 Howard St, offers a touch of elegance. Lunches ($5–13) include sandwiches, soups, and salads, quiche of the day, cottage pie, and their trademark cheesy chicken crunch, a southern casserole topped with potato chips and served with potato salad. Coming in for tea? Order tea for one

or two (served with scones), or try a tidbit tray of assorted desserts. After lunch, visit the gift shop for a timeless treasure.

Bartow

With early-bird specials, all-you-can-eat crab legs, and all-you-can-drink draft beer nights, it's no wonder **Catfish Country** (863-646-6767), 2400 EF Griffin Rd (US 98 N), is always hopping. If you're hankering for catfish or gator, you'll find it here, served up with a Cajun flair.

Davenport

The Hotel Tea Room & Flower Corner (863-421-0827), 301 W Maple St. The Flower Corner is full of gifts and collectibles, home to ladies' Red Hat teas, and soon to be a bed & breakfast. The Hotel Tea Room offers an ever-changing menu. Lunch includes a selection of salads, an entrée, sourdough rolls, beverage, and dessert of the day. Afternoon tea served Mon–Fri, reservations requested.

Dundee

Melonie's Café (863-439-5416), 209 Main St. Open since 1987, this local establishment displays an eclectic bit of roadside Americana. And although there is no white-water rafting near Dundee, that won't stop Melonie or her stepsons from talking about their trips. Photos of their adventures—along with a kayak hung from the ceiling—encourage discussion. Lunch includes soups, salads, burgers, and sandwiches ($3 and up). Top the meal off with Natahalla Crunch, a hot fudge ice cream delight. Breakfast and lunch Mon–Sat.

Frostproof

🍴 An unassuming old-fashioned eatery, the **Frostproof Family**

Restaurant (863-635-6595), 133 S Scenic Hwy, has quite the following for breakfast or lunch. I stopped in after the rush and had a mighty fine burger and sweet tea, but their Family's Special Sandwich, a triple-decker club with grilled ham, chicken salad, tomato and mayonnaise, sure looked tempting. Open Mon–Sat, lunches $6–9, dinner entrées ($8–15) range from broiled steak tips to Alaskan snow crab legs, and include a super salad bar and side.

Haines City
Home of the original "slawburger," **Lawhorn's Corner Café** (863-421-2665), 115 N Sixth St, is a local institution, a family diner serving downhome vittles since 1948. Stop in for a big country breakfast or their famous burgers.

Lake Alfred
Part of Barn & Stable Antiques (see *Selective Shopping*), the **Back Porch Restaurant & Tea Room** presents a delightful picnic lunch 11–3 daily. Fill your basket with your choice of soup or salad, sandwich, and dessert, and you'll be served in the elegant garden room or outdoors on a porch overlooking a lily pond.

Gary's Oyster Bar & Seafood House (863-956-5055), 670 E US 17-92, is the oldest oyster bar in Polk County. The house-special platter represents Florida's aquatic bounty—fried catfish, shrimp, scallops, oyster, turtle, gator tail, and frog legs; I've enjoyed the broiled seafood sampler with snow crab, petite lobster tail, Gulf flounder, and sautéed scallops. Dinner served daily, $9–22.

Lavender & Lace Tearoom and Gift Shop (863-956-3998; www .lavenderandlacetearoom.com), 430 N

Lakeshore Way, is a proper Victorian tearoom serving upscale lunches ($9–10). It's decorated in grape and hyacinth arbors; one entire room is lined floor to ceiling with tea sets. But what caught my attention was the choice of eight desserts (starting at $4), including a three-layer Hummingbird Cake with bananas, nuts, pineapple, and cream cheese. Yum! Mon–Sat 11–3:30.

Lake Hamilton
❧ Grab a bite to eat at the **Gift Mill Grille** (863-439-5075), 823 US 27, inside the Gift Mill (see *Selective Shopping*), serving fresh food fast in a nostalgic setting. Massive salads, stews, and soups are served in freshly baked bread bowls; sandwiches come with your choice of fresh side and a crisp dill pickle. Order up a bottomless root beer from the old-fashioned soda fountain, and don't forget a scoop of homemade ice cream, like peppermint chocolate chip or sugarfree butter pecan. Lunch bowls and sandwiches cost $6–8; now open for steak and seafood dinners Mon–Thu until 8:30, Sat until 9. Lunch 11–3 on Sun. Their new coffee shop offers espresso and breakfast pastries starting at 7.

Lake Wales
❧ At **Cherry Pocket Seafood Shak**, Old Florida meets gourmet chef: When chef Rich Eten's father bought a funky 1947 fish camp (see *Fish Camps*), he convinced his Prudhomme-trained son to come along for the ride. And what a ride it is! Pull in the drive, and you'd assume it's a biker bar; the atmosphere is pure fish camp with a few dressy touches hidden inside. Dinner specials might include frog legs, mahi-mahi, or grouper, all prepared in Creole

fashion with lots of starches and sauces; my plate of Key West grouper held enough food for several meals. Entrées run $10–24, and it's not just seafood: You'll find filet mignon and steak Oscar, as well as lemon-pepper chicken and fettuccine dishes. It's hard to find, you'll wait for an hour or two on weekends, and the restrooms are up on the hill, but it's an experience you won't want to miss.

In the historic downtown, the **Stuart Avenue Café** (863-676-9000; www .historiclakewales.com/stuartcafe), 216 Stuart Ave, serves up freshly prepared meals with a menu that spans the globe—grab an Italian sub, a wet burrito (my fave), Irish Reuben with corned beef on bucket rye, a gyro, or an all-American burger for lunch ($6–8). Dinner is served after 4 and includes clams scampi over angelhair, shrimp Creole, osso buco, and more, $15–19.

Lakeland

Lakeland is where it all began for **Crispers** (863-682-7708; www .crispers.com), 217 N Kentucky Ave, a Florida chain that's a gourmet extension of Publix supermarkets, housed here in a historic setting. Creative soups, sandwiches, and salads like Thai fusion, Nicoise, and Greek are freshly made ($5 and up); don't miss the tasty fresh-baked mile-high carrot cake and specialty cheesecakes. Open daily, lunch and dinner.

I just plain love **Fred's Market Restaurant** (863-603-7080; www .fredsmarket.com), 2120 Harden Blvd, for good country cooking with only the freshest local produce. This is their second restaurant in the region (the original is on the grounds of the State Farmer's Market in nearby Plant City, see "Tampa Bay"). The

buffet spread is simply amazing, offering vegetarians a broad choice of creatively cooked veggies and for the rest of us, fabulous meatloaf, catfish, fried chicken, and more. Sure, you could order off the menu, but why bother? The buffets are $12 adult, $11 seniors. Open Mon–Sat 6:30–8:30, Sun 8–3.

The **Garden Bistro** (863-686-3332), 702 E Orange St, feels like an extension of adjacent Hollis Gardens, with hand-painted ivy on the interior walls, garden tables and benches to dine at, and outdoor seating overlooking Lake Mirror's promenade. Open for breakfast and lunch, the restaurant's menu reflects creativity and simplicity, with selections like Belgian waffles, sushi salad, hummus pita, and pretzel-wrapped franks.

Harry's Seafood Bar & Grille (863-686-2228), 101 N Kentucky Ave, is one of those perennial Florida chains you'll find in other downtowns; in Lakeland, the New Orleans party atmosphere is infectious. I was unable to finish a heaping order (three!) of pan-seared crab cakes with creamy smashed potatoes, but I still had to try a slice of Lulu's Louisiana Mud Pie: It was heaven for this chocoholic. Open for lunch and dinner, entrées and platters $8 and up.

The aroma will lead you straight to **Jimbo's Pit BBQ** (863-683-3777), 1215 E Memorial Blvd (US 92), serving Lakeland since 1964. Savor tender, real pit barbecue for reasonable prices ($4 and up) for lunch and dinner—if you don't fill up on the free bowl of kosher dills and hot cherry peppers on your picnic table first!

JJ's Cafe (863-683-5267), 132 S Kentucky Ave, offers fresh salads, char-grilled sandwiches, burgers, quesadillas, subs, wraps, and panini in a relaxed downtown atmosphere, $5–9. Stop in for a muffin and coffee in the morning, or enjoy a fresh steak sandwich (neatly trimmed sirloin tips, no less!) for lunch.

At the **Rib House** (863-687-8260), 2918 S Florida Ave, it's like eating with family—the waitresses know the regulars, and everyone banters about what's up with whom. I stopped in for breakfast and was blown away by their creative rendition of stuffed French toast (a special that day). The extensive breakfast menu runs $3–8 for eggs, omelets, scramblers, sandwiches, and pancakes and French toast; lunch and dinner focus on barbecue and deli favorites. Open daily at 7.

Since 1947, the **Silver Ring Café** (386-687-3283), 106 N Tennessee Ave, has been Lakeland's home of authentic Cuban sandwiches. Try the mini, regular, or special ($4–5) and a hot devil crab roll on the side.

Polk City

The **Compass Rose Diner** at Fantasy of Flight (see *Attractions*), takes you back to a 1940s airport commissary, with a display case full of tempting pies and the availability of fresh milkshakes affecting your menu choice right off the bat: Will it be burgers, salads, or sandwiches, with your choice of fries or soup? Open 11–3 daily, $6 and up.

Winter Haven

Since 1951, **Andy's Drive-In Restaurant** (863-293-0019), 703 Third St, has been a local landmark for sweet treats and American comfort food—burgers, dogs, slaw, fries ($2–5), and in the evenings they serve catfish, shrimp, scallops, and oysters ($5–8) in heaping servings with veg-

etables. Breakfast served 9–11 for under $4.

No matter what you choose at **El Norteño** (863-298-0993), 1925 Sixth St NW, it'll be great; I loved the enchiladas here. Serving authentic Mexican food and drinks in a casual atmosphere: burritos, enchiladas, tacos, and platters for $6–14 (dinner) and $4–6 (lunch).

Tsunami Sushi (863-293-2395), 317 W Central Ave, is a five-star downtown sushi bar with a bistro feel. Order sushi rolls, or try sashimi and tempura platters; items can be ordered à la carte. Open for dinner.

BAKERIES, COFFEE SHOPS, DELIS, AND ICE CREAM

Bartow

A sign posted inside **The Cookie Jar Bake Shop** (863-519-3333), 305 E Main St, proclaims A BALANCED DIET IS A COOKIE IN EACH HAND, and they have a great selection available, including snickerdoodles and First Lady Laura Bush's own cowboy cookies. But they are most famous for their wedding and specialty cakes. Try a slice of the red velvet or lemon coconut with lemon curd. The attrac-

BARTOW'S COOL SHOPPE

Sandra Friend

tive retro café, with the large mural of Main St on the back wall, also serves a light lunch ($4–8)—"croissantwiches" in two sizes, or chicken or ham and cheese in spinach or sun-dried tomato wraps. Barnie's coffee coolers, cappuccino, and flavored coffees are also offered.

Take a break from the heat at the popular **Cool Shoppe Ice Cream** (863-533-1635), 135 S Central Ave, where 24 flavors come in a National Historic Register building wrapper, with tin ceilings and terrazzo floors. They serve some lunch items, but ice cream's the thing! Open until 8 PM.

Frostproof

I love the name! **Frostbite** (863-635-4222), 801 Scenic Hwy N, is a genuine 1950s ice cream stand with hamburgers and hot dogs, too.

Lakeland

ᵀ **Black and Brew** (863-682-1210; www.blackandbrew.com), 205 E Main St, has that hip urban feel, and is a gathering place where friends sip latte and chat politics. Their menu includes unusual twists like the spicy Thai peanut panini; sandwiches and salads, $3–7.

🐾 Mountains of ice cream await at the **Main Street Creamery** (863-683-0105), 128 E Main St, where the menu includes creations ($4–5) like The Architect, teetering with scoops of Hershey's Ice Cream and assorted syrups. There are only a few booths in this original ice cream parlor, but most folks take their amply stuffed cones ($2–5) with them. Serving lunch items, too—subs, burgers, dogs, and classic deli sandwiches, $3–7.

ᵀ Kick back at **Mitchell's Coffee House** (863-680-2944), 235 N Kentucky Ave, with a cup of coffee and a muffin in the morning, or a "create your own" deli sandwich in the afternoon ($5–7, 11–2) and a plate of their luscious four-cheese macaroni. Specialty coffees include Almond Joy and I Dream of Jeannie; try one with a slice of Coca-Cola cake.

Winter Haven

Andy's Igloo at Andy's Drive In (see *Eating Out*) is a walk-up window serving the sweetest treats this side of Lakeland, with 12 flavors of milkshakes (fruit salad, pineapple, and butterscotch among them) and ice cream treats and cones with your choice of Grandma's homemade fruit toppings. Until 11 PM Mon–Sat.

✳ Selective Shopping

Auburndale

International Market World (941-665-0062; www.intlmarketworld.com), 1052 US 92 W, an enormous flea market and auction at the US 17-92 junction, has a large covered building bustling with excitement every weekend as more than 800 vendors set out their wares. It's also home to Genesis Zoological & Wildlife Rehabilitation Center (see *Zoological Parks*), and hosts concerts and festivals; check the Web site. Open Fri–Sun 8–4.

Bartow

Poke around downtown Bartow for antiques: go to **Apple Seeds** (863-533-6400), 115 E Main St, for country gifts, furniture, and a great Christmas display. The two-story circa-1893 brick structure at 125 S Central Ave houses **Chinoiserie Antiques** (863-534-8534), 110 W Broadway, but it was used as Lovett's Grocery for 20 years, then Lizzie Epperson's Millinery from 1913 until 1939. **Thom Downs Antiques** (863-519-

0395; www.thomdownsantiques.com),
750 E Main St, has garden accessories
and fountains alongside classy European antique furnishings.

Dundee
Southern Comfort Antiques (863-
439-4944), 29119 US 27 N, houses a
couple of dozen antiques and collectibles dealers in 4,000 square feet
of air-conditioned comfort.

Haines City
South by Southwest Innovations
(863-419-1056; www.sbyswest
innovations.com), 600 E Hinson Ave.
When Jan Bowen moved back to
Florida from Taos, she brought the
Southwest she loved with her. Native
American originals—hand-painted
pottery, sculpture, ceremonial rat-
tles—fill the nooks of this expansive
shop, the largest southwestern outlet
in Florida.

Lake Alfred
**Barn Antiques and The Stable
Gifts** (863-956-2227; www.barn
antiques.biz), FL 557 at FL 557A.
Since 1970, this rambling collection of
red buildings on a family ranch has
housed one of the best-kept shopping
secrets in Florida—the quality
antique furnishings here are cheaper
than buying new from most furniture
stores! In addition to chairs, tables,
love seats, and armoires, you'll find
classic stained glass, two gift shops
with home decor items (one seasonal,
the other Far Eastern in tone), a
nursery, and the Back Porch Restaurant & Tea Room (see *Eating Out*).
Take your time and browse a while;
this is one place I'd drive out of my
way for.

At **Biggar Antiques** (863-956-4853;
www.biggarantiques.com), 140 W
Haines Blvd, everything is bigger—

this 40-year-old family business is the
home of huge advertising items, like
Pop-Tarts boxes you could crawl into
and giant Bayer Aspirin bottles. Great
selection of advertising signs and
posters, too!

Gourmet goodies abound at **Potpourri Antiques** (863-956-5535), 144
W Haines Blvd, where seasonal gift
items accent glassware, dishes, and
home decor.

Lake Hamilton
In the two small cottages at **Century
Cottage Antiques & Gifts** (863-439-
0203), 29890 US 27, browse through
the well-kept rooms for great prices
on blue lace glass, Victorian lamps,
jewelry, and furnishings.

Gift Mill Grille (see *Eating Out*). It's
hard to believe this place started as a
clothing manufacturing company's
outlet store. Since 1992, the shop has
exploded in size, and is stocked with
everything from fur coats to wind
chimes, chocolate-covered blueberries, creative cookbooks, and, yes,
Exclusively Pegi Goff clothing, with
the original design appliqués manu-
factured on site.

Lake Wales
Local and national artists' work can be
purchased in the fine arts and crafts
gift shop at the **Lake Wales Arts
Center** (see *Art Galleries*).

It's at **Chalet Suzanne** (see *Dining
Out*) that you'll find ceramicist Boz
creating colorful ceramic soup dishes
in the Norwegian style. The famed
"Moon Soup" is served on his creations in the restaurant. Wander
around the grounds; many famous
celebrity autographs can be found in
the sunken Autograph Garden.
Browse through the gift shop inside
the inn's lobby or stroll down the

brick walkway to the soup cannery, where you can go on a free guided tour, complete with soup and sauce sampling. Open daily.

Historic Downtown Lake Wales (www.historiclakewales.com; see *Historic Sites* and *Special Events*) will take you back to the 1920s with vintage shops and eclectic eateries. For rare books or forgotten decorating accents, stop by **Bittersweet Memories** (863-676-4778), 247 E Park Ave. Pick out a new bauble at **B S D Galleries** (863-679-2787), 208 E Stuart Ave. You'll find a nice variety of antiques and collectibles at **Inglenook Antiques** (863-678-1641), 3607 N Scenic Hwy (FL 17), which also sells herbal products and alternative-health books in a quaint pre-1920s home.

Lakeland

At **Brooke Pottery** (863-688-6844; www.brookepottery.com), 223 N Kentucky Ave, I was swept away by the sensual shapes and bold colors of this functional art—but then, I'm a sucker

LAKELAND'S DOWNTOWN SHOPPING DISTRICT

Sandra Friend

for pottery. This fine craft shop is the cornerstone of the downtown shopping district, a mainstay for 15 years, filled with beautiful items like raku fish, witch balls, and spoons carved from wild cherry.

Lloyds of Lakeland (863-682-2787), 301 N Kentucky Ave, offers two floors stuffed with antiques and collectibles, including an incredible collection of glass: Fenton, cobalt, ruby, pressed, and more.

For more than 50 years, **Nathan's Men's Store** (863-682-2811), 221 E Main St, has been the place to go for men to look their best. Debonair chapeaus, classy slacks, dressy dinner jackets, tuxedo rental, even a Boy Scout section—it's all here. Open Mon–Sat.

The fine mahogany tables at **Peacock Antiques** (863-686-7947), 234 N Kentucky Ave, look like they've been set for dinner, with curios, tea sets, and classic glassware.

East of downtown Lakeland, look for **Second Hand Rose** (863-665-0755), 600 S Combee Ave, where dealer booths contain retro toys, old Florida postcards, glassware, and other ephemera; radio-controlled model airplanes take up one corner of the first floor.

Winter Haven

Andy Thornal Expedition Outfitter (863-299-9999 or 1-800-499-9890; www.andythornal.com), 336 Magnolia Ave SW. Whether you're planning a backpacking trip on the Florida Trail or looking for technical clothes and lures for your next fishing trip, this is the place to come: Their selection encompasses all outdoor sports, and they run fly-casting and fly-tying schools.

Filling two floors of a 1928 country store and gas station, **Antique Mall Village** (863-293-5618), 3170 US 17 N, is a local landmark, a favorite for antiques shoppers since 1977 and complete with its own haunt: the ghost of an owner who died while counting the day's receipts. Mountains of saltshakers, piles of paintings, brass and tin and aluminum items, advertising signs, record albums—you name it, it's here. Closed Sun.

Classic Collectibles & Antiques (863-294-6866), 279 W Central Ave, is a sprawling complex of dealer booths with a nice selection of art glass and collectible glassware (Carnival, Fenton, Depression, and ruby) as well as unique furnishings like a circa-1790 deacon's bench in English oak.

You can't miss **Sherman's Antiques** (863-224-0395; www.shermans antiques.net), 2750 US 17 N. It'll delight the inner child with toys from your past (or mine, at least) like tin cars, windup walkers, Chatty Cathy, and Holly Hobbie; some of the wares are displayed on a 200-year-old ox yoke table. Bring your dolls for careful repair at the doll hospital.

CITRUS STANDS AND FARMER'S MARKETS During the winter citrus season, expect to see roadside fruit sellers along US 27 and SR 60 with temporary stands and pickup trucks.

Auburndale
Walker Groves (1-800-887-1253), 580 FL 559. With citrus groves and pine forests perched above Lake Juliana, the Walker family has one of the most historic orange stands in the state: They've been handing out samples of fresh-squeezed orange juice since 1884. Stop by for a sample and walk away with a bagful of fresh fruit.

Davenport
Webb's Candy (863-422-1051 or 1-800-289-9322; www.citruscandy.com), 250 US 27 S. Open daily 9:30–6:30. Call for tour information. Florida's oldest citrus-packing and candy factory was started in the 1920s by two friends, Miss Blogett and Miss Stilman, who still live nearby. Their unique recipe for "citrus candies" is the same one used today by the Webb family. Paul and Nadine Webb, no strangers to candy making, brought with them over 100 chocolate and fudge recipes, including their silky goat's-milk fudge. Take a tour of the candy factory, where the yummy confections are still made by hand in the original copper kettles and water-welled cooled tables. Free gift wrapping. Shipping available.

Dundee
Davidson of Dundee (863-687-3869 or1-800-654-0647; www.davidsonof dundee.com), US 27. Open daily. Watch while citrus candy, chocolates, marmalades, and jellies are made right in the factory kitchen. Then sample such fresh delights as pecan orangettes, creamy nougat, and Key lime truffles. Shop the enormous gift store for fresh citrus (in-season), attractive candy baskets, and marmalades. Shipping available.

Fruitree Fruit Shop (863-439-1396), US 27. Fruits, candies, and Florida souvenirs all at a great price. This is the place for authentic cypress-knee crafts. Cypress roots can no longer be harvested, so these will soon become rare. Beautiful cypress clocks $10–150.

Haines City
At the **Haines City Farmers Market** (863-421-3773), amble around

Railroad Park on Wed 8–5 to choose from fresh local produce, baked goods, and craft items. The **Orange Ring** (863-422-1938), 35969 US 27, featuring Indian River citrus, has been a local fixture since the 1970s— I remember stopping there for fruit on the way home from Cypress Gardens.

Lakeland

Since 1949, **Dereus Groves** (863-688-8893 or 1-800-311-7455; www .dereusgroves.com), 510 N Florida Ave, has been a fixture in downtown, selling local produce by the bag along with all the classic accoutrements— juice, souvenirs, jelly and marmalade, and gourmet Florida foods. They ship citrus, too.

Selling produce from a little green shed since 1979, **Pam's Fruit Stand** (863-647-3695), 434 Pipkin St, carries seasonal regional fruits and veggies like collard greens, pumpkins, and strawberries from nearby Plant City; open 8–6.

Lake Wales

Local produce farmers and students from Roosevelt School offer quality fruits, vegetables, and herb plants at the **MarketPlace** in Historic Downtown Lake Wales (see *Historic Places*) each Fri 8–2.

Winter Haven

Pinecrest Farms (863-293-6518), 2750 US 17 N, sells fresh organic produce and herbs.

✴ Entertainment

Since 1978, the **Lake Wales Little Theatre, Inc**. (863-676-1266; www .lwlt.org), 411 N Third St, Lake Wales, has been in continuous operation, bringing high-quality entertainment to patrons from near and far away. Tickets $12 adults, $9 under 18.

Affordable, quality live theater can be found at the **Lakeland Community Theatre** (863-603-7529; www.lake landcommunitytheatre.com), Lake Mirror Center Theatre, 121 S Lake Ave, Lakeland, established in 1984. Productions include well-known musicals, comedies, and Pulitzer Prize–winning dramas. $20 and up.

One of the last remaining themed theaters in the United States, the **Polk Theatre** (863-682-7553; www .polktheatre.org), 127 S Florida Ave, Lakeland, has that grand cinema magic lacking nowadays in the multi-screen cineplex; after all, the Munchkins danced here on the 50th anniversary of *The Wizard of Oz*! Seats slope gently down to the red-velvet-curtained stage; the balcony section has twinkling stars overhead. Films, primarily independent productions, are shown on weekends ($6 adults, $4 students, $3 children), with a slate of live performances running Nov–Apr, when you can catch performers like Roger Williams, Bea Arthur, the Coasters, and the Royal Shakespeare Company.

Theatre Winter Haven (863-294-SHOW; www.theatrewinterhaven .com) at Chain O'Lakes Park offers at least six quality stage productions— musicals, plays, and dramatic readings—every season. Performances run Thu–Sun evenings; individual tickets $20.

✴ Special Events

The "Polkpourri" of festivals and events throughout the county include several art exhibitions, antiques shows, and heritage festivals.

January: **Festival of the Buffalo Pow Wow** (863-665-0062; www .intlmarketworld.com), International Market World, 1052 W US 92, Auburndale. Experience the heritage and culture of Native Americans at this 3-day celebration of traditional food, arts, crafts, dance, drumming, dancing, storytellers, and live buffalo. Special events for children on Fri 9–2. Fee.

Alafia River Rendezvous—Visitor Days (863-965-0386; www.florida frontiersmen.org), Homeland. Just south of Bartow, where mountain men once met to trade wares, this pre-1840 living history event features food vendors, shooting competitions, knife throwing, and more. $6.

February: **Annual Mardi Gras Festival** (863-638-2686; www.lakewales mardigras.com), Lake Wales. This annual event is on the Saturday prior to Fat Tuesday and features musical entertainment, gala balls, and a colorful parade through Historic Downtown Lake Wales.

Annual Lake Wales Fine Arts Show, the Lake Wales Arts Center (863-676-8426; www.lakewalesarts center.org), 1099 SR 60 E. This annual arts show, nearly 40 years running, hosts more than 24,000 visitors. Fine art and entertainment on the shores of Lake Wales.

April: **Bloomin' Arts Festival** (863-644-4907 or 863-533-2600; www .bartowchamber.com), 1240 E Main St, Bartow. One of Florida's premier arts shows, drawing some of the finest artists throughout Florida and the Southeast. Brought to you by the Bartow Art Guild, this spring arts and flower show exhibits the works of 175 artists and craftspeople and offers a student art exhibit, quilt show, antique car show, food, and more.

More than 35 years old, the weeklong **Sun 'n Fun Fly In** (863-644-2431; www.sun-n-fun.org) held in early Apr at the Florida Air Museum, Lakeland (see *Museums*), is the second-largest general aviation event of its kind in the world. Expert aviators and eager participants fly in from more than 80 countries to exchange information via more than 400 forums, seminars, and workshops on aviation. Some 500 commercial exhibitors strut their wares, and daily air shows entertain the throng of more than 600,000 visitors during the week. If you love aviation, everything you ever wanted to learn is here—don't miss it!

October: **Crickette Club Annual Halloween Parade & Carnival** (863-534-0120; www.bartowchamber .com), IMC Park, Bartow. This old-fashioned fall event has been around since 1941 and is one of the largest costumed events in Central Florida.

Fall Festival (863-421-3773), Historic Railroad Park, Haines City. Crafts, food, entertainment, children's costume contest, and auction.

Cracker Story Telling Festival (863-284-4268), Homeland Heritage Park, Bartow. Polished storytellers weave tall tales of Florida history at this fun and educational event. Walk the grounds while local musicians fill the air with Florida folk music. Food vendors and crafters. Cracker whip contest on Sat. $6 adults, $4 children.

Annual Pioneer Days (863-678-4209). A celebration of Lake Wales history at the Depot Museum and around Lake Wales. Historical reenactments and antique car parade along South Scenic Hwy (US Alt 27), with lots of crafts, artisans, food, and entertainment.

Annual Downtown Bartow Winter Craft Fair (863-533-7125 or 863-534-4030; www.bartowchamber.com). This outgrowth of the Bloomin' Arts Festival has over 160 craft booths, produce, plants, children's activities, and food, helping you get an early start on holiday shopping.

Quilts and Tea (863-419-4797), Davenport Historic District. Throughout the historic district, the Heart & Sew Quilters of Davenport features more than 100 antique quilts and their history. Certified quilt appraiser on-site. Call in advance for tickets ($7) to the afternoon tea or brunch.

The Lake Wales Ridge Folk Art Festival (863-676-4778), the Market-Place in Historic Downtown Lake Wales (see *Historic Sites*), celebrates American music with live bluegrass, country, and gospel. You'll find traditional crafts, food, and old-fashioned children's games, and at night everyone joins in the fun at the Evening Circle Dance.

November–January: **City Lights—Cypress Nights**, a countywide holiday lighting festival, is an annual tradition throughout Polk County. Each town has its own lighting theme. Auburndale is the city of wreaths; Bartow, the city of nostalgia; Davenport, the city of holly; Dundee, the city of friends; Eagle Lake, the city of mistletoe; Fort Meade, the city of trees; Frostproof, the city of snowflakes; Haines City, the city of angels; Lake Alfred, Toyland; Lake Wales, the city of bells; Lakeland, the city of swans; Mulberry, a winter wonderland; Polk City, the city of deer; and Winter Haven, the city of poinsettias. Take in the lights in Bartow from a 42-seat horse-drawn wagon or play in the snow in Haines City.

Christmas at Pinewood (863-676-1408; www.boksanctuary.org), Historic Bok Sanctuary (see *Historic Sites*). Tour includes Bok Sanctuary admission. All 20 rooms in the 1930s Mediterranean Revival mansion are lavishly decorated in the spirit of Christmas.

December: **Seasonal Carillon Music** (863-676-1408; www.boksanctuary .org), Bok Tower Gardens (see *Historic Sites*). Holiday songs played on the 60-bell carillon at half-hour intervals. Includes admission to Bok Tower Gardens.

Life of Christ Passion Play (863-676-9300), 970 Passion Play Rd, Lake Wales. The birth of Jesus Christ, the baptism of John the Baptist, and more is performed live with spectacular costumes, lighting, and special effects on one of the largest sets in the country. Order tickets early, as this one sells out fast. $20 adults, $15 children. Group rates available.

Parade of Trees (863-533-7125), Polk County Historical Museum, Old Courthouse Bldg, Bartow. $1 adults, free to children 12 and under. Visitors—not trees—parade down Candy Cane Lane among beautifully decorated Christmas trees. Vote for your favorite themed tree by placing "A Penny for Your Thoughts" in the jingling penny jar in front of each tree.

Glitter, Glisten and Snow (863-421-3773), Historic Railroad Park, Haines City. The city transforms into a magical winter wonderland, including a mountain of snow to play in! This flurry of an event is free and features chestnuts, cider, cookies, entertainment, and Santa.

LAKE COUNTY

C entral Florida's sparkling lakes provide a natural backdrop to small towns and villages scattered across the gently rolling Central Highlands. The name is no misnomer: Lake County has more than 1,000 lakes, many renowned for their bass fishing. During the post–Civil War Reconstruction period, settlers streamed into Central Florida, eager to nab land grants. Named the seat of Lake County in 1872, **Astatula** was founded on the shores of Little Lake Harris. But the subsequent shift of population to the railroad corridor forced the county seat to move to its present location, **Tavares**, on the western shore of Lake Dora. Established on a knoll on the eastern shore of **Lake Dora**, the 1880s village of Royellou became Mount Dora, named for Dora Ann Drawdy, its first permanent homesteader. Its growth, fueled by early steamboat traffic, accelerated after the first steam train pulled into town. Known as Florida's antiques capital, Mount Dora retains that turn-of-the-20th-century feel—and has hilly streets reminiscent of a New England village. Unexpectedly hilly, thanks to ancient sinkholes turned to lakes, **Clermont** saw its first residents in 1884; the historic district is now off the beaten path (FL 50) at Eighth St. **Leesburg** dates back to 1853, and its history is reflected in its charming downtown.

As in much of Florida, developers shaped the modern landscape. After devastating freezes in the 1980s, the sweet fragrance of orange blossoms in spring was replaced by a carpet of nearly treeless subdivisions and landscaped retirement villages along US 27 around Clermont and **Lady Lake**. In the early 1900s, developers in on the Florida land boom created genteel lakeside communities like **Howey-in-the-Hills** and **Eustis**. While Eustis is small, it has a gorgeous turn-of-the-20th-century downtown, accentuated by the beauty of lakeside Ferran Park; Magnolia Ave forms the core of its downtown district. **Umatilla** shows off its heritage as a citrus town—not only are the lakes still surrounded by orange groves, but a large citrus-packing plant dominates the town as well. Umatilla is the gateway to the Ocala National Forest. To the west of Clermont, the towns of **Groveland** and **Mascotte** grew up around cattle ranching on the fringe of the vast Green Swamp, and Groveland retains that frontier-town feel. **GUIDANCE** The **Lake County Visitor's Center**, 20763 US 27, sits on the west side of US 27 between Leesburg and Clermont, near Florida's Turnpike; open 8–5 daily, offering free orange juice and lots of helpful information. In Mount

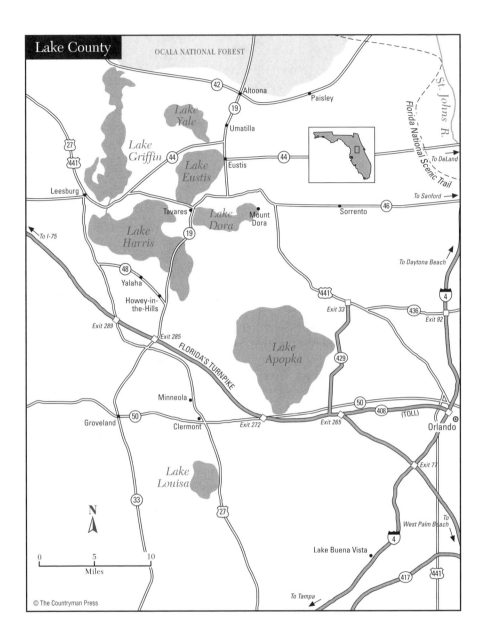

Lake County

Dora, stop in the old ACL railroad station, now the **Mount Dora Chamber of Commerce**, for flyers on local accommodations and shops. You may also contact Lake County Economic Development & Tourism (1-800-798-1071, www.lake countyfl.com), 315 W Main St, Tavares 32778.

GETTING THERE *By car:* **US 441**, **US 27**, **FL 19**, and **FL 33** provide north–south access through most of Lake County's communities; **Florida's Turnpike** has two Lake County exits near Leesburg and Clermont.

By air: **Orlando International Airport** provides the closest commuter service for Lake County.

By bus: **Greyhound** (352-787-4782) stops at 1006 S 14th St and US 27 in Leesburg.

PARKING In addition to plenty of street parking and small municipal lots throughout **Mount Dora**, there's covered parking at the end of Donnelly Street by the railroad tracks; all free and unlimited in time. **Clermont** offers free street parking with 2-hour limits, as does **Eustis**; find one of the small surface lots if you want to park longer.

PUBLIC RESTROOMS A rare find in Florida, but Lake County has them. In **Mount Dora**, they're in Childs Park, adjacent to the railroad depot; in downtown **Clermont**, at the corner of Minneola and Eighth St.

MEDICAL EMERGENCIES Major hospitals include **Florida Hospital Waterman** (352-253-3388; www.fhwat.org), US 441, Tavares, and **Leesburg Regional Medical Center** (352-323-5762), 600 E Dixie Ave, Leesburg.

✳ To See

ART GALLERIES

Eustis

Lake Eustis Museum of Art (352-357-4952; www.lakeeustismuseumofart.org), 113 N Bay St. Local artists shine in this public venue that hosts traveling art exhibits, showcases fine arts from its permanent collection, and holds quarterly juried art competitions. Open Mon–Sat noon–4. Drawn from the collections of the Lake Eustis Museum of Art, the **City Hall Gallery of Art** is open to the public during business hours, Mon–Fri 8–5. Both galleries are free; donations appreciated.

Mount Dora

Mount Dora Center for the Arts (352-383-0880; www.mountdoracenterfor thearts.org), 138 E Fifth Ave. Regional art and cultural center presenting rotating monthly exhibits in the gallery and sculpture garden, and well known for their annual arts festival. The center sponsors 4th Thursdays May–Aug, with tastings, live music, and artistic demonstrations in the evenings. Open and staffed by volunteers Mon–Fri 10–4, Sat 10–2.

ATTRACTIONS The Citrus Tower (352-394-4061; www.citrustower.com), 141 N US 27, still stands high above Clermont, but the view just isn't what it was when I first took the elevator to the top in the 1960s. On a clear day, you have great vistas of Lakes Apopka, Louisa, and Minneola, but the rolling sandhills topped with blossoming orange trees are now carpeted in rooftops of subdivisions. Just marking their 50th anniversary, this classic attraction showcases a history museum on their Web site. Open 9–6 Mon–Thu, 9–7 Fri–Sat; fee. At the base of the tower, the **National House of Presidents** (352-394-2836), 123 N US 27, showcases the "White House in Miniature," a scale model, and rooms thickly packed with presidential paraphernalia for $10 adults, $5 children.

GHOST TOWNS Five miles east of Eustis, the town of **Seneca** once had hotels, churches, a sawmill, and orange groves. During the Seminole Wars, an army payroll was supposedly hidden near the springs and never recovered.

HISTORIC SITES Most of Lake County's cities are historic districts—visit downtown Clermont, Eustis, Leesburg, Mount Dora, and Tavares for a taste of Florida between the 1890s and 1920s. In Mount Dora the **McDonald Stone House**, circa 1883, is a beautiful home on the corner of Seventh Ave and McDonald St. The **Community Congregational Church** is Mount Dora's oldest place of worship, dating back to 1887. In 1893, Pittsburgh native John P. Donnelly moved to Mount Dora and built an imposing Queen Anne Victorian (Donnelly St, between Fifth and Sixth Aves) that now houses the **Masonic Temple**. In downtown Leesburg, the **Mote-Morris House** (352-315-1800; www.leesburgflorida .gov/history/mote_morris.aspx) 1195 W Magnolia St, is of special note, built in 1892 for Leesburg's eight-term mayor Edward H. Mote. With its turrets and bay windows, it's an excellent example of late-era Victorian architecture. While it is primarily used for civic functions and weddings, the home is open for public tours on the second and fourth Sat of each month from 10–2, free.

HISTORIC TOURS Departing the Lakeside Inn (see *Lodging*), the **Mount Dora Road Trolley** (352-357-9123) offers narrated 1-hour historic tours, $10.75 adults, $8.75 children. Closed Sun.

MUSEUMS

Altoona
✔ **McTureous Homestead and Museum**, FL 19. This little Cracker homestead called Aunt Bessie's Place was the childhood home of Private Robert McTureous Jr., who received a USMC Medal of Honor during World War II. The adjacent park has picnic tables and a playground.

Eustis
✔ At the genteel Clifford House, an 18-room National Historic Landmark from 1910, the **Eustis Historical Museum** (352-483-0046; www.eustishistorical museum.com), 536 N Bay St, sits on the shores of Lake Eustis and surprises you with its contents, such as the only independently housed citrus museum in the state of Florida—celebrating a time when Eustis was the "Orange Capital of the World," and an extensive exhibit on Dr. Edgar Banks, billed as the "original Indiana Jones." Dr. Banks was a professor and archeologist, the first to search for the Ark of the Covenant, and after many storied adventures he retired to Eustis in 1921. Open Mon–Fri 1–5 and the first Sat of each month 12–4. Free; donations appreciated.

Groveland
When the ribbon was cut on July 4, 2007, Groveland celebrated the grand opening of the **Groveland Historical Museum** (352-429-4521; www.groveland history.org), 243 S Lake Ave, which focuses on preserving local history in this cattle and citrus outpost and delves deeply into the history of Groveland High School. Open 11–1 on Sat, free.

Lady Lake

Born from the former Austin Carriage Museum, the new nonprofit **Florida Carriage Museum & Resort** (352-750-5550; www.fcmr.org), 3000 Marion County Rd, Weirsdale, has as its mission "To educate, celebrate and preserve the history of the horse and its role in shaping world civilizations and changing lives." With more than 150 classic horse carriages ranging from an 1850 Arm-bruster dress chariot owned by Emperor Franz Joseph of Austria to a World War I horse-drawn supply wagon, it's one of the world's most elaborate collection of carriages, and you can experience history yourself on a carriage ride around the 400-acre estate. Open Tue–Sat 10–4, Sun 12–4; $10 adults, $5 ages 5–18.

In the small, historic train depot downtown, the **Lady Lake Historical Society and Museum** (352-753-1159), 107 S Old Dixie Hwy, packs in details about the town's past, from the railroad days to the citrus industry and local Civil War connections. Now surrounded by The Villages, this small town is a piece of old Florida where the history is real, unlike the saga of "Spanish Springs" proffered by its nearby neighbor. Open Tue 9–12 and Sat 11–3; free.

Leesburg

In the historic Women's Club Building, the **Leesburg Heritage Society and Museum** (352-365-0053; www.leesburgflorida.gov/history/museum.aspx), 111 S Sixth St, overflows with ephemera recounting the history of Leesburg, from citrus packing to classic hotels and the annual Watermelon Festival. Open Mon–Fri 9–4:30, free.

Mount Dora

Mount Dora Museum of Speed (352-385-1945; www.classicdreamcars.com), 206 N Highland St, showcases a private collection of automobile memorabilia and classic muscle cars. Open 10–5 Mon–Fri, $9; admittance available for groups of two or more.

At the **Mt. Dora History Museum** (352-383-0006), 450 Royellou Lane, learn the history of Mount Dora, as presented in the old city jail by the local historical society. Thu–Sat 1–4; fee.

Tavares

✎ The **Lake County Historical Museum** (352-343-9600; www.lakecountyfl.gov/historical_museum), 317 W Main St, covers everything from ghost towns to giant alligators, and is the home of the Annual Pickle Festival (see *Special Events*). Exhibits on regional history rotate through the museum on a regular basis, so there is always something new to see. Open Mon–Fri 8:30–5, free.

A CAMARO Z28 AT THE MOUNT DORA MUSEUM OF SPEED
Courtesy Lake County BCC

RAILROADIANA In 1886 the **Jacksonville, Tampa & Key West Railway** first steamed into Mount Dora; active rail service continued until 1973 under the auspices of the Seaboard Coast Railway. Remnants of the town's railroad heyday remain: several quaint low-clearance **Florida Central Railroad trestles**, and the **ACL passenger depot** (now the chamber of commerce), a narrow building on Alexander St. In Umatilla a bright orange **SCL caboose** sits on a siding outside the public library along FL 19. See *Railroad Excursions* for more train-related fun.

WINERY At **Lakeridge Winery & Vineyards** (1-800-768-WINE; www.lake ridgewinery.com), 19239 US 27 N, Clermont, guided tours begin every 15 minutes with a video on the winemaking process, then move out to a catwalk over the barrels and tanks. As the tour takes you outside, you overlook acres of grapes, both hybrids and muscadine, on the 127-acre estate. Finish off with tasting four types of wine. In addition to house-label items, the winery store has gourmet foods and gift items. Check the calendar for monthly special events like free jazz and blues festivals out on the green hillsides. Open Mon–Sat 10–5, Sun 11–5. Free.

ZOOLOGICAL PARKS AND ANIMAL REHABILITATION *✿* Show the kids some real barnyard critters at **Uncle Donald's Farm, Inc.** (352-753-2882), 2713 Griffin Ave, Lady Lake, where they can milk a goat, pet a horse, feed the chickens,

AT AMAZING EXOTICS

Sandra Friend

bounce around on a hayride, and visit with rehabilitating wild animals and birds. Admission $8 adults, $7.50 children and seniors; includes animal feed and hayrides, pony rides extra. Open Thu–Sat 10–4; in Feb–Apr, also Sun noon–4.

✿ For the wilder side of life, visit **Amazing Exotics** (352-821-1234; www.amazingexotics.com), 17951 SE CR 452, Umatilla, a working zoological education center, exotic animal rescue facility, and retirement home for animal actors. Just weeks after I watched one of the trainers petting and feeding a white-faced gibbon, the gibbon and other primates appeared with Jay Leno on *The Tonight Show*. Fifteen tigers and a complement of chimpanzees go about their paces in large enclosures on the hillside, while the lower section of the compound features lemurs, white wolves, a clouded leopard, and other rare and

interesting animals. Visitors on the daily tour cover the 100-acre ranch by foot and tram with a knowledgeable guide; tours run $54–94, depending on the amount of hands-on time with the larger mammals. Reservations required. The facility also offers hands-on classes for students learning exotic-animal management.

✳ To Do

AVIATION **Seminole-Lake Gliderport** (352-394-5450; www.soarfl.com), 4024 Soaring Lane, Clermont 34714. As the towrope dropped off our glider, I felt a sudden pang of fear: At more than 3,000 feet, I'd never been this high before without the assistance of an engine. Knut Kjenslie, owner/pilot/flight instructor, asked if I wanted to take the controls. "I'll let you drive," I said, and settled back for the ride. With a bubble of Plexiglas around my head, I could see as far as the birds could—and could see what the birds were up to. Chasing after climbing hawks, Knut had us rising up a column of air in a lazy spiral. "Do you like roller coasters?" he asked. I nodded. Within moments, he had us plunging on a track-less ride with serious g-forces—what a blast! I expected the quiet, but I'd never imagined gliders to be so maneuverable. Now this was an experience I'll never forget. Rides and instruction starts at $95; rentals for certified pilots at $35 per hour. Glider instruction and FAA certification courses offered, too.

BALLOONING Since 1978, **Hot Air Balloon Tours** (352-243-7865; www.hotair balloontourscentralflorida.com), 21432 CR 455, has taken passengers up, up and away on champagne flights over southern Lake County, launching near Sugarloaf Mountain, the high point for Lake County at 308 feet. Your float above the Florida landscape costs $185 per person, $150 for children 12 and under, and should be reserved in advance; flights are dependent on weather.

BIRDING Thousands of migrating birds stop at the impoundments of **Emeralda Marsh Conservation Area** between Lakes Yale and Griffin in Umatilla, between CR 42 and 44. Looking for rare birds? It's the place to go. On a single day I counted several bald eagles, more than a dozen limpkins, and numerous purple gallinules. For casual birding, you won't go wrong in **Mount Dora**; all of the lakeside parks offer excellent birding, especially at dusk. Check *Green Space* for more opportunities; every lakefront park has its resident egrets, ospreys, and herons. Ospreys nest in the tall cypresses along the **Dead River**, and are best seen on an ecotour (see *Ecotours*)

A GLIDER'S-EYE VIEW OF SEMINOLE-LAKE GLIDERPORT

Sandra Friend

BOATING At the *Mission Inn* (see *Resorts*), a pontoon boat rental is $210 for four hours, on the Harris Chain of Lakes; a guided bass boat, $260 for 2 hours. The marina is open Wed–Sun. In addition, several operators run ecotours (see *Ecotours*) along the Harris Chain.

CARRIAGE RIDES ∞ **A Hitch In Time** (352-394-8851; www.ahitchntime.com), 20301 Sugarloaf Mountain Rd, takes you on 20-minute narrated tours by horse and carriage around the streets of Mount Dora in the evening, Fri–Sat $14 adult, $12 senior, $10 children. On weekday evenings, there's a $2 discount. For a romantic twist, you can rent the carriage for yourself for a $80 "Lover's Lane" experience, a 30–minute ride between your chosen destinations.

DIVING C&N Divers & Snorkeling (407-735-5040; www.cndivers.com), 20211 US 441, Mount Dora, can set you up with gear to snorkel nearby Kelly Park or explore Wekiwa Springs, just over the border in Orange County (see "North of Orlando"). They also offer diving classes, and you can "rent a buddy" for a guided tour of nearby dive spots for $50.

Wekiva Falls Resort (see *Campgrounds*) runs hour-long narrated "jungle cruises"

AN OTTER SITS ON A LOG IN THE DORA CANAL

ECOTOURS ♿ 🐾 In the capable company of Captain Reg and Judy Bale, I cruised with a boatload of friends on the *Captain Doolittle*, part of the fleet of **Premier Boat Tours** (352-205-5552 or 1-866-269-6584; www.captaincharlie .home.vol.com), out of the Lakeside Inn in Mount Dora for a trip down the Dora Canal. It had been nearly 5 years since my last visit, and I'd forgotten what a wonderland of ancient cypresses is hiding in there. You can hardly fathom you're just a mile from busy US 441.

The afternoon was overcast and bitter cold on the water for the Lake Dora crossing, but the wildlife didn't mind, and we bundled ourselves in blankets along the wild and scenic Wekiva River. Enjoy the peaceful journey in a quiet electric boat through the most natural stretch of river in the Orlando metro area. Daily 9–4 on the hour; $15 adults, $10 ages 2–11.

At **Showcase of Citrus** (352-267-2597; www.showcaseofcitrus.com/ecotour.asp), 5010 US 27, near US 192 and just 10 minutes from Disney World, take an hour-long narrated tour on a monster tiger-striped 4x4 across a 2,500-acre cattle ranch through citrus groves, sandhills, cattle pastures, scrub, and marshes in search of deer and sandhill cranes; $20 adults, $10 children 4–12, reservations required—call ahead.

FISHING With two lengthy chains of lakes offering up some of the best trophy bass in the state, you can bet fishing is on the mind of many visitors to Lake County. Grab bait and tackle and put in your boat at any of the local parks with boat ramps (see *Parks*) or at one of the many fish camps (see *Fish Camps*). In addition to largemouth bass, you'll find the **Harris Chain of Lakes** (which includes more than 76,000 acres of water across Lake Griffin, Lake Harris, Little Lake Harris, Lake Eustis, and Lake Dora) brimming with bream, shellcracker, and bluegill. Fishing along the **Clermont Chain of Lakes**, a series of 13 lakes

provided by the crew. In addition to ubiquitous great blue herons, we spotted a nesting pair of bald eagles, some tri-colored herons, numerous egrets, and a yellow-crowned night heron. Judy pointed out historic homes along the shoreline, and we drew close to shore to see bald eagles. This was a new approach to the canal for me, through a narrow passage lined with old-time snowbird cottages, one with a garden of gnomes and a lighthouse with Hummel figurines behind glass. Entering the cypress-lined wilds, we took a side channel to a secret place where Reg pointed out a massive gator den and we cruised close by a black-crowned night heron peacefully roosting in a tree. Feeling like we'd boarded the *African Queen*, we continued down the Dora Canal between the giant cypresses and their giant knees, watching an otter race our boat along the waterway as if he were a dolphin, scrambling up and over logs that were in his way.

Premier Boat Tours offers three different ways to see the Dora Canal: launching with A Day on the Water's *Captain Doolittle* from the Lakeside Inn in Mount Dora, Blue Heron Tours' *Sea Haven* from Tavares' Gator Inlet along US 441, or Heritage Lake Tours' *Miss Dora* from the Harborside Restaurant in Tavares. Each of the quiet electric pontoons provides a interpretive guide and captain; you sit back and keep your camera steady as the wildlife slips by. Cruises are offered daily except Christmas, Easter, New Year's Day, Sep 11, and Nov 11, and cost $15 adults, $10 children, with special excursions (sunset, Halloween, Christmas lights) for an additional fee. Call ahead for reservations and departure times.

fed by the Green Swamp with waters flowing northward to form the Ocklawaha River, is more laid back; you won't find as many powerboats. Among the largest of the lakes are Lake Minneola, Lake Louisa, and Lake Palatlakaha.

GOLF Golfing is big in Lake County, where the rolling greens make for challenging courses. Most of the county's 26 courses are semiprivate, such as the renowned **El Campeón** at the Mission Inn (see *Hotels, Motels & Resorts*). One of the top 25 courses in the state, it's the third oldest resort golf course in Florida, established in 1926, and features rolling hills along cypress-lined lakes. The public **Clerbrook Resort** (see *Campgrounds*) has green fees starting at $18; watch out for the sandhill cranes! Check with the visitors center (see *Guidance*) for a brochure outlining all public golf courses in the county.

HANG GLIDING **Quest Air Hang Gliding** (352-429-0213 or 1-877-FLY-QUEST; www.questairforce.com), 6548 Groveland Airport Rd, Groveland, offers tandem hang gliding and hang-gliding training with certified instructors; flights start 2,500 feet above the ground. Tent and RV camping is available on site ($5–15).

HIKING For backpackers, the **Florida Trail** (www.floridatrail.org) is still the prime destination, crossing the county for nearly 40 miles through Seminole State Forest into the Ocala National Forest, where the trail's first blazes were established here at Clearwater Lake Recreation Area in Paisley back in 1966. Day hikers have an ever-growing variety of destinations: every time I check, another hiking trail opens in Lake County. Some of my favorites include Palm Island Park in Mount Dora, Tavares Nature Park in Tavares, Mason Nature Preserve in Howey-in-the-Hills, and Flat Island Preserve near Leesburg (see *Green Space*).

RAILROAD EXCURSIONS ⅃ For an excursion into the past, hop aboard the **Inland Lakes Railway** (352-589-4300; www.inlandlakesrailway.com), 51 W Magnolia Ave, Eustis. They run a variety of trains between Lake County destinations, including two dinner trains, a lunch train, trains to Orlando for the Magic basketball games, and their pride and joy, the Flagg Coal Express, a steam train. Departure stations, excursion lengths, and ticket prices vary, so call or visit the Web site for their schedule. Enjoy an elegant dinner excursion ($59 for dinner and a ride) on the **Orange Blossom Dinner Train** in the *Silver Spur*, a restored 1948 stainless dining car, or drop $10 extra to ride in the 1947 Vista dome car, the *Silver Bridle*. You'll dine on entrées like roast pork loin stuffed with dried berries and seafood-stuffed baked tilapia. Reservations required; this particular excursion departs from downtown Eustis and runs three hours.

SCENIC DRIVES For immersion into Old Florida, drive along **CR 42** (County Line Rd) at the northern edge of the county between the Ocklawaha River and Paisley, and follow scenic **CR 561**, which winds south from Astatula through Minneola and Clermont, looping around the lakes before it ends south of Groveland on FL 33.

SPORTS TRAINING Training for a marathon or more? Visit the 300-acre campus at the **USA Triathlon National Training Center** (1-888-841-7995; www.usa t-ntc.com), 1099 Citrus Tower Blvd, Clermont, where athletes can evaluate their abilities in the Human Performance Lab, work out in a state-of-the-art fitness center, and practice at the aquatic center with its 70-meter heated pool, plus a track-and-field complex with a 400-meter track.

TRAIL RIDING **Rocking Horse Stables** (352-669-9982; www.rockinghorseht .com), 44200 FL 19, Altoona, offers trail riding into the southern portion of the

PADDLING Newly signposted and open for paddling, the **Lake County Blue-ways** (www.lakecountyfl.gov/boating/blueways.aspx) program features eight different paddling trails encompassing 130 miles on the water. Each has distinct waymarking and signposts as well as designated campsites. The Blueways trails include three loops in the Ocala National Forest (see that chapter) and five on the chains of lakes, including the lengthy Palat-lakaha and Lake Harris Runs (requiring overnight camping), a short Helena Run for beginners, and the Golden Triangle Run, which hugs the north shore of Lake Dora and leads you through the wild Dora Canal. Two tips on this trip: No matter how tempted you are, don't try to step out of your canoe along the edges of the Dora Canal. The floating islands of peat and muck won't support your weight. Also, if you take to the Dora Canal under your own power, do so either early or late on a weekday to avoid the messy motorboat congestion that occurs every weekend.

Explore these waterways with your own watercraft or consider a rental at a livery. There are several in the county, including two county pre-serves—Flat Island Preserve and Lake Norris Conservation Area—where a $50 refundable deposit gets you a canoe for as long as you want it for marshy explorations; **Wekiva Falls Resort** (see *Campgrounds*), where for $5 per day you can enjoy the Wekiva River; and **Lake Griffin State Park** (see *Green Space*), where $3 per hour gets you out paddling through dense marshes into Lake Griffin and sightings of serious-sized alligators.

If paddling within sight of alligators gives you the willies, go with a guide. **Central Florida Nature Adventures** (www.centralfloridakayaktours .com), run by natives Kenny and Jenny Boyd, leads you into the wilds on tours like Li'l Amazon—which covers one of my all-time favorite birding spots, Emeralda Marsh—and the crystalline 8-mile Rock Springs Run, one of my favorite paddling trips, where my partner and I portaged over a sandbar within sight of a monster gator. Their guided tours, $59–99, include kayak rental and transportation, and encompass all experience levels.

Ocala National Forest, and accepts overnight campers with horses, as does **Fiddler's Green Ranch** (see *Ocala National Forest*). **Rock Springs Run Riding Ranch** (352-735-6266; www.rsrranch.com) 31700 CR 433, Sorrento, leads lengthy trail rides into surrounding Rock Springs Run Reserve in the Wekiva River basin, with more than 14,000 acres to explore. Excursions run from $10 per person for a 30-minute wagon ride to $150 for an all-day wilderness adventure with lunch on the trail. Nearby Seminole State Forest (see *Wild Places*) offers more riding opportunities, but you must bring your own horse.

WATER SPORTS With all its lakes, Lake County draws international attention for its water sports. Learn to water ski at accredited schools, including **Sunset Lakes Tournament Skiing** (1-800-732-2755; www.jacktravers.com), Okahumpa; and **Swiss Ski School** (352-429-2178; www.swissskischool.com), Clermont. Wakeboard enthusiasts can hone their skills at **Hansen's World Wakeboard Center** (352-429-3574; www.worldwakeboardcenter.com), Groveland; and P. J. Marks Wakeboard Camp (352-394-8899; www.wakeboardcamp .com), a popular training spot in downtown Clermont that's fun to watch from the waterfront parks.

✳ Green Space

GARDENS **Discovery Gardens** (352-343-4101; http://discoverygardens.ifas .ufl.edu), 30205 FL 19, Tavares. Roam 20 themed gardens in this educational resource supporting hands-on gardener training, including a special Children's Garden, colonial brick Courtyard Gardens, and a formal rose garden. Mon–Sat 9–4; free.

GREENWAYS Rail-trail corridors under development in Lake County include the **Lake Minneola Trail**, which presently has a ribbon of pavement ideal for biking from downtown Clermont through Minneola; the **Fruitland Park Trail**, which will run from Griffin Rd to Lake Ella Rd in Fruitland Park; and the **Tav-Lee Trail**, planned between Tavares and downtown Leesburg.

NATURE CENTER Just east of Eustis, **Trout Lake Nature Center** (352-357-7536), 520 E CR 44, offers interpretive exhibits and nature tours Oct–Apr, Fri and Sat 9–4, Sun noon–4. Free.

PARKS

Clermont
At the end of Third St, **Clermont Waterfront Park** has a playground, sheltered picnic benches, and a fishing pier, all for a daily parking fee of $2.

Lake Louisa State Park (352-394-3969; www.floridastateparks.org/lakelouisa), 12549 State Park Dr, Clermont, protects 4,500 acres around Lake Louisa, the largest of the Palatlakaha Chain of Lakes, fed by the Green Swamp, with paddling, hiking, and a developed campground. Active restoration is turning abandoned citrus groves back into natural longleaf pine and wiregrass habitat.

Eustis

The green expanse of **Ferran Park** along Lake Eustis is the southern terminus of the Eustis Lake Walk, a 0.25-mile boardwalk providing a great lakeside stroll. Although surrounded by subdivisions, **Hidden Waters Preserve** (352-343-3777; www.lcwa.org), Country Club Rd, feels more like a wild place than not. In this 90-acre park, the ground slopes steeply down to a giant sinkhole, with a trail paralleling a fern-lined stream rushing down the steep slope.

Fruitland Park

In a shady hammock sloping down toward the lake, **Lake Griffin State Park** (352-360-6760), 3089 US 27-441, provides access for paddlers (on-site rentals) and boaters out to the Chain of Lakes through a marsh filled with floating islands of vegetation. Hikers can amble the short nature trail; a pleasant campground is tucked under the oaks.

Howey-in-the-Hills

Griffin Stormwater Park on S Lakeshore Dr follows the shoreline of Little Lake Harris, offering a paved lakeside walking and biking trail, picnic area, playground, fishing pier, and a connecting walk in the woods to nearby **Mason Nature Preserve**, with boardwalks out to the lake. **Hickory Point** (352-343-3777; www.lcwa.org), a Lake County Water Authority recreational facility off FL 19 on Little Lake Harris, has a swimming beach, fishing pier, and nature boardwalk; fee.

Leesburg

A new 88-acre park on Lake Griffin, **Bourlay Historic Nature Park** (352-343-3777; www.lcwa.org), 910 Canal St, encompasses important moments in local history. It includes the site of the first steamboat landing in Leesburg, the site of the first Methodist church service, and was once owned by the Lee family, pioneer founders of the city. Hiking and bicycle trails let you explore the lakefront preserve.

∞ I have a newfound appreciation for city-owned **Venetian Gardens** along FL 44, a favorite spot for my sister to capture flowers as art and now a fond memory for me as the site of my wedding in spring 2005, beneath the grand old oaks with the azaleas ablaze on the central island. It was here, too, that my now-husband Rob popped the question beneath the twinkling array of lights that decks this park in a colorful celebration of Christmas every year. Each island along the shore of Lake Harris is linked by bridges, allowing you to stroll and watch the birds or sit and enjoy the sunshine from a bench. A marina, boat ramp, restrooms, and public swimming pool round out the public amenities; we used the community center on-site for our reception.

Herlong Park, off US 441 on Lake Griffin, has a picnic area and boat ramp with fishing opportunities.

Mount Dora

A ribbon of green runs along Lake Dora's eastern shore: **Gilbert Park** encompasses a landscaped version of Alexander Creek, which burbles downhill into the lake at Grantham Point, where the "Port of Mount Dora" and Mount Dora

Lighthouse are located. Next door is the wonderfully wild **Palm Island Park**, with a mile of trails along lakeside boardwalks out to wooded Palm Island. To the north, a lakeside walking and fitness trail leads around to **Evans Park**, another grassy spot for picnicking.

Tavares

Running between the railroad and Lake Dora in downtown Tavares, **Wooten Park** provides a gentle waterfront walking trail, picnic facilities, fishing platforms, and a playground for the kids.

WILD PLACES

Cassia

Protecting the western shoreline of Lake Norris, the **Lake Norris Conservation Area** (352-343-3777; www.lcwa.org) off CR 44-A now offers hiking in addition to kayaking beneath the shoreline cypresses, and has camping available as well. Covering 2,228 acres, it is home to several endangered species, including burrowing owls—not commonly seen in this part of Florida.

Leesburg

Surrounded by the vast Okahumpa Marsh, two deeply forested islands create the biological haven that is **Flat Island Preserve**, CR 25A, where orchids and colorful fungi flourish beneath ancient live oaks. A 4-mile trail with backpacking campsite circles the preserve, and you can rent canoes to paddle out into the marsh. This wilderness area is best visited during winter—the mosquitoes can be vicious the remainder of the year.

Sorrento

At the southeastern tip of the county, **Rock Springs Run State Reserve** (352-383-3311), FL 46, protects 14,000 acres of prime bear habitat at the confluence of Rock Springs Run and the Wekiva River. Hiking, biking, and equestrian trails crisscross the preserve, and seasonal hunting is permitted. Adjacent **Seminole State Forest** (352-360-6675; www.fl-dof.com/state_forests/Seminole.htm) encompasses more than 25,000 acres along the Wekiva River Basin, forming an important greenway connector for bear migration to the Ocala National Forest. The Florida Trail runs through the forest, and paddlers can enjoy a rugged trip on Blackwater Creek.

KAYAKING IN THE LAKE NORRIS CONSERVATION AREA

Lake County BCC

Umatilla

One of my top picks in Florida for birding, the **Emeralda Marsh Conservation Area** (see *Birding*) is barely off the beaten path but still remains a secret. Check out the details in *50 Hikes in Central Florida* and bring your life list.

Sawgrass Island Preserve (352-343-3777; www.lcwa.org) off CR 450, Umatilla, appeals to equestrians with its miles of trails along Lake Yale; hikers and birders can also amble the 1,100-acre preserve with its vast sawgrass marsh.

Sunnyhill Restoration Area (386-329-4404), CR 42 at the Ocklawaha River. Overlooked by many because it's just a little off the beaten path, this wilderness tract (once a cattle ranch) protects 9 miles of the Ocklawaha River floodplain, encompassing vast marshes along the scenic Lower Ocklawaha as well as uplands of scrubby flatwoods and scrub. Trails cater to hikers, bikers, and equestrians; the Levee Trail provides your best birding opportunities.

✳ Lodging

BED & BREAKFASTS

Mount Dora 32757

☙ **Christopher's Inn** (352-383-2244; www.christophersinn.net), 539 Liberty Ave. Just up the street from Mount Dora's beautiful lakeside parks, hospitality awaits in an 1887 home with beaded pine walls and ceilings. Decorated in a lush Victorian style with an eye to antiques lovers (note the 1940s *Reader's Digests* and the saltshaker collection in the parlor), Christopher's offers four cozy rooms with bath. $95–125, including full breakfast.

Coconut Cottage Inn (352-383-2627; www.coconutcottageinn.com), 1027 McDonald St. World traveler? Here's a place to bring back the memories! From the Zen Den with its serene Japanese furnishings to the Arabia Room, Coconut Cottage features the decor of faraway lands, inspired by the innkeepers' travels. $149, including expanded continental breakfast.

⚘ **Farnsworth House** (352-735-1894; www.farnsworthhousebnb.com), 1029 E Fifth Ave. Off the beaten path but attracting a regular clientele, this Superior Small Lodging dates back to 1886, offering three very spacious, well-decorated suites with kitchen and bath, plus two themed efficiency apartments in the detached Carriage House. Relax outdoors on the porch swing, or take a soak in the hot tub. Maximum rates $150–165, including expanded continental breakfast.

Mount Dora Historic Inn (1-800-927-6344; www.mountdorahistoricinn.com), 221 E Fourth Ave. In a cozy, convivial setting, Lindsay and Nancy Richards showcase their love of antiques in their 1886 home on the edge of the shopping district, with four lavishly decorated rooms and a full gourmet breakfast. $145–190.

☙ **Simpson's** (352-383-2087; www.simpsonsbnb.com), 441 N Donnelly St. Formerly the historic Simpson Hotel, this vibrant B&B sits right in the center of the action, in the heart of the shopping district. Each of the six comfortable and roomy suites ($130–150) has a small kitchen and private bath. You'll find a continental breakfast of fruit and bread, presented with a bouquet of roses, inside your refrigerator, but you can always graze the snack tray of chocolate chip cookies, peanuts, and popcorn if you can't wait until morning.

Tavares 32778

⌒ Built in 1926, the **Duncan House Bed & Breakfast Plantation** (352-343-0046 or 1-877-477-0739; www .theduncanhouse.com), 426 Lake Dora Dr, is a regal structure along the Lake Dora shoreline, noted by tour boats and simply splendid to look at, a three-story red brick mansion with grand pillars on a front porch that faces the lake. There are four rooms in this National Historic Landmark, all with quintessential southern charm. In the 1930s, Buddy Ebsen and his father taught dance lessons on the wooden floor of what is now the Third Floor Suite, a large and very private getaway; $199–285.

HOTELS, MOTELS, AND RESORTS

Howey-in-the-Hills 34737

&. ⁖⌒ **The Mission Inn** (1-800-874-9053; www.missioninnresort .com), 10400 CR 48, pitches itself as a "Golfer's Paradise," and with 36 holes they can certainly back up that claim. But golf isn't the only game at this resort, run by the same family for more than three decades. Spanish colonial architecture, replete with for-

THE DUNCAN HOUSE BED & BREAKFAST PLANTATION

Lake County BCC

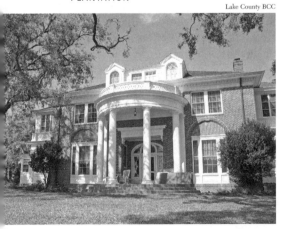

mal courtyards and fountains, accents the well-landscaped grounds with its many facilities: eight tennis courts, a full-service marina with rental boats, cruises, and fishing guides, and five restaurants and lounges, including La Hacienda, with its expansive breakfast buffet, and El Conquistador, serving intimate fine dinners in a luxurious setting, with a focus on prime steaks and wines. With 176 spacious standard rooms and suites, there are lodgings to fit every preference and budget. Rates start at $165, with numerous golfing and fishing packages and specials available; on-site bicycle rentals.

Mount Dora 32757

⌒ ⁖ **Lakeside Inn** (352-383-4101 or1-800-556-5016; www.lakeside-inn .com), 100 N Alexander St. Step back in time to a peaceful place, where guests play cards in the spacious lobby and sit out on the rocking chairs on the front porch, taking in the view of Lake Dora. Since 1883, the Lakeside Inn has been catering to those looking for a quiet getaway—including guests like President Calvin Coolidge, who wintered here in 1930. Built to accommodate tourists coming by steamboat and buggy, the original 10-room hotel consisted of a portion of the main building, which now includes the lobby, guest rooms, and two eateries: the Tremont (a classy lounge) and the Beauclaire (see *Dining Out*). It's quintessential Florida— as evening falls, a lone osprey cries from its perch above the swimming pool; couples stroll out on the dock to watch the shimmering lake turn to silver. Expanded several times through the 1930s to take advantage of the increasing tourist traffic via steam trains, this historic hotel now consists of five separate guest lodges, all with the graceful ambience of that period and, of course, the quirkiness that comes with older rooms. $99–189, including continental breakfast; a variety of room types and package deals are available. Canoes and paddle boats available for rent; lake cruises depart from the adjacent dock. Within an easy walk of downtown and the lakeside parks.

Tavares 32778
Inn on the Green (352-343-6373 or 1-800-935-2935; www.innonthegreen.net), 700 E Burleigh Blvd. Beautifully situated on the edge of a lake, this independent motel has the atmosphere of a golf resort, from its poolside putting greens and pleasant landscaping to the white-and-green motif of the buildings. Guests gather in a large, comfortable room overlooking the greens for continental breakfast. The spacious rooms have a touch of class and are a real value for the price, $89–129; golf packages available.

Umatilla 32784
Fox Den Country Inn (352-669-2151; www.foxdencountryinn.com), 27 S Central Ave. Featuring 10 units in a classic 1950s motel plus a 1925 home and a 1909 five-bedroom home for rent, this small family operation has pleasant small rooms outfitted with antiques; guests can wander through the orange groves down to Lake Umatilla. $60–185; reservations recommended.

WORKING RANCH

Weirsdale 32195
At the county line with "horse country," the **Florida Carriage Museum Resort** (352-750-5500; www.fcmr.org), 3000 Marion County Rd, is a

Lake County BCC

THE MISSION INN AND ITS GOLF COURSE, THE RENOWNED EL CAMPEÓN

working horse farm that opens its doors to visiting equestrians, with paddocks for your horses and pleasant cottages for you and your family, $97–172 (depending on size; check the Web site for full details). Riding lessons start at $65 (with your horse) or $85 (with theirs), or just kick back and relax on casual rides around the farm. Grassy RV sites with water and 30- or 50-amp hookups cost $15. The ranch is also home to the Florida Carriage Museum (see *Museums*).

FISH CAMPS

Leesburg 34788
With access to Haines Creek, **Black Bass Fishing Resort** (352-314-2123), 10402 CR 44, lets you motor out to Lake Griffin or Lake Eustis–your pick on any given lazy fishing day. $3 boat ramp charge, and accommodations $35–45.

Bring in the RV ($35 and up) or rent a waterfront mobile home ($110 and up) at **Footloose RV Resort** (352-253-1111; www.footlooseresort.com), 11711 Ocklawaha Dr, also situated on Haines Creek; boat rentals available.

Nelson's Fish Camp (352-821-3474), on the Ocklawaha River, CR 42. Providing prime access to this scenic river basin for anglers and paddlers, Nelson's offers campsites ($10–15 tent, $25 RV) and rustic cabins under a canopy of grand old live oaks; full-service marina with slips, gas pumps, boat rentals (plus tax and fuel): jon boats $35 half-day, $50 full day; pontoon $100 half-day, $165 full day. A small grill room inside the camp store serves up the basics.

CAMPGROUNDS

Clermont 34711

Bee's RV Resort (352-429-2116; www.thebeesresort.com), 20260 US 27. Pick your spot, shade or sun, and set up your tent, pop-up, or trailer for a relaxing stay, $20–30; enjoy the swimming area and recreation hall, nine-hole miniature golf, and on-site nature trail. New: rent yourself a tidy little cottage for $250–300 per week.

Clerbrook Golf and RV Resort (1-800-440-3801; www.clerbrook.com), 20005 US 27. With more than 1,200 full-hookup spots on 287 acres, this is one whopping campground, and a favorite of many snowbirds—the natural landscaping attracts wintering flocks of sandhill cranes. Nab an RV space ($30 and up) or tent site ($15 and up) or go upscale with villa rentals ($81 and up). Their on-site 18-hole golf course has a resident golf pro, and this complex is huge, with three swimming pools and four spas, beauty salon and barbershop, and even its own post office.

Lake Louisa State Park (see *Parks*) now has cabins . . . and these aren't the rustic camping cabins you grew up with. More like giant log homes, they can handle an extended family on an extended outing. The cabins overlook the lake and feature fine

woodworking, comfortable furnishings, and two bedrooms, $123.

Leesburg 34748

Holiday Travel Resort (1-800-428-5334; www.holidaytravelresort.com), 28229 CR 33. Ah, the life: an indoor pool and spa, a nine-hole golf course, shuffleboard and tennis courts, and a marina. Focused on long-term stays (but with room for vacationers), this massive campground has large pull-through sites ($34) with full hookups, on-site groceries, and three recreation halls managed by a social director.

Sorrento 32776

Extraordinarily convenient to the northern Orlando metro area, **Wekiva Falls Resort** (352-383-8055), 30700 Wekiva River Rd, isn't just about camping; it's a destination, on the wild and scenic Wekiva River, with canoe rentals, a swimming area, and guided ecotours along with more than 800 sites, from tent camping to full RV hookups, $19–21.

Tavares 32778

Banana Cove Marina (352-343-7951; www.bananacovemarina.com), 28725 FL 19, which dates to the 1960s, underwent a serious transformation in 2004 from old-time fish camp to modern RV resort. RV sites have 30- or 50-amp service, city water, septic, and cable TV ($38). Ramp fee $5 unless you're renting a boat slip on this cove on the south end of Lake Harris.

A serious seasonal destination for RVers, **Lake Harris Resort** (352-343-1233 or 1-800-254-9993; www.lakeharrisresort.com), surrounds 336 top-notch RV sites with a nine-hole golf course and a marina on a quiet cove off Lake Harris. All sites are full hookup and start at $35.

✳ Where to Eat

DINING OUT

Leesburg

Vic's Embers Supper Club (352-728-8989; www.vicsembers.com), 7940 US Hwy 441, takes you back to the 1950s with supper-club ambience; you'll expect Dean Martin to step out of the shadows. The entrées here are straightforward classics, from 12-ounce blackened prime rib rubbed in Creole seasonings to filet mignon with crab legs. Caesar salad is prepared tableside, and appetizers include such standards as oysters Rockefeller, stuffed mushrooms, and escargot. Prices are upper crust, too: $11–33, with two "steak for two" options, $39–50.

Mount Dora

Beauclaire (352-383-4101), 100 N Alexander St. Step back into the 1920s at the Lakeside Inn's classy dining room, where wait staff drift through to fill your glasses and take your orders in an atmosphere with a *Great Gatsby* feel. Entrées $17–27; the tasty Maryland crab cakes come with Zellwood corn fritters from the famed nearby farming district, and the chicken pot pie is homemade. Open for all meals daily. Dress for dinner, and make a reservation!

Goblin Market (352-735-0059; www.goblinmarketrestaurant.com), 331-B Donnelly St. Classical music drifts through the dining rooms, where you're surrounded by shelves lined with books—as an author, I felt right at home. And the food is fabulous. Served Tue–Sat 11–3, lunch is a bargain for the quality: Try the Irish whiskey onion soup for a twist on an old favorite, or the potato-crusted grouper sandwich. Return at dinner

for fine-dining choices like wasabi-crusted salmon, coquilles St. Jacques, or New Zealand rack of lamb. This is the "in" place in Lake County; reservations highly recommended. Dinner Tue–Thu 5–9 and Fri–Sat 5–10.

Tavares

Angelo's Italian Restaurant (352-343-2757; www.angelositalianrestaurant.net), 2270 Vinedale Rd, appeals with fine dining in a relaxed atmosphere and fine family cooking. Traditional Italian dishes like caprese salad, stuffed shells, shrimp scampi, and baked ziti comprise their traditional lunch menu ($7–9), with the addition of more refined entrées in the evenings such as chicken Sorrento and flounder al forno ($8–17). They prepare pizza and calzones, too.

EATING OUT

Clermont

☙ The Chef's Table (352-242-1264; www.clermontchefstable.com), 796 W Minneola Ave, is a busy lunchtime stop for deli sandwiches, salads, and ice cream delights. Sandwiches come in heaping baskets; chef's signature specialties include the country meatloaf sandwich, homemade hot sausage, and muffuletta. Lunch $4–7; closed Sun.

The Sunset Grille (352-394-6911; www.sunsetgrillandcomedyclub.com), 801 W Montrose St, serves up an extensive traditional menu with everything from mini-burgers and "flamingo" wings to fried oysters, prime rib, baby back ribs, grouper, and rack of lamb. Nab lunch or dinner for $6–19, and stick around for the comedy club.

Leesburg

I stopped in **Phyllis' Kountry Kitchen** (352-787-9500), 708 S 14th

St, one morning while waiting for the county offices to open. It's a tiny place, but my breakfast was down-home southern and certainly satisfying. Open for breakfast and lunch only.

It's easy to nab a hearty meal at **Wolfy's** (352-787-6777), 918 N 14th St, no matter which meal, for less than $10 per person. Diner-style and friendly, they serve up comfort food like pot roast and roast beef just like their sister restaurant in Ocala.

Mount Dora

Follow the garden path off S Donnelly to **Al E. Gators Pub** (352-735-5203), Third Ave Alley, a spacious bar and grill with outside deck, a comfy place to kick back with a few beers and top it off with a burger or burrito; serving lunch and dinner, $5–7.

With its broad doors open to the street, **Eduardo's Station** (352-735-1711), 100 E Fourth Ave, reminds me of a Caribbean sidewalk café, where Latin music spills out into the antiques district. Spicy Tex-Mex favorites dominate the lunch and dinner menu, $7–16.

🍴 At the **Frosty Mug Icelandic Restaurant & Pub** (352-383-1696), 411 N Donnelly St, descend into a European rathskeller with tables arranged around a bar right out of the Old World. Never mind the choice of imported beers on tap: The food is just plain heavenly to a Nordic gal like me. Appetizers include gravlax (Icelandic cured salmon), *sveppa strimlar* (beer-battered portobello), and crunchy stuffed olives. The pan-seared Icelandic haddock is their signature dish, but other artfully presented entrées ($12–22) like schnitzel and Atlantic salmon will surely tempt. And for dessert . . . can you imagine Icelandic fried ice cream? It's called *saet fjalla brie*, and it's fabulous. Live jazz piano and creative sculptures by local artists add to the very different atmosphere; it's an unexpected treat in the heart of Florida, serving lunch and dinner daily.

🍴 Watch the world wander past at **The Gables Restaurant** (352-383-8993; www.mtdora.org), 322 N Alexander St, where tasty salads, burgers, and creative entrées ($8–10) like coconut-crusted grouper and Cajun seafood ragout complement daily soups and dessert specials. My pick: the Maryland-style crab cake with garlic lime mayonnaise, presented with a perfect potato salad on baby greens. The comfy dining room is filled with antiques, and the fresh bread at your table (different every day: I had kalamata and feta, and sunflower wheat) comes from the adjoining **Sunshine Mountain Bakery**, 115 W Third Ave.

Garden Gate Tea Room (352-735-2158), 142 E Fourth Ave. Duck through the arbor to enter this lacy, frilly bower of femininity and sample an asparagus sandwich (asparagus, Jack cheese, purple onion, fresh Thousand Island dressing on grilled pumpernickel) or the quiche of the day, $7–8.

Palm Tree Grill (352-735-1936), 351 N Donnelly St. A street-corner Italian restaurant with a patio atmosphere, accentuated with gorgeous murals inside; large windows let you watch the passersby. The menu encompasses both traditional Italian dishes and more creative endeavors like eggplant rollatini and stuffed shells Florentine, with salads starting at $9, pasta entrées at $10; serving lunch and dinner.

Windsor Rose Tea Room (352-735-2551), 142 W Fourth Ave. A proper British tearoom in the heart of Mount Dora, serving full English tea ($20, or $8 for one) all day, with fresh-made trifles, tarts, and cakes ($2–4) that you'll find hard to pass over. For lunch, try British favorites like cottage pie, Cornish pasty, Scotch eggs, and ploughman's lunch ($7–8, with salad). Open 10–6, Sun 11–6.

Tavares

❧ **Magoo's Deli** (352-253-0475), 390 W US 441. I grabbed a hearty country-style breakfast for under $5 at this family restaurant one Saturday morning, glad that I'd ordered the short stack of pancakes because they were so filling! Serving breakfast and lunch (under $6), 5:30–3.

Umatilla

Now that I've had breakfast from **Haystax** (352-669-1555), 526 Umatilla Blvd, I can proclaim "yum!" They catered an event I attended, and the restaurant is always packed in the morning, so I know they're doing things right. Hearty breakfast offerings include smoked pork chops and eggs and a variety of omelettes, $4–8. Open for lunch and dinner too, with an all-you-can-eat fish fry on Fridays ($8).

The Mason Jar (352-589-2535), 37534 FL 19. I've been driving past here for years, and rare is the day I don't see the massive parking lot packed at mealtime. Serving up good old-fashioned country cooking like fried chicken, cheese grits, and yams, the Mason Jar provides fast, friendly service in a comfortable family atmosphere. Sandwiches $3–5, dinners $5–8. Open daily for breakfast, lunch, and dinner.

Old Crow Real Pit BBQ (352-669-3922), 41100 FL 19, came recommended from several barbecue lovers before I had a chance to try them myself; I was very impressed with their smoked ham. Open Thu–Sat evenings.

Yalaha

Bodacious barbecue awaits at **BC's General Store** (352-324-3730), 8730 CR 48, where the Coca-Cola signs and the pigs decorating this simple shack let you know you're in for a down-home treat—that and the aroma that'll have you pulling over. It's West Tennessee style, slow-cooked, and you'd best arrive at lunch, because when it's gone, it's gone. Open Wed–Sat, takeout (with a couple of picnic tables outside).

BAKERIES AND ICE CREAM

Eustis

Strawberry's Dessert Parlor (352-589-2313), 24 E Magnolia Ave. Ice cream and lunch specials, fresh cookies, and eight kinds of hot dogs.

Tavares

Twist-tee Treat (352-343-6177), 397 N US 441. Shaped like a giant ice cream cone, it's your quick stop for a cold treat. There's an additional location in Clermont off US 27 near FL 50—just look for the outrageously large cone!

Yalaha

❧ **Yalaha Country Bakery** (352-324-3366; www.yalahabakery.com), 8210 CR 48. From the loving hands of pastry chefs straight from the Black Forest, these fresh-baked breads and incredible pastries are made with spring water, but not preservatives. Visitors arrive by the busload to walk away with authentic olive bread, napoleons, and Bavarian custard tarts ($1–3) from the two-story Bavarian building gaily painted with flowers and trees. On Saturday the complex bustles with activity, thanks to free folk music concerts out on the lawn. In addition to the luscious baked goods, the bakery serves up sandwiches, salads, and pizza for lunch. Open Mon–Sat 8–5; shipping baked goods worldwide!

✳ Entertainment

Mount Dora

Hankering for Broadway musicals? Check out the **Bay Street Players** (352-357-7777; www.baystreetplayers .org), 109 N Bay St, Eustis, a 33-year-old repertory group presenting six musicals each season in a playhouse reminiscent of a small London theater. The **Mount Dora Theatre Company** (352-383-4616; www .icehousetheatre.com) presents Shakespeare, cutting-edge plays, and old standbys.

Yalaha

Bring your lawn chair down to **Yalaha Country Bakery** (see *Bakeries*) on

FRESH LOAVES AT THE YALAHA BAKERY
Lake County BCC

Saturday at 10 AM to enjoy free folk, blues, acoustic rock, and the occasional oompah band. For a monthly list of performances, check www.edelweiss music.net or call 352-324-3366.

✳ Selective Shopping

Clermont

The Vintage View (352-243-9977), 780 W Montrose St. It's like browsing Grandma's house, with 14 dealers showcasing dishes, vintage clothing, glassware, and more. Closed Sun and Mon.

The Clermont Herb Shoppe & Day Spa (1-888-568-HERB; www .herbpantry.com), 702 W Montrose St. I went in for flaxseed and booked a same-day appointment for a long-overdue massage. Natural foods, vitamins, massage therapy, and an aromatherapy bar.

Eustis

Old South Stained Glass & Antique Mall (352-589-0034), 320 S Grove St. Where better to house a stained-glass studio than in a former church? But the studio, with its elegant artwork, supplies, and classes, is just one facet of the business—every themed room brims with antiques, from primitives to Coca-Cola.

Peddler's Wagon (352-483-2797), 25 E Magnolia Ave. Enticing fragrances fill this home decor shop, from sprays of flowers, dried flower wreaths, and candles; regional art graces the walls.

Porter's (352-357-2540), 120 E Magnolia Ave, is an independent camera shop with professional-grade film and processing, international electrical adaptors, and other important necessities for photographers on the road; don't miss their back corner gallery of fine art photography of local subjects.

Fruitland Park

North Lake Flea Market (352-326-9335; www.northlakefleamarket.com), 2557 US 27-441. Around for more than 20 years, this busy weekend flea market has a garage sale atmosphere; open year-round, Fri–Sun.

Lady Lake

South Wind Trading Post (352-753-0500), 835 US 27. I have to list this one—I remember stopping here as a kid in the 1960s. It has all the touristy stuff like citrus candies, T-shirts, and alligator heads, plus quite a range of Native American items.

Leesburg

Leesburg has a pleasant historic downtown with a nice selection of shops. You'll find most businesses on Main Street and the town square, where a fountain burbles in front of city hall. All downtown shops are closed Sunday.

In addition to its gifts and home decor, **Distinct Innovations** (352-365-1717), 706 Main St, serves up lattes and espresso in their snazzy little coffeehouse; pick up some gourmet goodies to take home.

Grace's Books & Records (352-315-0867), 309 W Main St. Dealing in used books and records, with an excellent selection to browse through. Open Tue–Sat.

Victoria's Antique Warehouse (352-728-8668), 113 N Seventh St, focuses on antique furnishings and garden accessories spread throughout a large warehouse; look here for large items.

Victorian Rose (352-728-8388), 600 Main St, is a large, neatly arranged store specializing in Victoriana, including furnishings and jewelry.

South of downtown, **Morning Glori**

Antique Mall (352-365-9977; www.morningglori.com), 111 S 14th St, has more than 60 dealers with quilts and primitives, coins and postcards, and plenty of fine antique furniture. Open daily.

Minneola

Uncommon Market (352-242-4699), 200-B S US 27. Gourmet foods, European imports, specialty meats (ostrich, buffalo, rabbit, and the like), and a fine selection of wines; weekly wine tasting Fri evening, $7. Open 11–6 Mon–Fri, 11–4 Sat.

Mount Dora

The corner of Fifth Ave (Old US 441) and Donnelly St marks the epicenter of Mount Dora's renowned shopping district, which stretches on for several blocks in all directions. From pottery to books, antique furnishings to gourmet foods, you'll find it here! Here's a sampling of Florida's largest selection of shops in one small downtown:

Barbara B's (352-385-7207), 411 N Donnelly St #107. Eclectic home decor, featuring playful Indonesian wood carvings, wooden spoons and masks, and animal carvings.

Noni Home Imports (352-383-1242), 438 N Donnelly St. Proprietor Lori Davis wanders the world for folk art like Rajasthani wall hangings, Thai daybeds, and "vegetable ivory" carvings; world music transports you to the Far East.

Old Towne Bookshop (352-383-0878), 127 W Fifth Ave. From floor to ceiling, books line the walls of this tiny shop filled with rarities and nostalgia.

Oliver's Twist Antiques (352-735-3337), 404 N Donnelly St. Always busy, with a wide selection of antique furnishings, glassware, and large home decor items.

Princess Antique Mall (1-800-637-2394), 130 W Fifth Ave. Explore this mini mall with two stories of collectibles and antiques in dealer booths, plus a café and fudge shop.

Purple Pineapple Antique Mall (1-888-735-2190), 317 N Donnelly. Full of fun niches to explore, these dealer booths contain a little bit of everything, from stained glass to Red Hat items.

Uncle Al's Time Capsule (352-383-1958; www.sign-here.com), 140 E Fourth Ave. Music from the 1940s drifts through this memorabilia shop, setting the tone for the movie collectibles inside.

Yesterday, Today, and Tomorrow (352-735-1887), 427 N Donnelly St. Floral paintings spill across the storefront and down the sides, inviting you to step inside and browse through showy vintage clothing and jewelry.

South of downtown, don't miss **Renninger's Antique and Flea Market** (352-383-8393), 20651 US 441. Open weekends only, this expansive complex has a split personality. Hang a right, and you drive down to the sedate ambience of antiques dealers with permanent booths inside a large air-conditioned mall as well as a village of permanent shops around the edge of the complex. Turn left and drive up the hill to the busy buzz of thousands of people combing through hundreds of flea market stalls selling everything from inexpensive used books to antique reproduction signs, live birds, local produce, and garage sale items. Renninger's also holds huge special events, like a motorcycle and car swap meet on the second Sun of every month, and an annual Civil War reenactment. This is a don't-miss stop if you enjoy spending hours and hours browsing, and the flea market prices are pretty darn good.

Sorrento
Cypress Things (352-383-3864), 28625 FL 46. The cigar-store Indian on the porch startled me, it was so lifelike. Joe, Shane, and Ethel Chavis carve cypress and other woods into works of art, from life-sized bears and fine furnishings to totem poles.

Umatilla
Umatilla Antique Markets (352-669-3202), 811 N FL 19. Sift through dealer tables for antiques and flea market items. Open Thu–Sat 9–4.

CITRUS STANDS AND FARMER'S MARKETS

Clermont
Every Sunday, head down to downtown for the finest local produce at the **Downtown Clermont Farmer's Market** (www.clermontdowntown partnership.com), where you'll also find Yalaha baked goodies, kettle korn, and houseplants.

Showcase of Citrus (352-394-4377; www.showcaseofcitrus.com), 5010 US 27. With a yellow-and-black-striped safari swamp buggy parked in front, you can't miss this seasonal citrus stand that boasts a citrus museum, live trees for sale, swamp buggy rides through the groves, and, of course, citrus for sale.

Eustis
Buy your food direct from the source at the **Lake County Farmers Market** (352-357-9692), every Thursday (except legal holidays) at the Lake County Expo Grounds, FL 19 N.

January: **Antique Boat and Car Show** (352-483-5460), showcasing the holdings of the local antique and classic boat society, held in Eustis along the shore of Lake Eustis at Ferran Park; third weekend.

February: One of the biggest events of the year, the **Annual Mount Dora Art Festival** (352-383-0880; www .mountdoracenterforthearts.org) wraps this historic village in arts and crafts from 285 top-notch artists and thousands of visitors; first weekend.

On the third weekend, the **Austin Horse Park Pleasure Driving Competition** (1-866-500-2237; www .fcmr.org/pdste), showcases spectacular horse-drawn carriages from around the United States competing for prizes and the joy of carriage driving; fee.

Georgefest (352-357-3434; www .eustisgeorgefest.com), third weekend, Ferran Park, Eustis, is the state's oldest continuous festival (since 1901), celebrating George Washington's birthday with a parade, fun events like a citrus squeeze and pie-eating contest, and patriotic fireworks over the lake. Free.

March: **Leesburg Art Festival** (352-787-0000; http://leesburgartfestival .com), last weekend. More than 30 years old, this annual festival brings in more than 100 fine artists and craftspeople.

April: **Mount Dora Regatta** (352-383-3188), first weekend. Every Apr, the Mount Dora Yacht Club hosts the Mount Dora Regatta, a showy display of yachtsmanship across Lake Dora; 2008 marks their 55th year.

October: ✍ The **International Pickle Festival** (352-343-9600), hosted by the Lake County Historical Museum (see *Museums*), celebrates the end product of one of the county's historic crops—in the 1920s, Lake County was a leading producer and shipper of cucumbers. Fun and silly; free.

✍ **Umatilla Black Bear Festival** (www.flblackbearfestival.org), first or second Sat. An educational festival celebrating Florida's endemic bruin with environmental presentations and field trips into bear habitat. Bring your injured teddy bear to the Bear Repair Clinic! Free.

December: **Eustis Art League Winter Art Show** (352-357-5031), first weekend, at the Eustis Art League, downtown. Since 1956, this celebration of the arts features the talented members of the local art league.

Venetian Gardens Light Up (352-365-0053), Leesburg. More than half a million twinkling lights in this waterfront public park create one of the most delightful Christmas displays in the region; open 6 PM nightly all month; free.

NATURE COAST

CITRUS, HERNANDO, PASCO, AND SUMTER COUNTIES

Encompassing the most accessible part of the Gulf Coast in Central Florida, the counties of the Nature Coast provide unparalleled outdoor recreation opportunities amid Old Florida towns (dating back to the 1840s) that provide quiet respite from their bustling neighbors to the south and east. Where the Withlacoochee River winds northward from the Green Swamp, its floodplain forests and feeder lakes define the interior of the region; vast estuaries along the Gulf of Mexico fringe its western border. Roam through hundreds of square miles of the Withlacoochee State Forest and adjoining public lands, paddle the Withlacoochee River, or bike the Withlacoochee State Trail, which runs the length of the region. Kick back at **Lake Panasoffkee**, where you can catch an 11-pound largemouth bass right off a dock, or kayak the maze of estuary waterways from **Hernando Beach** to **Crystal River**. Seek out busy little **Webster**, home of the state's largest farmer's and flea market, or head for the antiques shops of **Inverness, Brooksville**, and **Dade City**. Steeped in history, the region was a battleground during the Seminole Wars and the Civil War. Get off the beaten path and wander the back roads to connect with the people and places that make up this fascinating and beautiful region of rivers and coastal estuaries.

GUIDANCE **Citrus County** (352-628-9305 or 1-800-587-6667; www.visitcitrus .com), 9225 W Fishbowl Dr, Homosassa Springs, has a cozy visitors center adjacent to Homosassa Springs State Park's main entrance, where you can pick up brochures, book a room, or ask questions to plan your trip. In downtown Brooksville, the **Hernando County Tourist Development Office** (1-800-601-4580; www.co.hernando.fl.us/visit) 30305 Cortez Blvd, can help with trip planning in the county, including Brooksville, Spring Hill, and Weeki Wachee. Contact the **Pasco County Office of Tourism** (1-800-842-1873; www.visit pasco.net), 7530 Little Rd, New Port Richey, for information about Dade City, New Port Richey, Holiday, and Hudson. You can walk right into the **Dade City Chamber of Commerce** (352-567-3769; www.dadecitychamber.org), 14112 Eighth St, during business hours to pick up tourism brochures, and the **Sumter**

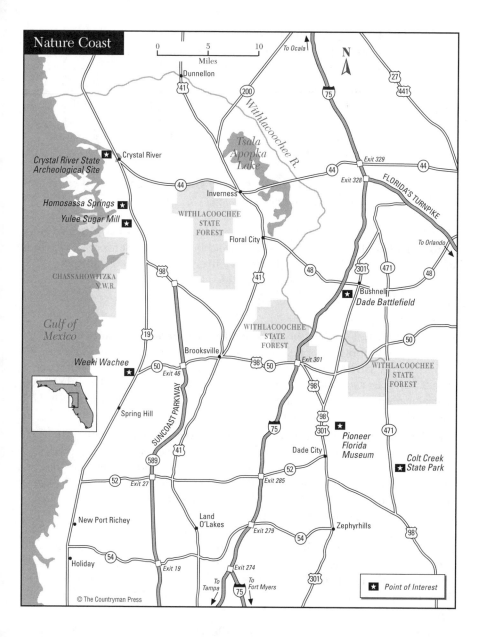

County Chamber of Commerce (352-793-3099; www.sumterchamber.org), 225 US 301 S, Sumterville, to learn about their quiet rural communities and thousands of acres of farms and forests.

GETTING THERE *By air*: For the quickest access to the Nature Coast region, fly into **Tampa International Airport** (see "Tampa") and drive up the new Suncoast Pkwy (FL 589), a toll road cutting through the heart of the region to reach the coast at Chassahowitzka.

By car: Both the **Suncoast Pkwy** and **I-75** provide quick access to the region; use **FL 52**, **FL 50**, and **FL 44** to make east–west connections with **US 301**, **US 41**, and **US 19**.

By bus: **Greyhound** (1-800-229-9424; www.greyhound.com) runs through Brooksville, Crystal River, Dade City, New Port Richey, and Spring Hill.

PARKING You'll find free public parking in all of the towns along the Nature Coast; some spaces are limited-term.

PUBLIC RESTROOMS Look for them in **Dade City** at the chamber of commerce building off Church Ave (see *Guidance*).

MEDICAL EMERGENCIES Two major regional hospitals are **Seven Rivers Community Hospital** (352-795-6560; www.srrmc.com), 6201 N Suncoast Blvd, Crystal River, and **Pasco Regional Medical Center** (352-521-1100; www.pasco regionalmc.com), 13100 Fort King Rd, Dade City.

✳ To See

ARCHEOLOGICAL SITES At the **Crystal River Archeological State Park** (352-795-3817; www.floridastateparks.org/crystalriver), 3400 N Museum Pointe, a paved interpretive trail winds around a ceremonial mound complex built more than 2,500 years ago; evidence of human use of this site dates back nearly 10,000 years, encompassing four cultural periods in Florida's history. A tour boat at the site provides birding tours along the Crystal River. Fee.

The **Fort Island Beach Archeological Site**, a Weedon Island culture site, adjoins the public beach (see *Beaches*); explore via a new series of boardwalks that winds through the hammocks. Another Weedon Island Culture site, the **Oeslner Mound**, Sunset Blvd, New Port Richey, is all that remains of a village settled around A.D. 1000 and occupied for several hundred years; Smithsonian archeologists analyzed the site in 1879.

ART GALLERIES **Brooksville City Art Gallery** (352-596-2443; www.cityof brooksville.org/artgallery), 201 Howell Ave, features rotating exhibits from local artisans in quilting, photography, painting, and more, and is the permanent home of the Hernando County Historical Quilt. Open 8–5 Mon–Fri, closed holidays.

On the downtown square in Inverness, **Galleria San Sebastian** (352-344-3838), 107-A W Main St, sparkles with art glass and pottery creations from local artists. Open Tue–Sat 11–8.

Pasco Fine Arts Center (727-846-7322; www.pascoart.org), 5744 Moog Rd, Holiday. Galleries showcase the works of locally and nationally renowned artists in all media, with an adjoining artists' co-op gift shop. Open Tue–Sat 9–4; free.

ATTRACTIONS ✐ **Boyett's Citrus Grove and Attraction** (352-796-2298 or 1-800-780-2296; www.boyettsgrove.brooksvillebusiness.com), 4355 Spring Lake

Hwy, Brooksville. In the tradition of old-time Florida roadside attractions, Boyett's thrills the kids with its wildlife park, 14,000-gallon saltwater fish tank, touristy gift shop, and ice cream parlor. Paved paths wander through the wildlife complex, but this is a working citrus packer, too—during season (Oct–Apr), peek through the windows watch the citrus being washed, waxed, polished, and sorted into crates. Open daily 9–5; free.

Weeki Wachee Springs (352-596-2062; www.weekiwachee.com), corner of US 19 and FL 50, Weeki Wachee. What little girl wouldn't be awed by real live mermaids? I know I was back in 1968, and that was well before Disney cornered the attraction market. Newt Perry's classic 1947 roadside attraction still centers on underwater choreography à la Esther Williams in sparkling Weekiwachee Spring, where the gals never have a bad hair day. Relying on specialized air hoses, the mermaids hold their breath for up to 3 minutes at a time. A little bird-watching on the quiet electric Wilderness River Cruise will introduce you to one of the most beautiful rivers in Florida as hungry pelicans tap dance on the canopied roof, and a walk down the Tranquility Trail immerses you in the native hardwood hammock on the river's edge. $14 adults, $11 ages 3–10, plus $3 parking; rates increase to $25 and $17 when their water park, Buccaneer Bay, opens for the season. It's been a rough ride during the past few years for this beloved Old Florida attraction, but the future is now well in hand—it's becoming a Florida State Park by November 2008. Watch their Web site for details. If you'd like to explore this crystalline river on your own, check out Weeki Wachee Canoe & Kayak Rental (see *Paddling*) or Dive Weeki Wachee (see *Diving*) for more details.

GHOST TOWNS One of the largest sawmills in Florida operated in busy **Centralia** between 1910 and 1921, until loggers depleted the virgin cypress stands. Abandoned in the 1930s, the remains of the town hide under vegetation along US 19 in Chassahowitzka National Wildlife Refuge (see *Wild Places*).

HISTORIC SITES

Brooksville

∞ **Chinsegut Hill** (352-796-6254; www.auxsvc.usf.edu/chinsegut.htm), prominently perched at the top of the hill above SR 481, is a grand mansion that was once the center of a 2,080-acre plantation. A gentleman from South Carolina, Colonel Pearson, staked his claim to the high rolling hills north of what would become Brooksville in 1842, and built a fine

THE FAMOUS WEEKI WACHEE MERMAIDS
Sandra Friend

manor house prior to the outbreak of the Civil War. By 1924, the manor and its lands passed into the hands of Col. Raymond Robins, who dubbed it *Chinsegut Hill* after the Inuit word for "spirit of lost things," years after he returned from the Klondike with enough gold to settle down and live a life of ease. Mrs. Robins loved gardening, and created extensive formal gardens around the house. A social economist, Colonel Robins moved in the upper echelons of politics and business and entertained folks such as Thomas Edison, J.C. Penney, and Harold Ickes at the mansion. By 1932, the Robins donated their land to the federal government to use as a wildlife refuge and agricultural experimental station. The mansion is owned and operated by the University of South Florida and can be booked for retreats and weddings. The surrounding plantation, including a significant stand of virgin longleaf pine, is managed by the Florida Fish and Wildlife Conservation Commission as Chinsegut Wildlife & Environmental Area (see *Wild Places*).

Chills ran down my spine when the ghost of Ransom Clark stood before us to speak. "This is where they killed us all," he said, striding out of the piney woods to meet us. "And I got to keep coming back." The Second Seminole War began amid the longleaf pines at **Dade Battlefield Historic State Park** (352-793-4781; www.floridastateparks.org/dadebattlefield), 7200 CR 603, Bushnell, where on December 25, 1835, Major Francis Dade left Fort Brooke (located in what would become Tampa) and led his troops north on the military road to Fort King, Ocala. Several days out, the troops fell into an unexpected trap at this very site: 180 Seminole warriors waited, angered by the federal Indian removal policy. After six hours and two waves of attacks, more than 100 soldiers lay dying. Only three escaped; Ransom Clark recounted the story when found. Every December, the reenactment of the battle is a colorful testament to Florida history, unfolding in a drama narrated by an actor playing the ghost of Ransom Clark. If you enjoy living history, this is one spectacle—the pageantry of the Seminole horsemen, the gallant fight of the dying soldiers—you must not miss. During the event (held the weekend after Christmas), a sutler's encampment springs up in the piney woods, filled with the clang of metal and the aroma of fresh-smoked meat, with old-fashioned foods and handmade early pioneer crafts for sale. The rest of the year, the park is a quiet place, where a path leads you from a small history museum devoted to the story of the battle through a walking tour of the battlefield, past monuments erected to mark the fall of each of the officers in the unit. Walk across the road, past the picnic tables and play area, and you'll find a nature trail winding deep into the pine forest, immersing you in what this place has felt like for millennia. It's a park for reflection, for remembrance. Open daily 8–sunset; fee.

Downtown Dade City dates back to the 1890s; a walking tour (see *Walking Tours*) of historical sites introduces Victorian dwellings like the McIntosh and Starr houses as well as neoclassical and Florida boom architecture, all within a few city blocks along Meridian Ave.

Elfers

Baker House (727-849-1628), 5740 Moog Rd. The centerpiece of Centennial Park, this is the oldest Florida Cracker home in western Pasco County, constructed in 1882 in a traditional dogtrot style, with a center corridor separating the living areas. Open for tours Sat 11–3.

Inverness

Fort Cooper State Park (352-726-0315; www.floridastateparks/fortcooper), 3100 S Old Floral City Rd, marks the site of another page in the history of the Seminole Wars, where a bedraggled battalion of sick and injured soldiers walking to Tampa stopped to regroup and recuperate after a month-long battle at the Cove of the Withlacoochee; they hastily built a wooden fort to defend themselves in April 1836 when the Seminoles attacked. An annual reenactment relives the event.

New Port Richey

Explore the **revitalized 1920s downtown** (see *Walking Tours*) for a look at landmarks like the **1926 Meighan Theater**, a former movie theater named for a silent film great and reborn as the Richey Suncoast Theatre, and **The Hacienda**, a 55-room 1927 hotel that attracted the crème of the Hollywood film industry.

St. Leo

St. Leo College dates back to 1890, and its grounds hold some interesting treasures. Built from local stone, **Our Lady of Lourdes Grotto** (across FL 52 from the St. Leo Abbey) was completed in 1916. Florida coral rock and stained glass make up the adjoining **Garden of Gethsemane Grotto** from 1938. The distinctive Romanesque-style **St. Leo Abbey Church** has beams of cedar from trees harvested at the college; it opened for worship in 1948. The oldest building on campus is the **St. Leo Abbey**, originally dedicated as a Benedictine monastery in 1902.

MEMORIALS At the **Florida National Cemetery** (352-793-7740; www.cem.va .gov/CEMs/nchp/florida.asp), 6502 SW 102nd Ave, west of Bushnell, you'll find the Memorial Trail, a paved footpath running past memorial plaques honoring veterans of the US armed forces. This is the only National Cemetery for veterans in Florida.

MUSEUMS

Brooksville

Hernando Heritage Museum (352-799-0129; www.hernandoheritagemuseum .com), 601 Museum Court. A 12-room Victorian home built in 1856 on an original land grant, the **May-Stringer House** boasts more than 10,000 regional-history artifacts on display. Open Tue–Fri noon–3 for 45-minute guided tours; fee.

Crystal River

Coastal Heritage Museum (352-795-1755), 532 Citrus Ave. Tucked inside the original town hall, a WPA project from 1939, this small museum is crammed with little-known historical facts about the maritime towns of Citrus County. An award-winning diorama depicts downtown Crystal River in 1927; displays cover such offbeat topics as school boats used to reach island schoolhouses, the oyster-canning industry, and the cedar pencil industry. Open Tue–Fri 11–3, closed July; free.

Dade City

Starting in 1961 with a donation of 37 antique farm vehicles, the collection of the **Pioneer Florida Museum** (352-567-0262; www.pioneerfloridamuseum .org), 15602 Pioneer Museum Rd, has grown to cover 20 acres. Eight historical buildings typical of early pioneers are spaced for leisurely exploring. Check out the Trilby Depot, circa 1896, complete with a 1913 Porter steam engine; pretend to shop in the 1920s C.C. Smith General Store; and go back to school in a 1930s one-room schoolhouse. Don't miss the First Ladies of Florida doll collection, or the doctor's room outfitted with memorabilia from an office of a local doctor and dentist, in the Main Building. My favorite? The citrus packing house. There's enough here to keep you busy for an afternoon or more. Open 10–5 Tue–Sat, fee. Nearby, **Withlacoochee River Park** (see *Parks*) hosts living history events in its replica Creek Indian and Florida Cracker villages.

Homosassa

The **Olde Mill House Gallery & Printing Museum** (352-628-1081; ww.visitcitrus.com/museumitem.asp?companyID=272), 10466 W Yulee Dr, is a small museum devoted to a vanishing art—typesetting. In addition to its displays of letterpresses and movable type, this museum offers hands-on experience with its antique machines, under the tutelage of curator Jim Anderson (call ahead to arrange). The museum also hosts a café (see *Eating Out*) popular for its real Cuban sandwiches. Open Thu–Sat 10–2.

AT THE PIONEER FLORIDA MUSEUM
Sandra Friend

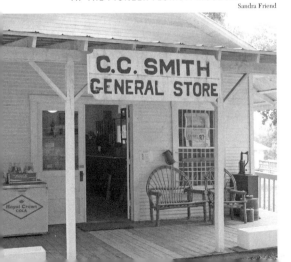

Inverness

Historic Courthouse Museum (352-637-9928; www.citrushistorical .org/cchshome.asp), 1 Courthouse Square. From the outside, it looks like a prop from *Back to the Future*, and it was featured in Elvis's *Follow That Dream*. But this 1912 courthouse is authentic, and exhibits inside tell the story of Citrus County. Free.

OLD HOMOSASSA Yulee Sugar Mill Ruins Historic State Park (352-795-3817), Yulee Dr. In the 1850s David Levy Yulee had already made quite a name for himself. Born in St. Thomas, he was brought to the Florida Territory in 1817 by his family and attended law school in St. Augustine. After attending Florida's first constitutional convention, he was elected a territorial delegate to the US Congress, and became Florida's first US senator when Florida achieved statehood in 1845. All the while he managed businesses ranging from the Atlantic & Gulf Railroad to his 5,100-acre sugar plantation, Margarita, on the Homosassa River, with his mansion set on Tiger Tail Island and connected to the mainland by a plank road. By 1851 the sugar mill had 1,000 workers, primarily slaves. Yulee joined the Confederate Congress when Florida seceded, and used his mansion as a storehouse for ammunition and supplies. So it was no great surprise that the Union Blockading Squadron targeted the plantation. In May 1864, after a failed attempt at ambushing Yulee on the road from Homosassa to Archer, a federal naval detachment burned the mansion to the ground. The mill, standing inland, escaped damage but fell into ruin as the plantation was abandoned. Now partially restored, the original machinery stands in place; walk through the complex to learn the historic process of turning sugarcane to sugar, which Yulee adapted from his Caribbean birthplace.

THE YULEE SUGAR MILL AT OLD HOMOSASSA

Sandra Friend

Sandra Friend

TYPEWRITERS AND OTHER EPHEMERA
ON DISPLAY AT THE OLDE MILL HOUSE
PRINTING MUSEUM

New Port Richey

In what was once a two-room school-house from 1916, the **West Pasco Historical Society** (727-847-0680; www.rootsweb.com/~flwphs/about _us.html), 6431 Circle Blvd, contains artifacts and papers on early area businesses and local history, including genealogical records; the Indian Gallery contains artifacts from Seminole and Timucua sites. Open Fri and Sat 1–4; free.

Zephyrhills

The **Zephyrhills Depot Museum** (813-780-0067; www.zephyrhills .net/depotmuseum.html), 39110 South Ave, inside the restored 1927 Atlantic Coast Line railroad depot, opened in 1998. Four exhibit rooms showcase the history of trains with artifacts from the original depot. Genealogists will want to check out the Family Room for local family history. Open Tue–Sat 10–2. Free.

RAILROADIANA In addition to the **Zephyrhills Depot** (see *Museums*), look for the Seaboard Coast Line freight station in Inverness along the Withlacoochee Rail Trail, down Apopka Ave east of the Old County Courthouse. The **last remaining Atlantic Coast Line depot on the Orange Belt Railway**, circa 1948, can be seen in San Antonio (www.sanantoniofla.com/depot) with its accompanying ACL caboose. The **Crystal River Railroad Depot**, with Seaboard Air Line rolling stock, adjoins Crystal St one block south of Citrus Ave. The **Citrus County Model Railroad Association** maintains a public display of their model-railroad layouts at the Citrus County Fairgrounds (US 41, south of Inverness), open Saturday during flea market hours.

AN ATLANTIC COAST LINE CABOOSE AT
THE SAN ANTONIO DEPOT
Sandra Friend

WINERIES Florida Estates Winery (813-996-2113; www.floridaestates wines.com), 25241 FL 52, Land O'Lakes. Set on a 3,600-acre working cattle ranch, this newcomer to the winery business shines with an intriguing array of specialty and dessert wines such as strawberry port, Key lime, and orange; I was impressed by the tasty Plantation Spice wine, which pairs well with chocolate. Most of their products are fermented and bottled at their sister winery, Eden Vineyards, but all contain some Florida grapes. Open 11–6 daily, with a new retail outlet in downtown St. Petersburg (see "St. Petersburg").

ZOOLOGICAL PARK AND WILDLIFE REHABILITATION Homosassa Springs Wildlife State Park (352-628-5343; www.floridastateparks.org/homosassa springs), 4150 S Suncoast Blvd, Homosassa. It's a blast from my past—a former roadside attraction now serving as a zoological park featuring Florida's native wildlife (excepting Lucifer the hippo, who was made a citizen of Florida to legally remain in his longtime home). Stroll the forested grounds and enjoy the rambling and slithering of Florida's wildlife; many of the animals are here for rehab, or because they cannot be reintroduced into the wild. In the underwater observatory, you descend into an inside-out aquarium, where you look through plate-glass windows at swirls of fish and manatees drifting around the first-magnitude, 45-foot-deep crevice of Homosassa Springs. $9 ages 12 and up, $5 children 3–12. Daily 9–5:30, ticket counter closes at 4.

✳ To Do

AIRBOATING At **Wild Bill's Airboat Tours** (352-726-6060; www.wildbillsairboatrides.com), 12430 E Gulf to Lake Hwy (FL 44), Inverness, take a 10-mile spin up the Withlacoochee River for a look at this wild, twisting waterway edged by dark floodplain forests.

BICYCLING Bike rentals are available at two **Suncoast Bicycles Plus** (1-800-296-1010; www.suncoastbikes.com) locations, each convenient to a trail: 1 mile from the **Fort Island Beach Trail** at 471 NE First Terrace, Crystal River (1 block east of US 19); and 322 N Pine St, Inverness, on the **Withlacoochee State Trail** (see *Greenways*), where you'll also find rentals at **Hampton's Edge** (352-799-4979), trailside in Istachatta.

Cyclists have more than 12 miles of trail to roam at the **Crystal River Preserve State Park** (see *Wild Places*), just north of Crystal River, and can bike a couple of miles on the **Pepper Creek Trail** at Homosassa Springs (see *Zoological Park*). The two long-distance trails in the region are the **Withlacoochee State Trail** and the **Suncoast Trail**, connecting the Nature Coast to the Tampa Bay area (see *Greenways*); for off-road fun on 32 miles of forested trails, visit the **Croom Off-Road Bicycle Trails** off Croom Rd, north of Brooksville off US 41, in Withlacoochee State Forest (see *Wild Places*).

INSIDE THE UNDERWATER OBSERVATORY AT HOMOSASSA SPRINGS

Sandra Friend

BIRDING Birders will delight at the whooping cranes that inhabit Chassahowitz-ka National Wildlife Refuge (see *Wild Places*) in the winter, but birding must be done by boat. This is the destination for the famed flock that wings its way south from Wisconsin following a bird-shaped ultralight. Flocks of black skimmers often hang out at **Fort Island Beach** (see *Beaches*); at **Fort Island Trail Park** (see *Parks*) on Crystal River, watch for wading birds. Great blue herons roost in the trees at **Homosassa Springs Wildlife State Park** (see *Zoological Park*); the park's free **Pepper Creek Trail** attracts birders looking for warblers. Bird-watching is also superb at **Weeki Wachee Preserve**, off Shoal Line Rd in Hernando Beach, where more than 230 species have been recorded, including a nesting colony of least terns. All of the Green Space entries will net you great birding, but **Key Vista Nature Park** (see *Parks*) is a top site for ospreys and bald eagles. For many more sites, visit the **Citrus Birding Trail** at www.citrus birdingtrail.com.

DINOSAUR SPOTTING More than a decade ago an Istachatta sculptor named Herwede created life-sized dinosaur sculptures to populate a park. Look for his remaining **half a brontosaurus** along CR 476 west of Nobleton. On US 19 in Spring Hill, a monstrous **1960 Sinclair Oil gray dinosaur** houses Harold's Auto, and a **pink dinosaur** stands roadside a few miles farther south.

DIVING

Crystal River

Bird's Underwater Dive Center (1-800-771-2763; www.birdsunderwater .com), 320 NW US 19, is a certified PADI five-star dive center with a 4-day open-water class (minimum age 10), $275. **Crystal Lodge Dive Center** (352-795-6798; www.manatee-central.com), 525 NW Seventh Ave, at the Best Western Crystal River Resort (see *Lodging*), is a full-service dive shop with on-site instructors, offering guided snorkeling or sightseeing tours on Crystal River and the nearby Rainbow River (see "Marion County"). **Crystal River Manatee Dive & Tour** (352-795-1333; www.manateetouranddive.com), 267 NW Third St, has cold air, boat, and equipment rentals; diving or snorkel tours. **Plantation Dive Shop** (352-795-5797; www.crystalriverdivers.com) at the Plantation Inn and Golf Resort (see *Resorts*) takes divers out on guided trips, offers instruction, and rents boats and gear; popular King Spring, 75 feet deep, is just a few hundred yards from their back door.

New Port Richey

Sunny Seas Scuba (727-849-2478; www.sunnyseasscuba.com), 7115 US 19 S, runs full- and half-day expeditions into the Gulf, and has rentals, sales, instruction, and nitrox; **Super Sports & Scuba** (727-848-7122), 7129 US 19, takes divers out into the Gulf for dives of 45 to 75 feet, with classes from open water to dive master available.

Weeki Wachee

Dive Weeki Wachee (407-592-8175; www.diveweeki.com). Yes, you can when the mermaids are off-duty. This is the park's official dive coordinator—get in touch to set up your dive ($55–85), which includes park admission fee. Additionally, other local dive shops do lead guided trips to the Weekiwachee Spring.

ECOTOURS

Crystal River
Bird's Underwater Dive Center offers winter tours of manatee habitats, as well as guided dives and snorkeling trips on the Crystal River and the Rainbow River, as does Crystal Lodge Dive Center (see *Diving* for both).

Homosassa
River Safaris and Gulf Charters (352-628-5222 or1-800-758-FISH; www .riversafaris.com), 10823 Yulee Dr. Offering narrated cruises on the Homosassa River ($18–39) and out into the Gulf of Mexico ($30), snorkeling ($30) airboat rides ($28–75) and boat rentals, it's your one-stop shop for exploration of the natural wonders of the Homosassa River and its surrounding estuaries.

Captain Mike's Sunshine River Tours (352-628-3450 or 1-866-645-5727; www.sunshinerivertours.com) take you out on a pontoon boat to go snorkeling with the manatees at Bluewater Springs ($50); birding trips, scalloping trips, airboat rides, and custom-tailored ecotours are also available.

FAMILY ACTIVITIES ✔ **Adventureland** (352-726-7001), US 41 between Floral City and Inverness, has a nicely landscaped miniature golf course and adjacent driving range. On US 19, **Crazy Eddie's Go-Karts** (352-563-1167) isn't just about go-carts: Let the kids try out the bumper boats, mini golf, and water balloon stations as well. For indoor fun on a rainy day, try the **Sportsmen's Bowl** (352-726-2873; www.sportsmensbowl.com), 100 N Florida Ave in Inverness, the **Roller Barn** (352-726-2044), 1740 US 41 north of Inverness, or **Jimmy's Skating Center** (352-793-3570), 5260 US 301 between Sumterville and Bushnell.

FISHING In addition to world-class bass, you can reel in a steady stream of panfish from **Lake Panasoffkee** for your evening repast—the lake is so clean, there's no limit. See *Fish Camps* for places to cast. Inshore and flats fishing is big all along the Nature Coast, with snook, tarpon, cobia, and Spanish mackerel. Charters run $300 and up for a full day, and you'll find eager guides all the way from Crystal River down to Holiday; stop in and ask around at the marinas. Anglers who want a taste of old-time Florida fishing shouldn't miss **Aripeka**, a historic fishing village off US 19 at the Pasco-Hernando county line, and Old Homosassa, at the end of Yulee Drive.

FISHING IS ALWAYS POPULAR ON THE NATURE COAST

Sandra Friend

Crystal River

Plantation Inn & Golf Resort (see *Hotels, Motels & Resorts*) has 27 holes of championship golf on a Mark Mahanah–designed course that's stood the test of time for nearly 50 years. Flowing around naturally landscaped water holes, it's also a haven for alligators and wading birds, a pleasant spot for nongolfers to take a stroll.

St. Leo

Lake Jovita Golf & Country Club (352-588-2233; www.lakejovita.com), 12900 Lake Jovita Blvd, features an extraordinary challenge—the longest natural drop of any golf course in Florida, 94 feet from tee to green on the 11th hole. The undulating landscape is reminiscent of the Carolina foothills; the course was designed by PGA pro Tom Lehman.

The 18 holes of **St. Leo Abbey Golf Course** (813-588-2016), 33640 FL 52, are great for beginners. Spread over 80 acres of rolling countryside, the open fairways and fast greens are sure to add just the right challenge. Full pro shop on site; rental clubs available.

Sumterville

From US 301, you can see the expanse of **Shady Brook Golf & RV Resort** (352-568-2244; www.shadybrookgolfandrv.com), 178 N US 301, a public 18-hole course (par 72, $14–16) adjoined by an RV park of grassy sites under a smattering of pine trees; the park is frequented by snowbirds, but you can inquire at the pro shop regarding overnight and weekend stays. Each hole has an interpretive sign giving the lay of the land. After a round, golfers gather at the Shady Brook Grille, just outside the pro shop.

Wesley Chapel

Challenge your skills amid tall cypress trees and tranquil lagoons at **Saddlebrook Resort** (813-973-1111; www.saddlebrook.com/golf.html), 4750 Fox Hunt Dr. Located on 480 acres of rolling terrain, this semiprivate course provides two 18-hole championship courses designed by Arnold Palmer. You'll learn the four basics—swing fundamentals, the scoring zone, course strategy, and how to practice like a pro—at their golf academy. Several packages are available, including a 30-minute individual lesson or a personal analysis of your swing, which includes a take-home video of your performance.

HIKING Although you'll stumble across signs for great little hikes like **Crystal River Ecowalk** and **Churchfield Hammock Trail** off US 19 at Crystal River State Buffer Preserve (352-563-0450), hiking opportunities on the Nature Coast mainly center on the many tracts of **Withlacoochee State Forest** (see *Wild Places*). The 43-mile **Citrus Trail** and 26-mile **Richloam Loop**, both part of the **Florida Trail**, are the best places to backpack; day hikers shouldn't miss the **Croom Hiking Trail** (off FL 50 at Ridge Manor) and the **Johnson Pond Trail** (off CR 33 south of Citrus Springs).

MANATEE-WATCHING The Nature Coast prides itself on being Manatee Central, where hundreds of these gentle giants come to winter in the many warm springs along the coast. A permanent population resides in rehab at **Homosassa Springs State Wildlife Park** (see *Zoological Park*), but if you're up for a little adventure, **Crystal River National Wildlife Refuge** (see *Springs*) is the place to take to the water in a kayak or with snorkeling or diving equipment. In Crystal River, ask your outfitter for a map or directions to some of the area's sweet spots for manatee sightings, like Magnolia, Three Sisters, Mullet, and Kings Springs. Stay out-

Sandra Friend

KAYAKING ON THE HOMOSASSA RIVER

side the roped boundaries of the manatee preserves along the river and do not touch or chase these massive creatures: Harassment of a manatee is a felony. Ecotour operators (see *Ecotours*) can also take you up close to the wintering manatee population.

PADDLING The Nature Coast is a top paddling destination in Florida, thanks to its many winding channels and extensive estuaries. Paddling is the best way to explore **Chassahowitzka National Wildlife Refuge**; the main put-in is at the Chassahowitzka River Campground and Recreational Area (see *Campgrounds*), where they also rent canoes and kayaks.

For exploration of the crystalline **Homosassa River**, grab your rentals at either the Marguerita Grill (352-628-1336), 10200 W Halls River Rd, **Riversport Kayaks** (1-877-660-0929; www.flakayak.com), 2300 S Suncoast Blvd, or **River Safaris** (see *Ecotours*).

Reservations are suggested for rentals to paddle the popular and pristine 8-mile route along the Weekiwachee River; stop in at **Weekiwachee Canoe & Kayak Rental** (352-597-0360; www.floridacanoe.com), behind the Weeki Wachee attraction, for rentals, $22–31. At Crystal River all the dive shops (see *Diving*) rent canoes and kayaks. My personal experience on the river says go for a sea kayak: It can slip into tight spots between the islands and yet stays perfectly stable when you're out in the broad channel, where you'll meet a lot of motorboats.

Navigable just north of Dade City, the **Withlacoochee River** flows north through the region and provides a fabulous multiday trip for paddlers. Rent canoes and kayaks at the **Nobleton Outpost** (1-800-783-5284; www.nobleton outpost.com), 29295 CR 476, under new management with Corrine Berry and Marsha Warner; they also have new riverside cabins ($60–75) and camping, and

SKYDIVING Always my adventure child, Sherri convinced me to do a mother–daughter jump for part of my research. "How can you write about it if you don't experience it?" So I found myself on a cool spring morning pulling on a brightly colored jumpsuit at ZHills Skydive City. As the instructors attached our harnesses, we nervously listened to the necessary instructions for a safe jump. Sherri now wore a somber look, but neither one of us were backing out. We boarded the Twin Otter aircraft, stripped of its seats, and sat on the floor; the instructor attached us to a rail inside the plane. Looking around, I noticed that everyone had a parachute—except us. Ours, it would appear, were attached to our tandem instructors. I double-checked my connection to the railing. As we climbed to over 13,000 feet we both grew increasingly quiet. The adrenaline-pumped jumpers were rooting for us, shouting "Redheads Rule!" Then one by one they left the plane and shot toward the earth at alarming speed. I leaned against JC as he attached the tandem harness in four places, checked it, and then checked it again. "Are you ready?" he yelled, as we toddled toward the open door. I nodded, as there wasn't a drop of spit in my mouth left for vocalizing. As we hung on the door I was thinking only one thing—Don't scream; it's all on camera!

We counted one–two–three, and then we were airborne. And I was free. The fear left me instantly and it was awesome. A surreal feeling enveloped me and I was surprised that I had no sense of falling, just a lot of wind in a very large open space. Pure freedom. We flew up to and probably over 120 mph for what seemed like minutes, but was just shy of 60 seconds. Then we deployed the parachute and I found myself gently sitting in my swinglike harness with JC still securely attached. It was so quiet, and I could see for miles. The ground still didn't look any closer. I breathed in the cool air as we glided in the remaining 5,000 feet. Not once did I get vertigo, and not once did my fear return. Both Sherri and I felt safe the entire time— tandem accidents are rare. The gear was checked and rechecked, and we were instructed clearly and repeatedly in not only what we needed to do, but also what was going to happen at each stage so there really were no surprises. Were we scared? Yeah, the video doesn't lie. Would we do it again? Race you to the drop zone!

Take the jump and get in with a whole new league of people at **ZHills Skydive City** (1-800-404-9399; www.skydivecity.com), 4241 Skydive Ln, Zephyrhills, where the thrills start at 13,500 feet. Let the wind whip past you as you fly at 120 mph, then deploy your parachute and glide into the drop zone for a perfect landing. This is one of the best places for tandem jumps. If you want to learn more, the experienced instructors will teach you how to fly by starting with either static line deployment or instructor-assisted deployment. Weight limit for tandem jumps is 220 pounds. Tandem free fall $195.

a Paddler's Pub with snack bar and cold drinks. They offer shuttles (for kayakers and hikers) in the area.

SCENIC DRIVES There are plenty of quiet back roads throughout the Nature Coast, so it all depends on the scenery you're looking for. For a taste of the Old South, head up **Istachatta Rd** (CR 39) from Nobleton to Floral City, driving through tunnels of live oaks, passing farms and colorful floodplain forests. Turn left on **FL 44** and continue into Floral City, marveling at the ancient oaks shading the town. For a drive through the Gulf estuary, follow the **Fort Island Trail** from Crystal River west to its terminus at Fort Island Beach; enjoy the vast expanse of salt marsh broken up by islands of cabbage palms. Through rolling hills topped with cattle ranches and horse farms, **US 41** passes through small-town Florida on its route through the Nature Coast, as does **US 301**: You'll see few strip malls and chain restaurants along these routes, and US 41 traces the route of Spanish explorer Hernando de Soto through the region.

SPAS Step into paradise at **The Spa at Saddlebrook Resort** (813-907-4419 or 1-800-729-8383; www.saddlebrook.com/spa_and_fitness.html). Your attendant will escort you to the dressing room, where you wrap yourself in luxury with a spa robe and slippers. Take an aromatherapy steam, sauna, or whirlpool before (or after) your services, then relax over a cup of tea. Your therapist will then take you to a private oasis for your personally selected body treatment. Choose a Relaxation on the Rocks stone massage, or revive and rejuvenate with a Citrus Herbal Body Scrub or a Wild Lavender Body Facial topped off with a unique glycolic peppermint crème. Products from the spa are available to continue your experience at home. Spa and salon open daily 9–8.

SWIMMING See *Beaches* for saltwater swimming throughout the region; for freshwater fun, hit **Hernando Beach** off US 41 in Hernando, with sandy shores on Lake Tsala Apopka, and **Lake Holathlikaha** at Fort Cooper State Park (see *Historic Sites*), or **Buccaneer Bay** (see *Water Park*).

TRAIL RIDING **Just Horsin' Around** (352-637-2206), on FL 44 west of the Withlacoochee River, offers trail rides on the shady forest roads in Flying Eagle Wildlife Management Area along the river. **Rymar Ranch** (352-382-4761) in Lecanto leads trail rides into Withlacoochee State Forest's Citrus Tract; by appointment only. And if you just plain enjoy being around horses, sleep above the stables at **Cypress House** (see *Lodging*), where guests can join in on guided trail rides.

WALKING TOURS *Citrus County's Heritage* introduces visitors to historic sites on walking tours of **downtown Crystal River, Inverness,** and **Floral City**; an overview map spotlights additional sites throughout the county. Contact the Citrus County Office of Historical Resources (352-637-9929) for a copy. *Historical New Port Richey* from Greater **New Port Richey Main Street** Inc. (727-842-8066; www.newportricheymainstreet.com) showcases the 1920s boomtown established by Hollywood bigwigs; Gloria Swanson and Alfred Hitchcock maintained seasonal residences here. *Visit Dade City* outlines a walking tour of historic sites from the 1880s through 1926; contact the Greater **Dade City** Chamber of Commerce (352-567-3769; www.dadecitychamber.org) for a copy. **Brooksville** also offers a walking tour of historic homes; pick up a brochure at the chamber of commerce or check the Web site at www.brooksvillemuralsoc.org.

WATER PARK With water slides and swimming in one of the clearest rivers in Florida, **Buccaneer Bay** at Weeki Wachee Springs (see *Attractions*) is included in summer ticket prices to the park; open from the end of March through Labor Day weekend.

✳ Green Space

BEACHES Fringed with estuaries, the Nature Coast isn't known for its beaches. But at **Fort Island Beach**, west of Crystal River at the end of Fort Island Rd, you can stretch out on the sand and enjoy the sun, or dive into the Gulf for a swim. At **Pine Island Park**, east of Weeki Wachee at the end of CR 550, enjoy Hernando County's only sandy strand, open 8–7 and perfect for sunset-watching, with Willy's Tropical Breeze Cafe providing munchies; fee. **Hudson Beach**, off US 19 south of Hudson, provides a small sandy shore (limited swimming) on the Gulf at Robert A. Strickland Memorial Park, and **Robert K. Rees Park** in Port Richey has 45 acres of shell-fringed beaches. Both parks are off US 19; follow the BEACH signs. If you have a boat, head for **Anclote Key Preserve State Park** (727-469-5942; www.floridastateparks.org/anclotekey), off Anclote, where paradise awaits along 4 miles of the most secluded beaches on the coast.

GARDENS Nature Coast Botanical Gardens (352-683-9933; www.nature coastbotanicalgardens.com), 1489 Parker Ave, Spring Hill. This peaceful 3.5-acre retreat has 17 themed spaces, including a butterfly garden, herb garden, and waterfall. Open daily; free.

GREENWAYS With its northern terminus at US 98 near Chassahowitzka and its southern terminus at Lutz, the **Suncoast State Trail** (1-800-749-PIKE; www.dep.state.fl.us/gwt/guide/regions/westcentral/trails/suncoast.htm) is one heck of a long ride. Built in conjunction with the Suncoast Parkway, the 42-mile ribbon of pavement parallels this new highway right into suburban northern Tampa. Occasional rest stops have restrooms; benches are scattered along the route. There's little to no shade, but I still see more bikers on the trail than cars on the highway when I drive to Tampa. The **Withlacoochee State Trail** (352-726-0315;

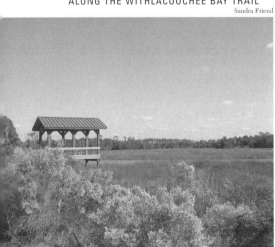

ALONG THE WITHLACOOCHEE BAY TRAIL
Sandra Friend

www.dep.state.fl.us/gwt/state/with/), 3100 S Old Floral City Rd, stretches 46 miles between Trilby, north of Dade City, to Dunnellon, ending just before you reach the Marion County line. It's a favorite of long-distance bicyclists, with lodgings in Hernando and Inverness, plus several campgrounds along the way.

NATURE CENTERS North of Brooksville off US 41, **Chisengut Nature Center** (352-796-6524; www.auxsvc.usf.edu/chisengut) at Chisengut Hill (see *Historic Sites*) has six interpretive trails radiating out from an educational center operated by the Florida Fish and Wildlife Conservation Commission. Open daily, with limited weekend hours.

PARKS In addition to the parks mentioned under *Beaches*, coastal parks along the Nature Coast include **Fort Island Trail**, a small park along its namesake road, with a boat ramp and fishing pier where you can watch manatees swim past in Crystal River; **Jenkins Creek Park**, Shoal Line Rd in Hernando Beach, with boat ramps, a boardwalk, and an observation tower overlooking fabulous sunsets over the Gulf estuary; and **Key Vista Nature Park**, 2700 Bailey's Bluff Blvd, Holiday, where nature trails provide wildlife-watching opportunities along the Gulf of Mexico.

In Pasco County (727-847-2411, ext 1260), 14 miles of backpacking, biking, and equestrian trails span a vast wilderness between the Pithlachascotee and Anclote Rivers at **Starkey Wilderness Park**, Wilderness Rd, which also has picnic pavilions and a developed campground. Get out into the wilds at **Crews Lake Park**, 16739 Crews Lake Dr, on a mile-long nature trail with special migratory bird and butterfly observation areas. **Withlacoochee River Park**, 12449 River Rd, has camping, hiking, and replicas of an 1800s Florida pioneer settlement and a 1700s Native American village.

Hernando County has **Lake Townsend Regional Park**, providing picnic facilities and trailhead access to the Withlacoochee State Trail in Nobleton at CR 476. In Sumter County, off CR 470, **Marsh Bend County Park** provides anglers a place to cast off an old railroad bridge on the Outlet River.

SPRINGS Thirty springs protected by **Crystal River National Wildlife Refuge** (352-563-2088; www.nccentral.com/fcnwr.htm) in Crystal River serve as critical wintering grounds for nearly 20 percent of the nation's manatee population. Stop by the Manatee Education Center on US 19 next to Homosassa Springs Wildlife State Park (see *Zoological Park*) for interpretive information; if you're paddling into the refuge (it's made up of river bottom and a handful of islands), tie off at the pontoon anchored near Banana Island.

WILD PLACES I'll never forget the image of whooping cranes following an ultralight airplane from Nebraska to **Chassahowitzka National Wildlife Refuge** (352-563-2088; www.nccentral.com/fcnwr.htm), one of the wildest places the Nature Coast has to offer. You can't get there on foot: Most of the refuge is the fringe of estuary along the Gulf Coast. Grab a paddle and head out on the water from the **Chassahowitzka River Campground and Recreational Area** (see

Campgrounds) for bird-watching and spectacular scenery, like the cabbage palm hammock at Seven Cabbage Cut. **St. Martin's Marsh Aquatic Preserve** (352-563-0450; www.dep.state.fl.us/coastal/sites/stmartins) and **Crystal River Preserve State Park** (352-563-0450; www.floridastateparks.org/crystalriver preserve) also protect a broad swath of the Gulf Coast estuary at Crystal River. The region has several wildlife management areas and water management areas that encompass floodplain forests along the Withlacoochee River, such as **Half Moon**, **Flying Eagle**, and **Lake Panasoffkee**; when it's not hunting season, the forest roads provide a place for exploration of these jungle-like forests. But the largest wild region along the Nature Coast is the **Green Swamp**, the birthplace of the Withlacoochee, Ocklawaha, Hillsborough, and Peace Rivers, accessed via hiking trails and forest roads west of Ridge Manor and Dade City in Pasco County.

The Nature Coast is also home to Florida's most expansive state forest, **Withlacoochee State Forest** (352-754-6896; www.fl-dof.com/state_forests/withlacoochee.html) which is broken into a smattering of separate tracts scattered across the region. In addition to being a popular destination for deer hunters each winter, the forest has a little something for everyone. Campers flock to several developed camping areas, including the beautiful **Hog Island** and **River Junction** recreation areas in the Croom Tract, and **Holder Mine** and **Mutual Mine** campgrounds in the Citrus Tract. Most equestrians head for **Tillis Hill**, a horse camping area in the heart of the trail system in the Citrus Tract. Stop at the Withlacoochee State Forest Recreation and Visitors Center (352-754-6896), 15003 Broad St, Brooksville, for maps and information on all of the tracts.

✴ Lodging
BED & BREAKFASTS

Bushnell 33513
🌱 **Cypress House** (352-568-0909 or 1-888-568-1666; www.bbonline.com/fl/cypresshouse), 5175 W 90th Blvd. If you love the outdoors, you must visit this very special B&B in the rural rolling hills of Sumter County, where Jan Fessler caters to folks looking for outdoor recreation—whether it be a trail ride with her horses, bicycling on the Withlacoochee State Trail, kayaking down the Withlacoochee River, or hiking the Florida Trail in Withlacoochee State Forest. Set under ancient live oaks, the lodge has five country-themed rooms and suites, $70–120; they'll board your horses (space permitting) for an additional fee.

Chassahowitzka 34448
🐾 ♿ **Chassahowitzka Hotel** (352-382-2075; www.chazhotel.com), 8551 W Miss Maggie Dr. From the outside, you'd never suspect this hotel dated back to 1910—that's how thorough David Strickland's renovations have been. His grandfather ran this as the area's premier resort for anglers, and David reopened it in 2001 to cater to those heading out on the water; a boat ramp and canoe livery are just down the street. It's classy for the outdoor recreation crowd: seven beautifully refinished rooms long on practicality, with multiple beds and common multiple-stall, multiple-shower bathrooms

at either end of the upper floor. The ground-floor room is fully wheelchair accessible. A den with an overflowing toy bin will keep the kids busy, and there's a television in the large living room, or you can sit out on the quiet porch and lose yourself in a book. Room rates ($40–80) include a continental breakfast; cooked breakfast or your catch prepared for dinner for an additional charge. Dinner available three days a week; call ahead for reservations, and ask about their fishing guide service.

Inverness 34450

Inverness Place (352-637-3104; www.invernessplace.com), 811 Zephyr St. Two spacious rooms ($109–125) with roomy private bath open onto a broad porch in one of the "grand old dames" of Inverness; each room is invitingly decorated with antiques and period reproductions. Downstairs, a cozy sunporch awaits readers, or curl up in the warm parlor with a good book. Full breakfasts include such delights as skillet frittatas and French toast.

San Antonio 33576

St. Charles Inn (352-588-4130; www.stcharlesinnbedandbreakfast .com), 12503 Curley Rd. Built as the St. Charles Hotel in 1913 to meet the needs of the Orange Belt Railroad line, this charming B&B run by Ted and Ann Stephens adjoins an orange grove. You'll want to spend as much time outside as in, tempted by the rocking chairs on the wraparound porch overlooking a garden shaded by an ancient cedar. Choose from two bright, airy rooms (one with twin beds) or a suite, $125–150.

Crystal River 34428

🐾 🐟 ♿ 🌺 **Best Western Crystal River Resort** (1-800-435-4409; www.crystalriverresort.com), 614 NW US 19. While the rooms sparkle with the cleanliness you'd expect from a major chain, this is not your typical chain motel. Guests enjoy complimentary cruises around Kings Bay every afternoon from the on-site marina, and have free use of the boat ramp and dock. The swimming pool and hot tub overlook Kings Bay, and are adjoined by Crystal Lodge Dive Center (see *Diving*)—a full-service dive shop that offers instruction, rental equipment, and guided trips—and Cravings on the Water (see *Eating Out*), a comfy waterfront tiki bar and restaurant. Spread out over four buildings, the smartly decorated rooms ($90 and up) include a coffeemaker, ironing board, and hair dryer; efficiencies available. Adjoining the lobby, the Sea Treasures gift shop includes a broad selection of fishing rods and reels. Small, attended pets permitted.

THE PLANTATION INN & GOLF RESORT

Sandra Friend

&. "¶" ⊙ The roots of **Plantation Inn & Golf Resort** (1-800-632-6262; www.plantationinn.com), 9301 W Fort Island Trail, go back to a 1950s hunting and fishing lodge, expanded upon to meet family needs. Now the inn is a major destination resort. Most of the guest rooms ($140 and up) are housed in grand structures with a southern plantation feel, overlooking Crystal River. Extras include a marina and dive shop with instruction, manatee tours, and an 18-hole golf course with a guaranteed gator in every water hazard. Don't worry, they're friendly—and if you stay in the two-story golf course villas (sleeps six, full kitchen, two baths), you'll be tempted to amble the fairways for some prime bird-watching: coots and herons on the water, sandhill cranes on the greens. Under construction in 2008: a new destination spa. I can't wait!

Homosassa 34448

McRae's of Homosassa (352-628-2602), 5300 S Cherokee Way. Kick back on a rocking chair overlooking the Homosassa River, or wander down to the marina to enjoy live music at the tiki bar. It's your choice at laid-back McRae's, a perfect launch point for boaters headed out to the Gulf, with large, clean, basic rooms. $55–125, kitchenettes available.

Hudson Beach 34667

Inn on the Gulf (1-877-840-8321; www.innonthegulf.com), 6330 Clark St. This family-owned motel has one of the best views in Pasco County, overlooking the Gulf of Mexico and several marinas. Eighteen kitchenette suites, $55–85, with older furnishings; caters to smokers, with all rooms permitting smoking, although the Sunset Room (see *Eating Out*) does not.

Inverness 34450

🦐 ✎ &. **Central Motel** (1-800-554-7241; www.centralmotel.com), 721 US 41 S. One of the nicest family motels in the region: Each enormous room sports a desk and a table (phones have dataports) as well as a coffeemaker and small refrigerator; there's a popular pool area and easy access to the Withlacoochee State Trail (pedal right on out of the back of the parking lot!). Reservations recommended, especially on weekends. $45–75.

Wesley Chapel 33543

⊙ "¶" **Saddlebrook Resort** (1-800-729-8383; www.saddlebrook.com), 5700 Saddlebrook Way. What I found at this impeccably groomed resort was six-star service. Yes, six stars! From the bellman to the front desk to house-keeping to the gift shop attendant, no matter where I went I was greeted with the best service I have ever received—anywhere. The courteous, professional staff are what makes this place so special. Once you check into your spacious suite ($145 and up), take a stroll through the Walking Village, where you can stop for a bite to eat at the Terrace on the Green, listen to live music at the Polo Lounge, perfect your backhand at the Tennis Shop, relax in the Spa, or take a dip in the 500,000-gallon SuperPool. Greet each morning with a lavish buffet breakfast in the Cypress Restaurant, where you'll find the best Belgian waffles and hearty scrambled eggs with cheese. I loved the granola yogurt and fruit served in a martini glass. And coffee to go is a nice touch. When the day winds down, you'll want to dine at the richly appointed Dempsey's Steak House or watch your favorite sporting event on oversized screens at TD's Sports Bar. Whatever you do at Saddlebrook, you won't need your car.

CABINS

Homosassa 34448
Nature's Resort (see *Campgrounds*), offers beautiful waterfront A-frame chalets as well as park models that are basic and clean, with full kitchens and room to sleep four; $100.

Lake Panasoffkee 33538
Tracy's Point Fish Camp (352-793-8060; www.tracyspoint.com), CR 437, has very pleasant "brand new rustic" cabins ($75–85), all within a few feet of the lake. Grab your bait and tackle from their shop, rent a boat, and hit the water for some serious bass fishing.

🐾 ✿ ♿ In addition to lakeside camping, **Werda-Hecamiat** (see *Campgrounds*) has several units that impressed the heck out of me: a duplex with two spacious rooms, each with full kitchen and all new appliances, perfect for families; and the Banana, a little old fish-camp-style cabin renovated to a T. $85–175, with a 2-night minimum.

CAMPGROUNDS

Chassahowitzka 34448
Run by Citrus County, the **Chassahowitzka River Campground and Recreational Area** (352-382-2200; www.swfwmd.state.fl.us/recreation/areas/chassahowitzka.html), 8600 W Miss Maggie Dr, offers both full-hookup and primitive campsites surrounded by the jungle-like floodplain forests of the Chassahowitzka River. There's a camp store and canoe livery; daily charge for non-campers to park at the boat ramp.

Crystal River 34428
Lake Rousseau RV Park (352-795-6336; www.lakerousseaurvpark.com),

10811 N Coveview Terr. Hidden along a quiet cypress-lined cove of Lake Rousseau, prime bass fishing territory, this snowbird retreat gets busy in winter, with more than 100 sites and two sets of boat docks; full hookup, $29; no tents.

Quail Roost RV Campground (352-563-0404; www.quailroostcampground.com), 9835 N Citrus Ave. Ten acres of camping with 72 full-hookup sites ($32), sparkling heated swimming pool, and recreational hall with fireplace; nice mix of sunny and shady sites.

Homosassa 34448
🐾 ✿ **Camp N' Water RV Resort** (352-628-2000), 11465 W Priest Lane. Follow the signs from Yulee Dr to find this campground tucked away on the Homosassa River, with well-shaded full-hookup sites with picnic tables, $28. Nice riverside swimming pool, dining area, and lounge; dockage and boat ramp available to guests.

🐾 ✿ **Nature's Resort** (1-800-301-7880; www.naturesresortfla.com), 10359 W Halls River Rd. Campsites along the entry road are bounded on both sides by thick forest, and large hardwoods provide a shady canopy overhead. Prefer the waterfront? Full-hookup sites ($30) face the estuary, with easy access for paddlers; tie a motorboat up right in front of your camper. Their on-site marina has a waterfront bar and grill with pool tables, and rents canoes and kayaks as well as pontoon boats. A large clubhouse provides a gathering place for the camping community, with swimming pool and shuffleboard. Bathhouse provided for tent campers ($25); small nondenominational church near the camp store and office.

Turtle Creek Campground (352-628-2928; www.turtlecreekrvresort .com), 10200 W Fish Bowl Dr. Nestled in the river hammock floodplain of the Homosassa River, this expansive campground (part shade, part sun) includes full hookups, heated swimming pool, and air-conditioned recreation hall. RVs, trailers, and tents welcome, $27; convenient to Homosassa Springs Wildlife State Park (see *Zoological Park*), boat ramps, and restaurants.

Inverness 34450

Riverside Lodge & RV Resort (1-888-404-8332; www.riversidelodgerv .com), 12561 E Gulf to Lake Hwy. In a shady hammock on the Withlacoochee River, this pleasant resort offers RV campsites ($35–40) and cabins ($60–120) with easy access to the water for boating and fishing.

Lake Panasoffkee 33538

Werda-Hecamiat RV Park & Marina (1-877-793-8137; www.myfish lodge.net), 965 CR 439. Sunrises and cool breezes off the best panfish lake in the region: That's what you'll find

at this great little "where the heck am I at?" family campground with sunny grassy spots ($25) and cabins, spontaneous fish fries, a proper camp store, and a covered boat slip.

DIVE RESORTS

Crystal River 34429

☙ Elvis slept at the **Port Hotel & Marina** (352-795-3111; www.port hotelandmarina.com), 1610 SE Paradise Circle. Honest! In 1959 he filmed *Follow That Dream* in and around Citrus County, and this was his home away from home. It's a great venue for water sports enthusiasts— every room ($65–75) faces the Crystal River Aquatic Preserve, where manatees gather en masse each winter seeking the warmth of the springs. Push your kayak in right from the grassy lawn outside your room, or grab a snorkel and swim out to the ropes to watch these gentle giants feeding. On-site dive shop, boat rentals, boat ramp, swimming pool, waterfront bar, and Ale House restaurant.

FISH CAMPS

Lake Panasoffkee 33538

🐾 **Idlewild Lodge and RV Park** (352-793-7057; www.idlewildlodge .com), 4110 CR 400. Providing great access to the wild spaces of Lake Panasoffkee's northern shore, this fish camp has shady RV spaces with paved pads and full hookups ($25), modest cottages ($79–105), and a pool for the kids to hang out at while the family angler is chasing bass. Launch fee waived if you're a guest, and all guests have access to a nice boardwalk out on the lake to a fishing platform.

DOCKING AT THE PORT HOTEL & MARINA
Sandra Friend

Pana Vista Lodge (352-793-2061; www.panavistalodge.com), 3417 CR 421. One of Florida's oldest fish camps, dating back to the 1880s, Pana Vista attracts folks looking for peace, quiet, and fishing. Situated on the Outlet River between the lake and the Withlacoochee River, it's an ideal place to plunk down your RV or tent ($15–25) under the tall magnolias and cabbage palms before prepping for a day on the water. Looking for more amenities? Try the modest fish-camp-style duplex cottages ($75–100) with air-conditioning and heating; linens and utensils furnished. Pontoon boat rentals, full-service bait-and-tackle shop, live well, fishing guides available.

✷ Where to Eat
DINING OUT

Brooksville
🍴 **Victoria's Steak House & Lounge** (352-799-8985), 11738 Broad St. An emphasis on hand-cut prime rib, porterhouse, filet mignon, New York strip, and T-bone, accentuated with more than a dozen seafood entrées, forms the meat of this local favorite—and the meat is excellent! Open daily for lunch and dinner, entrées $11 and up; adjoining lounge hosts live country music on weekends.

Crystal River
Charlie's Fish House Restaurant (352-795-3949), US 19. Perched on the edge of Kings Bay, Charlie's is an old standard in town, a family-run operation for more than 40 years. You won't be disappointed with any selection from the menu; I'm partial to the local mullet, escalloped oysters, and grouper. Sandwiches start at $4; entrées, $9 and up. Stop in their

adjoining fish market to nab smoked mullet and mullet dip. Lunch and dinner served.

Dade City
Lunch on Limoges (352-567-5685), 14139 Seventh St. I've never seen a place with so much southern pizzazz—waitresses in sparkling white uniforms bring you tall glasses of iced tea, and the daily menu is on a chalkboard carried from table to table. The tall cakes rival any you'd find in a fine bakery. It's the place to see and be seen at lunchtime, serving sandwiches, salads, and entrées ($10–15) like shrimp salad, pecan grouper, and Tuscan shrimp with pasta. The YaYa Sisterhood would find it just divine; I sure did!

Hernando Beach
Bare Bones (352-596-9403; www .bareboneshernandobeach.com), 3192 Shoal Line Blvd. Tom and Karen McEachern preside over this intimate fine-dining experience noted for its classy tableside preparation of fresh seafood and steaks ($12–25). Closed Mon, serving dinner 4–9.

Homosassa
Misty River Seafood House (352-628-6288), 4135 S Suncoast Blvd, features fresh seafood in tasteful preparations such as shrimp imperial, lemon-pepper fish, and coconut shrimp (entrées $10 and up), as well as several selections of steak, pork, and chicken for landlubbers. Watch for stone crab claw specials! Open for lunch and dinner; daily Sunset Specials 3–6.

Lake Panasoffkee
Harbor Lights Restaurant (352-793-7058), CR 470. Well off the beaten path, this restaurant has a fabulous view of the lake and has been a local

fixture since 1982, featuring all-you-care-to-eat buffets with crab legs, sirloin steak, roast beef, baked ham, and more. Open for dinner Thu–Sun; lunch on Sun.

Ozello

🦞 **Pecks Old Port Cove** (352-795-2806), W Ozello Trail (CR 494). At the end of a 9-mile drive leading to the Gulf of Mexico, Pecks's specialty is crab—garlic, soft-shell, snow, stone, and steamed—and plenty of it, thanks to their crab farm out back. But you'll find all the seafood fresh, not frozen, from the scallops and oysters to the calamari appetizers. Expect monster portions for a reasonable price. Entrées start at $7.93, with daily all-you-can-eat specials. Bring cash—no credit cards accepted. Open daily 11–10; reservations suggested.

Port Richey

Catches (727-849-2208), 7811 Bay View Ave. Perched above the Pithlachascotee River, this roomy restaurant with a New England feel features more than a dozen types of seafood, including coconut shrimp and giant Caribbean lobster tail (market price); lunch and dinner, $15 and up.

EATING OUT

Brooksville

Main Street Eatery (352-799-2789), 101 N Main St. The Buzzard Breath Chili tempted, but I settled on Bill's Special, piled high with ham, bacon, and three cheeses, with black beans and yellow rice on the side. Borrowing from several cuisines, this friendly local favorite lunch stop ($4 and up) shines. Closed Sun.

In the historic Hawkins House across from Roger's Christmas Village (see *Selective Shopping*), **Mallie Kyla's**

Café (352-796-7174; www.mallie kylas.com), 510 E Liberty St, is an award-winning eatery renowned for salad dressings. Try their Southern Spinach Salad, with dried cranberries, purple onions, mandarin oranges, feta cheese, and toasted pecans drizzled with citrus dressing. They bake exquisite desserts like coconut silk pie and hummingbird cake, available by the slice or by the whole. Open for lunch ($7–8) 11–3, Mon–Sat.

Crystal River

Cafe on the Avenue (352-795-3656), 631 N Citrus Ave. At Heritage Village, an artful presentation of salads, sandwiches, and entrées in a country garden atmosphere. Their signature dish is a Greek salad piled high with shrimps and anchovies; I was impressed by the fresh mini sweetbreads and smooth mushroom-crab bisque. Lunch favorites $8 and up, dinner entrées $14 and up.

Serving up Cuban favorites from Grandma Mimi's special recipes and seafood fare at the Best Western Crystal River (see *Resorts*), **Cravings on the Water** (352-795-2027; www .cravingsonthewater.com), a casual open-air dockside restaurant and bar, is a great place to kick back and enjoy a drink while watching the ospreys dive into Kings Bay. Enjoy black beans and rice, picadillo, or any of numerous other Cuban favorites prepared by Chef Alberto. Open 7–9, serving breakfast, lunch, and dinner; entertainment on weekends includes live music and Parrothead parties.

🦞 **Grannie's Country Cookin'** (352-795-8884), corner of US 19 and Fort Island Trail. This place is hopping every time I stop by—park in the strip mall behind it if you can't find a space. Expect the waitresses to call you "sweetheart" and "darlin' " as they dish up southern comfort food at prices that date back to the 1960s: You can grab a full meal for under $5. Breakfast served all day; breakfast, lunch, and dinner specials are posted on the board. The strawberry biscuit (for dessert or breakfast) is a real gem. Open 5 AM–9 PM daily.

Dade City

A Matter of Taste Café & Tea Room (352-567-5100), 14121 Seventh St. A family favorite with huge sandwiches and creative salads (shrimp chef, California cool plate, their famous Pineapple Boat, and more) served in large baskets, $7 and up. Open Mon–Sat, 11–8.

Since 1957, **George & Gladys' Barbecue** (352-567-6229), 19215 US 301, has been "nothing new, nothing fancy, just good bar-b-q." I can vouch for breakfast, too, as this little diner serves up a hearty set of eggs, grits, and toast for under $3. The barbecue beef and pork is chipped, with sandwiches and burgers under $3, too.

Kafé Kokopelli (352-523-0055), 37940 Live Oak Ave. This unique restaurant melds the best of the Southwest with traditional southern hospitality. Sample the chicken curry or go for the cedar-planked salmon; daily house specials include homemade spaghetti and meatballs and pot roast. Serving lunch and dinner, with entrées $9–17.

Floral City

At **Jeanette's Little Restaurant** (352-637-0555), 6689 S Florida Ave, they do mean "little"—this family diner only has eight tables, bathed in sunlight and just a few steps from the Withlacoochee State Trail (see *Greenways*). Breakfasts (served all day, to

Sandra Friend

JEANETTE'S LITTLE RESTAURANT

$10) include hearty items like eggs Benedict, corned beef hash, and country-fried steak, while big burgers and their "Brisketilla"—brisket dressed with wasabi, cucumber, sour cream, pepper, onion, tomato, and lettuce on a Mediterranean wrap— are on the lunch menu ($7–10) along with entrées like pot roast, chicken liver, and fried chicken. Open Tue–Fri until 8, Sat–Sun until 3.

The aromas are heavenly when you enter the **Old World Restaurant** (352-344-4443), 8370 S Florida Ave, thanks to the tureens of soup and fresh-baked German bread that all are welcome to enjoy with their entrée ($9–27); the diverse menu encompasses seafood, roast duck, osso buco, stuffed cabbage, *kassler rippchen* with spaetzle, rainbow trout, and even frog legs. The owners are Romanian and have been a local favorite since 1981, creating decadent desserts like Black Forest chocolate torte and apple strudel. Open for dinner Wed–Sun at 3.

Shamrock Inn (352-726-6414), 8343 E Florida Ave. "Good friends, good food, good times" is their motto, and as you step through the doorway painted with a giant leprechaun into this Irish-themed bar and grill, you'll feel at home. In addition to great American standbys like burgers, salads, and the best wings in the area, you'll find some offbeat items like Wiener schnitzel and spinach dip with chips. Serving breakfast, lunch, and dinner.

Hernando

❦ **Frank's Family Restaurant** (352-344-2911), Hernando Plaza, US 41 at FL 200. Think real blueberry pancakes, waffles with fruit, and omelets all the way. Frank's has on-the-ball service, and good food, attracting a steady local clientele. Serving all meals at bargain prices.

Homosassa

Dan's Clam Stand (352-628-9588), 7364 Grover Cleveland Blvd. It's small and off the beaten path, but for those who love freshly fried fish, Dan's serves up heaping helpings. The top attraction: whole belly clams ($13), with much more clam meat than clam strips. Open for lunch and dinner; no credit cards. A second, roomier location is in Crystal River on FL 44 E.

Museum Café (352-628-1081), 10466 W Yulee Dr. Adjacent to the Yulee Sugar Mill (see *Historic Sites*), the Museum Cafe serves up authentic Ybor City Cuban sandwiches piled with salami, ham, spiced pork, and Swiss cheese. Stop in to see the restored 1924 Model T in the middle of the dining room, and peek into the Olde Mill House Gallery and Printing Museum (see *Museums*), which shares the building.

Old Homosassa Smokehouse (352-628-6663), W Yulee Dr. There's hardly enough room inside to swing a mullet, but the aroma will draw you

right in. Grab some ribs or a smoked meat sandwich ($5 and up) with sides, and retreat to the picnic table outside for a feast, or choose the house specialty—smoked mullet (and smoked mullet dip, yum).

Hudson

Sunset Room at Inn on the Gulf (see *Lodging*). Never mind the killer sunset view: the chocolate desserts will grab your attention, like the mountainous Vesuvius. Seafood is the standard here, with a side of Hellas: saganaki, calamari, and (if you ask nicely) traditional Greek village salad. Sandwiches and entrées $7–38.

Inverness

Cinnamon Sticks Restaurant and Bakery (352-726-7333), 2120 W FL 44. Boasting the "Best Breakfast in Citrus County," served all day, this local family-run favorite is always humming. In addition to traditional favorites and omelets, you can order several types of crêpes or a fruit blintz, as well as skillet breakfasts piled high atop seasoned home fries; you won't go away hungry! Dinners include down-home favorites like meatloaf, southern-fried country steak, and Thanksgiving dinner with all the trimmings ($6–11).

❦ **Cockadoodles Café** (352-637-0335), 206 W Tompkins St. From cheese blintzes with strawberries to an 8-ounce rib eye with eggs, this downtown café (open 7–2) serves one heck of a breakfast ($2–7). Lunch includes house-special platters like meatloaf, open-faced roast beef sandwiches, and chicken livers ($3–7). Great food, great service!

❦ **Fisherman's Restaurant** (352-637-5888), 12311 E Gulf to Lake Hwy. Don't drive too fast: You might miss this tiny cottage along FL 44 near the Withlacoochee River. But stop for a taste of chef Bob Root's seafood, and he'll reel you in for good. Their massive fried shrimp are lightly breaded with a delicate hint of pepper, and their lime pie is one of the best I've had. Choose from a nice range of fresh seafood entrées, including grouper, scallops, and oysters, or from several prime cuts of steak. Serving lunch and dinner ($7–30); closed Mon.

🏵 **Stumpknockers on the Square** (352-726-2212; www.stumpknockers .net/Inverness_Downtown.html), 110 W Main St. Like its sister restaurant in Marion County, Stumpknockers delivers excellent seafood dinners ($10–18) and the best freshly fried mushrooms in Florida (monster portion served with dipping sauce). Housed in a historic building, the downtown location makes it a great lunch stop when you're browsing the shops. Open for lunch and dinner; closed Mon.

Istachatta
The **Istachatta Country Store** (352-544-1017), 28198 Magnon Dr, along the Withlacoochee State Trail, offers simple country breakfast and lunch items 7–2 daily, or show up for the Friday evening all-you-can-eat fish fry and famous Saturday evening shrimp platters, accompanied by live music 5:30–7:30.

Lake Panasoffkee
Catfish Johnny's (352-793-2083), CR 470, looks like a barbecue place but, hey, this is Lake Panasoffkee—fish dominates the menu, in baskets, grilled, and fried. Dinner specials include home-cooked entrées like country-fried steak and catfish, or choose a seafood platter for two,

$9–22. Homemade desserts like coconut cake and peanut butter pie will tempt. All-you-can-eat catfish served Fri.

Spring Hill
Pit Boss BBQ (352-688-BOSS; www .pit-boss.com), 2270 US 19. In a gambling mood? This Vegas-themed open-pit barbecue smells delicious, and the food is as good as the aromas off the fireplace—I was impressed by the freshly made burger on a toasted bun with thick-cut fries on the side. Ribs are their specialty, and you'll be tempted by banana-split cake for dessert. Serving lunch and dinner, $6–15.

A CHOCOLATIER AND ICE CREAM

Crystal River
Dockside Ice Cream Shoppe (1-800-844-0867), 300 N US 19. In addition to an excellent selection of flavors (cookie dough and coconut are two favorites), the venue is superb: Step outside onto the deck for a sweeping vista of Kings Bay and watch the marina traffic putter by. You might even spy a manatee during the winter months!

Hernando
Having moved into larger quarters, **Denny-Lynn's Fudge Factory** (352-637-3438), 2746 N Florida Ave, isn't so crammed full of chocolate as it used to be, but now you can see everything—and see some of it made. This family-run store aims to please with plenty of homemade creations, including their signature old-fashioned seafoam candy. Try freshly dipped fruits, fresh fudge, sugar-free candies, a rainbow of Jelly Belly flavors, and an amazing array of chocolates; you scoop from penny candy jars.

🖐 Right along the Withlacoochee State Trail, **Sabina's Hernando Diner** (352-637-1308), 2400 N Florida Ave, is a classic old-fashioned diner with red cushioned seats, a great place to stop for an ice cream cone or a banana split when you're out on a long bike ride. Open for breakfast, lunch, and dinner ($3 and up); breakfast served all day.

✳ Selective Shopping

Brooksville

Antique Sampler Mall (352-797-9330; www.antiquesamplermall.com), 31 Main St. Victorian furniture, glassware and china displayed on vintage dining room tables, and a lot of jewelry—free antique jewelry appraisals second Sat monthly. Closed Sun.

The Broken Mold (352-796-6979; www.thebrokenmold.com), 100 Brooksville Ave, has themed rooms of home decor items—nautical, Native American, Far East, and more.

Native American arts, crafts, and music are the centerpiece of **Peace Tree Trading** (352- 797-7886; www.peace treetrading.com), 770 E. Jefferson Street, where silver and turquoise jewelry shimmer inside the small log cabin.

Chassahowitzka

Naber's Doll World (352-382-1001; www.naberkids.com), 8915 S Suncoast Blvd. In a building reminiscent of the Black Forest, German-born Harald Naber displays more than three decades of craftsmanship with his collection of hand-carved wooden collectible dolls. Popular with collectors around the world, new limited-edition one-of-a-kind creations ($200–250, with summer clearance specials as low as $99) are also produced here; the

---

✄ ♿ At **Rogers' Christmas House & Village** (1-877-312-5046; www.rogers christmashouse.com), 103 S Saxton Ave, it's always Christmas in this sprawling complex of historic buildings in downtown Brooksville. Walk into a wonderland of Christmas trees and collectibles to enter the dream of Margaret Ghitto Rogers, who opened her first all-Christmas shop downtown in 1969 and in the 1980s was able to start acquiring and moving historic homes to this site canopied by grand old live oaks. Each building has its own unique theme, with one of the favorites being Storybook Land, where toy-themed ornaments are surrounded by dioramas of *The Wizard of Oz, Jack and the Giant, Sleeping Beauty, Alice in Wonderland,* and a real full-sized sleigh as well as European legends like the "Spider of the Ukraine." The Cottage is full of ornaments and gifts that are a little bit country, a little bit beach. The Magnolia House is grandiose, with an enormous Christmas tree in the foyer, but it was the kitchen that kept us busy with gourmet treats and cookbooks. Dogwoods, magnolias, and azalea line the garden paths between the six houses, with poinsettia growing to enormous heights as it does in the wild. Open daily 9:30–5 except Christmas and Thanksgiving.

fine wood grain shows beneath each realistically painted face. A former bush pilot, Naber started his carving in Alaska, and returns to those roots with at least one Eskimo doll series annually. An on-site doll hospital can restore your aging antiques to their original glory, and if you've ever wanted a miniature of your grandkids, a local porcelain doll artist affiliated with Naber creates lifelike portrait dolls ($289). Visit soon: the store will be closing in January 2009.

Howards Flea Market (1-800-832-3477 or 352-628-3532; www.howards fleamarket.com), 6373 S Suncoast Blvd. Featuring Mr. Ed's Books and a bunch of other weekend vendors, this roadside flea market on US 19 attracts a lot of browsers. Open Fri 7–2, Sat–Sun 7–3.

Coleman

Bobby's Antique Village (352-330-2220), US 301, a collection of late-1800s and early-1900s buildings, has plenty to delight antiques aficionados, from the classic exteriors to the bottles, tools, and ephemera packed inside.

Crystal River

Crystal River Antiques (352-563-1121), 756 NE US 19. Glassware and dishes pack the windows of this antiques shop along busy US 19.

Dockside Trading Company (1-800-844-0867), 300 N US 19. A shop featuring nautically themed gifts and souvenirs: seashells, carvings of manatees, T-shirts with Guy Harvey's excellent artwork, and a nice selection of children's books.

Heritage Village, 631 N Citrus Avenue. A collection of shops that meet a variety of interests, from clothing to home decor, in a village of historic buildings along Citrus Ave; free parking. My favorite is the playful Manatee Toy Company (352-795-6126; www.manateestore.com), which features a little bit of everything fun about maritime Florida, from books and stuffed animals to T-shirts and Jimmy Buffett music.

Magical Senses (352-795-9994), 560 N Citrus Ave. In addition to incense, cleansing candles, and aromatherapy, this decidedly offbeat shop features a full wall of packaged herbs for potion making, and books with a Wiccan theme. Closed Sun and Mon.

The Shoppe for Something Else (352-795-2015), 650 N Citrus Ave. Stroll through an exotic wonderland of home decor with a touch of Africa and the Far East, just across from Heritage Village.

Dade City

Downtown Dade City boasts an extraordinary antiques district, with more than 20 thriving shops catering to a full range of tastes. It's a shopper's getaway for the Tampa crowd, and I guarantee you'll be hooked the first time you visit. Park once, walk everywhere. Here's a sample of what caught my eye; most shops are open Mon–Sat.

At **Annetta's Attic** (352-567-5809), 14144 Eighth St, I stumbled across a kewpie doll and a rhino made from elephant skin, and noticed the Currier & Ives prints on the walls. There's a little bit of everything collectible here, with more in their walk-up attic.

Classic toys like a Flash Gordon propeller pop up in **Antiques on the Main Street** (352-523-0999), 14122 Seventh St, where you'll also find folk art, country primitives, and classic books.

The Book Shack (352-567-5001), 14407 Seventh St, carries a nice stock of used titles.

The Corner Emporium (352-567-8966), 37838 Pasco Ave, isn't really on the corner, but it's full of Far Eastern home decor, Fenton glass, and gourmet goodies, with a bargain attic upstairs.

Distinctive crystalline copper-toned pottery fills the window at **Glades Pottery and Gallery** (352-523-0992), 14145 Seventh St, where they showcase art from more than 20 American artists.

Ivy Cottage (352-523-0019), 14110 Seventh St, boasts an entire wall of Little Golden Books as well as architectural and farmstead antiques, beads, and Civil War ephemera.

South of downtown, **Ms. Charlotte's Antiques** (352-567-6717), 11124 US 98, is a multidealer antiques mall with primitives, furniture, glassware, vintage clothing, and more. Open Thu–Sat.

Floral City

Suzanne's Antiques and Collectibles Corner (352-344-4711), 8294 E Orange Ave. Although there's a heavy emphasis on antique glassware and small curio items, you'll also find shelves of books to browse, vintage clothing and furnishings, and accoutrements worthy of the Red Hat Ladies.

Homosassa

Mason Bleu Uni-ques (352-682-6676), 8445 W Homosassa Trail. The stagecoach outside this bright blue house will catch your attention; inside, shelves filled with antiques and collectibles.

River Safaris Gallery (1-800-758-FISH; www.riversafaris.com), 10823 Yulee Dr. Although the store serves their brisk ecotour business (see *Ecotours*), it also displays fine arts: The owner is a potter; her husband, a sculptor. From pottery and glasswork to copper sculpture, their art (and that of many other local artists showcased in the gallery) explores natural maritime themes.

Inverness

Book Worm (352-726-9141), 105 Dampier St. I'd never realized the connection between book cover design and genre until I saw the walls of paperbacks filling this popular used-book store. The romance section gleamed in pastels; the suspense and horror section looked foreboding in shades of red and black. Closed Sun; closed Mon in summer.

Maine-ly Antiques (352-637-3133), 1259 S Elmwood Dr. Their sign will surely catch your eye: a Victorian lady astride a giant lobster! "Recycled history" is the name of the game here, where spacious dealer booths gleam with goodies; a heavy emphasis on items from 1900 to 1940, from Coca-Cola tins and jewelry to an unexpectedly large stock of 1940s hardcover novels. Jewelry repair shop on-site.

Rainy Day Editions (352-637-3440), 202 Tompkins St. A tall bookcase filled with new books on Florida greets you when you enter this mostly used-book store with an excellent selection of hardcover and paperback by genre; dig through, and you'll find some real treasures.

Ritzy Rags & Glitzy Jewels, Etc. (352-637-6333), 105 Courthouse Square. The sign says it's the ROLLS ROYCE OF CONSIGNMENT SHOPS, and the owners tell me they're the "theme park of Inverness . . . people stop here before they visit with relatives!"

The 1940s music, funky flamingos, and a giant high-heeled chair say it all: classy yet eclectic. In addition to a fine selection of vintage clothing and jewelry, you'll find unusual home decor items and playful paintings from local artists.

Vanishing Breeds (352-726-6614), 105 W Main St. Featuring a nice selection of beautiful wildlife art, from classy copper sculptures to limited-edition carvings of birds, as well as conservation-minded gift items, cards, puzzles, games, T-shirts, and wildlife books.

New Port Richey

Looking for a gift? **Karen's Gifts** (727-841-0207), 6232 Grand Blvd, has choices large and small, from a mountain of stuffed bears to Christmas ornaments and Heritage Lace.

Port Richey

Wolding Fine Art Gallery & Gifts (727-869-9006; www.woldingstudios .com), 10128 US HWY 19, Unit A, in the Outback Plaza. A little bit nautical, a little bit jungle: the bold, bright colors of acrylics, stained glass, and metal art will draw you right into this vibrant display of more than a dozen local artists, where sea turtles, lizards, and manatees cavort on the walls.

Webster

Webster Flea Market/Sumter County Farmer's Market (352-793-2021; www.sumtercountyfarmers market.com), 516 NW Third St, off CR 478; use I-75 exit 309. No other flea market in Florida tops this bonanza of 4,000 vendors spread out over 40 acres. In peak season it's a madhouse with more than 10,000 people buzzing around. But the bargains at Webster are legendary: Pick up cheap produce, pore over antiques, buy a classic car, beat the prices on Asian imports, and catch some excellent crafts. From poodles to Porsches, you'll find it at Webster—and don't be shy about haggling. Open Mon only, 6–3; closed on Christmas.

Wildwood

Russell Stover Factory Outlet (352-748-6282), 950 Industrial Dr, off FL 44 just east of I-75. It's every kid's dream come true—step into a grocery store, and the shelves are lined with nothing but gobs of candy. At the "world's largest candy outlet," you'll find a fabulous selection of cut-rate candy (seconds, seasonal, and slightly discounted standards), from traditional fancy chocolates to jelly beans, licorice sticks, and jellies.

CITRUS STANDS, FARMER'S MARKETS, AND FRESH SEAFOOD

Bushnell

Halls Produce and Seafood (352-568-2498), corner of CR 476 and US 301, has fresh fruit and seafood, by the bushel or pound. Don't miss their smoked mullet!

Crystal River

Charlie's (see *Eating Out*) has an adjoining fresh seafood outlet with smoked mullet dip, and **Real Crystal Seafood** (352-795-3311), Citrus Ave, offers huge Gulf shrimp, mullet, and grouper.

Dade City

Browse an array of the freshest local produce, jams, and baked goods at the **Dade City Farmer's Market** (352-521-0766) on the second Saturday of each month, Oct–Apr, in downtown around the courthouse.

Floral City

Both **Sparracino's Produce** (352-637-2001) and **Ferris Groves** (352-860-0366) on US 41 north of town offer just-picked citrus and other regional fruits.

Hernando

The **Farmer's Market** (352-637-5323), US 41 S, sells "quality produce at reasonable prices," with shipping available.

Homosassa

Stormans Produce (352-628-3766), 3862 S Suncoast Blvd, proffers the freshest stuff under the tarps of their permanent stand on US 19; stop at the Old Homosassa Smokehouse (see *Eating Out*) for succulent smoked fish.

Inverness

Buzbee's Farm Fresh Produce (352-726-3867), 850 N US 41. Check out their nursery items, herbs, and plentiful local produce at reasonable prices.

Land O'Lakes

Fresh Market at Florida Estates Winery (see *Wineries*), held the second and fourth Saturday, Dec–Feb. Enjoy live music while browsing vendor booths with fresh fruit, baked goods, crafts, and spices; don't miss the wine tasting!

Oxford

Brown's Country Fresh Produce, corner of CR 102 and US 301, is a popular local stop for farm-fresh produce—peppers, potatoes, tomatoes, beans, and other crops in-season—right on the county line. **Jennings Citrus Packers** (1-800-344-2531), on US 301, wholesales but is open to the public (in-season) for sales of Indian River citrus fruit and juice; will ship.

Webster

The **Sumter County Farmer's Market** (see *Selective Shopping*) brings in the crowds every Monday morning; shop early for the freshest produce and baked goods.

✳ Entertainment

Weekends bring live music to many area restaurants, including **Sam's Hudson Beach Bar** (look for the miniature village on the roof!) on the Gulf. For large live concerts, check the schedule at **Rock Crusher Canyon** (352-795-1313; www.rock crushercanyon.com), housed in a former quarry west of Inverness.

Show Palace Dinner Theatre (727-863-7949; www.showpalace.net), US 19, Hudson, features Screen Actors Guild players in fabulous comedies and musicals like *Guys and Dolls* and *Mame*; I was impressed by the roomy stage setup, and the food certainly satisfied. Reservations required.

✳ Special Events

January: **Florida Manatee Festival, Crystal River**. Attracting manatee enthusiasts from around the country, this massive first-weekend event celebrates the Nature Coast's signature mammal with manatee-sighting trips, arts and crafts vendors, and fun activities for the entire family.

Brooksville Raid (352-799-0129, www.brooksvilleraid.com), Hernando County, third weekend. Relive the Civil War during one of the top reenactments in the state, including a full encampment, sutlers, Blue/Gray Ball, and a re-creation of the Brooksville Raid.

Annual Quilt and Antique Shoe Sale, which is held in conjunction with the Dade City **Kumquat Festival** (352-567-3769; www.dade citychamber.org) on the Pioneer Florida Museum grounds, last Sat. Taste dishes made from this small, tangy citrus fruit and experience the beauty of small-town life when you watch the kids vie for Kumquat Princess and Best Kumquat Costume; adults can participate in the recipe contest and 5- and 10K runs.

February: **Annual Heritage Day Festival**, May-Stringer House, Brooks ville. Living history demonstrations of weaving and crafts, Native American dance, and country music.

Pasco County Fair, FL 52, third week. Approaching its 60th year, this traditional county fair celebrates local produce, livestock, arts and crafts, and is the proud host of the Heart of Florida Folk Festival.

March: **Fort Cooper Days**, Inverness. Reenactment of Second Seminole War battle between the Seminoles and the ambushed federal troops who hastily constructed Fort Cooper for protection; a weekend's worth of living history demonstrations.

Strawberry Festival, Floral City. Held at Floral Park along US 41, this popular festival celebrates the incoming strawberry crop with fun activities and the State Fiddling Championship.

Swamp Fest, Weeki Wachee, first weekend. Entertainment, swamp foods, and an excellent display of local arts.

April: **Hernando County Fair**, fairgrounds. A weeklong traditional county fair with rides, games, food,

informative displays, musical entertainment, and the judging of local crafts and livestock.

Jump into the **Spring Magnolia Festival and Garden Show** on the grounds at Pioneer Florida Museum (352-567-0262), where you will find many vendors of various subjects connected to gardening and landscaping.

May: **Cotee River Seafood Festival and Boat Show**, New Port Richey. At Sims Park in the historic district, this festival features fresh Gulf seafood and regional artists.

September: Travel back through time at the annual Labor Day weekend **Pioneer Days Festival** at Pioneer Florida Museum, where you can experience Civil War battle reenactments and see craft demonstrations, pioneer exhibits, antique cars, even pony rides for the kids.

October: **Rattlesnake Festival** (www.rattlesnakefestival.com), San Antonio, third Sat. Dating back to 1967, this scary-sounding event celebrates Florida's reptiles with snake shows, gopher races, reptile demonstrations, and more. There's barbecue and games to boot . . . and no, they don't round up rattlesnakes anymore.

November: **Old Homosassa Arts & Crafts Seafood Festival**, second weekend. Now three decades old, this extravaganza of art and food brings in fine artists from around the country to share the limelight with some of the Nature Coast's top wildlife artists.

December: **Dade's Battle Reenactment**, last weekend at Dade Battlefield Historic State Park (see *Historic Sites*). Massive Seminole War reenactment held at 2 PM each day, encampments and trade fair all weekend. Fee.

OCALA AND MARION COUNTY

L akes, forests, and farms define the landscape of Marion County, the center of Florida's thoroughbred industry, with more than 600 horse farms scattered across the county. Established in 1827, Fort King served as a trading post and outpost for the US Army. Several months after General Wiley Thompson, the US Army agent responsible for removing the Seminoles from Florida, embarrassed Chief Osceola by placing him in leg irons at the fort for "insolent remarks," Osceola shot and killed Thompson and another man walking past Fort King in late 1835. That same day, Indians attacked Major Francis Dade's troops along the military trail between Fort Brooke and Fort King; these two incidents sparked the lengthy Second Seminole War.

Incorporated in 1844, the county saw a steady stream of settlers in response to the Armed Occupation Act. Dubbed Brick City when it was rebuilt in brick after a devastating fire, **Ocala** is a modest-sized city, established in 1846, radiating from a quaint downtown. Nearby **Silver Springs**, home of the world's largest freshwater spring, has attracted tourists since the late 1800s; today's tourists enjoy glass-bottomed boat rides along the crystalline stream, where schools of fish whirl around the many spring vents. At the south end of the county, **Ocklawaha** and **Weirsdale** sit on the edge of scenic Lake Weir. Ocklawaha lives in infamy as the home of Ma Barker and her gang, whereas Weirsdale has the distinction of still being surrounded by working orange groves. Historic **Belleview**, founded in 1884, is the county's second largest city, centered around Lake Lillian. In **Dunnellon**, settlers arrived in droves in the 1890s in Florida's equivalent of the gold rush—the boom sparked by the first discovery of phosphate in Florida by Alburtus Vogt in 1889. Victorian architecture defines the original residential district a few blocks from the Withlacoochee River, now a haven for eclectic shops and galleries.

Heading north from Ocala on US 301 or US 441, you'll encounter small-town life in villages like **Citra**, **Orange Lake**, **Irvine**, and **Reddick**. Victorian **McIntosh** turns on the charm with narrow paved streets shaded by grand old moss-draped oaks. Home of the annual 1890s Festival, this former railroad and citrus packing town is a peaceful place to explore.

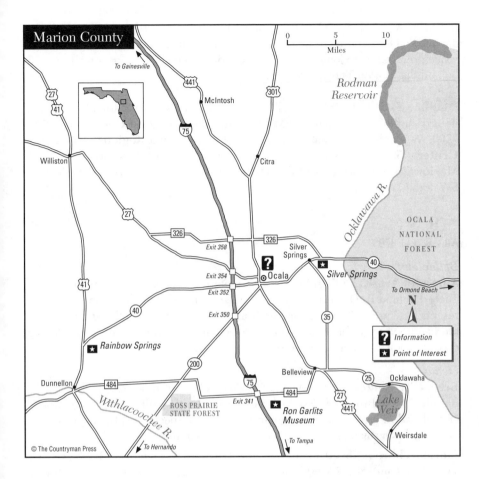

GUIDANCE Ocala/Marion County Chamber of Commerce (352-629-8051; www.ocalacc.com), 110 E Silver Springs Blvd, Ocala 34470, is downtown on the square, open Mon–Fri 8–5, Sat 10–4. Stop in to pick up maps and brochures and to see their regular fine-art displays. Online, www.ocalamarion.com represents the **Ocala-Marion County Convention & Visitors Bureau**, providing an up-to-date calendar of events and detailed travel information.

GETTING THERE *By air:* Ocala is 1½ hours north of **Orlando International Airport** via I-75 and Florida's Turnpike, and 45 minutes south of **Gainesville Regional Airport**. Ocala International Airport supports a steady stream of private pilots but as of yet does not offer commuter service.

By car: Six exits off **I-75** provide access to Marion County's communities. **US 27**, **301**, and **441** all meet in the middle of Ocala, passing north–south through the county; **FL 40** ties together the east–west corridor.

By bus: **Greyhound** (1-800-229-9424) also stops in Ocala at the historic railroad station along North Magnolia Ave, enabling easy transfers.

PARKING All of Marion County's communities have free street parking. In downtown Ocala there are time limitations (normally 2 hours) on many of the spaces, but there are longer-term metered lots at the chamber of commerce and behind the Marion Theatre in downtown.

MEDICAL EMERGENCIES Several Ocala-area hospitals serve Marion County and its surrounding rural neighbors: **Munroe Regional Medical Center** (352-351-7200; www.munroeregional.com), 131 SW 15th St; **Ocala Regional Medical Center** (352-401-1000; www.ocalaregional.com), 1431 SW First Ave; and **West Marion Community Hospital** (352-291-3000; www.westmarion.com), 4600 SW 46th Court.

✳ To See

ART GALLERIES

Belleview

All About Art (352-307-9774; www.allaboutartcenter.com), 5162 US 441. Tucked behind B. D. Bean's Coffee Co. (see *Coffee Shops*), this cooperative represents local artists in media ranging from oils and acrylics to photography, textiles, and pottery, offering an excellent selection of fine arts as well as regular art classes. Open Tue–Sat 11–5. Free.

Ocala

Brick City Center for the Arts (352-840-9521; www.mcaocala.com/brickcity .shtml), 23 SW Broadway. Exhibit space for local artists affiliated with the Marion Cultural Alliance; features regular juried shows, special events, and art classes, as well as a small gift shop. Open Tue–Sat 10–5, free.

Florida Thoroughbred Breeders' and Owners' Association (352-629-2160; www.ftboa.com), 801 SW 60th Ave. View original art and artifacts from Florida's horse industry inside the offices of this busy equine business complex; Mon–Fri 8:30–4:30. Free.

Gallery East (352-236-6992; www.galleryeastocala.com), 4901 E Silver Springs Blvd. A nonprofit artists' cooperative with exhibits by member artists, who also teach regular art classes. Exhibited items in various media are for sale. Open Mon–Sat 10–5. Free.

CFCC Webber Exhibit Center (352-873-5809; www.cfcc.cc.fl.us/departments/ instruction/las/webber/webber_gallery.htm), 3001 SW College Rd. Featuring rotating exhibits ranging from an annual model railroad display to environmental education to presentations by local artists. Open Tue–Fri 11–5, Sat 10–2. Free.

McIntosh

Ice House Gallery (352-591-5930), US 441 and Ave C. Enjoy fine arts and sculpture by regional artists, displayed in the town's historic icehouse; antiques collectors will find the vintage tools interesting. Open Sat–Sun 12–5, call for appointment on weekdays.

Once a family citrus shop, the store on the high hilltop overlooking Orange Lake has been converted into the **Windmill Gallery**, featuring the works of Sean M.

Dowie, a naturalist and freelance wildlife photographer, as well as paintings from area artists.

ATTRACTIONS ✆ ♿ **Silver Springs** (352-236-2121; www.silversprings.com), 5656 E Silver Springs Blvd. In the 1960s this was my family's top Florida vacation destination, Florida's first real tourist attraction. It started in 1878 with the invention of a new device called a glass-bottomed boat, used to ferry visitors down the crystalline waters of the Silver River to observe one of the world's largest springs. Real Florida lurks around every bend. Alligators sun on the grassy garden slopes, raccoons slink between the cypress knees, and millions of fish swim in swirling schools around the river's many spring vents. Beautiful formal gardens line the northern shore of the river, tucked beneath grand old cypresses and oaks. Jazz drifts through the trees from hidden speakers. Wander through the gardens to discover treats like the **World of Bears**, the only place in Florida to see Kodiak and grizzly bears; the **Jeep Safari**, a ride through wildlife habitats with giraffes, zebras, and lemurs; and the **Lost River Voyage**, a cruise along the river's floodplain forests. Kids will enjoy the **Kids Ahoy! Playland**, which includes a small petting zoo and a wild animal carousel.

In recent years one of the biggest draws for the park has been the concerts held at **Twin Oaks**, an outdoor amphitheater with a faux southern mansion stage, where top baby-boomer favorites like Frankie Vallee, Loretta Lynn, and the Smothers Brothers play to overflowing crowds between January and April; lights twinkling in the live oaks and cabbage palms create a fairyland atmosphere after dark. On Ross Allen Island, boardwalks neatly fitted around the trees of a natural floodplain forest lead you through habitats that support native Florida reptiles and amphibians, as well as species from around the world. Florida's most critical endangered species, the Florida panther, rates its own large exhibit. From Fort King Landing, the **Jungle Cruise** takes you down a natural waterway through more wildlife habitats.

A GLASS-BOTTOM BOAT AT SILVER SPRINGS

Sandra Friend

Silver Springs has changed ownership many times since I modeled an indigo snake at the Ross Allen Reptile Institute, but some things haven't changed. A kid can still walk into the Dockside Emporium and buy a seashell for a dime, you can still sit on the lucky horseshoe cabbage palm under the watchful gaze of Chief Osceola, and the alligators continue to crawl up onto the neatly manicured lawns to sun themselves. Retaining its unspoiled natural appeal, Silver

Springs remains one of my favorite places. $34 adults, $31 seniors, $25 ages 3–10, with many discounts and affordable multiday passes available, plus a combination ticket with Wild Waters; $8 parking fee. One caveat: the park owners have instituted an odd schedule of hours and days open, so check ahead on their Web site to ensure the park will be open during your visit.

Don Garlits Museums (1-877-271-3278; www.garlits.com), 13700 SW 16th Ave, Belleview. The famed funny car driver with a place in the Smithsonian Museum of American History shows off his personal drag-racing and classic car collections, totaling nearly 200 vehicles. Open daily 9–5, closed Christmas. $15 adults, $13 seniors and ages 13–18, $6 ages 5–12.

HISTORIC SITES Stop in at the Ocala Chamber of Commerce (see *Guidance*) for the *Marion County Historical Tour Sites* booklet, which provides a map with locations of the county's most significant historic sites. The towns of **Citra**, **McIntosh**, and **Reddick** date back to 1881 and 1882, with architecture to match; **Belleview** and **Weirsdale** hide circa 1885 Victorian districts in their downtowns. But one of the region's most significant sites is **Fort King**, SE Fort King St east of SE 36th Ave, a major stop on the military trail in 1827 and the sparking point of the First Seminole War. The site is still undeveloped, but you can park and wander through it.

MUSEUMS Based on a foundation of industrialist Arthur I. Appleton's large personal collection of Oriental art, the **Appleton Museum of Art** (352-236-7100; www.appletonmuseum.org), 4333 E Silver Springs Blvd, Ocala, is a work of art itself in Italian marble. One gallery features European masterworks from the 1800s, including the *The Knitter* by William-Adolphe Bouguereau and *Daphnis and Chloe* by his wife, Elizabeth Jane Gardner, both circa 1888. The Victor DuBois Collection of West African Art, with its many intriguing masks and figurines, adjoins a pre-Columbian exhibit of bowls, pendants, vessels, and other artifacts. Upstairs, galleries feature changing exhibits of national significance. At 1 PM weekdays, enjoy a docent-led tour of the galleries. Fee.

DON GARLITS MUSEUMS

Sandra Friend

Marion County Museum of History (352-629-2773), 307 SE 26th Terrace in the McPherson Government Complex, Ocala. This museum features artwork and artifacts from early Marion County, including a 1,500-year-old canoe, farming equipment, and historical photos. Open Fri and Sat 10–2; fee.

Silver River Museum and Environmental Education Center (352-236-5401; www.silverrivermuseum .com), 1445 NE 58th Ave. In Silver River State Park (see *Parks*), this classy natural and cultural history museum shows off the bones of prehistoric creatures, Seminole artifacts, Spanish cannons, and more; outside, roam a replica Cracker village and see an original glass-bottomed boat used at Silver Springs. Open weekends and holidays 9–5; fee.

RAILROADIANA It's hoped the old **Dunnellon Depot** will someday be a museum and visitor center, but in the meantime at least the turn-of-the-20th-century building has been preserved—it's along US 41 across from city hall. The **McIntosh Depot** houses the local historical society museum.

HORSE FARMS AND COMPETITIONS With more than 225 horse farms, Ocala's nickname of "**Horse Capital of the World**" is well-earned, as Marion County led the country in number of horses in residence during the last USDA census. During the winter months, equestrians from around the United States descend on Ocala for world-class riding and jumping competitions, including the ever-popular seven-week-long HITS (Horse Shows In The Sun, www.hitsshows.com) series of hunter/jumper competitions at **Post Time Farm** (352-620-2275), 13710 US 27; spectators free Wed–Sat, $5 Sun. At the **Florida Horse Park** (352- 307-6699; www.flhorsepark.com), 11008 S SR 475, ongoing Olympic Trials–style competition means more spectator fun; check their online calendar for upcoming events.

Ocala is home to the **Florida Thoroughbred Breeders & Owners Association** (352-629-2160; www.ftboa.com), 801 SW 60th Ave, with museum exhibits related to the industry, open 8:30–4:30 Mon–Fri. At **Ocala Breeders Sales** (352-237-2154; www.obssales.com), there is a memorial at the grave of 1956 Kentucky Derby and Belmont Stakes winner Needles. You can watch the thoroughbred auctions in action, visit the racetrack to see horses put through their paces, or jump into the fray with intertrack wagering (see *Gaming*). Take a road trip (see *Scenic Drives*) to see hundreds of horse farms amid the rolling hills. **Young's Paso Fino Ranch** (352-867-5305; www.youngspasofino.com), 8075 NW FL 326, is one of few in the area that is open to the public for farm tours of the working ranch, $7.50 per person. At the **New England Shire Centre** (352-873-3005; www.newenglandshirecentre .com), it's $20 per person for tours of a draft-horse farm that has some thoroughbreds, offered Mon–Sat 1–3:30.

Horses not only roam the fields, you'll find them in town, too. Grab a copy of the visitor's guide from the chamber of commerce for a driving tour of **Horse Fever** locations, where you can spot (and pose with) 27 life-sized horse sculptures remaining in the county after a fund-raising auction for the arts.

For more horse-related places to visit and things to do, see *Carriage Tours, Gaming, Trail Riding, Selective Shopping,* and *Special Events.*

BICYCLING Built by the Ocala Mountain Biking Association, the wild rides of the **Santos Biking Trails** are geared for high-speed pedaling on singletrack through the lush forests of the Cross Florida Greenway. Choose from rides like the Canopy Trail, under the shade of massive live oaks, or the Sinkhole Trail, which loops around a giant sink. Blazes denote three levels of difficulty: gentle (yellow), moderate (blue), and oh-my-God (red), which includes the quarry drops. Don't forget the helmet! Rent bikes at the nearby **Santos Trailhead Bicycle Shop** (352-307-2453; www.santosbikeshop.com), 8900 S US 441, or **Streit's Cyclery Ocala** (352-629-2612), 1274 E Silver Springs Blvd.

The **Ross Allen Loop** at Silver River State Park (see *Parks*) runs 5 miles along old forest roads near the campground. Just south of Dunnellon, the **Withlacoochee State Trail** heads south through the Nature Coast region for a 46-mile ride ending at Dade City, passing through Old Florida towns with plenty of facilities.

CARRIAGE TOURS Ocala Carriage Tours (1-877-99-OCALA; www.ocala carriage.com), 4776 NW 110th Ave. For a refined visit to Ocala's horse farms, enjoy a formal horse-drawn carriage tour along the back roads of horse country.

DIVING Paradise Springs (352-368-5746), 4040 SE 84th Lane Rd, a privately owned sinkhole, combines dive training with a picture-perfect window into the Floridan Aquifer. Pick up your open-water and cave certifications in their classes, or stop by to dive the springs. The site is up for sale, so check first before arriving. Certified cave divers will want to check out **Hal Watts Forty Fathom Grotto** (352-368-7974; www.40fathomgrotto.com), 9487 NW 115th Ave, for practice in technical deep diving, open by reservation only; the cavern is more than 100 feet deep in places.

For open-water diving, try a drift dive on the **Rainbow River** from the KP Hole (see *Swimming*) or on the **Silver River** (put in at Ray Wayside Park on FL 40).

ECOTOURS Captain Mike's Lazy River Cruises (352-637-2726; www.lazy rivercruises.com), departing from Stumpknockers on the Withlacoochee (see *Eating Out*) and the Dunnellon City boat ramp at US 41 and the Withlacoochee Bridge. Enjoy a leisurely float on a pontoon boat with a certified eco-heritage guide along the cypress-lined Withlacoochee and Rainbow Rivers. Call for reservations; specify length of trip (1–5 hours), number of participants, and any activities you'd like to concentrate on (diving, snorkeling, birding, swimming). These three factors will determine price ($12.50–22 per person, minimum trip 6 people).

On the **Singing River Tours** (352-804-1573; www.singingrivertours.com), Florida folk singer Captain Jon Semmes presents a pontoon cruise down the Rainbow and Withlacoochee Rivers in Dunnellon with an environmentally-minded live soundtrack and naturalist commentary. Cruises are most Sat but can also be booked weekdays, call to reserve. Captain Jon departs Angler's Family Resort(see *Fishing*), and it costs $10 per person for the almost two hours on the water.

FAMILY ACTIVITIES ✐ At Brick City Park, the **Discovery Science & Outdoor Center** (352-401-3900), 1211 SE 22nd Rd, has hands-on science and nature exhibits for the kids, including an outdoor dinosaur "bone dig," fun physics activities, and scavenger hunts; open Tue–Fri 9–4, Sat 10–2, fee. At **Easy Street Family Fun Center** (352-861-9700; www.ocalaeasystreet.com), 2727 SW 27th Ave near the Paddock Mall, play mini golf and race go-carts until the wee hours.

FISHING Angler's Family Resort (352-489-2397), US 41, Dunnellon, caters to anglers heading out on the Withlacoochee River; visit Carney Island Park (see *Parks*) for access to Lake Weir. **McIntosh Fish Camp** (352-591-1302), 5479 Ave H, is a great place to launch an expedition on Orange Lake, with boat rentals, bait and tackle, and basic lodging. There's plenty more fishing in Marion County—see "Ocala National Forest."

GAMING Next to the racetrack at Ocala Breeder's Sales, **Champions Restaurant & OTB Facility** (352-237-4144; www.obssales.com), SW 60th Ave, has parimutuel wagering, harness racing, and off-track betting in the ITW Teletheatre. Open at 11 daily; free after 6 PM. Ocala Jai Alai at Orange Lake presents a high-speed lacrosse-like sport with wagering on players.

GOLF The granddaddy of public courses is the **Ocala Municipal Golf Course** (352-622-8681), 3130 E Silver Springs Blvd, which opened in 1920; at the 18th hole tee, you'll encounter a granddaddy live oak closing in on the millennium mark. **Golden Ocala Golf and Country Club** (352-622-2245; www.goldenocala.com), 7340 N US 27, a semiprivate course, stakes its reputation on popular replica holes from top courses around the world, and the nearby **Golden Hills Golf & Turf Club** (352-629-7980; www.goldenhillscc.com), 4782 NW 80th Ave off US 27, a par-72 championship course, is owned in part by golf architect Rees Jones.

HIKING Enjoy more than 30 continuous miles of the **Florida Trail** along the Cross Florida Greenway (see *Greenways*), where you hike with history along the relict remains of the Cross Florida Barge Canal, reforested over the past 70 years. The 2-mile Land Bridge Loop (off CR 475A, north of CR 484, at the Land Bridge

WITHLACOOCHEE RIVER

Sandra Friend

Trailhead) and 3.5-mile Ross Prairie Loop (off SR 200 at the Ross Prairie Trailhead) are popular day hikes along the route.

PADDLING In addition to popular canoe routes on the **Rainbow River** (put in either at Rainbow Springs State Park or at the FL 484 bridge, 6 miles downstream) and **Silver River** (put in at Ocala Boat Basin, Ray Wayside Park, FL 40), the nearby **Ocala National Forest** (see the next chapter) offers beautiful wilderness paddling. To paddle on the lovely **Rainbow River**, rent canoes and kayaks at Rainbow Springs State Park (see *Springs*). In Dunnellon both **Dragonfly Watersports** (1-800-919-9579; www.dragonflywatersports.com), 20336 E Pennsylvania Ave, and **Rainbow River Canoe and Kayak** (352-489-7854; www.rainbowrivercanoeandkayak.com), 12121 Riverview Dr, handle rentals and shuttling along the Rainbow and Withlacoochee Rivers. At **Brasington's** (see *Selective Shopping*), you can rent a kayak and take it with you to explore area rivers and lakes.

RETREAT CENTER Crone's Cradle Conserve (352-595-3377; www.crones cradleconserve.com), PO Box 535, Orange Springs 32182, is a unique private preserve 6.4 miles west of Citra off CR 318. Watch for the sign along the highway and turn north on an unpaved road that leads you into the woods, emerging at a grassy area along a lake, a tranquil spot with meandering pathways, gardens, a playground, and porch swings. It's a retreat center focusing on women's issues, and an active organic farm with a large shop offering garden items, seedlings and herbs, seasonal produce, and books for nurturing the soul. Open until 3 daily.

SCENIC DRIVES Head into the country west of I-75 to enjoy Marion County's many horse farms. While you'll see quite a few between Ocala and Dunnellon on FL 40, getting off the beaten path is more fun. **CR 225** and **CR 326** provide excellent scenic drives through the heart of Horse Country.

SILVER RIVER

Sandra Friend

SWIMMING For a splash in cold but clear water, visit the popular swimming area at **Rainbow Springs State Park** (see *Springs*). Downstream, swimmers go with the flow at **KP Hole County Park** (352-489-3055), 9435 SW 190 Ave Rd, and **Dunnellon Beach**, a city park tucked away in the residential area south of CR 484 near the confluence of the Rainbow and Withlacoochee Rivers; fee. Warmer waters wait in **Lake Weir** at Carney Island (see *Parks*), which is also a favorite launch point for water skiers.

TRAIL RIDING **Young's Paso Fino Ranch** (see *Horse Farms*) offers trail riding and riding lessons on their farm. On the west side of the county, **North Star Acres** (352-489-9848; www.dunnellonbusiness.com/northstar.htm) provides guided trail rides of up to 3 hours along some of the state's most beautiful riding trails in Goethe State Forest.

TUBING **Dragonfly Watersports** (see *Paddling*) supports 4-hour tubing trips down the crystal-clear Rainbow River from KP Hole County Park to the CR 484 take-out.

WALKING TOURS Check with the Marion County Chamber of Commerce (see *Guidance*) for dates and ticket fees for its annual **Heritage Tour of Homes**, which allows public access to homes in Ocala's historic districts. In Dunnellon (www.dunnellon.org), take a walk around the **Historic Village** (see Selective *Shopping*), where interpretive markers explain the history of homes dating back to 1902.

WATER PARK **Wild Waters** (1-800-234-7458; www.wildwaterspark.com), corner of FL 40 and CR 35, adjoining Silver Springs. A densely knit canopy of live oaks shades four speeds of rides on eight very different slides in one of Florida's original water parks. Let the kids run wild in Cool Kids Cove, squirting, splashing, and pouring water through a complex of pipes and wheels, or grab a raft and hit the wave pool. Open Memorial Day–Labor Day, $40 season pass, kids 2 and under free, plus a combination ticket with Silver Springs available; $8 parking fee.

WATER-SKIING **Lake Weir** is Water-Ski Central for the region, where many a barefoot skier has gotten his or her training; access via Carney Island (see *Parks*).

✳ Green Space

BEACHES Swim at Lake Weir at several beaches popular for more than a century. **Johnson's Beach** is right at Gator Joe's (see *Eating Out*), and the beach at **Carney Island Park** (see *Parks*) is especially popular during the summer months. At **Hampton Beach** off CR 25 between Ocklawaha and Weirsdale, you can picnic under the live oaks and splash in the fresh water; fee.

GARDENS Not quite an acre but extremely colorful, **Taylor Garden** (352-671-8400), 2232 NE Jacksonville Rd, Ocala, is a demonstration garden for the Florida Master Gardener Program, showcasing different types of gardens—from butterfly to vegetable—that can be planned in your own backyard space.

Don't miss azalea season (Feb–Mar) at **Rainbow Springs State Park** (see *Springs*), a vintage Florida botanical garden attraction turned state park with extensive, mature plantings along the Rainbow River.

GREENWAYS The **Marjorie Harris Carr Cross Florida Greenway** is a 110-mile corridor cutting across Marion County into adjoining Putnam and Levy, from the St. Johns River to the Gulf of Mexico. Florida's premier greenway project owes its existence to the failed Cross Florida Barge Canal, a 1920s project resurrected in the 1960s and fought off by environmentalists. The mile-wide corridor provides separate hiking, biking, and equestrian trail systems as well as access for anglers to prime fishing in Lake Rousseau and Rodman Lake; there are numerous trailheads along the corridor. For maps and information, contact the Office of Greenways and Trails Ocala Field Office (352-236-7143), 8282 SE CR 314, or stop in weekdays; the office adjoins the Marshall Swamp Trailhead.

PARKS In **Brick City Park** (352-401-3900), 1211 SE 22nd Rd, Ocala, a boardwalk trail loops around a historic limestone quarry laced with caverns. **Carney Island Park** (352-288-8999), 13275 SE 115 Ave, offers Lake Weir access for swimming, boating, picnicking, and hiking. **Silver River State Park** (352-236-7148; www.floridastateparks.com/silverriver), 1425 NE 58th Ave, has one of the nicest campgrounds in the region, with upscale cabins and one of the busiest hiking trail systems in Florida. A replica Florida Cracker village sits just outside the Silver River Museum and Environmental Education Center (see *Museums*), adjacent to a large picnic grove.

BIRTH OF A RIVER: VIEW OF THE HEAD-SPRING AT RAINBOW SPRINGS

Sandra Friend

At privately-owned **Sholom Park** (352-854-7435; www.sholompark.org), 6840 SW 80th Ave, enter the labyrinth for a peaceful walking meditation, or walk the rambling trails through rose gardens, shady forests, open fields, and around the koi pond. Open daily, free.

SPRINGS Rainbow Springs State Park (352-489-8503; www.floridastateparks.com/rainbowsprings), US 41 north of Dunnellon, protects the first-magnitude spring and hundreds of smaller bubblers that make up the headwaters of the Rainbow River. Unusually rugged slopes around the river are due to 1890s phosphate mining tailings; this former theme park still sports its botanical gardens with azalea-covered slopes (visit in late February for optimum blooms) and tall artificial waterfalls. Canoeing and kayaking (on-site outfitter), swimming, hiking, and picnicking are all part of the fun; a shady campground downriver provides river access.

WILD PLACES Encompassing more than half a million acres, the **Ocala National Forest** (see the next chapter) takes up most of the eastern half of Marion County and just recently celebrated its first century. **Ross Prairie State Forest** (352-732-1201) adjoins the Cross Florida Greenway off FL 200 south of CR 484, with new hiking and horse trails opening to the public via the Ross Prairie Trailhead. West of Dunnellon, **Goethe State Forest** (352-447-2202; www.fl-dof .com/state_forests/goethe.html), 8250 SE CR 336, spills across the Marion–Levy border, with 50,000 acres of longleaf pine forests open to hunting, horseback riding, and hiking.

✳ Lodging

BED & BREAKFASTS

McIntosh 32664

🦢 **Merrily** (352-591-1180), Ave G. Built in 1888, this beautiful Victorian home has been open to guests for more than 12 years. "I'm not going to heat it for just me and my dog," says Margie Karow, "so I'm happy to visit with people." There are three rooms ($70) with shared sitting rooms and bath, each tastefully decorated; the room with twin beds is popular with ladies traveling together. Period furnishings downstairs accent the polished hardwood floors. A light breakfast featuring muffins and fresh fruit is served in the grand dining room. Relax on the spacious porch in a rocker or on the swing and take in the lush landscaping under the ancient oak trees.

Ocala

♿ Set in the heart of Horse Country, **Heritage Country Inn** (352-489-0023; www.heritagecountryinn.com), 14343 W FL 40, Ocala 34430, has six

THE CRACKER VILLAGE AT SILVER RIVER STATE PARK

rooms ($99–199) with unique Florida themes, from an 1800s plantation to Florida's springs, and features wood-burning fireplaces, single Jacuzzis, and separate private entrances.

The Inn at Jumbolair (352-401-1990; www.jumbolair.com/inn.htm), 1201 NE 77th St, Ocala 34479, caters to equestrian-minded travelers. It's in the rural northeast of the county, at a fly-in community where John Travolta and Kelly Preston have lived for nearly a decade. The inn features five luxurious apartment-sized suites ($225 and up) named for prize steeds, a pool and fitness center, and an equestrian facility.

Weirsdale 32195

🦢 **Shamrock Thistle and Crown** (1-800-425-2763; www.shamrockbb .com), PO Box 624, CR 42. You'll delight at this quiet three-story Victorian (the 1887 Thomas B. Snook house), once the manor house for an orange grove empire. Owners Brantley and Anne Overcash infuse the residence with a Scots-Irish theme; each comfortable suite tells a story. A romantic cottage overlooking the pool makes a great honeymoon getaway. Whirlpool suites with fireplaces are available; TV and VCR are provided in every room. Full breakfast served. Rates range $95–210, depending on season and amenities; modest dress requested.

HOTELS, MOTELS, AND RESORTS

Dunnellon 34432

❦ **Two Rivers Inn** (352-489-2300; www.tworiversinn.com), 20719 W Pennsylvania Ave. An old-fashioned motor court resurrected as a snazzy little inn—what a treat! And what a storied history. Originally built as officers' quarters for the Dunnellon Air Field (where glider pilots trained) during World War II, these cottages were moved into town after the war to become Davis Motor Court. Each of the 15 spacious rooms and suites ($55–65) is fully updated and decorated with an interesting theme—the Safari, the River, the Savannah—and each has a fridge, microwave, toaster, and coffeemaker.

Ocala 34481

Numerous small chain motels cluster at Ocala's I-75 exits; those on US 27 offer rates as low as $40 for a single. The **Ramada Conference Center Ocala** (352-732-3131 or 1-800-272-6232), 3810 NW Blichton Rd, is owned by George Steinbrenner, a longtime Ocala-area snowbird with his own horse farm. Baseball fans will love the Yankees memorabilia throughout the common spaces and a chance to see George or some of his players who pop in during winter; $79 and up.

Amid the choices at the FL 200 exit of I-75, the **Ocala Hilton** (352-854-1400 or 1-877-602-4023; www.hilton ocala.com), 3600 SW 38th Ave, Ocala's only themed hotel, shines. Visit the paddock out back, and you'll feel a part of Florida's thoroughbred capital. Rates vary from $109–209; packages available for trail rides, horseback lessons, hayrides, horse farm tours, and boarding your horse.

Silver Springs 34488

The retro sunny sign under the grand old oaks at the **Sun Plaza Motel** (352-236-2343), 5461 E Silver Springs Blvd, is just as it was back in the early '60s when my parents started staying here every year on our trips to Florida, eventually settling on room #50. I remember pulling cold Cokes out of the 1940s soda machine and playing on the same playground equipment that is here today . . . and yes, it is well-maintained. If you grab one of the rooms in the back nonsmoking section, you'll find them a great blast from the past, neatly kept, $69 and up.

CAMPGROUNDS Both of Marion County's state parks—Silver River and Rainbow Springs—offer comfortable campsites and cabins in a forested setting (see *Green Space*). Beyond the bounds of this chapter, the Ocala National Forest (see next chapter) has dozens of places for those roughing it. The following choices are a bit more urban.

Ocala 34474

Ocala RV Camp Resort (352-237-2138; www.ocalarvcampresort.com), 3200 SW 38th Ave. Nestled in a pleasant wooded setting (albeit along I-75), this full-service campground has camping cabins ($56), hot tub, and a swimming pool plus full-hookup sites ($30–46). Tents welcome, $25

Ocala Sun RV Resort (1-877-809-1100; www.ocalaranchrv.com), 2559 SW CR 484. A family-owned and -operated park with top ratings from Woodall's; more than 150 spaces including large pull-throughs. Full hookups, heated swimming pool, clubhouse; fills up quickly for the winter months, but a handful of overnight spots are reserved for drop-in guests during the snowbird season. $27–54, no tents.

Silver Springs 34488

With 618 spaces, **The Springs RV Resort** (352-236-5250; www.rvresorts .com/resort17.htm), 2950 NE 52nd Court, caters to snowbirds but has a daily rate of $27 for full-hookup sites. The grassy open area is anchored by a large picnic pavilion and clubhouse with pool; two bathhouses provide hot showers.

✳ Where to Eat

DINING OUT

Ocala

While most patrons come by for the daily lunch specials, the **Amrit Palace** (352-873-8500), 2635 SW College Rd, offers the best Indian cuisine in the region, $12–20. Of special note are the vegetarian entrées, including a proper mushroom *bhajee*.

Most fine restaurants feature a dessert tray. But **Felix's** (352-629-0339), 917 E Silver Springs Blvd, catches your attention streetside with signs touting their DESSERT ROOM! They're best known for their aged buckhead beef ($37–43), and are one of the few restaurants around that let you order a half serving, known as their petite entrées ($8–12),

of delights like Asian duck breast, Chilean sea bass, eggplant rollatini, and Thai pepper shrimp. For heftier appetites, try "Comfort Food with Attitude" such as Swedish meatballs (100 percent Angus beef) over homemade fettuccini, country-fried filet mignon, and slow-roasted prime rib ($13–24). It's a romantic setting, in this 1890 Victorian gingerbread home, perfect for that special night out.

Tony's Sushi Japanese Steakhouse (352-237-3151), 3405 SW College Rd. From traditional bento box lunches to perfect sashimi, Chef Tony presents Asian favorites that please both your artistic and culinary senses. Enjoy tableside preparations, or sit down at the bar to watch sushi chefs at work. Sushi $3–11 per roll, platters $15; dinners $9–25.

THE WONDERFULLY RETRO SIGN AT THE SUN PLAZA MOTEL

Sandra Friend

Belleview

🐾 **La Casa Del Pollo** (352-307-0555), 10819 SE Abshier Blvd. Known locally as "Chicken Time," this authentic Cuban restaurant is tops in the region, going well beyond the mainstays of Cuban sandwiches and chicken, black beans and rice, to offer numerous hot pressed sandwiches ($6–8) such as the Puerto Rican Tripela (a house specialty, with roast pork, deli ham, Swiss cheese, seasoned Cuban steak, and pickles), empandillas, homemade soups, vegetarian options, and delicious entrées ($6–28) like chicken Caribe, lobster Creole, and picadillo à la Cubana. Never tried Cuban food? Your best bet is the Cuban Classic Sampler for two, a combination platter with a little bit of everything. Open for lunch and dinner; closed Sun and Mon.

Lassie's Restaurant (352-245-4318), 5068 SE Abshier Blvd. It's rare these days to find a 24-hour nonchain diner, but that's Lassie's, with basic home-cooked fare like stuffed cabbage, hot roast beef and mashed potatoes, ravioli, and grilled cheese. Prices range from $1 for a hot dog to $18 for the all-you-can-eat stone crab claws, so there's something for everyone, especially with breakfast served any hour of the day.

Dunnellon

The Front Porch Restaurant and Pie Shop (352-489-4708), 12039 N Florida Ave. Murals bring the outdoors in at this popular family-owned restaurant, a local fixture since 1986, offering up regional favorites like Ybor City Cuban sandwiches, gator tail, fried yam sticks, chicken gizzards, cheese grits, and okra. Serving breakfast, lunch, and dinner, but the capper is dessert—their famous piled-high pies, $2 a slice. Closed Mon.

Stumpknockers on the River (352-854-2288; www.stumpknockers.net), 13821 SW FL 200 at the Withlacoochee River Bridge. Barely an evening goes by when the parking lot isn't packed—except on Monday, when they're closed. Featuring seafood of all stripes, Stumpknockers sits right on the cypress-lined Withlacoochee River. Giant portions make it tough to take on the appetizers, but don't miss the fried mushrooms, freshly battered and served in an overflowing basket with accompanying dipping sauces. Nightly specials ($12–25) feature local seafood, such as grouper amandine or lobster Newburg, but hearty appetites won't go wrong with the all-you-can-eat catfish, the crabmeat-stuffed flounder, or the seafood platter. If you haven't tried alligator yet, here's the place, with three different preparations of gator steaks or

A SIGN FOR GREAT SEAFOOD

Sandra Friend

crispy gator nuggets. Serving dinner Tue–Sat, lunch and dinner on Sun.

McIntosh

Jim's Pit BBQ (352-591-2479), I-75 and CR 318. You might not assume it's a restaurant from the gas pumps, citrus stand, and selection of touristy gifts near the cashier, but head to the back of the building for some real pit barbecue, served up in this locale by Jim for more than 20 years. In addition to barbecue dinners ($7–13, with barbecue beans, coleslaw, and garlic bread) and sandwiches ($3–8), they serve up breakfast ($3–6) and ice cream as well.

Ocala

Abio's Italian Restaurant (352-629-4886; www.abiospizza.com), 2377 SW College Rd. For a green olive fanatic like me, tiny Abio's hits the spot with their New Jersey Joy calzone: mozzarella, ricotta, sausage, onion, green peppers, and green and black olives stuffed into a pizza crust and baked with sauce. Subs, baked Italian dishes, and pizza, $5–10. Closed Sun.

At **Champions** (352-237-4667), 1701 SW 60th Ave, dine while watching the thoroughbreds step through their paces at the Ocala Breeder's Sales track; lunch, $6–8, in an off-track betting facility (see *Gaming*).

❦ **Charlie Horse Restaurant** (352-622-4050), 2426 E Silver Springs Blvd. It's a casual place to gather with friends, with a sports-bar atmosphere, and the appetizers are great (potato skins, yum!), with more than a dozen choices; the burgers, wings, and Charlie's specially topped steaks are the reason to stop here. Entrées $6–22; stick around after 9 for open-mike karaoke!

Crossroads Country Kitchen (352-237-1250), 7947 FL 40, is a great

country breakfast stop (under $8) with tasty pancakes in five flavors; they do lunch and dinner, too (entrées under $12), with daily specials and live music on Fri evenings 5–9.

On the square, **Harry's** (352-840-0900; www.hookedonharrys.com), 24 SE First Ave, feeds Ocala's need for a vibrant downtown. Popular with the late-night crowd, this upscale Florida chain bar and grill serves up pan-seared crab cakes thick with blue crabmeat, red beans and rice Cajun style, and tasty Gulf Coast oysters among its many entrée choices ($8–12); lunch and dinner.

Open for breakfast and lunch, **Mango's** (352-402-9822), 20 SW Broadway, features Caribbean cuisine, vegetarian specialties, and fabulous old-fashioned homemade root beer floats—free root beer refills! Try the Beach Quesadilla, a tasty mix of cheeses and veggies with fresh salsa, or the Sunshine Salad, fresh fruit, carrots, and almonds piled high and topped with creamy strawberry-mango dressing. Most of the offerings contain mango. Subs, salads, and sandwiches, $7 and up.

Downtown and always busy for breakfast and lunch, **Richard's Place** (352-351-2233), 316 E Silver Springs Blvd, is a local institution where I used to grab lunch when I worked across the street 20 years ago. My husband declared his pork chop and eggs superb, and I was quite happy with my pancakes. Meals start at $3. We will be back!

At the **Veranda Gallery and Tea Room** (352-622-0007; www.veranda gallery.com), 416 SE Fort King St, enjoy a quiet weekday lunch in genteel Old Ocala, with sandwiches and salads $8–10.

❧ **Wolfie's** (352-622-5008), 2159 E Silver Springs Blvd. An Ocala tradition since the 1960s, Wolfie's attracts a crowd of regulars. The servers know their patrons well, and you'll swear they can read your mind. Offering daily specials such as all-you-can-eat fried fish, spaghetti, pot roast, and meatloaf dinners. Bountiful salads run $4–8. Sandwiches include New York classics like kielbasa, Reuben, club, and pita ($3–5), plus burgers and dogs "grilled to order." Breakfast served all day. Open Mon–Sat 6–9, closed Sun.

Ocklawaha

❧ **Gator Joe's Beach Bar & Grill** (352-288-3100), 12431 SE 135th Ave. Riding the coattails of Ma and Pa Barker's infamous shootout with the FBI in 1937 (see *Special Events*), the restaurant takes its name from Old Joe, a massive alligator who lived along this shoreline and was mentioned in one of the Barkers' letters. This funky Florida seafood restaurant is perched on Johnson's Beach with walls of windows overlooking the grand sweep of Lake Weir, serving up huge lunch sandwiches ($6–8), and dinner entrées ($9–13) like Joe's Kick-in' Frog Legs, Barker's Ribeye, and grouper nuggets. Special kids' menu and live calypso music on Sat 2–6; closed Mon.

Silver Springs

Back in the '60s, a Old West "whoop 'em up" attraction called Six Gun Territory was a big draw for tourists coming from Ocala to Silver Springs, and around it popped up lots of western-themed motels and restaurants. The attraction is long gone, and so are most of the spinoffs, but the **Stage Stop Restaurant** (352-236-1115), 5131 E Silver Springs Blvd, still has that cowboy feel and serves up a nice southern breakfast for under $6.

BAKERIES, COFFEE SHOPS, DELIS, AND ICE CREAM

Belleview

Fun and funky, playful and painted **B. D. Beans Coffee Co.** (352-245-3077), 5148 SE Abshier Blvd. sparkles with artistic flair in both its surroundings and its menu selections: creative and healthful quiches, salads, and sandwiches, $4–7, with daily specials; smoothie lovers will rejoice at the wide selection, including coconut, toasted almond, and chai. Java junkies have their day, too, with nearly a dozen choices. When I'm in a veggie mood, I go for the succulent portobello mushroom sandwich or the tasty veggie melt; the grilled Havarti sandwich is one of my favorites. Serving coffee and muffins at breakfast, lunch items until 5. Closed Sun. Don't miss the restrooms!

Ms. Steve's Dairy D Lite, corner of FL 484 and US 27-301-441. A busy drive-through (or walk-up, but parking is nearly impossible) family ice cream shop with hot dogs ($1.35) and

B.D. BEANS COFFEE CO.

Sandra Friend

a wide variety of dessert selections: cones $1–2, sundaes $2, shakes $2–3.

Citra

At the **Olde Tyme Bread House** (352-595-2012), 2390 E FL 318, I was stopping in for a muffin when they made me a convert to their chicken salad—and I've never even liked chicken salad. But this was fine stuff and that day's special. Grab fresh-baked breads and pies, and stop for lunch for a BLT or Angus steak burger ($3–5); open for breakfast, too.

McIntosh

Antique Deli (352-591-1436), US 441 and Ave G. Stop in for the sweet tea, stay for a sandwich ($2–5) or fresh-made salad and a great southern dessert like old-fashioned banana pudding ($1) or a frozen Mississippi mud pie ($2). Features root beer floats ($2) and ice cream ($1), too! Gift and craft items and a smattering of antiques line the walls. Open for lunch and dinner.

Ocala

⁹₁⁹ A prime hangout for us and our friends is **Chelsea Coffee** (352-351-JAVA), where I enjoy a tasty chai or mocha cappuchino while working on my latest novel-in-progress. Stacks of aromatic coffee, colorful mugs, and local art means you can shop for gifts, too!

⁹₁⁹ Two stories of bakery and art: that's the **Primary Oven Handmade Bakery** (352-390-6881; www.primary oven.com), 306 SW Broadway St, a delightful bakery with fresh breads, muffins, and pastries downstairs and a big gallery space upstairs filled with local art and enough tables to get a bunch of friends together to chat. Come early for the freshest bread; coffee, too. Open Tue–Fri 6–4.

It's tough to find an independent doughnut maker, which makes **Tas-t-O's Donuts** (352-622-7657) 2205 E Silver Springs Blvd, worth looking for. Stare at the fresh-baked doughnuts through the plate glass and order at the little window. Show up at daybreak for the best selection. When they're gone, they're gone! My favorite: coconut. They have an additional location on US 27-301-441 in Belleview, too.

✳ Selective Shopping

Belleview

More than 1,000 vendors keep the **Market of Marion** (352-245-6766), 12888 SE US 441, one of the busiest flea markets in the region, with great buys on produce, clothing, and garage sale items; they host special events, too. Open Sat and Sun year-round, and Fri Oct–Apr.

Off US 301 just south of town, **Mossy Oaks Antique Mall** (352-307-0090), 6260 SE 118th Place, represents 25 dealers. It's a joy to browse through the neatly arranged displays of art glass, saltcellars, quilts, and furnishings; I was delighted to find a good selection of books on Florida. You'll find the eclectic here, too: One dealer specializes in refurbished antique gas pumps, another dealer shows off retro chairs and stools, and a custom furniture maker takes up the back of the place. Closed Sun.

Citra

✎ **The Orange Shop** (1-800-672-6439; www.floridaorangeshop.com), US 301. Step into the wayback machine and take a trip to when fresh-squeezed orange juice flowed free for every tourist cruising through Florida. Opened in 1936, the Orange

Shop still has that old-time appeal with lots of scented and kitschy souvenirs and, of course, oranges ready to ship nationwide.

Dunnellon

Spread across several blocks of the 1890s boomtown district in downtown Dunnellon, the **Historic Village Shops** occupy classic Victorian and Cracker houses bursting at the seams with antiques, fine arts, and gifts. With more than a dozen shops to choose from, leave yourself plenty of browsing time! Some you shouldn't miss:

Grumbles House Antiques & Specialty Shops (352-465-1460; www .grumbleshouseantiques.com), 20799 Walnut St. In this showy southern mansion, rooms overflow with a mix of old and new. Step down the breezeway to its sister shop, **The Barracks**, which places an emphasis on antique glassware.

✐ **Our Florida Bookstore and Art Gallery** (352-489-3114), 20709 W Pennsylvania Ave. It's the perfect place to immerse in what's so special about Florida—an entire bookstore devoted to the subject. From mysteries by Carl Hiaasen and Randy Wayne White to history tomes by Michael

Gannon and yours truly, Sandra Friend, this Florida-centric bookstore covers the state in every possible way. There's even a room for the kids, entirely devoted to children's literature on the Sunshine State. Truly a one-of-a-kind place, decorated with fine Florida art, including the primitive folk art of Ruby C. Williams, as well as fossils gathered by the owner's husband.

Pop in **The Stitch Niche** (352-465-8000), 20780 Walnut St, for an amazing rainbow of fancy yarns perfect for those special knitting projects. It's inside the historic Parker House, which also hosts **Cottonbelle Cottons** quilt shop and the **Book Nook**, filled with used books.

Two Sisters Antique and Gift Gallery (352-465-6982), 20721 W Pennsylvania Ave. When the shopkeeper hands you a glass of icy pink lemonade, how can you not keep browsing? Feathered with fine furniture, linens, jewelry, and more, this friendly feminine nest screams girl stuff and is an ideal place to find the perfect gift for Mom or Sis.

Irvine

In a giant old barn, **A Antique Mall** (352-591-0588), 17990 NW 77th Ave, towers over the interstate, with two floors packed full of dealer booths which are each packed full of antiques. During one afternoon's browse, I worked my way through the maze of shelves to stumble across brass jugs, stacks of old maps, and bisque collectibles.

McIntosh

Dianna Van Horn Antiques (352-339-6864), US 441 and Ave B; (352-591-1185), Ave G and Third St. At

OUTSIDE CITRA'S ORANGE SHOP

Sandra Friend

her US 441 storefront, the focus is on glassware and pottery and other small collectibles. Head back to Dianna's second location in the large tin-roofed barn (the old packing house) across from the McIntosh Depot, and you'll find a little bit of everything and a lot of classic furniture, with a heavy turnover of items weekly.

Ocala

Getting ready for a big adventure in the Ocala National Forest, on the Cross Florida Greenway, or on one of Ocala's many scenic rivers? Gear up at **Brasington's Adventure Outfitters** (352-861-8022 or 1-888-454-1991; www.brasingtons.com), 406 E Silver Springs Blvd, where you'll find Florida-appropriate outdoor clothing, camping supplies, and kayak rentals amid a flood of technical equipment.

If you love to tinker in the kitchen, do visit **Bakers & Cooks** (352-789-6020; www.bakersandcooks.com), 128 SW Broadway, where they have a broad selection of top-notch kitchenware, including fancy peppermills, showy copper cookie cutters, and classy Le Creuset cookware and bakeware. And if you don't cook? Stop in for a free cup of coffee and a chat, and take home some gourmet foods from the front of the store, including the always-fun Gullah Gourmet mixes and Earth & Vine tropical jams like apricot-pineapple-tangerine and banana rum. Open Mon–Sat.

Fletchbilt Handbag & Shoe Outlet (352-629-0134; www.handbag-factory .com), 1927 SW College Rd, offers discounts up to 50 percent off retail for leather purses in every style imaginable; their fine stock of shoes includes sandals for $10 and moccasins for $25.

Open on weekends and popular with locals, the **I-75 Super Flea Market** (352-351-9220), 3132 NW 44th Ave, is fun to browse; you'll find garage sale items, permanent booths with collectibles, and the usual array of cheap gimcracks and gadgets imported from Asia.

The **Ocala Wine Experience** (352-369-9858; www.wineexperience.cc), 36 SW First Ave, offers up gourmet pizza, coffee, and desserts during the daylight hours, and segues into fine wines and cigars as the day progresses. Part shop, part café, they're open until midnight on Friday and Saturday and feature tasty gourmet gifts along with their mainstay wines and cigars.

Orange Lake

Bulging with ephemera, the funky **Orange Lake Trading Post** (352-591-0307), 19063 N US 441, has everything from architectural pieces and farm tools to nuts and bolts.

FRUIT STANDS AND U-PICK

Belleview

Frank's Fruit Shoppe (352-245-2370), 5625 SE Abshier Blvd, carries fresh citrus (they will ship!) and the best fresh veggies in-season.

Citra

Watch along US 301 for a whole bevy of roadside stands with local produce. At **Steve's Famous**, produce is laid out neatly in a pole barn (they sell pole barns) next to a green space covered in lawn art (they sell lawn art, too), and the signs tell you what's fresh today, from watermelons and cantaloupe to strawberries and Vidalia onions. A line of banana trees front **Paul's Fresh Grove**, US 301 N, where the big "Indian River Citrus" signs lets you know what to expect.

Stop and pick your own organic citrus fruit at **Johnson's Farm** (352-595-7842; www.localharvest.org/farms/M12369), 1460 NE 180th St, just south of Citra.

Notable for their national awards for organic produce and beef, **Rosas Farms** (1-888-353-9912; www.alrosas .com), 13450 N US 301, sits in the curve between the US 301/441 split and offers retail organic food from Chef Al Rosas.

It was the Silver Springs Groves packing house when I was a kid, but then the frosts came and wiped out most of the county's citrus groves. Now, the building is **Waldron Farms** (352-

TACK SHOPS & WESTERN GEAR Ocala's status as "Horse Capital of the World" means a broad variety of shops you won't find anywhere else in Florida—and in many cases, anywhere else on the East Coast. Along SW 60th Ave near Ocala Breeders Sales (see *Horse Farms and Competitions*) and the airport are businesses catering to working horse farms, including feed stores and farriers. Downtown, the only shop in Horse Country solely dedicated to equine-related gifts, **Paddock Room Galleries** (352-629-3723), 226 E Silver Springs Blvd, has everything from fine art to home decor and casual throws. But along US 27 (Blitchton Rd) near I-75 is where you'll find the greatest concentration of western shops. Starting north to south, **Rustic Ranch Furniture** (352-351-9663), 4211 NW Blitchton Rd, has lovely slab benches and tables, swings and chairs made from heavy interwoven vines, and handcrafted wood accent pieces for your home. The big boot outside should give you a clue that **Skip's Western Outlet** (352-629-4266), 3890 NW Blitchton Rd, sells Nocona and Tony Lama boots as well as related western wear for men, women, and children. At **Western Roundup / Accent West** (352-351-4498), 3130 NW Blitchton Rd, you'll find home decor to make your house seem truly western, as well as a broad range of clothing and boots. But the big daddy of them all is **Wishful Thinking Western World** (352-629-7676; www.wishfulthinking-westernworld.lbu.com), a complex so huge that they call it a "cowboy superstore" and they are not kidding—I haven't seen a western store this big since a visit to Utah. From the outside, it looks like it was dropped in from Durango, and inside, the aroma of leather pervades. Ladies will appreciate the big selection of rhinestone-studded leather handbags and clutches, and the Breyer collectible horses perfect for young riders. One full room in the back is full of tack, including saddles set up for inspection, and the array of fancy Laredo boots is like looking at a work of art. The hat section ranges from straw to Stetson, and there are more Wrangler jeans and tops here than you'll find anywhere else. And yes, you can buy western jewelry as well. Open daily.

595-5591), 17750 N US 301, and they'll sell you green peanuts straight from the fields.

Ocala

Get your green peanuts at **Seiler's Produce** (352-732-2742), 7711 US 441 N, a large stand with Indian River citrus and fresh Georgia peaches in-season.

✳ Entertainment

Dunnellon

Catch Florida **acoustic folk musicians in a weekly concert series** every second Sunday from 2:30–4:45 at the Historical Dunnellon Theatre on Park Ave (352-489-3766).

Ocala

The **Marion Cultural Alliance** (352-369-1500), 110 E Silver Springs Blvd, Suite B, Ocala, represents such cultural offerings as the Central Florida Symphony Orchestra (352-351-1606), 416 SE Fort King St, with a season of Oct–Apr; the Central Florida Master Choir (1-877-996-2252), performing at regional venues in Oct and Nov; and the Central Florida Philharmonic Orchestra (352-873-4347), with performances in three venues Oct–Apr. The **Ocala Civic Theatre** (352-236-2274), 4337 E Silver Springs Blvd, is more than 50 years old (I saw *Dial M for Murder* here as a teen), and presents a broad repertoire of plays during its Sep–June season.

After a long hiatus and several incarnations as various businesses, the circa-1940 **Marion Theatre** (352- 622-1247; www.themariontheatre.org), 50 S Magnolia Ave, is now open with intimate concerts, comedy, and film screenings.

Jokeboys (352-368-JOKE; www.joke boys.com), 18 SW Broadway, is a new comedy club in downtown Ocala fea-

turing live acts like Kelly MacFarland, Dwight York, Chris Mancini, and Mark Sweeney.

Silver Springs

The Silver Springs Concert Series (see *Attractions*) features major country acts like Loretta Lynn, Lee Greenwood, and Alan Jackson, and baby-boomer favorites like Frankie Vallee and the Smothers Brothers. Concert price is included in admission on concert dates, and is part of the price of the annual pass.

Weirsdale

Orange Blossom Opry (352-821-1201; www.obopry.com), 13939 CR 42, is an old-fashioned foot-stompin' country music mall set amid the orange groves around Lake Weir, with its own opry cast and visiting headliners like Bobby Bare and the Blackwoods. Shows are Thu–Sat evenings at 7; Thu is always a country jam session (bring your own instrument!). Tickets $13–15 for headliners.

✳ Special Events

January: **Mustang/Ford Roundup** (352-236-2121), second weekend, Silver Springs. In a town like this, you'd think it was a horse gathering, but no—it's a roundup of more than 400 classic Fords, a mecca for serious antique-auto buffs. Fee.

Ma Barker Day (352-288-3751), Ocklawaha. Meet Marion County's historic terrorists: Ma Barker and her gang, who had their little shootout with the FBI in the sleepy village of Ocklawaha in 1937. Everyone wakes up with a bang on the second Saturday, with three reenactments of the classic gun battle.

Feburary: **Taste of Ocala** (352-237-1221), Ocala. Looking for a quick way to sample Ocala's wide range of dining? This annual benefit fund-raiser for Central Florida Community College is just the ticket. Diners gather at the Paddock Mall on the last Saturday of the month for an evening's worth of grazing. Fee.

April: The **Will McLean Music Festival** (352-465-7208; www.willmclean.com), first weekend, Dunnellon, provides a weekend's worth of the finest Florida folk music along with poetry, storytelling, and workshops on songwriting, guitar, banjo, and dulcimer. Bring your lawn chairs! Held at the Withlacoochee Campground ($10–15 for sites). Weekend tickets $25 in advance, $30 at the gate; children under 12 free.

Boomtown Days (352-489-2320), Dunnellon, third week. Celebrating its roots as a turn-of-the-20th-century mining boomtown, Dunnellon kicks up its heels in mid-April with pageantry, music, crafts, and canoe races down the Rainbow River.

May: **African-American Arts Festival** (352-629-8051), Webb Stadium at Dr. Martin Luther King Jr. Blvd, Ocala. First weekend. This three-day celebration of the African American community is still going strong after a dozen years.

August: **Ocala Shrine Club Rodeo** (352-694-1515), Ocala, weekend before Labor Day. In some cities, they ride funny cars. Not here in Ocala. Here, it's a wild ride around the Southeast Livestock Pavilion as the Shriners take on the meanest cattle this side of Kissimmee.

September: The **Marion County Springs Festival** (www.springsfest.org), held at various locations on the third weekend, is the only such of its

kind—celebrating our beautiful springs through educational workshops, field trips, and exploration.

October: **McIntosh 1890s Festival** (352-591-4038; www.friendsofmcintosh.org), McIntosh, last Sat. Step into yesteryear with a visit to McIntosh during the annual 1890s festival, now in its third decade of all things Victorian: arts, crafts, and food booths.

FAFO Images in Art (352-622-7263), Ocala, last Sat. Without a doubt the largest annual display and sale of fine arts in Marion County, featuring 250 juried artists, at the McPherson Government Complex, SE 25th Ave.

November: **Ocklawaha River Raid** (352-288-3751), Lake Weir, first weekend. Although Marion County saw its fair share of Civil War skirmishes, only one true battle raged: The local militia, the Ocklawaha Rangers, fought off a Union army invasion. Step into the Union and Confederate camps, or visit the sutler's village for an old-time treat.

Ocala Scottish Games and Irish Feis (352-347-2873), Ocala, second Sat. A gathering of the clans from which the region's original European settlers came, with Highland and Irish step dancing for all; stop by for the pipers, stay for the caber toss. Events held at the Ocala Regional Sportsplex, 3500 SW 67th Ave.

December: **Festival of Lights** (352-236-2121), Silver Springs. Of the many special events held at Silver Springs (see *Attractions*), the annual Festival of Lights delights the most—millions of twinkling lights illuminating the gardens along the Silver River. Fee; holiday buffet available.

OCALA NATIONAL FOREST

When President Theodore Roosevelt designated 160,000 acres of the Big Scrub as the Ocala National Forest on November 24, 1908, he created the first national forest east of the Mississippi River. To those of us who live nearby and cross it often, it's simply "the Forest." But this is a forest unlike any other. Encompassing parts of Lake, Putnam, and Volusia Counties, and most of eastern Marion County, it has grown to more than half a million acres in the past century. It protects the world's largest continuous scrub forest, a desert-like environment of ancient sand dunes capped with vegetation adapted to a lack of water. Yet within these rolling hills hide vast wet prairies and crystalline springs that pour forth millions of gallons of fresh water from the Floridan Aquifer. On his explorations of the St. Johns River, botanist William Bartram wrote about Salt Springs in 1774, describing its 52-million-gallon-per-minute flow as an "amazing crystal fountain." The Ocala National Forest is the stronghold of the Florida black bear, and the home of the largest Florida scrub-jay population in the world. Its communities predate the establishment of the national forest, when settlers moved into the region in the 1840s to homestead in frontier towns like **Astor**, ideally situated as a trading post along the St. Johns River; **Paisley**, not far from Alexander Springs, and **Fort McCoy**, established during the Seminole Wars. It is the largest and southernmost of the three National Forests in Florida.

GUIDANCE After you preplan your trip via the extensive Ocala National Forest Web site (www.fs.fed.us/r8) presented by the US Forest Service, you'll find helpful and accommodating staff at four visitors centers throughout the Forest. The busiest and easiest-to-access location (just east of Silver Springs off FL 40) is the **Ocklawaha Visitors Center** (352-236-0288), 3199 NE CR 315. If you're headed south from Palatka on FL 19, stop at the **Buckman Lock Visitors Center**, open Mon–Wed 7–5, Thu–Sun 9–5. Coming north from Altoona on FL 19, the **Pittman Visitors Center** (352-669-7495) is inside the Seminole District Ranger Station. The **Salt Springs Visitors Center** (352-685-3070), 14100 N FL 19, is centrally located within the Forest at Salt Springs. Detailed maps of the entire Forest and its recreation areas are available for $7 at each center.

Most communities in the Forest do not have their own post office but rely on postal service from outside (such as Ocklawaha and Silver Springs), which makes

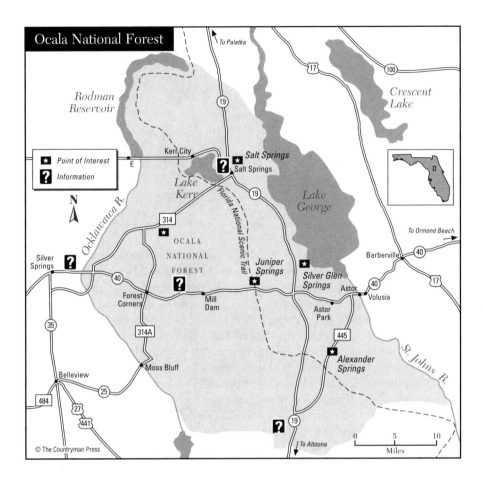

Ocala National Forest

Rodman Reservoir

Crescent Lake

Kerr City

★ Salt Springs
? Salt Springs

★ Point of Interest
? Information

E

N

Ocklawaha R.

Lake Kerr

Lake George

Florida National Scenic Trail

To Palatka

To Ormond Beach

To Altoona

Silver Springs ?

314 ★

OCALA
NATIONAL
FOREST

?

★ Juniper Springs

★ Silver Glen Springs

Barberville

40

40 ★

Astor

Volusia

Forest Corners

Mill Dam

Astor Park

35

314A

445

Belleview

Moss Bluff

Alexander Springs ★

St. Johns R.

484

27

441

25

? 19

© The Countryman Press

0   5   10
Miles

finding a place based on its address confusing. To help ease this confusion, I've grouped services under their communities rather than mailing addresses.

GETTING THERE *By car*: **FL 40**, the Florida Black Bear Scenic Byway, runs east–west from Ormond Beach to Silver Springs, and is considered the main route through the Forest. This is a heavily trafficked two-lane road (with sporadic passing zones) through large stretches of wilderness; drive carefully. **FL 315** runs north from FL 40 west of the Ocklawaha River to Fort McCoy and Orange Springs. **FL 314** runs north from FL 40 at Nuby's Corner (just east of the Ocklawaha River) to FL 19 at Salt Springs. **FL 19**, designated the Backwoods Trail, is a scenic drive passing through the heart of the Big Scrub and is the primary north–south road through the area, heading north from Altoona to meet Palatka above the northern edge of the Forest. **CR 42** provides another scenic drive along the southeastern edge of the Forest, connecting a string of small Lake County communities like Deerhaven and Paisley.

MEDICAL EMERGENCIES No medical facilities are available within the confines of the Ocala National Forest and its communities. The nearest hospitals are in Ocala (to the west) and Palatka (to the north). Cell phone service is sporadic to nonexistent throughout the Forest: Do not count on your phone to summon help for an emergency.

✳ To See

GHOST TOWNS Numerous small villages in the region disappeared shortly after the deep freeze of 1889, which convinced fledgling citrus growers that the Big Scrub was too far north to grow their crops. The town of **Kismet**, complete with a hotel, sawmill, tavern, and school, attracted northern settlers to the area near Alexander Springs (see *Green Space*) in the 1880s. After the freeze, the hotel's relocation to Altoona sounded the town's death knell. Only a cemetery remains along CR 445, where Duke Alexander, for whom the springs are named, still rests. The 1875 village of **Acron** along Acron Lake vanished with the end of steamboat traffic, as did the thriving riverfront town of **St. Francis** along the St. Johns River; the town's remains can be visited along the St. Francis Hiking Trail. Many other small settlements were abandoned as part of the establishment of the Ocala National Forest in 1908.

WORKING LOCK An integral part of the 1960s development of the Cross Florida Barge Canal, the **H. H. Buckman Lock** (386-329-3575) now provides a portal for anglers headed from the St. Johns River to Rodman Reservoir. Operations are visible from parks on both sides of the lock, but an overlook on the north side lets you get the best view; access via FL 19 and Buckman Lock Rd.

✳ To Do

BICYCLING Making a 22-mile loop between trailheads at Paisley and Alexander Springs, the **Paisley Woods Bicycle Trail** provides an excellent off-road experience for mountain bikers looking to get out into the sand pine scrub, rolling sandhills, and hardwood swamp of the southern portion of the Forest. Marked with yellow diamonds, the trail has an option of a shorter loop at the halfway point. Best access is at Clearwater Lake Recreation Area.

DANCE OF THE SANDHILL CRANE
Sandra Friend

BIRDING You'll see and hear birds everywhere along hiking trails and the edges of lakes in this vast wilderness, but my top pick for bird-watching goes to the **Ocklawaha Prairie Restoration Area** (352-821-2066; www.sjrwmd.com/recreationguide/ w07_ocklawaha_prairie_RA.html) at Moss Bluff, CR 314A, where thousands of blue-winged teals and hundreds of sandhill cranes spend each winter. For sightings of Florida scrub-jays, head to the **Florida Trail through Juniper Prairie Wilderness** or through the scrub north of CR 314.

BOATING Rent jon boats ($30–50 plus fuel) at the south end of the Forest at **Nelson's Outdoor Resort** (see *Fish Camps*), or at the north end at **Salt Springs Run Marina** (352-685-2255; www.saltspringsmarina.com), where pontoon boats run $70–110, powerskiffs $28–45 (plus gas). If you're running under your own power, tie up and stay a while at the Astor Bridge Marina (see *Motels*) with its 68 wet slips along the St. Johns, or put your own boat in at one of the many boat ramps throughout the Forest. Check the official national forest map for boat ramp locations.

ECOTOURS **Guided Tours with Captain Peggy** (352-591-1508; www.golden images-photo-scuba.com). Outdoor photographer Captain Peggy Goldberg leads custom-tailored photo safaris (surface and scuba) and tour charters on the Silver and Ocklawaha Rivers, as well as kayak trips along Juniper and Alexander Runs. Customized tours run $112 for photo tours, $180 for scuba tours, and accommodate up to four people.

FERRYBOAT Since its first incarnation in 1856, the **Fort Gates Ferry** remains the only crossing of the St. Johns River between Astor and Palatka. It runs 7–5:30; closed Tue. The western terminus is 7 miles east of Salt Springs on a rough dirt road nearly impassable during the rainy summer season; the ferry runs to Welaka on the eastern shore of the St. Johns River.

FISHING Where better to cast a line than the St. Johns River? **Lake George** has some of the best bass fishing in the state; ask around at the Astor Bridge Marina (see *Motels*) for fishing guides. There are dozens of sparkling lakes throughout the Forest just waiting for quiet bank fishing—places like **Hopkins Prairie**, **Halfmoon Lake**, **Grasshopper Lake**, and **Lake Kerr** beckon. Pull out the national forest map and pick yourself a sweet spot!

HIKING Hiking trails established by the USFS within the national forest include the **Yearling Trail** (off FL 19), which loops around historic Pat's Island, where Marjorie Kinnan Rawlings met the family who became the basis of her Pulitzer Prize–winning novel; the **Lake Eaton Trails** (off CR 314), showcasing a giant sinkhole in the scrub; and the **Salt Springs Loop** (off FL 19), taking you through the scrub down to beautiful Salt Spring. Four of the national forest recreation areas (see *Recreation Areas*) also have don't-miss hiking and nature trails. The Florida Trail Association maintains a 7.7-mile loop trail, the **St. Francis Hiking Trail**, through the Alexander Springs Wilderness. Access is from FL 42 just west of FL 44 at River Forest Campground. For more hikes in this bountiful wilderness region, see *50 Hikes in North Florida* and *50 Hikes in Central Florida*.

THE FLORIDA TRAIL When Jim Kern and friends painted their first blaze at FL 42 in Paisley in October 1966, they brought a new concept to the Sunshine State: backpacking in Florida. Envisioned by Kern as a southern counterpart to the Appalachian Trail, the **Florida Trail** now runs more than 1,400 miles from the Big Cypress Preserve on the edge of the Everglades north to Fort Pickens on Pensacola Beach, and is one of America's National Scenic Trails. Established in the late 1960s, the Ocala Trail was the first hiking trail blazed by the Florida Trail Association, and still draws more backpackers than any other part of the Florida Trail. It runs more than 70 miles straight through the heart of the Ocala National Forest. Starting at Clearwater Lake Recreation Area in Paisley, it passes within hike-in distance of the Alexander Springs, Juniper Springs, and Salt Springs Recreation Areas before reaching Buckman Lock at the north end of the Forest. Backpackers seek out beauty spots like Farles Prairie, Hidden Pond, Hopkins Prairie, and Grassy Pond to settle down for the night. The new Western Connector heads southwest from Kerr Island to connect to the Cross Florida Greenway, adding another 35 miles of backpacking within the Forest. For maps and guidebooks, contact the Florida Trail Association (1-877-HIKE-FLA; www .floridatrail.org), 5415 SW 13th St, Gainesville 32608.

HUNTING The Ocala National Forest remains one of Florida's most popular hunting grounds during deer hunting season in fall and turkey hunting season in spring. For information on hunting seasons and regulations, check the Florida Fish and Wildlife Conservation Commission Web site (www.floridaconservation .org). Several times a year, the commission offers classes to introduce ladies to activities in the great outdoors at their **Ocala Conservation Center** on Lake Eaton. Dubbed "Becoming an Outdoors Woman," the program presents such diverse offerings as archery, backpacking, birding, and fly-fishing (561-625-5126; http://myfwc.com/huntered/bow).

PADDLING Juniper Run is one of Florida's most beautiful waterways, winding nearly 6 miles through the scenic Juniper Prairie Wilderness with a single take-out rest stop along the way. Rent a canoe at the concession at Juniper Springs Recreation Area (see *Green Space*) and they'll pick you up at the end of the trip. The concessionaire at Alexander Springs Recreation Area is similarly accommodating, and the spring run is very different: Where Juniper Run is mostly a shallow, narrow, winding channel canopied by overhanging trees, **Alexander Run** is a broad, slow-moving, and deep waterway with islands creating side channels.

JUNIPER SPRINGS

Sandra Friend

At Silver Glen Springs Recreation Area (see *Green Space*), rent canoes or kayaks for an out-and-back paddle down crystalline **Silver Glen Run** to Lake George; Salt Springs Recreation Area (see *Green Space*) provides rentals for you to paddle **Salt Springs Run**, retracing the route of William Bartram as he explored this wilderness channel flowing into Lake George; also check in at Salt Springs Run Marina (see *Boating*) for rentals. Canoe and kayak rentals at Ocklawaha Canoe Outpost & Resort (see *Cabins*) allow you to put in along the wild and scenic **Ocklawaha River**, with easy access to the Silver River upstream; they lead guided trips from an 8-mile half-day trip to overnight excursion and post an excellent map of the river online (http://outpostresort.com/rivermap.html). You'll also find several public put-ins where you can launch your own craft for free, including the hidden treasure of **Redwater Lake Scenic Site** (off FL 40, Lynne) and the Upper Ocklawaha River at the FL 19 bridge.

SCENIC DRIVES A recent addition to the Florida Scenic Highway program is the **Florida Black Bear Scenic Byway** (www.flbbb.org), stretching from Silver Springs to Ormond Beach along FL 40, with a scenic loop through the Forest surrounding Alexander Springs. Visit the Web site for details about the communities along the route, which celebrates the core habitat of the endangered Florida black bear. **FL 19** also provides an excellent scenic drive through the Ocala National Forest, but if you really want to immerse in the Big Scrub, take **FR 11** (formerly FR 88, and one of the few paved forest roads) from FL 40 to FL 314. If you have four-wheel drive, there are hundreds of sand and clay forest roads to get yourself lost on. *Very important note*: All Forest Roads were renumbered by the US Forest Service in 2008. Pick up an updated road map at any of the ranger stations (see *Guidance*).

SWIMMING Swimmers can enjoy a dip in several major springs, including **Alexander**, **Juniper**, **Salt**, and **Silver Glen Springs** (see *Recreation Areas*). Bring your snorkeling gear, as the water at all of the springs is crystal clear and shimmering with fish; water temperatures hover around 72 degrees year-round. For a sandy beach on a large lake, stop at **Mill Dam Recreational Area** along FL 40; this day-use picnic and swimming facility was a CCC camp in the 1930s.

TRAIL RIDING **Rocking Horse Stables** (352-669-9982; www.rockinghorseht .com), 44200 FL 19, Altoona, offers trail riding into the southern portion of the Ocala National Forest, and accepts overnight campers with horses ($10–25) on their 150 acres, as does **Fiddler's Green Ranch** (see *Working Ranch*), where you can take riding lessons ($45 per hour; multilesson packages available), or enjoy a 2-hour ($50) or full-day ($175, includes lunch) trail ride.

Bringing your own horse? Try the trail systems at **Sunnyhill Restoration Area** and the **Ocklawaha Prairie Restoration Area** (see *Restoration Areas*) along the southern edge of the Forest at Moss Bluff. For serious outings, the **Ocala One Hundred Mile Horse Trail** loops through the Big Scrub, with a trailhead at Swim Pond on FR 573. Stop by a visitors center (see *Guidance*) for a map of the route, which includes the 40-mile Flatwoods Trail, the 40-mile Prairie Trail, and the 20-mile Baptist Lake Trail. Free.

✳ Green Space

GREENWAYS The **Marjorie Harris Carr Cross Florida Greenway** is a 110-mile corridor from the St. Johns River to the Gulf of Mexico, encompassing Rodman Reservoir at the north end of the Forest. For maps and information, contact the Office of Greenways and Trails Ocala Field Office (352-236-7143), 8282 SE CR 314; there is a visitors center at the Buckman Lock off FL 19, open daily. Free.

RECREATION AREAS On CR 445A, **Alexander Springs Recreation Area** borders Alexander Spring and Alexander Run, where archeological evidence of Timucua culture dating to A.D. 1000 has been uncovered. Rent a canoe and float down the run, or take a swim in the chilly clear waters. A blue-blazed trail leads to the Florida Trail, while a short nature trail leads you through hammocks near the spring. Fee.

Off FL 42 in Paisley, **Clearwater Lake Recreation Area** is the gateway to the Paisley Woods Bicycle Trail (see *Bicycling*) and the Florida Trail (see *Hiking*), and offers fishing and canoeing. Fee.

Along CR 314, **Fore Lake Recreation Area** on Fore Lake offers swimming, fishing, and a pleasant picnic area. Fee.

One of the Forest's most popular destinations is **Juniper Springs Recreation Area** along FL 40 near FL 19. Developed in the 1930s, it centers on Juniper Springs (where you'll see eels shimmering in the depths) and Fern Hammock Spring, where sands dance in aquamarine shimmers beneath the glassy surface. The paddling trip down Juniper Run is one of the best in the state. Access the Florida Trail through the Juniper Prairie Wilderness from here. Fee.

If you're looking for a weekend's worth of outdoor activities to keep the whole family busy, head over to **Salt Springs Recreation Area** (1-877-444-6777; www.saltspringscampground.com), FL 19. Set up camp under the moss-draped oaks and take off in every direction: Explore the little-known **Bear Swamp Trail** with its giant cypresses, head out fishing on Salt Springs Run, rent a canoe or kayak to paddle the pristine waters, or snorkel across crystalline Salt Spring.

Silver Glen Springs Recreation Area, FL 19, provides a place for swimming and snorkeling as well as picnicking, paddling, and wandering along the hiking trails that parallel Lake George. Fee.

Wildcat Lake Recreation Area along FL 40 near Astor Park has fishing and canoeing; the alligators are pretty thick in here, so you won't want to take a dip in the lake. Fee.

RESTORATION AREAS Managed by the St. Johns Water Management District, both **Ocklawaha Prairie Restoration Area** (entrance on CR 314A, Moss Bluff) and **Sunnyhill Restoration Area** (entrance on CR 42, Moss Bluff) provide large open areas in which the Ocklawaha River is being restored to its natural meanders through wetlands. Birding is superb along the riverside levees, which serve as multiuse trails for hikers, bikers, and equestrians.

SPRINGS Numerous crystal-clear springs bubble up in the Ocala National Forest, forming some of the state's most pristine spring runs: The major springs lie within recreation areas. All are open to swimming and paddlesports, but paddling is best at **Juniper** and **Alexander Springs**; swimming, at **Silver Glen** and **Salt Springs**. Don't miss spectacular **Fern Hammock Springs** at the end of the nature trail at Juniper Springs Recreation Area; you can't swim in it, but you'll be mesmerized by the variety of unusual spring vents, from liquid pools like turquoise paint to swirling underwater dust storms.

WILD PLACES Designated wilderness areas are places of beauty: No roads mar the wilderness experience for hikers, and wildlife abounds. Along the Florida Trail, you'll pass through the wilds of the **Alexander Springs Wilderness**, south of Alexander Springs, which showcases wet flatwoods and bayheads; in **Juniper Prairie Wilderness**, prepare to immerse in the Big Scrub of the Ocala National Forest, where you'll be surprised to see crystal-clear streams and ponds in one of Florida's driest environments. Both wilderness areas can also be paddled; Juniper Run is one of the best canoe trips in the state.

Caravelle Ranch Wildlife Management Area (352-732-1225), FL 19 near the Ocklawaha River, is primarily managed for hunting but also has a network of forest roads marked for hiking.

One of the lesser-known wonders of the Forest is the **Mormon Branch Botanical Area**, off FL 19 north of SR 40. Accessible only on foot (walk in on FR 71), this watershed area drains into the lower portion of Juniper Run and is home to a wide variety of extremely rare and endangered flora, including Florida willow and yellow star-anise, and is home to a champion stand of Atlantic White Cedar trees.

MORMON BRANCH BOTANICAL AREA
Sandra Friend

✳ Lodging

Lodging in the Ocala National Forest tends to be rustic, as it caters to folks interested in the outdoors. Camping is the norm, although there are small family-run motels near Salt Springs and Astor and fish camps along the lakes.

MOTEL

Astor 32102
✾ **Astor Bridge Marina** (866-BD-POTTS; www.astorbridgemarina.com), 1575 W FL 40. Zipping past on the Astor Bridge, you'd assume this is just another nondescript fish camp. But Hall's Lodge, built in the 1940s, has undergone serious renovation under the care of owners Dale Potts and Betsy Dunn. Although the exterior still

has that 1940s feel, these units impress. Four are tidy but small motel rooms, sharing a waterfront porch for sitting or fishing, but the six "cottages" (essentially efficiency apartments) facing the St. Johns River showcase classy furnishings in spacious suites ($79–99); guests arriving by water have their slip fee included; guests bringing their boats enjoy boat ramp use. Encompassing 8 acres, the marina also includes a waterfront café (see *Eating Out*) and docks, a ship's store, gas pumps, and 68 wet slips with electric power and pump-out service.

WORKING RANCH

Altoona 32702
Bring your horse or borrow one of theirs at **Fiddler's Green** (1-800-94-RANCH; www.fiddlersgreenranch .com), 42725 W Altoona Rd, a working ranch focused on training mounted police. Owner Glenn Barnard oversees 2-week clinics for riding instruction, but daily guests are welcome to enjoy the spacious facilities, which include several multibedroom villas ($110–215), an efficiency ($80–115), and RV sites ($20). Guests share a swimming pool, private lake, and tennis court, and can arrange for guided trail rides into the nearby Ocala National Forest. It's an enchanting place, deeply shaded by ancient live oaks, providing respite for equestrians and their steeds.

CABINS
Ocklawaha Canoe Outpost & Resort (1-866-236-4606; www.outpostresort.com), 15260 NE 152nd Place, Fort McCoy 32134, is just off CR 314 along the wild and scenic Ocklawaha River, a perfect place to arrange a paddling trip (see *Paddling*). Their luxurious log cabins

ASTOR BRIDGE
Sandra Friend

($79–109) sleep up to nine guests and boast kitchenette, cable TV, and a screened porch; enjoy a complimentary continental breakfast. Tent camping (with bathhouse) available; bring your gear or rent theirs.

Elite Resorts at Salt Springs (see *Campgrounds*) has the largest collection of indoor lodging in the Forest, with more than 30 cottages spread across their oak-shaded property. Each comes with sheets, towels, and dishes, including basic pots and pans; visitors have access to all amenities that the campers do, including the pool, and you get cable TV to

BOARD YOUR HORSE AND YOURSELF AT FIDDLER'S GREEN
Sandra Friend

boot. $80–125, two-night minimum stay; call ahead to reserve a pet-friendly cottage (extra charge).

&. **Lake in the Forest Estates & RV Resort** (see *Campgrounds*). You can't imagine a more tranquil retreat, tucked under live oaks with a view of Half Moon Lake. The rental cabin (more planned for the future) feels like it dropped right out of the Appalachian Mountains—a roomy log retreat with screened porch, cozy sleeping loft, and full kitchen, fully wheelchair accessible; $79, sleeps seven.

🐾 **St. Johns River Campground** (see *Campgrounds*) has lovely little lodges with screened porches, $55–95, depending on size (sleeps 4–9); bring your own towels, all other linens, dishes, and pots and pans provided. Each cabin has cable TV and a microwave.

CAMPGROUNDS

Altoona
Ocala Forest Campground (352-669-3888), 26301 SE CR 42, Umatilla 32784, sits on the south border of the Forest, with a nice mix of wooded and sunny sites, concrete pads and pull-throughs, and tent spaces. A small marsh with a boardwalk gives the kids somewhere to drop in a line and wait for a catfish to nibble. Recreation room, swimming pool, and camp store; sites start at $19 tent, $21 full hookup for 2.

Astor 32102
🐾 &. Whether you're looking for a cedar log cabin or modern mobile home, or just want to pitch your tent, at **Parramore's Fantastic Fish Camp & Family Resort** (386-749-2721 or 1-800-516-2386; www .parramores.com), 1675 S Moon Rd,

is a great place for families, with a large pool and playground. Cast your line and catch your own dinner. The campground offers one- to four-bed-room cabins ($114–190), some on the water; tent sites and full hookups ($33–37).

🐾 At **St. Johns River Campground** (386-749-3995; www.stjohnsrivercamp ground.com) 1520 SR 40, choose from cabins, RV sites, or tent camping ($26–28) in a nicely shaded setting not far from the river. This is a family-oriented place, with playground, shuf-fleboard, horseshoes, and a recreation room.

Lynne
🐾 **Ben's Hitching Post** (352-625-4213; www.benshitchingpost.com), 2440 NE 115th Avenue, Silver Springs 34488. Located up a short stretch of dirt road, this is a pleasant, partially wooded campground with 56 full-hookup sites (some pull-through), a sparkling pool, heated spa, and club-house. Tents and RVs, $25

🐾 **Whispering Pines RV Park** (352-625-1295; www.wprvp.com), 1700 NE 115th Avenue, Silver Springs 34488. At the south end of the same some-times-bumpy dirt road, another pleas-ant choice set under the semishade of tall pines; ring the giant cowbell at the office for service! 56 full hookups (some pull-through), all large camp-sites, $22; amenities include recre-ation hall, two bathhouses, on-site coin laundry, picnic tables at each site.

🐾 &. **Lake Waldena Resort** (352-625-2851 or 1-800-748-7898; www .lakewaldena.com), 13582 East FL 40, Silver Springs 34488. One of the larg-er campgrounds in the area: 104 sites, virtually all in the shade of beautiful old hardwood trees. Full hookups $22–25, includes use of swimming area, fishing and boat dock, and playground on Lake Waldena. The office also houses a camp store and recreation room.

Mill Dam

☀ ♿ **Lake in the Forest Estates & RV Resort** (1-877-LIFES-OK; www.lakeintheforest.com), 19115 SE 44th St, Ocklawaha 32179. Set well off the beaten path off 183rd Ave Rd, this expansive campground shaded by grand live oaks slopes down to the edge of Half Moon Lake, with roomy spaces and full hookups. Pull-through spaces are in a sunny field. Each site has its own picnic table and fire ring; wheelchair-accessible restrooms and showers in clubhouse. Rental boats for fishing or paddling. Sites $30, minimum two-day stay; special discounts for Florida residents.

☀ **Mill Dam Lake Resort** (352-625-4500; www.milldamlake.com), 18975 E FL 40, Silver Springs 34488. An angler's delight—large campsites right on the edge of one of the larger lakes in the Ocala National Forest. Swim in the lake, or kick back in the screened pavilion; play shuffleboard, horseshoes, and other games, or pop in at the grocery store with deli on-site. Partial hookups; dump station/shower fee $5. RV or tent $24. Lakefront park models ($75) sleep four.

Salt Springs 32134

Elite Resorts at Salt Springs (1-800-356-2460; www.eliteresorts.com), 14100 N SR 19. Top-rated 70-acre camping resort with 465 paved full-hookup spaces, 40 furnished cottages, clubhouse, heated pool and spa, 18-hole mini golf, and many other amenities, including gated access and organized activities. Caters to snowbirds but accepts overnight guests; RV sites $32–37, cottages $60–75.

USFS CAMPING Camping in the Ocala National Forest falls into three categories: developed (run by concessionaires), limited facility, and primitive. Individual sites at developed and limited-facility campgrounds are on a first-come, first-served basis. Fees vary. Primitive camping is allowed anywhere in the Forest (limit two weeks in one spot) for free, but campers must stay at designated campsites or established hunt camps during hunting season. Listed here are a handful of the 26 campgrounds available; visit the Forest Web site for a complete list (www.fs.fed.us/r8).

Developed campgrounds

Juniper Springs (352-625-3147), FL 40 west of FL 19, Silver Springs 34488. More than 70 shady trailer and tent sites, $17; hot showers, dump station, swimming area and canoe rental, camp store, access to Florida Trail and nature trails.

♨ **Salt Springs** (352-685-2048; www.saltspringscampground.com), FL 19, Salt Springs 32134. Full-hookup sites in full shade ($20 paved, back-in) under beautiful moss-draped oaks and pines, separate primitive camping area ($14), recreation barn and hiking trail (see *Hiking*). Includes access to one of the best swimming holes (see *Swimming*) in the region. Reservations accepted (www.reserveamerica.com).

Limited-facility campgrounds

Clearwater Lake, CR 42, Paisley. Forty-two campsites ($14) in two loops, flush toilets and warm showers, access to Florida Trail and Paisley Woods Bicycle Trail.

Fore Lake, CR 314A. Thirty-one lushly shaded sites ($10) with spaces up to 35 feet, no hookups. Access to lake with canoe put-in and fishing pier; pit toilets, no showers.

Hopkins Prairie, FR 86, off FL 19 north of Silver Glen Springs. Twenty-one sites ($6) with a spectacular view across the prairie. Pitcher pump, pit toilets not always open. Boat ramp accesses some of the best bass fishing in the Forest. Open Oct 1–Jun 1.

Lake Delancy East, N FR 75, off FL 19 north of Salt Springs. Fifty-nine sites in two campgrounds around the lake, $6. Pit toilets, no showers. Open Oct 1–Jun 1.

Lake Dorr, FL 19 north of Pittman. Thirty-four secluded sites hidden in the palmettos, $8. Warm showers, rest-rooms. Boating and fishing on the lake.

Lake Eaton, CR 314. Fourteen sites, $6–8. Fishing pier and boat ramp on Lake Eaton. No showers or dump station. Open Oct 1–Jun 1.

Designated primitive campsites
During hunting season, primitive campers can pitch a tent only at the 23 designated primitive campsites in the Forest, including Little Lake Bryant, Clay Lake, Echo Pond, and Trout Lake; pick up a locator map at a visitors center (see *Guidance*).

FISH CAMPS

Astor 32102
There are no RVs at **Front Street Bait & Tackle** (352-759-2795; www.frontstreetbait.com), 55522 Front St. Just seven comfy cabins along the St. Johns River—all with refrigerator, stove, and everything you need to fry up big bass or catfish. If you can't eat fish every day, the Beans BBQ is open 11–6 weekends, serving platters ($5–14) of pork ribs, beef, chicken, and good ol' country beans. Come by river; one covered boat slip comes with each cabin. Well-stocked bait shop on-site. $70–100 night; $375–500 week.

Umatilla 32784
Nelson's Outdoor Resort (352-821-FISH; www.nelsonsoutdoorresort.com), 19400 FL 42. Right on the Ocklawaha River at FL 42, this good old-fashioned fish camp dates back to the 1950s and has fabulous access to Lake Griffin and the wild marshes along the river heading north. Nelson's Store serves up its famous pork BBQ sandwiches, sells fishing tackle and bait, and even has venison and alligator in-season. Rustic cabins come with fully equipped kitchens and fresh linens, $50–159; many have river views and range up to three bed-rooms. Full-hookup RV sites and campsites with electric and water are $25; tent sites, $10–15. Boat rentals and boat slips available.

✳ Where to Eat

DINING OUT Blackwater Inn Restaurant & Lounge (1-888-533-3422; www.blackwaterinn.com), 55716 Front St, Astor. Fine dining on the St. Johns River; tie up at the dock and enjoy fresh seafood entrées ($10–26) including rainbow trout, crab legs, frog legs, deviled crabs, and Canadian sea scallops as well as massive fried and broiled seafood platters. Opens 4:30 Tue–Fri, 11:30 Sat–Sun; closed Mon. William's Landing, atop the Blackwater Inn, opens at 11:30, serving lunch and dinner in a more casual setting with the same riverfront view.

It's about as duded up as this part of the Forest gets, but the **Salt Springs Seafood Restaurant** (386-467-9930), 2932 FL 19, is one kickin' location for seafood. You wouldn't expect it in the middle of the Big Scrub, but a birth-day celebration here convinced me otherwise. This casual restaurant offers all-you-can-eat catfish, gator

BLACKWATER INN RESTAURANT

Sandra Friend

tail, and other country delights, $10–27. Also sharing the locale is the Frontier Saloon, a hot spot for country dancing and bands on weekends.

EATING OUT

Forest Corners
Jake's Place (352-625-3133), 16725 E FL 40. Barbecue is the claim to fame at Jake's, where they serve up chicken, baby back ribs, and tender sliced beef available to go for a picnic or right here at your seat, specials $6. Chef's seafood specials on Friday nights include rainbow trout, sauteeed scallops, red snapper, and flounder, to $15. Open daily 7–8.

Moss Bluff
🦆 **Duck's Dam Diner** (352-288-8332), 9748 SE CR 464-C. One of my favorites, the Dam Diner is a hot spot for home cooking, pure and simple, and lots of it. I love the real 1950s diner atmosphere—no replica here—from the black-and-white-tiled floor to the lunch counter. Breakfast includes cheesesteak omelets, their famous biscuits and gravy, and French toast, $3–9; lunch runs the gamut from barbecue to salad, and dinner (served Fri 3–8) might be an all-you-can-eat fish fry one week, spaghetti the next. Open 6–2 daily.

Mill Dam
Lena's (352-625-6489) 18478 E FL 40, grabs your attention with the giant sign A WHALE OF A MEAL! and I finally caught them open one day. The owners run a sister restaurant up in Cape Cod during the summer, and when they return to the Forest, they grace us with awesome clam and lobster rolls and other New England–style seafood delights, including homemade fish chowder. Open 11–8, closed Jul–Sept; no credit cards.

Nuby's Corner
Roger's Barbecue (352-625-2020), FL 40 and FL 314. Enjoy tasty barbecue in hefty servings at budget prices: under $5 for a sliced pork dinner with all the fixin's. Take-out available. Daily specials. Open weekdays 10:30–8:30, weekends 10:30–9. Cash only.

Paisley
Big Oak Italian Restaurant and Pizza (352-669-4296; www.bigoak italianrestaurant.com), 24929 CR 42. Eat in and enjoy a pizza or lasagna in the spacious dining room, or take out a sandwich and head to nearby Clearwater Lake for a picnic in the Forest. Lunch and dinner $6–15; closed Sun.

DUCK'S DAM DINER

Sandra Friend

Salt Springs

Square Meal (352- 685-2288), 14100 NE FL 19, is a great lunch stop after a morning's hike or paddle. Entrées include down-home favorites like meatloaf, ham steak, fried chicken, and country-fried steak, $7–9. Open lunch and dinner, Tue–Sun.

Volusia

Stop in the **Astor Bridge Marina Bar & Grill** (see *Motels*) for burgers, sandwiches, salads, and spicy hot wings ($4–9) with a side of the St. Johns River. Open for lunch and dinner.

I've always been pleased with my breakfasts at **O'Brien's Café** (386-749-1999) 1455 East FL 40, where a cup o' joe and a stack of pancakes keeps me going. Open at 6:30 AM, serves breakfast, lunch, and dinner, with daily specials; closed Wed.

At **Essex Seafood II** (386-749-1557), 1360 W FL 40, they tout their whole belly clams and, being the clam aficionado that I am, I had to take them up on it. The owners are from Essex, Massachusetts, and do their seafood New England style. It's a small place, but great food, and always busy for lunch, $11 and under. A picnic table on the back porch accommodates smokers.

✳ Entertainment

Live music can be found in many of the bars on weekends, at places like **Cactus Jack's** (352-685-2244), 23740 NE CR 314 in Salt Springs, where you might catch a rock band or live acoustic country, and the **Frontier Saloon** (see *Dining Out*). At **The 88 Store** (352-685-9015), FR 11 at Lake Kerr, catch live performers most Friday and Saturday nights, strumming bluegrass or singing country tunes to an appreciative local audience.

✳ Selective Shopping

Both the **Ocklawaha** and **Salt Springs Visitors Centers** (see *Guidance*) carry excellent selections of books about the region—for both children and adults—including many guidebooks by yours truly, Sandra Friend.

✳ Special Events

April: **Chambers Farm Spring Pow Wow** (352-625-2764), Orange Springs. Each spring, Native Americans from around the nation come together in celebration at a site near the Ocala National Forest; 2008 marked their 29th year. Open to outsiders, the powwow features tribal dancing, food, and crafts.

September: The **Marion County Springs Festival** (www.springsfest .org) swings back and forth across the county, but often has a component focused on the beautiful springs of the Ocala National Forest, with presentations and activities for all ages.

October: For more than 18 years, the **Salt Springs Festival** (352-685-2954) has featured music, arts, and crafts in the middle of the Ocala National Forest . . . and don't forget the barbecue! First Saturday.

Atlantic Coast 3

DAYTONA BEACH AND VOLUSIA
COUNTY

THE SPACE COAST: BREVARD
COUNTY

Sandra Friend

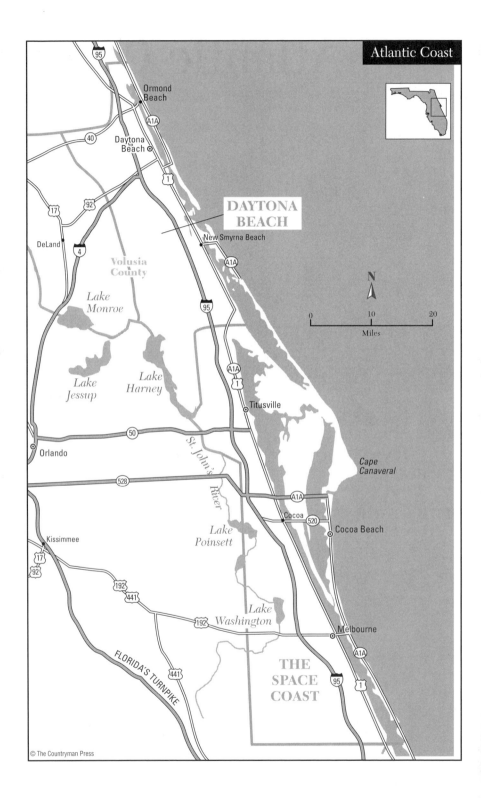

Atlantic Coast

95

Ormond
Beach

A1A

40   Daytona
Beach

1

17   92

DAYTONA
BEACH

DeLand   New Smyrna Beach

4   A1A

Volusia
County   N

Lake
Monroe   95

0   10   20
Miles

A1A
1

Lake   Lake
Jessup   Harney

Titusville

50

Orlando   Cape
Canaveral

528

Lake
Poinsett   A1A

Kissimmee   Cocoa   520
Cocoa Beach
17
92

192
441

Lake
192   Washington

Melbourne

A1A

THE
SPACE   95
441
COAST   1

© The Countryman Press

DAYTONA BEACH AND
VOLUSIA COUNTY

When you think "auto racing" or "Florida beach," chances are that **Daytona Beach** comes to mind. This coastline, the official Birthplace of Speed, attracts a fun-loving crowd for spectacular Speed Week and Bike Week, as well as millions looking to stretch out and hang out on the "world's most famous beach."

But Volusia County has its wild side, too. The St. Johns River provides a western coast, a languid flow of water through chains of lakes surrounded by floodplain forests and teeming with wildlife. The River of Lakes Heritage Corridor (US 17) connects historic communities in an interface of wild and rural lands stretching from **Pierson** at the north end to **New Smyrna Beach** in the south. Here you'll find offbeat places like **Orange Park**, with the highest concentration of wintering manatees in the state, and **Cassadega**, with the highest concentration of psychics in Florida.

Archeological finds along the St. Johns River and the Atlantic Ocean indicate that this region has been occupied for thousands of years. Near Ponce Inlet, the **Green Mound** is one of the largest pre-Columbian middens in Florida. Along with **Turtle Mound** on the Mosquito Lagoon, these sizable piles of ancient oyster shells indicate settlements of the late period St. Johns cultures, circa A.D. 800. Many middens have been uncovered along the riverbanks and barrier islands of Volusia County. Timucuan villages existed concurrent with the first European exploration of the area, until European diseases wiped out the natives. After Spanish sovereignty over Florida was established in 1565, the king of Spain parceled out land grants along the coastline, but few settlers came. An ill-fated British colony established by Andrew Turnbull in 1768 at what is now New Smyrna Beach relied on indentured servants from Greece, Minorca, and other parts of the Mediterranean; it fell apart as colonists struggled to survive along the harsh shoreline and British protection evaporated after the American Revolution. But in 1804, Englishman Samuel Williams obtained a Spanish land grant which encompassed the bulk of today's Daytona Beach. He and his son oversaw a successful sugar mill and plantation, which was destroyed in 1836 during the Second Seminole War. The land lay fallow and wild until 1870, when Ohio speculator Matthias Day Jr. purchased a large portion of it and started a new settlement, which had its own post office, sawmill, and 20 homes within three years. Day couldn't attract enough buyers, and lost the mortgage, but Daytona, the community named in his honor, persisted and flourished when Henry Flagler's Florida East Coast Railroad steamed into town in 1886. Close on its heels was the Dixie Highway, built to accommodate those brand-new automobiles in the early 1900s. Cashing in on a massive post–World War II land boom that drew thousands of new residents to the region, the communities of Daytona, Daytona Beach, and Seabreeze decided to merge as Daytona Beach in 1926. Meanwhile, the cities of Ormond Beach, New Smyrna Beach, and Deland experienced their own turn-of-the-century growth, and all are fortunate to have echoes that exuberant past in their historic downtowns today.

In 1903, the smooth, hard-packed sands of Ormond Beach attracted automobile inventors wanting to test their vehicles. The "Birthplace of Speed" slogan comes from 1906, when Fred Marriott set the world land-speed record in his Stanley Rocket Racer, clocking in at 127.659 miles per hour. His record stood for four years. By 1911, racing moved to Indianapolis, but continued in Daytona Beach from 1936 to 1958, utilizing the beachfront and A1A to create an oval that began at Atlantic Avenue and stretched 2 miles south to Beach Street. When NASCAR was founded in Daytona Beach in 1959, the race moved from the beach to became the Daytona 500 at the new International Speedway, a racing tradition that continues to this day.

GUIDANCE The visitor information centers of the **Daytona Beach Area Convention & Visitors Bureau** (1-800-854-1234; www.daytonabeach.com), 126 E Orange Ave, Daytona Beach 32114, can be found at the Daytona Beach International Airport, Destination Daytona (see *Motorsports*), and the Daytona 500 Experience (see *Motorsports*). The **Ormond Beach Welcome Center** (386-677-7005) and museum is in the MacDonald House at 39 E Granada Blvd. The Web site is an excellent planning tool. You'll also find regional tourism information at the **Southeast Volusia Chamber of Commerce** (386-428-2449 or 1-877-460-8410; www.sevchamber.com), 115 Canal St, New Smyrna Beach 32168, with a visitors center open Mon–Thu 9–5, Fri 9–4. Online, visit the **River of Lakes Heritage Corridor** (www.riveroflakesheritagecorridor.com) to learn more about western Volusia County.

GETTING THERE *By air*: **Daytona Beach International Airport** (386-248-8069; www.flydaytonafirst.com) is the primary airport for the region and offers a broad variety of carriers.

By bus: **Greyhound** (386-255-7076 or 1-800-231-2222; www.greyhound.com), 138 S Ridgewood Ave, offers service 9 AM to 10 PM daily.

By car: Most of Volusia County lies within an easy drive of **I-95**. For Ormond Beach, exit at **FL 40** and head east. For Daytona Beach, exit at **International Speedway Blvd** (**US 92**) and head east. For New Smyrna Beach, exit at **FL 44** and head east. If you head west of any of these three major highways, you'll reach **US 17**, the north–south route between communities along the St. Johns River.

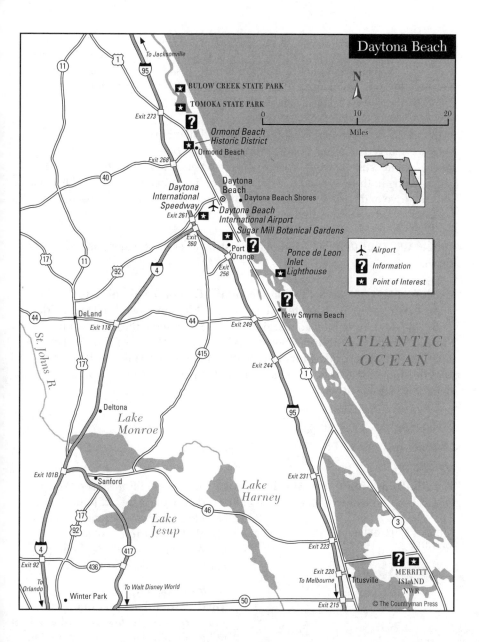

Daytona Beach

To Jacksonville

BULOW CREEK STATE PARK

TOMOKA STATE PARK

Exit 273

Ormond Beach
Historic District

Ormond Beach

Exit 268

Daytona
International
Speedway

Daytona
Beach

Daytona Beach Shores

Exit 261

Daytona Beach
International Airport

Sugar Mill Botanical Gardens

Exit
260

Port
Orange

Ponce de Leon
Inlet

Exit
256

Lighthouse

DeLand

Exit 118

New Smyrna Beach

Exit 249

ATLANTIC
OCEAN

Exit 244

St. Johns R.

Deltona

Lake
Monroe

Exit 101B

Sanford

Lake
Harney

Exit 231

Lake
Jesup

Exit 223

Exit 92

To
Orlando

Winter Park

To Walt Disney World

Exit 220
To Melbourne

Titusville

MERRITT
ISLAND
NWR

Exit 215

© The Countryman Press

N

0   10   20
Miles

✈   Airport

?   Information

★   Point of Interest

GETTING AROUND **Votran** (386-756-7496; www.volusia.org/votran) is the county's public transit service, with buses in Daytona Beach, Southeast Volusia, and West Volusia. View schedules and maps online; fares run $1.25 adult single-ride, 60¢ seniors, children under 6 free. Passes are a great bargain (all-day pass $3, 3-day $6, 7-day $12, and monthly $40). On the water, you can connect Ponce Inlet and New Smyrna Beach with the City of **New Smyrna Beach Water Taxi** (386-428-4828; www.nsbtaxi.com), which runs to five different stops—the

Marine Discovery Center, Down the Hatch Restaurant, Inlet Harbor Restaurant, Grille at Riverview, and Riverside Park—on a schedule between 11 AM and 8:45 PM daily, with additional runs on weekends. It saves you a 45-minute drive between these destinations ($10 adult, $5 ages 4–12, or $25 per family for a round-trip, one-way tickets available too).

PARKING Most beach parking lots are free, and filled first-come, first-served. Fees are charged at access points to drive onto the beach. Volusia is the only Florida county still allowing beach driving, a practice rooted in the history of beach racing in the early 1900s. Still, there are limitations of where and how far you can drive and park. Downtown Daytona Beach, New Smyrna Beach, and DeLand have free or metered time-limited parking.

PUBLIC RESTROOMS You'll find public restrooms at most major parks along the beach.

MEDICAL EMERGENCIES **Florida Hospital—Ormond Memorial** (386-676-6000; www.fhmd.com), 875 Sterthaus Ave, and **Florida Hospital–Oceanside** (386-676-6444; www.fhmd.com), 264 S Atlantic Ave, serve the coast, while **Florida Hospital–DeLand** (386-943-4522; www.fhdeland.org), 701 W Plymouth Ave, DeLand, and **Florida Hospital–Fish Memorial** (386-917-5000; www.fhfishmemorial.org), 1055 Saxon Blvd, Orange City, serve communities along the St. Johns River.

✳ To See
ARCHEOLOGICAL SITES

Barberville
The **Bluffton Mound and Midden** at Lake George State Forest (see *Wild Places*) is a remnant from the ancient cultures that roamed the St. Johns River corridor. Early settlers and explorers like William Bartram noted the existence of these mounds of shells, primarily tiny snails, near the river.

YOU CAN STILL DRIVE ON THE BEACH AT DAYTONA
Sandra Friend

Bethune Beach
Turtle Mound at Canaveral National Seashore (see *Beaches*) is considered to be the third largest shell mound in the United States. Rising 50 feet tall, with an excellent view of both the Atlantic Ocean and Mosquito Lagoon, it's been used as a navigational landmark for centuries, and can be accessed by a short but steep boardwalk trail to an observation platform on the top.

At **Hontoon Island** (see *Parks*), Florida's only intact aboriginal totem pole was pulled out of the muck of the St. Johns River during construction of a ferryboat dock for the state park in 1955. Created by the Timucua, who fished and farmed and piled up a massive midden—which can be seen at the end of the Indian Mound Trail—these artifacts included a large owl carved from a single log, an otter holding a fish, and a pelican. Replica of the owl and otter totems are in the picnic area; the originals are in museums.

New Smyrna Beach

In 1854, construction workers found massive coquina walls beneath the ground right in downtown new Smyrna Beach, sparking a debate as to the exact location of **the Turnbull Colony** (www.volusiahistory.com/turnbull.htm) the ill-fated first settlement south of St. Augustine, established in 1768 by Englishman Andrew Turnbull and his retinue of mostly indentured Greeks, Minorcans, Italians, French, Corsicans, and Turks. Many of the immigrants died on the sea voyage, and when they arrived at this coastal spot, the colonists suffered through poor diets, ill health, scary weather, and deadly mosquito-borne diseases. In building a plantation for Turnbull, these Europeans worked under overseers used to handling slaves. The colony disintegrated in 1777, when British rule evaporated from Florida after the American Revolution; the survivors made their way back to St. Augustine to seek their own destiny, and form some of the oldest lineages in that city today. By the 1950s, archeologists determined that the downtown coquina walls were part of a fort. But it wasn't until excavations in the 1990s uncovered tabby floors and British colonial artifacts at **Old Fort Park** that the discovery of the original colony truly began. More tabby walls and Colonial-era foundations were uncovered throughout the city of New Smyrna Beach, with nearly 40 sites from the Turnbull Colony now identified and undergoing extensive research.

Ormond Beach

Many middens have been found throughout the residential areas along Granada Blvd, and the location of the ancient village of **Nocoroco**, once a thriving Timacuan community on the shores of the Tomoka River, points to the region as a hotbed of early Florida cultures. Visit Tomoka State Park (see *Parks*) to learn more about the region's peoples.

Ponce Inlet

The **Green Mound** is one of the largest pre-Columbian middens in Florida, and can be explored on the trail system through Ponce Preserve (see *Parks*). The mound is thought to have been built by late St. Johns period cultures, after A.D. 800, and was greatly disturbed prior to the 1940s—as many middens were—by removal of materials for roadfill. Excavations in the midden have uncovered evidence of a village, including postholes marking the corners of raised houses.

ART GALLERIES

Daytona Beach

& Founded in 1929, the **Art League of Daytona Beach** (386-258-3856; www .artleague.org), 433 S Palmetto Ave, showcases local talent through monthly exhibits and workshops and offers an art video library. Open Tue–Sun 1–4.

DeLand

At Stetson University, the **Duncan Gallery of Art** (386-822-7266; www.stetson
.edu/artsci/art), 421 N Woodland Blvd, features student art from the Art School
as well as rotating exhibits from visiting artists. Open Mon–Fri 10–4, Sun 1–4, in
Sampson Hall. Free.

Deltona

The area's rich historical heritage comes alive at the **Deltona Arts & Historical
Center** (386-575-2601; www.deltonaarts.com), 682 Deltona Blvd, with paintings
and art classes by local artists.

New Smyrna Beach

Canal Street (in town) and Flagler Avenue (at the beach) are the central points
for this arts-minded community, with many retail galleries (see *Selective Shopping*) the centerpiece of the shopping districts. Since 1957, **Artists' Workshop,
Inc.**, has been the cheerleader for this arts community, and they run a co-op in a
little yellow brick building downtown, **Art Gallery and Studio** (www.artists
workshopinc.com), 115 Canal St, open Mon–Fri 11–3, where classes and workshops are opened and the members' works of art are for sale. They also participate with other galleries along Canal Street in a Gallery Walk, first Saturday each
month, 4–8 PM.

Arts on Douglas (386-428-1133; www.artsondouglas.net), 123 Douglas St, represents more than 50 Florida artists with a broad range of interpretations and
media; on my visit, I saw wood slab benches, lapidary, art glass, and pottery as
well as bold modern acrylic pop art and gentle oils depicting Florida scenes.
Open Tue–Fri 11–6, Sat 10–2.

Part of the **Atlantic Center for the Arts**, the historic **Harris House** (386-423-
1753; www.atlanticcenterforthearts.org) 214 Riverside Dr, offers creative space
for working artists and hosts rotating exhibits open to the public, open Tue–Fri
10–4, Sat 10–2.

Galleri di Vetro (386-409-0402; www.galleriadivetro.com), 310 Flagler Ave,
evokes the artistry of Dale Chihuly, with its blown glass and art glass sculptures
in natural forms. They feature special
gallery shows with works from artists
all across America and teach classes in
glass.

FLAGLER AVENUE IN NEW SMYRNA BEACH
Sandra Friend

DRIVE-IN CHURCH In an area dedicated to cars, it comes as no surprise
that there's a **drive-in Christian
church**. You'll park in an old drive-in
theater while listening to sermons
from the comfort of your car. Toot
your horn during choir sing-alongs.
Located at 3140 S Atlantic Blvd (FL
A1A) in Port Orange.

Cassadaga

New Yorker George Colby founded the **Cassadaga Spiritualist Camp** (386-228-3171), 355 Cassadaga Rd, in 1895 after being told in a seance that it was his destiny. The community, established as a winter retreat for spiritualists, encompasses more than 60 historic buildings circa 1895–1938. At the Colby Memorial Temple you can experience a Candlelight Healing (see *Psychic Readings*) and attend a Sunday service that recognizes all religions.

Daytona Beach

Built during the Great Depression, the **Daytona Beach Bandshell** opened on July 4, 1937. While it's now crowded against the oceanfront by a series of new condos and a shopping mall, it's still a delight to behold, constructed of native coquina with unique embellishments. During the summer months, concerts keep the place hopping like they did when the bandshell was built. It connects to what remains of the historic **Daytona Beach Boardwalk** and **Main Street Pier** via a series of oceanfront parks with memorials to racing.

Howard Thurman Home, 614 Whitehall St. The 1899 two-story frame vernacular childhood home of Dr. Howard Thurman, a mentor of Dr. Martin Luther King Jr., is also listed on the Florida Black Heritage Trail. Open by appointment.

Baseball legend Jackie Robinson broke the color barrier in pro sports right here at **Jackie Robinson Ballpark** (386-257-3172), 105 E Orange Ave, and is honored with a bronze statue, on permanent display at the entrance.

⊙ The **Ormond Memorial Art Museum & Gardens** (386-676-3347; www.ormondartmuseum.org), 78 E Granada Blvd, Ormond Beach, provide a two-fold aesthetic experience. The gardens, established in the 1940s as a war memorial, designed by Chicago landscape architect Henry Stockman, are atop sand dunes. With lush native plantings, winding pathways, a waterfall, and multiple levels with ponds where turtles sun, it's a visual and aromatic delight. Benches in quiet spots provide places for relaxation and reflection, and there's a touch of history in one corner—the 1885 Emmons Cottage, which was moved here from Beach St. Built of heart pine, this pioneer structure withstood many a hurricane and the ravages of the salt breeze; it is open Wed–Fri 11–2 and features fine art from local artists. At the other corner of the gardens, the art museum began with the donation of 56 religious paintings by Canadian artist Malcolm Fraser in 1946, which sparked a community-wide effort to fund a museum. Originally called the Ormond War Memorial Art Gallery, it was the first Florida memorial to honor World War II veterans. The museum has expanded from its original space to include a new building with rotating exhibits by regional artists. Museum open Mon–Fri 10–4, Sat–Sun 12–4, donation; gardens open sunrise–sunset, free.

DAYTONA'S MAIN ST PIER

An important educator in African American history, **Mary McLeod Bethune** established a school for young girls with only $1.50 and a few packing crates. Her persistent efforts led to the 1923 Bethune-Cookman College, now an accredited university. The **Mary McLeod Bethune Home and Gravesite** (386-481-2122; www.bethune.cookman.edu), 640 Mary McLeod Bethune Blvd, is open Mon–Fri 9–4, weekends by appointment. Free.

Housed in Bethune-Cookman University's Carl S. Swisher Library, the **"New Deal" Permanent Exhibit** (386-481-2180), 640 Mary McLeod Bethune Blvd, showcases President Franklin D. Roosevelt's "Black Cabinet" and depicts the life in the community of Rosewood from 1845 to the infamous massacre of 1923. Tue and Thu 11–1. Free.

DeBary

∞ **DeBary Hall** (386-668-3840; www.debaryhall.com), 210 Sunrise Blvd, is a beautifully restored two-story Italianate mansion that was the winter retreat of entrepreneur wine importer Samuel Fredrick DeBary, built in 1871. The complex also includes an icehouse, a stable with kennels for hunting dogs, and several small working houses. The two-story southern plantation home has stunning verandas on both floors around three of its sides. Open Thu–Sat 10–4, Sun noon–4, with guided tours until 3:30; fee.

DeLand

Thinking it would be a nice place for his kids to go to college, Henry A. DeLand opened **Deland Academy** in 1884. By 1889, Mr. DeLand's friend, the Philadelphia hat manufacturer John B. Stetson, was forced to rescue the financially strained academy and renamed it **Stetson University** (www.stetson.edu), now one of the top-ranked universities in the southeast. **DeLand Hall** is the oldest Florida structure in continuous use for higher education. You'll find the **1886 John B. Stetson House** on 1031 Camphor Lane.

Although Deland was founded in 1882, downtown Deland's historic **Main Street District** (www.mainstreetdeland.com), like many others in Florida, is a product of rebuilding in brick after a fire wiped out most of the city in 1886. The oldest remaining building is at 100 N Woodland Blvd, built as Miller's Hardware in 1887. Most of the architecture downtown dates back to the 1930s and before.

Lake Helen

Take a drive or stroll through the quaint neighborhood of the **Lake Helen Historic District**. The town, named for Henry DeLand's daughter, was intended to be the "prettiest and pleasantest" town in Florida. And I have to agree. Start your tour on Euclid Avenue under canopies of live oak decorated with Spanish moss, then cross back and forth along the side streets of this residential community. You'll find more than 70 formal homes built for wealthy businessmen of the era in the designs of Queen Anne, Classic and Gothic Revival, and Italianate. Pick up *A Walking Tour of Euclid Ave* at the Lake Helen public library, which details 13 of these homes.

New Smyrna Beach

The mostly forgotten community of **Eldora** existed along the Mosquito Lagoon on the barrier island now protected by Canaveral National Seashore (see *Beaches*). It's a stop along the road within the park worthy of a walk down the trail and a visit to one remaining structure, the **Eldora State House**, open for tours 10–4 Sat–Sun and now a museum and manatee research center.

Orange City

A postage stamp of a philatelic museum, the **U.S. Postal Service Museum** (386-774-8849), 1876 Heritage Inn, 300 S Volusia Ave, Orange City, offers a unique perspective on Florida by displaying Postal Service artifacts and history from around the state. Young stamp collectors will appreciate the freebie canceled stamps at the front desk. Open daily 9–4, Sat 9–noon. Free.

Built in 1872, the **Thursby Home** is on the grounds of Blue Spring State Park (see *Springs*). It has been undergoing renovation for many years, but is not yet open for tours. You can walk around the exterior to see the beauty of a hewn-cypress home built for practical family needs in the Florida wilderness.

Ormond Beach

The former winter retreat of John D. Rockefeller, **The Casements** (386-676-3216), 25 Riverside Dr, is named for its charming windows. On the National Register of Historic Places, it now serves the community as a cultural center. **The Boy Scout Historical Exhibit** has been a permanent display since 1980. The home is open for tours Mon–Fri 10–3, Sat 10–noon.

Measuring 24 feet in circumference, the **Fairchild Oak** is the 15th largest tree in Florida. It can be seen in all its majesty on the east side of Old Dixie Hwy in Bulow Creek State Park (see *Parks*).

At **Fortunato Park** on the northeast end of Granada Bridge sits the **Hotel Ormond Cupola**. The red-roofed cupola sat atop the Hotel Ormond for 204 years. Thousands of visitors stop by to sign the guest book. A mural and memorabilia of the era are shown on Wed, Sat, and Sun 2–4.

Port Orange

At **Gamble Place** at Spruce Creek Environmental Preserve (386-255-0285; www.moas.org/gamble%20place.html), 1819 Taylor Rd, the 150-acre preserve features historic buildings, including a 1907 "Cracker" house built by James Gamble (of Proctor and Gamble fame) as his hunting and fishing retreat. Also on the grounds is a 1907 citrus packing house and two unusual structures built in 1938—the Snow White Cottage and the Witch's Hut, modeled after Disney's animated film. Open Thu–Sun 8–5; free, but fee for guided tours of the house.

HORSE RACING The largest horse training facility in the world is in Paris, France. The second largest is tucked back off the road in De Leon Springs, but you'll think you're in Kentucky. The **Spring Garden Ranch Training Center** (386-985-5654), 900 Spring Garden Ranch Rd, started life as a turn-of-the-20th-century dairy farm. Housing fewer than 100 horses in 1949, it now holds more than 600 standardbred horses in state-of-the-art barns. Watch from the observation deck as up-and-coming horses, as well as legends, train on the 1-mile clay track. The restaurant offers a front-seat view (see *Eating Out*).

LIGHTHOUSES Get a workout climbing Florida's tallest lighthouse. Even the fittest athletes were huffing and puffing as they worked their way up all 203 steps in the **Ponce de Leon Inlet Lighthouse** (386-761-1821; www.ponce inlet.org), 4931 S Peninsula Dr, Ponce Inlet. Completed in 1887, the beacon soars 175 feet high, tapering to just 12 feet at the top. Take it slow; once you get there the view is unsurpassed, and you'll want to enjoy it. The extensive complex also warrants equal attention, from the original lighthouse keeper's dwelling to a museum featuring pirates' treasures and teacups from many of the ships passing through the area. Nature trails meander through coastal habitats, where you'll run across a cemetery of the light keeper's cats. The lens exhibit houses a magnificent, fully restored Fresnel lens that was used at Cape Canaveral until 1993. Open daily 10–5, until 9 in summer. Fee.

MEMORIALS & MONUMENTS

Daytona Beach
Unless you meander along the waterfront off the Main Street Pier, you won't see this series of interesting monuments. First, a new palm-lined **walkway** commemorates world **land-speed records** set on the sandy strand at Daytona Beach. The nearby **coquina clock tower** honors Sir Malcolm Campbell's achievement of 276.82 MPH "on these sands" in 1935. And a modern marble monument along the edge of the bandshell is engraved with historic photos of the **Daytona 200 motorcycle races** held here circa 1937–1960, with images of the winners for each year.

DAYTONA BEACH'S LAND-SPEED RECORD MONUMENT

Sandra Friend

New Smyrna Beach
At Riverside Park, at the end of Canal Street, there are two monuments of note on this grassy expanse overlooking the Intracoastal Waterway. The **Pancretan Greek Monument**, a white structure topped with stained glass inlaid with symbols, commemorates the arrival of the first Greeks in

Florida on these foreign shores as part of the Turnbull Colony, 1768–1777. Near-by, an older **coquina monument** honors American veterans of foreign wars.

Ormond Beach

Nine miles north of Granada Blvd on Old Dixie Hwy is the tomb of James Ormond, for whom the town is named, in **Ormond Tomb Park** (386-257-6000, ext. 5953). At the Birthplace of Speed Park (see *Motorsports*), look for a monument commemorating the **first land speed record** set with an automobile, clocked right here in 1906.

MOTOR SPORTS Known throughout the world as a top-line racetrack, the **Daytona International Speedway** (386-253-7223; www.daytonainternational speedway.com), 1801 W International Speedway Blvd, Daytona Beach, is where professional AMA Superbikes and NASCAR stock cars race up to 190 mph at such events as the annual Daytona 500. The track is also a venue for concerts, athletic events, and testing and development of race cars. Take a tour of the track and get a better view of the 31-degree banked turns.

✧ Race fans will want to spend some time at the **Daytona 500 Experience** (386-947-6800; www.daytona500experience.com), 1801 W International Speed-way Blvd, Daytona Beach, where you can test your skill changing tires at the timed pit stop, or buckle up in Acceleration Alley for a simulated ride of pure speed. Other interactive games, simulators, and historical exhibits are found at this official NASCAR attraction. Open daily 9–7. Track tours available every half hour until 5, except on race days.

Admission $24 adults, $19 seniors and ages 6–12; the VIP Hot Pass provides admission plus a personal track tour, lunch at the Budweiser Bistro, discounts on merchandise, and vouchers for Acceleration Alley, $50. Various annual passes are also available. On site is the **Richard Petty Driving Experience** (386-947-6530 or 1-800-BE-PETTY; www.1800bepetty.com), where you can ride as a passenger going 150 mph while banking 31-degree turns as you travel around the famed 2.5-mile Daytona racetrack, $149 for one lap. Want to drive the legendary banks yourself? You'll need to call to see if you qualify.

Destination Daytona (www .destinationdaytona.com), 1635 N US 1, Ormond Beach, is the newest entrant to race-themed fun, this time, for motorcycle enthusiasts, with 150 acres devoted to motorcycles—

THE DALE EARNHARDT STATUE AT DAYTONA SPEEDWAY

themed restaurants, bars and pubs, gear shops, an on-site hotel, and a cluster of motorcycle dealers, including the world's largest Harley-Davidson Store.

You can find great NASCAR-sanctioned auto racing, at reasonable prices, just 15 miles west of Ormond Beach at **Volusia Speedway Park** (386-985-4402; www .volusiaspeedwaypark.com), 1500 E FL 40, De Leon Springs (5 miles east of Barberville). Watch as late-model and street stock cars speed around the 0.5-mile clay oval dirt track taking turns on the on the 9-degree semibanked corners. And as if one track wasn't enough, the speedway also has a 0.4-mile semibanked asphalt oval for special events. Free parking at both tracks, and go-cart racing for fun!

MURALS The **DeLand Mural Walk** is a fine compliment to the Historic Main Street District and is "like flipping the pages through a history book about DeLand." *Pioneers at the Parceland* depicts the early life of settlers in the up-and-coming town, complete with a steam locomotive. *Manatees* is behind a waterfall at a downtown bank and is a glass art mural honoring the creature that appears here en masse every winter. In Painter's Park, a new mural depicts the origins of the pioneering African American community. For more information on the mural program, contact Main Street DeLand (386-738-0649).

MUSEUMS

Barberville

✏ At the **Pioneer Settlement for the Creative Arts** (386-749-2959; www .pioneersettlement.org), 1776 Lightfoot Ln, you'll discover what life was like around the turn of the 20th century. Dedicated to preserving the past, this pioneer community not only has historic buildings and artifacts, but also demonstrates and offers classes on candle dipping, batiking, basket weaving, blacksmithing, quilting, and even dancing. Walk through the settlement and discover the past through historic farm equipment and buildings, such as an 1885 post office and 1920s pottery shed. The exposed turpentine quarters where slaves were forced to live will alarm you. The modest admission includes an informative tour with a guide; fee.

THE OLD GENERAL STORE AT THE PIONEER SETTLEMENT
Sandra Friend

Daytona Beach

✏ ♿ Located on the beautiful Tuscawilla Nature Preserve, the **Museum of Arts and Sciences** (904-255-0285; www.moas.org), 1040 Museum Blvd, offers an outstanding and varied collection of fine art, scientific, and historical items. It's hard to believe that the 130,000-year-old, 13-foot giant ground sloth came from right here in Florida. The Root family's collection showcases Americana, containing two fully restored railroad cars, a 19th-century apothecary, and hundreds of teddy bears. Coca-Cola fans will love the Coca-Cola exhibit with bottles, memorabilia, and machinery used to bottle the popular soda. The Cuban Museum collection spans 500 years of Cuban history with more than 200 objects of Cuban fine and folk art, allowing all cultures a rare glimpse of material not usually seen outside Havana. A fine collection of African art features ceremonial masks and sculpted figures and is also part of the Black Heritage Trail. Soon to come is the Charles and Linda Williams Children's Museum, with 9,300 square feet of interactive children's exhibits. Open Mon–Sat 9–5, Sun 11–5; $13 adults, $11 seniors and students, $7 ages 6–17.

& One of the newest entrants on the local arts scene is the **Southeast Museum of Photography** (386-506-4475; www.smponline.org), 1200 W International Speedway Blvd, in the School of Hospitality at Daytona Beach College. This nationally significant gallery is the largest in Florida to focus on photography. Massive gallery spaces provide a backdrop for photographic studies such as Steve McCurry's *The Path to Buddha*, which presented images evoking the grace and brilliant color of the peoples of the Himalaya. Exhibits change quarterly, with at least four major photographers featured. Open Tue–Fri 11–5, until 7 Wed, Sat-Sun 1–5.

✎ One of the finest presentations of regional history in Florida, the very authentic **Halifax Historical Museum** (386-255-6976; www.halifaxhistorical .org), 252 S Beach St, is housed in the former Merchant's National Bank building, still resplendent with its marble columns, teller's cages, Tiffany lamps, and massive murals with Florida scenes from the 1950s. Exhibits in the center of the building change every few months, but the back of the museum hosts a permanent exhibit of the history of racing, with detailed historical models created by Lawson Diggett, a longtime volunteer. One of the more interesting models is that of the Daytona Beach boardwalk circa 1938. An astounding array of artifacts is tucked away in the corners, including an 1860s dress worn at Abraham Lincoln's inauguration by Mary Todd Lincoln's sister and left behind at a hotel of the era; handcrafted surfboards from the 1940s; a solid mahogany plantation table from the 1880s, rescued from the steamship *Veracruz*; and Grandma's Attic, an upstairs room full of classic toys that the kids (and you) can play with. Researchers will appreciate the extensive library, with volumes of records, plat books, photos, and postcards. And the building is haunted. Curators speak of smelling the scent of barn animals, or flowers, or cigars behind this building in the downtown district, of an elephant that "just wouldn't stay put" in the gift shop, and of a little girl who occasionally appears atop a desk in the main hall. It's a fascinating place, full of details. Open Tue–Sat 1–4, fee; donation on Thu; children free Sat.

Since its opening in 1995, the **African American Museum of the Arts** (386-736-4004; www.africanmuseumdeland.org), 325 S Clara Ave, has slowly built a collection of more than 150 artifacts, including sculptures and masks from several African countries, including Zimbabwe, Madagascar, and Kenya. The only museum in the area devoted to African American and Caribbean American cultures, it also houses a revolving gallery of established and emerging artists. Open Wed–Sat 10–4, fee.

Interestingly enough, the **Henry A. DeLand House Museum** (386-740-6813; www.delandhouse.com), 137 W Michigan Ave, was owned by several leaders of the community, but never by Mr. DeLand. He sold the piece of land where the house sits to the city's first attorney, George Hamlin, who then passed it on to John Stetson for university faculty housing. The home changed ownership several times, and during the Civil War was divided into apartments. Nearly 100 years later, the Conrads (see Elephant Fantasyland, below) rescued the house and donated it to the city. The home is filled with period furniture and accessories, along with the history of western Volusia County depicted in period photographs. Behind the house is a gazebo in the center of a small garden. This monument commemorates Lou Gim Gong the Citrus Wizard, who is credited with developing a new citrus orange resistant to cold. An immigrant from China, his dedication to the groves also produced a new grapefruit. Some of the original trees are still there on the grounds. The **Robert M. Conrad Educational and Research Center** (386-740-6813) is also found on the grounds, open Tue–Sat 10–4.

At the **DeLand Memorial Museum** (386-734-5333), 230 N Stone St, housed in DeLand's 1920s-era hospital, you'll find an unusual array of museums. Look into a real 1920s surgical room, and you'll also find historical medical equipment (some a bit barbaric), and a hospital dispensary. DeLand became the first city in Florida to enjoy an electrical system in 1887, so another gallery presents one of the few electrical collections in the country: The **Gallery of Ice and Electricity** is filled with rare artifacts from the late 1800s, like the colorful rainbow of insulators. The **Black Heritage Exhibit** portrays life when the first freed slaves settled in the West Volusia community. The exhibit, housed in a small building behind the main museum, portrays life in the black community through photographs, personal artifacts, and memorabilia. It took more than 40 years for Hawtense (Fuzzy) Conrad to amass **Elephant Fantasyland**, a collection of pachyderms, some dating back to the 1940s. More than 1,000 pieces are on display, from cloth to blown glass. The complex is open Wed–Sat 10–3; donation.

With works from national exhibitions, like Ansel Adams, Audubon Treasure, and celebrated local artists, the **DeLand Museum of Art** (386-734-4371; www.delandmuseum.com), 600 N Woodland Blvd, provides cultural enrichment to the surrounding community. The museum shop is a great place to find beautiful handcrafted works and unique gifts. Open Tue–Sat 10–4.

World War I dive-bomber pilots trained right here in DeLand, flying the Douglas Dauntless SBD. At the DeLand Airport, the **DeLand Naval Air Station Museum** (386-738-4149; www.delandnavalairstation.org), 910 Biscayne Ave, displays naval uniforms, photos, and other memorabilia. Down the street the Historic Hangar, 1380 Flightline Blvd, features a MASH helicopter and 1914–1918 Curtis JN4 "Jenny" World War I trainer.

On the campus of Stetson University, the **Gillespie Museum of Minerals** (386-822-7330; www.gillespiemuseum.stetson.edu) is Florida's only museum entirely devoted to minerals—and yes, there's more to Florida than limestone. In addition to native microminerals and crystals, check out the gemstone and fluoOpen Tue–Fri 10–4 during school sessions; free.

New Smyrna Beach
The **New Smyrna Museum of History** (386-478-0052; www.nsbhistory.org), 120 Sams Ave, provides a timeline walk through the settlement of this deeply rooted city, founded prior to the American Revolution and abandoned for a time thereafter. The Turnbull Colony is but one of the many stories illustrated here. Open Tue–Sat 10–4, free. A small bookstore features regional and local history and guidebooks; adjacent to the museum is the Maryland Shuffleboard Club, with courts evocative of the 1940s.

RAILROADIANA On the grounds of the Holly Hill City Hall, 1065 Ridgewood Ave, is a **Merci boxcar**, received from the people of France in 1949 as a token of appreciation for the efforts of our World War II veterans. Built between 1872 and 1885, each boxcar could hold 40 men or 8 horses, and were used for transport during the war.

WILDLIFE VIEWING Many endangered species roam freely in their natural habitat throughout the county. Lake Woodruff National Wildlife Refuge (see *Wild Places*) and Gemini Springs Park (see *Springs*) are two of the best places to view endangered species, such as the **bald eagle, manatee, eastern indigo snake, American alligator, wood stork**, and **snail kite**. Lyonia Preserve (see *Parks*) provides a perfect habitat to view the threatened **Florida scrub-jay** and **gopher tortoise**; I've yet to be disappointed in a visit, as this is the number-one place in Florida to see a scrub-jay up close in the wild. During the winter months, the **manatee** population soars to more than 150 in the crystal-clear waters of Blue Spring State Park (see *Springs*).

WINERY Indulge your palate at the **Ormond Beach Winery** (386-671-2636; www.ormondbeachwinery.com), 388 S Atlantic Ave, where they've won more than 200 medals in competitions with their premium fruit wines. Complimentary tastings are offered Mon–Fri 10–6, Sat 11–5, Sun 12–5.

ZOOLOGICAL AND MARINE PARKS ♪ Near the Ponce de Leon Inlet Lighthouse is the **Marine Science Center** (386-304-5545; www.marinesciencecenter.com), 100 Lighthouse Dr, Ponce Inlet. At this true working science center, you'll get to see rehabilitation in action from the turtle terrace; if you're lucky, you may be around for a beach release of various sea turtles, perhaps even a loggerhead. A tour guide takes you through turtle rehabilitation, where you'll learn about the different endangered marine species, and then on to the exhibit gallery, where you'll see dioramas of Florida ecosystems, a 5,000-gallon artificial reef, marine mammal bones, and the largest mosquito you'll never want to meet. The small marine park is just right for a quiet day of exploration. Outside, you can take a walk on the nature trail or relax on the scrub oak observation deck admiring the view of the lighthouse. Tue–Sat 10–4, Sun noon–4. Fee.

✳ To Do

BEACH CRUISING Drive your own car from dawn until dusk on 16 miles of the famous Daytona Beach—but there'll be no racing, as the speed limit is strictly enforced. Access points are all along FL A1A, including a historic 1920s access point *underneath* the Plaza Resort & Spa (see *Resorts*) at Atlantic Ave and Seabreeze Blvd. Fee.

BOAT TOURS

Daytona Beach
Select a narrated tour of the Halifax River and admire dolphins, the exquisite riverfront estates, and historic treasures, or try a sunset cruise with Captain Jim on **A Tiny Cruise Line** (386-226-2343; www.visitdaytona.com/tinycruise), Halifax Harbor Marina, Show Dock, 425 S Beach St. Cruises last 1–2 hours ($13–19, with reduced rates for kids) and have a variety of themes. Mon–Sat; call for times.

DeLeon Springs
Cruise on the *Acuera* (386-837-5537) on a 45-minute eco-history journey to Spring Garden Lake, or a 1½ hour trip to Lake Woodruff, at DeLeon Springs State Park (see *Springs*). Reservations required in advance. 45-minute trips run at 10 and 2:30, longer trips at 11 and 1.

RELEASED SEA TURTLE

Kathy Wolf

Orange City
❧ Captain Ron Woxberg and his crew at **St. Johns River Cruises** (407-330-1612; www.flashsolutions.us/reserveatour/sjrc/index.html), 2100 W French Ave, provide two hour pontoon boat tours on the St. Johns River out of Blue Spring State Park (see *Springs*) on a smooth-riding, quiet boat. Having enjoyed their presentation several times, I can tell you these folks will go out of their way for you to get a great photo of our native Florida wildlife, of which you'll see much along the journey. Two tours daily, 10 and 1; $20 adults, $18 seniors, $14 ages 3–12.

Ponce Inlet

Join the **Manatee** (386-428-0201 or 1-800-881-BOAT; www.manateecruise.com) for a 2-hour scenic tour of the Intracoastal Waterway between Ponce Inlet and New Smyrna Beach. Departs at 10, 1, and 4 from Inlet Harbor Marina and Restaurant (see *Eating Out*), with a special sunset cruise at 7, Jun–Sept. Reservations required; $25 adults, $22 seniors, $16 children under 12.

Port Orange

Cracker Creek Canoeing (see *Paddling*) provides popular eco-history tours aboard a pontoon boat Thu–Sun at 11 and 2 from Gamble Place (see *Historic Sites*); fee.

CHOCOLATE TOUR Satisfy your sweet tooth at **Angell & Phelps Chocolate Factory** (386-252-6531 or 1-800-969-2634; www.angellandphelps.com), 154 S Beach St, Daytona Beach. The confectioner offers free tours of their handmade-chocolate factory, with sample! The half-hour tours run about every hour Mon–Fri, with the last tour at 4. Make sure you bring home bags of chocolate (see *Selective Shopping*).

CONTRA DANCING ✐ While I chatted with two local ladies at dinner one night, they asked if I was going to the **Cassadaga Contra Dance** (386-255-6286 or 386-943-9142; www.members.aol.com/OTownFOFF/Cassadaga.html), and I thought: Why not get into the spirit of things! So I followed them to the Andrew Jackson Davis Building opposite the Cassadaga Hotel to find out what this was all about. Nothing at all like country line or square dancing, this fun-for-all activity is comparable to the Victorian dances of the great English balls—though you'll want to wear casual clothes and sneakers, and it's a lot faster. You don't need a partner for this, either, so it's a great opportunity to meet and talk with the townspeople. Most of the dance patterns are very simple; the caller walks you through a few times before the live band, playing tunes with Scottish and Irish roots, picks up the pace. A great way to work off your vacation pounds, the nonsmoking, nondrinking activity is perfect for families and a hometown treat. Second Saturday of the month 8–11; fee.

ST. JOHNS RIVER

Sandra Friend

DIVING Swim alongside dolphins; see tropical fish, sharks, and barracudas as you scuba and snorkel with eco-friendly **Discover Diving Center** (386-860-3483; www.divefl.com), 92 Dunlawton Ave, Port Orange. They are a full-service PADI certification school and offer dive trips throughout the region, as well as snorkeling trips to regional springs.

ECOTOURS ✿ At New Smyrna Beach, the **Marine Discovery Center** (386-428-4828; www.marinediscoverycenter.org), 162 N Causeway, is right on the Indian River Lagoon, which is the focus of its mission—to promote a healthy marine environment within this critically imperiled lagoon. A nonprofit organization, they provide ecotours on their 36-foot pontoon boat ($25 adult, $20 seniors and students, $10 ages 4–12) and lead guided kayak tours on the lagoon, plus offer rentals starting at $15. They offer summer camps for children and lead Master Naturalist programs for coastal habitats. There is also a small gift shop and a stopping point for the water taxi (see *Getting Around*).

FAMILY ACTIVITIES

Daytona Beach
✿ Play miniature golf at **Congo River Golf Adventure Golf** (386-258-6808; www.congoriver.com/daytona/dindex.html), 2100 S Atlantic Ave, in the company of live gators, or hang out with ye maties at **Pirate's Island Golf** (386-767-9397; www.piratesislandgolf.com), 3420 S Atlantic Ave; $12 to play all day or $9 adult, $8 children per round.

✿ Chill out with some ice skating (yep, ice skating!) at **Sunshine Park Ice Arena** (386-304-8400), 2400 S Ridgewood Ave, a destination for US Figure Skating training.

✿ Go from 0 to 75 mph in under 3 seconds on drag-racing go-carts at **Speed Park Motorsports** (386-253-3278; www.speedparkdaytona.com), 201 Fentress Blvd. Cars run on a track. Riders must be 58 inches tall.

FISHING

Daytona Beach
An important remaining remnant of the original Daytona Beach Boardwalk is the **Main Street Pier** (386-253-1212), 1200 Main St, stretching 1,000 feet over the Atlantic Ocean. Open from 6 AM–11 PM daily, it remains a great place to fish near shore. Bring your own rod and reel or rent theirs; fee. The **Sunglow Pier** (386-788-3364; www.sunglowpier.com); 3701 S Atlantic Ave, is the home of Crabby Joe's restaurant, but also has rentals and bait for you to walk out to the end and cast a hopeful line in search of pompano, tarpon, and sharks; fee.

Ponce Inlet
Critter Fleet (386-767-7676 or 1-800-338-0850; www.critterfleet.com) takes you on their 57-foot *Critter Gitter* bottom fishing or trolling, and **Sea Spirit Deep Sea Fishing** (386-763-4388; www.seaspiritfishing.com) is an offshore party boat—half day $50 adults, $30 ages 6–12; full day $75 adults, $45 ages 6–12.

St. Johns River
From the novice fisherman to the serious bass angler, the **St. Johns River** offers a variety of fishing adventures. Many top names in fishing have cast in these waters, landing trophy bass, stripers, and speckled perch. Dotting the banks of the river are many fish camps (see *Fish Camps*) and marinas that will rent you

everything you need, from bait to gear to boat. If you want the inside scoop on where to find the best fish, consider hiring a local fishing guide, who will gladly help you weave your own special fish tale. Many guides are available and can be found at almost any marina. Here are some recommended by locals: Captain Larry Blakeslee (386-736-9151), Captain Roger Dillon (352-759-2446), Captain Jeff Duval (386-789-3914), Captain Bill Flowers (386-734-5211), Captain Red Flowers (386-734-6656), Captain Robert Hees (386-649-4185), Captain James Hillman (386-734-2334), Captain Curtis E. Lucas (386-749-2707 or 386-749-2505), Captains Rick and Ron Rawlins (386-734-2334 or 1-800-525-3477), Captain Mark Smith (386-738-1836), and Captain Bob Stonewater (386-736-7120).

GHOST TOURS **Daytona Beach Ghost Walk** (386-253-6034; www.hauntsof daytona.com) is one of the rare ghost tours owned and operated by a certified paranormal investigator, blending science and folklore. You'll meet at sunset at the Quick Stop near the Boot Hill Saloon, then take a walking tour through the area while your ghost hunter, Dusty, weaves comical, sad, romantic, and sometimes macabre tales of local "inhabitants." You can't help but come away with a new appreciation of the paranormal in this articulately presented historical overview of past residents. $8 adults, children are free.

HIKING Volusia County offers numerous state and county parks and vast stretches of public land with hiking trails, some of which are detailed in *50 Hikes in Central Florida*. See *Green Space* for more on hiking trails in the various parks, beaches, wild places, and springs.

MOTORCYCLE RIDING Rent an Electric Glide or Road King by the day or week at **Daytona Harley-Davidson** (386-253-2453 or 1-800-307-4464; www.hdrental .com and www.daytonaharleydavidson.com), 290 N Beach St, Daytona Beach; must have a valid motorcycle license.

PADDLING **Cracker Creek Canoeing** (386-304-0778; www.oldfloridapioneer .com), 1795 Taylor Rd, Port Orange, offers kayak and canoe rentals Thu–Sun at Gamble Place (see *Historic Sites*). You can also rent a canoe ($20 per hour, $50 per day) or kayak ($15 per hour, $50 per day) anytime to explore the winding estuary of Spruce Creek; PFDs and paddles provided.

PARASAILING **Daytona Beach Parasail, Inc**. (386-547-6067; www.daytona parasailing.com), has four locations on the beach to take you up, up and away over the Atlantic, with flights from 800 to 2,200 feet, single, tandem, or triple.

PSYCHIC READINGS You won't find witchcraft or black magic at **Cassadaga Spiritualist Camp** (www.cassadaga.org), or anywhere else in Cassadaga; that's not what this spiritualist community of psychic mediums and healers is all about. What it is about has more to do with your own instincts. Based on the philosophy that we are more than our physical body, mediums "channel" information from outside the physical realm, bringing in bits of information that relate to your individuality. I experienced this with a thud. Sitting in the Candlelight

HOUSEBOATING Holly Bluff Marina (1-800-237-5105; www.hollybluff.com), 2280 Hontoon Rd, DeLand. For 20 frustrating minutes, I cast into the shallows on the edge of the Hontoon Dead River, where the bass have been surfacing, nibbling at flies, since we anchored. It's my first attempt at using a rod and reel; nothing bites. Around us, the river awakens as the sun slips behind Hontoon Island. A kingfisher chatters as it swoops low across the placid water. Two anhingas find a perch in the high branches of a cypress. Deer crash through the woods. White ibises honk as they settle down on a tall Carolina willow. With the generator cut off, all is still. It could be 2000 B.C., when the Timucua slipped down this channel in canoes made from hollowed-out cypress logs. It could be 1765, when botanist and explorer William Bartram paddled along the St. Johns. Then the roar of a jet taking off from the Sanford Airport breaks the twilight stillness. We open the sliding glass door to step back into the mosquito-free comfort of our houseboat.

To immerse yourself in the primeval environment that is the St. Johns River between DeLand and Palatka, consider a houseboat rental. No special boating license is required to pilot a houseboat, but if your skills are limited, you may want to hire a captain. These massive craft putter along like a box on water, but it only took me and my crew a day to get the hang of steering and navigation. Houseboats range in size from 38 feet for one-bedroom models to 53 feet for four bedrooms, and have air-conditioning, heat, and hot water for your shower. All linens, utensils, and cookware are supplied, and each boat comes with a fully equipped kitchen, and a gas grill on the front deck. Other amenities include a television, VCR, and deck chairs. Prices vary by season, time of week, and size of boat, but generally run $750–2,700 for a 2- to 4-day outing, plus the cost of fuel. A $500 security deposit is required.

HOUSEBOATING IS A GREAT WAY TO SEE THE ST. JOHNS RIVER

Sandra Friend

Healing in the Colby Memorial Temple, I was in a state of total relaxation. The meditation and calm music enveloped me like a warm, soft blanket. Toward the end of the ceremony, participants are invited to come forward while members of the spiritualist community channel healing energy. I was a bit hesitant but finally went forward. Sitting on a stool, my healer touched my head and shoulder; I could feel the warmth radiate from her hands. It was very comforting and put me at ease. After a few moments she leaned over and told me that a woman wrapped in a quilt wanted me to know that this will be a very exciting year for me. Hmmm? Sitting back in the pew I pondered who the woman might be—my grandmother maybe? Then I felt an invisible thud and voice proclaiming, "No you idiot, it's me!" I immediately knew it was my recently deceased friend Sunny, who no doubt would have whacked me in the head to get my attention. And indeed it has been a very exciting year.

The Candlelight Healing service is at 7:30 on the second Friday of each month. For an individual reading, first walk through the town and feel the energy permeate from the historic homes. One of these will stand out and feel comfortable to you. Those with mediums typically have a name and phone number posted outside. Depending on their availability, you may have to schedule your reading for another day. For those who can't wait, there's a list of certified mediums on call at the Camp Bookstore (see *Selective Shopping*); one is sure to stand out. You may not experience what I did, but you will most definitely receive insightful information and leave relaxed and rejuvenated. Readings $40–60 for about half an hour; or check out the monthly mini readings for $20.

Cassadega's reputation as a psychic center brings in the curious from around the globe. Some visitors steer toward the warmth of the spiritualist camp, but many take their chances with readings offered at various shops around the village. What's the allure of these modern-day fortune-tellers? Curious, I signed up for a reading with the Reverend Galen at Purple Rose (see *Selective Shopping*). Entering through a beaded curtain, I sat down in a darkened room where New Age music and incense set the mood.

After shaking my hand, Galen "channels the spirit," telling me what she sees. I ask about romance and finances, and the things she says fit like pieces of a jigsaw puzzle. I marvel: How could she know these details about the men in my life, or the projects I am pursuing, when I haven't said a word about myself? I realize, of course, that the mind grasps to make order from chaos, and her words can be fit into my frame of reference, but I still find the experience intriguing—especially when I return a few months later and discover continuity in predictions made during the last visit. Whether you call it entertainment or guidance from beyond, it's an experience you won't forget.

SCENIC DRIVES Itineraries for **self-guided driving tours** are available from the Tourist Information Center at the DeLand Area Chamber of Commerce.

The newest scenic drive in the region is the **Florida Black Bear Scenic Byway** (www.flbbb.org), connecting the edge of Ormond Beach with Silver Springs (see "Ocala National Forest") along FL 40. Highlights in Volusia County include the many natural lands the byway passes through, including Tiger Bay State Forest,

Heart Island Conservation Area, and Lake George State Forest (see *Wild Places*), along with the Pioneer Settlement for the Creative Arts (see *Museums*). The **River of Lakes Heritage Corridor** (www.riveroflakesheritagecorridor .com) intersects at Barberville, and is a 116-mile corridor paralleling the St. Johns River from the Putnam County line south to Enterprise, primarily along US 17.

Don't miss the scenic drive the locals call **The Loop**. There have been concerted efforts to save this 22-mile country drive from encroaching developers, and I hope they succeed; even after driving a couple of hundred miles to get there I was revitalized by cruising this section. Begin on John Anderson Drive at the Granada Bridge in Ormond Beach and head north alongside the Halifax River. You'll pass through a historic residential area, and then the view turns to countryside, with several places to stop and take in the natural beauty. Continue on the winding road and then take a left (west) at Highbridge Road over the Intracoastal Waterway. Make another turn on Walter Boardman Road to go farther west to Old Dixie Highway, where you'll take another left and go south back toward Ormond Beach. The canopy of oaks is enchanted as you reach Tomoka State Park (see *Parks*). Here you'll find one of the oldest oak trees in Florida, the Fairchild Oak.

SCENIC TOURS The Ormond Beach Historic Trust, Inc., 38 East Granada Blvd, offers self-guided historic scenic tours (386-677-7005; www.obht.org) of the Ormond Beach area. Ask for the publication *Historic Scenic Tours for Walking–Driving–Biking Beautiful Ormond Beach* to learn more about the homes, ruins, and Indian mounds along Granada Boulevard, John Anderson Drive, US 1, Beach Street, and Orchard Lane.

SPAS At the Plaza Resort & Spa (see *Resorts*), the **Ocean Waters Spa** (386-267-1660, www.oceanwatersspa.com) offers a relaxing escape from the hubbub of the world's most famous beach. Try their signature 4-layer facial, sea spa body glow and foot exfoliator, honey body polish with Vichy shower, stone therapy, or traditional deep tissue and Swedish massages, which I could go for after a long day of collecting information. Facials start at $85, massage $90, and a full day of indulgence, $225. Open Mon–Wed 8–7, Thu–Sat 8–8, Sun 10–5.

Deep inside the Daytona Shores Resort & Spa (see *Resorts*), **Indulge** (www .shoresresort.com/florida-spa-resorts.php) offers a getaway within a getaway. Once you step into this world of muted light, pleasant aromas, and soft music, your treatment room is your room—complete with shower and bath. A classy couples room can be booked for dual treatments. Sip a Shirley Temple or margarita as you relax and are pampered.

In New Smyrna Beach, **The Spa at Riverview** (386-424-6262; www.riverview hotel.com), 103 Flagler Ave, is a stand-alone facility adjoining the historic Riverview Hotel (see *Hotels*), with a signature treatment, the Riverview Stone Massage, that combines two of my favorites—Swedish and stone massage. Other special treatments include Watsu, an aquatic massage in a heated mineral pool, and cranial-sacral therapy, a massage with a gentle touch which helped me recover from an auto accident. Treatments start at $70. Open Mon–Thu 9–7, Fri–Sat 9–8, Sun 12–6.

SKYDIVING Whether your rush is free fall or tandem, **Skydive DeLand** (386-738-3539; www.skydivedeland), 1600 Flightline Blvd, will take you to new heights. The adrenaline soars at a high altitude at this world-class diving center where the best of the best practice and compete. Bring your binoculars—all the action is well over 5,000 feet in the air. Fretting family members and nonfliers can watch the drop zone from the spacious observation deck. And yes, this is the place where Cruise and Kidman learned to dive while filming *Days of Thunder*.

WALKING TOURS Take a walk down at least one street in each of the three **National Historic Districts** in DeLand, Lake Helen, and Cassadaga. Walking tour maps providing descriptions of historic, turn-of-the-20th century architecture, can be picked up at the DeLand Chamber of Commerce (386-734-4331), 336 N Woodland Blvd; the Cassadaga Spiritualist Camp Bookstore and Information Center (386-228-2880), 1112 Stevens St; or the Lake Helen City Hall (386-228-2121).

✷ Green Space

BEACHES Beach access parking is generally free along this coast, which brings the big crowds out in summertime. From north to south between Ormond Beach and Ponce Inlet, major county parks (386-257-6000 ext 5953) with parking access and lifeguards include **Bicentennial Park**, 1800 N Oceanshore Blvd, Ormond Beach, a pedestrian-only strand with restrooms and sports facilities; **Sun Splash Park,** 611 S Atlantic Ave, Daytona Beach, where small children will love the interactive water fountains; and **Frank Rendon Park**, 2705 Atlantic Ave, Daytona Shores, with picnic area, playground, and picnic shelters. There are many more access points; one of the largest I saw was in Wilbur-by-the-Sea, a residential community south of Daytona Shores, with free off-beach parking along FL A1A in several places and a large lot with portable toilets across from the drive-on beach access at Toronita Ave.

New Smyrna Beach

Bethune Beach Park, 6656 S Atlantic Ave, offers beach access with a playground and bathhouse on site.

Canaveral National Seashore (386-428-3384; www.nps.gov/cana), 7611 S Atlantic Ave, is one of the rare places in America where you can backpack along the Atlantic Ocean, where surf and sand meet along a narrow strip of barrier island along the Mosquito Lagoon. Climb the midden at Turtle Mound for a sweeping view of the lagoon, or walk the shifting sands to quiet campsites along the beach. In the shadow of Kennedy Space Center, this protected seashore provides a place for solitude and beach fishing, sunning, and camping. Access the Turtle Mound area via FL A1A, New Smyrna Beach, where you'll find the official visitors center.

&. ❦ Tucked away at the northern tip of New Smyrna Beach, the 250-acre preserve of **Smyrna Dunes Park** (386-424-2935; www.volusia.org/park), Peninsula Blvd, protects several fragile coastal environments from the ongoing encroachment of development that has marred most of Central Florida's beaches. No signs lead you to this park, and the lot holds less than 50 cars, but Smyrna Dunes provides several significant types of recreation—hiking, fishing, and the enjoyment of an unspoiled beach; fee.

GARDENS At **Sugar Mill Botanical Gardens** (386-767-1735; www.dunlawton sugarmillgardens.org), 950 Old Sugar Mill Rd, Port Orange, enjoy a tranquil stroll with the family through this 40-year-old park past a reconstructed 19th-century English sugar mill, statues of dinosaurs, and butterfly gardens. Walking under canopies of live oaks, past bromeliads and towering birds of paradise, you'll suddenly notice one of the four dinosaur statues made by Dr. Manny Lawrence in the early 1950s when the gardens were known as Bongoland, and you'll feel like you're back in prehistoric times. The 10-acre gardens are listed on the National Register of Historic Places. Please note that this is not a picnic area and food is not allowed in the park. Free; donations appreciated. Gift shop open Wed and Sat.

GREENWAYS The **Spring to Spring Trail** (386-736-5953), a 1.3-mile multiuse trail, links DeBary with Gemini Springs via a shady paved path; park at the trailhead at US 17-92 at Dirksen Drive in DeBary. A new countywide greenway is in the works, the East Central Regional Rail-Trail (ECRRT), which will provide a 51-mile biking experience that will parallel the River to Lakes Heritage Corridor (see *Scenic Drives*) as part of the **East Coast Greenway** from Putnam County to Enterprise.

PARKS

Cassadaga

Just east of the center of Cassadaga off Colby Lane you'll find **Colby Alderman Park** and Lake Colby (386-736-5953), 1099 Massachusetts St. The casual footpath travels from the Cassadaga Spiritualist Camp past a small citrus grove with tangerine, grapefruit, and orange trees, then a healing spring next to Lake Colby where George Colby is said to have drunk and then recovered from a near-fatal illness. Moving north through a beautiful cluster of live oaks, you may spot two resident gopher tortoises, Mabel and Gertrude, then head up to Lake Macy. The path is self-guided, but a map with more details can be picked up at the bookstore (see *Selective Shopping*).

Daytona Beach

Across from the downtown strip, **Riverfront Park** overlooks the Intracoastal Waterway and Jackie Robinson Stadium. Park of the park includes a historic garden complex with unusual stone bridges, and it is here that "Brownie, the town dog," an icon of old Daytona Beach, has been buried since 1954.

DeLand

Bill Dreggors Park, 230 N Stone St. Local celebrity, town storyteller, and his-

torian Bill Dreggors was honored in 1991 with his own park. The kids will love
Freedom Playground, while the adults will enjoy the DeLand Memorial Hospital
(see *Museums*), containing eight galleries and exhibits.

Hontoon Island State Park (386-736-5309; www.floridastateparks.org/hontoon
island), 2309 River Ridge Rd. Florida's state park system includes several island
preserves, but Hontoon Island State Park is the only one surrounded by fresh
water, and the only one to which the state provides a free ferry. Once on the
island, walk out to an ancient Timucua shell midden at the end of the Indian
Mound Trail, or carry your gear back to the campground for a quiet night's
sleep. The two Timucua totem poles represent originals dredged out of the mud
offshore, the only aboriginal totem poles found in the United States outside the
Pacific Northwest. The park also offers picnicking, a marina, a nature center, and
miles of forest roads to walk or bike. Fee.

Deltona

Lyonia Preserve (407-736-5927; www.lyoniapreserve.com), 2150 Eustace Ave,
is indisputably the best place in Florida to come face to face with a rare species:
the endemic Florida scrub-jay. Covering 400 acres of relict sand dunes, this preserve is very hilly and includes Volusia County's high point, at 75 feet above sea
level. Walk the trails in the early-morning hours, and you're guaranteed to see
not just one or two of these colorful blue-and-white birds but dozens of them,
flitting through the oak scrub in search of breakfast. Free.

Ormond Beach

The first auto racing began right here, with the Winton Bullet breaking the
world land-speed record at 65 miles an hour in 1903. The historic **Birthplace of
Speed Park** commemorates this event at the corner of Ocean Shore Blvd (FL
A1A) and Granada Blvd, with replica automobiles in a beachside picnic park.

Bulow Creek State Park (386-676-4050; www.floridastateparks.org/bulow
creek), off Old Dixie Hwy, protects one of the South's oldest and largest live oak
trees, the Fairchild Oak, thought to be more than 2,000 years old. A 7-mile hiking trail connects this preserve with
its springs, ancient forests, and pine
plantations to adjacent Bulow Plantation Ruins Historic State Park. Free.

At **Bulow Plantation Ruins Historic State Park** (386-517-2084;
www.floridastateparks.org/bulow
plantation), CR 2001/Old Kings Highway, the rough road beneath ancient
oaks leads you back in time to an
1821 sugar plantation along Bulow
Creek, where the ruins of the sugar-
processing equipment, slave cabins,
and spring will have you marveling at
the ingenuity of Florida's pioneer settlers at making a living from the land.

FLORIDA SCRUB-JAYS ARE A COMMON
SIGHT AT LYONIA PRESERVE

Sandra Friend

The Bulow Creek Trail parallels the creek and its tributaries, leading through one of the oldest forests remaining on Florida's east coast. Canoe rentals available for paddling Bulow Creek. The park is open for day use only, and straddles the county line with Flagler County; fee.

At **Tomoka State Park** (386-676-4050; www.floridastateparks.org/tomoka), 2099 N Beach St, walk in the footsteps of the Timucua as you explore the ancient village site of Nocoroco, once a thriving community on the shores of the Tomoka River. The park offers canoe rentals, a boat ramp, picnicking, fishing, and an extensive shady campground with 100 sites (all hookups except sewer; dump station available).

Ponce Inlet

In addition to protecting the archeologically significant Green Mound (see *Archeological Sites*), 155-acre **Ponce Preserve** (386-236-2150), 4400 Peninsula Drive, offers more than a mile of rugged hiking trails ambling up and over folded dunes dense with vegetation, and out a system of boardwalks to scenic views along the estuaries on the Halifax River. A parking lot with restrooms provides access to both trail systems; the boardwalk is across the street.

Port Orange

At **Spruce Creek Park** (386-322-5133; www.volusia.org/parks), 6250 S Ridgewood Ave, you can camp amid a coastal hammock blessed with breezes off the estuary, or roam the trails through a string of hammock islands for views of the marshes.

THE FAIRCHILD OAK, THOUGHT TO BE TWO MILLENNIA OLD

Sandra Friend

SPRINGS ✦ **Blue Spring State Park** (386-775-3663; www.floridastateparks .org/bluespring), 2100 W French Ave, Orange City, is one of Florida's don't-miss state parks. In addition to its abundant wildlife, camping and swimming facilities, picnic grounds, and historic treasures, it hosts two trails that provide two very different looks at habitats along the St. Johns River. Ideal for families, the riverside boardwalk parallels beautiful Blue Spring Run as it flows from deep Blue Spring, where swimmers and divers can play. The rugged Pine Island Hiking Trail attracts backpackers with its pristine primitive campsites along the St. Johns River at the end of a 3.6-mile trek. Rent a canoe and paddle the run, or take a tour of the Thursby House, one of the original plantation homes on the St. Johns, circa 1872. In winter months this is the top site in Florida to see manatees—more than 150 cluster in the warmth of the spring run. Fee.

De Leon Springs State Park (386-985-4212; www.floridastateparks.org/deleonsprings), 601 Ponce de Leon and Burt Parks Rds, De Leon Springs. It was the wintering ground for the Clyde Beatty Circus, and it was the plantation owned by Colonial Orlando Rees before he died by the shores of Lake Eola. But more important, it might have been Ponce de León's famed Fountain of Youth. Exploring the St. Johns River, De León discovered this spring in 1513, a place "which the Indians call 'Healing Waters.' " In springtime the azalea are in bloom; all year long, the hiking trails treat you to the deep shade of the floodplain forests of Spring Creek Run. Swim in the spring, take a quiet hike, paddle down the run (rentals available), or pile up the pancakes at the Old Spanish Sugar Mill (see *Eating Out*).

☙ **Gemini Springs Park** (www.volusia.org/parks/gemini.htm), 37 Dirksen Dr, DeBary is centered around the spectacular spring (swimming not permitted) and features nature trails, canoeing, and a dog park.

WILD PLACES The **St. Johns Water Management District** (386-329-4883; sjr.state.fl.us) is responsible for conservation areas that serve as buffers to the St. Johns River and its tributaries. In western Volusia, their lands include **Crescent Lake Conservation Area**, off US 17 at Crescent Lake, with several miles of trails through pine flatwoods open to hiking, biking, and equestrians; and **Heart Island Conservation Area**, between FL 40 in Barberville, US 17, and FL 10 in DeLand, a massive preserve of wetlands and wet flatwoods where you're welcome to walk the forest roads.

Looking for sandhill cranes? You'll find them at **Lake Woodruff National Wildlife Refuge** (386-985-4673; www.fws.gov/lakewoodruff), 2045 Mudlake Rd, De Leon Springs. One of the region's top birding sites, the refuge was established in 1964 and encompasses more than 20,000 acres of water and marshes along the St. Johns River. Walk the dikes slowly to watch for alligators, gallinules, and deer; this is an excellent place for wildlife-watching, with more than 6 miles of hiking trails. The visitors center and bookstore is open 8–4:30 Mon–Fri.

Lake George State Forest (www.fl-dof.com/state_forests/lake_george.html) comprises bottomland forests along the edge of the St. Johns River and its largest lake. There are trails for hiking, biking, and equestrian use, and primitive overnight camping is allowed with a permit. At the Bluffton Recreation Area, you'll learn about the rich history of this region through the middens left by ancient peoples.

Tiger Bay State Forest (904-226-0250; www.fl-dof.com/state_forests/tiger_bay .html), US 92, Daytona Beach. It's called Tiger Bay because it's a wet place— more than 11,000 acres of boggy pine flatwoods and cypress swamps draining into the Tomoka River. The forest roads are open to hunting, biking, equestrian use, and hiking; the 2-mile Buncombe Hill interpretive trail introduces you to the forest and its history from a trailhead at Indian Lake, off Rima Ridge Rd. Pop a kayak in the lake and tour the wetlands, too!

✳ Lodging

BED & BREAKFASTS

Daytona Beach 32118

♿ ⁽†⁾ Built in 1896 as a guest house adjoining the original J. N. Gamble estate, the **August Seven Inn** (1-877-79-SEVEN; www.jpaugust.net), 1209 South Peninsula Dr, is a classy vintage destination with modern accoutrements. The shared parlor offers a large-screen TV surrounded by French Provincial seating; an adjacent Florida room has two heavenly full-body massage chairs. Each of the rooms in this historic two-story home is specially themed, and numbered for specific important dates in the owners' lives. The 819 has green and red accents and a king bed with a river view; the original brick chimney is exposed in the bath. The 1022 is a palatial space with earth tones, leopard-dappled exotic decor, and a heart-shaped tub. Occupying the bottom floor of the former carriage house, the 1221 has a big-screen TV, roll-in shower, fridge, and microwave, and makes a great base camp for longer stays. Guests can choose a rate plan that avails them of a gourmet breakfast with such delights as crustless quiche, overnight French toast, or pancakes with homemade raspberry and brown sugar syrup. All guests have access to a communal fridge as well as movies and popcorn; coffee is served at 6 AM in the butler pantry. Behind the house is a courtyard bar, which rocks out on Wednesday and Saturday nights until late. They're only a few blocks from the beach, too. Weekday rates $125–145, weekends $140–180, with à la carte options starting at $105 or $120.

🐾 ☃ The dog-friendly **Coquina Inn** (386-254-4969 or 1-800-805-7533; www.coquinainn.com), 544 S Palmetto Ave, feels like a treehouse, surrounded as it is by some of the grandest old oaks and pines in the Olde Daytona National Historic District, but this 1912 residence is made of the compressed-seashell stone unique to Florida's Atlantic coastal ridge. Innkeepers Steve and Rhonda Hunt and their dog, Godiva, welcome you with dog biscuits at reception, and offer you port and sherry on the bright, airy sunporch in the afternoons. Outside, a gazebo with hot tub awaits. There are three common rooms, and four rooms for guests. Florida artists are featured on the walls. Each room has crisp decor accenting the original beadboard walls. I could move right into the Hibiscus Room and be happy—the windowed walls allow sunlight to pour in, and the upper story is cradled in the live oak canopy, so it feels like you're sleeping in a garden. The airy bath space has a clawfoot tub, and the private balcony surrounded by live oaks limbs is a recipe for romance. The Hunts present a full five-course breakfast each morning. One special secret: you can see the space shuttle launch from the upper front balcony. It's a peaceful retreat, just 1.5 miles from the beach, with rates $99–139, and corporate special (multiday stay), $89.

Having undergone a recent transformation, the **Live Oaks Inn** (386-252-0449 or 1-866-LIV-OAKS; www .liveoaksinn.com), 444 S Beach St, regains its former stature as a grand old lady of Daytona Beach. It's the oldest occupied structure in the area, with 14 guestrooms comprising a complex once the domain of Matthias Day, the "Day" part of Daytona

Beach. An Ohio speculator, he came to Florida after the Civil War and started selling the land surrounding this spot. Decor is neat and modern, and accommodations come in three classes—Classic ($129–149), Deluxe ($149–174), and Luxury ($169–199), which come with in-room Jacuzzi; romance, honeymoon, girls' night out, and golf packages available. A European-style continental breakfast is offered at your leisure.

The Villa (386-248-2020; www.the villabb.com), 801 N Peninsula Dr, on the National Register of Historic Places, is set in a Spanish mansion in the heart of Daytona Beach. The luxurious home is only three or four blocks from the beach in a quiet neighborhood. You'll feel like royalty and won't want to leave the comfortable ambience of this private residence; room rates ($125–300) include continental breakfast.

Lake Helen 32744
Cabin on the Lake B&B (386-228-2878; www.cabinonthelake.com), 222 Tangerine Ave. This cozy cabin has it all! Take in the beauty of the butterfly garden, grape arbor, azaleas, and grand oaks. Explore the area with a leisurely bicycle ride down the street to the historic districts of Lake Helen or over to Cassadaga for a spiritual reading. Then return to relax on the porch overlooking the lake. Slip a canoe into the water for a sunset paddle. This B&B is all about relaxation. The first-floor Captain's Room has French doors that open to a private porch, with its own hot tub. The second-floor Island and Antique Rooms each have private bath. In the morning you'll wake up to a full country breakfast served in the front room on the plank farm table or outside on the deck. Ask about the in-house psychic readings! $115–145.

∞ Red rocking chairs greet you from the porch at the **Ann Stevens House** (386-228-0310; www.annstevenshouse .com), 201 E Kicklighter Rd. Ann hosts you at this two-story National Register of Historic Places (circa 1895) inn with warmth and camaraderie. You don't visit this place—you come home. And you won't want to leave. Hot coffee and friendly conversation are served early in the country kitchen; then guests move to the main dining room, where delectable delights such as poached pears and baked Italian omelets are dished up on warmed plates. The carriage house, although built 100 years later, stays true to the period. All rooms have king or queen beds; some also have daybeds. Every carriage house room has a private screened porch. There are eight rooms to choose from—some with Jacuzzi tub—including the English garden Windsor with rich floral fabrics, hardwood floor, and antiques; the homey Cross Creek, with handmade quilts and wicker in the Old Florida style; and the Laredo, a log cabin room complete with cowboy and western antiques, a ranch house bathtub, and a unique king-sized log bed with all the romance of the Old West. In the gazebo you'll find a hot tub to sooth your aching muscles after bicycling down to Cassadaga for spiritual renewal or walking along the Cross Volusia Trail past Lake Colby and beyond. Rooms $130–170.

New Smyrna Beach 32168
"♦" Step back to 1906 at the **Night Swan** (386-423-4940; www.nightswan .com), 512 S Riverside Dr, overlooking the Indian River Lagoon. This his-

toric home and cottage complex features 15 comfortable guestrooms, some with private Jacuzzi bath, with wireless Internet throughout. Guests have access to a 160-foot dock on the lagoon, and it's an easy stroll to shopping and dining, $110–200.

HOTELS, MOTELS, AND RESORTS

Daytona Beach 32118

The **Cove Motel** (1-800-828-3251; www.motelcove.com), 1306 N Atlantic Ave, is an older property (circa 1958) designed by architect David A. Leete. The classic curves provide an oceanfront view for everyone, and the pool is oceanfront, too. The large rooms are perfect for beachgoers—step right out of your room and walk down to the surf. The facility is popular with foreign visitors, so signs are in English and French. Rates $35–85.

🦞 ♿ 🐾 📷 ⚓ At **Perry's Ocean Edge** (386-255-0581; www.perrys oceanedge.com), 2209 S Atlantic Ave, every nook and cranny is magical. You just can't tell from the highway how massive this sprawling complex is, with its variety of options (rooms, suites, efficiencies, and cottages) with spacious floorplans. I was especially impressed by the rooms with a separate children's nook filled with bunk beds and play area, but traveling without children, I'd go for an efficiency in the building with the two-story tropical oasis atrium with indoor pool and spa. Every room I visited was sparkling clean. There are two oceanfront pools with a tiki bar between, Perry's Gifts with beachwear and boogie boards, a doughnut lounge for early morning coffee drinkers, and a nice old-fashioned diner (see *Eating Out*) near the front office. If you and your big family want space to sprawl,

ask for #19, a massive oceanfront suite with full kitchen, living room, dining and kitchen area, and two bathrooms. Pet lovers get to choose from the pink cottages, which are pretty sweet, too. Move in here for your entire vacation; it's that good. Rates start at a low $89.

⚓ ♿ 📷 🍽 After a century of continuous operation, the **Plaza Resort & Spa** (386-255-4471 or 1-800-225-0329; www.daytonahotels.com/Plaza) 600 N Atlantic Ave, has undergone a complete transformation to return to her former glory as the grand dame of the beach. Now mind you, this place was Spring Break central when I was in college; years of that abuse took its toll. But recent new ownership poured more than $70 million dollars into polishing this gem till it shines, and what a difference. It's at once Old World elegant and sleek and modern. A new entrance brings guests in adjacent to the grand marble-pillared Colonnade, which is now part of the convention complex, restored to showcase its friezes and the original marble fireplace. The original beach underpass still goes under the hotel. Its pool deck is the largest on the beach, with a 10-foot-deep pool shimmering next to the Atlantic Ocean. Each spacious standard room features a 42-inch flat-screen TV, a niche with mini fridge, microwave, and coffeemaker, and classy contemporary furnishings. The Riverview side offers a sunset view, with city lights and highway bridges twinkling after dark, while Oceanside has the pounding of the surf—throw open your sliding glass doors and fall asleep to the rhythm (but turn off the air conditioning first, to honor the efforts of this certified Green Lodging). Guests have rooms, suites, and efficiencies to choose from; the corner suites feel like apartments and have spacious balconies on both sides of the room, with a fully outfitted full-size kitchen. There is a world-class spa, Ocean Waters (see *Spas*) on the ocean level, and Magnolia's Restaurant (see *Dining Out*) for all meals. After 5, it's fun to hang out at the Veranda Lounge and enjoy creative martinis and live music on Friday and Saturday night, and no matter when you're hungry, the first floor Mercado Marketessan has not just sundries and beach supplies, but juices, salads, sandwiches, beer, wine, and liquor. Best of all, it's a small price for elegant surroundings—off-season rates run for $129–189 for a standard room, add $100 for suites.

✿ ⛄ Being of Scandinavian descent, I couldn't help but pull into the **Sun Viking Lodge** (386-252-6252 or 1-800-815-2846; www.sunviking.com), 2411 S Atlantic Ave, when I saw the massive Viking longboat emerging from the front of the hotel. It's an oldie-but-goodie with generations of repeat guests who bring their whole families. The complex is extremely family-oriented, with two heated pools (indoors and out), one with a 60-foot waterslide, playground, and old-fashioned shuffleboard. For couples, the oceanfront hot tub is a nice amenity, and what would a Scandinavian place be without a sauna? Rates start $69 low season, $97 high.

✿ Brightly colored like the feathers of a macaw, **Tropical Manor** (386-252-4920 or 1-800-253-4920; www.tropical manor.com), 2237 S Atlantic Ave, is a fun place to stay with the kids. One of the nicest beachfront motels, this place really shines. The tropical feel is

everywhere from the picturesque murals to the grassy lawn overlooking the heated king-sized swimming pool and beach. There's also a kiddie pool for the little tykes. Choose from one- to three-bedroom apartments, efficiencies, and regular motel rooms; rates start at $75 off-season, $90 in-season.

Daytona Shores 32118

🦐 ⛄ 🐾 With only 49 rooms at the **Atlantic Ocean Palm Inn** (1-800-634-0098; www.atlanticoceanpalm .com), 3247 S Atlantic Ave, it's intimate enough for a quiet getaway, and, as a Superior Small Lodging, offers an assortment of recently renovated, well-maintained bright and cheery standard rooms, many with tiled floors (perfect for keeping up with beach sand). Families can get adjoining rooms with a full kitchen (fridge, stove, sink, microwave, and all kitchenware) in one of them. There

THE NEWLY RESTORED FAÇADE OF THE PLAZA RESORT & SPA

Sandra Friend

Daytona Shores

THE OCEAN VIEW AT DAYTONA SHORES

are three very large beachfront rooms to choose from: I'd pick #301, which has a heart-shaped tub overlooking the sea. The rooms directly above the office are apartment-sized suites, perfect for large families to settle in for a week, which many do year after year. Rates are very reasonable, starting around $70 off-season, $80 in-season for a large efficiency.

♋ ⚬ ℗ Right upon check-in, **The Shores Resort & Spa** (386-767-7350 or 1-866-934-SHORES; www.shores resort.com), 2637 S Atlantic Ave, creates an aura of relaxation. As I enter this rejuvenated former chain hotel, I'm greeted at the front door by staff behind little podiums in a cozy space, the rich woods offset by vibrant yellows and orange. Around me, the furniture groupings create intimate spaces to gather with friends around the fountain. There's a boutique with little black dresses and cute purses as well as sundry items. And then I arrive at the room. Oceanfront, it is a massive 500 square feet, has a 42–inch flat-screen TV with built-in CD/DVD player (and complimentary lending library at my fingertips), that all-

important writing desk, plush furnishings, and oversized balconies. The canopied pillowtop bed has high-thread-count sheets and feels like a dream. The spacious bath boasts an Italian marble shower and spiffy Kohler sinks. So why would I leave this room? Well, there's the Indulge Spa (see *Spas*), for one. And we can pick up s'mores kits for the fire pit, a beachfront gathering place after dark. There's a fitness center, and, of course, the oceanfront pool. The staff treats you like family. During the restoration, the trompe l'oeil painted wallpaper in the hallways was painted by the employees, who feel a great deal of pride in the place. Rates start at $99 in the winter months, $189 in summer. While valet parking is available, there's a free flat lot. Internet access costs extra.

DeLand 32720

DeLand Artisan Inn (386-736-3484; www.delandartisaninn.com), 215 S Woodland Blvd. This small three-story hotel, located in the heart of downtown DeLand, has only eight suites, so you are assured individual attention. Each suite in the 1924 Mediterranean Revival building is located on the third floor, providing a great view of the historic district. Decorated in a different theme and named for local pioneers, suites like the literary John Batterson Stetson reflect their namesakes' personalities and accomplishments. On the first floor, live entertainment and good conversation can be found in the full-service lounge.

Ormond Beach 32176

⚬ ❦ ℗ The **Castillo Del Sol Hotel** (386-672-6711 or 1-800-874-9910; www.castillodelsolhotel.com), 206 S Atlantic Ave, is a Best Western affiliate with impeccable taste. This is a don't-judge-a-book-by-its-cover hotel; from the highway, it looks like a typical older beachfront high-rise. But inside, the rooms really sparkle, and they are immense—the King had a wet bar the size of my home kitchen. Each room features a large flat-screen television with built-in DVD, cordless phones, small fridge, and remote controls for the air-conditioning. Side rooms have triangular balconies to afford a glimpse of the beach, while oceanfront rooms on the ground floor have picnic tables. There is a large pool with a fire pit and plenty of room for oceanfront sunning. The in-house restaurant is open 7–11 AM, offering a $5 breakfast. Pets are welcome but must be pre-approved; mention them when you call. Rates start as low as $59 off-season.

Simple and safe beachfront lodging is found at the **Symphony Beach Club** (386-672-7373; www.visitdaytona .com/symphony), 453 S Atlantic Ave. The clean efficiencies have everything you need, and the Murphy bed allows extra room during the waking hours. The heated pool is small but inviting. You'll find solitude and comfort, as this place doesn't allow wild parties. $65–125.

New Smyrna Beach 32168

♠ ⓧ ⁱ Built as the bridge-tenders home in 1888, the **Riverview Hotel** (386-428-5858 or 1-800-945-7416; www.riverviewhotel.com), 103 Flagler Ave, began its life as a guest destination in 1900. Christa and Jim Kelsey have been tending to this beautiful historic inn for nearly 20 years, and it's such a delight that they allow you to browse the cozy rooms and their classic baths—if a door is standing open in the hall, you can

peek in. Color schemes and furnishings reflect a vintage, practical Caribbean feel. There is a heated pool, wireless Internet, and an expanded continental breakfast. Room rates run $115–165, with an adjacent spa (see *Spas*) and restaurant (see *Dining Out*) and the entirety of Flagler Street within easy walking distance. Even better, the beach isn't far by foot!

♠ ⁱ Circa 1956, the **Seahorse Inn** (386-428-8081; www.seahorseinn florida.com), 423 Flagler Ave, is a vintage motel from my road-trip youth, an Old Florida delight with terrazzo floors and dark knotty-pine walls. Impeccably kept, each room has retro pink-and-black tiled bath, TV, fridge, microwave, coffeepot, and wireless Internet. Rooms come in a variety of configurations, including ones with full kitchens or extra beds. Only a block from the beach, it's a real steal at $65–135.

Pierson 32180

Sunny Sands Naturist Resort (386-749-2233; www.sunnysands.com), 502

RIVERVIEW HOTEL

Sandra Friend

Central Blvd. Where else but in the "Fern Capital of the World" would you find a nudist resort? This secluded not-for-everyone resort offers 35 acres of natural beauty. Private mobile home trailers can be rented for $113 a night or $98 with ANA membership. Sun lovers will enjoy the privacy of the heated swimming pool and hot tub. Take in some golf on the nine-hole chipping course or go on a leisurely hike on the nature trail. Restaurant open weekends. Gated security.

CAMPGROUNDS AND FISH CAMPS

Daytona Beach 32124
International RV Park (386-239-0249 or 1-866-261-3698; www.inter nationalrvdaytona.com), 3175 W International Speedway Blvd, set along the edge of a pine forest, offers tent sites for $22 and standard sites for $30; rates jump to $105 during the big event weekends. There is a large pond for fishing and playground equipment for the kids.

DeBary 32713
&. Bring your RV or tent to **Highbanks Marina & Camp Resort** (386-668-4491; www.campresort .com), 488 W Highbanks Rd, a 25-acre RV campground nestled along 2,300 feet of the St. Johns River. Then relax on a guided tour of the river on their *River Queen*. Don't have an RV ($45) or tent ($25, May–Sep only)? Rent an air-conditioned RV "cabin." Cable TV, playground, and swimming pool are just some of the many amenities.

DeLand 32720
Cast off for the backwaters at **Highland Park Fish Camp** (386-734-2334; www.hpfishcamp.com), 2640 W

Highland Park Road, where it seems everything is biting. Since 1962, this has been a launch point for anglers headed into the wilds along the St. Johns River. On the boundaries of Lake Woodruff National Wildlife Refuge (see *Wild Places*), you'll be fishing some of the best spawning sites around. Tents $18, RVs $22, and fabulous little cabins $75 (seasonally). Boat rentals $40 and up.

You'll see the wonders of natural Florida on your own houseboat from **Holly Bluff Marina** (see *Houseboating*). Alligators line the banks, while eagles and ospreys soar above. You may even see a Florida sea cow (manatee) in the crystal-clear waters.

There's more than fish stories at **Hontoon Landing Resort & Marina** (386-734-2474; www.hontoon.com), 2317 River Ridge Rd. Resident celebrity Stumpy, a true Florida "snow bird," returns each year to this resort. One year he was rescued from a fishing accident, and I guess he knows where his fish is fried! Standing on his only leg, this great white egret has been the resident mascot for more than a decade. And he's selected a fine place. The immaculate motel is right on the water, with rooms from $125, and an executive suite, $195. Or rent a houseboat (in-dock only, $295) and pile on the family and friends. The resort also has a charming hummingbird garden and gorgeous pool.

You'll want to roll right into the RV sites in the family-owned **Tropical Resort & Marina** (386-734-3080; www.tropicalresortandmarina.com), 1485 Lakeview Dr on Lake Beresford. The lush natural landscape has full hookups; those without RV can stay in one of the 14 spacious suites.

Pool, marina, boat rentals, and bait shop. Suites $75–180; they have houseboat rentals, too.

✳ Where to Eat
DINING OUT

Daytona Beach
Adjoining their signature chocolate factory (see *Chocolate Tour*), the **Angell & Phelps Café** (386-257-2677; www.angellandphelpscafe.com), 156 S Beach St, is infused with the tantalizing aroma of chocolate. But you can't eat chocolate for lunch (wait for dessert), so order a deep, rich raspberry iced tea and start pondering the menu. On a lunch visit ($4–10), I discovered the Island Chicken Salad, with banana slices, grapes, Gorgonzola, nuts, and creamy zucchini dressing on spring lettuce. There is live jazz Thursday through Saturday eves, certainly a reason to indulge in dinner, with Black Angus beef a centerpiece of this very classy eatery. Entrées $17–28.

Inside the Plaza Hotel (see *Resorts*), rich dark woods, dark wicker and florals evoke Caribbean colonial dining at the **Magnolia Grill**, and the chandeliers and wall lamps reminded me of pitcher plants. I came for breakfast, and what a breakfast! There's a weekend buffet ($10), but I was afraid that would be too much for me, and had a tough time choosing from the menu, what with southern biscuits and gravy, blueberry pancakes, the Plaza Benedict, brioche French toast with Hawaiian banana sauce, and island-style grapefruit—a broiled half with honey. My eggs were scrambled with a hint of cream, my coffee full-bodied, and the platter was amply garnished with fresh fruit. Breakfast $4–10; lunch and dinner tends toward entrées ($13–29) like prime New York strip, locally caught macadamia nut grouper served with fresh fruit and coconut-rum sauce, and gnocchi pasta with spoon spinach, wild mushrooms, pine nuts, and fresh raspberries.

Daytona Shores
At the Shores Resort & Spa (see *Resorts*), Executive Chef Lonny Huot has carved out a high-end niche with **Azure**, the only AAA four-diamond restaurant in the region. Open from 7–2 for breakfast and lunch, it segues into a fine dining experience in the evenings, with a sweeping view of the beach across the pool from within a Bahamian colonial room. Fine cuts of meat and locally grown organic produce form the foundation for creations like Bronzed Diver Scallops, served with creamy mascarpone stone-milled grits and a blood orange vinaigrette; and Five Pepper Rubbed Filet Mignon, with truffle-infused red potatoes, rainbow chard, white asparagus, honey-roasted garlic, and a Gentleman Jack demi-glace. Entrées $28–46.

DeLand
Emmy's Time Out Tavern (386-734-0756), 2069 Old New York Ave, offers food from her Germanic roots—rouladen, goulash, pork chops, and schnitzels—in a convivial atmosphere that'll have you singing *zige zake zige zake ho ho ho!* Sides include red cabbage, potato dumplings, German potato salad, applesauce, and spaetzle. If you're not into the authentic Old Country food, locals swear the prime rib here is the best in town, and there are seafood and chicken entrées to choose from, too. Four special German dinners served Wed. Enjoy live music in the lounge at 9 PM Friday and Saturday.

Step down the stairs to **MainStreet Grill** (386-740-9535; www.mainstreet grilldeland.com), 100 E New York Ave, just to view the waterfall cascading over the tiled manatee mural. This upscale grill serves mouthwatering steaks and a long list of seafood. Open for lunch and dinner daily, with a popular Sunday brunch.

New Smyrna Beach

Dine along the waterfront at **The Grille at Riverview** (386-428-1865; www.riverviewhotel.com/restaurant), 103 Flagler Ave, in a warm brick-and-wood dining room with massive windows overlooking the boat traffic. Savor delights like macadamia nut and banana-crusted grouper, Riverview seafood jambalaya, or gratineé of seafood ravoli entrée. Entrées $15–39.

Right in front of the airport, **Stella's Skyline Café** (386-426-5777; www

.stellasskyline.com), 2004 N Dixie Freeway, catches your attention with its classy wrapping—that windowed cottage began its life as an officer's club in the 1940s and 1950s. A spinoff of one of my hometown favorites, the Swamp in Gainesville, this restaurant offers an extensive menu that caters to every taste. At lunch, try the herb-encrusted tuna salad, made with ahi tuna, or the succulent lobster roll, done just like the Maine classic. Dinner entrées ($16–28) turn to baked seafood Italiano, lobster and shrimp Augustine, and New York strip.

Ormond Beach

At **Billy's Tap Room** (386-672-1910; www.billys-tap.com), 58 E Granada Blvd, old Ormond Beach still lives in the wooden walls and floors built in 1922, the walls crowded with photos from the past, especially images of the much-revered and much-missed grand Ormond Hotel, for which this was the classy tea room. It has the feel of a British pub, with the same air of refinement, but offers casual fine dining with daily wine or cocktail specials. When you are seated for dinner, you're greeted with a basket of warm sourdough bread. The menu includes twilight dinner specials (3–5:30) and two-for-one drinks; the entrées ($15–26) are top-notch, with offerings like fresh Gulf shrimp with red sauce, chateaubriand for two, and chicken à la orange. Open Mon–Sat for lunch and dinner (no lunch served on Sat).

The original **Stonewood Tavern and Grill** (386-671-1200; www.stonewood grill.com), 100 S Atlantic Ave, started right here along Ormond Beach. Their mainstay is oakwood-grilled chicken and steaks and fresh seafood, but do give the baked Brie a try. Stick

BILLY'S TAP ROOM

Sandra Friend

to your healthful diet with a garden entrée salad ($5–15) like oak grilled steak, vine-ripened tomatoes and fresh mozzarella, or grilled asparagus and Brie. Half portions are available on some menu items. Open nightly for dinner; entrées $20–25.

EATING OUT

Daytona Beach

Okay, I succumbed to **Bubba Gump Shrimp Company** (386-947-8433; www.bubbagump.com), 250 N Atlantic Ave, in the Oceanwalk Shoppes. It's a chain, so my expectations weren't all that high. But I was excited about the ambience—the outside seating abuts the historic Daytona Beach Bandshell (see *Historic Sites*). And I was surprised to discover that my New Orleans Shrimp was downright kickin' with green onions and a spice I just couldn't identify, until the kind waitress gave away the secret. I went away full and happy. It's a busy family hot spot, with entrées $14–19.

The lively tropics greet you at the door at **Caribbean Jacks** (386-253-5557 or 1-877-525-2257; www.caribbeanjacks.com), 721 Ballough Rd, with a gorgeous view of the Indian River Lagoon and reasonable prices; open for lunch and dinner.

Healthy breakfasts and lunches are served at the **Dancing Avocado Kitchen** (386-947-2022; www.avocadokitchen.net), 110 S Beach St, with crazy bread pizzas, sandwiches, wraps, and veggie burgers all $3–10. They have a fresh-squeezed juice bar, too!

Get off your hog and settle into a half-pound burger at **Daytona Diner** (386-258-8488), 2901 N Beach St

(located in the rear of the Daytona Harley-Davidson dealership). Open Mon–Sat for breakfast and lunch.

This little brick building on the corner looks like it's been here since the 1940s, and indeed, the **Gateway Restaurant** (386-252-1262), 219 E International Speedway Blvd, is a gathering place for residents, a slice of Hellas in the thick of a Greek neighborhood just two blocks from the beach, where the banter between old friends is still in the mother tongue. Since they serve breakfast all day, I was tempted by the "almost famous" pecan waffles, but our waitress raved about the gyros—"I take them home for dinner every Thursday"—so I had to try one. It overflowed with tzatziki and a garnish of chopped onions and tomatoes, fresh and delectable. Breakfast $2–6; lunch $4–8. Open 7–2 daily, cash only.

Our friends bragged about the delightful breakfasts at **Molly's Café and Gift Shop** (386-760-3948), 1728 Nova Rd, so we had to stop in. The parking lot was packed at Sunday brunchtime, and this cozy diner was humming with orders for blueberry pancakes, eggs and scrapple, pecan Belgian waffles, and Spanish omelets. Breakfast all day ($2–7), open 6–2.

As you walk into the **Starlite Diner** (386-255-9555), 401 N Atlantic Ave, a jukebox might belt out an Elvis song. Old Americana graces the walls with aged *Time, Life,* and *Saturday Evening Post* magazine covers of the 1950s. You'll want to get there early on Friday for the all-you-can-eat fish fry.

DeLand

A favorite with the college crowd, **Bellybusters** (386-734-1611), 930

Woodland Blvd, dishes up enormous sandwiches at reasonable prices. Ask for your sandwich "all the way," with mayonnaise, slaw, onions, sweet pickles, and their special sauce.

Ahoy mates, stow ye appetite and get ye to **J. C.'s Lobster Pot** (386-734-7459; www.jcslobsterpot.com), 2888 W FL 44, open for lunch and dinner, where platters ($18–24) come with chowder, hushpuppies, and lots and lots of seafood. From the butcher block, there's chicken, ribs, and steaks ($18–21). My usual: the Coquille St. J.C.'s (aka "That Dish Here"), where shrimp, scallops, crabmeat, and lobster are baked up with three cheeses and white wine, yum!

De Leon Springs

🦐 🐾 It's one of Florida's most unusual and fun family dining experiences: Cook your own pancakes made from stone-ground flour on the griddle built into your table. You'll find it at the **Old Spanish Sugar Mill & Griddle House** (386-985-5644), DeLeon Springs State Park (see *Springs*).

Trot up to the breakfast buffet at **Spring Garden Ranch Restaurant** (see *Horse Racing*) while watching standardbred racing at the second largest training facility in the world. The hot roast beef Breeder's Crown served open faced with mashed potatoes and the Shady Daisy Reuben are just two of the winners lined up on the menu. Open daily. Breakfast buffet on weekends and for special events.

New Smyrna Beach

Healthful eats await at **Heavenly Sandwiches and Smoothies** (386-427-7475), 115 Flagler Ave, purveyors of more than 30 types of smoothies ($5–6), from Beachside Blast to Wipeout, and gourmet good-for-you lunch and dinner items ($7–9) like hummus and veggie roll-ups, Tuscan pesto chicken, and hot portobella basil salad. Pizza and soups, too—including my favorites, lobster bisque and corn-and-crab chowder.

🦐 Ask anyone in town where the best seafood is, and they'll point you to **JB's Fish Camp** (386-427-5747; www.jbsfishcamp.com), 859 Pompano Ave. It's off FL A1A en route to Canaveral National Seashore (see *Wild Places*) and right along Mosquito Lagoon; I've seen manatees hanging out at the dock, playing under the flow of water out of hoses. This was a post-hike hangout for me when I lived an hour away. It's no frills, paper plates and beer or margaritas in disposable cups, sit down at a picnic table packed tight with your closest friends (or you will be, by the end of the meal) to savor fresh local fixings like their savory oyster stew (an original recipe) and Bethune seafood gumbo. Blue and stone crab are river fresh, and the steamed platters come with an ear of corn next to fresh oysters, clams, crab, and shrimp. They even serve up rock shrimp, a delicacy in these parts. Ain't nothing more authentic and the place is always packed on weekends—may I suggest a weekday visit for your first time? Entrées are under $20, except for surf and turf, and the sandwiches and baskets are less than $10. Open daily 11:30–9:30.

At **Malony's Steam Kettle Cooking Pub** (386-424-1312), 147 Canal St, it's all about the shellfish, simmered in steam pipe kettles to make a mean handcrafted bisque of shrimp, oyster, and clams, and their own Brunswick stew. Since 1997, they've served authentic soups based on organic broths; no fried foods here. The seafood is fresh, there are always veggies available, and happy hour kicks off back in the biergarten. Soups, sandwiches, $6–8, closed Sun.

🍽 Since 1970, **Pappa's Drive In** (386-427-0633), 1103 N Dixie Freeway along US 1, has offered good old drive-up curb service for everything from their "famous burgers" to Greek salads, spinach pie, gyros, spaghetti, and clam strips. You can sit inside, too, and savor a slice of coconut or chocolate cream pie. Managed by three generations of the same family, it's a don't-miss local icon. Sandwiches, meals, and shakes, $2–8.

Orange City
With its wagon-wheel lamps, wood bench seats, and enormous fireplace, you'd assume **Pier 16's Fish House** (386-775-2664), 1081 N Volusia Ave, was a steakhouse. And indeed, steaks are on the menu. But seafood is their strong suit—this is the home of the best lunch value in Orange City, where you can pick up a heaping plateful of breaded fish or popcorn shrimp, Texas toast or hushpuppies, and coleslaw for under $5.

Ponce Inlet
You'll find a colorful Caribbean nautical playground for adults at the very busy **Inlet Harbor Marina and Restaurant** (386-767-5590; www .inletharbor.com), 133 Inlet Harbor Rd. With folks lifting piña coladas in monkey-shaped coconuts and saluting the steel drum band on stage, it almost feels like a slice of the Bahamas. Fresh local seafood is the cornerstone of the menu, but hot baked bread with Key lime butter comes first, followed by such delights as fresh island sea scallops, Jamaican-

Mon Chicken Breast, juicy prime rib, and peel-and-eat shrimp. It's like dining in the middle of a party; the marina has constant boat traffic. Entrées $9–23.

🍽 ✪ NASCAR fans will race to the booth named after their favorite driver—"Hey, Dad, someone already got Jeff Gordon!"—and marvel at the authentic racing memorabilia on the walls, from car hoods to historic photos that show the original context of this eatery, **Racing's North Turn** (386-322-3258, www.racingsnorth turn.com), 4511 S Atlantic Ave, at the south end of the track where racing began in 1936. The photo library at the entrance recaps this history of this spot, the original Daytona Speedway, which encompassed the beach and the highway. But you don't have to love racing to enjoy the setting, with its oceanfront seating and outdoor bar with live music. It's family-friendly eats with a focus on seafood, including a just-spicy-enough conch chowder, fresh oysters, peel-and-eat shrimp, bacon-wrapped scallops, and a catch of the day. Meat lovers can opt for an ample rib-eye or strip steak, "Vicki Wood" cheesesteak, or build-your-own half-pound burger. Open daily for lunch and dinner; entrées $7–21.

Port Orange
In 1984 Tim and Linda Booth started a small pub-style restaurant, **Booth's Bowery** (386-761-9464; www.booths bowery.com), 3657 S Nova Rd at Herbert St, with only six employees. Two decades later they have 120 employees and a hoppin' family place. The food is what keeps everyone coming back. Keeping with fresh ingredients and making everything from scratch, they offer just about anything you can

think of—shrimp Parmesan, broiled or blackened grouper, "hunger-buster" sandwiches—but they are famous for their Buffalo wings. The kids will enjoy the game room while waiting.

BAKERIES, COFFEE SHOPS, CHOCOLATES, AND ICE CREAM

Daytona Beach

When you're done with the chocolate tour at **Angell & Phelps** (see *Chocolate Tour*), you'll spend a lot of time in the chocolate shop debating exactly what to bring home. There is a featured candy of the week, and the delicious aromas and exotic flavors are just heavenly for chocoholics like us. As I sit here nibbling on coconut-covered dark chocolate truffles, I can tell you that whatever you pick—be it lemon or maple crème dark chocolates, chocolate ginger, peppermint or pecan bark, or a molded chocolate leaf that looks like a work of art—it's bound to be good. Grab lunch and dinner next door with live jazz Thu–Sat at the Angell & Phelps Café (see *Dining Out*).

Hidden in the commercial district just north of downtown, **Flamingo Homemade Ice Cream** (386-255-8090), 559 N Beach St, has been a local favorite since 1946. They tout "the best shakes in town" and offer a full range of creamy delights, from coconut to rum raisin.

My husband insisted we go to **Krispy Kreme** (386-253-0499; www.krispy kreme.com), 980 International Speedway Blvd, where "hot fresh doughnuts" are indicated by a neon sign in the front window of this little white brick building, and when it's lit, they're hot. It's one of the oldest Krispy Kreme stores in Florida, so

stop by for a coffee and a doughnut as you're passing through. Most importantly, everyone knows where it is, and directions around here are given in distances from the Krispy Kreme.

Zeno's Boardwalk Sweet Shop (386-253-4563; www.zenoscandy .com), 38 S Atlantic Ave, has a fabulous backstory behind that giant taffy puller in the window. This sweet shop came about thanks to a Greek immigrant who left Thessoliniki and made his way to Daytona Beach. He opened up this confectionary in 1948 along the entrance to the Main Street Pier and passed it on to his nephew, Zeno, who took over at age 21 and has since passed it on to his son. Their chocolates come from homemade recipes, handed down through the family; they make their own fudge and delectable candy creations, including the tasty caterpillar—several marshmallows poked on a skewer and swirled in caramel—and pecan balls. They also

ZENO'S BOARDWALK SWEET SHOP HAS BEEN IN BUSINESS SINCE 1948.

Sandra Friend

make their own ice cream, and are now wholesaling it to others—including Angell & Phelps. Flavors tempt just by name, with Cake Batter, Caramel Caribou, Mud Pie, and Death By Chocolate in the freezer when we visited. Trust me, you cannot leave this shop without succumbing to your sweet tooth.

Daytona Shores

✏ I couldn't resist a stop at **Cow Licks** (386-761-1316), 2624 S Atlantic Ave, where those black and white Holsteins pop out against an aqua sign as you drive by. They have 26 regular flavors plus five specialty items, with your choice of toppings and syrups on splits and sundaes ($3–6). A limited snack menu includes burgers, dogs, and chips, and there's a video arcade and pinball machines to round out the experience.

New Smyrna Beach

Along US 1, the **Dairy Queen** (386-428-8066), 729 North Dixie Hwy, is an authentic oldie, a tiny walk-up window with original 1950s sign. Its parking lot is greatly expanded to accommodate frequent classic car shows and the crowds of weekend ice cream lovers who enjoy their treats on the picnic tables scattered beneath the palm trees.

Sip a latte on the deck at the **Flagler Avenue Coffeehouse** (386-426-0098), 411 Flagler Ave, and savor the sound of the surf. Featuring coffee favorites, smoothies, hot dogs, and more, $2 and up.

The Little Drug Co (386-428-9041; www.littledrug.com), 412 Canal St, has one of Florida's few remaining vintage soda fountains. The original store opened in 1922 and relocated a block down the street to this spot in 1965. The soda fountain and counter service is just like I remember from childhood excursions with Mom to a similar five-and-dime, with towering thick milkshakes and great BLTs. Breakfasts include standards like pancakes, eggs, and omelets; lunch brings on comfort sandwiches and platters. Open Mon–Fri 8–6, Sat 8–2.

FARMER'S MARKETS AND FRUIT STANDS Since 1922, **Davidson Brothers** (386-252-7462 or 1-877-378-4848; www.indianrivercitrusgifts .com), 248 S Beach St, has been a downtown purveyor of fine tree-ripened Indian River citrus. Grab a bag or two while you're here. You can sample them before you buy, or stock up on citrus sweets and jams and jellies.

Stock your cupboards December through July with fresh local produce picked at the **West Volusia Farmers Market** (386-734-9514 or 386-734-1613; www.volusiacountyfair.com), Volusia County Fairgrounds, FL 44, where you will also find a large variety of garage sale items.

✳ Selective Shopping

Cassadaga

Cassadaga Spiritualist Camp Bookstore and Information Center (386-228-2880; www.cassadaga .org), 1112 Stevens St, in the Andrew Jackson Davis Building. Not only will you find a large collection of books from spiritualism to metaphysics, and gifts from crystals to meditation tapes, but this building is also your first stop for all the activities in town (see *Special Events*). Open daily till 5, later on Mediums Nights.

Purple Rose (386-228-3315; www
.cassadaga-purplerose.com), 1079
Stevens St. In addition to featuring a
wide selection of minerals at reasonable prices, the warm and relaxing
Purple Rose offers down-to-earth
items such as dream catchers, bub-
bling fountains, stone jewelry, and
New Age books. Several psychics
offer readings of the past, present,
and future for you to get in touch
with your inner self, or you can ask
for a demonstration of the aura-
cleansing crystal bowls.

Daytona Beach

In business here since 1925, **Beach
Photo** (386-252-0577 or 1-800-874-
2115; www.beachphoto.com), 604
Main St, is one of those rarely found
photo shops still carrying film and pro
equipment, including lighting and
photography books, as well as cameras. They offer one-hour film and
digital processing, and video rental
equipment.

Historic Daytona prints and evocative
Florida scenes are a major part of the
mix at **Bennett's Framing Gallery**
(386-255-1233), 242 S Beach St,
where they can frame your finds right
on the spot.

**Daytona Flea and Farmers Mar-
ket** (386-253-3330; www.daytonaflea
market.com), 2987 Bellevue Ave, has
new and used bargains galore and
fresh produce.

With more than 150,000 books in
stock, **Mandala Books** (386-255-
6728 or 1-888-318-9696), 127 W
International Speedway Blvd, will
keep you busy browsing their stacks
for hours. Segmented with hand-lettered signs, the collection rambles
through many rooms of floor-to-ceiling shelves, including one devoted to

children's books. Bibliophiles amble
in and out past stacks of posters and
art prints, through the faintest hint of
incense, to seek out their favorite section. Open daily.

Four stories of shopping, dining, and
entertainment awaits at **Ocean Walk
Village** (www.oceanwalkvillage.com),
250 N Atlantic Ave, scrunched up
against the historic bandshell along
the Atlantic Ocean. There's a 10-
screen movie theatre, a Maui Nix surf
shop, and the Boardwalk Beach
Bazaar, with all sorts of creative take-
home souvenirs. The complex connects to what's left of the famed
Daytona Beach boardwalk and the
Main Street Pier via a series of oceanfront parks.

Spend the afternoon in the quaint
downtown area at boutiques, antiques
and collectibles shops, and intimate
restaurants at the **Riverfront Marketplace** (386-671-3272; www.river
frontmarketplace.com), 262 S–190 N
Beach St. A few highlights:

Balinese frog carvings almost as tall as
I am flanked the entrance to
Carousel Antiques (386-255-1132),
110 N Beach St, the entrance to a former Cartier Jewelers, now home to a
vast array of costume jewelry and fine
art; on the second floor, fabulous vintage furnishings, primitives, and
paintings for that retro look.

**Dancing Dragon Fly's Whimsical
Gift Gallery** (386-239-0147; www
.dancingdragonflys.com), 226-A S
Beach St, is full of fun, inexpensive
gifts like candles and bath beads,
magnets and cards, fairies and stuffed
animals. They have a nice selection of
hand-crocheted clothes for your wee
ones as well.

You'll find an extravagance of antiques at **Nicole's Beach Street Mall** (386-252-3033), 140 N Beach St, a former department store filled with dealer booths with something for everyone. On a quick sweep through, I saw movie posters and trolls, vintage jewelry and glassware, a collection of Toby jugs, and an original Victorian dresser.

Park Mara Galleries (386-258-3414), 110 S Beach St, drew me in with fantastical art glass—fluid trout, octopi in millefiori, dangling funky lights, and bright giclée sea scenes by Robert Thomas. There's a coffee shop in the gallery, too, with gourmet Florida foods on the shelves, including spices, pastas, bread mixes, and Florida wines.

DeLand

You could spend all day shopping throughout the historic downtown area. From Woodland Blvd to just a few steps down a side street, you'll find a variety of antiquities, bric-a-brac, galleries, eateries, and boutiques. More than 50 dealer displays cover three floors at the **Rivertown Antique Mall** (386-738-5111) 114 S Woodland Blvd, with a half dozen antique shops within a block or two. Concerned with the demolition of architecturally significant properties, Mark Shuttleworth (also mayor of Lake Helen) started to salvage the building materials from these houses and opened **Florida Victorian Architectural Antiques** (386-734-9300; www.floridavictorian.com), 112 W Georgia Ave. If you've been remodeling your vintage home and you just can't seem to find the right trim molding or hardwood flooring—or you just want a unique doorknob or stained-glass window—you'll most likely find it here. Leave the kids at

home, as a lot of materials are lying around. Open Mon–Sat 9–5 or by appointment.

Several fine galleries are almost within the same block on Woodland Blvd. You can stop by and see Mike at **Gold Leaf Gallery and Framing** (386-943-4001; www.goldleafgalleryand framing.com), 110 N, for fine art limited-edition prints and custom framing. Ceramic works are showcased at **Clay Pigeons** (386-734-1100), 120 S Woodland Blvd #C, a hands-on craft shop with pottery painting studio.

Bibliophiles will enjoy **The Muse Book Shop** (386-734-0278; www .themusebookshop.com), 112 S Woodland Blvd, an independent bookseller specializing in antiquarian books and topographical maps.

I stepped inside the **Quilt Shop of DeLand, Inc**. (386-734-8782; www .quiltshopofdeland.com), 116 E Rich Ave, and looked at all the walls of beautiful fabric, and immediately wanted to start a quilt, but didn't know how. And that was okay, because they'll teach you everything you need to know so you can make your own family heirloom. From fabric selection to rotary cutting and finishing, the talented women of this quilt shop will guide you every stitch of the way.

Stop by **Danny's Shoe Service** (386-734-1645), 206 N Woodland Blvd, just to view the vintage cobbler tools. Danny loves to chat and can tell you just about anything about his hometown.

Wild and wonderful, **Primitive Expressions** (386-740-0022; www .primitiveexpressions.com), 118 N Woodland Blvd, has amazing exotic home decor from all over the globe—

African masks, imported furniture, textiles, you name it.

Can't wait to get those vacation pics developed? Shutterbugs will want to stop into the **Camera Store & Studio** (386-736-1307; www.camera storeandstudio.net), 122 E Rich Ave, for one-hour developing—and you can frame it here, too!

Lake Helen

Delight in artistic creations of colorful daylilies through hybridization at **Art Gallery Gardens** (386-228-3010; www.artgallerygardens.com), 203 Oakapple Trl, and yes, these perfect hybrids are real, and ready to be planted in your garden.

Holly Hill

It's not a store—it's a city block. **Magnolia House Antique Village** (386-252-8086), 1078 Ridgewood Ave, is an extensive complex of vintage homes showcasing 20 dealers. Colorful

Anamese garden pots overflow the front courtyard, stacked in artful displays. Each home provides a glimpse into more treasures—restoration hardware pieces, kitchen items, glassware, vintage pottery, figurines, ceramic critters, Highwayman paintings, you name it. Out back is **Schley's Bonsai and Supplies**, with carefully sculpted cedars, baldcypress, and Mikawa pine; they sell orchids and carnivorous pitcher plants, too. Way back tucked under the oaks is the **III Oaks Nursery**, with more garden accoutrements, water features, potted palms, and flowering plants.

If you're looking for vintage furnishings, head to **Our Old Stuff** (386-238-7207), 1005 Ridgewood Ave, where bamboo and wicker sit side by side with classic European antique dressers and sofas. Closed Mon.

New Smyrna Beach

There are two distinct shopping districts in this historic city—the shops of Canal Street, between US 1 and the Halifax River, and the shops of Flagler Ave, on the barrier island across the river at the beach. A paved bike path connects the two along Flagler, but most visitors park at one or the other while doing their browsing. Saturdays are lively, so come early!

New Smyrna Beach—Canal Street Shops

The new age shop **A Lotta Scents** (386-423-9190; www.alottascents .com), 511 Canal St, has a broad variety of aromatherapy oils and essences, as well as books and sacred symbols, fairies, and mermaids.

Gallery 925 (386-478-0306), 508 Canal St, showcases a variety of local and nationally known artists in fine

A FEW OF THE WARES AVAILABLE AT MAGNOLIA HOUSE ANTIQUE VILLAGE

Sandra Friend

jewelry and contemporary crafts like bronze art chairs and sea-life tables.

Costume jewelry, flatware, and glassware are everywhere at **Jeff's Antiques on Canal** (386-428-4958), 405 Canal Street, in an unmistakable grand old turn-of-the-century residence now full of vintage silver, china, furnishings, and rugs.

One step into **Mosquito Mud Pottery** (386-409-7240; www.mosquito mudpottery.com), 141 Canal St, and I was destined to walk away with a few choice pieces of fine art pottery—it's art with a natural twist, clay formed into fun shapes echoing objects found in nature, on forest floors and in the depths of the sea. There are also wood and glass sculptures by regional artists, and fiber arts.

Iron soldiers, glassware, and art caught my attention at **The Palms** (386-409-5232), 328 Canal St, where collectibles and "shabby chic" crowd the rooms.

At **The Pink Palm Tree** (386-426-1800), 149 Canal St. Original oils by Elizabeth Barr reflect impressionist interpretations of Florida, and are set upon the antique furnishings and hung on the walls. The store primary features vintage furniture, but the paintings are truly haunting.

Southern and sea meet snow at **The Shops at 421** (386-426-2002), 421 Canal St, where a palm tree stands in for a Christmas tree, delightfully accented with mini beach pails amid this home decor store with a by-the-beach flair.

New Smyrna Beach—Flagler Avenue Shops

It's color in motion at **Garden Arts** (386-427-8221), 405B-1 Flagler Ave, with the sea breeze sending wind-

socks flapping, pinwheels whirling, hanging baskets swaying, and chimes tinkling in this haven for outdoor art.

Jonah's Cat's Art Gallery (386-428-2150), 220 Flagler Ave, is a haven for artists like John Hostetter, who enjoy creating bright, splashy, playful works of art starring cats, fish, and other critters in scenes evocative of children's picture books.

It was quite the surprise to discover **New Smyrna Rock and Gem** (386-424-0041), 394 Flagler Ave, all a-sparkle and within whistling distance of the beach. Filled with lovely lapidary, uncut stones, and specimen-quality minerals, it's a gem of a find.

Since 1969, **Nichols Surf Shop** (386-427-5050, www.nicholssurfshop.com), 411 Flagler Ave, has been serving serious surfers looking for top-notch surfboards and surf togs. No touristy stuff here—it's a 1910-vintage shed with sleek-looking boards outside, from Hobie and Dreamtime to collectible antiques. Best of all, they rent it all: surfboards, bodyboards, kayaks, wetsuits, bicycles, you name it, plus one-on-one surf lessons available for $75.

See it made by hand at **Palms Up Pottery** (1-800-405-3726, www.palm suppottery.com), 413 Flagler Ave, a working clay studio since 1987 and home of master potter Richard Collison. His "funpots" feature silly sea creatures, and his "Frog Hollow" series has frogs and toads I love. The fruits of artistic labors extend to blown and stained glass, art glass, and gaily-painted boxes, but the main focus is pottery, including eight six-week classes offered each year.

Tucked into the **Shops of the Cloisters**, a little side alley at 307 Flagler

Ave, are **Janie's Indian River Bazaar** (386-426-2556; www.janieson line.com), Suite 102, with tropical island dresses, slinky wraps, fun purses, blouses, and shoes; and **Gyftz** (387-409-9336; www.gyftz.com), Suite 103, with tempting gourmet foods mingled amid home decor items.

Ta Da Gallery and Gift Shop (386-428-1770), 113 Flagler Ave, is just plain fun. There's fancy nautical art snug up against shell-encrusted mirrors, clay crosses, and pottery that looks like fish (or vice versa).

In their distinctly lilac cottage, the **Wicker Basket Boutique** (386-427-3732; www.wickerbasketboutique .com), 401 Flagler Ave, has been part of the beach scene since 1969, offering elegant but casual wraps and dresses, sandals, and gifts.

Ormond Beach

The **Fountain Square Shopping Village** (386-677-3845), 1445 E Granada Blvd, provides a collection of petite upscale boutiques clustered around a garden courtyard. Among them are **Bon! Gourmet**, with wines and cheeses, aromatic coffees, and a tea bar; **The Inkwell Home**, featuring Vera Bradley purses; and **Adornment**, with designer dresses and shoes.

The Pelican's Pouch (386-441-6765), 1546 Ocean Shore Blvd, is a cute and kitschy seaside shop that isn't part of a chain, offering books and T-shirts, nautically themed gifts, and kites for flying on the breezy beach across the street.

At **Wall-y-World Gallery** (386-673-2916), 173 S Yonge St, I was smitten with a slightly surrealistic view of Old Ormond in *Walk with Palms,* by Doug Cavanaugh, which draws you

into a world of giant oaks and fern-draped jungly cypress. The oil on masonsite *Moon Over Bulow,* by Don Ambrose, with its soft silhouette of palms, had an equal pull. The art is original, by eight regional artists, and depicts the unique flavor of the region.

Ponce Inlet

The **Lighthouse Gift Shop** (see *Lighthouse*) has interesting educational toys and puzzles along with T-shirts and items commemorating the historic Ponce Inlet lighthouse.

At Inlet Harbor Marina (see *Eating Out*), the **Pelican Landing** gift shop and ship's store is where kids can bring their menu, colored nicely, to trade for something from the treasure chest. Besides the usual souvenirs, you'll find regional books, T-shirts, dolls, tackle, and boat repair items.

✸ Entertainment

Take in a show at the **Sands Theater Center** at the Cultural Arts Center (box office 386-738-7456; www.sands theatercenter.com), 600 N Woodland Blvd, DeLand. This venue offers professionally directed theatrical productions for all ages and tastes. Enjoy classic or contemporary on either the Main Stage or the more intimate Stage II. **Children's Storybook Theater** keeps the kids entertained with classics and interactive performances. DeLand's own community orchestra—the **DeLand Little Symphony**—is also on-site.

✐ **Shoestring Theater** (386-228-3777), 380 S Goodwin St, Lake Helen. Check out the local talent in a 150-seat theater housed in an old schoolhouse. Geared toward families, with productions Sept–May.

✳ Special Events

Year-round, last Thursday of the month: The downtown DeLand galleries open their doors 6–9 with great art, wine, and snacks during the **Gallery Stroll**.

Year-round, second Friday of the month: **Candlelight Healing Service**, Colby Memorial Temple, Cassadaga, is at 7:30 PM (see *Psychic Readings*).

January: For everything you always wanted to know about the Florida sea cow, the **Blue Spring Manatee Festival** (386-804-6171; www.themanatee festival.com), Valentine Park, French Avenue, Orange City, is the place to go. A complimentary bus takes you to the park so you can view manatees in their natural habitat. Lots of environmental exhibits, food, and music. Fee.

More than 200 dealers ride in to the **Annual Railroad Show** (407-656-5056), Volusia County Fairgrounds, to display and sell model trains and collectibles.

February: **Speedweeks** (386-253-7223; www.daytonainternationalspeed way.com) features qualifying events culminating in the **Daytona 500**. Harleys and Hondas cruise into **Bike Week** (1-800-854-1234; www.official bikeweek.com), the world's largest motorcycle event. Racing at Daytona Speedway, concerts, exhibits, and street festivals dominate the scene for nearly two weeks.

🐾 DeLand has great tail-wagging fun at **the Canine Cabaret Parade and Mardi Gras** on Main St (386-734-4243), Woodland Blvd. Dogs and owners dress up and march down the center of town in the largest parade of the year. Dog-gone activities galore,

and awards for both dogs and their human companions.

Buckler Craft Show (407-860-0092; www.volusiacountyfair.com), Volusia County Fairgrounds. Two hundred award-winning Volusia County craftspeople come here to exhibit and sell.

Speed Week Dirt Racing, Volusia Speedway Park (386-985-4402; www .volusiaspeedwaypark.com), 1500 E FL 40, De Leon Springs (5 miles east of Barberville).

The Pioneer Settlement for the Creative Arts (see *Museums*) offers mini workshops in many of the folk art fields at **Pass It On Folk Art Days** (386-749-2959). You'll learn all about such long-ago skills as basket weaving and blacksmithing at this two-day event.

March: **Semiannual Birthplace of Speed Celebration** (386-677-3454; www.ormondchamber.com). The first sanctioned time trials of auto racing actually took place on Ormond Beach. This event celebrates that memorable event, featuring reenactments of the historic beach race. Also in Nov.

Hear from Florida authors from all over the state as they read and discuss their writings at the **Annual Florida Author's Book Fair** (386-228-0174), Hopkins Hall, Lake Helen. The free event also has a silent auction and a café.

For more than 25 years the annual **Motorcycle Swapmeet & Special Bike Show** (301-336-2100; www .volusiacountyfair.com), Volusia County Fairgrounds, has put on a blast of a show full of stunts, thrills, and bikes, bikes, bikes, all for only $8.

Families from all over the United States come to **Daytona Beach Spring Family Beach Break**

(1-800-854-1234) for sun and fun, and an escape with the kids.

Hot rods ride in with chrome and style at the **Spring Break Car Show and Swap Meet** (386-255-7355).

July: One of the few races that run at night, the **NASCAR Coke Zero 400** (386-253-7223; www.daytonainter nationalspeedway.com) is one of the summer's best, with concerts, festivals, and fireworks surrounding the annual event.

October: An international event, with bikers riding coming down from Canada and over from Europe, **Biketoberfest** (1-800-854-1234; www .biketoberfest.org) gives riders one last time to ride before putting the bike up for the winter. This family event takes place throughout Daytona with street festivals, charity events, and wholesome fun.

Volusia County Fair, Volusia County Fairgrounds, FL 44, DeLand. This large county fair shows breeding and market livestock: goats, sheep, swine, poultry, rabbits, and cattle. Entertainment includes nationally recognized talent, live bands, a petting zoo, puppet shows, a pie-eating contest, and

the Little Miss, Mr., and Senior Fair Queen contests. Admission $7 adults, $3 children 6–12. All-you-can-ride bracelets for midway amusements can be purchased for $12–15 with special sponsor coupons.

One of the largest events around, the annual juried **DeLand Fall Festival of the Arts** attracts more than 200 talented artisans, who exhibit their talents all along Woodland Blvd.

November: **Semiannual Birthplace of Speed Celebration** (see *March*).

Annual Fall Country Jamboree (386-749-2959) celebrates a weekend of Florida pioneer life at the Pioneer Settlement for the Creative Arts (see *Museums*). Continuous folk music, lively storytellers, and creative activities like indigo dyeing and cane grinding are just some of the activities. Juried arts show, crafts, and antique autos. Call for admission prices.

December: The whole community of DeLand comes out for one of the largest, and longest (2½ hours), **holiday parades**—half the town is in it, the other half watches. Woodland Blvd.

THE SPACE COAST:
BREVARD COUNTY

While the Space Coast is best known for the Kennedy Space Center, NASA, and decades of rocket and space shuttle launches, the history of the region dates back more than 8,000 years, with proof uncovered of an ancient people who buried their own in a peat bog south of Titusville. When Ponce de León came to Florida, the Ais Indians were the dominant culture along this part of the coastline, evidenced both by the middens they left and an encounter between the explorer and the natives sometime between 1513 and 1565 at a small village just south of **Cape Canaveral**. Unlike the peaceable Timucua to their north, the Ais were thought to be warriors, skilled at surviving off the bounty of the Indian River Lagoon, and cannibalistic to boot. In October 1565, the founder of St. Augustine, Pedro Menéndez de Avilés, marched his troops south after they massacred the French colony in Florida along the St. Johns River and brought them to the Indian River along what is now commemorated as the Spanish Military Trail, a portion of which still exists in Titusville. Encountering numerous Ais villages and the chief of the Ais, Menéndez left behind a force of men to colonize the area; no doubt understanding the peril they were in, they mutinied and departed soon after he left. The region remained under Spanish rule for nearly 200 years, but by the time any serious European settlement occurred in the area, the Ais had vanished—perhaps of European-introduced diseases, perhaps of inter-tribal warfare. Cape Canaveral, named "cape of canes" because sailors thought they saw native sugar cane growing along the shore, became a significant landmark for the dangerous ocean currents in the area; numerous shipwrecks are found from this point south.

One of the earliest homesteads in the region was that of Captain Douglas D. Dummitt, who established a grove and home on Merritt Island at what is now the Hammock Trails. By 1828, Dummitt was shipping citrus to northern markets from his groves along the Indian River, kicking off the long history of Indian River Citrus, to this day a mark of the finest fruits. The area's temperatures, moderated by the Indian River, proved perfect for citrus-growing, which spread throughout the region. In 1855, Brevard County was officially established—long and thin, along the length of the Indian River Lagoon. Settlement was sporadic,

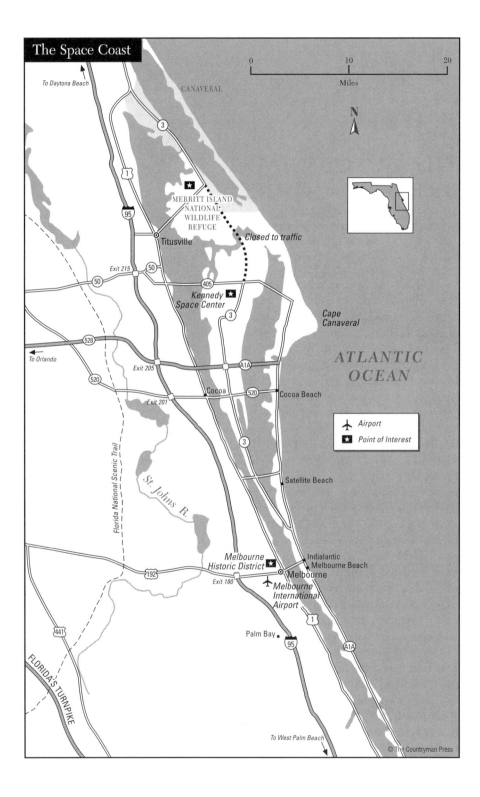

as all of the small communities and plantations—sugar cane and pineapple joining the citrus growers—relied on the waterways for transportation. Not until after the Civil War did regular steamboat service connect North Florida cities with Titusville and Melbourne. When Henry Flagler's Florida East Coast Railway came through in the 1890s, the towns of **Titusville, Cocoa, Rockledge, Eau Gallie,** and **Melbourne**—all to the west of the Indian River Lagoon—began to flourish. It wasn't until the land boom of the 1920s that the population expanded to the barrier islands. In 1949, Brevard County launched into the space program at Cape Canaveral, one of the world's few quadruple-mode ports—sea, land, air, and space.

GUIDANCE Walk right in to the **Space Coast Office of Tourism** (1-877-572-3224 or 321-433-4470; www.space-coast.com), 430 Brevard Ave, Suite 150, Cocoa Village, 32922, Mon–Fri 8–5. Their main entrance is on Delannoy Boulevard, but the cool mural of the history of the region is on the Brevard Avenue side.

Explore the possibilities in **Cocoa Beach** (321-459-2200 or 1-877-321-VISIT; www.visitcocoabeach.com), 400 Fortenberry Rd, Merritt Island, FL 32952, or **Melbourne and Palm Bay** (321-724-5400; www.melpb-chamber.org), 1005 E Strawbridge Ave, Melbourne 32901. In **Titusville** (321-267-3036; www.titusville .org or www.spacecityFLusa.com), 2000 S Washington Ave 32780, the chamber of commerce is downtown and offers information during business hours.

GETTING THERE *By air:* Only an hour from **Orlando International Airport** via FL 528 ("The Bee Line" or "The Beachline," depending who you talk to), Melbourne is also served by **Melbourne International Airport** (321-723-6227; www.mlbair.com).

By bus: **Greyhound** rumbles down US 1 with stops in Titusville (321-267-8760), Cocoa Beach (321-636-6531), and Melbourne (321-723-4323), as well as a terminal conveniently located at the Melbourne International Airport.

By car: From I-95, head east on **FL 520** or **FL 528**.

GETTING AROUND *By bus and beach trolley:* **Space Coast Area Transit** (SCAT; 321-633-1878; www.ridescat.com). Buses run Mon–Fri 6 AM–6:45 PM from Mims to Micco. Weekend service is available in some areas. The beach trolley runs Mon–Sat 7 AM–9 PM, Sun 8–5, from Port Canaveral to 13th Street in Cocoa Beach. $1 full fare, 50¢ half fare (seniors, handicapped, and students). The **I-4–FL 520 Connector** takes you from the beach (FL A1A) along FL 520 over to Cocoa Village. There's no extra charge for transfers or for bikes and surfboards. Unlimited monthly passes $28.

By taxi: Melbourne (321-676-3100); Titusville (321-267-7061); Cocoa Beach (321-720-4342).

PUBLIC RESTROOMS All major beachfront parks (and many along the Indian River Lagoon) have public restrooms, but there are no restrooms at beach crossovers. You'll also find public restrooms in Cocoa Village at Taylor Park (8–6:30) and adjacent to the municipal parking lot.

LIFEGUARD STATIONS Stations are staffed at public parks Memorial Day–Labor Day only. Jetty Park (see *Parks*) has a lifeguard on watch year-round.

LAUNCH REPORTS NASA launches are listed on a recorded phone message (321-867-4636). For more information, go to www.kennedyspacecenter.com or www.ksc.nasa.gov.

SURF REPORTS Call ahead to check surf conditions and tides. For a live voice, call Cocoa Beach Surf Company (321-783-1530) or any of these recorded surf lines:

Cocoa Beach: **Natural Art Surf Report** (321-784-2400); **Ron Jon Surf Report** (321-799-8888, ext 3, then press 7).

Indialantic: **Groove Tube Surf's Up Line** (321-723-3879); **Spectrum Surf Shop** (321-725-5905).

MEDICAL EMERGENCIES **Cape Canaveral Hospital** (321-799-7111); **Health First, Inc.** (321-868-8313), Cocoa Beach; Jetty Park (321-434-7000) and **Wuesthoff Medical Center** (321-752-1200), Melbourne; **Health First, Inc., Palm Bay Community Hospital** (321-434-8000), Palm Bay; **Parrish Medical Center** (321-268-6111), Titusville.

✴ To See

ARCHEOLOGICAL SITES Several middens (ancient Indian garbage dumps) are located in the vicinity of Rockledge. **Persimmons Mound** is on the east bank of a former channel of the St. Johns River about 10 miles from Rockledge. Standing a little over 4 feet, the 165-by-100-foot mound is said to date back to 4000 B.C.

In 1982, a backhoe operator found human remains in a peat bog pond in Titusville and contacted the authorities. After the county medical examiner proclaimed them "very old," the developers contacted Florida State University and the archeological marvel that is **Windover** opened a new window into Florida history. Preserved in peat and tannic water, the unearthed human remains are 7,000 to 8,000 years old, and include an intact 3-year-old buried holding her toys—a wooden pestle-like object and a turtle carapace. Over a six-month dig, 91 skulls were found to contain intact brain tissue. Some bodies had the remains of meals in their stomachs. After the survey of the Windover Bog People was complete, the pond was returned to its original state, still holding the remains of hundreds of this region's earliest inhabitants. There is no formal interpretation of the site, which is in a subdivision.

ART GALLERIES

Cocoa

More than 60 award-winning Florida artists strut their stuff at **Art Vue Galerie** (321-637-2787; www.artvuegallery.com) in over 6,000 feet of space. This is one monster gallery, the largest in the county, with life-sized sculptures of palm trees, tiny masterpieces in art glass, pop-art acrylics, colorful pottery, and wearable art.

It's the pulp fiction novel cover, Florida-themed, that sets off the tone of the **Bad Birds Gallery** (302-218-6204; www.badbirdsgallery.com), 518 Delannoy Ave, a fun gallery full of nautical- and coastal-inspired pop art, with drunken flamingos a common theme (see *Dining Out*). John Kalinowski, the working artist in residence, appreciates your appreciation, but do not disturb the artist at work. Open 12–6, Tue–Sun.

✂ Carolyn Seiler's art is whimsical and fun, and that's why you need to peek into **Boatyard Studios** (321-637-0444), 118 Harrison St, where you can see her unique interpretations of palms in pastels, folk art paintings, funky clay sculptures, and cards. On Saturday and Wednesday, Carolyn teaches drop-in art classes for children ($10), no preregistration needed, just stop by and see what today's project will be!

Melbourne

Creative art exhibits and premier productions are found at the **Henegar Center for the Arts** (321-723-8698; www.henegar.org), 625 E New Haven Ave. Located in the heart of Historic Downtown Melbourne, it is also listed on the National Register of Historic Places.

Titusville

The **Downtown Gallery** (321-268-0122), 335 S Washington Ave, features local artists.

DINOSAURS At **The Dinosaur Store** (407-783-7300; www.dinosaurstore.com), 299 W Cocoa Beach Causeway (FL 520), I couldn't decide whether this was a store or a museum! What you'll find here is a fabulous collection of rare museum-quality fossils and minerals, amber, meteorites, dinosaur eggs, nests, and skeletons (many from right here in Florida). Several items are often on loan to museums. Knowledgeable owners Steve and Donna are real dino hunters and would be happy to discuss their various paleontological expeditions. From serious to novice collectors, everyone has the opportunity to take home a historical treasure, priced from a few dollars to several thousand. Closed Sun.

HISTORIC SITES

Cape Canaveral

The 1848 **Cape Canaveral Lighthouse** stands 160 feet tall and has been automated since 1967. The US Air Force is the current keeper and on rare occasions will open it for special groups like the Florida Lighthouse Association (www .floridalighthouses.org). It can be viewed from Canaveral Harbor Road or looking southward from the beach at Cocoa Beach.

Cocoa

The entire **Cocoa Village Historic District** is a step back to the turn of the last century, with homes and shops from the late 1800s through 1920s. **Porcher House** (321-639-3500), 434 Delannoy Ave in the heart of the district, was built by E. P. Porcher, a pioneer citrus grower and founder of Deerfield Citrus Groves. The beautifully restored, elegant 1916 coquina and wood mansion is an excellent example of Classical Revival adapted for the Florida environment. The semicircular portico with four fluted Ionic columns is absolutely breathtaking. Just a block away, the **Florida Historical Society** (321-690-1971; www.florida -historical-soc.org), 435 Brevard Ave, calls the WPA-constructed Art Deco **1939 Post Office** its home. They have the most comprehensive Florida history bookstore in the state (see *Selective Shopping*), and extensive archives available for scholarly research. Their library is open Tue–Sat 10–4:30.

Step back in time to 1885 at **Travis Hardware**. The oldest hardware business from Jacksonville to Key West, this shop has been operated by the Travis family since 1897. As a kid, I remember going to the hardware store with my dad. This place retains much of the same charm with its bins of nails and nuts, now placed next to modern electrical tools.

Cocoa Beach

Originally built in 1962, the **Cocoa Beach Pier** stretches out 800 feet over the Atlantic Ocean; cars used to drive along its boardwalk planks and park at the end. Now a gathering spot of restaurants and shops, the pier is the social hub of the college crowd during spring break.

Grant

Arriving in pieces by riverboat from Jacksonville in 1916, the home of Clara Christensen Bensen is now the **Grant Historical House** (321-723-8543), 5795 US 1, at Fisherman's Landing Park.

Melbourne

Founded in 1880, Melbourne's downtown developed along Front Street on the Indian River, as the only means of commerce at the time was by ship. Henry Flagler's Florida East Coast Railroad steamed into town in 1893. After a 1919 fire that destroyed the frame buildings, the entire downtown districted shifted west to the train depot, with businesses rebuilt in brick. Today's **Historic Downtown Melbourne** (www.downtownmelbourne.com) is the result of a concerted community effort started in 1980 to restore and revitalize the downtown district.

The 1905 **Nannie Lee House**, 1218 E New Haven Ave, was often the center for social events and still is, as the fine-dining restaurant called Strawberry Mansion (see *Dining Out*).

Titusville

Old Haulover Canal, on the north side of Merritt Island, is so named because Indians and traders actually had to portage (or haul) their canoes over a narrow strip of land at the current location of the 725-foot canal, dug in 1843. It's a great spot for kayaking and manatee viewing.

An imposing three-story Queen Anne Victorian, the 1891 **Pritchard House**, at the corner of Pine and Washington, is under renovation to open it for community use. The Pritchard family moved to Titusville in 1886. Captain James Pritchard, a Confederate veteran, organized the first bank in Titusville, the Indi-

Honoring the men and women who have visited outer space and the programs that supported them, the City of Titusville's **Space View Park** (www.titusville.com) 219 Indian River Ave, is in downtown Titusville at CR 402 and US 1. Stretching from US 1 to the Indian River Lagoon across a block and a half, the park offers an insightful walk through the history of the space program. Closest to US 1 is the Apollo monument, with a splashing pool and fountain and a sculpture of the moon with detailed topography. Monuments flank both sides of a small inlet. Cross Indian River Avenue to walk down to the Gemini monument, adjoining an apartment building; tiles inlaid into the sidewalk list the missions of this program. On the other side of

the inlet, walk through the history of space travel, from Chinese rockets in 300 B.C. to Space Station Freedom. At the *Mercury 7* monument, which looks like a massive modified Egyptian ankh, you'll find handprints and signatures captured in bronze from astronauts who were my childhood heroes—Gus Grissom, John Glenn, Scott Carpenter, Wally Schirra, Deke Slayton, Gordon Cooper, and Alan Shepard. Step to the right and you can see the Vehicle Assembly Building and space shuttle launch pads at the Kennedy Space Center complex across the lagoon in Complex 39, established in 1965. The boardwalk and sidewalk along the lagoon is a popular launch-viewing area;

THE GEMINI MONUMENT IN SPACE VIEW PARK

Sandra Friend

look down, and you'll see a constellation's worth of tiny fish shimmering in the sea grass beds. During launches, live audio from NASA Mission Control is broadcast throughout the park. Around the corner, the **US Space Walk of Fame Museum** (321-264-0434; www.spacewalkoffame.com), 4 Main St, is the nonprofit responsible for this memorial, the only one of its kind in the United States. Open 10–5 Mon–Fri, they have artifacts from the space program and a small gift shop; free.

an River Bank, which opened in 1889. Constructed of heart pine, their home rose on a plot of land bought from Mary Titus.

MEMORIALS The **Melbourne Military Memorial Park** (www.melbourne florida.org/news/memorial.htm) 1601 Oak St, honors veterans from ten American wars and is adjacent to the Honor America Liberty Bell Museum (see *Museums*). The park is centered around a memorial to 63 pilots and two enlisted men who died in flight training activities in the area.

MUSEUMS

Cocoa

At the **Brevard Museum of History & Natural Science** (321-632-1830; www.brevardmuseum.com), 2201 Michigan Ave, learn about the early inhabitants of Brevard County through hands-on activities and exhibits. Step into the archeological field and uncover fossils and artifacts. Then take a stroll in the 22-acre nature preserve. Open 10–4 Mon–Sat; fee.

Melbourne

✒ Walk through seven galleries at the **Brevard Museum of Art & Science** (321-242-0737; www.artandscience.org), 1463 Highland Ave, which features ever-changing exhibits of internationally and nationally recognized artists. The Children's Science Center allows kids to touch, feel, and discover through hands-on exhibits. Fee.

Under the Melbourne water tower, the **Honor America Liberty Bell Museum** (321-727-1776; http://home.att.net/~honorAmerica), 1601 Hickory St, displays a full-sized replica of the famed bell along with 300 years of historical artifacts; visitors may ring the bell with a padded hammer. Open Mon–Fri 10–4; free.

Titusville

Operated by the Historical Society of North Brevard, Inc., the **North Brevard Historical Museum** (321-269-3658), 301 S Washington Ave, started collecting regional ephemera in 1966, including the bank safe from the city's first bank, ladies clothing from the early 1900s, a Seminole Indian display, and much more. Open 10–3, Tue–Sat, donation.

Founded in 1960, the **American Police Hall of Fame & Museum** (321-264-0911; www.aphf.org), 6350 Horizon Dr, is the nation's first museum honoring all police—federal, state, county, and local departments. The solid marble wall memorializes over 60,000 officers who fell in the line of duty. See an electric chair, gas chamber, and the original police vehicle from the movie *Blade Runner*, along with more than 10,000 pieces of historical memorabilia. Have your photo taken in a real jail cell. The interactive and hands-on exhibits allow you to enter the world of forensics and test your detective skills, and the new indoor pistol range is now open to the public. Open daily 10–6. $12 adults; $8 ages 4–12, military, and senior citizens. Admission is free to law enforcement officers and survivors' families.

At **Valiant Air Command** (321-268-1941; www.vacwarbirds.org), 6600 Tico Rd, World War II memorabilia and vintage warplanes are on display. See a T-28, Mig-17D, F-14A Tomcat, the VAC flagship Douglas C-47A, and more. Open daily 9–5; $12 adults, $10 seniors and military, $5 children 4–12.

PLANETARIUM ♿ ✐ When on the Space Coast, think space! The **BCC Planetarium and Observatory** (321-433-7373; www.brevardcc.edu/planet), 1519 Clearlake Rd, Cocoa, does just that, opening its doors to the public to its fully accessible observatory, hands-on demonstration hall, and iWerks movie theater. At their rooftop observatory after dark, you can peer through the 12- and 24-inch reflectors and 6-inch refractor to see the rings of Saturn and the moons of Jupiter. The 70-foot planetarium dome features star shows and late-night laser light shows. Admission $6, open Fri–Sat 6:30 PM–10 PM, Wed 1:30–4 PM; observatory open Fri and Sat nights, weather permitting.

ZOOLOGICAL PARK ✐ **The Brevard Zoo** (321-254-9453; www.brevardzoo.org), 8225 N Wickham Rd, Melbourne, is unlike any zoo I have ever been to. Recently celebrating its 10th anniversary, this small community zoo has grown under the support of local residents and currently hosts more than 460 animals from Latin America, Australia, Florida, and the newest addition, Expedition Africa, where you can pet and feed the giraffes Raffiki, Doc, and Duncan and watch rhinos Howard and Max from the observation deck. Among my favorite animals in the zoo are the rare and endangered breeding pair of native red wolves. Over the past decade several attempts have been made to reintroduce the red wolf into the wild, to one key location on a secluded Florida island. Brevard is one of a handful of zoos working with the American Zoological Association and Species Survival Plan to increase their numbers and reintroduce them into their natural habitat.

KAYAKING THROUGH THE BREVARD ZOO
Kathy Wolf

The innovative Brevard Zoo is also the only zoo that kayaks! Paddle through the Florida Wetlands Outpost and learn about the "breakfast nook," where your guide tells you how to make pancakes and hash browns from native plants. Go on a journey through Expedition Africa, where you paddle past rhinos, giraffes, cotton-top tamarins, and gazelles on the African plains. Then pull your kayaks up on a sandy beach and climb the lookout tower to pet and feed the friendly giraffes as these gentle giants bat their long eyelashes, begging for your affection. You can also go beyond the park and take a

4-hour kayak ecotour into the Merritt Island natural areas with an expert naturalist. Wild Encounter tours ($75) get you up close and personal with Howard the white rhino, anteaters, gray foxes, aviary birds, flying fox (or fruit) bats, and more. The history of the zoo and its animals is also explained in this once-a-day limited tour. The zoo is open daily 10–5, with last entrance at 4:15. Regular admission $11.50 adults, $10.50 seniors, $8.50 ages 2–12. Add-ons: Wetlands Outpost or Expedition Africa 20-minute kayak tours ($6) and the Cape to Cairo Express train ride ($3).

✳ To Do

AIRBOATS Grasshopper Airboat Ecotours (321-631-2990; www.airboateco tours.com), FL 520 at the St. Johns River (4.5 miles west of I-95 on FL 520), Cocoa. USCG captain Rick Thrift takes you on a journey through the grassy marshes of the St. Johns River in his 60-to-90-minute ecotour. Small groups (less than 12 people) learn about the history of the river and its wildlife inhabitants through the eyes and mind of Rick, who comes with botanical and zoological background. See alligators and eagles, *and* learn about their habitats. Elevated seats and complimentary binoculars make sure you don't miss a thing. This is the "limo" airboat ride, not the "taxi" version. Rick provides for your comfort with beverages, and blankets when it's chilly. But for those who want a little thrill, you'll still get the adventure of an airboat without hanging on to your heart. Seasons dictate what time the boat goes out for best wildlife viewing and guest comfort, so call ahead for times; reservations are required. $45, ages 8 and up only.

At Lone Cabbage Fish Camp (see *Eating Out*), **Twister Airboats** (321-632-4199; www.twisterairboatrides.com), FL 520 at St. Johns River, Cocoa, will have you hanging on to your hat on a twisting, turning thrill ride in these large watercraft. Round a turn to surprise an alligator, pass cattle in the field, and watch the grassy marshes carefully, as you just might see the bleached white skeleton of an alligator that lost the battle for his territory. Rates vary by trip length: $20 adults, $12 children for 30 minutes; $45 and $25 for 60 minutes; $65 and $35 for 90 minutes. Call ahead—reservations are required.

ATTRACTIONS ✍ Dedicated to bravery of American astronauts, the **US Astronaut Hall of Fame** (321-269-6101; www.kennedyspacecenter.com/visitKSC/attractions/fame.asp), 6225 Vectorspace Blvd, Titusville, lets you experience hands-on astronaut training. Suit up and get ready to blast off; you'll also enjoy exploring actual space capsules and viewing astronaut artifacts in this interactive exhibit, home of US Space Camp Florida. Open daily. $17 adults, $13 children; combine with a visit to Kennedy Space Center for greater savings.

✍ At the **Kennedy Space Center Visitor Complex** (KSC; 321-449-4444; www.kennedyspacecenter.com), off FL 405, you can walk through a full-sized replica of the *Explorer* shuttle, touch a real Mars rock, see *The Dream Is Alive* and the new *Space Station 3D* at the IMAX theater, take a stroll among giants in the Rocket Garden, then meet and talk with a real astronaut at the Astronaut Encounter. You'll also want to purchase the add-on NASA Up Close guided tour ($21 adult, $15 child), which will take you out past the Vehicle Assembly Building (VAB) to the launch pads for a breathtaking view of the island, and also includes admission to the Astronaut Hall of Fame. The VAB is one of the world's largest buildings in cubic volume, having as much interior space as nearly four Empire State Buildings and covering more ground area than six football fields. It's so large, in fact, that the micro atmosphere inside is closely watched—it

Sandra Friend

A REPLICA OF *EXPLORER* AT KENNEDY SPACE CENTER

has actually rained inside the building. The KSC is also a successful National Wildlife Preserve managed by the Department of the Interior. It has more 220 miles of waterways, marshes, and beaches, home to more than 500 species, many of which will be pointed out to you on the guided tour. If you don't take the add-on tour, then check out the informative Nature Exhibit showcasing various Florida wildlife species. Art enthusiasts will also want to check out the Space Shuttle Collection (see *Art Galleries*). The best time to visit KSC is on the weekends, when the 70,000-plus employees are off and the roads are not as congested. Admission ($38 adult, $28 children ages 3–11) includes access to the Astronaut Hall of Fame, IMAX shows, and all simulators. An annual pass is $50 adult, $40 child, so if you're going to stay more than a day, it's the best deal. For those truly adventurous souls, the new 2-day Astronaut Training Experience immerses the entire family in hands-on training with mentoring from an astronaut, $250 per person.

BIRDING With more than 330 bird species in the Space Coast region, you'll want to take along a knowledgeable guide. **Birding & Photography Guide Services** (321-383-3088; www.cfbw.com), CFBW Enterprises, Inc., Titusville, offers half- and full-day guided tours through several diverse ecosystems such as wetlands, highlands, pinelands, grass plains, and scrub. You'll see everything from songbirds to raptors while exploring in small groups. Birding on your own? You'll find few better places in Florida than **Merritt Island National Wildlife Refuge**, especially on the berms and levee walks along Black Point Drive. See *Wild Places* for this and other suggestions. And don't miss the annual **Space Coast Wildlife & Birding Festival** (see *Special Events*), one of the top birding events in the country.

GREEN HERON IN THE LAUNCH COMPLEX 39 AREA

NASA/Jim Grossmann

CRUISING Port Canaveral (321-783-7831; www.portcanaveral.org), the second largest port in the world, docks some amazing cruise ships, like **Carnival Cruise Line** (1-800-839-6955; www.carnival.com) and **Disney Cruise Line** (1-800-511-1333; www.disneycruise.com). Board partial-day gaming cruises such as **Sterling Casino Lines** (1-800-765-5711; www.sterlingcasino.com), which provides you free passage with a complimentary buffet and live Vegas entertainment. Watch these glamorous vessels set sail from **Jetty Park** (see *Parks*) or several restaurants along Port Canaveral's shoreline.

ECOTOURS At **Island Boat Lines** (321-454-7414; www.islandboatlines.com), former Miss Florida Penny Flaherty is now known as Penny-the-Boat-Lady. Her pontoon boats (brightly decorated with Miss Florida colors of cherry red, lemon yellow, apple green, and orchid purple) have been sailing the Indian River Lagoon since 2002. Her most popular tour, the "Cocoa Beach 1,000 Islands 'In Search of Wildlife' " explores a manatee sanctuary, where amid the Thousand Islands, endangered sea cows graze on the Serengeti of the sea. You'll graze, too, on free chips and salsa, nuts, and fresh fruit as you pass stately homes, Indian shell mounds, and hundreds of islands in the tidal delta. Beer and soft drinks are also available for purchase. This boat tour will satisfy everyone in your party with wildlife off the port and "wild life" off the stern. Offered daily at 10 and 1, boarding at South Banana River Marina, 1357 South Banana River Drive, Merritt Island, trips cost $25 adults, $23 seniors and military, $20 ages 2–12, and must be reserved in advance. Penny also offers more casual sightseeing cruises of the port, or you can rent one of her boats, with captain, for a private party.

Boarding at the Cocoa Village Marina, 90 Delannoy Ave, the ***Indian River Queen*** (www.indianriverqueen.com/html/public_cruises.html) is Penny's classic southern sternwheeler, which debuted in the 2003 movie *Out of Time* with Denzel Washington. It features a historical photo gallery and crew dressed in period costumes. Check the Web site for public boarding opportunities, which typically include dinner cruises; the boat is frequently rented out for functions.

AT ANCHOR IN INDIAN RIVER LAGOON
Sandra Friend

FAMILY ACTIVITIES ✍ Ride bumper boats, play miniature golf, or race go-carts at **Andretti Thrill Park** (321-956-6706; www.andrettithrillpark.com), 3960 S Babcock St, Melbourne.

✍ **TRAXX at Jungle Village** (321-783-0595), 8801 Astronaut Blvd, Cape Canaveral. Go-carts, batting cages, laser tag, miniature golf, and arcade games. Open daily 10 AM–11 PM.

Off the jetty

Jetty Park Bait Shop (321-783-2771; www.jettypark.org), 400 E Jetty Dr, Cape Canaveral, has fishing pole rentals and all the bait necessary to fish off the pier or from shore.

Charter

Sail 20 to 40 miles offshore in a 28-foot Bertram with **Gettin' There II Sportfishing Charters** (321-784-2279; www.gettinthere.com), 201 International Dr #734, Cape Canaveral. The USCG-licensed captain and crew are great with both professionals and beginners. Full day $800, half-day $600.

My buddy and fellow writer Captain John Kumiski runs **Spotted Tail Charters** (407-977-5207; www.spottedtail.com) on the Indian River Lagoon; his specialty is teaching how to land the giant redfish found in the lagoon "on the fly." All trips are sight fishing, light tackle or fly-fishing, for a relaxing experience. You can fish from a skiff, or try a canoe or kayak. Trips within the Indian River Lagoon run $250 for kayak fishing (5 hours) or $375 half day, $450 full day for skiff or kayak.

Party boat

Miss Cape Canaveral (321-783-5274; www.misscape.com). This 85-foot boat takes up to 100 people for a lively day of great fishing for everyone. The daily special includes a hot breakfast, lunch, soda, coffee, beer, rod and reel, bait and tackle, and fishing license.

GOLF **The Habitat** (321-952-4588; www.brevardparks.com), 3591 Fairgreen St in Valkaria, is an 18-hole, par-72 course in a completely natural environment. Greens and fairways meld with the flow of the land, utilizing rolling elevation changes and topographical features to challenge golfers. Non-resident fees run $21 for 9 holes, $35 for 18.

At **Royal Oak Resort and Golf Club** (321-269-4500; www.royaloakgolfresort .com), 2150 Country Club Dr, you'll play a course designed in 1963 by Dick Wilson, who also designed Bay Hill near Orlando. It's well off the beaten path, surrounded by residential communities, encompassing 170 acres with eight lakes. Public fees run $26–33 per round.

HISTORIC CRUISE ♿ The North Brevard Historical Museum (see *Museums*) sponsors the **Indian River Historical Cruise** (321-267-4551) aboard the *Skimmer*, a 44-passenger canopied pontoon boat that glides across the Indian River Lagoon as your period-dressed crew recounts the exciting history of this waterway, from Seminole encampments and Confederate blockade runners through the founding of Titusville and the creation of NASA's spaceport. Departing one hour before sunset on Friday evenings from the historic Indian River Steamboat Wharf at Space View Park, Titusville, for a 45-minute sunset journey. $12 adults, $9 under 12.

KAYAKING **A Day Away Kayak Tours** (321-268-2655; www.adayawaykayak tours.com), 3532 Royal Oak Drive, Titusville. I can't say enough about my day with Rick Shafer and Laurilee Thompson. Call it a kayaking tour or an ecotour, I learned so much about the natural inhabitants of the Mosquito Lagoon while paddling around the bird rookery and in and out of inlets where manatees nosed right up to my the kayak with interest. The 3- to 4-foot lagoon makes a perfect kayak adventure for novices. And the crystal-clear water is full of exciting creatures like fish, tiny crabs, rays, and jellyfish. I exclaimed that they had everything here but seahorses and Laurilee said, "Keep looking—they're there, too!" I loved this area so much, I've brought my own kayaks back for several trips. Day tours (of which they provide a wide variety) start at $32. Ask about the opportunity for nighttime bioluminescent kayaking trips in summer starting at Haulover Canal; the lagoon's health is certainly on the rise in this area, as it is once again possible to see what Laurilee describes as "underwater fireworks."

Paddle the Thousand Islands tidal delta in either canoe or kayak with **Adventure Kayak of Cocoa Beach** (321-480-8632 or 321-453-6952; www.advkayak .com), 4755 Orchid Lane, Merritt Island, exploring mangrove islands. Paddle next to manatees and dolphins while white and brown pelicans sail by on the 2- to 3-hour trip. $25 adults, $15 ages 8–16.

Go kayaking at the **Brevard Zoo**! Discover a natural nursery for fish in the 20-minute Florida Wetlands tour, where resident otters may come out to play early in the day, or go on an expedition through Africa past rhinos and giraffes. These add-ons to the regular park admission (see *Zoological Park*) are a bargain at only $6.

The skilled staff at **Village Outfitters** (321-633-7245; www.villageoutfitters .com), 229 Forrest Avenue, Cocoa, offer tours locally or to faraway destinations like the Bahamas, Costa Rica, and even Alaska. Local half-day tours through the Thousand Islands, Canaveral National Seashore, Merritt Island Wildlife Refuge, and more start at $30; call for reservations.

SPAS **Essential Massage** (321-631-5678; www.emassagecocoa.com), 311 Brevard Ave, Cocoa. Put a roof on an alley and what do you get? Essential Massage makes use of the 6-foot wide, 70-foot long floor space, and the soothing aroma will draw you in from across the street. Display cases reaching the ceiling are filled with oil scents, aromatherapy candles made with pure palm and beeswax, painted glass bottles by Linda Elian, beaded necklaces, and beaded chain pulls for ceiling fans or lamps. Liquid castile soaps are scented with essential oils, and custom bar soaps come with a tiny vial of essential oil for your complete aromatherapy experience. Massage therapist on-site offering a decadent foot massage for $40.

SCENIC DRIVE The **Indian River Lagoon Scenic Highway** forms a 166-mile loop through the Space Coast, starting and ending at Merritt Island National Wildlife Refuge (see *Wild Places*). It encompasses a variety of roads, dipping as far south as Sebastian and providing a scenic way to see it all along the Space Coast.

As you drive north from **Satellite Beach** through Patrick Air Force Base along FL A1A, there is a beautiful stretch of untrammeled waterfront framed by sea grapes and sea oats, courtesy of the Air Force base. Similarly, **FL A1A north** on Merritt Island (north of Cape Canaveral and Titusville), from Merritt Island National Wildlife Refuge to where it rejoins US 1, offers truly natural views of the oceanfront, especially at the **Haulover Canal Bridge**.

WINDSURFING **Calema Windsurfing & Kayak Lessons, Rentals, and Pro Shop** (321-453-3223; www.calema.com), 2550 N Banana River Dr, Merritt Island. Tinho and Susie Dornellas have been teaching windsurfing for more than 20 years. You'll set out from Kelly Park to sail next to dolphins in the Banana River Lagoon. This sport is easy to master and great for all ages, but you'll need a few days to really get it right. The Beginner's Clinic ($299) is 4 days and will guide you through all the basics with on-land simulators, lightweight equipment, and step-by-step technique. Board rentals are also available to experienced sailors for partial or full days.

SAILING Learn how to sail at **Performance Sail & Sport** (321-253-3737; www.performancesailandsport.com), 6055 N US 1, Melbourne, or **Boater's Exchange** (321-638-0090; www.boatersexchange.com), 2101 S US 1, Rockledge, and then rent a Hobie Cat, Sunfish, or larger sailboat and glide alongside dolphins in the lagoon.

SKYDIVING At **Skydive Space Center** (321-267-0016 or 1-800-823-0016; www.skydivespacecenter.com), 476 N Williams Dr, Titusville, they'll take you to new heights. How high can you go? All jumps are 15,000 feet (the highest in Florida), or you can request the 18,000-foot jump—the highest tandem skydive offered anywhere in the world! Count me in, Patty! During the minute-and-a-half flight you'll see the Atlantic Coast, Indian River Lagoon, and an awe-inspiring view of the Kennedy Space Center. You'll fly as close to the Space Center runway and launch pads as NASA will allow. Not everyone in your group ready for a jump? A scenic ride is offered to those non-jumpers who want to see you step out of a perfectly good airplane. Open daily. A 15,000-foot tandem jump runs $174; the world's highest tandem $199; add video and photos for $90.

SURFING Who says you can't surf? I was up catching waves in less than 30 minutes! They love beginners. Under the guidance of professional surfer Craig Carroll and his staff at the **Ron Jon Surf School** (321-868-1980; www.cocoabeach surfingschool.com), 150 E Columbia Lane, Cocoa Beach, you, too, will be riding in, on long or short boards. First you'll learn the necessary marine safety awareness, from shark and stingrays to riptides. Then you'll practice your "snap" and positioning while in the air-conditioned comfort of the training school. In just a short time you'll hit the water, where your instructor will stay by your side the entire time while offering positive support and guidance. Surf lessons are scheduled with the incoming tides, so call in advance of your trip for times. Private 1-hour lessons $60; semiprivate (two students/one instructor) 1-hour $45, 2-hour $60, 3-hour $80 per person. Not ready for the wide-open ocean? Craig also

RON JON SURF SHOP

Sandra Friend

teaches over at Disney's Typhoon Lagoon Wave Pool (see "Theme Parks").

WALKING TOURS **Historic Titusville** outlines a walking tour of more than a dozen sites in this circa-1880 outpost on the Indian River; pick up a brochure at the local Titusville Chamber of Commerce (see *Guidance*). Throughout town, historic panels provide details about the community and its growth.

✴ Green Space

BEACHES

Cocoa Beach

Alan Shepard Park is at the east end of FL 520 on the ocean. The 2-acre park was named for astronaut Alan Shepard and provides an excellent view of space launches. The park has a picnic area, barbecues, and restrooms with showers; fee. **Sidney Fischer Park** (321-868-3274), in the 2100 block of FL A1A, was named for Sidney Fischer, who served as the mayor of Cocoa Beach from 1956 to 1960. The 10-acre oceanfront park has shower and restroom facilities; fee. ❀ ✍ The 32.5-acre **Lori Wilson Park** (321-455-1380), 1500 N Atlantic Ave, is bordered by I Dream of Jeannie Boulevard and has its own dog park. The parking areas flank a shady maritime hammock with interpretive boardwalk. Beach access, up and over the dunes, includes picnic tables, showers, pavilions, playground, volleyball court, and seasonal lifeguards; free.

Melbourne Beach

&. Search out seashells at **Coconut Point Park** (321-952-4650), FL A1A. The popular surfing spot with picnic area and showers is also home to several sea turtle nests, so observe marked-off sections. Open dawn–dusk.

Straddling a human-made cut through the barrier island that runs from Melbourne Beach to Vero Beach, **Sebastian Inlet State Park** (321-984-4852; www.floridastateparks.org/sebastianinlet), 9700 S FL A1A, Melbourne Beach, offers beach access on the Atlantic side and nature trails and fishing along the Intracoastal Waterway, where a campground overlooks the Indian River Lagoon. It's a popular launch point for fishing and diving trips. The McLarty Treasure Museum, featuring Spanish doubloons and other treasures brought up from offshore wrecks, is open daily 10–4:30; fee except for nature trails.

Titusville

Canaveral National Seashore (321-267-1110; www.nps.gov/cana), 308 Julia St, is one of the rare places in America where you can backpack along the Atlantic

Ocean, where surf and sand meet on a narrow strip of barrier island along the Mosquito Lagoon. In the shadow of Kennedy Space Center, this protected seashore provides a place for solitude and beach fishing, sunning, and camping. Access **Playalinda Beach**, a popular swimming beach, from Merritt Island National Wildlife Refuge. Playalinda has a local reputation for nudity, which is not sanctioned by park management. The park may close during space shuttle launches for security reasons.

GARDENS The 30-acre **Florida Tech Botanical Gardens** (321-674-8000; www .fit.edu), 150 W University Blvd, Melbourne, has one of the largest collections of palms in the state. The lush hammock contains oaks, maples, and hickories. A plant guide and nature trail map is available at the adjacent Evans Library, but you'll have to wrangle a parking pass from the college officials, or park off-campus and walk in.

PARKS

Cape Canaveral
Jetty Park (321-783-7111), 400 E Jetty Rd, Cape Canaveral. Off the FL 528 Causeway. The newly renovated boardwalk along the jetty makes a great place to view cruise ships or shuttle launches. Campsites, fishing, pavilions, beach, barbecue grills. Open 7 AM–9 PM. Parking $1 for cars, $5 for RVs. At nearby **Kelly Park**, Banana River Dr off FL 528, grab a picnic lunch and watch the many sailboarders (see *Windsurfing*).

Cocoa
Established in 1920, **Taylor Park** (321-639-3500), Delannoy & Harrison Avenues, right behind City Hall and the Civic Center, is the original park in the historic district, with a playground shaded by grand old oaks, and also a rose garden, and provides public restrooms. A 2001 addition expands on this expanse of green with the **Cocoa Riverfront Park**, offering a riverwalk boardwalk on the Intracoastal Waterway with access to a marina and a new grassy amphitheater for special events. There are special celebrations here at Mardi Gras and Christmas, an alcohol-free New Years Eve family event, and even Friday night movies in the park—bring a lawn chair!

Melbourne
At **Promenade Park**, 1005 E Melbourne Ave, walk along the boardwalk at this prime manatee-viewing area along Crane Creek, a freshwater tributary flowing into the Indian River Lagoon. Kids will want to climb on

THE BOARDWALK THROUGH LORI WILSON PARK

Sandra Friend

the colorful manatee statues at tiny, unassuming **Holmes Park**, at the corner of Melbourne Ave and Melbourne Court, near Historic Downtown Melbourne.

Palm Bay

Turkey Creek Sanctuary (321-952-3433), 1502 Port Malabar Blvd, treats visitors to a boardwalk through sand pine-scrub and along Turkey Creek, a popular kayaking route. Tall cliffs above the creek provide scenic views; look up in the canopy overhead for bromeliads and orchids. At the entrance you'll find a butterfly garden and the Margaret Hames Nature Center, with interpretive displays, research materials, and restrooms. Open 7–sunset; free.

Satellite Beach

A kayaker's secret sweet spot, **Sampson's Island** (321-773-6458; www.satellite beach.org) is a 52-acre oasis in the Banana River, with nature trails, picnic areas, and primitive camping. On Sundays, you can hop a free city boat (first come, first served) at 1 PM from the dock behind the Satellite Beach Fire Station, 1390 S Patrick Dr, to explore the park; the boat returns at 4.

🐾 Who let the dogs out? Not the **Satellite Beach Dog Park** (321-773-6458; www.satellitebeach.org), 750 Jamaica Blvd, where pets are safely contained in a free-roaming, pet-friendly, landscaped environment. Canines love the unrestricted social interaction. The new dog park has some specific rules and requires your current shot documentation. Free dog clinics and events are scheduled throughout the year. $2 admits up to three vaccinated dogs and two of their human companions (who don't need shots).

Titusville

Enchanted Forest Nature Sanctuary (321-264-5185; www.brevardparks.com/eel/enchforest), 444 Columbia Blvd off FL 405, is at once a forest preserve and a history lesson on Florida's settlement. The entrance road follows the Hernandez-Capron Trail, a military trail built by General Joseph Hernandez and his men in 1837 to link US Army fortresses at St. Augustine and Fort Pierce. The Coquina Quarry at the south edge of the preserve slices into the Anastasia Formation of the Atlantic Coastal Ridge, and the creek that the trail system follows is the Addison Canal, created in 1912 to drain the extensive wetlands between the St. Johns River and the Indian River Lagoon for development. Ancient oaks and magnolias form a dense forest on one corner of the preserve. Before you walk the hiking trails, stop in at the educational pavilion to browse the interpretive displays; the building also houses a gift shop. Open Tue–Sun 9–5; free.

WILD PLACES Thanks to the Brevard County's Environmentally Endangered Lands (EEL) program (321-255-4466; www.eelbrevard.com), the Space Coast has a patchwork of wilderness areas breaking up the urban mass. In addition to its flagship project, the **Enchanted Forest Nature Sanctuary** (see *Parks*), Brevard's EEL lands (primarily accessible only for hiking and biking) include **Buck Lake Conservation Area** off FL 46, with a network of forest roads for hiking, biking, and horseback riding along the prairies edging the St. Johns River; **Malabar Scrub Sanctuary**, off Malabar Rd, a quiet 400-acre tract just south of Palm Bay, where early-bird visitors enjoy bird sightings amid flatwoods and

scrub; **Micco Scrub Sanctuary**, off Micco Rd, a 1,300-acre scrub preserve; and
Pine Island Conservation Area, on Pine Island Rd just south of Kennedy
Space Center, a great place to watch for manatees in summer along Sam's Creek.
On the barrier island south of Melbourne Beach, enjoy exploring the coastal
scrub on hiking trails through **Coconut Point Sanctuary** (just south of the Melbourne Beach Publix), where the trail leads through a variety of habitats along
the Indian River Lagoon, and **Maritime Hammock Sanctuary**, South Beach,
where orchids abound in the oak hammocks and you can watch wading birds
from a mangrove-rimmed platform on the lagoon.

Adjoining Kennedy Space Center along the Indian River Lagoon, **Merritt
Island National Wildlife Refuge** (321-861-0667; www.merrittisland.fws.gov),
east of Titusville on FL 402, offers some of the best bird-watching opportunities
in Florida. Stop by the visitors center before you explore the refuge for information and maps. Renowned for its diversity of species, the park offers several hiking trails on which you'll want to bring your binoculars and camera for an
opportunity to see some of the 310 different types of birds, including Florida
scrub-jays, bald eagles, black-necked stilts, and roseate spoonbills. **Black Point
Wildlife Drive** is a must-see one-way scenic drive out into the marshes of the
Indian River Lagoon. The visitors center is closed on Sun Apr–Oct; the park may
be entirely closed during space shuttle launches. Free.

St. Johns Water Management District (321-329-4500; www.sjr.state.fl.us) is
responsible for a string of conservation areas that serve as buffers to the St.
Johns River and its tributaries. Most are open for fishing and paddling; some are
open to hiking, equestrian use, and hunting. Check their Web site for the *Recreation Guide to District Lands*, which will lead you to preserves like **Blue
Cypress**, **Three Forks**, and **River Lakes**.

With nearly 23,000 acres, **St. Sebastian River Preserve State Park** (321-953-
5005; www.floridastateparks.org/stsebastian), 1000 Buffer Preserve Dr, Fells-
mere, straddles two counties. You can backpack or ride horses on nearly 40 miles
of trails through pine flatwoods and scrub, or walk the nature trail along the river
to watch manatees; up to 100 have been seen in the river at one time.

✳ Lodging
BED & BREAKFASTS

Indialantic 32903
❝❡❞ ⊙ The beachfront **Windemere
Inn by the Sea** (321-728-9334 or 1-
800-224-6853; www.windemere
inn.com), 815 S Miramar Ave, was
built only in 1998, but was made to
look like a house from the turn of the
20th century. Romance and relaxation
abound as Thomas and Vivien Hay
bring southern hospitality to the
coral-colored mansion. Three buildings compose the inn. You might
choose to stay in the Main House in
the Enchantment Room with pearl
and mocha coloring, a mahogany
poster bed, and a Jacuzzi bath; or in
the Windward Cottage, where the sun
greets you each morning in the natural decor of the Honeysuckle Room,
with a wicker-and-twig queen-sized
bed, twin daybed, Jacuzzi bath, and
separate outside entrance. Each
evening sherry is served with freshly
baked dessert treats of the day. Then

fall off to sleep to the sounds of the surf just outside your window. 149–262; suites $338–390 for up to 4 people.

Melbourne, Historic Downtown 32901

☙ The beautiful 1925 **Crane Creek Inn B&B** (321-768-6416; www .cranecreekinn.com), 907 E Melbourne Ave, is decorated in the casual style of Old Key West and situated on the Indian River tributary Crane Creek, right at the edge of Historic Downtown Melbourne. Innkeepers Gillian and Bob Shearer know how to make you feel right at home and will chat with you about local wildlife and the downtown historic area or just let you relax in your own space. Take a moment to unwind at the gorgeous waterfront pool or hot tub, and then canoe along the creek to discover the varied wildlife—waterfowl, blue-shell crabs, and even manatees. In the evening you might see or smell the blooming queen of the night, or night-blooming cereus, a cactus growing off the many palms on the property. Park your car or come by boat and moor at the dock. This is one of the few B&Bs that allow pets; both Gillian and Bob welcome and adore well-behaved canine companions. $100–199.

Mims 32754

The 1860 **Dickens Inn** (321-269-4595; www.dickens-inn.com), 2398 N Singleton Ave, was built as a grand manor house for a thriving citrus plantation. Several orange and grapefruit trees still stand on the property, assuring fresh seasonal juices. Innkeepers Ursula and Bill Dickens want you to feel right at home and combine southern and Old World

hospitality with the vibrancy of this millennium. The natural decor is comfy, not stuffy, with touches of Old Florida and Ursula's homeland, Germany. After staying with this active couple, you'll leave feeling relaxed and rejuvenated. That is, if you really want to leave. $100–115.

Titusville 32780

🐾 "▮" ∞ It's a world unto its own, just a couple of blocks from the Indian River Lagoon, an enormous 1927 coquina rock mansion painted with murals and standing three stories tall. **Casa Coquina** (321-268-4653 or 1-877-684-8341; www.casacoquina .com), 4010 Coquina Ave, is at once a quirky museum and a relaxing retreat, a place inviting you to have some fun, where a knight in shining armor sits atop a horse in the main hall, a British pub and wedding chapel compete for atmosphere, and every surface in the common rooms is crowded with antiques, all available for purchase. Rooms along the eastern side of the building, like the Diamond Suite with its hardwood floors, fireplace and whirlpool, and massage chair, also have sundecks overlooking the Vehicle Assembly Building at NASA, with a perfect view of the space shuttle launches. There are eight suites in all, many of them with a separate bed, perfect for traveling with girlfriends, siblings, or parents. Each has its own distinct character, and none so rich as the Black Pearl, the penthouse on the third floor, where the Oriental trappings include a 17th-century Ming Dynasty marriage bed (for show— your bed is much grander). Outdoors, the mansion is flanked by niche gardens with koi ponds and a hot tub. Why pay motel rates when suites here start at $79 weekdays, $109 weekends—and you have the run of the manor? Rates include a full breakfast, complimentary beer and wine in the evenings, wireless Internet, and your own big suite with private bath.

HOTELS, MOTELS, AND RESORTS

Cocoa Beach 32931

& 🕈 All rooms at **Cocoa Beach Oceanside Inn** (321-784-3126; www .cocoabeachoceansideinn.com), 1 Hendry Ave, have an ocean view, and what a view—you can look right over the Cocoa Beach Pier! You'll love the tropical Rain Forest Room for just hanging out. A deck atop this high-rise hotel offers a ringside seat for space shuttle launches. All rooms have a tropical feel, with colorful island decor, and each has its own private balcony. Rates start at $99.

↤ & "🍴" A certified Florida Green Lodging, the **Courtyard by Marriott Cocoa Beach** (321-784-4800; www.courtyardcocoabeach.com), 3435 N Atlantic Ave, goes beyond the typical chain resort by being the first in Brevard County to be honored for actively conserving energy, recycling most waste, and utilizing eco-friendly products in the day to day operation of the hotel. The complex includes a full-service restaurant (with room service 4–10 PM), a snack bar called the Moonwalker Café, a heated pool and hot tub, and free wireless Internet. All rooms are environmentally friendly, and the hotel offers special accommodations for allergy sufferers. Standard rooms come with desks, a mini fridge, and balconies for you to sit outside and enjoy the sea breeze. A walkway to the ocean is right at the edge of the parking lot shared with their sister Green Lodging, the **Hampton Inn and Suites** (321-799-

4099; www.hamptoninn.com), and while most rooms are not oceanfront, there is no extra charge for the rooms that are! Rates start at $149; I suggest booking room 717, a standard king corner, with an incredible panorama of the Cocoa Beach strip that you can view from bed or from your own sitting room.

The funky **Fawlty Towers Motel** (321-784-3870; www.fawltytowers resort.com), 100 E Cocoa Beach Causeway, is owned by a couple of Brits and, yes, named for the British TV show. Just a few steps from the beach, the Caribbean-themed motel—which you can't miss, thanks to its pink turrets with aqua roofs— has a heated pool surrounded by lush tropical gardens and an authentic tiki bar featuring European beers and ciders. $69–129.

↤ & 🕈 "🍴" Another keen Green Lodging, with a prominent façade that looks like a giant bongo drum, the **Four Points by Sheraton Cocoa Beach** (321-783-8717; www.starwoodhotels.com/fourpoints), 4001 N Atlantic Ave, is a surfer's dream, a three-story surfing megaplex under one roof. From participating in surfing lessons to staring into the 5,600-gallon shark and exotic fish aquarium in the Shark Pit Bar & Grill, you'll feel surrounded by the sea. The spiffy rooms have a calming blue decor with surfing photos, a desk with free Wi-Fi, microwave, mini fridge, and coffeemaker, $85 and up. An enclosed, heated pool is part of the complex, too, but the beach beckons only a block away!

The Inn at Cocoa Beach (1-800-343-5307; www.theinnatcocoabeach .com), 4300 Ocean Beach Blvd, could also be called a B&B if not for the 50 rooms. This wonderful European-style hotel offers fresh fruit, warm moist muffins, and rich coffee and teas each morning. Eat indoors or out on the beautiful patio, where you can visit with Tangee, the sociable tropical macaw. The inn is located across from Ron Jon Surf Shop, so you may want to rent a kayak and get innkeeper/seasoned kayaker Karen Simpler to go for a paddle with you! $150 and up for the uniquely appointed rooms, each with a view of the sea, some with Jacuzzi tubs.

The family-owned and -operated **Luna Sea Bed & Breakfast Motel** (321-783-0500; www.lunaseacocoabeach.com), 3185 N Atlantic Ave, has guest rooms ($60 and up) with a tropical flair; each comes with a mini fridge, desk or recliner, and new beds. There is a heated pool and book borrowing library, and guests receive coupons for a free hot breakfast at a nearby diner.

🐾 Bringing a touch of Key West to these surfer shores, **Sea Esta Villas** (321-783-1739 or 1-800-872-9444; www.seaestavillas.homestead.com), NW Corner Seventh St, is across from the beach with fully equipped kitchens and one- or two-bedroom suites, $159 nightly or $999 per week.

🐾 🖉 A vintage seaside hotel, just like I used to remember them, **South Beach Inn-on-the-Sea** (321-784-3333 or 1-800-546-6835; www.southbeachinn.com), 1701 S Atlantic Ave, has 18 one- or two-bedroom suites ($90 and up) with fully equipped kitchens, and welcomes your pet.

🖉 Built in 1948 by Norman Greenwald, a Greenwich Village native with a dream that got him through World War II, the **Surf Studio Beach Resort** (321-783-7100; www.surf-studio.com), 1801 S Atlantic Ave, feels like a vintage Florida beach experience, because the hotel stayed in the family all these years. The rooms (with efficiencies and full kitchens, $95–210) are lined up across an immaculate oceanfront lawn. Slip into the oceanfront pool, lie in a hammock, or take your board to the beach.

Rockledge 32955

♿ 🖉 The **Swiss Inn & Tennis Center** (321-631-9445 or 1-866-SWISS-GO; www.swissinntennis.com), 3220 Fiske Blvd, is a small, independent hotel with large, bright and cheerful rooms ($70–85) with a wet bar, microwave and mini fridge, and a basic bathroom. It's an older place, but it's a mecca for tennis fanatics who just have to play on red clay courts; there are six lighted ones out back behind the pool and palm-lined pond. Breakfast is included, served in their spacious breakfast room; small pets welcome.

CAMPGROUNDS

Bellwood 32780

Pitch your tent or pull in your RV beneath the lush canopy of oaks at **Manatee Hammock Campground** (321-264-5105; www.nbbd.com/godo/prec/ManateeCamp), 7275 S US 1, inside a 26-acre county park along the Indian River Lagoon. With an unimpeded view of launches at Cape Canaveral, it's a rare find. Campers enjoy their own private pool, along with a reception hall, shuffleboard court, horseshoe pit, and a fishing pier shared with day visitors. 177 campsites, with 147 full hookups.

Mims 32754

Opened in the 1950s, **Loughman**

Lake Lodge (321-268-2277; www
.loughmanlake.com), 1955 Hatbill Rd,
sits surrounded by watery wilderness
along one of the unusual saline lakes
of the upper St. Johns River. There
are cabins ($90), RV sites ($35), and
tent sites ($15) at this Old Flori-
da–style getaway.

Rockledge 32955
⁰🎯⁰ At **Space Coast RV Resort** (321-
636-2873 or 1-800-982-4233; www
.spacecoastrv.net), 820 Barnes Blvd,
camp among the pines just 15 minutes
from Cocoa Beach while enjoying a
heated swimming pool, recreation
building, shuffleboard, and Wi-Fi. $25
for tents, $55 for RVs, discount for
Woodalls and Good Sam members,
and for longer stays.

Titusville 32780
Perched on the edge of a vast marsh
created by the floodplain of the St.
Johns River, **The Great Outdoors
RV Nature & Golf Resort** (321-269-
5004 or 1-800-621-2267; www.tgo
resort.com), 125 Plantation Dr (along
FL 50), is just plain huge. Set in a
pine forest, it features beautiful lakes,
a golf course, a restaurant, bank, and
shopping on-site. This oasis is for RV
owners only; sites have level concrete
pads with 30- and 50-amp hookups.
In-season $45, off-season (summer)
$35, with discounts for longer stays.

✳ Where to Eat
DINING OUT

Cocoa
The Black Tulip (321-631-1133;
www.theblacktulip.net), 207 Brevard
Ave, began the revitalization of Historic Cocoa Village when they opened
in 1981, and we have that to thank
them for by stopping in for a fine
meal before a show at the Phoenix

Theatre or Historic Cocoa Village
Playhouse (see *Entertainment*). Their
signature dish is roast duckling with a
semi-sweet apple cashew sauce. Open
for lunch and dinner, entrées $16–27.

At **Café Flamant** (www.cafeflamant
.com), Delannoy Ave—unmistakable
with the sax-playing flamingo outside
courtesy of the Bad Birds Gallery (see
Art Galleries)—relax and enjoy
Drunken Flamingo wine and live
music. Executive Chef Huie Martin
runs a catering business, and this is
his other creative outlet. The menu
ranges from lobster ravioli to tiramisu
to hot dogs, so you know it's eclectic!

For an elegant French dinner, **Café
Margaux Restaurant** (321-639-
8343; www.margaux.com), 222 Brevard Ave, is just the ticket. Starters
include continental delights such as
garlic butter-sautéed snails on lemon
saffron angelhair, and fine duck liver
and peppercorn paté. Move to the
salad course, which might be French
goat cheese rolled in macadamias,
glazed with lavender honey and mixed
greens with a citrus Pernod vinaigrette. Then, the pièce de résistance,
your entrée—perhaps a spice-rubbed
seared ostrich tenderloin, or Chicken
Margaux wrapped in bacon, stuffed
with prosciutto, asparagus, and feta
with a crimini mushroom sauce. The
multicourse production, à la carte,
will run about $50 per person, and
can be paired with a fine wine.

Cocoa Beach
You can't beat the view at the
Atlantic Ocean Grille (321-783-
7549) 401 Meade Ave, on the Cocoa
Beach Pier. Since 1962, this historic
landmark has served up great dishes
in a comfortable setting with a nautical theme, surrounded by warm,
wood-paneled walls. Start with grilled

alligator or oysters Rockefeller, then order from a variety of fresh Florida seafood ($17–22)—but save room for their famous desserts, like Key lime pie and Kahlua cake.

Pompano Grille (321-784-9005), 110 N Brevard Ave. Mark Siljestrom and Vicki Cooper whip up some tasty dishes in this unlikely location. You've got to explore to find them, tucked in a bland strip mall off on a side street, but this is one perfect gem. The former South Florida chef moved up the coast, and Cocoa Beach should be thrilled to have him. Mark's sister, Pam, greets everyone at the door, and with less than a dozen tables, you are assured prompt attention as you settle into intimate surroundings. The French Continental and northern Italian cuisine is accented with cozy recessed arches displaying natural pieces and fine art. With selections like blackened shrimp with creamy dill sauce, sea scallops in brandy cream, boneless breast of chicken layered with sautéed apples, and pasta capellini el pesto—made with fresh basil, pine nuts, and garlic in virgin olive oil, partnered with pesto vegetable curry with fresh vegetables, raisins, and apples over rice pilaf—I didn't know where to start. But I knew where to end, and saved enough room for their homemade Oreo ice cream and moist chocolate cake. They also offer a nice selection of fine wines. Opens at 5:30 for dinner, entrées $14 and up; dinner served Tue–Sat. in season, Thu–Sun in summer.

With Norwegian salmon, baked Brie, Wiener schnitzel, and jaegerbraten, it's a taste of the Old Country at the **German Heidelberg Restaurant**, 7 N Orlando Ave (FL A1A), served in elegant European-style surroundings. Entrées $15–21, open Tue–Sat. Adjoining is Heidi's Jazz Club, a hip local hangout since 1992 (see *Entertainment*).

Malabar

The beautiful **Yellow Dog Café** (321-956-3334; www.yellowdogcafe .net), 905 US 1, is the same place that Stuart Woods writes about in his books. The elegant building overlooking the Indian River serves light lunches ($8 and up) like grilled portobello Caesar salad, and the California Dreamer sandwich with melted Brie, sliced tomatoes, alfalfa sprouts, and scallions on top of fresh foccacia, along with sumptuous dinners like onion-crusted chicken with caramel citrus glaze. Closed Mon; reservations suggested.

Melbourne

A snazzy showcase for local artists, **Bellas** (321-723-5001; www.meet meatbellas.com), 1904 Municipal Ln, serves up great pasta dishes ($12 and up) like Amica Loretta (a meat tortellini sauteed with creamy Alfredo sauce and prosciutto) and Mama Anna's Traditional Lasagna with three imported cheeses, Bella's marinara sauce, and lots of beef. Settle into the romantic setting and browse the wine list first.

At Nannie Lee's Strawberry Mansion, **Mister Beaujean's Bar-Grille & Breakfast** (321-723-1900; www .strawberrys.com) offers a relaxing garden courtyard with a backstory: This 1986 addition to the mansion property honors Claude Beaujean, a carpenter who fashioned the lovely oak staircase, bay window, and gingerbread trim back in the day. His family operated the Atlantic Ferry Service, crossing the Indian River Lagoon five times daily to the Melbourne Beach Pier before the first bridge opened. While the mansion is used for special event banquets, you can get a taste of it here at Mister Beaujean's by stopping in for a sumptuous breakfast omelet or eggs Benedict, old-fashioned flapjacks with their famous caramel syrup, or lunch munchies like Buzzard's Breath or Truck Stop Chili.

Rockledge

A landmark since the 1920s, the distinctive Tudor roadhouse that now hosts **Ashley's** (321-636-6430), 1609 US 1, comes with its own haunts—read the menu for the eerie details. The menu appeals to a broad array of palates, with entrée-sized salads ($7–9), baskets ($7–8), and entrées ($8–18) ranging from bacon-wrapped and chargrilled filet mignon to honey-fried chicken, tilapia filets, All-American burgers, and a chimichanga.

Titusville

Starting out as a small roadside smokehouse, **Paul's Smokehouse** (321-267-3663), 3665 S Washington Ave, has grown into a fabulous dining establishment. But don't let the gorgeous architecture scare you away: The prices are reasonable ($8–22), the view of the Indian River is breathtaking, and you can't beat the location for viewing launches. Among the highlights of their menu are beef burgundy, a filet sautéed in burgundy and topped with Swiss cheese and mushroom sauce; shrimp sauté, featuring chargrilled shrimp with sautéed mushrooms served over fettuccine with a lightly herbed sauce; and thin-sliced hickory-smoked barbecued pork or ribs. Opens 4 PM.

Cape Canaveral

A fun place to go to watch the cruise ships or the eclectic crowd is **Grill's Seafood Deck & Tiki Bar** (321-868-2226; www.visitgrills.com), 505 Glen Creek Dr, Cape Canaveral. Famous for their fantastic grilled fish of the day ($17), they get my vote! Also offering entrées like grilled tropical chicken kebabs and grilled seafood Alfredo. You'll want to try the spicy brown Bahamian chowder or creamy traditional clam chowder ($3–4). For not-so-light meals there's a variety of juicy sandwiches and the famous Hurricane Burger.

Come casual right off the boat at **Rusty's Seafood and Oyster Bar** (321-783-2033; www.rustysseafood .com), 628 Glen Creek Dr, where your jumbo scallops can be rustled up Jamaican jerk style, but the true southern approach to seafood is their Steamed Seafood Platter, with ¼ pound of shrimp, 6 oysters, ½ pound of scallops and ½ pound clams, served with parsley potatoes, and corn on the cob, $21.

Cocoa

The retro sign above **Arbetters** (321-636-0763), 816 Dixon Blvd, caught our attention from US 1, so we backtracked to check out the sweet stuff. For nearly 25 years, they've been churning out thick shakes, sundaes, and hot dogs of all stripes, including chili dogs, kraut dogs, chimi dogs, and even pizza dogs, $1 and up. Burgers and gyros, too!

Cold beer and swamp food attracts a steady parade of bikers, anglers, and tourists to the rustic **Lone Cabbage Fish Camp** (321-632-4199), 8199 FL

520. It's been there in some form or fashion for more than a century, right on the St. Johns River, and serves up critters like gator, frogs (the legs), and catfish ($8 and up) plus sampler combos. You'll want to come out for the Sunday fish fry with live band. Save room for Key lime pie!

Murdock's Bistro and Char Bar (321-633-0600), 600 Brevard Ave, has a classy tap room inside and picnic table seating along the sidewalk. One salad is especially tempting: slices of Granny Smith apples (my favorite) on baby field greens, topped with walnuts, Gorgonzola, and red onions. House specialties include the Fried Yardbird, with four pieces of crispy southern-fried chicken, and tender home-cooked pot roast; entrées, sandwiches, and burgers ($8–13) come with your choice of sides like southern turnip greens, macaroni and cheese, and red-skinned mashed potatoes with gravy.

Cocoa Beach

You'll find several hot spots on the **Cocoa Beach Pier** (321-784-4409; www.cocoabeachpier.com), 401 Meade Ave. The **Marlins Good Times Bar and Grill** is a favorite of the college crowd with Buffalo wings, fish sandwiches, and burgers ($6–8). **Oh Shucks Seafood Bar** (321-783-7549) is world famous for their finger foods and has live reggae bands every Wed night. At the end of the pier, the **Atlantic Ocean Grille** (321-783-7549; also see *Dining Out*) offers finer dining with a breathtaking ocean view. Nightly entertainment can be anything from soft guitar at the open bar to lively reggae depending on the season. The college crowd dominates during spring break and the annual Easter spring surfing festival.

The attractive muraled walls, by local artist Vern Matiolli, soften the sports-bar image in the comfortable **Rum Runners Grill** (321-868-2020), 695 N Atlantic Ave. This restaurant didn't waste any time putting their clam "chowdah" to the test with this native New Englander. Their version of the traditional New England chowder, made with real butter and heavy cream, not only won them a caseful of medals but also garnered my award. For a new twist, they offer cocktail sherry on the side, which gives it an unexpected kick. They also dish up some of the best crab cakes any-where—delicate and full of crab, held together with just a few Ritz cracker crumbs. Don't miss their annual event, on the first Saturday of May, where they fly in official glasses of the Kentucky Derby to fill with mint juleps.

Stop by **Simply Delicious Café & Bakery** (321-783-2012), 125 North Orlando Ave (FL A1A southbound), for a fabulous breakfast with such items as malted waffles and eggs Benedict, or lunches like the grilled mahi sandwich and crispy Oriental salad. Get there early—the best muffins, like pistachio and fresh peach, go fast. You'll enjoy sitting in the colorful rooms of this historic beach house while sipping cappuccinos and lattes.

Indian Harbor Beach

Great sandwiches and gourmet foods are found at the **Green Turtle Market** (321-773-2001; www.brevardnow.com/greenturtle.htm), 855 E Eau Gallie Blvd. Much of their menu changes daily, based on the fresh local produce and seafood available, but includes a vast array of creative salads ($3–7 per pound) such as marinated asparagus (fresh asparagus in a special blend of balsamic vinaigrette and olive oil with diced walnuts and black pepper) and their signature Tim's Pesto Pasta (bowtie pastas with sun-dried tomatoes, fresh basil, garlic, and toasted pine nuts).

Melbourne
Not only does the **Greenhouse Gallery Cafe** (321-676-1243), 705 E New Haven Ave, offer great salads, deli sandwiches, and suitable lunches for kids, but it also hosts a variety of local artists' works. The front garden patio makes for a great spot for relaxing while secluded behind the garden trellis.

'Tis a grand Irish pub, **Meg O'Malleys** (321-952-5510; www.meg omalleys.com), 812 E New Haven Ave, which offers traditional dishes ($4–10) such as rosemary-scented Irish stew, corned beef and cabbage, and fish-and-chips. A cup of the Irish Parliament Bean Soup is still served for 18¢, same as it is at Parliament. For dessert, Bushmill's bread pudding ($5) is made with the traditional recipe, served on a pool of sweet Irish whiskey cream with raspberry sauce or doused with their "drunken" raisin sauce. Stick around and have them pour you a pint while you listen to the live entertainment.

Titusville
Stop by the "almost famous" **Dogs R' Us Grill and Bar** (321-269-9050), 4200 S Washington Ave, for gourmet hamburgers and hot dogs. This fun and funky place also serves dinners and a great selection of desserts. A second location is in Port St. John along US 1 near Faye Blvd.

🦞 ℐ **The Coffee Shoppe** (321-267-9902), Baldwin Plaza, 125 Broad St. A down-home family restaurant with tasty, inexpensive breakfasts ($2–5) served 6–2, lunch sandwiches, and entrées (veal cutlet, grilled Salisbury steak) that run $3–9.

ℐ **Hope's Tea Room & Treasures** (321-259-9158), 814B S Washington Ave. Imagine my delight at stumbling across this family restaurant jam-packed with antiques and country crafts, many for sale! No matter what you order for breakfast—and the selection is huge; I recommend the crêpes—Hope greets you with a bucket of fresh-baked mini muffins. The creative morning menu (served Sunday only) includes orange cream cheese bagels, chocolate Belgian waffles, and fruit ambrosia; in addition to wraps, sandwiches, and salads for lunch ($5–8), try the Victorian Flair with your friends—dainty tea sandwiches, fruit, and bakery delights ($13–30) with a hot pot of herbal tea. Closed Sat.

🦞 ℐ Find your way into **Kloiber's Cobbler Eatery** (321-383-0689), 337 Washington Ave, for Joe's soup of the day ($3–4), quiche, and a variety of salads and sandwiches ($3–6). Joe also makes his fresh fruit cobbler from scratch *every* day. Hey, they have peanut butter and jelly on the menu. How much more down-home can you get?

🦞 ℐ You just can't help stopping at the **Moonlight Drive In Restaurant** (321-267-8222), 1515 S Washington Ave, when you see the big neon moon sign. Since 1964, it's been family owned and operated, and is an excellent example of the restaurants that used to line US 1 during the hey-day of the early space program. The cozy restaurant evokes a sock hop, with its '50s and '60s pop icons and black-and-white tiled floor, but you

Sandra Friend

MR. ROCK SHOWS OFF THE MENU AT DIXIE CROSS-
ROADS

🦐 🛶 If there's one place that defines Titusville, it's **Dixie Crossroads Seafood Restaurant** (321-268-5000; www.dixiecrossroads .com), 1475 Garden St, a success story to warm the heart. I've heard owner Laurilee Thompson tell it several times, but it never ceases to amaze me how she came up with the idea of cooking rock shrimp – long known as "peanuts," "trash," or "hardheads," to Atlantic shrimpers—by splitting and broiling them like lobster at a time her father was struggling to pay off his new shrimp boat. In 1983, the restaurant opened to feature these unusually tasty shrimp, with just thirty seats. Today, they can handle hundreds at a time—and they do. On any visit to the coast, we make a beeline here, and it's not just because it's the rock shrimp capital of the world (and I always order it), but it's the savvy, conservation-minded Captain Laurilee, who's always fun to talk to about her latest project to show-case the region's natural treasures, be it ramping up plans for the upcoming Space Coast Wildlife and Birding Festival (see *Festivals*), which she helped found, or heading out on a kayak trip by moonlight to see bioluminescence in the Indian River Lagoon. That's the dedication you get from a family with six

can also eat your meals right at your car with their curbside service. Choose from comfort sandwiches ($1–5)—BLTs, burgers, roast beef, and subs—or dinners of shrimp, clams, or fish-and-chips ($7–10). But the big reason it gets busy here are the milkshakes, which come in 16 flavors, and the ice cream goodies, ranging from soft-serve cones and sundaes to parfaits and banana splits.

🦐 Watch cooks rustle up mountains of biscuits, big bowls of gravy, and piles of sausage links at this bustling short-order favorite, **Your Place Restaurant** (321-268-1811), 605 Hopkins Ave, where they serve breakfast all day—and grits worth the visit. Items like corned beef hash, sirloin and egg, chicken-fried steak, country-fried steak, and ham are among the mainstays, along with overstuffed three egg omelets, French toast, and pancakes. $3–8, cash only.

generations of roots right here. The restaurant complex is an experience in itself. Mazy pathways lead through a jungle-like garden on one side of the parking lot, and next to the building is a giant pond where imported Egyptian fish swim. Colorful murals of natural Florida are everywhere, and there are Mr. and Mrs. Rock Shrimp, life size and in living pink, for you to take your picture with. If you have to wait for a table (and you often do), don't worry; there's plenty to see, and the staff may hand out hot corn fritters (another family favorite) to keep those tummy grumbles down. Once inside, you'll notice the lively, rustic rooms flanked with colorful murals as well as original wildlife paintings from local artists. As you sit down, you are immediately greeted with more corn fritters! Don't fill up, because the dinner portions are generous, and this is where you'll find the largest selection of shrimp anywhere. Dixie Crossroads shrimp come straight off their own fleet of commercial shrimpers and are then processed only a few blocks away at their own Wild Ocean Seafood Market (see *Seafood Market*). The assortment of shrimp is outstanding; you'll wonder why you haven't seen these varieties before now. Choose from pinks, hoppers, brownies, whites, royal reds, Cape Canaveral browns, and the shrimp that made them famous—the rock shrimp. This crustacean looks a bit prehistoric, but tastes like a mini lobster. And they'll cook them any way you like—blackened, fried, sautéed, broiled, and even crunchy with coconut. Dip them in homemade sauces like spicy orange mango (great with rock shrimp) or mandarin orange sesame (goes well with blue crab claws). Shrimp is their forte, of course, but the restaurant also serves a huge selection of freshly caught fish; steaks and chicken are there for the landlubbers in your party. Open daily. Beef entrées ($13–34) include a 20-ounce porterhouse and lobster dinners; fish ($9–17), from salmon to cod and tilapia; shellfish ($9–35), with all-you-can-eat snow crab; and the famous shrimp ($11–35) served by the dozen, prepped your way; combos and platters available too. Yes, there is a kid's menu—and my husband drew the artwork for it *years* before we met.

BAKERIES, COFFEE SHOPS, CHOCOLATES, AND ICE CREAM

Cocoa

There was quite a line along the sidewalk for **Ossorio** (321-639-2423), 316 Brevard Ave, thanks to the delectable ice cream inside this colorful coffee shop and ice cream parlor. They serve flatbread pizza and sandwiches, too, but you have to get in the door, first!

Since 1975, the **Village Ice Cream and Sandwich Shop** (321-632-2311), 120 Harrison St, has keep the wandering villagers of Cocoa happy. They feature Thumann's deli products and serve sandwiches as well as 30 flavors of organic ice cream in cones, shakes, and sundaes. Grab a cappuccino here, too!

Cocoa Beach

Great fitness shakes, smoothies, and coffees are at the **Juice 'N' Java Café**

(321-784-4044), 20 N Brevard Ave, which also serves healthy soups and sandwiches.

At the Cocoa Beach Pier, grab a cool treat at **Ricky's Ice Cream Parlor** (321-868-2990), then play some video games in the arcade. Ricky's sundaes, malts, and shakes ($3–5) are made with Edy's Ice Cream.

Melbourne

The 905 Café (321-952-1672), 905 E New Haven Ave, is primarily a coffee shop with espresso drinks, beer and wine, and a great assortment of interesting desserts, but they also serve light salads and sandwiches on croissants, bagels, wraps, or wheat, white, or rye breads.

Titusville

One bite of a chocolate decadence brownie at **Caffe Chocolat** (321-267-1713; www.caffechocolat.com), 304 S Washington Ave, and I was in fudgy love. They make their own fudge and truffles, and prepare a special Chocolate Fondue Tray (call 24 hours ahead, $10 per person), a do-it-yourself decadent treat loaded with fresh fruits, graham crackers, pretzels, chips, angel-food or pound cake, and marshmallows ready to dip into melted Belgian chocolate. Coffee drinks include creative twists like hazelnut biscotti latte and caramel hazelnut divinity. Now it's not *just* about the chocolate here—they have a section devoted to gourmet foods, including specialty beers and wines, and prepare breakfast quiches, burritos, and scones ($1–7) and lunch sandwiches, salads, soups, wraps, and panini ($5–8)—portobello mushroom on ciabatta, anyone? Closed Sun.

At the **Sunrise Bread Company** (321-268-1009; www.nbbd.com/ bakery), 315 S Hopkins Ave, the hardest part is deciding which of a dozen-plus handcrafted breads you want to take with you. The mural-wrapped bakery offers Old World Spelt, Raspberry Swirl made with unbleached white flour, Wild Rice & Sweet Onion, and so many more, $4–6.

❋ Selective Shopping

Cocoa

The downtown historic district of the City of Cocoa, **Historic Cocoa Village** (321-631-9075; www.cocoavillage .com), is a true Main Street USA. Stroll throughout the tree-lined streets, stopping in on the charming mix of shops and boutiques— antiques, jewelry, arts, crafts—and fabulous gourmet restaurants. Saunter down the brick walkways to the waterfront park. Take a tour through 20th-century Classic Revival architecture at the **Porcher House** (see *Historic Sites*) on the walking tour. You will want to spend the day here to take it all in. Some suggested stops:

You don't have to be a kid to love **Annie's Toy Chest** (321-632-5890), 405 Brevard Ave, for elegant dolls, plush animals, and wacky wind-up toys.

Antiques and Collectibles Too! (321-632-9924), 115 Harrison St, captured my husband's attention for the better part of an hour. It's crammed throughout its rooms with dealers' booths filled with just about everything, including something you won't find in most antique malls—lots of ephemera and collectibles associated with space exploration.

An appealing array of scents surrounds you at **The Bath Cottage** (321-690-BATH; www.bathcottage

.com), 425 Brevard St, where you'll find candles, gels, and bath accessories.

The Book Xchg (321-639-5624), 604 Brevard Ave, has a cozy nook to read in while your friends are perusing the tall shelves piled up with paperbacks. It's a mix of new and used, including Sunshine State Standards books, and greeting cards.

Bushveld (321-427-3085, 321-363-4334, or 1-800-386-7407), 26 Oleander St, displays an artful collection of African crafts, including furniture and fabrics.

Country Craft Corner (321-639-3189), 117 Harrison St, has Christmas miniatures, vintage tchotchkes, vases, and fine glassware.

Downtown Divas (321-433-0727; www.downtowndivas.com), 411 Brevard St, offers elegant, chic fashions.

Inside the old Post Office, the **Florida Historical Society Print Shoppe** (321-690-0099; www.floridabooks .net), 435 Brevard Ave, contains the largest selection of Florida history books you'll find in a single bookstore in the entire state. Only the Florida State Archives and other university collections have access to more books on Florida's lengthy past.

I found "hiker casual" wear at **Green Apples Boutique** (321-635-8728), 111 Harrison St, including Life is good, Merrell footwear, Grassroots shirts, and dressy eco-friendly gear.

✈ At **Knit & Stitch** (321-632-4579), 15 Stone St, colorful skeins of yarn are piled up, inviting closer inspection of both raw materials and finished pieces.

A young lad pulled a card trick on me at **Magic Dove** (321-433-1130), 639 Brevard Ave, and I'm not sure I figured it out yet. Or is there such a thing as a marked deck? Open daily, this is a fun little shop full of magic tricks, novelty items, and secrets from magicians. Learn a trick or two, bring the kids for free animal balloons and face painting, and grab a bag of popcorn—you're about to be entertained.

Nature's Haven (321-632-1221; http://2006.naturespirit.com), 602 Brevard Ave, cured my sinus headache with an aromatherapy tonic, and that made for a happier afternoon of browsing the shops. They have a large selection of pure botanical essence oils and their own blends. With an accent of New Age books and minerals, and shawls and covers direct from Rajasthan—it's mystical, moody, and fun.

The rich red and gold exterior draws you toward **Something Different** (321-633-0113), 121 Harrison St, an elegant home decor shop with thematic floral pillows and vases.

Threadneedle Street Mall, 402 Brevard Ave, is an old-fashioned 1920s arcade building filled with shops like Candles by G (321-638-4131), with wind chimes and handbags; and Lin's Collectibles (321-639-2829), with vintage lamps and home decor. There's an Old Time Photo studio, too!

A co-op for local artists since 1990, **Space Coast Crafters** (321-632-6553), 410 Brevard Ave, has woodturning and wearable art, fused dichroic glass, ceramics and photography, and Karen Jasiunas's handpainted wine glasses, turntables, and mugs.

Since 1973, **The Strawberry Patch** (321-632-5991), 423 Brevard Ave, has carried fine gifts, greeting cards, and vintage furnishings.

Good things are in small packages at **The Toybox** (321-632-2411), 419 Brevard Ave, where the dollhouses and miniatures are tiny bits of perfection; I love the scale model lighthouse with jelly jar light.

What You Love to Do (321-504-0304; www.whatyoulovetodo.com), 602 Brevard Ave, is just that—a shop for the artistically minded by artists. "Open the door to all possibilities," says the vermillion door, and inside, captivating pieces by local artists, including Kevin Doyle's amazing one-of-a-kind mosaic guitar and mosaic mirrors. Smaller objects, like the handcrafted leather books, make affordable and beautiful gifts.

Woods and Water (321-433-2077), 304 Brevard Ave, sells Wild Cotton tees decorated with Florida wildlife designs, boat ornaments, hiking sticks, and Jimmy Buffet T-shirts, too.

From the outside, **What Not's Old Time General Store** (321-258-3888), 409B Delannoy Ave, looks like they're selling kitchenware circa 1949, with Pyrex, Corning, and Fireware plates, platters, and glass-covered baking dishes lining the shelves and sitting atop antique stoves and countertops. But it's a tiny grocery store, too, with cold drinks, snacks, and enough consumables to feed folks who come in from the marina looking to restock their pantries.

Cocoa Beach

The Dinosaur Store (407-783-7300; www.dinosaurstore.com), 299 W Cocoa Beach Causeway (FL 520), has a large selection of museum-quality dinosaur fossils, along with minerals, amber, and meteorites (see *Dinosaurs*).

On a trip to the beach in the early 80s, it was the biggest thrill to step into

Ron Jon Surf Shop (321-799-8888; www.ronjons.com), 4151 N Atlantic Ave, and pick out my own collectible tropical "World Famous Ron Jon T-shirt" from the rainbow of colors along the wall. These folks pretty much defined the Cocoa Beach scene back then, with the largest selection of surf clothes, surfboards, surf gear, swimsuits, and tropical print shirts you could find under one giant roof. Okay, so today they have some competition in the "big surf shop" market, but they're the rockin' granddaddy of them all, and they're still downright impressive. They call it the Surf Palace—an art deco creation of 52,000 square feet with a waterfall and a great glass elevator inside, surfing celebrities dropping in for autographs, surf school, rentals for your beach vacation, and best of all, open 24 hours every day, just like the beach.

Frontenac

Between Cocoa and Titusville along US 1, the **Space Coast Flea Market** (321-631-0241) brings in hundreds of dealers with everything from farm fresh produce (especially citrus) to sports memorabilia, art, and the usual hordes of cheap Asian goods. Open Fri 8–5, Sat–Sun 7–5.

Indialantic

Eclectic shops and surfer stores are found in Indialantic, like **Kite World** (321-725-8336; www.kiteworld.com), 109 S Miramar Ave, which has a large selection of unique kites and can also teach you kiteboarding; and the **Longboard House** (321-951-0730), 101 Fifth Ave, which has a great selection of surfboards and beachwear. They opened in 1961, and now have more than 1,000 boards in stock of all shapes and sizes.

Melbourne

The mega-monster of local flea markets is the **Super Flea & Farmers Market** (321-242-9124; www.super fleamarket.com), 4835 W Eau Gallie Blvd, visible from I-95. Open Fri–Sun 9–4, with vendors hawking gemstones, silk and live trees, handbags, puppies and birds, new and used books, and a lot more.

Melbourne, Historic Downtown

A great selection of specialty shops, antiques stores, restaurants, and art studios is found all along New Haven and Strawbridge Aves. **Apple Barrel Gifts** (321-956-0026), 901 E New Haven Ave, has gourmet foods and gift baskets. **Antiques by Heidi** (321-722-2112), 821 E New Haven Ave, and **Seldom Scene** (321-768-8442), 724 E New Haven, have your grandmother's antiques and collectibles. Interesting creations by local artists are at **Heart Strings** (321-724-0111), 802 E New Haven Ave. Fine ladies' apparel, evening wear, and Brighton shoes and purses are at **Isabella's Ladies Apparel** (321-952-4489), 845 E New Haven Ave. You'll enjoy stopping in for some Turkish tea at **Shading International** (321-951-7560), 812 E Strawbridge, which has a fabulous collection of Turkish and Oriental rugs and Bursa silk scarves. The **Indian River Soap Co.** (321-723-6464), 804 E New Haven Ave, makes their own natural soaps on the premises, and the **Baby Patch** (321-676-7590; www.e-babypatch.com), 800 E New Haven Ave, is the place to go for complete layette and nursery furniture; individual themed vignettes are displayed. The real find at Baby Patch is Tropical Rockers, which has handcrafted wooden rocking helicopters, motorcycles, giraffes, alligators, dragons, and, of course, horses.

Satellite Beach

Karen & Charles L. Smith (321-773-0506), 309 Gemini Dr, often show their landscape and portrait oils at galleries along the Space Coast, but you can also see their works by appointment.

Titusville

You'll find a neatly organized selection of used books at **The Book Rack** (321-264-0808), 346 S Washington, awaiting perusal 10–6 weekdays, 10–4 Sat.

With two stories and 40-plus dealers in a vintage downtown home, **Dusty Rose Antique Mall** (321-269-5526; www.dustyroseantiques.com), 1101 S Washington Ave, hands-down has more ephemera packed in per square inch here than any other store in town, especially after 25 years in business. I found a Victrola with record albums, sheet music, fine china, Vaseline and carnival glass, and that was just on a quick browse. Plan to spend some time sifting for treasures in this shop.

Find your dream home in miniature at **Jim's Dollhouses & Gifts** (321-267-4995), 329 S Washington Ave, featuring "real good toys" and lovely lifestyles at 1-inch scale, the handcrafted furnishings ranging from casual to fine. A hobby store shares the space, so browse for model planes, trains, and automobiles as well.

The classiest presentation of antiques I've seen yet, **Inventory** (321-269-7175), 305 S Washington Ave, showcases thematic groupings of vintage platters and cafeteria trays, cookbooks, skeins of yarn, and children's toys. An artful use of space creates an extremely appealing place to shop.

ANTIQUES IN TITUSVILLE

At **River Road Mercantile** (321-264-2064), 219 S Washington Ave, I've found delightful Old Florida ephemera with which to delight my hubby. On this visit, the thick pottery bowls caught my eye, but you never know what you might find—their new location lends itself to more outdoor and garden art.

"For surfers, by surfers," is the motto of **Stickee Surf Shop** (321-269-2203; www.stickeesurfshop.com), 326 S Washington Ave, the place to gear up before you head out to Canaveral National Seashore.

FARMERS MARKETS, FRUIT STAND AND SEAFOOD MARKET Looking for fresh local produce? Head down to the Myrt Tharpe Square Gazebo in Historic **Cocoa Village** for the weekly farmer's market, held each Wednesday 11:30–3, where fresh-baked breads, pies, and cookies accent the fresh produce and flowers.

The second Saturday of each month, the city of **Palm Bay** brings together farmers, crafters, and antique sellers for a grand farmer's and flea market

(321-952-3441) with live entertainment, bounce house for the kids, munchies, and more.

I couldn't help but grab a bag of Ruby Red grapefruit at **Harvey's Groves** (321-636-6072 or 1-800-327-9312; www.harveysgroves.com), 3700 US 1, Rockledge, one of Florida's classic citrus shops. It still has that 1940s feel, complete with an authentic packing house. The family owns more than 400 acres of citrus groves on Merritt Island, so you know you're taking home authentic Indian River fruit, grown right along the lagoon, where they started their business in 1924. All fruit is handpicked and hand-packed, and yes, they'll offer you samples of fruit and orange juice when you stop in. You'll also find delectable candies, fudge, and Florida souvenir items in their signature shop along US 1; there are two satellite locations in high-traffic areas along FL A1A in Cocoa Beach, and along US 192 in Melbourne. Open daily during season, and they do ship.

Founded as the Cape Canaveral Shrimp Company, **Wild Ocean Seafood Market** (321-269-1116 or 1-866-WILD-OCEAN; www.wildocean market.com), 688 Park Ave, Titusville, is where Dixie Crossroads (see *Eating Out*) gets their shrimp—it's all in the Thompson family. Now you can take some home to cook, too! A second location is now open in Cape Canaveral at 710 Scallop Drive (321-783-2300); open daily.

✳ **Entertainment**

Cocoa
Built in 1924, the 500-seat **Historic Cocoa Village Playhouse** (321-636-5050; www.cocoavillage.com), 300 Brevard Ave, is a quaint theater in the

heart of the village shopping district, and listed on the National Register of Historic Places. You can also take in a play or musical at the intimate **Phoenix Theatre** (321-777-8936), 817 E Strawbridge Ave.

Cocoa Beach
The fabulous 289-seat **Surfside Playhouse** (321-783-3127; www.surfside players.com), Fifth St S and Brevard Ave, Cocoa Beach, has been around since 1959 and is the only live theater on the barrier islands.

Spend an evening enjoying cool drinks and smooth jazz at **Heidi's Jazz Club** (321-783-4559; www .heidisjazzclub.com), 7 N Orlando Ave, a happening place where performers like Phil Flanagan, Boots Randolph, and Steve Cox show up to play. Open 3 PM–1 AM; open jam nights on Sunday evenings after 7 PM.

Melbourne
The Maxwell C. King Center for the Performing Arts (321-242-2219; www.kingcenter.com), 3865 Wickham Rd, offers Broadway shows, dance, opera, and children's theater in a spacious 2,000-seat facility.

Titusville
The historic **Emma Parrish Theater**, 301 Julia St, is home to the **Titusville Players** (321-268-3711; www.nbbd .com/godo/tpi), who started their troupe in 1962 and continue to dazzle today with productions like *Ragtime* and *Arsenic and Old Lace*.

❋ Special Events
Year-round, first Friday of the month: Listen to some music at **Jazz Friday** at the Brevard Museum of Art & Science (www.artandscience.org/events .html; see *Museums*).

Year-round, second Friday of the month: The shops stay open late, so saunter down to Historic Cocoa Village for **Friday Fest**, an evening of shopping, browsing, music, and art.

January: Now, after a decade, one of the largest birding events in the United States, the annual **Space Coast Birding and Wildlife Festival** (321-268-5224) is one of the largest regional events of the year, with more than 30 field trips, seminars, and workshops; I'm pleased to say I've presented a few over the years. This nature-based trade show draws a large crowd of birders from miles around. Boating, kayak, and hiking trips take you into significant natural areas of Florida's Space Coast, home of the largest collection of endangered wildlife and plants in the continental United States.

February: The **Grant Seafood Festival** (www.grantseafoodfestival.com), held the third weekend in the tiny south Brevard County village of Grant, serves up good eats while benefiting community projects such as the restoration and care of the Grant Historical Home and Grant Library. Enjoy more than 100 crafters and succulent seafood, presented entirely by local volunteers; free admission

March: The annual **Cocoa Village Spring Gallery Walk** fills the historic district with fine arts and crafts.

April: The harbinger of spring, the annual **Ron Jon Easter Surf Festival** (321-453-5352) is held at Shepard Park at the foot of FL 520 and the Cocoa Beach Pier. The event features the best professional surfing along with amateur competitions and various vendors, and has been going strong since 1964!

Since 1976, the **Indian River Festival** (321-267-3036; www.nbbd.com/festivals/IRF) has been just good old-fashioned family fun in Titusville, with an arts and crafts show, live national and local entertainment, duck race, river raft race, antique and custom car shows.

Out of 3,000 artists who apply, only 250 are selected to display their crafts and artistry at the annual **Melbourne Art Festival** (321-722-1964; www.melbournearts.org).

June–July: Turtle hatchlings race from their sandy nest to the ocean in a ritual that has been performed for millions of years. A 12-mile strip from Melbourne Beach to Sebastian Inlet is heavily monitored, as this is the largest nesting site in the United States. To see this natural phenomenon, go on a **Turtle Walk**. The reservations-only 2-mile walk lasts from 9 PM until about midnight. Contact the Sea Turtle Preservation Society (321-676-1701; www.seaturtlespacecoast.org) or Sebastian Inlet State Park (see *Parks*) for more information. If you walk on your own, do not shine flashlights or use flash photography, as this disorients the hatchlings.

August–September: More than 500 surfers converge for a competition on the waves off Lori Wilson Park in Cocoa Beach for the annual **Cocoa Beach Surf Company/National Kidney Foundation Pro-Am Surf Festival** (1-800-927-9659; www.kidneyfla.org), Labor Day Weekend.

October: **Boo at the Zoo**, mid-October. Bring the kids for this slightly scary special event at the Brevard Zoo (see *Zoo*).

With more than a hundred artisans displaying their creations all weekend, start your Christmas shopping early at the **Fall Arts & Crafts Festival**, Historic Downtown Melbourne (321-724-1741; www.downtownmelbourne.com), mid-October.

November: **Space Coast State Fair** (321-639-1204; www.cocoaexpo.com/fair). Held for 10 days in mid-November, this large-scale county fair features all the critters you can think of, unlimited rides on the midway for thrills, live acts like Robinson's World Famous Racing Pigs, and musical guests. Held at the Andretti Thrill Park, Melbourne.

Now in its 45th year, the **Space Coast Arts Festival** (321-784-3322; www.spacecoastartfestival.com) is the biggest art gathering on the Central Florida coast.

December: Get more shopping in during the **Downtown Cocoa Village Winter Craft Fair** (321-631-9075), first Saturday, with hundreds of artists displaying their wares in an already shopper-friendly venue.

Ring in the New Year with the whole family at the **First Night** celebration in downtown Cocoa Village, a family-friendly celebration of the arts; fee.

Tampa Bay 4

TAMPA AND HILLSBOROUGH
COUNTY

PINELLAS COUNTY:
ST. PETERSBURG, CLEARWATER
AND TARPON SPRINGS

TAMPA BAY

From land, air, or sea, there is no missing Tampa Bay. It is one of Florida's most distinctive geologic features, the largest open-water estuary in the state, a shallow basin 12 feet deep on average, yet covering 400 square miles. Its barrier islands showcase a 35-mile ribbon of white-sand beaches on the Gulf of Mexico. Ancient tribes settled on its shores, building ceremonial and village mounds in protected coves from which they could launch their longboats to ply the bounteous waters for fish. Europeans first reached its waters in the early 1500s— Pánfilo de Narváez, Hernando de Soto, and others; Spanish conquistadors intent on discovering gold. As the Dutch and English followed, they explored and mapped the channels and rivers flowing into the bay. After the American Revolution, the United States purchased Florida from Spain in 1821, and European settlers began to trickle into the region, founding a settlement around Fort Brooke.

In the 1850s Tampa served as the end of the line for cattle drovers in North and Central Florida, who brought their herds to the docks for Captain James McKay to supervise shipping to Cuba in exchange for gold. As a result, Tampa Bay was a major target for the Union Blockading Squadron during the civil war, as many successful Confederate blockade runners hid their ships in the countless channels and estuaries, seeking the opportunity to break for open water and escape. Bringing goods back to the region, they helped support Florida's war effort. Union gunboats shelled downtown Tampa on several occasions, damaging the hotel and surrounding shopping district. The region's growth accelerated in 1884 when industrialist Henry Plant extended his railroad, determining that Tampa Bay would make a perfect port for his export operations. Jules Verne foresaw Florida's future in space travel when he set *From the Earth to the Moon* along the bay's shores.

As in most parts of Florida, the development of air and naval bases during World War II accelerated the region's population growth when servicemen decided to settle their families near the bases after their tour of duty was complete. The advent of television showcased vibrant downtown St. Petersburg and the sparkling sands of Clearwater and Treasure Island, enticing visitors. Best known for its beach destinations, the Tampa Bay area has much to offer the traveler eager to explore.

TAMPA AND HILLSBOROUGH COUNTY

C overing more than 1,000 square miles of Florida's west coast, Hillsborough County forms an arc around the northern and eastern sides of Tampa Bay. Dutch cartographer Bernard Romans named this region and its major river in 1772 in honor of Lord Willis Hills, secretary of state for the British colonies. Soon after Florida became a US territory, the federal government established Fort Brooke as a frontier outpost, and the surrounding settlement became the town of **Tampa** in 1855.

After Henry Plant brought his railroad to the region, he invested heavily in Tampa. He started a steamship line from Tampa to Key West and Havana and opened a grand $3-million-dollar, 511-room Moorish-themed hotel downtown in 1891. This grand structure is topped with distinctive minarets and is now a museum honoring Plant's legacy and a National Historic Landmark. Plant continued his rail line east through the county, where **Plant City** was founded. Now known as the Strawberry Capital of the World, this bustling city is worth a visit for its excellent fresh produce, fine family restaurants, and distinctive historic downtown shopping district.

In 1885 Don Vicente Martinez Ybor, an exiled Spanish cigar manufacturer from Cuba, moved his business from Key West to a hammock east of Tampa; soon, many factories and workers followed. The surrounding settlement became **Ybor City** (pronounced *EE-bore*), a community of Spanish, German, Italian, and Cuban families with nearly twelve thousand people working in more than two hundred factories. Ybor City remained the Cigar Capital of the World until Cuban tobacco was embargoed when Fidel Castro came to power.

Tampa's first developer, O. H. Platt, created **Hyde Park** in 1886. It's a neighborhood of bungalows and Queen Anne–style architecture that retains its old-time charm today within **South Tampa**. Since then, it seems that the land boom around the bay never stopped. In 1924, David P. Davis "rebuilt" two natural islands at the mouth of the Hillsborough River to create the **Davis Islands.** A similar fill project connects **Rocky Point** to Clearwater via the Courtney Campbell Causeway. Two major World War II airfields, MacDill Air Force Base and Drew Airfield, were responsible for a huge influx of residents that increased the

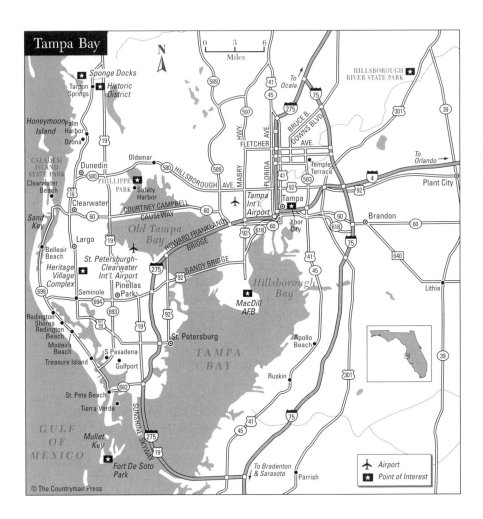

population density, creating **Brandon** to the east and **Town & Country** and **Temple Terrace** surrounding **North Tampa. Lutz** is a community to the northwest established by German immigrants.

Farming is still an important part of life on the eastern side of the county. There are the rural communities of **Thonotosassa** along the Hillsborough River on US 301, **Alafia** and **Lithia** along the Alafia River on FL 39 south of Plant City, and **Mango** and **Ruskin,** known worldwide for tomatoes, on US 301 south. Also in the southeastern section of the county are the residential communities of **Riverview** and **Sun City Center** along US 301. South on US 41, **Apollo Beach** provides waterfront access for visitors, and **Gibsonton** has a storied history as a "carny village" where many off-season circus performers have lived.

GUIDANCE In downtown Tampa you'll find all of your questions answered at the large **Tampa Bay & Company & Gift Shop** (813-223-2752 or 1-800-44-TAMPA; www.VisitTampaBay.com), 615 Channelside Dr, Suite 108A. In Ybor City stop by the **Ybor City Visitor Information Center** (813-248-3712 or 1-877-9-FIESTA), 1600 E Eighth Ave, Suite B104; and in Plant City pick up information (including a walking tour brochure) at the **Greater Plant City Chamber of Commerce** (813-754-7045; www.plantcity.org), 1702 N Park Rd.

GETTING THERE *By car:* Most major regional highways intersect in Tampa. **I-4** provides an eastern connection from Orlando, while **I-75** links the region to North Florida and the remainder of the Gulf Coast. **I-275** leads drivers down into the heart of the city and over to St. Petersburg. The **Veterans Expressway,** heading north from Tampa International Airport, becomes the **Suncoast Parkway,** which ties into Pasco, Hernando, and Citrus Counties to the north.

By air: **Tampa International Airport** (813-870-8700 or 1-800-767-8882; www .TampaAirport.com) offers continual flights to national and international destinations, with major carriers such as AirTran, America, Delta, Frontier, Song, Spirit, United, US Airways, British Airways, AirCanada, and more. Located at the intersection of FL 60 and the Veterans Expressway, the airport borders Tampa Bay just west of downtown.

By rail: **AMTRAK** (813-221-7600) has a passenger station in the historic Union Station in downtown Tampa, 601 N Nebraska Ave.

By bus: **Greyhound** (813-229-2174 or 1-800-231-2222) stops in downtown Tampa at 610 Polk St.

GETTING AROUND *By car:* Finding your way around downtown Tampa can be confusing due to all the one-way streets and flyover ramps. Thankfully, there are many directional signs to guide you toward Channelside and Ybor City.

US 41 and **US 92** (Dale Mabry) slice right through the city's neighborhoods, while **US 301** keeps to the city's rural eastern fringe, paralleling both **I-75** and **US 41,** which stays close to the bay as it heads south through Gibsonton, Apollo Beach, and Ruskin. **FL 60** provides access between Brandon through South Tampa and the Airport/Westside Area, becoming the Courtney Campbell Causeway to Clearwater, and **CR 39** ties together the rural communities of Plant City and Alafia on the county's eastern border. **US 92** connects Plant City with Lakeland and Tampa.

By bus: **HARTline** (Hillsborough Area Regional Transit Authority, 813-975-2160; www.hartline.org) runs 207 buses on 26 city routes. The rubber-tired In Town Trolley runs north–south through downtown (50¢) and connects to the electric streetcar system.

By streetcar: Great for a downtown tour, the **TECO Line Streetcar System** (813-254-4278; www.tecolinestreetcar.org) offers 11 stops that link downtown to the Port of Tampa at Channelside and Ybor City. Fares are cash only ($2 per trip), but you can buy a day pass ($4) or multiday pass; seniors and kids are half-price. It's a fun trip, too! See *Streetcar Rides.*

By taxi: **United Cab of Tampa** (813-251-5555; www.unitedtaxicab.com) and **Yellow Cab Company of Tampa** (813-253-3590). Taxis must be called in advance from your location. The average cost of a taxi fare from the airport to downtown is $20. Most of the major hotels offer shuttles to the airport and attractions.

PARKING There is metered street parking throughout **downtown Tampa,** but finding a space can be downright difficult except on Sunday. Try one of the many parking garages, including those on Ashley Street and at Channelside. In **Ybor City** you'll find parking garages, flat lots, and metered street parking on most of the in-town streets; fee.

MEDICAL EMERGENCIES For emergency care visit **Tampa General Hospital** (813-844-7000; www.tgh.org), One Davis Boulevard, downtown; they have a trauma unit and emergency room.

✳ To See

ARCHEOLOGICAL SITES **Fort Brooke** was the end of the line on the Fort King Military Trail from Ocala to Tampa Bay, and a crucial outpost during the Seminole Wars of the early 1800s where the Hillsborough River empties into the bay. Unfortunately, it and other archeological sites in downtown Tampa vanished under centuries of building. Walk up Franklin Street and through the plazas to see many blue signs that explain what was once there and is now buried beneath concrete and steel.

ART GALLERIES

Tampa—Airport/Westside
At the **Tampa International Airport** (see *Getting There*), visitors enjoy a diverse mix of tapestries, sculptures, and paintings throughout the high-traffic areas. Airside E is the home of seven original historic Works Progress Administration murals painted by George Snow Hill in 1939, depicting mythical and historic figures that contributed to the history of human-powered flight, from Icarus and Daedalus to Tony Jannus, the pilot who made the world's first commercial flight—between St. Petersburg and Tampa, in 1914.

A TECO STREETCAR STOPS FOR PASSENGERS IN YBOR CITY

Sandra Friend

Tampa—Downtown and Vicinity
Artists Unlimited (813-229-5958), 223 N 12th St, encompasses working studios and gallery space, as well as a sculpture garden. Open Mon–Fri 9–6, Sat by appointment.

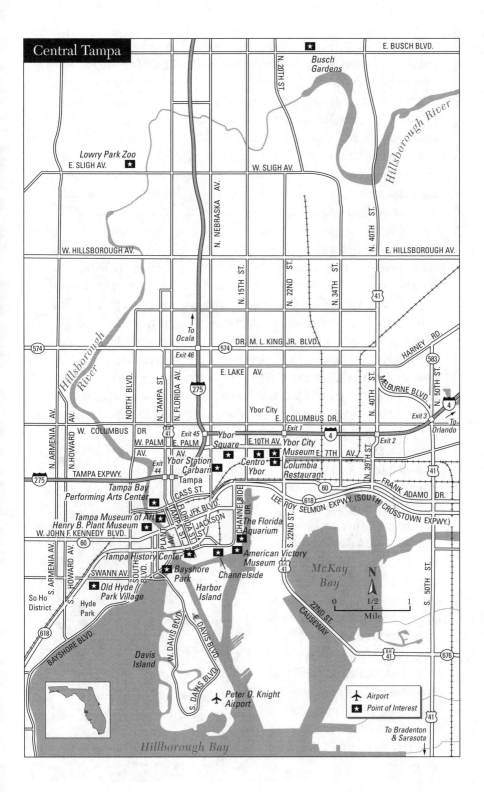

Central Tampa

E. BUSCH BLVD.

Busch Gardens

E. SLIGH AV.

Lowry Park Zoo
E. SLIGH AV.

W. SLIGH AV.

W. HILLSBOROUGH AV.

E. HILLSBOROUGH AV.

N. 20TH ST.
N. NEBRASKA AV.
N. 15TH ST.
N. 22ND ST.
N. 34TH ST.
N. 40TH ST.

Hillsborough River

574

Hillsborough River

To Ocala

Exit 46

DR. M. L. KING JR. BLVD.

574

E. LAKE AV.

HARNEY RD.

583

275

NORTH BLVD.
N. TAMPA ST.
N. FLORIDA AV.

Ybor City

E. COLUMBUS DR.

Exit 1

N. 40TH ST.

MELBURNE BLVD.

Exit 3

N. 50TH ST.

4

To Orlando

N. ARMENIA AV.
N. HOWARD AV.

W. COLUMBUS DR
W. PALM AV.
E. PALM AV.

Exit 45

Ybor Square

E.10TH AV.

Ybor City Museum

E 7TH AV.

Exit 2

N. 39TH ST.

41

275

TAMPA EXPWY.

Exit 44

Ybor Station
Carbarn
Tampa

CASS ST.

Centro Ybor

Columbia Restaurant

60

FRANK ADAMO DR.

Tampa Bay Performing Arts Center

JFK BLVD.

CHANNELSIDE DR.

LEE ROY SELMON EXPWY. (SOUTH CROSSTOWN EXPWY.)

618

Tampa Museum of Art
Henry B. Plant Museum
W. JOHN F. KENNEDY BLVD.

TAMPA ST.
FLORIDA AV.

JACKSON ST.

The Florida Aquarium

S. 22ND ST.

60

S. 50TH ST.

S. ARMENIA AV.
S. HOWARD AV.

Tampa History Center

Bayshore Park

American Victory Museum

Channelside

McKay Bay

N

SWANN AV.

SOUTH BLVD.

Harbor Island

B.R. 41

0   1/2   1
Mile

So Ho District

Hyde Park

Old Hyde Park Village

618

W. DAVIS BLVD.
E. DAVIS BLVD.

Davis Island

22ND ST. CAUSEWAY

B.R. 41

676

BAYSHORE BLVD.

S. DAVIS BLVD.

Peter O. Knight Airport

41

To Bradenton & Sarasota

Hillborough Bay

✈ Airport
★ Point of Interest

AQUARIUMS ♿ ✎ With its creative, showy educational displays of regional and world marine life, **The Florida Aquarium** (813-273-4000 or 1-800-FL-FISH1; www.flaquarium.org), 701 Channelside Dr, Tampa, entertains and educates as it tells the story of Florida's unique water cycle, involving aquifers and springs, freshwater and saltwater. The multistory complex starts with an eerie entrance through a cave, where fish swim far above your head. You walk past alligators, turtles, and other freshwater creatures from our rivers and streams, reaching the mangrove estuary, where native birds flit above salt water teeming with fish. Climb up to the lookout to learn about exotic plants and animals in Florida, and then follow the path into the heart of the building for a nose-to-nose encounter with stingrays, massive groupers, and spiny lobsters. Descend into a coral reef grotto, with picture windows across the Coral Reef Gallery, modeled after a real reef in Florida's Dry Tortugas, so large that you feel like you're under the sea. Special exhibits house unusual sea creatures such as sea dragons and cuttlefish. Walk through Shark Bay, a 93,000 gallon saltwater exhibit, in a tunnel surrounded by sea turtles and sharks before you reach the lobby, where a massive touch tank lets you feel invertebrate sea life, and the outdoor Explore a Shore provides a wet playground for kids to let off steam. African black-footed penguins promenade with a trainer at 10, 1, and 3 daily and may grab your shoelaces! Browse through the large gift shop, and grab a snack at the restaurant. Interactive programs include "Swim with the Fishes," a SCUBA experience inside the Coral Reef Gallery where you wear the gear but stay at snorkeling depths; no SCUBA experience required, $75. Certifed SCUBA divers can "Dive with the Sharks" in the Shark Bay exhibit, $150. Daily Behind the Scenes Tours ($10 and up) let you tag along with biologists and trainers to the back side of the exhibits. Ecotours are also offered on the *Bay Spirit* (see *Ecotours*) into Tampa Bay. Open 9:30–5 daily except major holidays; adults $18, seniors 60 and over $15, children 3–12 $13, under 3 free.

CHILDREN AWAIT A CHANCE TO TOUCH A STINGRAY AT THE TOUCH TANK INSIDE THE FLORIDA AQUARIUM.

Sandra Friend

Tampa—Ybor City

In the artists' village (see *Selective Shopping*), watch Arnold Martinez perfect his craft at the **Arnold Martinez Art Gallery** (813-248-9572), 1909 N 19th St. He paints striking scenes of Tampa and Tampa history using media unique to Ybor City culture—Cuban coffee and tobacco juice.

The **Brad Cooper Gallery** (813-248-6098; www.bradcoopergallery.com), 1712 E Seventh Ave, showcases the works of established, mid-career and new contemporary artists in a large gallery space.

Look for whimsical creations at **Creatures of Delight** (813-248-4167; www.creaturesofdelightstudio.com), 1901 N 15th St.

Tampa—North Tampa

University of South Florida Contemporary Art Museum (813-974-4133; www.usfcam.usf.edu), 4202 E Fowler Ave, showcases scholarly exhibitions of contemporary art, hosts workshops and lectures, and organizes visiting artist presentations. Permanent holdings include an exquisite collection of African art as well as graphics and sculpture by acclaimed artists Roy Lichtenstein and James Rosenquist. Open Mon–Fri 10–5, Sat 1–4; free, parking $2.50.

ATTRACTIONS ♿ ✐ **Busch Gardens Tampa Bay** (813-987-5805 or 1-888-800-5447; www.buschgardens.com), 3605 E Bougainvillea Ave, Temple Terrace, is the region's only theme park and one I remember fondly from my youth when it was just a bird garden and a brewery tour. The brewery is long gone, but the expansions and renovations over the decades have transformed this 335-acre park into one of Florida's most fun family theme park destinations, mingling a zoological experience with thrill rides and elaborate stage productions. I loved it years ago when they added the Stanley Falls log flume and Congo River Rapids rides, and now the park is really hopping. The newest addition is Jungala, a 3-story family play area with mazes, climbing nets, tunnels, a zip line, orangutans, and Bengal tigers. Ride some of the world's top-rated roller coasters—Kumba, Montu, and Gwazi (a mammoth wooden coaster), as well as SheiKra, the first dive coaster in the United States, twisting and turning on its half-mile track like an African hawk at speeds up to 70 miles per hour. If rides aren't for you, never fear—the Serengeti Plain, the core of this park, has always made it an attraction to those who love to view wildlife. Seen from walkways, the Serengeti Express train ride, or the Skyride, this 65-acre habitat features hundreds of free-roaming African animals in open landscapes; Jambo Station lets you interact with them. The Myombe Preserve re-creates a rain forest

A GIRAFFE DELIGHTS VISITORS TO THE SERENGETI PLAIN AT BUSCH GARDENS TAMPA BAY

Busch Gardens Tampa Bay.

habitat for a tribe of great apes. The Bird Gardens are still here, too, with more than five hundred tropical birds in aviaries and enclosures. And yes, you can still pose with the famous Budweiser Clydesdale team. The little ones will love Land of the Dragons, a wet and dry playground with fanciful rides and a three-story treehouse; the Egypt area has a replica of King Tut's tomb and an archeological dig for kids. Combine this all with spectacular shows such as *KaTonga: Musical Tales From the Jungle,* a Broadway-quality spectacle with massive puppets, vibrant music, and African storytelling, and you'll see why a single day just isn't enough to take it all in. Adults $68, ages 3–9 $58, includes a second-day admission free; combination tickets with Adventure Island (see *Water Parks*), Sea-World, and Aquatica available. Parking fees of $9-10, depending on vehicle size.

🐾 ✍ Every time I pass **Dinosaur World** (813-717-9865; www.dinoworld.net), 5145 Harvey Tew Rd, Plant City, on my drive down I-4, I think about the Sinclair Dinoland exhibit I visited at the 1964 World's Fair. Today there's no larger exhibit of model dinosaurs in the world than you'll find here, towering over the pathways of a 12-acre forest. The irony, of course, is that dinosaurs never roamed Florida—it was under water at the time. After visiting the museum for some background on the Age of Dinosaurs, wander around and marvel at these massive, scientifically accurate models. Open 9–6 daily; adults $13, seniors $11, children 3–12 $10, with passes available.

BASEBALL Each March, the **New York Yankees** (813-879-2244 or 1-800-96-YANKS; www.legendsfieldtampa.com), One Steinbrenner Dr, Tampa, take over Legends Field for spring training, followed by their farm team affiliate, the **Tampa Yankees,** Apr–Aug.

CIGARS Cigar-making is a fine art perfected in Ybor City, so aficionados have several spots to pause, sample, and enjoy a tour. At **Gonzales y Martinez Cigar Company** (813-248-8210), 2103 E Seventh Ave (in the Columbia Restaurant building), learn about the area's tradition of cigar rolling. Visit the **King Corona Cigar Factory** (813-241-9109; www.kingcoronacigars.com), 1523 Seventh Ave, to sample the product of five generations of cigar crafters. You'll find Arturo Fuente products at the **Tampa Sweetheart Cigar Company** (813-247-3880; www.tampasweetheart.com), 1310 N 22nd St.

HISTORIC SITES Downtown **Ybor City** is a piece of Florida frozen in time from more than a century ago, with beautiful Spanish architecture. At Bird Ave and Florida Ave, River Tower Park (not currently open to the public) contains one of the region's oldest landmarks, the **Sulphur Spring Water Tower** along the Hillsborough River. Drive the streets of **Hyde Park** to enjoy homes ranging from Victorian gingerbread to 1920s bungalows.

MUSEUMS

Tampa—Downtown and Vicinity
✍ The SS *American Victory* is a floating slice of history, a World War II merchant marine ship under restoration as the **American Victory Mariners**

The region's largest and most grandiose historic site, circa 1891, is the **Tampa Bay Hotel**, 401 W Kennedy Blvd, built by railroad tycoon Henry Plant to draw tourists to Tampa on his rail line. The Henry B. Plant Museum (see *Museums*) offers public access to this immense structure along the Hillsborough River downtown; part of it also serves as the University of Tampa campus. In its heyday, the hotel had five hundred rooms and sprawled over 6 acres, with numerous outbuildings, such as a boathouse and casino. Plant appointed his hotel with 41 trainloads of French furnishings from Paris, and his wife sought out exotic tropical plants for the botanical garden along the river—still there for you to stroll through today. The hotel had Florida's very first elevator and an indoor pool when it opened on February 4, 1891. Serving nearly four thousand guests the first year, it put the then tiny city of Tampa on the map. But Plant's magical destination never quite caught on, and as it continued to lose money, he used his political influence to draw the base of operations for the Spanish-American War on-site. In 1898 troops camped around the hotel, and luminaries such as Teddy Roosevelt, Clara Barton, and Frederic Remington strode the grounds. After Plant died, his heirs sold the building to the city of Tampa. The first Florida State Fair was held on the grounds in 1904. Walk the ground-level halls of Tampa University to see the hotel's intriguing Moorish architecture; free.

Memorial & Museum Ship (813-228-8766; www.americanvictory.org), 705 Channelside Dr, adjoining the Florida Aquarium (see *Aquariums*). Admission adults $8, children $4, for self-guided tours Tue–Sat 10–4, Sun 12–4.

& ♂ Although the Florida State Fair is open in February only (see *Special Events*), the permanent **Cracker Country Folk Life Museum** (813-627-4225 or 1-800-345-3247 www.crackercountry.org) at the fairgrounds (5100 Orient Rd) celebrates rural Florida history and is open all year, Mon–Fri 8–5, with living-history exhibits and buildings from 1870 to 1912. See old-fashioned toys and candies, Octagon soap, and glass minnow traps at J. R. Terry Dry Goods, or visit the model railroad inside the Seaboard Air Line depot. Fee.

& A glimpse into the Gilded Age, the **Henry B. Plant Museum** (813-254-1891; www.plantmuseum.com), 401 W Kennedy Blvd, is the world's only railroad hotel museum, celebrating Plant's Tampa Bay Hotel (see *Historic Sites*). While most of the building and grounds now house Tampa University, the museum's niche allows them to showcase what travelers experienced back in Florida's first tourism boom. The distinctive mix of Moorish architecture and Victorian gingerbread makes this a one-of-a-kind historic building.

Start your tour with a 14-minute video that lays the backdrop for this grand hotel, and then walk the halls to immerse yourself in European opulence and to peek into rooms with original furniture in place. Notice the attention to detail, even in the balustrades and period lighting with Edison electric filament bulbs. In the Reading Room, almost every piece is original to the hotel, from the ebony woodwork to the inkwells and ceramic tile fireplace. The Museum Store offers original art, history books, and reproductions of the hotel's plates and coasters. As one of only two remaining Plant System hotels (the other, the Belleview Biltmore, is still in operation in Bellaire—see "Pinellas County"), it is a grand reminder of an era long past and well worth a visit. Open Tue–Sat 10–4, Sun noon–4; donation. Free parking available at the garage at North Blvd and North B Street.

& ✄ At the **Tampa Bay History Center** (813-228-0097; www.tampabayhistory center.org), 225 S Franklin St, browse through rolling collection cases and drawers with interpreted artifacts from the many periods of the city's history, such as the keel pin from the *Scottish Chief,* Captain McKay's blockade runner during the War Between the States, and Cuesta Ray cigar boxes from Ybor City's past. In addition to a Cracker homestead with computer stations, there are numerous hands-on activities and workstations for kids. Open Tue–Sat 10–5. Free.

Tampa—North Tampa

& ✄ The largest science center in the Southeast, the **Museum of Science & Industry** (813-987-6000 or 1-800-995-MOSI; www.mosi.org), 4801 E Fowler Ave, has an impressive array of hands-on science exhibits. Want to know what hurricane season is like? Step into the Gulf Coast Hurricane Chamber for a dose of 74-mile-per-hour winds. Or dare yourself to pedal the high-wire bicycle 30 feet above the ground. If you love dinosaurs, the *Diplodocus* skeletons that stand three stories tall won't disappoint. In addition to numerous permanent and rotating exhibits, MOSI offers a unique IMAX dome movie theater for a separate admission. Open Mon–Fri 9–5, Sat–Sun 9–6; adults $21, seniors $19, children 2–12 $17, under 2 free.

Tampa—Ybor City

& ✄ At the **Ybor City Museum State Park** (813-247-1434; www.ybor museum.org), 1818 E Ninth Ave, learn about this tight-knit community of cigar workers and their families by immersing into the past. A preserved half block includes three restored *casitas,* the traditional shotgun-style homes of cigar workers, with more undergoing restoration. The main museum is in the historic Ferlita Bakery building and focuses on the colorful history of the area. Walking tours of the city (see *Walking Tours*) depart the museum on Saturday at 10:30 AM; fee.

DEPICTION OF A CIGAR FACTORY FLOOR AT THE YBOR CITY MUSEUM

Sandra Friend

RAILROADIANA Henry Bradley Plant opened a new frontier when he brought the **Plant System** railroad into Tampa in 1884, linking his freight and passenger lines with a steamboat to Havana. All of the region's railroad history is tied to Plant, from the stately **Atlantic Coast Line depots** in Dunedin and Tarpon Springs to the amazing **Tampa Bay Hotel** (see *Historic Sites*), which Plant built as a tourist destination. As compensation for laying railroad track in Florida, the state gave Plant more than 750,000 acres of land, which was developed into cities such as **Plant City**; its depot, **Union Station,** 102 N Palmer St, is on the National Register of Historic Places. In 1901 the Plant System encompassed 1,196 miles of main line valued at $7.4 million, versus East Coast railroad magnate Henry Flagler's 466 miles of main line worth $2.7 million.

Sandra Friend

THE HISTORIC RAILROAD STATION IN PLANT CITY

ZOOLOGICAL PARKS & ANIMAL REHAB ♿ ✎ At **Big Cat Rescue** (813-920-4130; www.bigcatrescue.org), 12802 Easy St, the focus is on the care of exotic felines. After visiting a fur farm where wild cats were bred for slaughter à la *101 Dalmatians,* founder Carole Baskin bought them all and brought them home. She became a strong voice against breeding these exotic cats for the pet, fur, and entertainment industries, bringing in photographers and stars such as Jack Hanna to promote the need to care for these abandoned and abused creatures. Staffed by eager volunteers, this nonprofit organization now cares for more than two hundred cats, including tigers, lynx, bobcats, servals, snow leopards, and more, and must turn away more than three hundred abused cats a year. They run entirely on donations and will awaken your sense of responsibility toward the exotic pet trade. Tour cost varies as to length and interactive nature of the tour; the simplest tour is a guided walking tour of the facility at 9 AM and 3 PM, Mon–Fri or Sat at 9, 11:30, and 1:30, $25, ages 10 and over only.

♿ ✎ Visit the **Lowry Park Zoo** (813-935-8552; www.lowryparkzoo.com), 1101 Sligh Ave, and marvel at the many themed sections radiating out from the wildlife carousel—it will take quite a while to explore them all. In Australia kids can romp through the squirt ponds, ride ponies, or climb through the Woolshed; the entire family can walk through the Kangaroo Walkabout or past emus and fruit bats. Descend into Africa through a broad tunnel or take the Skyfari ride to see large open enclosures with warthogs and antelopes, and savannas where giraffes, zebras, and elephants roam. My family's favorite part of the zoo is Florida, a more traditional boardwalk through enclosures where you'll see our favorite neighbors—Florida panthers, roseate spoonbills, sandhill cranes, gopher tortoises, American bison, and more. You'll walk past one of only three manatee rehabilitation hospitals in Florida and into an aquarium where you can stand nose to snout with these massive mammals, or stroke a stingray at Stingray Bay. Finally, the Asia exhibit transports you above enclosures where tigers lurk beneath a waterfall, lemurs and chimps chatter, and rhinos ramble along rocky cliffs. Open 9:30–5 daily; adults $19, seniors $18, children 3–11 $14.50; special combination tickets for the River Odyssey Ecotour (see *Ecotours*) available.

✳ To Do

BEHIND-THE-SCENES TOURS Tampa offers several eclectic behind-the-scenes tours (www.seefloridaonline.com/_tampa/tours.html) of real-life businesses. The **Port of Tampa Tour** (813-905-5131), departing from the Main Port office on Wynkoop Rd, showcases the inner workings of the largest port in the Southeast, with more than 1 million passengers departing on cruise ships each year. If theater is your love, try a free backstage tour of the Southeast's largest performing-arts center, the **Tampa Bay Performing Arts Center** (813-222-1065; see *Entertainment*), or a tour of the **Tampa Theatre** (813-274-8981; see *Entertainment*), one of the last remaining grand movie palaces in the United States; donation. Sports fans can take a trip behind the scenes at **Raymond James Stadium** (813-350-6576), Dale Mabry Hwy, on Tuesday, Wednesday, and Thursday each week; tour highlights include the locker room, the press box, and a walk on the field where the Tampa Bay Buccaneers play. Reservations required; call in advance for times.

BICYCLING Off-road biking is at its best along the river wilderness areas of Hillsborough County. Launch your trip along the Hillsborough River basin at **Wilderness Trail** (813-987-6200), 12550 Morris Bridge Rd, Thonotosassa, and follow 20 miles of winding singletrack through pine flatwoods and oak scrub. At **Alderman's Ford Park** (813-757-3801), CR 39, Lithia, a maze of shady paved and unpaved trails strings together developed picnic areas along the Alafia River.

BIRDING Tampa Bay's islands and shoreline are important stopping points for migratory birds headed to and from Central and South America in fall and spring. Viewable only by boat, piping plovers and flocks of red knots can be seen on **Shell Key** and **Three Rooker Island,** both refuges in the south part of the bay. Flocks of white pelicans pass through in the fall and can be seen at **McKay Bay Nature Park** (813-274-8615), 134 N 34th St; and **Apollo Beach Nature Park,** Apollo Beach, is a popular bird-watching site at the mouth of the Alafia River on the eastern shore of the bay.

CRUISES The **Port of Tampa** (813-905-PORT; www.tampaport.com) is departure central for dozens of popular cruises, slow boats to paradise in Mexico, the Caribbean, and Key West. **Carnival Cruise Lines** (305-599-2600; www.carnival .com) offers four ships weekly with four-, five-, and seven-night Caribbean cruises. **Holland America Line** (206-281-3535; www.hollandamerica.com) offers 7–14 nights in the Caribbean with weekly departures. **Royal Caribbean International** (1-800-327-6700; www.royalcaribbean.com) whisks you away to Cozumel or Belize on three weekly four- or five-day cruises, and offers a seven-day cruise to Honduras, December–April. Terminal parking is across the street, and most of the terminals are at Channelside. See the port's Web site for specific directions to each terminal.

ECOTOURS ✐ The Florida Aquarium (see *Aquariums*), takes passengers out on the *Bay Spirit*, a 64-foot catamaran ideal for spotting bottlenose dolphins and West Indian manatees in the shallow waters of Tampa Bay; adults $20, seniors 60 and over $19, children under 12 $15. Lowry Park Zoo offers **River Odyssey Ecotour** (see *Zoological Parks*), a one-hour narrated tour along the Hillsborough River, with a naturalist pointing out wildlife. The *Sirenia* makes five cruises a day, Wednesday–Sunday. Adults $14, seniors $13, children $10; can be combined with zoo admission.

FAMILY ACTIVITIES ♿ ✐ **Kid City** (813-935-8441; www.flchildrensmuseum .com), 7550 North Blvd, North Tampa, is a miniature outdoor city for young children to explore, from City Hall to a doctor's office and apartments. Children are encouraged to role-play along the city streets and in the buildings while parents tag along or relax in the shade at a picnic table. Open daily; fee.

✐ At **Malibu Grand Prix** (813-977-6272; www.malibugrandprix.com), 14320 N Nebraska Ave, enjoy miniature golf with the entire family or let the kids challenge each other on the Grand Prix racecourse. There are batting cages, go-carts, and video games, too.

FISHING Take your tackle down to the reservoir at **Edward Medard Park** (813-757-3802), off FL 60 west of Plant City, or hit one of the fishing piers at one of the many parks on Tampa Bay (see *Parks*).

GAMING The **Seminole Hard Rock Hotel & Casino** (see *Lodging*) is a top destination for Las Vegas–style action with video gaming, poker, and high-stakes bingo 24 hours a day. The complex includes several outstanding restaurants, a food court, shops, and row upon row of popular slot machines. For more than 80 years, **Tampa Bay Downs Thoroughbred Racing** (813-855-4401 or 1-800-200-4434; www.tampabaydowns.com), 11225 Racetrack Rd, has held live horse racing December–May; they showed up as the racetrack in a scene from *Ocean's 11*. For greyhound racing, head to the **Tampa Greyhound Track** (813-932-4313; www.tampadogs.com), 8300 N Nebraska Ave, where races are held Monday–Saturday, Jai Alai is scheduled year-round, and they now have a poker room.

GENEALOGICAL RESEARCH Housed in the historic 1914 Plant City High School, the **Quintilla Geer Bruton Archives Center** (813-754-7031; www .rootsweb.com/~flqgbac), 605 N Collins St, offers researchers a treasure trove of more than 3,500 books on genealogy as well as census records, family history, genealogical files, and old newspapers for Hillsborough County. Open Tue 10–5, Wed 1–5, Thu–Sat 1–5.

GOLF The top challenge in Hillsborough County is **The Golf Club at Cypress Creek** (813-634-8888; www.cypresscreekgolfclub.com), 1011 Cypress Village

Rd, Ruskin, a semiprivate 18-hole course winding around more than 600 acres of protected wetlands. Recently renovated, it features pros from the PGA and LPGA on staff. Wildlife sightings are common just up the road at the public **Apollo Beach Golf Club** (813-645-6212; www.apollobeachgolf.com), 801 Golf and Sea Blvd, Apollo Beach, the only Robert Trent Jones Sr. signature golf course on Florida's west coast. On the county's northwest edge in Lutz, visit the rambling cypress-edged greens of **Heritage Harbor Golf & Country Club** (813-949-4886; www.heritageharborgolf.com), 19502 Heritage Harbor Pkwy, and the **Tournament Players Club of Tampa Bay** (1-866-PLAY-TPC; www.tpc tampabay.com), 5300 W Lutz Lake Fern Rd, the only PGA tour–owned and –operated course in the region. In Temple Terrace, **The Claw at USF** (813-632-6893; http://usfweb2.usf.edu/TheClaw) offers long, tight fairways with towering moss-draped trees. And near the airport, tee off at the scenic **Rocky Point Golf Course** (813-673-4316; www.tampasportsauthority.com/golf/rockypoint .htm), 4151 Dana Shores Dr, where water is a hazard on 12 of the 18 holes.

HIKING There are numerous parks in the county that offer short hikes and boardwalks, but one of my favorite leg-stretchers is the **Little Manatee Hiking Trail** at **Little Manatee River State Park** (see *Parks*). Stop at the ranger station for a trail map, gate combination, and directions to the hiker's entrance, which is on the north side of the river. The 6-mile loop traverses an incredible variety of habitats, including beautiful Cypress Creek, and offers a 3-mile loop for those less inclined for a long walk. A primitive campsite beckons campers out for a quiet weekend. Other great hikes in the area include the Florida Trail system in **Hillsborough River State Park** (see *Parks*) and the network of trails in **Alderman's Ford Park** in Alafia.

ICE SKATING Those Stanley Cup winners had to skate somewhere, and you can, too. **The Ice Sports Forum** (813-684-7825; www.theicesportsforum.com), 10222 Elizabeth Pl, offers an NHL regulation rink for figure skating and hockey practice. ✆ Or take the kids to **Countryside Mall** (727-796-1079), 27001 US 19 N in nearby Clearwater, for fun on the ice.

MANATEE WATCHING ✆ During the manatee's winter migration into Tampa Bay, you can see them by the dozens at the **TECO Big Bend Power Station Manatee Viewing Center** (813-228-4289; www.tampaelectric.com/manatee), off Big Bend Rd at Dickman Rd, from an observation platform with exhibits, murals, videos, and other educational materials. Open Nov 1–Apr 15. Free.

PADDLING Join **Canoe Escape** (813-986-2067; www.canoeescape.com), 9335 E Fowler Ave, on a wilderness paddling trip along the Hillsborough River, where alligator sightings are guaranteed. Trips run from two hours to a full day, starting at $50 per person in a tandem, $75 single.

SCENIC DRIVES **Bayshore Boulevard,** with its extensive waterfront views, is one of the prettiest drives in the region and should not be missed. The views from the **Courtney Campbell Causeway** (FL 60) are pretty incredible, too.

SCENIC WALKS How about a waterfront view for 4.5 miles? That's what you'll get walking the **world's longest continuous sidewalk** along **Bayshore Boulevard,** overlooking the sparkling waters of Tampa Bay. Or walk *over the water* on the old Gandy Bridge, now called the **Friendship Trail Bridge,** which links Picnic Island Park in Hillsborough County to Weedon Island Preserve near St. Pete, a 12-mile paved trek with 2.6 miles over the bay.

STREETCAR RIDES ⛓ ✿ When I took my dad, a lifelong streetcar aficionado, down to Channelside to ride the **TECO Line Streetcar System** (www.tecoline streetcar.org), little did I suspect there would be dozens of tourists there doing the same exact thing. The original line existed from 1892 through 1946; the new line opened several years ago on a much more limited scale. Staffed by operators in vintage uniforms, these replica Birney Safety Cars transport you into the past, offering a 20-minute ride with 11 stops that link downtown to the Port of Tampa at Channelside and end in Ybor City, with a rare railroad-streetcar crossing along the way. Fares are cash only, but you can buy a pass ($4) good for the day, which gives you the opportunity to enjoy the ride and utilize the streetcar for what it's meant to be, after all—clean, comfortable, eco-friendly public transportation. And if you ask and they have the staff to handle your request, you may be able to tour the streetcar barn in Ybor City, where one of the restored Birneys is on display.

TRAIL RIDING ⛓ At **In the Breeze Horseback Riding Ranch** (813-264-1919; www.breezestables.hypermart.net), 7514 Gardner Rd, near the airport, the trails wind through 300 acres of real Florida hammocks, hardwood forests, and scrub. Trail rides are offered all day, and hayrides and bonfires at night. There is a petting zoo and swimming hole on the premises, making this a great family outing. Trail rides start at $29; hayrides for $3. ⛓ In Lutz, the **Bakas Riding Center** (813-264-3890; www.bakasridingcenter.com) at Lake Park, 17302 N Dale Mabry, offers special facilities for wheelchair-bound riders.

Bringing your own horse? An extensive network of equestrian trails crisscrosses **Alfia River State Park** (813-987-6771; www.floridastateparks.org/alafiariver), accessed from CR 39 southeast of Brandon, and you can also take to the trails on the south side of **Little Manatee River State Park** (see *Parks*).

WALKING TOURS Ybor City Walking Tours, departing from Ybor City Museum State Park (see *Museums*) at 10:30 AM each Sat, include admission to the museum and a guided stroll along Seventh Ave. Fee. Self-guided tour brochures are available at the museum. In Plant City grab a **Downtown Walking Map** from the chamber of commerce to explore the city's many historic sites, including the 1914 High School & Museum at 605 North Collins Street.

WATER PARKS ⛓ Immerse into a Key West theme at **Adventure Island** (813-987-5600 or 1-888-800-5447; www.adventureisland.com), 4500 Bougainvillea Ave, a 30-acre wet playground adjoining Busch Gardens (see *Attractions*), where tropical plantings accent swimming pools and waterfalls, the wave pool, and slides that will have your heart pounding. Open daily late Mar–early Sep; weekends mid-Feb to Mar and mid-Sep through late Oct. Adults $38, children $35, plus parking fee; can be combined with a ticket to Busch Gardens.

✳ Green Space

BEACHES While the region's best beaches are in Pinellas County (see that chapter), Hillsborough County beaches (813-931-2121) still provide a few miles on Tampa Bay to catch some rays. Along FL 60 west of the airport, the Courtney Campbell Causeway, crowds gather on weekends to enjoy the slender strips of bayside beach at **Ben T. Davis Beach.** Over on the Davis Islands you'll find **Davis Islands Beach,** open during daylight hours. At **Picnic Island Park,** 7409 Picnic Island Blvd, the bay surrounds you, with a connecting trail (see *Scenic Walks*) to Weedon Island, as well as a fishing pier, picnic shelters, and playgrounds.

GARDENS It's an oasis in this urban area: Meander the boardwalks and trellised walks through 31 acres of woodlands at **Eureka Springs** (813-744-5536), 6400 Eureka Springs Rd. The springs are not open to swimming, but you can walk around the rim and follow the boardwalk off into a lush wetland filled with ferns, tall bay trees, maples, and cypresses; enjoy the fernery and orchid room along the pond. To find this little-known park, exit I-4 at US 301 and go north to the first traffic light, Sligh Avenue. Turn right, then right at the T, and follow the signs. Free.

More than 3,000 species of flora are packed into just 7 acres at the **University of South Florida Botanical Gardens** (813-974-2329; www.cas.usf .edu/garden), 4202 E Fowler Ave at Alumni Dr and Pine Dr, just off Bruce B. Downs Pkwy. Enter through the archway and follow meandering pathways past well-identified plants in a variety of habitats from an oak hammock with a lush floor of ferns to a sunny formal garden, an orchid room, and a bamboo walkway lined with bonsai. Open 9–5 Mon–Fri, 9–4 Sat, noon–4 Sun. Free.

ST. FRANCIS WITH LIZARD IN THE USF BOTANICAL GARDENS

Sandra Friend

GREENWAYS The **Town & Country Greenway** (813-264-8511), 7311 Baseball Ave, is a paved path with trailhead access on the east side of Hanley Road, between Hillsborough Avenue and Waters Avenue. The **Upper Tampa Bay Trail,** along Ehrlich Rd, runs from Wilsky Road north.

PARKS One of the most popular state parks in Florida, **Hillsborough River State Park** (813-987-6771; www.floridastateparks.org/hillsboroughriver), protects a beautiful section of the river, including the state's southernmost stretch of rapids. Paddlers ply the short stretch of whitewater, hikers trek miles of backcountry trails in shady river hammocks, and campers appreciate the two full-service campgrounds tucked in the woods. There's even a giant swimming pool! Newly opened; a "make your own" pancake restaurant just like DeLeon Springs (see *Daytona Beach and Volusia County*.) **Little Manatee River State Park** (813-671-5005; www.floridastateparks.org/littlemanateeriver), US 301, south of Sun City Center, offers horse trails, hiking trails, and river access for paddling.

Literary fanatics—head to South Tampa to see **Ballast Point Park & Pier** (813-274-8615), 5300 Interbay Rd, the setting for Jules Verne's classic *From the Earth to the Moon.* Most folks stop here to picnic along the bay or fish on the pier, but there's also a "Jules Verne Park" historical marker and a mural blending Jules Verne's fantasy with the wildlife along the bay. 🐾 Dogs can romp free in the dog park at **Al Lopez Park,** 4810 N Himes, a 120-acre city park with nature trails, playgrounds, a fishing pier, paved walking trails, and dozens of picnic tables and grills for a nice family outing. **Centennial Park,** 1800 Eighth Ave, Ybor City, is a gathering place with picnic tables, home to the Saturday-morning farmer's market. **Cotanchobee Park,** 601 Ice Palace Dr, downtown, sits along Garrison Channel. It has a fishing pier and playground, and centers on a memorial to the Seminole Wars. **Plant Park,** on the University of Tampa campus, protects 6.9 acres along the Hillsborough River. In Ybor City the tiny **Parque Amigos de Martí** is a sliver of Cuba in the United States. Cuba owns title to this piece of land, which contains a statue of José Martí and soil from all of the provinces of Cuba—considered the only free Cuban soil in the world. For City of Tampa parks information, call 813-274-8615.

In the county, **E. G. Simmons Park** (813-671-7655), 2401 19th Ave NW, Ruskin, encompasses nearly 500 acres on Tampa Bay, perfect for boating, swimming, bird-watching, and fishing. There is also a campground on-site. This park hosts many regional festivals. At **Lettuce Lake Park** (813-987-6204), 6920 Fletcher Ave, a series of boardwalks leads you out along the Hillsborough River to an observation tower, and the picnic pavilions provide scenic views. **Upper Tampa Bay Park** (813-855-1765) protects more than 2,100 acres and has walking trails, an environmental study center, and picnic groves along the shores of Tampa Bay.

SPRINGS A swim's the thing at **Lithia Springs** (813-744-5572), 3932 Lithia

RAPIDS ALONG THE HILLSBOROUGH RIVER IN HILLSBOROUGH RIVER STATE PARK

Sandra Friend

Springs Rd, a 200-acre park surrounding a second-magnitude spring edged with cypresses and bay trees. A small swimming beach and roped-off area for the kids provide access to the 72°F waters. Open 8–7 Mon–Fri, 8–8 weekends. Fee.

WILD PLACES North of Tampa along the Hillsborough River, **Wilderness Park** includes a chain of parks connected by a ribbon of protected land, where hikers, bicyclists, and paddlers can explore miles of unbroken wilderness. Trailheads are at **Flatwoods Wilderness Park & Trail** (813-987-6211), 16400 Morris Bridge Rd, Thonotosassa, and Bruce B. Downs Blvd, New Tampa; **Trout Creek Wilderness Park** (813-987-6200), 12550 Morris Bridge Rd; and **Morris Bridge Wilderness Park** (813-987-6209), 13330 Morris Bridge Rd. Paddlers can also access the river's tributaries via wilderness parks off US 301: **Dead River Wilderness Park** (813-987-6210), 15098 Dead River Rd; **John B. Sargeant Sr. Memorial Wilderness Park** (813-987-6208), 12702 US 301; and **Veteran's Memorial Wilderness Park** (813-744-5502), 3602 US 301.

✳ Lodging
BED & BREAKFASTS

Brandon 33511
🍴 An unexpected find in Florida: A shaker saltbox evoking New England. **Behind the Fence Inn** (813-685-8201), 1400 Viola Dr, provides a touch of Amish hospitality in a relaxing setting. Innkeeper Larry Yoss was raised in an Amish home but left the community when he married his wife, Carolyn, who had been raised on a historic farm. Together, they bring rural hospitality to the fringe of the big city, their home artfully decorated with treasured finds from their days in the antiques business. The house has three guest rooms with private bath ($89), and two cottage rooms next to the pool. Rates include continental breakfast with homemade Amish sweet rolls. The innkeepers host tours for schoolchildren showcasing 18th-century life, and each Christmas, local artisans showcase their crafts-making at the house.

Tampa—Ybor City 33605
A fully equipped 1908 bungalow, the **Casita de la Verdad** (813-654-6087; www.yborcityguesthouse.com), 1609 E Sixth Ave, offers the comforts of home with a location central to the nightlife that Ybor City is famous for. The bungalow has two bedrooms, each with a queen-size bed, and a restored clawfoot tub in the marble-floored bath, as well as a full kitchen and outdoor grilling space. Rates run $180 Sun–Thu, $250 Fri–Sat, and $350 during special events.

HOTELS, MOTELS, AND RESORTS

Tampa—Airport/Westshore 33607
♿ For a romantic escape head to the **Renaissance Tampa Hotel** (813-877-9200 or 1-800-644-2685; www.marriott.com/hotels/travel/tpaim-renaissance-tampa-hotel-international-plaza), 4200 Jim Walter Blvd, where delightful Mediterranean decor will sweep you off your feet, thanks to the influence of Gabriella and Sergio Pesce. Gabriella, who inherited her family's Ybor City cigar business, fell in love with Sergio while vacationing

on the Spanish Riviera. The faux turn-of-the-20th-century architecture is enchanting, and who can resist the tray of fresh olives available to guests in the lobby? In this relatively new Marriott property, the rooms (starting at $179) and suites reflect the overall elegance of the theme. It's a short walk to shopping at International Plaza (see *Selective Shopping*). The hotel offers both complimentary on-site parking and valet parking.

&. "ı" Overlooking the sparkling expanse of Tampa Bay, the **Sailport Waterfront Suites** (813-281-9599 or 1-800-255-9599; www.sailport.com), 2506 N Rocky Point Dr, provides all the comforts of home. One- and two-bedroom suites ($99 and up) include a full kitchen, making this an ideal location for long-term stays. A pool and sunning beach let you soak in some bayside rays. Complimentary covered parking and free airport shuttle.

Tampa—Downtown 33602
&. "ı" In the heart of the busy Channelside district, the **Tampa Marriott Waterside Hotel & Marina** (813-221-4900 or 1-888-268-1616; www.marriott.com/hotels/travel/tpamc-tampa-marriott-waterside-hotel-and-marina), 700 S Florida Ave, adjoins the St. Pete Times Forum and has one end of the TECO streetcar line out front. The spacious rooms have luxurious cherrywood furnishings and classy art, dedicated work space with high-speed Internet, and fabulous views across the Hillsborough River. There is an on-site spa, several restaurants, and concierge floors with upscale suites, including the Presidential Suite. Standard rooms start at $169; on-site (fee) and valet parking.

CD &. "ı" At the **Sheraton Tampa Riverwalk Hotel** (813-223-2222; www.tampariverwalkhotel.com), 200 N Ashley Dr, settle into a comfortable room that evokes the city's Spanish heritage, with muted earth tones, wrought-iron lamps, and a marble coffee table. Towering over the Hillsborough River, the hotel offers great views of Henry Plant's classic 1891 Tampa Bay Hotel. Standard rooms $149 and up; the spacious suites are larger than most one-bedroom apartments and include a massive walk-through closet/vanity area, microwave, mini fridge, and large writing desk. Valet parking only.

Tampa—East 33610
&. "ı" Having attended a business meeting at the **Seminole Hard Rock Hotel & Casino** (1-866-502-PLAY; www.hardrockhotelcasinotampa.com), 5223N Orient Rd, I can attest to the "wow" factor of their hotel rooms—I felt like I'd slipped into a chic version of *The Jetsons*. Each spacious room ($179 and up) comes with its own stereo system (I was supplied a CD upon check-in; others can be purchased in the stores in the casino complex), massive television, ultra-modern furnishings, mini bar, comfortable bed, and roomy bath area with separate tub and shower. Guests enjoy a tropical art deco pool area, fitness center, and spa on the hotel side of this massive entertainment complex.

Tampa—North Tampa 33612
While **Embassy Suites USF** (813-977-7066; www.embassysuitesusf.com), 3705 Spectrum Blvd, caters to business travelers with all the usual amenities, it is also an excellent place to stay on a visit to Busch Gardens

(see *Attractions*), which is 2 miles away; special package deals and complimentary shuttle available. One- and two-bedroom suites ($139 and up) include a cooked-to-order breakfast.

Tampa—Ybor City 33605

∞ In a building constructed in 1895 by the founder of Ybor City as a clinic and hospital, the **Don Vicente de Ybor Historic Inn** (813-241-4545; www.donvicenteinn.com), 1915 Republica de Cuba, offers a step back in time through its 16 boutique rooms ($139–179). The common areas evoke the splendor of Renaissance Europe, with gilded paneling and lush draperies, while each room offers elegant furnishings, floor-to-ceiling windows, and writing desks. Breakfast and parking are complimentary.

& "▐" Adjoining the historic village at the Ybor City Museum State Park (see *Museums*), the **Hilton Garden Inn Tampa Ybor Historic District** (813-769-9267), 1700 E Ninth Ave, blends in seamlessly with its Latin Quarter surroundings. Rooms $139 and up. From here it's an easy walk to Centro Ybor, or you can catch a streetcar to Channelside and downtown.

Temple Terrace 33637

& "▐" Set in a quiet nature preserve near a bustling business district, **Hilton Garden Inn Tampa North** (813-342-5000; www.tampanorth .gardeninn.com), 600 Tampa Oaks Blvd, provides everything a business traveler needs: The clean, comfortable rooms ($127 and up) include a large work desk. Families will appreciate this location as a getaway for visiting local attractions—Busch Gardens and the Museum of Science & Industry are only a few miles away.

CAMPGROUNDS

Dover 33527

Green Acres Campground & RV Travel Park (813-659-0002), 12720 E US 92, offers seven hundred grassy sites, from full hookup to primitive, and amenities including a heated swimming pool, playground, laundry room, recreation hall, and golf course.

Ruskin 33570

🐾 Enjoy gorgeous natural scenery along the Little Manatee River at **Hide-A-Way RV Resort** (813-645-6037 or 1-800-607-2532), where it costs $32 daily (water and electric; $16 Passport America holders) for you to pull your trailer or RV under the oaks. Enjoy the RV lifestyle with clubhouse, scheduled activities, heated pool, and great access to the river for fishing.

🐾 Enter through the red barn at **Manatee RV Park** (813-645-7652), 6302 US 41 S, to discover a nicely forested campground with its own mini-golf course, shuffleboard, clubhouse and pool, and a large pond busy with birds. Sites include water and electric; pets permitted in designated areas.

Thonotosassa 33592

Sheltered by massive live oaks, **Spanish Main RV Resort** (813-986-2415), 12110 Spanish Main Resort Trl, US 301 N, is an appealing place to set up camp for the night, with a playground, pool, and shuffleboard. RV sites are $29 and include full hookups.

✳ Where to Eat

DINING OUT

Tampa—Airport/Westshore

The classy **Tampa Bay Palm Restaurant** (813-849-7256; www.the

palm.com), 205 Westshore Dr, is a spinoff of the original New York City steakhouse that opened in 1926, but with its own Tampa twist: The walls are decorated with caricatures of local celebrities, from newspaper columnists to politicians and business executives. Featuring jumbo Nova Scotia lobsters and prime Angus steaks as well as nearly a dozen choices of fresh veggies served family-style, it's a serious place for fine dining. Open for lunch and dinner, with a $16 business lunch. Reservations recommended.

Tampa—Downtown and Vicinity

Dine along the Hillsborough River at the **Ashley Street Grille** (813-226-4400), 200 N Ashley Ave, inside the Tampa Riverwalk Hotel (see *Lodging*), where Chef Mike Pagliari presides over a well-pedigreed kitchen, which has won various awards from *Wine Spectator* magazine over the past decade. Entrées showcase fresh local vegetables and seafood in creations such as chile-rubbed salmon, seafood St. Jacques, and my selection, the Mediterranean penne, a garden-fresh mix of veggies, kalamata olives, and goat cheese reminiscent of the Greek islands. If you're tempted by the dessert tray, don't hesitate—the Key lime pie is just the right measure of tart. Serving breakfast, lunch, and dinner, and offering menu items via room service throughout the hotel.

Donatello (813-875-6660; www .donatellorestaurant.com), 232 N Dale Mabry, is a favorite of *Wine Spectator* magazine for the extensive wine list that complements their northern Italian and other innovative cuisines, including fresh oysters cooked with cream and spinach, fresh salmon with asparagus, and Angus beef with homemade pâté. Open for dinner at 6 PM

daily, lunch 11:30–2:30 Monday–Friday, with lighter fare like their Donatello Salad with crispy romaine, broccoli, fresh mushrooms, asparagus, heart of palms and avocado, $10.

Tampa—South Tampa

🍸 A Tampa legend, **Bern's Steak House** (813-251-2421; www.berns steakhouse.com), 1208 S Howard Ave, doesn't do anything by halves. Their famous cut-to-order steaks come with the world's largest wine list (the size of a small laptop computer—and how can they help it, with a half million bottles of wine in stock?) and a 65-page dessert menu to complement their dessert room. Stepping into the restaurant, you feel as if you've entered a medieval castle, and each of the themed dining rooms are named for European wine districts, such as Bordeaux and Rhone. The intimate murmur of conversation flows throughout the room as you savor the art of dining. Our waiter, Jim, along with his peers, trained for at least a year before being permitted to work alone. He took the time to explain the different cuts of meat and how they are prepared. I settled on a New York strip from the hundreds of choices (in the steak category alone, $29 for a 6-ounce filet mignon to $233 for a 60-ounce strip sirloin) on the menu. Every entrée comes with French onion soup, salad, baked potato, and fresh onion rings. If you think you'll want dessert (and you will), ask your waiter to reserve your space *before* you begin your main course. The vegetables come straight from the family farm near north Tampa Bay and are perfectly crisp; the macadamia nut–vanilla dressing gave the salad a uniquely sweet twist. As for the steak, the rarer the better! After dinner, we took the kitchen and wine cellar tour offered to all guests and marveled at the massive aquariums and the walls of fine wine in the wine cellar. Ushered upstairs to the Harry Waugh Dessert Room, we enjoyed intimate seating in a giant wine cask, each a soundproof booth with your choice of music. It was tough to settle between vanilla bean crème brûlée, orange chocolate-chip pecan pie, and Grand Marnier chocolate mousse among dozens of choices, but we did our best. Our luxurious dining experience took about four hours—this is not a place you want to hurry through—and the bill for two topped $150, with a minimal amount of alcohol included. The Laxer family has nurtured their business from its humble beginnings as a sandwich shop in 1956 into a destination in itself, and are presently developing their old parking lot across the street into the Epicurean Hotel, slated to open late 2008. Reservations highly recommended for this fine dining experience.

Tampa—Ybor City
At **Bernini of Ybor** (813-248-0099; www.berniniofybor.com), 1702 E Seventh Ave, in the grand old Bank of Ybor City, "Taste is a Matter of Art." With a menu that changes constantly, this popular innovative Italian restaurant receives rave reviews on a national level. One evening's entrées included pork *saltimbocca, cioppino,* and veal lasagna ($15–24) and a selection of wood-fired pizzas ($10–15).

✍ The original **Columbia Restaurant** (813-248-4961; www.columbia restaurant.com), 2117 E Seventh Ave, a tradition for more than a century, is Florida's oldest continually operating restaurant. It defines the standard to which Spanish cooking in America is

held. I was honored to be present at an awards ceremony where Joe Roman, "the Singing Waiter," received a lifetime achievement award for customer service. Enjoy a flamenco dance show every night while you nibble on their incredible selection of tapas, and settle into a classic slow-cooked *paella* for dinner, or tender *ropa vieja* (a Cuban beef dish—one of my favorites) served with plantains and rice. While you'll find spinoffs of the this restaurant all across Florida, nothing compares to sitting in the grand interior courtyard of the 1905 original. Open for lunch and dinner; children's menu available.

EATING OUT
Plant City
🍴 Right in the regional farmer's market, **Fred's Market Restaurant** (813-752-7763), 1401 W Martin Luther King Jr Blvd, offers some of the best country cooking in the state. Southern fried chicken, perfect mashed potatoes, and flaky biscuits are all part of an extensive buffet for $11 per person, or you can order from the menu, $8–14. Open 6 AM–8:30 PM, closed Sun and holidays.

Grab a snack with your paperback at the **Manatee Bay Café** (813-707-1450), 119 S Collins St, where "adult fast food" comes surrounded by Mae's Book Store (see *Selective Shopping*). Open 8–4 Mon–Sat with tasty pressed sandwiches ($6), a mess of Cuban combos ($6–7), and good old standards like pastrami, BLT, and egg salad ($4–6).

At **Snellgroves Restaurant** (813-752-3652), 109 S Collins, you'll feel right at home with tasty home cooking in a down-home atmosphere. Breakfast starts at $3, with Tennessee country ham a featured side. Daily dinner specials ($7–17) come with an endless salad bar, and include country favorites like baked ham, boneless catfish, fried chicken gizzards, and meatloaf. Open daily.

Ruskin
A roadside stand with Old Florida appeal, the **Fish House** (813-641-9451), 1900 Shell Point Rd, features down-home seafood dinners such as smoked mullet and grits, fried oysters, and soft-shell crab. Take it to go, or eat outdoors at the shaded picnic tables. Open 11–8 Thu–Sat.

Tampa—Downtown and Vicinity
An Irish sports pub in a historic downtown building, **Hattricks** (813-225-HATT; www.hattrickstavern.com), 107 S Franklin St, shows off hockey jerseys up on the old brick walls and has the best wings in Tampa—but try the offbeat, too, such as sweet potato fries with maple syrup or lemon-pepper grouper nuggets ($4–9). Lunch and dinner options include salads, classic sandwiches and burgers, and pub fare such as fish-and-chips and meatloaf ($9–11).

It's not your ordinary dining experience. **Splitsville** (813-514-2695; www.splitsvillelanes.com), 615 Channelside Dr, is a funky, retro bowling alley and billiards hall where sushi sits side by side with ninepins. And it's fun! Choose from gourmet tapas or classics such as chicken wings and sandwiches ($8 and up), or entrées such as pork tenderloin Waikiki ($15 and up).

Tampa—Hyde Park
America's only thatched-roof Irish pub is in a Tampa neighborhood! Get your potato-leek soup and shepherd's pie while listening to traditional Irish musicians at **Four Green Fields**

(813-254-4444; www.fourgreenfields .com), 205 W Platt St, 11–3 daily.

Tampa—North Tampa
A taste of real Florida, **Skipper's Smokehouse and Oyster Bar** (813-971-0666; www.skipperssmokehouse .com), 910 Skipper Rd, serves up gator ribs, mudbugs (crawfish), conch chowder, and one heck of a black bean gator chili; fresh fish, too, with fare $3–14. No frills here—the digs are authentic, and it seemed fitting that the day we stopped by, Tampa author Tim Dorsey was hanging out signing his latest madcap novel. Enjoy live music most evenings in the "Skipperdome" under moss-draped live oaks.

Tampa—South Tampa
Under a canopy of ancient live oaks, **Kojak's House of Ribs** (813-837-3774; www.kojaksbbq.com), 2808 Gandy Blvd, offers lip-smackin' ribs and barbecue—and *fast!* I'm picky about ribs and must declare these some of the best I've ever had, and on my husband's choice of a combo dinner, the fresh sausage was kick-butt spicy and good. Entrées start at $6, and the best seating is out on the porch. The Forney family has been making barbecue here since 1978, with great service and killer food.

Tampa—Ybor City
Step back into a more genteel era in the **House of Two Sisters Tea Room** (813-258-8220; www.house oftwosisters.com), 1901 N 19th St, where afternoon tea is served. Reservation; Wed–Sat, from $6 to $17 per person with all the proper accoutrements.

The Spaghetti Warehouse (813-248-1720; www.meatballs.com) is a fun family Italian restaurant where you can dine inside a street-car. No matter whether you order spaghetti, lasagna, or a salad, the portions are big, but the prices make this a great family choice: lunch and dinner $6–14.

BAKERIES AND A COFFEE SHOP

Tampa—Downtown and Vicinity
🍴 One of my favorite places in Tampa is **Alessi Bakeries** (813-879-4544), 2909 W Cypress St, where it still looks and smells like the bakeries of my youth. A century's worth of loving care brings forth goodies like napoleons, éclairs, and banana bread. The deli sandwiches, salads, and entrées are world-class, too. Stop here for lunch. You'll keep coming back.

It's hard to pass by a French bakery, so don't pass up **Au Rendezvous** (813-221-4748), 200 E Madison St, when you're downtown—quiches, croissants, ooh la la! My picks are the rustic olive bread and aromatic rosemary bread.

⚟ **Joffrey's Coffee** (www.joffreys .com) is a local chain with numerous locations around Tampa Bay. The one I've hung out at is in Channelside, where you can grab a deli sandwich to go with your java or order up a dessert like frozen coffee drink.

Tampa—Ybor City
All of Ybor City, it seems, gets its fresh bread and rolls from **La Segunda Central Bakery** (813-248-1531), 2512 N 15th St, where you can pick up tasty pastries, too.

✴ Selective Shopping

Plant City
Look for primitives and tools at **Antiques & Treasures** (813-752-

4626), 107 N Collins St; the back room is filled with furniture and glassware.

You'll find an eclectic selection of dealer booths in an old McCrory's building at **Collins Street Junction** (813-659-2585), 117 N Collins St, with collectibles, ephemera, and glass.

Get lost in the dealers booths at **Frenchman's Market** (813-754-8388), 102 S Evers Street, where the aisles lead to collections of classy glassware, vintage clothing, and fine furniture.

More than 100,000 paperback books (grouped by genre) will keep you browsing at **Mae's Book Store** (813-707-1450), 119 S. Collins St, an adjunct to Manatee Bay Café, which serves a nice lunch (see *Eating Out*).

At **Pieces of Olde** (813-717-7731), 113 W Reynolds St, there is a room of tins and kitchenware, quilts, some primitives and books, and a "Mad Hatter" room.

At **Sisters & Co.** (813-754-0990), 104 E Reynolds St, I found some great books and toys to give as gifts and browsed the fun and colorful selection of clothing and purses.

Tampa—Airport/Westshore
Adjacent to the airport, **International Plaza and Bay Street** (813-342-3790; www.shopinternationalplaza .com), 2223 N Westshore Blvd, has more than two hundred shops anchored by Neiman Marcus, Nordstrom, and Dillard's, as well as an open-air village of boutique shops, Bay Street, and popular restaurants such as Blue Martini, the Cheesecake Factory, and TooJay's. Older, but still popular with shoppers, nearby **Westshore Plaza** (813-286-0790; www .westshoreplaza.com), 250 Westshore

Plaza, has more than one hundred specialty stores, including Banana Republic as well as several upscale chain restaurants.

Tampa—Downtown and Vicinity
Step into a historic Victorian home just outside downtown to enter the world of **Artsiphartsi** (813-348-4838; www.artsiphartsi.com), 2717 Kennedy Blvd, where more than five hundred nationally acclaimed artists are represented in various media, from contemporary quilts to fine furniture, metalwork, jewelry, and glass. Don't miss the sculpture garden! Mon–Fri 10–5.

Set right along the waterfront, where docked cruise ships dwarf the plaza, **Channelside** (813-223-4250; www .channelsidetampa.com), 615 Channelside Dr, combines dining and shopping with a quick walk to attractions like the Florida Aquarium. Browse streetfront shops such as **White House Gear** and **Cigars by Antonio,** or work your way into the complex for the cinema and more shops**.**

A top-notch independent bookstore, **Inkwood Books** (813-253-2638; www.inkwoodbooks.com), 216 S Armenia, has a great selection in my favorite niches—recent travel narrative, travel guides, and Florida authors, as well as the best modern trade paperbacks and Book Sense picks. They regularly host author visits.

Downtown, the **Old Tampa Book Company** (813-209-2151; www.old tampabookcompany.com), 507 N Tampa St, offers more than forty thousand used and collectible tomes—talk about some serious browsing! Owners Ellen and David Brown should be applauded for breathing some life into Tampa's

downtown, as theirs is one of few places to shop, featuring Florida books, fine-art collectibles, and more.

Tampa—Hyde Park
Touting themselves as a "cure for the common mall," **Old Hyde Park Village** (813-251-3500; www.oldhyde park.com), 748 S Village Cir, offers upscale favorites such as Restoration Hardware, Williams-Sonoma, Pottery Barn, and Crabtree & Evelyn in a parklike setting, with on-site theaters, coffee shops, and the popular Wine Exchange. For unique artsy gifts with a local touch, seek out **Nicholson House** (813-258-3991; www.nicholson house.net), 1605 Snow Ave, filled with whimsical functional art; **The Wild Orchid** (813-258-5004; www .wildorchidshop.com), 1631 W Snow Cir, a lush rain forest with live orchids, tropical home decor, garden ornaments, and gifts; and **A Source for the Home** (813-259-9999; www .asourceforthehome.com), where you'll find the perfect art glass, dinnerware, and lighting for your home. Free parking provided in several garages.

AN OPEN-AIR MALL ALONG THE HARBOR, CHANNELSIDE IS A SHOPPING AND DINING DESTINATION

Sandra Friend

Tampa—Ybor City

Rather than demolish a neighborhood of early-1900s bungalows, the city moved them from the path of I-4 to face Centennial Park (see *Parks*) as part of the Ybor City Museum State Park (see *Museums*). Painted in cheery colors, the homes are now an artists' village of shops and galleries, among them the **Arnold Martinez Art Gallery** (see *Art Galleries*) and the **Ybor City Museum Store** (813-241-6554; www.ybormuseum.org), 1820 E Ninth Ave, where you'll find cigar art, history books, and a unique line of "Trolley Kat" books and dolls for the kids.

Centro Ybor (813-242-4660; www.centroybor.com), 1600 E Eighth Ave, is the central shopping, dining, and entertainment district within historic Ybor City, anchored by the Centro Español social club.

Thonotosassa

Head east for bargains at the **Big Top Flea Market** (813-986-4004; www.bigtopfleamarket.com), 9250 E Fowler Ave, where more than a thousand dealer booths give you a choice of everything from cheap Asian goods to farm fresh local produce, fishing tackle, puppies, and garage-sale type items.

PRODUCE STANDS AND A FARMER'S MARKET

Plant City

Plant City is best known for its fabulous annual strawberry crop, and where better to buy strawberries than direct from the farm? At **Parkesdale Farm Market** (813-754-2704 or 1-888-311-1701; www.parkesdale.com), 3702 W Baker St, stop in for luscious strawberry shortcake and milkshakes, fresh strawberries, preserves, and

more. Closed Sunday–Monday. Driving south on CR 33 from Plant City to Alafia, you'll encounter dozens of roadside stands, most open during the winter growing season. Open daily.

Sun City

Follow the signs from US 41 to **Dooley Groves** (813-645-3256 or 1-800-522-6411; www.dooleygroves.com), 1651 Stephens Rd, where citrus is as fresh as it comes, right at the packing plant. Watch fresh orange juice being squeezed and breathe in the sweet aroma of orange blossoms. In addition to citrus, they have a gift shop full of Florida goodies. Open seasonally for nearly 40 years.

Tampa—Ybor City

Ybor City Fresh Market (813-241-2442; yborfreshmarket.ypguides.net) at Centennial Park (see *Parks*) offers fresh local produce, baked goods, and arts and crafts vendors every Saturday 9–3.

✳ Entertainment

FINE ARTS **Tampa Bay Performing Arts Center** (813-229-7827 or 1-800-955-1045; www.tbpac.org), 1010 W. C. MacInnes Pl N, is the largest performing-arts center in the Southeast and offers a broad range of entertainment, from the Florida Orchestra to Opera Tampa, Broadway shows, and dance. See their Web site for details and ticketing.

THEATER ⅙ An intimate Actor's Equity venue, the 76-seat **Gorilla Theatre** (813-879-2914; www.gorilla-theatre.com), 4419 N Hubert Ave, offers original works and classics, as well as workshops for young playwrights. Schedule varies by performance.

Enjoy movies as they were meant to be seen in the 1920s elegance of the **Tampa Theatre** (813-274-8982; www.tampatheatre.org), 711 Franklin St, where seasonal film festivals showcase the classics: Imagine watching *Casablanca* on the big screen in this plush venue from the past, replete with a pre-show Wurlitzer organ introduction. They also feature avant-garde films and documentaries you won't see at mainstream theaters, shown nightly.

SPORTS The **Tampa Bay Buccaneers** (813-879-BUCS or 1-800-795-BUCS; www.buccaneers.com) play football each fall at Raymond James Stadium, and the recent winners of the Stanley Cup, the **Tampa Bay Lightning** (813-301-6500; www.tampabaylightning.com), compete in fast-paced games on ice at the St. Pete Times Forum downtown.

✳ Special Events

February: The state's largest celebration of rural bounty is in an ironically urban setting at the **Florida State Fair** (813-621-7821 or 1-800-345-FAIR; www.floridastatefair.com), 4800 US 301 N, Tampa, just off I-4 near I-75. For more than a century, it's been a statewide showcase for agriculture, with exhibits on Florida wildlife (from the Fish & Wildlife Commission) and Florida's forestry industry (from the Department of Forestry), covering historic turpentine tapping, cypress logging, pine straw, and careers in modern forestry. Antique steam engines are shown off in their own barn. Inside the grand exhibit hall, see the "best of," from cakes to tapestries to rag dolls, from all over Florida. There's also a giant

midway to keep the kids busy, and concerts (extra fee) on some evenings during the 12-day gala.

One of Florida's wildest invasions, the **Gasparilla Pirate Fest** (813-353-8108; www.gasparillapiratefest.com), held the first Saturday, celebrates the taking of Tampa—by pirates. For more than a century, Ye Mystic Krewe of Gasparilla has sailed their pirate ship into downtown, swarming the city with more than a hundred other krewes before tossing beads and doubloons to the crowd in a colorful parade. The revelry continues all weekend at parties private and public and spills over to other special events—arts festival, marathon, road race, and more—throughout the remainder of the month.

Florida Strawberry Festival (813-754-1996; www.flstrawberryfestival.com), Plant City, is the world's largest celebration of strawberries right at the peak of harvest season. The exhibition halls are filled with everything from art to cakes, and livestock gets its own judging in the big tents.

MIDWAY RIDES AT THE FLORIDA STATE FAIR
Sandra Friend

The festival offers concerts almost every night, but it's packed on weekends, so try to visit on a weekday ($10)—and be sure to get in line for strawberry shortcake!

History comes alive at the **Fort Foster Rendezvous** at Fort Foster State Historic Site, Hillsborough River State Park (see *Parks*), where an encampment and skirmishes recall the days when soldiers attempted to keep the Seminoles from migrating north of the Hillsborough River in the early 1800s. Fee.

March: Enjoy arts, crafts, food, and a celebration of one of Tampa Bay's most beloved creatures at the **Apollo Beach Manatee Arts Festival** (813-645-1366; www.apollobeachchamber .com), Apollo Beach.

At the **Tampa Heritage Cigar Festival** (813-247-1434), Centennial Park, Ybor City, cigar vendors celebrate the city's rich tradition with demonstrations showcasing the history and cultural behind the business.

May: At the **Tampa Bay International Dragon Boat Races** (813-962-7163; www.TampaBayDragon Boats.com), corporate and community rowing teams race colorful dragon-decorated boats on the Hillsborough River downtown near Cotanchobee Park, by Channelside.

Celebrate the bounty of the earth at the **Ruskin Tomato Festival** (813-645-3808; www.ruskinchamber.org), held the first weekend, with musical entertainment, fresh produce, a Cinco de Mayo celebration, and all the sliced tomatoes you can eat. The festival is held at E. G. Simmons Park off US 41.

September: The **Mainstreet Arts & Crafts Series** (813-621-7121; www .cc-events.org/msartcraft), held mid-month in Ybor City at Centennial Park, features local and national artists, musical entertainment, and local produce and baked goods vendors. Free admission and parking; repeated in November.

October: One of the country's largest rallies of vintage autos, the **NSRA Southeast Street Rod Nationals** (303-776-7841; ww.nsra-usa.com) brings together more than 1,400 pre-1949 street rods from around the US at the Florida State Fairgrounds.

Guavaween (www.cc-events.org/gw), celebrated the Saturday before Halloween, brings together Tampa's nickname of "The Big Guava" with a Latin approach to this day of the dead, with outlandish costumes in a late-night street parade in Ybor City, overseen by "Mama Guava," who's taking the "bore" out of Ybor.

November: **Ruskin Seafood and Arts Festival** (813-645-3808; www .ruskinchamber.org), held the first weekend at E. G. Simmons Park, sates seafood appetites with dozens of vendors serving up Florida shrimp, conch, grouper, and more. Arts and crafts vendors and live entertainment round out a weekend of fun.

December: The **Victorian Christmas Stroll** (813-254-1891; www.plant museum.com) is a genteel walk through the old Tampa Bay Hotel, decked out as it was in the days of railroad magnate Henry Plant, December 1–23. Christmas fun continues downtown on the first Saturday at Curtis Hixon Park with **Santa Fest** and the **Holiday Parade,** and it continues on Saturdays up through Christmas with **Holidayfest** (813-223-7999), featuring events such as a lighted boat parade.

PINELLAS COUNTY: ST PETERSBURG, CLEARWATER AND TARPON SPRINGS

*P*unta Pinal, the point of pines, is what Spanish explorer Pánfilo de Narváez dubbed this long, thin peninsula in 1528, where he discovered a Tocobagan village on the shores of Tampa Bay and ransacked it looking for gold. Three centuries after the conquistadors moved on, settlers to the Pinellas peninsula came from around the globe, their touch reflected in the unique communities found to the west of Tampa and St. Petersburg along the Gulf of Mexico. After Florida became a state, pioneers sailed down the Gulf coast from outposts such as Cedar Key to establish homesteads. Frenchman Odet Phillippe came to **Safety Harbor** to establish a settlement in the early 1800s, centuries after Spanish explorer Pedro Menéndez de Avilés stopped in on a Native American village at the springs. Early residents in the wilderness of Pinellas County carved a living out of the pine flat-woods, establishing ranches and vegetable farms in the **Seminole** and **Largo** areas, and commercially harvested the rich fisheries off **Indian Rocks** and **Redington Beach.** After visiting the region in 1841, James Parramore McMullen and his six brothers settled along the "Clear Water Harbor," which evolved into the community of **Clearwater**. One of Florida's oldest West Coast cities, **Dunedin**, was founded in 1852 and has its roots in Edinburgh, Scotland. A thriving agricultural community built on cotton and later citrus, it once had the largest fleet of commercial sailing vessels in Florida. Greeks seeking fortune from the rich sponge beds of the Gulf came to **Tarpon Springs** in 1882, bringing with them hundreds of divers (and eventually their families) from islands in the southern Dodecanese. But it was General John Williams from Detroit who purchased 2,500 acres of Tampa Bay waterfront in 1875 with the express intent of creating a grand city. Development commenced, but with some competition—Hamilton Disston, the Philadelphia developer who in 1881 promised to drain Florida's swamplands and make them livable, nabbed thousands of nearby acres from the state on Boca Ciega Bay. Eyeing a settlement established by Civil War veteran Mames Barnett in 1867, Disston established Disston City at the southern end of the peninsula on Boca Ciega Bay. As the railroad barons pushed south, they decided the fate of the two competing cities. In 1888 Peter Demens, a Russian immigrant, brought his Orange Belt Railway right down to Williams's development, and the fledlging city was dubbed **St. Petersburg** in honor of his hometown. Meanwhile, developer

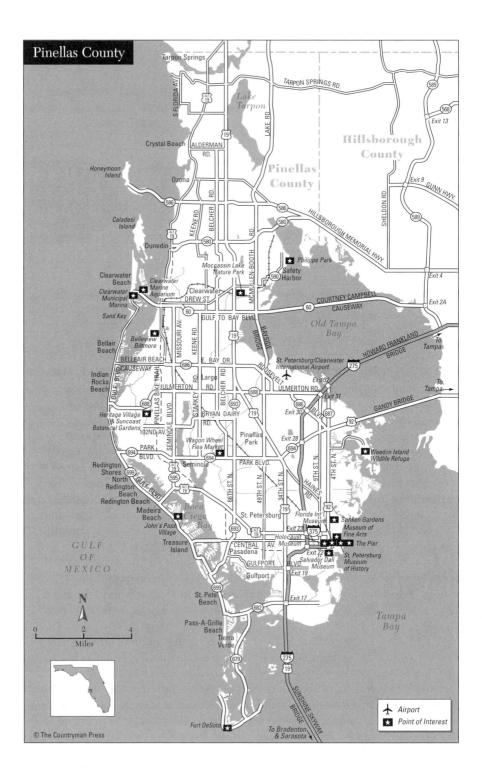

Pinellas County

Tarpon Springs

Lake Tarpon

TARPON SPRINGS RD.

Hillsborough County

Pinellas County

Crystal Beach ALDERMAN RD.

Honeymoon Island

Ozona

Caladesi Island

Dunedin

Moccassin Lake Nature Park

Philippe Park

Safety Harbor

Clearwater Beach

Clearwater Marine Aquarium

Clearwater Municipal Marina

Clearwater

DREW ST.

Sand Key

COURTNEY CAMPBELL CAUSEWAY

Old Tampa Bay

Bellair Beach

Belleview Biltmore

BELLEAIR BEACH

GULF TO BAY BLVD.

St. Petersburg/Clearwater International Airport

Indian Rocks Beach

E. BAY DR.

CAUSEWAY

Largo

ULMERTON RD.

Heritage Village & Suncoast Botanical Gardens

BRYAN DAIRY

Wagon Wheel Flea Market

Pinellas Park

Weedon Island Wildlife Refuge

Redington Shores

North Redington Beach

Redington Beach

PARK BLVD.

Seminole

Madeira Beach

Boca Ciega Bay

John's Pass Village

St. Petersburg

Florida Int'l Museum

Sunken Gardens Museum of Fine Arts

The Pier

GULF OF MEXICO

Treasure Island

CENTRAL AV.

Pasadena

GULFPORT BLVD.

Holocaust Museum

Salvador Dali Museum

St. Petersburg Museum of History

Gulfport

N

St. Pete Beach

Tampa Bay

0   2   4
Miles

Pass-A-Grille Beach

Tierra Verde

To Tampa

To Tampa

GANDY BRIDGE

HOWARD FRANKLAND BRIDGE

SUNSHINE SKYWAY BRIDGE

Fort DeSoto

To Bradenton & Sarasota

✈ Airport
★ Point of Interest

© The Countryman Press

Henry Plant connected the coastal cities with his railroad and built grandiose resort hotels, including the still-operational Belleview Biltmore (see *Lodging*) in 1897, establishing Clearwater as a destination. When Plant's railroad bypassed Disston City in favor of bustling St. Petersburg and its commercial shipping port, the development folded, and that area evolved into the quiet modern-day **Gulfport**, which boasts genteel neighborhoods of historic homes.

St. Petersburg started booming in earnest in 1911, with planned communities sprouting off the downtown business district along the many creeks and bayous draining into the bay. On New Year's Day 1914, history was made during the world's first commercial flight: Daredevil pilot Tony Jannus flew former mayor Ed Pheil from St. Petersburg Airport to Tampa for the princely sum of $400.

After the Florida boom went bust in the 1920s, the city remained a major destination for "Tin Can" tourists driving their jalopies down the eastern seaboard to escape the winter weather and camp out in the many parks around the city, which welcomed the influx of tourists. As that population aged, the region became known as a snowbird haven for retirees seeking to spend their winters in an inexpensive trailer court. Like most Florida cities, St. Petersburg experienced a population explosion immediately after World War II, when airmen assigned to the local bases decided to keep their families in Florida. **St. Pete Beach** broke off from the city and merged with its oceanfront neighbors to create a separate municipality in 1957, including **Pass-A-Grille**, an Old Florida fishing village that remains mostly residential. **Tierra Verde**, a collection of islands at the tip of the county, is the gateway to historic Fort De Soto. Art Deco hotels cropped up along the beachfronts, and the farms and fields yielded to sprawling suburban communities. The advent of television showcased the sparkling sands of Clearwater and Treasure Island, enticing more visitors to the region. Today's Pinellas County is the most densely populated of all of Florida's counties, its tourism infrastructure primarily a ribbon along the barrier islands and major highways.

GUIDANCE Overseeing the region's tourism is the **St. Petersburg/Clearwater Area Convention & Visitors Bureau** (727-464-7200 or 1-877-352-3224; www .floridasbeach.com), 13805 58th St N, Suite 2-200, Clearwater 33760. You'll find plenty of trip-planning information on their Web site.

Driving into Clearwater on FL 60, you'll see the **Clearwater/Pinellas Suncoast Welcome Center** (727-726-1547; www.visitclearwaterflorida.com), 3350 Courtney Campbell Cswy, open Mon–Sat 9–5, Sun 10–5 for brochures and travel information. For **Clearwater and Clearwater Beach** (727-447-7600 or 1-888-799-3199; www.beachchamber.com), stop at either the **Clearwater Chamber of Commerce Welcome Center** at 333 C Gulfview Blvd, open Mon–Fri 9–4, Sat 9–2, or the **Clearwater Beach Visitor Information Center**, 1 Causeway Blvd/Pier 60 Park, open daily 10–6 or longer. Both venues have brochures and someone to talk to about your needs.

In **Dunedin,** the Chamber of Commerce (727-733-3197; www.dunedin-fl.com) is downtown at 301 Main Street, and in **Tarpon Springs** (727-937-6109; www .tarponsprings.com) at 11 E Orange St.

In downtown St. Petersburg, you'll find the **St. Petersburg Chamber of Commerce** (727-821-4069; www.stpete.com), 100 Second Ave N, in front of bustling

Baywalk (see *Selective Shopping*). In Gulfport, ask for assistance at the **Gulfport Chamber of Commerce** (727-344-3711; www.gulfportchamberofcommerce .com), 2808 58th St S, and at the beach, stop in the **St. Pete Beach Chamber Information Center** (www.stpetebeach.com), 6990 Gulf Blvd.

GETTING THERE *By car:* Crossing the Sunshine Skyway northbound or the Howard Frankland Bridge southbound from Tampa, **I-275** provides primary north–south access. FL 60 west from Tampa connects with US 19 and Alt US 19 on the western side of the county. **I-275** and **US 19** provide primary access. **I-375** (exit 23A) leads you straight into downtown St. Petersburg.

By air: **Tampa International Airport** (see *Tampa and Hillsborough County*) is the closest option with the most choices. **St. Petersburg–Clearwater International Airport** (727-453-7800; www.fly2pie.com), 14700 Terminal Blvd, Clearwater, is off Roosevelt Boulevard on the north end of the Pinellas peninsula. They're home to Allegiant Air and USA 3000.

By bus: **Greyhound** (727-796-7315; www.greyhound.com), 2811 Gulf to Bay Blvd, Clearwater, and 180 Ninth St N, St. Petersburg (727-898-1496).

GETTING AROUND *By car:* This is a long linear beachfront county with not a lot of options for major highways. **I-275** slices through the eastern side of the county, south of Tampa, but most places you'll want to visit lie off either **Alt US 19, US 19,** or **CR 699** along the beach. **St. Petersburg** is laid out as a grid system, so finding your way around is a breeze. Avenues go east–west, streets go north–south. **Beach Blvd** follows the coastline from Vinoy Park past the Pier to the Basin. To find **Gulfport,** follow 22nd Ave S from either 54th St N or 49th St N. Keep going west to reach **St. Pete Beach.**

By bus: **Pinellas County Transit Authority** (727-530-9911; www.psta.net) offers several options, including the hourly Route 3 trolley from Treasure Island to St. Petersburg and Route 35 trolley from St. Pete Beach to St. Petersburg, and the ⅖ **Official Suncoast Beach Trolley** (www.psta.net/beachtrolley.htm) connects beach communities from Sand Key to Pass-A-Grille (average one hour, one way) every 20–30 minutes with well-marked bus stops; daily card, $3.50. The **City of Gulfport Trolley** runs Fri–Sat eve 6–10 PM. In Clearwater Beach, the **Jolley Trolley** (727-445-1200), 483 Mandalay Ave, offers trips at 10 AM to Sand Key and downtown Clearwater for $1, seniors and chidren, 50¢.

By taxi: Options include **Bats Taxi Company** (727-367-3702; www.BatsTaxi.com), 5201 Gulf Blvd, St. Pete Beach; in St. Petersburg, **Independent Taxi** (727-327-3444), 4121 Fifth Ave N; and **Pinellas Bay Taxi** (727-546-4955), 6800 49th St N.

PARKING When beachgoers swarm **Clearwater Beach**, parking can be tough to find, especially on weekends. For general parking information, call 727-562-4704. Metered lots run 75¢ to $1.25, attended lots up to $2 an hour, $10 a day max. Watch those meters carefully, as times vary. The largest lots at are 4 Rockaway Street and 51 Bay Esplanade on the north end, Pier 60 and the Marina in the middle, and 332 Gulfview Blvd on the south end. A savvy choice to avoid traffic is to park at **Sand Key Beach**, where there are more than 750 spaces, and catch the Suncoast Beach Trolley into Clearwater Beach. Farther south on Sand Key, you can park for free at Bay Park (no restrooms) with beach access across the street; the trolley stops there, too.

In **downtown St. Petersburg**, there is a lot of free parking, especially along Beach Boulevard, but it goes quickly. During the day your stay is limited to 90 minutes (8 AM–7 PM) and at night to 3 hours (7 PM–8 AM). And they *do* enforce it to the minute—you'll see the blinking golf carts of the parking authority enforcement officers zipping all over town. It's a very walkable city, so leave your car at your accommodations and hoof it, or pick one of the centrally located parking garages and keep it there while you explore. Street parking is free in **Gulfport** and virtually nonexistent in **St. Pete Beach**. As in Clearwater, beach parking packs a per-hour metered charge, varying by location.

Dunedin has lots of free street parking and several flat lots. At **John's Pass Village** in **Madeira Beach,** you'll pay $1 per hour—bring quarters! If you're lucky enough to find street parking in **Tarpon Springs**, it's free; otherwise, there are quite a few options for flat-fee flat-lot parking along Dodecanese Boulevard. Most shops and restaurants everywhere else offer free street parking or their own parking lots.

PUBLIC RESTROOMS In **Clearwater Beach** you'll find restrooms at Pier 60, along the roundabout. In **Dunedin,** look for them behind the caboose on Railroad Street. At **Madeira Beach** you'll find them adjacent to the parking area at John's Pass Village. In downtown **Tarpon Springs** they are midway down the block in the heart of the shopping district, while on Dodecanese Boulevard, you'll find them in the back of the Sponge Exchange. The classy architecture might let you slip right past without noticing the public restrooms at the corner of **Bayshore and Second Avenue NE,** next to the Museum of History, downtown St. Petersburg.

MEDICAL EMERGENCIES The largest medical center in the north portion of the county is **Morton Plant Hospital** (727-462-7500), 300 Pinellas St (Alt US 19), Clearwater, and to the south, **St. Petersburg General Hospital** (727-384-1414; www.stpetegeneral.com), 6500 38th Ave N, St. Petersburg.

✳ To See

AQUARIUMS ✐ Take a self-guided tour of the **Clearwater Marine Aquarium** (727-441-1790; www.cmaquarium.org), 249 Windward Passage, Clearwater, an educational and marine life rehabilitation facility with coral reef tanks, dolphins, and sea turtles. Trainers perform scheduled feedings. Adults $11, seniors $9, children 3–12 $7.50; open Mon–Sat 9–5, Sun 10–5.

✐ In Tarpon Springs, the centerpiece of the **Konger Tarpon Springs Aquarium** (727-938-5378; www.tarponspringsaquarium.com), 850 Dodecanese Blvd, is a 120,000-gallon main tank containing a living reef, which divers enter four times daily to feed the fish; there is also a touch tank room. Fee.

✐ ✇ A nonprofit marine education center, **The Pier Aquarium** (727-895-7437; www.pieraquarium.org), 800 Second Ave NE, is part of **The Pier** complex in St.

Petersburg (see *Attractions*) and is staffed by marine science students from local colleges. Habitats represented include Tampa Bay, California's kelp forests, and coral reefs of the Caribbean and Pacific Ocean. Children and adults alike will enjoy their many hands-on programs. Fee; free admission to all on Sunday.

ARCHEOLOGICAL SITES More than four thousand years ago, the **Safety Harbor Culture** built their homes on the bluffs overlooking northern Tampa Bay. The oldest park in Pinellas County, **Phillippe Park** (727-669-1947), 2525 Philippe Pkwy, Safety Harbor, preserves the site of some of the 1930s archeological finds that uncovered this ancient culture, as well as the site of the city and temple complex of Tocobaga, where Spanish explorer Pedro Menéndez de Avilés stopped in 1567. The park is named for Dr. Odet Phillippe, who founded the oldest settlement on the Pinellas Peninsula here in 1823, adjacent to Espiritu Santo Mineral Springs (see *Spas*).

At **Weedon Island Preserve** (727-453-6500; www.stpete.org/weedon.htm), 1500 Weedon Island Dr, St. Petersburg, explore the ancient cultures of Florida. In 1924 a Smithsonian Institution archeological dig led by J. Walter Fawkes discovered artifacts dated between A.D. 200 and 1000. Learn the story uncovered by these early researchers at the Learning Center, which explores the ten-thousand-year history of the island's peoples, and then walk the boardwalks and trails to immerse yourself in the landscape of mangrove forests, salt flats, and upland hammocks.

Along 1620 Park St N, St. Petersburg, a large **midden of oyster shells** bears this large hand-lettered sign: "HERE LANDED **PANFILO DE NARVAEZ,** APRIL 15, 1528." Tucked between residential lots, this archeological site (now on private land) was once an ancient village, and from this place, the Spanish explorer Narváez is credited with being the first European to launch an exploration of the North American continent. Please respect private property and view the site from the sidewalk.

ART GALLERIES

Belleair
I'll return soon to **The Miranda Gallery** (727-518-0071), 1764 Clearwater–Largo Rd, where Ellen Phaff's bold, bright tropical birds, fish, and palm trees shout "Florida!" and Frank Miranda's metal and wood sculptures capture the natural heart of our state. They plan to open a café out under the arbors, so stop by and visit. Since their mainstay is art shows, call ahead to ensure they're open.

Belleair Bluffs
In the airy **Art At The Plaza** (727-559-7767; www.artattheplaza.com), 100 Indian Rocks Rd N, you'll be enticed by works such as the marine life scenes of glassblower Chuck Boux, the large bronzes of Joe Rotella, and whimsical welded glass sculptures by Susan Pelish. Offering a nice mix of media, with many Florida artists represented.

Oil painting restoration is a unique art, and Laura Robinson Werner practices it

daily at **Wall Things, Etc**. (727-518-2032), 2617 Jewel Dr, her studio and
gallery space behind Traders Alley (see *Selective Shopping*). Laura also paints
vibrant watercolors and shares her space with antique glassware, glass art, the
distinctive portraiture of Edna Hibel, and an extensive collection of finely
detailed Civil War paintings by various artists.

Dunedin

At the **Dunedin Fine Art Center** (727-298-3322; www.dfac.org), 1143 Michigan Blvd, Dunedin, explore the galleries, visit the children's art museum (see
Family Activities), or sign up for a hands-on workshop in the visual arts.

Do not miss **The Painted Fish Gallery** (727-734-5060; www.paintedfish
gallery.com), 350 Main St, which features the creative spirit of Bill Renc as
expressed in colorful watercolor scenes of Florida landscapes, wading birds, and
fish—as paintings, drawings, and on ceramic tiles.

Gulfport

At **The Art Village** (727-459-1963; www.artvillagevoice.com), 2908–2914 Beach
Blvd, historic cottages surround a welcoming courtyard where there's live music
every weekend and working artists conduct classes outdoors. Call 727-344-3711
for information on Gallery Walks and Saturday Strolls. ✍ One prominent gallery
in the village is **Makin' Art** (727-323-4938; www.nancygable.com), 2914 Beach
Blvd, where artist Nancy Gable believes that art should be hands-on. "Touch
everything!" she told me, and then pointed out "celebration sticks" made from
fractured art reborn anew. Her creativity shines in a combination of common
items and found objects, with sticks and pottery becoming part of lamps and
chairs, paintings morphing into mosaics—creativity in motion. She encourages
her visitors, even the kids, to touch the art. If something breaks, no problem! It'll
become part of her newest work.

Largo

Part of the Pinewood Cultural Park, the **Gulf Coast Museum of Art** (727-518-
6833; www.gulfcoastmuseum.org), 12211 Walsingham Rd, offers nine permanent
collections and several changing galleries that focus on artistic contributions
from the southeastern states, plus a gift shop, sculpture gardens, and on-site studios with regular workshops. Open 10–4 Tue–Sat, noon–4 Sun; $8 adults, $7
seniors, $4 students, under 6 free.

Safety Harbor

Harborside Studios (727-723-8638), 176 Fifth Ave, is a working studio catering
to students with disabilities. Exhibits are on display year-round, showcasing bold
crimson pottery, paintings, and sculpture, with sales of art benefiting the students and the nonprofit studio.

St. Petersburg

St. Petersburg is truly a city of the arts, with more than 25 galleries in the downtown district. The nonprofit **Downtown Arts Association** (www.stpetearts.com)
arranges gallery walks the second Sat of each month until 9 PM. Contact the
DAA for a brochure and map detailing their member galleries. Here's a sampler
of what I saw while walking around downtown:

Part gallery, part shop, part classroom space, **The Arts Center** (727-822-7872; www.theartscenter.org), 719 Central Ave, offers demonstrations of fine arts, hands-on workshops for members (memberships start at $45 annually), and rotating exhibits of members' work in four classy galleries.

Florida Craftsmen Gallery (727-821-7391; www.floridacraftsmen.net), 501 Central Ave, features fine art for collectors, and has showcased members' work in all media for nearly two decades. Special exhibitions bring in fine-craft artists from around Florida.

Art glass appeals to my senses, and so I was drawn to the **Glass Canvas Gallery** (727-821-6767), 146 Second St N, a dazzling celebration of the fluid flow of this extraordinary medium, with swirls of color offered as sculpture à la Chihuly as well as more formally structured vases and bowls.

Red Cloud (727-821-5824; www.redcloudindianarts.com), 208 Beach Dr NE, showcases Native American arts, from dynamic ceramics to traditional masks, southwestern pottery, and ceremonial headdresses.

The **St. Petersburg Clay Company** (727-896-2529; www.stpeteclay.com), 420 22nd St S, in the historic train station, is the largest working clay studio and gallery in the Southeast, where you can buy finished art or raw supplies, rent a studio, attend a workshop, or sign up for hands-on private lessons.

The Studio @ 620 (727-895-6620; www.thestudioat620.com), 620 First Ave S, brings together local artists and their audience to celebrate the creative process. Kicking off with an exhibit of 100 Years of African-American Quilting, this newcomer to the local arts scene seeks to build bridges between the visual arts, music, poetry, theater, film, dance, and dialogue.

Studio Encanto (727-821-2959; www.encantoart.com), 209 First St N, showcases internationally collected artists as well as local talent such as Barry Nehr, whose painting of an egret in a cypress swamp stole my heart, and Monika Wilson with her mosaics. Owner and artist Esther M. Scott creates colorful painted tables, stained glass, and tiles.

ATTRACTIONS Part museum, part store, all blast from the past, the **Sponge-orama** (727-938-5366; www.spongeorama.com), 510 Dodecanese Blvd, takes you on a trip through Tarpon Springs's century-plus history of sponge diving, kicking off with a film on Florida's unique sponge industry, patterned after the Greek tradition of diving for sponges in the Dodecanese Islands. Dioramas showcase the various sponges found on the Gulf floor and their uses, and you can purchase your own to take home from the gift shop.

BASEBALL Spring training started nearly a century ago in the area and still packs the fans in at Clearwater's Bright House Field, 601 N Coachman Rd, where you'll catch the **Philadephia Phillies** (727-467-4457) in action along with their farm team, the **Clearwater Threshers** (www.threshersbaseball.com). The **Toronto Blue Jays** (727-733-0429) play in nearby Dunedin, as do their minor leaguers, the **Dunedin Blue Jays** (www.dunedinbluejays.com). The region's own Major League Baseball team, the **Tampa Bay Rays** (727-825-3137 or

The Pier (727-821-6164; www.stpete-pier.com), 800 Second Ave, is one of the city's oldest landmarks and unique in its inverted five-story design. It's been through several permutations over the years, established first by founding father Peter Demens in 1899, whose Orange Belt Railroad ran down a half-mile wharf. The first public pier opened in 1895, but most classic postcards show the "Million Dollar Pier" built in 1926, which was torn down in 1973 to create today's unusual structure. Housing a variety of shops (see *Selective Shopping*) and restaurants (see *Eating Out*), The Pier is also home to **The Pier Aquarium** (see *Aquarium*) and an observation deck with an excellent view of Tampa Bay. Parking costs $3 (optional valet $4), and a free shuttle runs between the parking lots and The Pier.

1-888-FANRAYS; www.raysbaseball.com), One Tropicana Dr, plays at Tropicana Field near downtown St. Petersburg.

HISTORIC SITES

Largo

✤ The history of Pinellas County through its early architecture is collected at **Pinewood Cultural Park** (727-582-2123; www.pinewoodculturalpark.org), 11909 125th St N, Largo, where a stroll into the piney woods takes you back in time to **Heritage Village,** a collection of original pioneer homes and early Pinellas County buildings such as the McMullen-Coachman Log Cabin, built in 1852 and the oldest existing structure in the county; the House of Seven Gables, a 13-room Victorian home from 1907; and the Safety Harbor Church from 1905. In all, there are more than 30 stops to visit, with living history docents to help you get the feel of frontier Florida. Open daily. Free; donations appreciated.

Pass-A-Grille

At **Fort De Soto Park** (see *Beaches*), explore the remains of Spanish-American War–era Fort De Soto, built by the federal government at the urging of railroad tycoon Henry Plant, who managed to also convince the government to use his Tampa Bay Hotel (see *Tampa and Hillsborough County*) as headquarters and departure point for troops headed to battles throughout the Caribbean. Built in 1898, the brick road along the battery now leads you down a historical trail, passing storehouses and living quarters

INSIDE THE OLD SULPHUR SPRINGS RAIL-ROAD STATION AT HERITAGE VILLAGE, LARGO

Sandra Friend

BELLEAIR To build his grand destination hotel, the **Belleview,** in 1895, railroad tycoon Henry Plant had nearly 1,000 acres overlooking Sand Key cleared of palmettos and pines, using mule-powered scrapers and hundreds of laborers. When Plant died in 1899, his son Morton took over the hotel's management. An avid golfer, Morton had the greens expanded from 6 to 18 holes by 1909, with a Donald J. Ross course that followed the natural features of this high bluff. Two wings—East and South—were also added to the hotel under Morton's direction. In 1919, the hotel became part of the Biltmore chain under John McEntee Bowman, and the name **Belleview Biltmore** (see *Lodging*) has stuck. According to early advertisements for the hotel, each bedroom had "3 incandescent lights, a polished cedar mantel and tiling around the fireplace, polished floors, and oak or cherrywood furniture." Between the wars, times were lean, and like other major hotels throughout the country, the Biltmore was taken over by the federal government to house soldiers, in this case the Army Air Corps, between 1942 and 1944. In 1947 the hotel reopened to guests. On a recent ghost tour of the hotel, the biggest surprise was that we were able to visit rooms that have remained closed off from guest use for more than 50 years, still containing artifacts from the military era, on floors and sections of floors that are never used. Imagine a hotel big enough you can just forget about operating parts of it! We were told, however, by the tour guide that sometimes the front desk gets calls from these long-forgotten rooms, which are not wired for electricity or phone. As you may imagine, this structure is full of ghost stories, including a haunted elevator.

It's heartening to see most visitors pause and look at the many historic displays along the main corridor on the first floor, recounting the story of the "White Queen of the Gulf." This is the last remaining destination resort hotel in Florida from the railroad tycoon era. The on-grounds Historical Museum contains vintage guest registers and photos, tools used around the hotel, guest history cards, and an original Istachatta Cypress Shingle Company shingle from the original roof. Each day at 11 AM, a fascinating historical tour highlights the Queen Anne decorative pieces, the Tiffany Room, Children's Private Dining Room, Sun Parlor Suite, and the fabled Underground Railway, used to wheel in luggage on handcars directly from the railroad tracks that once sat outside the hotel; fee. The ghost tour, now handled by an outside operator, only occurs on weekends and can be arranged through the concierge, $25 per person, cash only.

completed in 1906. Stairs enable you to climb atop Battery Laidley for a sweeping view of the bay. The army post included barracks, the mess hall, and 27 other buildings. By the time men were stationed at the fort, the war was over. During World War I, the heavy mortars installed to protect Tampa were dismounted and shipped to San Diego. Twenty-four men remained on duty, never needing to fire a shot. In 1922 the army decided that the forts were no longer needed for Florida's coastal defense. The island lay fallow and wave-battered for many years, used as a quarantine station and then a bombing range before the army sold the land back to Pinellas County. The county park opened to the public in 1963.

During the Civil War, **Egmont Key** (727-893-2627; www.floridastateparks.org/egmontkey), offshore from Fort DeSoto, served as an outpost for the Union Blockading Squadron as they played cat-and-mouse with Confederate blockade runners. It also housed a refugee camp for Confederate defectors, guarded by and eventually evacuated by the Union navy. The operational lighthouse, constructed in 1848 and open for tours, is surrounded by the brick streets of the ghost town of **Fort Dade,** built during the Spanish-American War. If you're a birder, bring your binoculars—Egmont is also a National Wildlife Refuge for migratory species. Egmont Key is an island, however, so approach is either by your own boat or commercial ferry service. ⚓ Departing from Fort De Soto Park (see *Beaches*) at 10 and 11 AM daily, the **Tampa Bay Ferry** (727-867-6569; www.hubbardsmarina.com) costs $15. The ferry also runs snorkel trips over the underwater ruins of Fort Dade ($10); rental of snorkeling equipment ($5) available.

St. Petersburg

Many historic buildings remain in **downtown St. Petersburg** (www.stpete.org/Landmarks1.htm) as residences and businesses, including many of the shops along Central Avenue, which was the city's 1920s boom "Main Street." There are also several designated residential historic districts, including **Granada Terrace** around Coffee Pot Bayou, Old Southeast, and Roser Park, all developed prior to 1926. Built in 1924 and thoroughly renovated in more recent times, **The Coliseum** (727-892-5202; www.stpete.org/coliseum.htm), 535 Fourth Ave, hosts major festivals and other special events, and was featured in the movie *Cocoon* as the dance hall. Another downtown site of interest is **Albert Whitted Municipal Airport** (www.stpete.org/air.htm), the site of the world's first commercial aviation flight in 1914, with scheduled service by National Airlines kicking off in 1934. Off the beaten path a little, look for **Admiral Farragut Naval Academy,** 501 Park St N, which started out as one of the region's original resort hotels, the Jungle Country Club, opened in 1926. Despite the exotic furnishings, it went bankrupt quickly and reopened as the academy in 1945. Despite the loss of many of the boom-era hotels, there are two nearby still in business and welcoming guests—the **Don CeSar** and the **Renaissance Vinoy Resort and Golf Club** (see *Lodging*).

Tarpon Springs

In the **Tarpon Springs Historic District,** visit the **Atlantic Coast Line Railroad Depot** (see *Railroadiana*) and wander down Tarpon Ave to **Spring Bayou** to see a grand array of Victorian homes, all turn-of-the-20th-century private residences. **Universalist Church** (727-937-4682; www.uutarpon.org), Grand Blvd and Read St, is home to the **Innis Paintings,** the world's largest collection of landscape paintings by George Innis Jr. For a step into Greece, visit the **St. Nicholas Greek Orthodox Church** (727-937-3540; www.epiphanycity.org) 36 N Pinellas Ave, which showcases the devotional detail of the Orthodox religion. One inscribed marble tablet was donated by settlers from Halki, an island of sponge divers near Rhodes. On Dodecanese Blvd, the **Sponge Exchange** (727-934-8758; www.thespongeexchange.com) and many of the buildings surrounding it date from 1908. In the early days, sponge boats would remain at sea for more than a month.

Built in 1883, **The Safford House** (727-937-1130; www.tarponarts.org), 23 Parkin Ct, is a beautiful example of early Florida vernacular architecture, built of virgin pine from the local sawmill. The original home was a typical dogtrot; when Anson Safford, one of the pioneering founders of Tarpon Springs, purchased it in 1887, he had it raised up and a second floor added underneath the original structure to accommodate the family's needs. In 1975 it was added to the National Register of Historic Places. The warm wooden rooms are decorated with furnishings evoking the period of Safford's residence. Docents lead tours to interpret the house's historic and architectural significance as well as the history surrounding the Safford family. Open 11–3 Wed and Fri and by appointment. Fee.

MUSEUMS

Dunedin
National Armed Services & Law Enforcement Memorial Museum (727-734-0700; www.naslemm.com), 500 Douglas Ave, commemorates the daily duties of the law enforcement and military officer, with exhibits ranging from a life-size electric chair to whiskey stills confiscated from Florida's piney woods during raids; fee.

Gulfport
At the **Gulfport Historical Museum** (727-327-0505; www.gulfporthistorical museum.homestead.com), 5301 28th Ave S, housed in a 1912 Methodist church, learn the history of this community founded in 1867 by a Civil War veteran and incorporated 20 years later as Disston City by developer Hamilton Disston as the largest incorporated town in Florida. Free; donations appreciated.

Safety Harbor
Filled with artifacts and exhibits interpreting the region's long history of more than ten thousand years of human occupation, the cozy **Safety Harbor Museum of Regional History** (727-726-1668; www.safetyharbormuseum.org), 329 S Bayshore Blvd, sits on the site of a Tocabaga shell mound along Old Tampa Bay. Open Tue–Fri 10–4; free.

St. Petersburg
Considered a top destination for lovers of the arts, the **Museum of Fine Arts** (727-896-2667; www.fine-arts.org), 255 Beach Dr NE, features world-class exhibi-

tions, such as the recent Monet's London: Artists' Reflections on the Thames, 1859–1914. Their comprehensive collection of more than four thousand works includes many French masters, from Cezanne to Renoir, and American artists such as Thomas Moran and Georgia O'Keeffe. Since 1965 they've showcased their masterworks in a plush setting akin to a grand home. Tue–Sat 10–5, Sun 1–5; fee.

 ♧ Experience the master of surrealism at the **Salvador Dalí Museum** (727-823-3767 or 1-800-442-3254; www.salvadordalimuseum.org), 1000 Third St S, which houses the world's largest collection of works by Dalí. Six of his 18 masterworks are housed in the museum, where curators offer detailed interpretation of the awe-inspiring canvases. There are more than 1,300 pieces in the permanent collection, displayed on a rotating basis. In a recent display of Dalí's commercial images, it was amusing to note his work appearing in 1950s advertisements for ladies hosiery and on the cover of a Jackie Gleason album. Boldly colored walls provide a backdrop to art that still surprises with sometimes delightful, sometimes disturbing, images. Opens 9:30 Mon–Sat, Thu until 8 PM, noon–5:30 Sun. Adults $15, seniors $13.50, ages 10–18 $10, ages 5–9 $4.

 ♧ One of the nation's largest, the **Florida Holocaust Museum** (727-820-0100; www.flhm2.org), 55 Fifth St S, humanizes the story of the 11 million who died in the Holocaust. Start your tour with a video that connects the horror of yesterday to the hate and prejudice faced by teens of today, and then follow the displays through a presentation of facts and figures to the Memory Wall, where in the open gallery you'll find the museum's centerpiece, boxcar #113 0695-5, which transported prisoners to Auschwitz. In the Court of Witnesses, experience an audiovisual presentation by survivors and liberators. Be sure to head upstairs for several changing galleries; I found the presentation Hitler's Soldiers in the Sunshine State particularly interesting since I knew very little about this chapter of Florida history—there were many POW camps in Florida, and prisoners harvested citrus and cut sugarcane during the war. As you exit, pop into the gift shop to browse history books and memorabilia. Open Mon–Sat 10–5; adults $12, under 18 $6, audio wand use free.

♧ A Smithsonian affiliate, the **Florida International Museum** (727-822-3693; www.floridamuseum.org), 100 Second St N, features rotating exhibits every few months. On my visit, I stepped into the '60s through a collection of vintage Barbie and her accessories, but I truly felt at home inside The Cuban Missile Crisis: When the Cold War Got Hot. I had chills listening to the crackly radio (". . . increases the likelihood of a nuclear war . . .") while walking through a kitchen not unlike my own from that era. The timeline swept me

ONE OF THE MANY PAINTINGS AT THE SALVADOR DALÍ MUSEUM
St. Petersburg/Clearwater Araea Convention & Visitors Bureau

St. Petersburg/Clearwater Araea Convention & Visitors Bureau

AVIATION EXHIBIT AT THE ST. PETERS-
BURG MUSEUM OF HISTORY

into a replica fallout shelter and, in an unexpected twist, a gallery of contemporary Cuban art. Open Mon–Sat 9–6, Sun 12–6; $20 adult, $17 senior, $15 military, $13 ages 6–12.

⚓ At the **St. Petersburg Museum of History** (727-894-1052; www.stpete museumofhistory.org), 335 Second Ave NE, history isn't just a thing of the past. Start your tour with a seven-minute historical overview video, and then let the interactive galleries take you on a walk through time, featuring touch-me artifacts such as a 1913 trolley car and an 1870 general store, as well as a canoe from the Tocobaga, who lived on the shores of Tampa Bay when the first Spanish conquistadors arrived in the 1500s. In the third-oldest historic museum in Florida, you'll learn a great deal about early aviation, the grand hotels of the 1920s boom, and St. Petersburg's many little-known historic neighborhoods. Open 10–5 Mon–Sat, 1–5 Sun; closed major holidays. Fee.

♿ ⚓ One of Florida's oldest science centers, **The Science Center of Pinellas County** (727-384-0027; www.sciencecenterofpinellas.com), 7701 22nd Ave N, showcases a marine-life room with a 600-gallon touch tank, an outdoor 16th-century Indian village, and for budding stargazers, the Minolta MediaGlobe planetarium and a powerful Meade 16-inch telescope. The gift shop is fun, too! It's a perfect place to take the kids. Open 9–4 Mon–Fri, fee.

Tarpon Springs
⚓ The **Leepa-Rattner Museum of Art** (727-712-5762; www.spjc.edu/central/museum), St. Petersburg College, 600 Klosterman Rd, is a hands-on gallery featuring the works of Abraham Rattner (1893–1978), a figurative expressionist, and Allen Leepa, Rattner's stepson, a retired professor of art. The collection includes pieces from Chagall, Picasso, Henry Miller, and other friends and contemporaries of Rattner, who is best known for his work on the Holocaust. The Challenge of Modern Art gallery is where kids (and adults) will have a blast stepping through a painting, standing within the elements of design, and working with media at a demonstration table. Closed Mon. Fee.

RAILROADIANA Depots on the **Atlantic Coast Line** in downtown Tarpon Springs and Dunedin were once part of the famous Plant System line that opened this region to commerce and tourism. Henry Plant's most famous contribution to the region, the opulent **Belleview Biltmore** (see *Lodging*), offers a daily historical tour that takes you beneath one of Florida's last of the grand railroad-era hotels to see where porters once pushed baggage carts down tracks connecting to the railroad sidings outside the building.

Were it not for the railroads, St. Petersburg might still be a sleepy little village by the bay. But the Orange Belt Railroad and Plant's grand system brought major commerce to the waterfront. Little remains from that era save the **Seaboard Coastline Railroad Station,** 420 22nd St S, which was built in 1926 for the Tampa and Gulf Coast Railroad, the second major player in the region. Home of the St. Petersburg Clay Company (see *Art Galleries*), it is open for tours, $10 per group.

✳ To Do

BICYCLING A paved ribbon in a green corridor stretching from Tarpon Springs to St. Petersburg, the **Fred Marquis Pinellas Trail** (see *Greenways*) provides bicyclists with nearly 34 miles of stress-free cruising, connecting communities and green space throughout the county along the route of the former Atlantic Coast Line. A free detailed map and guidebook can be downloaded off the Web site or ordered from the county to plan your adventure. Southern trailheads are at **Trail Head Park** in St. Petersburg on Fairfield Ave between 37th St S and 40th St S, and north of Pasadena at Azalea Park on 72nd St N. In Gulfport, rent your bikes at **Tropical Cycles** (727-463-7602), 2908 Beach Blvd, where they also rent surreys and beach cruisers for checking out the waterfront.

BIRDING Encompassing 31 acres in a heavily populated Largo, **Largo Central Park** (727-586-7415), 101 Central Park Dr, has three paved loops around man-made wetlands where you might spot roseate spoonbills from the observation tower or floating dock. In Seminole, **Boca Ciega Millennium Park** (see *Parks*) has a boardwalk along the bay, excellent for observing wading birds. Both **Caladesi Island State Park** and **Honeymoon Island State Park** (see *Beaches*) have hiking trails that bring you within easy viewing of nesting osprey and pelican colonies. And all along the beachfront, listen for the distinctive warbles of green conures, naturalized parrots that travel in flocks and can be seen emerging from holes in palm trunks. In St. Petersburg's **Granada Terrace,** herons and other wading birds flock to roost at sunset to an island off Coffee Pot Blvd. **Sawgrass Lake Park** (see *Parks*) is an excellent place to watch wading birds along the canals and osprey swooping over the lake. But the region's hot spot is **Egmont Key** (see *Historic Sites*)—it's a wildlife refuge devoted to migratory birds.

BICYCLISTS ON THE PINELLAS TRAIL
Sandra Friend

Clearwater Beach

Many cruises head out from the **Clearwater Municipal Marina** (727-462-6954), 25 Causeway Blvd, including the **Calypso Queen** (727-461-3113; www.showqueen.com), a giant floating piece of art billed as a "tropical party cruise," and the "world's largest speedboat," **Sea Screamer** (727-447-7200; www.sea screamer.com), which spouts an enormous wake as it cruises the bay in search of dolphins. And in case you were wondering about the pirate ship, there's ♂ **Captain Memo's Pirate Cruise** (727-446-2587; www.captainmemo.com), a long-standing nautical attraction. Take the kids on a two-hour daytime cruise, and save the evening Champagne Cruise for yourself; rates start at $33 adults, $28 seniors and juniors, $23 ages 3–12, and $8 for baby pirates (costume optional).

Gulfport

In Gulfport, dock your craft at the **Gulfport Municipal Marina** (727-893-1071), 4630 29th Ave, an easy walk from the business district.

St. Petersburg

Salt Creek Marina (727-821-5482), 107 15th Ave SE, is a popular option on the south side of downtown near the Dalí Museum, but the convenient-to-every-thing marina is at the bayfront near **The Pier**—the **St. Petersburg Municipal Marina** (727-893-7329; www.stpete.org/marina), 300 Second Ave SE. If you're looking to rent a boat, go to **The Electric Marina** (727-898-2628 or 1-888-898-BOAT; www.electricmarina.com), 372 Second Ave N, with electric watercraft so quiet you can slip right up behind dolphins. These 21-foot Duffy electric boats have a roof, CD/cassette, center dining area, and refrigerator and can be run bareboat or with a captain. Prices start at $40 per half hour, $75 per hour, seating up to 10.

ECOTOURS

Clearwater Beach

♂ On **Dolphin Encounter** (727-442-7433; www.dolphinencounter.org), cruise the Gulf of Mexico on the double-decker 125-passenger *Clearwater Express* to watch dolphins jumping in the surf and birds feeding on the shoreline. Multiple cruises daily, adults $21.50, ages 4–12 $11.45. Their claim is "you'll see a dolphin or your next trip is free!" Another great dolphin cruise is the **Little Toot** (727-446-5503; www.southernromance.com/littletoot/), a genuine tugboat that kicks up such a wake that the dolphins love to chase it; $17 adults, $11 children; tours at 11, 1, 3, 5, and sunset. **Sea Life Safari Nature Cruises** (727-462-2628; www.cmaquarium.org), departing from the Clearwater Municipal Marina and the Clearwater Marine Aquarium (see *Aquariums*), offers hands-on exploration of Tampa Bay with a biologist on board who pulls a trawl net for you to pick up and examine creatures of the bay. There's also an island stop where you can pick up seashells.

Tarpon Springs

♂ Enjoy a "sea"fari adventure on **Sun Line Cruises** (727-944-4468; www.sun linecruises.com), 776 Dodecanese Blvd, on a narrated tour of the Anclote River out to the Gulf of Mexico and surrounding bayous. A professional naturalist on board narrates local history, explains the sponge and shrimping industries, and points out wildlife along the way. It departs from the far west end of the sponge docks. Adults $16, seniors $15, children $9.

FAMILY ACTIVITIES

Clearwater

⚓ At **Pier 60 Park,** One Causeway Blvd (on the roundabout), let the kids go wild on the awesome collection of playground equipment, including a tugboat and giant slides within a massive canopied sandbox; a nearby concession stand and visitors center ensure that Mom and Dad have something to check out, too. Along Gulf Boulevard in both Indian Shores and Madeira Beach, **Smugglers Cove Adventure Golf** (727-398-7008; www.smugglersgolf.com) is a destination for playful mini golf. Feed the gators, too!

Dunedin

⚓ An outreach of the Dunedin Fine Art Center, the **David L. Mason Children's Art Museum** (727-298-3322; www.dfac.org/childmuseum.html), 1143 Michigan Blvd, provides special exhibits for kids, interactive workshops, and family programs.

St. Petersburg

⚓ At **Great Explorations: The Children's Museum** (727-821-8992; www.greatexplorations.org), 1925 Fourth St N, St. Petersburg, it's all about learning through exploring with play. Sail a ship, design your own robot, build a race car and race against your friends, or join in a workshop. Admission $9. Open 10–4:30 Mon–Sat, noon–4:30 Sun.

FISHING Check at the **Clearwater Municipal Marina** (see *Boating*) for numerous charter captains who'll take you on the flats or well offshore, including **Queen Fleet Deep Sea Fishing** (727-446-7666; www.queenfleet.com).

Recycling the old, the **Old Sunshine Skyway Bridge** (727-865-0668; www.floridastateparks.org/skyway), paralleling the Sunshine Skyway, provides a long linear state park from which to fish—the longest fishing pier in the world! Drop a line at **The Pier** (see *Attractions*), or join the crowd at the **Fort De Soto pier**. Offshore and flats fishing is hot, too—check in at the local marinas (see *Boating*) for an experienced guide.

GAMING The world's oldest continuously operating greyhound track is **Derby Lane** (727-812-3339; www.derbylane.com), 10490 Gandy Blvd, established in 1925. Open for live action greyhound races; simulcast thoroughbred racing; and the Derby Lane Poker Room.

GOLF In Largo, **Bardmoor Golf Course** (727-392-1234; www.bardmoorgolf.com), 7919 Bardmoor Blvd, is an 18-hole par 72 that used to host the JCPenney Classic on its well-landscaped grounds. Designed by Donald Ross, **Belleview Biltmore Golf Club** (727-581-5498 or 1-800-237-8947; www.belleview

biltmore.com), 1501 Indian Rocks Rd, is a classic Florida course dating from 1925 and part of the Belleview Biltmore (see *Lodging*) complex. Farther north in Clearwater, the **Chi Chi Rodriguez Golf Club** (727-726-4673), 3030 McMullen Booth Rd, offers a par 69 course with extensive landscaping to include more than 70 sand traps and a dozen water hazards.

The par 72 **Mangrove Bay Golf Course** (727-893-7800; www.stpete.org/golf/mangrove.htm), 875 62nd Ave NE, St. Petersburg, offers 18 holes of USGA championship golf on 180 well-maintained acres. Professional PGA lessons are available at this top-notch course, named one of the Top 100 most women-friendly golf courses by *Golf for Women* magazine.

Built in 1908, the **Tarpon Springs Golf Course** (727-937-6906; www.gulf coastflorida.com/tarpongolf), 1310 S Pinellas Ave, has classic styling with small, elevated greens.

HIKING In such an urban area, you wouldn't expect much hiking, but regional parks offer some beautiful boardwalks and a few natural surface trails though unspoiled habitats. At **Boyd Hill Nature Park** (see *Parks*), short nature trail loops lead from a paved path into a variety of habitats along Lake Maggiore. **Fort De Soto Park** (see *Beaches*) offers three short hiking trails—the Arrowhead Nature Trail is my favorite, leading to sweeping views along the bay. **Sawgrass Lake Park** (see *Parks*) has a mile's worth of boardwalk through a lush floodplain forest. In addition to the boardwalks at **Weedon Island Preserve** (see *Archeological Sites*), you'll find nearly 4 miles of trails following mangrove-lined levees and slicing through wet flatwoods. One of my favorite walks in the region is the quiet 3-mile loop on **Caladesi Island** (see *Beaches*), where hikers pass through several distinct habitats, including a virgin slash pine forest, mangrove forest, and coastal dunes. Explore more than 8,500 acres of wilderness at **Brooker Creek Preserve** (see *Wild Places*) on 4 miles of hiking trails.

PADDLING Saltwater kayaking is the major attraction in this region; my friend Sandy Huff, an authority on Florida paddling, puts in her craft at **Phillippe Park** (see *Archeological Sites*) to explore the wild mangrove fringe of northern Tampa Bay. Most waterfront parks and all beaches provide launch points to hit the surf, and for offshore places like **Caladesi Island** (see *Beaches*), paddling provides a way to get there and back on your own timetable. If you take the ferry to Caladesi Island, you can rent sea kayaks at **Café Caladesi** (727-443-4369)—$10 per hour or $35 per day single, $20 per hour or $60 per day tandem. For a day of freshwater paddling, head to **John Chesnut Sr. County Park** (see *Parks*) to explore the cypress-lined edges of massive Lake Tarpon and Brooker Creek, which flows into the lake. Launch your kayak at Soliders' Hole, **Fort De Soto Park** (see *Beaches*), for an intrepid exploration of the mangrove channels leading out to calm waters around the park's islands in Tampa Bay. A 2.3-mile marked canoe trail leads you through the maze, and rentals are available on-site.

SAILING Since 1964, Steve and Doris Colgate's **Offshore Sailing School** (1-800-221-4326; www.offshore-sailing.com) has trained students how to raise a sail, catch the wind, and then tack back to port, with a series of in-depth hands-on courses that turn landlubbers into live-aboards. In St. Pete, the Mansion House B&B (see *Lodging*) works in conjunction with Offshore Sailing School to wean you from land to sea, combining a downtown stay with a daily workout on the water until you're ready to cast off and cruise. Offered year-round, Learn to Sail courses run from three to nine days; check the Web site for seasonal pricing.

SPAS Espiritu Santo Mineral Springs, discovered by Hernando De Soto in 1539, has been a part of the **Safety Harbor Resort and Spa** (see *Resorts*) since the 1920s, a destination for "taking the waters" at the only natural mineral springs resort in Florida. Known as Green Springs in the 1850s, the springs were credited with healing the crippled, and the town of Safety Harbor became known as the "Health-Giving City" in the early 1900s, with each of the five springs credited with helping a different part of the body. The newly updated facility is an Aveda Concept Spa with a 50,000-square foot Spa Sanctuary containing 14 treatment rooms.

Among its many treatments, **Conscious Soul Day Spa** (727-725-3255; www .conscioussoul.com), 400 Second St N, offers an "All Wrapped Up in Chocolate" package, including a sugar body polish, 50-minute massage, facial, pedicure, and manicure—an afternoon of aromatherapy for chocolate lovers, $245.

Centered around a European spa pool, the **Belleview Biltmore Spa** (see *Lodging*) has luxe therapies for men and women, including the Golden Goddess with a sprinkling of gold dust and an 80-minute Hot Sea Shell Massage, $150 each.

✳ Green Space

BEACHES Pinellas County is well known for its famous strand stretching from **St. Pete Beach** north to **Clearwater Beach,** where white sand and aquamarine water beckons. St. Pete Beach is a destination for thousands of sun seekers, but most access the beach by stepping out the front door of their motel, condo, or cottage. There are no county parks along the beachfront, just public access points. At tiny **Gulfport,** there's a pretty public beach on Boca Ciega Bay, right along Shore Blvd, overlooking the line of condos on St. Pete Beach. **Fort De Soto Park** (727-582-2267; www.pinellascounty.org/park/05_Ft_DeSoto.htm), 3500 Pinellas Bayway S, Tierra Verde, hangs into Tampa Bay like a huge anchor on the map. Its 7 miles of isolated beachfront on five islands make up one of the top beaches in the continental United States. At the north end of the county, the Clearwater Beach waterfront appeals to families and folks streaming over from Tampa. So if you're looking for the quieter side, go north a little ways. It takes a very long walk or a ferryboat to get to **Caladesi Island State Park** (727-469-5918; www.floridastateparks.org/caladesiisland), but if you want solitude, there are miles of unspoiled beach to explore. 🐾 **Honeymoon Island State Park** (727-469-5918; www.floridastateparks.org/honeymoonisland), One Causeway Blvd, is the launch point for Caladesi Island and also offers uncluttered sandy shores with no condos in sight. **Caladesi Island Connection** (727-734-1501) provides the ferry, with shuttles beginning at 10 AM, $9 adults, $5.50 children; your stay is about four hours.

In Tarpon Springs, take Tarpon Avenue around Spring Bayou and follow the signs to **Fred Howard Park** (727-943-4081; www.pinellascounty.org /park/06_Howard.htm), 1700 Sunset Dr, a county park with picnic pavilions under the shade of the coastal scrub, a kayak trail, and a long, windswept causeway leading out to a palm-lined beach on the Gulf, where wheelchairs are available upon request for the physically challenged.

&. **Sand Key Park** (727-588-4852; www.pinellascounty.org/park/15_Sand_Key .htm), 100 Gulf Blvd, Sand Key, encompasses 95 acres at Clearwater Pass, with a beachfront that sweeps around to face the Clearwater strand. There are miles of walking trails, a dog park, picnic pavilions with grills, restrooms, and in-season lifeguards—everything you need to spend the whole day at the beach.

GARDENS

Largo

Florida Botanical Gardens (727-582-2100; www.flbg.org), 12175 125th St N, part of Pinewood Cultural Park, is a place to spend a couple of hours in quiet communion with the outdoors in a peaceful venue where art meets nature. Pathways meander between tasteful plantings of both native and tropical species, through forests of palm trees, past fountains and mosaics. Numerous benches make this a great destination for all ages, and gardeners will appreciate the detailed plant identification markers complete with information on water, light, and care needs of each species. A nature trail wanders off into one of the last untouched pine forests in this area. Walkways and bridges connect with the adjacent **Gulf Coast Museum of Art** (see *Art Galleries*) and **Heritage Village** (see *Historic Sites*). Open 7–7 daily. Free.

BANANA TREE IN BLOOM AT THE FLORIDA BOTANICAL GARDENS

Sandra Friend

St. Petersburg

Lose yourself in a forest of fronds at the **Gizella Kopsick Palm Arboretum** (727-893-7335; www.stpete.org/ palm.htm), North Shore Dr at 10th Ave NE, a 2-acre park with more than 300 palms and cycads showcasing more than 70 species, all well labeled for botanical enthusiasts. Free; adjacent free parking.

GREENWAYS The **Fred Marquis Pinellas Trail** (727-464-8200; www .pinellascounty.org/trailgd), 600 Cleveland St, Suite 750, Clearwater, is one of the busiest greenways in Florida, stretching from Tarpon Springs south to St. Petersburg and roughly parallel-

&. ✿ **Sunken Gardens** (727-551-3100; www.stpete.org/sunken), 1825 Fourth St N, is a Florida classic more than a century old, a sensory experience full of fragrances and colors, the burble of water and the play of sunlight through a virtual jungle of foliage. In 1903 local plumber George Turner Sr. began a tropical garden cascading down the slopes of an ancient sinkhole. In 1935 it officially opened as a tourist attraction, and by the 1950s it had a resident colony of flamingos, brilliant tropical macaws, and other wildlife complementing the winding paths through the lush forest. This quiet spot is still a true Florida treasure, a place to get lost under the canopy of trees and enjoy the well-maintained gardens. Best of all, the photo spots from the 1960s are still in place! Open 10–4:30 Mon–Sat, noon–4:30 Sun. Adults $8, seniors $6, children $4.

ing the route of Alt US 19. The **Clearwater Ream Wilson Trail** (727-562-4167) runs about 13 miles through residential and shopping areas, connecting Tampa Bay to Clearwater Beach, crossing the Pinellas Trail and heading across the Causeway to the beach.

NATURE CENTER ✿ In addition to its nature center full of activities and critters, **Moccasin Lake Nature Park** (727-462-6531), 2750 Park Trail Ln, Clearwater, has a nice 1-mile loop trail that crosses numerous fern-lined creeks. Fee.

PARKS

Largo
With 31 acres in the heart of the city, **Largo Central Park** (727-518-3047), 150 Highland Ave SE, is an urban getaway with almost a mile of paved trails and boardwalks winding through live oaks, wildflower and butterfly gardens, and across manmade marshes. A two-story observation tower is great for birding, and you can even kayak the waterways! ✿ **Walsingham Park** (727-549-6142; www.pinellascounty.org/park/22_Walsingham.htm), 12615 102nd Ave N, is a 354-acre county park with 4.5 miles of paved trails, plenty of picnic tables, a botanical area, and a paw playground.

Oldsmar
On the shores of Lake Tarpon, **John Chesnut Sr. County Park** (727-464-3347; www.pinellascounty.org/park/04_Chesnut.htm), 631 Chestnut Rd, offers picnicking and a boat launch, two waterfront boardwalks for exploring the shoreline, and a shady trail along Brooker Creek.

Safety Harbor
Safety Harbor City Marina, which includes **Veterans Memorial Marina Park and Muncipal Pier** (727-724-1545), 110 Veterans Memorial Ln, provides access to Tampa Bay for boats via a ramp and for visitors by a walk along the pier. Watch those anglers casting! An observation platform at the end of the pier

Sandra Friend

ALONG THE PIER IN SAFETY HARBOR

has a panoramic view of Tampa Bay, the Courtney Campbell Causeway, and the city of Tampa in the misty distance.

Seminole

🐾 Hugging Boca Ciega Bay, **Boca Ciega Millennium Park** (727-588-4882; pinellascounty.org/park/03_Boca_Ciega.htm), 12410 74th Ave N, Seminole, has numerous picnic pavilions, a boardwalk and tall observation tower along the bay, a rugged nature trail, canoe launch, and a paw playground for your pets.

St. Petersburg

Stroll the trails at **Boyd Hill Nature Park** (727-893-7326; www.stpete.org/boyd), 1101 Country Club Way S, to enjoy nearly 250 acres of natural habitats and cultivated gardens along the shores of Lake Maggiore. The paved Main Trail loops around the outer edge of the park, and numerous short loops lead off it to showcase specific environments, such as a willow marsh, sand pine scrub, and floodplain forest. A former zoo, the park also showcases raptors in an aviary near the entrance and provides exhibits on native habitats at the Lake Maggiore Environmental Education Center. Closed Mon. Fee.

Protecting nearly 400 acres of wetlands, **Sawgrass Lake Park** (727-526-3020; www.pinellascounty.org/park/16_Sawgrass.htm), 7400 25th St N, is an oasis of green along I-275 and the Pinellas Park border. Boardwalks lead through a red maple swamp, and you're guaranteed to see alligators and soft-shell turtles from the observation deck. A nature center at the parking area introduces the habitats and their residents.

AMID THE LIMBS OF AN ANCIENT LIVE OAK AT PHILLIPPE PARK

Thanks to William L. Straub, the editor of the *St. Petersburg Times* in 1909, nearly 7 miles of Tampa Bay's waterfront has been preserved in a string of parks through St. Petersburg, with its northern anchor **Vinoy Park,** a delightful village green beneath a shady canopy of oaks.

Tarpon Springs

A L Anderson Park (727-943-4085; www.pinellascounty.org/park/01_Anderson.htm), 39699 US 19 N, Tarpon Springs, covers more than 100 acres on the western shore of Lake Tarpon. It's a popular place for picnicking and fishing, and kids will love the playground. The Jungle and Lake Boardwalks provide great places to commune with nature.

SPRINGS With nearly 200 acres on the coast, **Wall Springs Park** (727-943-4653; www.pinellascounty.org/park/21_Wall_Springs.htm), 3725 De Soto Blvd, Palm Harbor, protects a small historic spring used as a spa and bathing area until the 1960s. The park provides access to the Fred Marquis Pinellas Trail (see *Greenways*), and now has quite a slate of features, including extensive boardwalks on the bayou and a tall observation tower, picnic shelters, a playground, and a memorial sundial. Swimming is not permitted in the spring.

WILD PLACES Lying 3 miles offshore, **Anclote Key Preserve State Park** (813-469-5918; www.floridastateparks.org/anclotekey) doesn't get a lot of visitors—which is what makes this barrier island extra special for beach lovers and birders alike. There are no established trails, so walking the beach is the way to spy ospreys nesting, eagles cruising along the coast, and American oystercatchers poking around for a meal. There is no formal ferry, so you must charter a boat (or pilot your own) to visit this unspoiled treasure. Easier to get to is **Brooker Creek Preserve** (727-453-6900; www.friendsofbrookercreekpreserve.org), 3620 Sletch Haven Dr, which protects more than 8,500 acres of unspoiled forests at the northern edge of the county.

A tangled jungle of mangroves along Tampa Bay, **Weedon Island Preserve** (see *Archeological Sites*) provides this area's only place to wander into the wild, where the whine of highway traffic is replaced by the whine of mosquitoes. Nearly 4 miles of trails wind through tunnels of mangroves and sometimes-flooded flatwoods. Stop by the visitors center to get the full picture of the rich prehistory of this site, and walk the (not-so-wild) boardwalks to an observation tower that provides a panorama of Tampa Bay and views of both downtown Tampa and St. Petersburg.

✳ Lodging

BED & BREAKFASTS

Gulfport 33707

"♈" ⊗ Blending the exotic with the historic, **Sea Breeze Manor** (727-343-4445 or 1-888-343-4445; www.seabreezemanor.com), 5701 Shore Blvd, is a place to relax. It appeals on many sensory levels, from its globe-trotting island decor and comfortable beds to each room's private balcony or porch catching the sea breeze off adjacent Gulfport Beach on Boca Ciega Bay. This 1923 Tudor features five massive well-appointed rooms with television, VCR, CD player, and wireless Internet access, plus two cottages on the courtyard ($155–180). Everyone in town knows innkeeper Lori Rosso, and she delights in letting you know the fun places to eat, drink, and shop. Enjoy a leisurely home-cooked breakfast on the main balcony overlooking the waterfront, and leave your car parked—everything you'll want to see and do is an easy walk down the street.

Redington Beach 33708

❧ I'm ready to move into the unique **Park Circle B&B** (727-394-8608; www.parkcircle.com), Seven Park Circle, an intimate neighborhood of original two- and three-bedroom 1940s bungalows. Renovated in 1997, these charming homes ($180 and up) feature original tile in the kitchens and baths and original kitchen cabinets with updated appliances. Each house has its own garage, screened porch, and grassy courtyard. Host Margaret Bourgeois serves up a tasty breakfast at the office each morning, and guests can mingle at the new communal pool and cabana area or keep to themselves in their roomy, romantic bedrooms. Take a virtual tour beforehand on their Web site, and choose your dream home.

Safety Harbor 34695

Conveniently located downtown within walking distance of shops and restaurants, **The Ibis** (727-723-9000; www.ibisbb.com), 856 Fifth St S, is a modern bed & breakfast that offers three pretty guest rooms ($125–165), each with private bath and unique quilts.

St. Petersburg 33701

Inn at the Bay (727-822-1700 or 1-888-873-2122; www.innatthebay.com), 126 Fourth Ave NE, is another success story of saving a historic structure—in this case, the oldest continuously occupied rooming house in St. Petersburg, established by Anna Morrison in 1910. Renovation wrapped up in 2001, and you can now enjoy the results—each of the 12 units ($155–240) has a uniquely Florida theme, like the Siesta Key, the Manatee, and the Lighthouse ($290—a third-floor honeymoon suite), and most come with a whirlpool for two.

Children older than eight welcome, but with the romantic ambiance of these rooms (and the buttery-soft robes), you'll want to leave them at home.

❧ ❀ A 1920s hotel abandoned to a crumbling neighborhood, **La Veranda B&B** (727-824-9997 or 1-800-484-8423; www.laverandabb.com), 111 Fifth Ave N, became the phoenix that put the surrounding community back on its feet, thanks to the efforts of Nancy Mayer, who took over the building in 1995 with "a passion to restore houses." Parts of the complex date from the 1890s and offer vintage charm—low doorframes and water-glass windows. All five rooms ($99–250) have private exterior entrances, unique period decor, and a large veranda for relaxing. I luxuriated in the roomy Cinnabar, enjoying a bath in the claw-foot tub—bath salts and candles included. The resident cats will join you for breakfast under the ivy trellis, and what a breakfast—I enjoyed the raisin French toast with apples and walnuts with a citrus granita.

Feel pampered at the **Mansion House B&B and The Courtyard on Fifth** (727-821-9391 or 1-800-274-7520; www.mansionbandb.com), 105 Fifth Ave NE, where a comfortable bed piled with pillows awaits. The first mayor of St. Petersburg, David Moffett, lived in the Mansion House, which in 1901 anchored the development of the Northeast District, just up the street from the Vinoy Park Hotel, in which he was a partner. This home, the adjoining Kemphurst (1904), and a carriage house are clustered around a private brick courtyard with a swimming pool and hot tub. Each house has an upstairs library—

and you know how we writers love libraries—plus the parlor and kitchen areas to mingle, or enjoy the intimacy of your well-appointed room with its polished hardwood floor. Original art from resident artist Marva Simpson and handmade bedding by Pat Berry grace the 12 individually themed rooms ($139–250), but I was most grateful for the antique writing desk in mine.

Now here's a charmer with an interesting story—the **Sunset Bay Inn** (727-896-6701 or 1-800-794-5133; www.sunsetbayinn.com), 635 Bay St NE, was the 1940s childhood home of Martha Bruce, who with her husband, Bob, acquired and renovated the house into a bed & breakfast in 1996. In this 1911 Colonial Revival, there are eight themed units ($150–270), including two in the carriage house, ranging from the elegant, masculine, golf-themed Augusta Room to Marthasville, with bright candy stripes, a skylight, and a claw-foot tub, to the elegant Monterey Suite with its Jacuzzi and mini kitchen.

Tarpon Springs 34689

An English Tudor mansion built in 1904, the **Bavarian Inn** (727-939-0850 or 1-800-520-4446; www .bavarianinnflorida.com), 427 E Tarpon Ave, became a bed & breakfast in 2000 and continues operation under the care of innkeepers Dave and Lynn. There are nine rooms on two floors, including spacious suites such as the Edelweiss (sleeps four, $95–180) and themed rooms such as the Tropical and Magnolia ($70–115). Historic touches include the original lighting system and a large common parlor, where guests can mingle and are welcome to borrow from the VHS library to watch movies in the privacy

of their own room. Older children welcome.

I felt like I'd stepped into my great-grandmother's house at the **Spring Bayou Inn** (727-938-9333; www.springbayouinn.com), 32 W Tarpon Ave, a 1905 Victorian in the middle of the Historic District, with tower rooms, gleaming heart-pine wood floors, and a 1920s baby grand piano in the parlor. History buffs take note: The home once served as staff quarters for the long-departed Tarpon Inn. Wood crowns accent the molding around the doors and windows in the three spacious rooms and two large suites ($99–159). I found the Orchid Suite just perfect for a working writer; wireless Internet access is free—just ask! Hosts Bill and Sherri Barzydlo provide a gourmet breakfast each morning; Bill completed Le Cordon Bleu Classic Cuisine. And talk about location! It's just a minute's walk up the street to the heart of the shopping district and a short stroll down to the waterfront. Well-behaved children welcome.

HOTELS, MOTELS, AND RESORTS

Belleair 33756

With the vintage shuffleboard courts out front, **Belleair Village Motel** (727-584-7131; www.belleair village.com), 1025 Clearwater-Largo Rd, is a retro look at our 1950s tourism roots, offering clean, roomy, vintage accommodations surrounding a sparkling pool. Motel rooms are $65–75, efficiencies and apartments rented by the week, $250–335.

When it opened in 1896, it was the jewel in the crown of Henry Plant's railroad hotel empire, the "White Queen of the Gulf," the ultimate destination for wealthy northeasterners seeking a tropical paradise at the end of a direct train from New York City. The oldest operating hotel in Florida, the **Belleview Biltmore** (727-373-3000; www.belle viewbiltmore.com), 25 Belleview Blvd, is on the National Register of Historic Places and, I am pleased to report, saved from demolition after the hard-working efforts of local preservationists. In May 2009, the hotel will close for a full restoration, including removal of portions of the hotel that are not true to its origins. But before it does, I encourage you—see it now!

I've made frequent visits to this historic site, and standing in a hallway, looking down the broad, never-ending corridor, it feels like you're in a very different world, where ladies stroll side-by-side in hoop skirts. This is the largest occupied wooden structure in the world, thanks to the naturally fire- and termite-resistant properties of heart pine and cypress wood used for the structural timbers. The hotel is reminiscent of the Grand Hotel of Mackinac Island, but on an even grander, larger scale. Polished wood plank floors, high ceilings with chandeliers, and transoms over the doors are all part of the vintage decor. You'll chuckle at the uneven upper floors, inevitable in a wooden building of this age, en route to your room, which has elegant touches such as wooden chair rails and baseboards, glass doorknobs, and a tiled bathroom. Although the furnishings have been updated, I found an antique luggage stand in the walk-in closet. Choose from standard rooms, junior suites, or suites; rates start at an affordable $79. Valet or free self-parking.

Down the main hall, a high-tech business lounge with complimentary Internet access sits across from Henry's Library, an intimate meeting room dominated by Plant's portrait and rows of bookshelves. The J. Harrison Smith Fine Art Gallery adjoins the Historic Museum. The Palm Grill (see *Dining Out*) is the resort-causal dining option in the hotel, with Maisie's Ice Cream Parlor down the hall serving sandwiches and sweets. The links (see *Golfing*) remain a top-notch destination for golfers. The main hotel complex offers an enormous pool, playground, and tennis court complex, but free shuttle service is also provided to their beachside property, the Cabana Grill (see *Dining Out*) on Sand Key, with its ocean-front pool and fine dining.

Clearwater Beach 33767

Like the beach motels of my youth, where the rooms have jalousie windows to let the sea breezes pour in, the **Amber Tides Motel** (727-445-1145; www.ambertides-motel.com), 420 Hamden Dr, is centered around a lush tropical courtyard surrounding the pool. From $55 for a standard room up to $105 for a one-bedroom

THE BELLEVIEW BILTMORE

Sandra Friend

apartment, it's a compact family-oriented getaway.

❝❡❞ The intimate **Beachouse** (727-461-4862; www.flbeachouse.com), 421 Hamden Dr, is nestled right along Clearwater Harbor with a plunge pool and spa offering a southern exposure perfect for sunbathing. This 1950s nonsmoking inn is family owned and operated and a Superior Small Lodging, offering large spacious rooms with solid cement walls—no hearing your neighbors here! Clean and quiet, it's a restful retreat, $95–105.

❝❡❞ The Art Deco **Palm Pavilion Inn** (727-446-6777; www.palmpavilion .com), 18 Bay Esplanade, is one of the most appealing Superior Small Lodgings choices on the beach. It's been in the preservation-conscious Hamilton family for years, a mainstay where other vintage lodgings have vanished. The 29 rooms ($100 and up) range from standard to one-bedroom apartments. Every room has an in-room safe and Internet access, and my comfortable choice included retro avocado doors and trim, a tiled bath, and a refrigerator. Given its central location, I was surprised how quiet it was late at night. Enjoy the heated outdoor pool or walk between the dunes to reach the beach in moments.

🐾 At the **Sands Point Motel & Suites** (727-446-5608 or 1-800-433-2362; www.sandspointmotel.com), 438 Coronado Dr, rooms overlook the pool, and the beach is just a block away. All rooms and suites ($50–120) are newly renovated, with efficiencies sporting a full kitchen/dining area; weekly rates top out at $650, so move right in!

♿ A 1952 landmark across from the Clearwater Marina, **Sea Captain Resort on the Bay** (727-446-7550 or 1-800-444-7488; www.seacaptain resort.com) has great curb appeal with their white walls, blue accents, and curving architecture so typical of the Greek Islands. Inside, you'll fall in love with this Superior Small Lodging's broad variety of configurations of rooms, from simple motel rooms to large efficiencies and suites, most with doors at both ends, $94–156. A few boat slips are available to guests, and the pool and spa look right over the action at the marina. Continental breakfast served weekends.

Dunedin 34698

♿ 🐾 After spending a weekend here to celebrate a friend's birthday, I just love the **Blue Moon Inn** (727-784-3719 or 1-800-345-7504; www.theblue mooninn.com), 2920 Alt US 19 N, with its spacious rooms and suites with large picture windows and patios overlooking sweeping green lawns, a heated pool, and a playground. There are only nine rooms, which makes this an intimate gem. The standard suites ($94–139) include two full-size beds; the deluxe suites ($119–169) offer a king-size bed, separate bedroom and living room areas, and a massive bathroom with Jacuzzi tub for two. All suites have a sleeper sofa, wet bar, microwave, coffeemaker, and numerous other amenities; a continental breakfast buffet is included.

🐾 Step into the 1950s at **Seaside Artisan Motel** (727-736-4657; www .ij.net/seasideartisan), 1064 Broadway, where the nine units ($60–80) have jalousie windows and tiled floors, full kitchens, and large showers—a real old-time road-trip motel, remodeled but retaining that genuine Florida flair.

♿ ❝❡❞ **Best Western Yacht Harbor Inn** (727-733-4121 or 1-800-447-4728; www.yachtharborinn.com), 150

Marina Plaza, is by no means a typical chain hotel. In the best tradition of Florida waterfront accommodations, these are superb rooms and suites ($125–180) with vintage architecture and an amazing location, surrounded by Clearwater Harbor and the Dunedin marina, and you with a patio or private balcony to enjoy the view. The on-site restaurant, Bon Appetit, (see *Dining Out*), is simply superb. And best of all, you're downtown—it's just a block to walk to the quaint historic downtown and all its shopping and art galleries.

Gulfport 33707

∞ "ɪ" The **Peninsula Inn & Spa** (727-346-9800; www.thepeninsulainn spa.com), 2937 Beach Blvd, evokes the grand adventures of British explorers in the 1800s. Karen and Bob Chapman finished renovations of this century-old hospital building in 2003, and the results are stunning. Climb the staircase or use a restored original elevator to reach your room, one of 11 well-appointed units, each with a uniquely themed decor. Some, like the Serengeti, are two- or three-room suites with a sitting room and bedroom; others, like the Nile, are smaller but just as elegant. Enjoy sleigh beds, cable TV, wireless Internet, child-sitting services, two fine restaurants (see *Dining Out*), and a full-service spa on the premises, all within an easy walk of all of Gulfport; $129–189 in-season.

Indian Rocks Beach 33785

Small and appealing, the seaside **Colonial Court Inn** (727-517-0902; www.colonialcourtinn.com), 318 Gulf Blvd, offers six different configurations of apartments (all with kitchen), a guest house, and a cottage, with

rates starting at $80 off-season, $110 in-season. Each unit is themed and has cable TV, microwave, stereo, VCR, and telephone. Pathways lead through the tropical arbor and butterfly gardens toward the beach.

The **Great Heron Inn** (727-593-5518; www.heroninn.com), 2008 Gulf Blvd, has a pool overlooking the beach, with most of the rooms centered around the pool and courtyard ($75–110). A few rooms have a direct view of the ocean ($90–145). Each unit is a small apartment with a sleeper sofa in the parlor, full kitchen, bedroom, and full bath, maximum five guests per unit. See a virtual tour of the rooms on their Web site.

Madeira Beach 33708

�--- Aspiring thespians note: A stay at the **Snug Harbor Inn** (727-395-9256; www.snugharborflorida.com), 13655 Gulf Blvd, will immerse you in the stage production of your choice. Hosts T. G. and Susan Gill parlay their years in the theater to theme their eight classic units after productions such as *On Golden Pond* (complete with play props and a screen door) and *Same Time Next Year* (a piano for your pleasure). Renovated in 2000, these 1950s apartment suites ($72 and up) include a full kitchen and sitting area.

Redington Beach 33708

�--- At the **Island House Resort Hotel** (727-392-2241; www.island houseresort.com), 17103 Gulf Blvd, the rooms surround a tropical pool. Built in the 1950s, these large units are a good value for the price ($50–80) and vary by size from a motel to a two-bedroom apartment. Beach access is next to the Hilton.

Safety Harbor 34695

"¶" ○○ ⅋ A destination resort since the 1920s, **Safety Harbor Resort and Spa** (727-237-8772 or 1-888-BEST-SPA; www.safetyharborspa .com), 105 N Bayshore Dr, offers a different take on Florida history— relax at an upscale spa with pools of mineral water emerging from springs discovered by Hernando De Soto in 1539. The hotel's spacious guest rooms overlook the expanse of Tampa Bay; rates start at $129, with numerous spa and entertainment packages available.

St. Pete Beach 33706

Enjoy your own village by the sea at **Beach Haven Villas** (727-367-8642; www.beachhavenvillas.com), 4980 Gulf Blvd, a 1950s motel with 18 units and plenty of charm. This Superior Small Lodging offers small but bright rooms with classic tiled baths in a mix of standard rooms and efficiencies ($83–175), each with a VCR in the room. The heated pool overlooks the ocean.

The **Bon-Aire Resort Motel** (727-360-5596; www.bonaireresort.com), 4350 Gulf Blvd, is a Florida classic circa 1953, an open rectangle with rooms facing the pool and beach. It's been in the same family for more than 45 years. The efficiencies and standard units ($63–155, discounts for full weekend bookings) have that '50s charm, and the baths are large for the era. Each kitchenette has a mini stove, mini fridge, coffeemaker, and dishes.

⅋ 🖉 🐾 ○○ "¶" The **Don CeSar Beach Resort & Spa** (727-360-1881 or 1-800-282-1116; www.doncesar .com), 3400 Gulf Blvd, the pink palace on the beach, is the quintes-

sential seaside resort, the 1926 creation of Thomas J. Rowe and a grand reminder of the Florida boom, on the register of the National Trust for Historic Preservation. But it wasn't always so. This grand dame was neglected, almost demolished. Despite its parade of celebrity guests, including the New York Yankees in the 1930s trying out the new concept of spring training in Florida, and F. Scott Fitzgerald taking Zelda for a jaunt in the wilderness—for it was truly wilderness back then—this 277-room hotel didn't last long. After Rowe died in 1943 and his heirs divested themselves of the property, the Don became a rest and relaxation center for recuperating servicemen, and then

THE DON CESAR HOTEL

Sandra Friend

a Veteran's Administration Hospital for 22 years. In 1967 the gutted building was abandoned; several years later, local resident June Hurley Brown started a "Save the Don" campaign. With $30 million in renovations, the hotel celebrated its grand reopening in 1973. Little of the original interior remains, but the re-creation of the hotel's grandeur is striking. On the fifth floor, the marble fountain that once graced the lobby was the meeting place of Rowe and the love of his life, his mistress, Maritana. Their ghosts are said to meet there still. Employees insist that Rowe, who breathed his last on the main floor, continues to watch over the hotel; his presence in a white suit and hat has been noted whenever a new set of renovations are under way. Now part of the Loew's family, the hotel offers family- and pet-friendly amenities in a world-class setting. Enjoy afternoon tea in the lobby, or kick back poolside at the Sea Porch Café. Swim in two oceanside pools with piped-in underwater music, or relax on the beautiful beach itself. The standard rooms offer a 1920s feel with modern sensibilities, including high-speed and wireless Internet access, and rates start around $214.

✑ Painted concrete pathways lead you through the appealing **Plaza Beach Resort** (727-367-2791 or 1-800-257-8998; www.plazabeach.com), 4506 Gulf Blvd, a family-owned motel where each kitchenette ($76–249) has a full fridge, and the rooms have big picture windows. The delightful patio area leading to the beach has a heated pool, shuffleboard, and life-size chess board along with a picnic area in sight of the sea. 🐾 Their sister property, the **Bayview Plaza Resort** (727-367-

2791 or 1-800-257-8998; www.thebay viewplaza.com), 4321 Gulf Blvd, offers fully equipped kitchens, daily housekeeping, and a private pier with dockage for guests, $59–189.

St. Petersburg 33701

A historic landmark set right across from the waterfront at Vinoy Park, the intimate **Grayl's Hotel** (727-896-1080 or 1-888-508-4448; www.grayls hotel.com), 340 Beach Blvd NE, conveys a sense of privacy while offering rooms and suites with tasteful decor evoking both St. Pete's hip present and the past—look for the antique radio in the corner. This 1922 apartment building was once so dilapidated-looking it was almost condemned, but the Grayl family stepped in more than a decade ago and coaxed a phoenix from the ashes. The results are stunning and well worth the room rate (30 units, $99–250, most with a separate kitchen area).

⇨ ⟐ ⊙ 🍽 Opened on New Year's Day 1926, the **Renaissance Vinoy Resort and Golf Club** (727-894-1000 or 1-888-303-4430; www .marriott.com/hotels/travel/tpasr -renaissance-vinoy-resort-and-golf -club), 501 Fifth Ave N, is a fanciful bayside destination with a blend of Mediterranean Revival and Moorish architecture. During the 1940s, soldiers occupied the hotel for rest and recuperation. The hotel has since been fully restored to its original elegance, and provides up-to-date amenities such as high-speed Internet access, fluffy robes, and VCRs. There are seven restaurants and lounges, a fitness center, day spa, and heated pool on-site. A complimentary shuttle takes guests to the beach. Rates begin around $209, with parking (valet or self) adding to the bill.

Treasure Island 33706

Relax in comfort at the intimate **Beach Side Palms** (727-360-1459; www.beachsidepalms.com), 10200 Gulf Blvd, where the six units ($75–165)—two studio efficiencies, three two-room apartments, and a five-room apartment—have direct access to the beach. Natural light floods each room to reveal classy furnishings and a full kitchen. Sit on the patio or play shuffleboard on an old-fashioned board. An outdoor grilling area overlooks the beach.

COTTAGES

Treasure Island 33706

🐾 **Seahorse Cottages** (727-367-7568 or 1-800-741-2291; www.seahorse -cottages.com), 10356 Gulf Blvd, are the way a trip to the beach used to be—peering out the windows of your little wood-frame cottage through the sea oats and sea grapes to drink in that incredible Gulf view. Natural light floods these delightful 1939 cottages, each with a full kitchen and a typical-for-the-era tiny bath and shower; $95–155, weekly rates available.

CAMPGROUNDS

Dunedin 34698

Behind the Blue Moon Inn (see *Hotels, Motels, and Resorts*), the **Dunedin RV Resort** (727-784-3719 or 1-800-345-7504; www.dunedinrv .com), 2920 Alt US 19 N, has a healthy winter snowbird population but offers overnight electric back-in sites for $32–43. Dump station available.

Palm Harbor 34683

With both shady and sunny sites, **Caladesi RV Park** (727-784-3622; www.caladesirvpark.com), 205

Dempsey Rd, has easy access to the Pinellas Trail (see *Greenways*) and an ice cream parlor out front. What more could a camper need? Nevertheless, you'll also get a heated pool and laundry room with your full-hookup site.

🐾 **Sherwood Forest RV Park** (727-784-4582; www.meetrobinhood.com), 175 Alt US 19, is one of the few campgrounds in the region to welcome tent campers ($35 for two people) on no-hookup spaces. Full-hookup spaces cost $55. The park has a mix of shady and sunny sites.

St. Petersburg 33708

🐾 Ready for your own private seaside view? Pick the right campsite at **Fort De Soto Park** (see *Beaches*), and you'll have an unimpeded view of where Tampa Bay meets the Gulf of Mexico. Each spot (water and electric) is shaded by tall Australian pines ($30–35). Pets accepted in certain campsites.

Hidden along a mangrove-lined bayou, the **St. Petersburg/Madeira Beach KOA Resort** (1-800-562-7714; www.koa.com/where/fl/09144/ index.htm), 5400 95th St N, is an appealing spot to set up camp and see the local attractions, with tent sites, full hookup sites, and Kamping Kabins with air-conditioning available.

✳ Where to Eat

DINING OUT

Belleair

In the Belleview Biltmore (see *Lodging*), the resort-casual **Palm Grill** offers long-standing classics in an elegant setting. The rich and creamy rock shrimp bisque has a hint of sherry, and kernels of corn to add crunch. I love the Biltmore Salad, made with mixed greens, tomatoes, goat cheese, candied pecans, and balsamic vinegar. Entrées run $14–30. Save room for a luxurious dessert, such as Bailey's mousse or Key lime pie.

Dunedin

∞ Savor the view of Clearwater Harbor from your waterfront table at **Bon Appetit** (727-733-2151; www.bon appetitrestaurant.com), 150 Marina Plaza, where Chef Stephen creates daily Three Course Specials ($19) around entrées such as osso buco of pork garni, petit filet mignon, and Gulf shrimp with artichokes and mushrooms. Or order à la carte twin jumbo lump crab cakes or pasta jambalaya. The long list of creative appetizers ($7–15), like smoked calamari salad and lobster cocktail, make it easy to select a bunch and share them around for a Greek mezze-style dinner. Reservations recommended.

✐ I first stumbled across **Kelly's Restaurant** (727-736-5284; www .kellyschicaboom.com), 319 Main St, while looking for breakfast en route to Honeymoon Island, and wow—what a breakfast: My platter overflowed with eggs and home fries. Parents will delight in the "pay what they weigh" option for kids. Virgel Kelly is the owner and executive chef overseeing this classy bistro with garden seating. Lunch offerings include grilled Brie with a baby lettuce salad, Jamaican jerk chicken, and rib-eye salad; the Gorgonzola-crusted rib eye is my dinner choice (entrées $13–23). Their adjoining Chic-a-Boom-Room "Martooni" Bar is a gathering place for locals, with live music most evenings.

Gulfport

Enjoy fine French cuisine at **La Côte Basque** (727-321-6888), 3104 Beach Blvd S, where veal and poultry dominate the menu in such classics as chicken Cordon Bleu, veal piccata, and Wiener schnitzel. Beef lovers will enjoy the fine chateaubriand, beef Wellington, and filet mignon.

Intimate elegance reigns at **Six Tables,** the signature restaurant of the Peninsula Inn & Spa (see *Lodgings*). Each evening at 7, Chef Thomas Rufin greets his guests and presents a selection of seven fine entrées such as chateaubriand, venison, and rack of lamb as the centerpiece of a six-course meal with intermezzos ($80 per person; reservations required). For those with tighter budgets but refined tastes, enjoy the globetrotting British Colonial ambiance of the **Palm Terrace,** either out on the porch or in at the well-stocked bar, with live music most nights and ethnic-themed buffets several times weekly.

Palm Harbor

🦐 The decor is old school, but the food is anything but—the **Old Schoolhouse Restaurant** (727-784-2585), 3419 Alt US 19, is indeed an old schoolhouse, built in 1910 and opened as a restaurant in 1982. Under executive chef Larry Lloyd's direction, the innovative menu includes fusion foods such as sesame ginger beef short ribs and crab-crusted salmon with basil cream sauce. Specials are posted on the blackboards. I enjoyed the creamy lobster bisque and was tempted by the toasted coconut (or pecan—take your pick!) ice cream ball, but I stuck to my New Year's resolution and finished off a plate of fried oysters for dinner.

Redington Shores

At **The Lobster Pot Restaurant**

(727-391-8592; www.lobsterpot restaurant.com), 17814 Gulf Blvd, shellfish is the focus of the menu, from the creamy lobster bisque to king and stone crab, escargot, and lobster delights from both Florida and Maine (entrées $20–39). Open for dinner only; reservations recommended.

Safety Harbor

Tiny **Cello's Char-House** (727-723-0909; www.celloscharhouse.com), 143 Seventh Ave N, a romantic restaurant with strains of Sinatra, provides ample portions with a parade of courses—their cup o' beer cheese soup, fresh veggies, house salad, potato dumplings, and hot flatbread—that come with your entrée ($11–23), which might be grilled filet mignon one visit, grilled portobello mushroom the next. Open for dinner, cash only, BYOB.

In a 1920s cottage downtown, the **Green Springs Bistro** (727-669-6762; www.greenspringsbistro.com), 122 Third Ave N, serves up "creative American food" accompanied by music and art to delight the senses. Specialties include gumbo, blue crab–stuffed portobello; sausage, shrimp, and grits; and the Florida cowboy–style rib-eye steak; entrées $17–26. Reservations suggested for dinner.

Sand Key

As orange and blue fade to black over the waters of the Gulf of Mexico, another sunset is savored over dinner at the **Cabana Grill** (727-595-1807; www.cabanagrill.com), 1590 Gulf Blvd, part of the Belleview Biltmore (see *Lodging*). After dark, smooth jazz fills the bistro space at the perfect volume for romantic conversation. Offering the only oceanfront dining

on Sand Key, this classy dining experience showcases the talents of Executive Chef Alain Martin with entrées like romaine-wrapped filet of salmon, served with lemon confit and roasted fresh fig, sliced roasted almond, and green peppercorn sauce. I savored my grilled Black Angus sirloin steak, neatly topped with imported Roquefort cream sauce; entrées $19–35. With ample portions, fine cuisine, and extremely attentive wait staff, this is a don't-miss dining experience. Arrive just before sunset (reservations recommended) for a spectacular show over the Gulf.

St. Pete Beach

Fine dining is a tradition at the **Don CeSar** (see *Hotels, Motels, and Resorts*), and in this classic resort, the place to dine is the **Maritana Grille** (727-360-1882), 3400 Gulf Blvd, named for J. Thomas Rowe's greatest love. "Floribbean" cuisine, a fusion of Florida Cracker and Florida Keys, is all the rage, with fresh-grilled fish prepared atop a pecan and cherry wood grill. Surrounded by thousands of gallons of saltwater aquariums,

CELLO'S CHAR-HOUSE

Sandra Friend

you'll feel immersed in the sea as you dine on specialties such as orange habañero barbecued gulf fish, pan-seared sea scallops, and grilled filet mignon ($30–38). Reservations recommended, especially if you'd like to dine at the Chef's Table in the kitchen. One major departure from the past: jackets not required.

St. Petersburg

One of the city's oldest restaurants, **The Garden** (727-896-3800), 217 Central Ave S, offers intimate indoor dining or a shady brick courtyard beneath a banyan tree, with creative entrées such as crab-stuffed grouper or chicken Boursin and assorted tapas offered à la carte or as a platter of the day.

From your perch on the fourth floor of The Pier (see *Attractions*), a leisurely dinner at the **Columbia Restaurant** (727-822-8000; www .columbiarestaurant.com), 800 Second Ave NE, brings together fabulous Spanish food with the best dining view in the city—a 360° panorama of the city and the open waters of Tampa Bay, its distant shore defined by twinkling lights after dark. I took my parents here for their anniversary, and they loved the array of options; I settled on Shrimp Criollo, an old family recipe where large white shrimp are sautéed in a hot skillet with extra virgin olive oil, garlic, green peppers, tomatoes, *platanos*, potatoes, spicy Spanish paprika, and vermouth. Items are à la carte, and a generous dinner will cost about $50 per person.

EATING OUT

Clearwater

Breakfast at **Angie's Restaurant** (727-461-2880), 725 Cleveland St—what a blur of activity! This home-town diner, opened in 1965, seats singles at the counter and families in booths, the kitchen behind a gleaming stainless-steel backdrop with colorful bottles of juice and cereal boxes. Photos of old Clearwater line the walls. With breakfast all day ($2–8), they're a popular neighborhood gathering spot, where friends chat over biscuits smothered in Grandma's sausage gravy, buttermilk pancakes, Texas French toast, and steak and pork chops with eggs. You won't go away hungry!

With the classic dark and intimate feel of an authentic Irish pub, **O'Keefe's** (727-442-9034; www .okeefestavernonline.com), 1219 S Fort Harrison Ave, has delighted local residents since 1961. Their menu includes some decidedly unusual items, such as the Yuk burger (topped with peanut butter, bacon, and lettuce) and sweet potato fries sprinkled with white chocolate and cinnamon. Eclectic entrées mingle with standards like fish-and-chips and shepherd's pie, $6–16.

I don't understand the connection between Egypt and Poland, but at the **Pierogi Grill** (727-216-3055; www .pierogigrill.com), 1535 Gulf to Bay Blvd, the decor is certainly wrapped in a lush Egyptian temple motif, like walking into an Indiana Jones movie. Classic Polish dishes ($3–13) are on the menu, including barley *kiszka* (black sausage), *golonko* (roasted pork shank), and the namesake pierogi, offered by the half-dozen and dozen. Open daily 11–10.

Clearwater Beach

Headed out early? Catch a cheap breakfast at the **Beach Shanty Café** (727-443-1616), 397 Mandalay Ave, where eggs, grits, and pancakes headline the menu.

♪ Right on the roundabout, **Crabby Bill's** (727-442-2163; www.crabbybills.com), 37 Causeway Blvd, is one location of many in a popular local chain with "fresh no-frills seafood" at cheap prices. Fresh off the local boats, nab crabs, oysters, clams, and more ($9–18), plus fresh crab and lobster at market prices.

Frenchy's Rockaway Grill (727-446-4844; www.frenchysonline.com), 7 Rockaway St, is one of four Frenchy's locations on the beach and best known for its signature seafood dishes, ranging from grouper sandwiches to seafood gumbo, smoked fish spread, and grouper Santorini; all fresh, nothing frozen ($5–16).

⊙ In a historic 1926 beach pavilion, **The Palm Pavilion Beachside Grill & Bar** (727-446-2642; www.palmpavilion.com), 10 Bay Esplanade, is simply the beachside place to be, revitalized in 1964 and still owned by the Hamilton family, adjoining their Palm Pavilion Inn (see *Lodging*). A family-oriented restaurant with an ample tropical beach bar, this perennial favorite caters to a very casual crowd walking right in off the beach to savor specialties like Florida shrimp and crab chowder, coconut shrimp, u-peel shrimp, the "Biggest Grouper Around" (which hangs off the hoagie roll, it's so immense), and the Famous Palm Burger, a half-pound seasoned and grilled to order. After your meal ($6–20), check out the original decking and arches of the pavilion in the bar area, and stop in the gift shop for some colorful T-shirts and souvenirs.

Dunedin

For excellent Mexican, **Casa Tina's** (727-734-9226; www.casatinas.com),

365 Main St, is a top pick for vegetarian palates, and the festive Mexican atmosphere makes it an easy choice. No lard is used in their preparations, and everything is fresh. Virtually anything on the menu can be created with the vegetarian in mind. My basic fare: el burrito, the classic wet burrito slathered in melted cheese. Entrées ($9–17) include numerous fresh fish options.

The walls are covered with covered bridge postcards at the **Covered Bridge Family Restaurant** (727-734-0808; www.thecoveredbridgerestaurant.com), 2070 Bayshore Blvd, where you can nab a hearty breakfast for less than $6 en route to Honeymoon Island. Open for breakfast and lunch daily, and dinner Wed–Sat.

Have some home brew at the **Dunedin Brewery Snug Pub** (727-736-0606; www.dunedinbrewery.com), 937 Douglas Ave, nestled in a microbrewery providing handcrafted beers to dozens of local restaurants. They serve pub fare, including burgers, sandwiches, wings, and pizza ($6–8), and their smooth Celtic Gold Ale goes down good! Open at 5 Tue–Sat, with live music Wed–Sat.

Gulfport

🦀 ♪ Several folks suggested I try the signature crab cakes at the funky little **Backfin Blue Café** (727-343-2583; www.backfinbluecafe.com), 2913 Beach Blvd; I'm glad I did—two of these big balls of flaky crab (with very little breading to hold them together and just the right amount of spice), plus a heaping mound of garlic mashed potatoes and a tasty tomato-artichoke salad filled me right up. They have a wine list, top-notch beers, and dressy desserts, too, if you save room. Closed Tue.

H. T. Kanes Beach Pub & Restaurant (727-347-6299), 5501 Shore Blvd, serves up Ipswich whole-belly fried clams in a roll or as a meal as well as the "best burger in town" ($5 and up, depending on toppings); grouper, catfish, shrimp, steak, and chicken round out the dinner menu.

Hot is hot at the **Pierhouse Grill and Pepper Co.** (727-322-1741), 5401 Shore Blvd, where the "Wall of Flame" celebrates diversity in hot sauces, including Manny's Monkey Butt, the house special. Enjoy great steaks, grouper tacos, and spicy numbers such as Reuben's Crusty Balls (can you believe corned beef, Swiss, and sauerkraut deep-fried?) and Cherry Bomb Chips (yup, deep-fried hot cherry pepper rings). All these and more creative offerings for lunch and dinner, with a killer waterfront view to boot.

Indian Rocks Beach

A local favorite since 1971, **Brewmaster Steak House** (727-595-2900; www.brewmastersonline.com), Gulf Blvd and Walsingham Rd, prides itself on its great steaks and the "magic glass" of free refills of beer and wine with your entrée, and live music on the tiki deck. Shaved prime rib, Delmonico, steak Diane, and ribs—you name it, they've got it, $11 and up for dinner.

Indian Shores

Along the travertine limestone outcroppings of Indian Shores, the **Salt Rock Grill** (727-593-7625; www.saltrockgrill.com), 19325 Gulf Blvd, offers a menu to meet the varied palate, with fine seafood and steaks, pork, and tuna. Entrées start at $13 for a mile-high meatloaf, and early-bird specials are offered 4–5 PM.

Largo

At the **Greek Islands Restaurant** (727-581-1767), 1501 Clearwater-Largo Rd, our *saganaki* was delivered with an *opa!* flourish, the starter to an excellent meal. Greek favorites like chicken *avgolemono* soup, *souvlaki*, *bifteki*, *kalamari*, and lamb chops make up much of the taverna-style menu. The faux archways look out on painted murals of Greece, and the blue-and-white checked tablecloths make you feel like you're dining oceanfront in Mykonos; lunch and dinner 11–9 daily, $6–13.

My fluffy creamy eggs were just the right start to the day at the **Suncoast Family Restaurant** (727-585-5459), 1901 W Bay Dr, a busy family-oriented diner in a small strip mall with breakfast specials from 7–11, open daily. Breakfast for two under $10.

Grab a filling breakfast or lunch ($3–6) at **Ted's Luncheonette** (727-584-2565), 1201 Clearwater-Largo Rd, an unpretentious family diner with big picture windows and fast, friendly service. Open 6–2:30 daily.

Madeira Beach

Sculley's Boardwalk Restaurant (727-393-7749), 190 Johns Pass Boardwalk, perched on John's Pass, has an old fish house atmosphere and offers up freshly caught amberjack, yellowfin, red grouper, and other house seafood favorites, including pistachio-crusted red grouper, as well as a handful of beef, chicken, and pasta entrées, $15 and up.

Ozona

The good times roll at **Molly Goodhead's** (727-786-6255), 400 Orange St, a popular raw bar and seafood house in this little historic village. The menu features grouper "right off the boat," steamed Gulf shrimp, calamari salad, grouper Reuben, and more, $6 and up.

The aroma of smoking meat made me walk into the **Ozona Pig** (727-773-0744), 311 Orange St, where southern-style barbecue ($5-17) is the order of the day: succulent pulled pork and beef on a bun, barbecue chicken, and ribs. Hot tamales, too! Call a day ahead to order a picnic basket of your favorites.

Pass-A-Grille

Kick back dockside at the **Sea Critters Café** (727-360-3706; www.sea critterscafe.com), 2007 Pass-A-Grille Way, recommended by locals and visitors alike. Fresh margaritas complement tasty offerings such as risotto scallops Rockefeller, lobster pasta, crab salad, and grouper Reuben ($8–24).

Take-out's the thing at **Shaner's Land & Sea Market** (727-367-4292), 2000 Pass-A-Grille Way, with hot and cold sandwiches to go, entrées such as crawfish and pasta or pot roast, and platters to feed a crowd.

Pinellas Park

For funky Louisiana fun, check out **Cajun Café on the Bayou** (727-546-6732; www.CajunCafeOnThe Bayou.olm.net), 8101 Park Blvd, where you overlook the mangroves while dining on spicy entrées such as red beans and rice, Creole gumbo, crawfish étouffée, blackened gator, and jambalaya, $8–16.

Safety Harbor

Lunch at **Brady's Backyard Barbecue** (727-712-3727; www.bradysback yardbbq.com), 122 Third Ave N, satisfied even my vegetarian friend with their array of fresh veggie sides; the

pulled pig and sweet tea done right suited me just fine. If you're not sure what to order, ask for "A Try" ($1); entrées include brisket, smoked chicken, pulled pork, spare ribs, baby back ribs, and riblets, $6–18.

Captain's Italian Restaurant (727-725-2846), 324 Main St, is a welcoming eatery reminiscent of a Greek taverna; surrounded by murals, I felt like we were dining in a garden. Owner Steve Capitanos is a native of Sparta with some Italian lineage, and he and wife meld the two to create wonderful casual Mediterranean meals like the Chicken Aristocrat, sautéed with eggplant and topped with a rich white sauce over pasta. Their "famous Greek salad" goes well with a platter of gyro, or order the crispy thin traditional homemade pan pizza. The Greek potato salad is wonderfully garlicky, and their bottomless lemonade is just perfect on a hot day. Open 9 AM–11 PM daily, with lunch specials 11–3 ($3–5), and entrées $9-14.

BRADY'S BARBECUE UNDER THE OAKS IN SAFETY HARBOR

Sandra Friend

Sand Key

Open 7–2, **Maggie Mae's** (727-595-1096), in the Shoppes on Sand Key (see *Selective Shopping*), has pride in making breakfast "just like Granny fixed it." Try the Eggs Benedict Arnold with real southern sausage gravy, or a decadent southern pecan waffle with Grand Marnier and Malibu Rum syrup. The toasted almond French toast is enough to make me drive down here. Dozens of breakfast delights, $3–7.

St. Pete Beach

With its award-winning entrées, the **Hurricane Seafood Restaurant** (727-360-9558; www.thehurricane.com), 807 Gulf Way, is sure to please. Select from crab several ways, including stone crab fresh from their own boats, snow crab flown in from Alaska, or crab cakes Maryland style, as well as hearty New York strip and filet mignon ($8–24). Enjoy sunset on the Gulf from their rooftop seating.

St. Petersburg

🦐 I enjoyed superb food and speedy service when I stopped in **Athenian Garden** (727-822-2000), 2900 Fourth St N, savoring a Greek salad and soft fresh bread in a comfortable indoor garden. Desserts are on display at the door so you'll make the proper selection to have room for them later. Entrées include Greek classics such as gyro, moussaka, *pastitsio*, and *dolmades*, plus sandwiches, seafood, and salads.

St. Petersburg—Downtown

Several folks pointed me toward **Café Alma** (727-502-5002; www.cafealma.com), 260 First Ave S, which has taken over a historic firehouse and turned it into a happening restaurant that segues into a club atmosphere after 10 PM. You can make a fun meal just from the starters, sampling goodies such as steak tartare and pepper-crusted beef carpaccio, sautéed calamari, and spiced butternut squash soup, but the entrées are awesome, too—black truffle gnocchi, paella, and three ethnic trio platters (Caribbean, Tuscan, and Spanish), $19–25. Dinner served Wed–Sat until 1 AM.

At breakfast, the line was out the door at **The Dome Grill** (727-823-5090), 561 Central Ave, where you stand in line to order off the big photo menus. Belgian waffles are a huge hit, and the daily special of eggs, home fries or grits, and toast will set you back less than $3. Served 11–2, lunch includes fresh pasta, ribs, gyro sandwiches, and other Greek specialties.

🦐 **The Moon Under Water** (727-896-6160) is at 332 Beach Dr NE, and I'm glad I wandered in. The ambiance is British Colonial with a hint of London curry shop, and the menu is something this world traveler gives a thumbs-up to. Natives of Wales, the Lucases (who once owned the Mansion House B&B) mingle British isles favorites with Greek, Indian, and Middle Eastern dishes, and a few "normal" entrées (blackened salmon, pork chops, pasta Alfredo, and burgers) thrown in for good measure ($8 and up). Where else can you order hummus, Greek olives, tabbouleh, raita, *and* potato-vegetable curry as sides? My soup of the night, she-crab bisque, was buttery and succulent, and the chicken tikka, a mild but piquant rub. Their signature dish is curry (choose your heat wisely), and you can take a jar of the aromatic sauce home with you. It's noisy in here, and there's plenty of beer, but the locals love this tavern—and you will, too.

Throughout downtown, look for distinctive **Sabrett Hot Dog** pushcarts serving up extra-long dogs with all the fixings. There's enough foot traffic around the city to warrant vendors to set up shop Monday–Saturday.

South Pasadena

🍴 One of my good friends grew up in Gulfport, and every time I headed down that way, she said, "Aren't you going to stop at Ted Peters?" Talk about a local institution. **Ted Peters Famous Smoked Fish** (727-381-7931), 1350 Pasadena Ave, will smoke up your catch or serve you up some of the best red snapper and mullet on earth, smoked in their red oak smoker, and they've been doing it for more than 50 years. Kick back outside and enjoy. Closed Tue.

Tarpon Springs—Downtown

At the **Greek Pizza Kitchen** (727-945-7337; www.greekpizzakitchen.com), 150 E Tarpon Ave, a decidedly romantic interior second-floor wrought-iron terrace perches diners over the spacious main room. Serving delicious taverna food (gyros, *kefetedes,* souvlaki, *horiatiki,* $8–11) and unique Greek-themed pizzas ($22–28), they are *the* choice for traditional food in the Historic District.

Tarpon Springs—Waterfront

A family favorite, **Hellas Restaurant** (727-943-2400), 785 Dodecanese Blvd, evokes the feel of the restaurants in the tourist districts of coastal Greece, with waiters who shout *"opa!"* as they serve your flaming *saganaki,* and colorful murals of the islands covering the walls. I've enjoyed everything I've ordered, from a basic gyro to *dolmades,* pastitsio, and moussaka; entrées $9 and up.

🍴 In the Sponge Exchange, **Mama's Greek Cuisine** (727-944-2888; www.mamasgreekcuisine.net), 735 Dodecanese Blvd #40–41, is the closest I've been to an authentic taverna in years. Their specialty is *lithrini*—whole snapper topped with olive oil, lemon, oregano, garlic, and spices, served with *horta*—but Mama's entrées ($8–19) include all the favorites, from charbroiled lamb chops to octopus, Greek shrimp, and *makaronada.*

BAKERIES, COFFEE SHOPS, AND SODA FOUNTAINS

Clearwater

🍴 Sit under the red-and-white-striped canopy at **Dairy Kurl** (727-446-1549), 1555 Gulf to Bay, on long picnic tables and try to keep that ice cream cone from dripping on you. This is a family favorite for locals, with a giant "medium" soft-serve cone for under $3 and plenty of different shakes, sundaes, and dips for your cones.

Dunedin

Make a whistle stop at **The Boxcar** (727-738-8550), 349A Main St, for coffee, cinnamon rolls, and the morning paper inside an authentic Orange Belt ACL boxcar, adjoining the Pinellas Trail downtown.

Gulfport

Hang out in the Art Village courtyard at **Java Nirvana Cafe** (727-323-5094; www.javanirvanacafe.com), 2908½ Beach Blvd, where the night I arrived the courtyard was hoppin' with the brassy sounds of The Fallopian Tubes, a brash local band that packs out the house. Enjoy live music with your cappuccino on Fri–Sat nights.

Palm Harbor

Dairy Rich (727-789-9285), 3109 Alt US 19, is a classic drive-up ice cream and hot dog stand where a burger basket costs $4. Just up the street, **J. J. Gandy's Famous Key Lime Pie** (727-938-PIES; www.jjgandyspies .com), 3725 Alt US 19, supplies more than a hundred local restaurants with their pies; choose from 20 tempting varieties 9–4 Mon–Sat.

Safety Harbor

A downtown landmark, the **Whistle Stop Grill & Udderly Cool Ice Cream** (727-726-1956; www.whistle stopgrill.com), 915 Main St, is just plain yummy. Enjoy frozen delights ($2–5) like the Sandlot Sundae or apple dumpling à la mode, or grab a veggie wrap or an order of fried green tomatoes.

Sand Key

You can't miss **Ryan's** (727-596-0006)—it's right in the middle promenade of the Shoppes on Sand Key (see *Selective Shopping*), and there's always a line for their gourmet ice creams, sorbets, and frozen yogurts. They'll fix you a fine coffee, too, good for savoring as you watch the sailboats on Clearwater Harbor from the boardwalk behind the shops.

St. Petersburg

Since 1975, **John & Noel's Central Coffee Shop** (727-550-8733), 530 Central Ave, has served up dependable breakfasts and lunches. On busy Beach Drive, **Marketplace Express** (727-894-3330), 284 Beach Dr NE, hums with java junkies and locals dropping in for a deli lunch or takeout—especially since it's right across from the Museum of Art.

Tarpon Springs

You won't go wrong with a stroll down Dodecanese Blvd, where the sight of trays of tempting *pastas* (think decadent cream-filled Greek pastries, *not* spaghetti) and baklava will pull you into many storefront bakeries, including **Parthenon** (727-939-7709), 751 Dodecanese Blvd; and **Hellas** (727-943-2400), 785 Dodecanese Blvd. I've yet to be disappointed at any of the stops I've made, so explore!

✳ Selective Shopping

Belleair

Greenbaum's Antiques (727-586-4043), 1797 Clearwater/ Largo Rd, has everything from an inlaid mother-of-pearl casket to hand-carved 19th-century Moorish chairs, military miniatures, and antique pottery. There's a Furniture Annex as well.

Belleair Bluffs

I'm a sucker for gourmet cooking stores, so **Beans About Cooking** (727-588-3303), 100 Indian Rocks Rd N, was fun to browse, and I couldn't help but walk away with some exotic spices and sushi bowls.

Jewel Antique Mall (727-441-3036), 2601 Jewel Rd, is a rabbit warren of dealer spaces that just go on and on and on. Keep looking, and you will find *something* you like! Open daily.

Traders Alley (727-584-4799), 596 N Indian Rocks Rd, boasts a collection of more than a dozen shops, each brimming with goodies. **Victoria's Parlor** (727-581-0519) is a grandmother's attic filled with glassware. **My Little Place** (727-584-4799) offers appealing country folk art.

Clearwater

It's always the holidays at **Robert's Christmas House** (727-797-1600 or 1-800-861-6389), 2951 Gulf to Bay, where a stop just before Christmas yielded both classic and whimsical ornaments, an incredible array of collectibles from Annalee dolls to Lenox, and a virtual forest, a sparkling wonderland with dozens of unique artificial trees to choose from. Gifts shipped daily. Open daily all year except major holidays.

Clearwater Beach

Walk Mandalay Avenue to check out the beach shops. At **Key West Express** (727-461-6462), 484 Mandalay Ave, nab soft flowing dresses in bright island colors and other comfy casual wear. Searching for beach gear and boogie boards? Try **Mandalay Surf & Sport** (727-443-3884), 499 Mandalay Ave, an original on the beach since 1979.

Dunedin

Dunedin is truly a shopper's paradise, with dozens of shops lining the quaint downtown streets, informational kiosks to show you what's where, and free parking nearby. Most shops are open Sundays. Here are some of my favorites:

Browse the dealer booths at **Amanda Austin** (727-736-0778), 365 Main St, for tasteful home decor, Depression glass, vintage children's books, and craft items.

Indulge yourself in the very feminine **Erika's Place** (727-733-0461), 714 Broadway, with its aromatic soaps, potpourri, and candles. I especially liked the retro powder-puff pink Christmas tree in the middle of the store, but it wasn't for sale—yet.

Seek out gifts from the Far East at **Kismat** (727-733-0040), 355 Main St, where I found camel bone boxes from India and Thai percussion animal carvings.

Not downtown but nearby, **Knot on Main** (727-738-8090), 2428 Bayshore Blvd, has a large number of dealer booths where you'll find antique lamps, collectible coins, ruby glass, Steubenville ware, some crafts and gifts, and much more.

You'll find classy collectibles and fine Florida art at **Objects & Accents** (727-738-4565), 340 Main St, a different kind of home and garden shop, where I was particularly intrigued by the faux orchids and white-topped pitcher plants.

The **Old Feed Store Antiques Mall** (727-736-8115), 735 Railroad St, yields some unique gifts for friends and family. The dealer booths aren't just full of old stuff—one of my previous finds, Catch the Drift (a driftwood art shop in North Florida) shows off their wares here, too.

It's a jungle inside **Palm Latitudes** (727-733-7343), 322 Main St—you can't see the ceiling for the forest of wind chimes and ornaments! It's your one-stop Jimmy Buffet–tiki bar–surfer–tropical kitsch connection.

Gulfport

Dream big at **Small Adventures Bookshop** (727-347-8732; www.small adventuresbookshop.com), 3107 Beach Blvd, where every nook and cranny is crammed with the literature you love, from genre paperbacks to philosophy, travel narrative, and Florida classics.

Largo

On a back street near the Pinellas Trail, **The Amish Country Store** (727-587-9657; www.theamishcountry store.com), 206 13th St SW, is a little grocery filled with Pennsylvania Dutch goodies, from birch beer and bulk spices, scrapple, and pretzels to

THE AMISH COUNTRY STORE

Sandra Friend

homemade shoo-fly pie in the bakery. Grab a sandwich and eat it on the porch. Open Tue–Sat.

Set under a canopy of live oak trees, **Karen's Korner** (727-581-2812), 506 First Ave SW, is a cottage filled with suites of furnishings, glassware, dishes, and collectibles at reasonable prices.

In the very roomy **Quaint Essential Antiques** (727-398-2228; www.quaintessential.com), 11890 Walsingham Rd, the dealer booths are nicely spaced and offer finds like antique fishing lures, McDonald's collectibles, and vintage glassware.

Chic, colorful clothing awaits at **Suzette's on the Rocks** (727-595-8700), 13042 Indian Rocks Rd.

Madeira Beach

A serious shopper's destination, **John's Pass Village** (727-397-1667; www.johnspass.com), Village Blvd, has both the typical beach shops and some truly unusual ones. Claiming more than fifteen thousand in stock, **Angel Haven** (727-399-8455), 13007 Village Blvd, is filled with angel figurines in every medium as well as angelic gifts. **The Artisan's Market** (727-394-2218), 124 John's Pass Boardwalk, has Mexican clay figurines, wall art, fountains, and more. **The Bronze Lady** (1-800-269-3412), 12955 Village Blvd, features distinctive collectibles, with their showpiece original art by Red Skelton. **Caribbean Jubilee** (727-399-0551), 13015-A Village Blvd, brims with colorful, playful plates and wall decor—just the sorts of gifts I buy for my siblings. Stop in at the **Florida Winery at John's Pass** (727-362-0008; www.thefloridawinery.com), 12945 Village Blvd, for free wine tastings, gourmet foods, fudge and chocolate, and Tropical Wine ice cream. **Tropic Shoppe** (727-397-4337), 12913 Village Blvd, has dressy tropical wear and sandals, as well as kids' clothing.

Pass-A-Grille

Vivid art catches your attention as you drive past the **Nancy Markoe Gallery** (727-360-0729; www.nancymarkoegallery.com), 3112 Pass-A-Grille Way. Stop and check out handmade arts and crafts by artists throughout America in a variety of media, including wood, fiber, and paper.

Pinellas Park

For flea market bargains, browse thousands of booths at the **Wagon Wheel Flea Market** (813-544-5319), 7801 Park Blvd, on weekends.

Safety Harbor

Seahorses and mermaids sparkle and shimmer at **Art Designs & Interiors** (727-726-8303), 344 Main St, an art shop with framed art and great gifts.

Fun and funky flamingos, flags, and garden art are at **Caribbean Kat's Trading Company** (727-796-5666), 230A Main St, whimsical delights for your garden and home.

Odile of Safety Harbor (727-791-6900; www.shop-odile.com), Main St, a chic boutique, has flax and fun fashions for women.

The pink salt crystal lamps drew me into **Illuminations Station** (727-797-4441; www.illuminationsstation.com), 130 Eighth Ave S, but once inside, I found a fabulous South Pacific drum to add to my sister's collection. Massage and reiki treaments offered, plus plenty of New Age gifts, books, incense, and original art.

In the **Safety Harbor Galleria** (727-799-1600), 123 Second Ave S, there is Charlestowne pottery with whimsical sea accents, organic dog and cat cookies, handbags, seed and bead necklaces, and even more crafty, creative gifts by local artisans. Stop in and say hello to April, who has launched this artists' showcase in a vintage home.

This Old Place (727-725-4242), 454 Main St, has a bit of everything in a 1914 landmark, from antique Imperial glass, sterling silver rings, and tea towels in the back to designer jewelry and home decor up front, including an entire bathroom in a picture window facing the street!

Sand Key

The **Shoppes on Sand Key** (727-596-8466), 1261 Gulf Blvd, include a mix of retail, restaurant, and commercial establishments on an island where, for thousands of people, it's the only place to grab a bite to eat or drop off stuff at the cleaners. What makes this a great stop is the boardwalk, stretching the length of the strip mall with an unimpeded view of Clearwater Harbor and its sailboats. At **The Merry Mouse Gift Shop** (727-595-5075), I found (and stocked up on) creative toys and fun gifts like a sushi-serving set for toddlers, plus T-shirts and plush toys, Florida souvenirs and gourmet snacks, and lots of beach towels.

St. Petersburg

Artistreet & Co. (727-895-5347), 221 First Ave NE, stays open late on weekends and is full of whimsical items to give as gifts or take home, from sushi platters and bowls to incense, wind chimes, Aspen Bay candles, and the gift for he who has it all—monogrammed toilet paper. Nearby, arts and crafts from the islands delight the senses at **Caribbean Artworks** (727-553-9213), 203 First Ave N, including playful toys, striking large sculptures, and fine jewelry.

Baywalk (www.yourbaywalk.com), 153 Second Ave N, is an outdoor mall with a modern Mediterranean flair and a choice of shops and restaurants reflecting hip urban lifestyles. Don't miss **Shapiro's Gallery** (727-894-2111; www.shapirogallery.com), 185 Second Ave N, as Michael Shapiro brings in unique American-made sculpture, pottery, fiber craft, art glass, and more from more than three hundred artists nationwide. Here you'll find Brian Andreas's endearing Story People, Alison Palmer's whimsical candlestick women, and other gifts sure to please—intarsia frames, Raku cats, even hand-dipped candles. Another intriguing shop is **Being: The Art of Urban Living** (727-922-6252), 115 Second Ave N, for chic home decor. **Ben & Jerry's** and **Too-Jay's** are among the options for a quick bite.

The **Beach Drive shopping district** tends toward the stylish, with upscale jewelers sandwiched between home-decor and fine-collectibles shops. At **Good Night Moon** (727-898-2801), 222 Beach Dr NE, *plush* plush is the rage, from adorable Lamaze for the little ones to sensual bedding for Mom and Dad.

A bibliophile's pilgrimage is not complete without a visit to **Haslam's Book Store** (727-822-8616; www .haslams.com), 2025 Central Ave, a destination in itself since 1933 with room upon room upon room of books—more than three hundred thousand, they say! You'll spend countless hours browsing the neatly arranged mix of new and used. In their fourth generation of family ownership and hands-on management, Haslam's does a great job of bringing in authors for signings. Open 10–6:30 Mon–Sat.

Have your fortune told at **Heavenly Things** (727-822-8938), 216 First Ave N, where gifts run "from art to Zen," including New Age books, witch balls, and amateur musical instruments.

With four floors of treasures, the **Gas Plant Antique Arcade** (727-895-0368), 1246 Central Ave, is the ultimate destination for ephemera collectors. The upper two stories are focused on fine antique furniture; on the lower floors, look for everything—from postcards and stereoscopes to Elvis memorabilia, autographs, glassware, and more.

Your antiquarian source in the region, **Lighthouse Books** (727-822-3278), 1735 First Ave N, offers a fine selection of rare books, prints, and maps, including a special selection of literature of the South.

At **The Pier** (see *Attractions*), you'll find a variety of shops to browse, including the **Crystal Mirage Gallery** (727-895-1166; www.crystal mirage.com), with its art glass perfume bottles, fancy stemware, and marine life cast in glass; **Rainforest Gifts** (727-821-1434), filled with tropical home decor and gift items; and **St. Petersburg Candle Gallery** (727-823-9299; www.stpetecandle.com), where they make candles on the spot.

Chocolate fiends should stop at **Schakolad** (727-892-2400), 401 Central Ave, where the aroma will draw you in, and there's always a special worth walking away with. In addition to fine handmade chocolates, they offer great fudge, too.

St. Pete Beach
Step back in time at the region's only remaining neighborhood five-and-dime store, the **Corey Avenue 5¢ and 10¢ Store** (727-360-8503; www.coreyave.com), 300 Corey Ave, established in 1949; their stock includes old-fashioned items and modern sportswear, sundries, and souvenirs.

Tarpon Springs—Downtown
Immerse in the local community through song—update your CD collection at **Greek Music Superstore & More** (727-939-8498; www.greek music.com), 11 Pinellas Ave, in what is likely the largest Greek-only music store in Florida. My pick: *anything* by Anna Vizzi.

Search for the unusual at **Tarpon Avenue Antiques** (727-938-0053), 161 Tarpon Ave, such as flash cards in Chinese and bookplates from the 1880s, along with many Teutonic-influenced items.

A bright red dragonfly Tiffany lamp drew me to **Unique Designs** (727-943-0440), 218 E Tarpon Ave, where the inventory tends toward the exotic with Asian masks and elephant pedestals as well as vintage furnishings and one-of-a-kind statuary.

Tarpon Springs—Waterfront

Dodecanese Boulevard is lined with shops, so you'll have no problem picking up something with a Greek flair. Circa 1912, the **Athens Gift Shop** (727-937-3514), 703 Dodecanese Blvd, has a unique cutaway corner that visitors like to pose in for photos. I always stop at **Gift World** (727-938-3225), 557 Dodecanese Blvd, for CDs, videos, and books in Greek.

Formerly a working sponge market, **The Sponge Exchange** (727-934-8758), 735 Dodecanese Blvd, is now a collection of shops and restaurants, and you can still pick up great natural sponges at the **Tarpon Sponge Company.** At **CJ's Nature Shop,** look for plush critters, shirts, and bags with wildlife prints. **Miracles of the Sea** has stained glass and sculptures and marine art.

Luxurious handmade olive oil soap, bath oils, and inspirational art await at **Getaguru** (727-937-8193; www.geta guru.com), 777 Dodecanese Blvd, one of my favorite Tarpon Springs shops.

In the shopping complex near the end of the street, **Thee Museum Shoppe** (727-934-6760; www.museumshoppe .com), 822 Dodecanese Blvd, has a classy selection of museum reproductions, the entire educational Dover coloring book series, and statuettes of just about any deity you can think of.

Treasure Island

The **Florida Shell Shop** (727-367-3215; www.thefloridashellshop.com), 9901 Gulf Blvd, is the oldest shop on Treasure Island, opened in 1955. It still retains that Old Florida charm,

Sandra Friend

ATHENS GIFT SHOP

filled with seashells, souvenirs, and nautical décor.

PRODUCE STANDS, FARMER'S MARKETS, AND SEAFOOD MARKETS

Along Alt US 19 between Tarpon Springs and Dunedin there are many small produce stands to choose from, such as **Johnny's Farm Fresh Produce** (which, like many of the stands, sells Greek favorites like fresh olives and feta) and **Steve's Produce** (fresh shrimp daily! Bananas 3 lbs for $1!). In Dunedin, every Fri Oct–Apr there's the **Dunedin Green Market**, downtown at Pioneer Park, 8–1, with local vendors bringing in fresh produce, flowers, and organic eats and clothing.

Walk into **Island Fish** (727-595-8777; www.islandfishseafood.com), 13042 Indian Rocks Rd, and you'll have to walk out with something. Smoked salmon? Fresh shrimp? Gourmet relishes? Seafood rub? Selling salads, bowls of gumbo, prime quality seafood, and freshly cut meats.

It's where the locals go for seafood,

Mid-Peninsula Seafood (727-327-8309), 400 49th St S, St. Petersburg, has been around for nearly 30 years, serving up fresh catches by the piece or by the pound. Nab fresh fish at their fish market, too!

The finest selection of produce and fresh fish in the area can be found at the **Saturday Morning Market** (727-455-4921; www.saturday morningmarket.com), corner Central Ave and Second St in downtown St. Petersburg, every Saturday 9–2. Live music and crafts vendors add color to this happening scene.

Ward's Seafood (727-581-2640 or 1-800-556-3761; www.wardsseafood .com), 1001 Belleair Rd, Clearwater, a local favorite since 1955, has the best of the local catch. Stop by for their succulent take-out, or have them ship some seafood home.

✳ Entertainment

DANCING A true Florida classic, the historic **Casino Ballroom** (727-893-1070), 5500 Shore Blvd, Gulfport, overlooks Boca Ciega Bay and the twinkling lights of St. Pete Beach in the distance. Step back into the 1930s and relive the days of ballroom dancing every Sunday, Tuesday, and Thursday, or jump into the swing of swing dancing on Wednesday.

MUSIC Up for a jam or some cool jazz? At the **Peninsula Inn & Spa** (see *Hotels, Motels, and Resorts*), join the folks out on the **Palm Terrace** for a near-nightly jam, or wander over to the Art Village across the street to see who's hot tonight. Artists also perform on weekends at **Yabba Dew Beachside Grille,** 5519 Shore Blvd, and **H. T. Kanes Beach Pub &**

Restaurant (see *Eating Out*) in Gulfport. In St. Petersburg, I caught live music on Friday night in the plaza at **Baywalk,** but for a guaranteed good time, catch the big names that play at **Jannus Landing Courtyard** (727-896-2276; www.jannuslanding concerts.com), 16 Second St—more than 75 concerts a year!

One of the time-honored venues for Florida folk music, the **Ka Tiki** (727-360-2272), 8801 W Gulf Blvd on Sunset Beach (S Treasure Island), draws appreciative crowds each Thursday night for its folk night, hosted by Sunset Beach Pete and featuring troubadours such as Frank Thomas, Raiford Starke, and Val Wisecracker. It's a don't-miss stop for serious lovers of Old Florida and of folk music.

PERFORMING ARTS **Ruth Eckerd Hall** (727-791-7400; www.rutheckerd hall.com), 1111 McMullen Booth Rd, Clearwater, is a favorite stop for top-name musical acts and comedians. Check their Web site for the current schedule and ticket prices.

In St. Petersburg, the vibrant non-profit **American Stage Theater** (727-823-1600; www.americanstage .org), 211 Third St S, offers a fresh slate of programs twice annually, with presentations ranging from classic drama such as *A Moon for the Misbegotten* to edgy comedy like the caustic *Santaland Diaries*. The **Florida Orchestra** (813-286-2403 or 1-800-662-7286; www.floridaorchestra.org), which has performed for almost 40 seasons, puts on more than 150 concerts each year. One of their regular venues is the **Mahaffey Theater** (727-892-5767; www.stpete.org/ mahaffey.htm), 400 First St S, a grand performing-arts center that also hosts

Broadway musicals and other unique events. The **Palladium Theater** (727-822-3590; www.mypalladium .org), 253 Fifth Ave N, a community center for the performing arts built in 1925, boasts a full-size Skinner Pipe Organ. Check their Web site for a calendar of their many musical events.

✳ Special Events

January: On the sixth, **Epiphany,** in Tarpon Springs, is an important devotional day in the Greek Orthodox faith that includes the blessing of the fleet and a dive for the Cross. Young men compete for the honor of retrieving the icon for a year of good luck.

February: **Greek Fest** (727-937-3540), St. Nicholas Orthodox Cathedral, Tarpon Springs, is a major event featuring Greek music and dancing, food, and children's activities. Admissions go to help families in need.

March: Just say *ohi* ("no") at the **Greek Independence Day Parade** (727-937-3540), Tarpon Springs, on the 20th at the sponge docks at 1 PM. Ask a participant why and you'll learn more about modern Greek history.

Since 1975, the **International Folk Fair** (727-552-1896; www.spiffs.org) lets you explore the customs and cuisines of more than 50 cultures, with continuous folk dancing and music on the center stage.

Pioneer Jamboree (727-866-6401), at the Pinewood Cultural Park's Heritage Village (see *Historic Sites*), Largo, on the second Saturday, is a celebration of pioneer life with folk music, antique tractors, and hayrides.

April: Nationally known blues acts gather annually for the **Tampa Bay Blues Festival** (727-502-5000; www .tampabaybluesfest.com), held along

the St. Petersburg waterfront at Vinoy Park.

The **St. Petersburg Grand Prix** (727-894-7749; www.gpstpete.com) brings classic autos through town on a 1.78-mile course along the waterfront and Albert Whitted Airport.

Started in 1921, the annual **Festival of the States** (727-898-3654; www .festivalofstates.com) is one of the largest civic celebrations in the South, with parades, concerts, sports, and a band competition.

✐ One of the nation's top art shows is the **Mainsail Arts Festival** (727-892-5885; www.mainsailartsfestival.org), drawing more than three hundred artists to set up their booths along the waterfront. The festival includes a lively children's arts activity center, a food court, and live entertainment.

A major arts event for more than 30 years, the **Tarpon Springs Arts & Crafts Festival** (727-937-6109), held the second weekend, is one of the nation's top art festivals, bringing in more than two hundred artists who compete for prizes. There's also food, exhibits, and entertainment.

In the tradition of Scotland, the **Dunedin Highlands Games and Military Tattoo** (727-733-3197; www.dunedinhighlandgames.com) held the first Saturday at Dunedin High School, features massed pipers, drummers, highland and country dancers, and the parade of clans. Tickets are $8 in advance, $12 at the gate, $4 children.

More than one hundred thousand people descend on the weeklong **Fun 'N Sun Festival** (727-562-4804), Clearwater, held the last weekend Apr–first weekend May. An event that's been going on annually since 1953, it features concerts, sports competition, food, arts and crafts, and the gala illuminated Fun 'N Sun Night Parade starting at Crest Lake Park.

June: The oldest African American festival in America, **Juneteenth** (727-823-5693; www.juneteenth.com) celebrates the Emancipation Proclamation with a candlelight vigil, inspirational music, and fun for the entire family.

November: For more than 30 years, the **Clearwater Jazz Holiday** (727-461-5200), held midmonth, has brought in top names from the jazz world for four days of free public concerts at Coachman Park in downtown Clearwater.

The **Dunedin Celtic Festival** (www.dunedinhighlandgames.com/celtfest.html) rallies local Scottish spirit, centered around concerts at Dunedin Community Center Auditorium, 1920 Pinehurst.

Chefs strut their stuff at **Ribfest** (727-528-3828; www.ribfest.org) at Vinoy Park, and we barbecue fans benefit from the top-notch competition, accompanied not just by spicy sauces but by top country and rock bands, too.

For more than 25 years, the **St. Petersburg Boat Show** (954-764-7642; www.showmanagement.com) has taken to the waterfront with a gathering of hundreds of happy boaters swapping stories and checking out the newest manufacturers' specials.

December: During **Light up the Bayou** (727-943-5523), stroll along Spring Bayou, Tarpon Springs, on Christmas Eve to enjoy the waterside luminaria in front of classic Victorian homes.

INDEX